Josh McDowell's

Handbook on Counseling Youth

By Josh McDowell and Bob Hostetler

JOSH MCDOWELL'S HANDBOOK ON COUNSELING YOUTH

*A Comprehensive Guide for Equipping
Youth Workers, Pastors, Teachers, and Parents*

By Josh McDowell and Bob Hostetler

WORD PUBLISHING
Dallas•London•Vancouver•Melbourne

Unless otherwise indicated, Scripture quotations used in this book are from The Holy Bible, New International Version (NIV). Copyright © 1973, 1978, 1984 International Bible Society. Used by permission of Zondervan Bible Publishers.

Other Scripture references are from the following sources:

The King James Version of the Bible (KJV).

The Amplified Bible (AMP): Old Testament, copyright © 1962, 1964 by Zondervan Publishing House (used by permission); and from The Amplified New Testament, copyright ©1958 by the Lockman Foundation (used by permission).

The New King James Version (NKJV), copyright © 1979, 1982, 1992, Thomas Nelson, Inc., Publisher

The New Revised Standard Version Bible (NRSV), copyright © 1989, by the Division of Christian Education of the National Council of the Churches of Christ in the United States of America. Published by Thomas Nelson, Inc., Nashville, Tennessee. Used by permission.

The Living Bible (TLB), copyright © 1971 by Tyndale House Publishers, Wheaton, Ill. Used by permission.

The New American Standard Bible, copyright © 1960, 1962, 1963, 1968, 1971, 1972, 1973, 1975, 1977 by the Lockman Foundation. Used by permission.

James Moffatt, A New Translation of the Bible (MOFFATT) ©1922, 1976, Published by Harper and Row.

Excerpts from the book Choices by Stacy and Paula Rinehart, copyright © 1983, are used by permission of NavPress, Colorado Springs, Colorado. All rights reserved.

Excerpts from the book Counseling Teenagers by Dr. G. Keith Olson, copyright © 1984, are used by permission of Group Publishing, Inc., Box 481, Loveland, CO 80539.

Some passages are taken from Advanced Peer Counseling in Youth Groups by Joan Sturkie and Siang-Yang Tan. Copyright © 1993 by Youth Specialties, Inc. Used by permission of Zondervan Publishing House.

Additional passages are taken from You're Someone Special by Bruce Narramore. Copyright © 1978 by The Zondervan Corporation. Used by permission of Zondervan Publishing House.

Anecdotes and case studies presented in this volume are composites of actual cases. Names and other details have been changed to protect identities.

The publications listed in "For Further Reading" at the end of each chapter are not necessarily endorsed by the authors but are presented to give readers an idea of the materials available. The Bible is the only book the authors endorse without reservation!

Library of Congress Cataloging-in-Publication Data

McDowell, Josh

[Handbook on counseling youth]

Josh McDowell's handbook on counseling youth: a comprehensive guide for equipping youth workers, pastors, teachers, and parents / by Josh McDowell and Bob Hostetler

        p.   cm.

ISBN 0-8499-1326-8

ISBN 0-8499-3236-X (pbk.)

        1. Youth—Pastoral counseling of.   2. Teenagers—Pastoral counseling of.   3. Youth—religious life.

4. Teenagers—religious life. I. Hostetler, Bob, 1958– .   II. Title

BV4447.M36   1996

259' .23–dc20   96-13517

    CIP

Printed in the United States of America.

6 7 8 0 1 2 3 4 9 RRD 9 8 7 6 5 4 3 2 1

Contents

Physical Issues

Vocational Issues

Acknowledgments

This book and its authors owe much to the extraordinary contribution and collaboration of many people, without whom its completion would have been impossible. We wish to thank:

Dale Bellis, who researched sixty-seven key issues and compiled sixty-seven hundred pages of research from over 250 resources.

Harry and Ginny Yates, who provided substantive and voluminous research for this project.

Bob Evans, for his technical expertise and selfless willingness to help, and to Rob Pickering, whose technical help at a crucial moment helped keep the project going.

Becky Bellis, for her review of key sections of the manuscript and her support in a myriad of practical ways;

Professional Contributors and Authors

Stephen Arterburn and the Minirth Meier New Life Clinics for valuable insight and editorial oversight, and for guiding us to helpful resources.

Rick Fowler, whose expert help with the chapters on coping with attention deficit disorder and long-term illness was invaluable.

Robert Whitcomb, for his contribution to the chapter on peer persecution and rejection.

Ken Wilgus, for his expertise on the subject of runaway threats and attempts.

Brian Newman, for his expert assistance with the chapters on overprotective parents and inattentive parents.

Guy Chandler, whose expertise contributed much to the chapter on ritual abuse.

Larry Stephens, for his expert help with the chapter on gambling.

Steve Brinkerhoff, whose contribution to the chapters on school dropouts and overachievement and underachievement was indispensable.

Bill Riley, whose frequent and substantive guidance prevented many early mistakes and helped devise a wise and workable model.

And to the many highly regarded professionals whose writings are indispensable to the help offered in this volume, among whom are:

William Backus, Ph.D., a pastor, author, and clinical psychologist. His books include *Telling Yourself the Truth* and *Telling the Truth to Troubled People*;

Dr. Gary R. Collins, a licensed psychologist with a Ph.D. in clinical psychology, and author of the widely respected *Christian Counseling: A Comprehensive Guide*;

Dr. Larry Crabb, who holds a Ph.D. in clinical psychology from the University of Illinois. Dr. Crabb is the author of *The Marriage Builder*, *Inside Out*, and others;

Frank Minirth, M.D., and Paul Meier, M.D., founders of the Minirth-Meier Clinics and authors of over thirty books;

Dr. G. Keith Olson, author of *Counseling Teenagers*, and a respected Christian psychologist.

Manuscript Evaluation and Critique

Ward Ballard, Mike Combs, Mike Erre, Ed Hackney, Ann Helwig, Rev. Darrell Jackson, Candi McGuiare, Bill Riley, Kathy Seal, and Boyd Warner, for reading the early draft, participating in the focus group, and providing keen insight and practical guidance, making this book an inestimably better tool than it otherwise would have been.

Editorial and Design

Joey Paul, whose guidance, leadership, and support brought this book through the long process from conception to realization;

Laura Kendall, for her devoted labor in wrestling this book into its final form and shepherding it through the editing and design process;

Sue Ann Jones, for her careful and thorough attention to the manuscript in preparing it for publication;

Kathryn Murray and Sabra Smith for their intensive labor and creative design, making this book both attractive and usable.

Finally, to the many experts and authors whose work is cited herein, making this book the fruit of many, many years of study and ministry, we say thanks.

Josh McDowell
Bob Hostetler

Introduction

I received a letter from a Christian father who had heard me speak. He said he and his wife had always done their best to be good parents. They were members of a good church and had always been proud of their children. But he told me they had just discovered something about their oldest daughter, something that brought their world crashing down around them. He described his daughter as a pretty girl, but he said she'd never been real popular with boys. Until recently.

She started dating one of the boys on the football team, and—this father had just learned—very early in the relationship she had sex with him. She went from that football player to another. Before long, she had slept with the whole football team! This tortured parent wrote me, "Josh, they were passing my little girl around as some sort of 'team girl'!"

That loving father poured his heart out to me in writing. He wanted to know what to do, what to say. He pleaded with me for answers. Some of his questions I could answer; some I couldn't, though I did my best.

I can't count how many times I've heard similar stories—firsthand—that would melt even the hardest heart. Parents, grandparents, teachers, pastors, and youth workers confide their frustrations and fears and their intense and urgent longings for help with the complex, critical issues youth face today.

That's the reason for this book.

Youth in Crisis

Research tells a statistical horror story of what is happening *every day* in America:[1]

- 1,000 unwed teenage girls become mothers

- 1,106 teenage girls get an abortion

- 4,219 teenagers contract a sexually transmitted disease

- 500 adolescents begin using drugs

- 1,000 adolescents begin drinking alcohol

- 135,000 kids bring a gun or other weapon to school

- 3,610 teens are assaulted; 80 are raped

- 2,200 teens drop out of high school

- 2,750 kids watch their parents separate or divorce

- 90 kids are taken from their parents' custody and placed in foster care, a group home, or institutional care

- 7 kids (ages 10–19) are murdered

- 7 juveniles age 17 and under are arrested for murder

- 6 teens commit suicide

Many of America's twenty-eight million teens face struggles and crises that most adults would find difficult to bear. For example, one in eight has an alcoholic parent.[2]

One in five lives in poverty. More than one in five (22 percent) live in single-parent homes. More than one in fifty live with no parent at all.[3]

Moreover, research—and experience—reveal that teens in evangelical churches are by no means immune to such problems. A survey of twenty-three national Christian youth leaders[4] involved in denominational and parachurch ministries identified such issues as premarital sex, pornography, sexual abuse, emotional abuse, abortion, parental divorce, alcoholism, drug addiction, and suicide as issues faced by their kids—churched youth, Christian youth—issues those leaders consider both important and urgent for today's youth . . . and the adults who care for them.

Those twenty-three national youth leaders helped us identify the fifty most basic, pressing problems faced by youth today, problems that range from emotional issues (like loneliness and depression) and relational issues (such as love, dating, and peer pressure) to sexual issues, abuse, addictions, disorders—even vocational issues (like finding God's will and choosing a career or ministry).

How to Use This Book

Josh McDowell's Handbook on Counseling Youth is one component in a series designed to provide parents, youth workers, pastors, and teachers—any caring adults who work with youth—a collection of resources that will help them prevent and address the crises that so many of today's youth face at one time or another. The series is comprised of three main resources:

- *Crisis manuals*
  The crisis manuals address the twenty-four most urgent and most threatening crises, prescribing appropriate responses for the first twenty-four to forty-eight hours after learning of the problem.
- *Cassette tapes*
  A set of cassette tapes has been designed for the concerned adult to loan or give to a young person in crisis. The tapes contain comfort and counsel aimed directly at the youth in crisis.
- *The Handbook*
  This book, *Josh McDowell's Handbook on Counseling Youth*, provides in-depth and extensive understanding of the issues youth face, helping the concerned parent or other adult gain a strong working knowledge of the issues and appropriate short- and long-term responses to each.

Each of the fifty chapters that follow focuses on a serious issue faced by adolescents (and sometimes preadolescents) and is intended to offer ready reference to that issue. A synopsis at the beginning of each chapter presents an overview of that chapter's contents, allowing quick location of specific topics or suggestions. Each chapter is constructed in the following way:

An opening case study, presenting an illustration of the problem, its symptoms, and characteristics in a true-to-life scenario. Many of the case studies are adapted from actual news accounts; others are based on case studies encountered by professionals who work with youth. Some are composites of several cases.

An overview of the problem and its prevalence among youth.

The primary causes and effects of the problem or issue, according to the experts in that particular field.

A biblical perspective of the problem, offering insight into the Bible's position on the subject.

The response that a pastor, youth worker, parent, or teacher may be able to take in preventing or addressing the issue. Each of the fifty chapters recommends a six-step response utilizing the acrostic "LEADER" (Listen, Empathize, Affirm, Direct, Enlist, and, when applicable, Refer). The acrostic is intended to help concerned adults remember and implement the suggestions readily and accurately.

A listing of further resources, including Scripture passages cited in the chapter, additional Scripture, and other books recommended for reading.

The research, expert opinions, recommendations, biblical background, and scriptural basis presented here can be an invaluable resource to a parent or other caring adult who wonders "What can I do?" "What should I say?" or "What do I need to know?" This book is structured to allow a concerned parent, pastor, youth pastor, teacher,

or other adult to open the book to the table of contents, locate the chapter that addresses the problem at hand, and in one sitting, gain a thorough understanding of the problem and how to respond to it. However, the design of this book will also allow a reader to turn to the synopsis at the beginning of a chapter and locate specific issues within the chapter. In addition, after careful reading of an entire chapter, a concerned adult can gain even more extensive insight and information by reviewing the additional Scripture and resources recommended at the end of each chapter.

The chapters that follow owe much to the expert opinions of many highly regarded Christian professionals. Among the most quoted are such persons as:

William Backus, Ph.D., a pastor, author, and clinical psychologist. His books include *Telling Yourself the Truth* and *Telling the Truth to Troubled People.*

Dr. Gary R. Collins, a licensed psychologist with a Ph.D. in clinical psychology. Dr. Collins is the author of the widely respected *Christian Counseling: A Comprehensive Guide.*

Dr. Larry Crabb, who holds a Ph.D. in clinical psychology from the University of Illinois. Dr. Crabb is the author of *The Marriage Builder, Inside Out,* and other books.

Frank Minirth, M.D., and **Paul Meier, M.D.**, founders of the Minirth Meier New Life Clinics and authors of over thirty books.

Dr. G. Keith Olson, a respected Christian psychologist and author of *Counseling Teenagers.*

Though the chapters in this book benefit from advice and information from the most respected authorities in Christian counseling, they are not meant to present a comprehensive or infallible treatment of each subject; whole books on each issue could not do that. Neither is this book intended to supplant—or even delay—the counsel of a Christian trained in counseling and crisis intervention. It is a recognition, however, of the fact that thousands of parents, teachers, pastors, and youth workers are already facing situations in which young men and women desperately need wise counsel.

This book is offered to those concerned adults who feel ill-equipped, who feel they are in over their heads, who long for a resource to help them help the kids who come to them. It is offered as a first line of defense for adults who hope to prevent or address the tragedies that too often afflict our youth.

Josh McDowell's Handbook on Counseling Youth presents a perspective that is not available in the many good books for sale in secular bookstores—a biblical, Christ-centered approach to helping teens, one that recognizes the harsh realities of a fallen world but also offers "the light of the knowledge of the glory of God."[5]

This handbook also provides something that is not available in the many excellent Christian books on counseling adults—a guide specifically designed for helping youth, one that recognizes the difficulties *and* possibilities of the adolescent years.

The physical and emotional tumult of the teen years have always presented multiple problems and challenges. But today's youth struggle with many issues that most of their parents and grandparents would find difficult to bear. Many of those teens show incredible resilience in the face of difficult circumstances. Some cope admirably, against all odds. Others, however, become casualties of the dangerous road to adulthood. This book is for all of those young people and for the adults who care about them.

Laying the Foundation

A momentous change has occurred in the church over the past fifty years.

A half-century ago, a great gulf seemed to stretch between the church—which was all about understanding God, Jesus, the Bible, salvation, and sanctification—and psychology, which was concerned with human behavior and helping men and women understand and cope with their problems. Many Christians viewed psychologists and psychotherapists with suspicion, and many psychologists regarded religion—and Christianity in particular—with skepticism or outright hostility.

In the 1950s and 1960s, however, a few Christians—Clyde Narramore, James Dobson, Larry Crabb, Frank Minirth, and Paul Meier among them—began exploring and developing Christian approaches to psychology. They began talking about understanding the tenets and techniques of modern psychology with the Bible's teaching, not substituting the Bible with these tenets and techniques but rather trying to better understand human emotions and relationships in the light of biblical analysis and solutions.

Today, writes Tim Stafford in *Christianity Today*:

> Christian psychology has moved to the center of evangelicalism. Psychologists write best-selling Christian books. Psychologists are prominent on Christian television and radio shows; they are the ones we look to for guidance on family problems and personal growth. . . . A 1991 *Christianity Today* reader survey suggests that evangelicals are far more likely to take problems to a counselor than to a pastor. (Thirty-three percent sought "professional" help, versus 10 percent who looked to a pastor.) . . . Pastors, too, have joined the surge, realizing that their congregations care more for homilies on "Healing the Hurts of the Inner Child" than on "The Missionary Mind of the Apostle Paul." Words like *addiction*, *self-esteem*, and *dysfunctional* sprinkle many Sunday morning sermons. Evangelical seminaries find their counseling departments growing fast. Wheaton College, a bastion of evangelical orthodoxy, is launching its first doctoral program, not in theology or biblical studies, but in psychology.[1]

Despite the growing acceptance of and interest in Christian counseling, however, problems—and protests, and rightly so—still arise, primarily due to one of two extremes.

Two Extreme Reactions

Some highly respected Christian voices attack various attempts to introduce psychological theories and counseling techniques into the church. Some would say, "Jesus is the answer. All we need to do is trust Him and pray more, and everything will be all right." Others might say, "God does not call us to understand our feelings; He calls us to know and obey the will of God."

Others take the opposite extreme. They believe that the only thing most people need is to "get in touch" with their past and everything will turn out okay. Deliverance is found in support groups and Twelve-Step programs. They may turn to the Bible to support their theories and may wrap their ideas in "Christian" terminology, but careful investigation will reveal that their approach is indistinguishable from that of a non-Christian.

The difficulty is that there is truth in both positions and justifiable fears behind their criticisms. Jesus *is* the answer, and obedience to the will of God *is* a key issue; on the other hand, understanding one's past is often revealing, and crises do often require help from other caring humans. But neither extreme—by itself—is biblical, because each approach only presents part of the picture.

Christian psychologist Gary R. Collins writes:

> According to the Bible, Christians are to teach *all* that Christ commanded and taught us. This surely includes doctrines about God, authority, salvation, spiritual growth, prayer, the church, the future, angels, demons and human nature. However, Jesus also taught about marriage, parent-child interactions, obedience, race relations, and freedom for both women and men. And he taught about personal issues such as sex, anxiety, fear, loneliness, doubt, pride, sin, and discouragement.
>
> All of these are issues which bring people for counseling today. When Jesus dealt with such people he frequently listened to the inquirers and accepted them before stimulating them to think or act differently. At times he told people what to do but he also led people to resolve their problems by skillful and divinely guided questioning.[2]

Christians who wish to emulate Jesus, who is our Model in all things, will not only recognize the benefit of preaching to large crowds but will also acknowledge the healing that can take place through one-on-one interactions in which careful listening and sensitive, biblically sound speaking can produce dramatic results.

Nor does the acknowledgement of valuable psychological research and techniques compromise the fact that ultimate healing and wholeness comes from God, through Christ, any more than consulting a physician betrays a lack of faith in God's sovereign love and ability. But just as God often works His wonders through men and women who are trained in medicine, He also frequently performs emotional and mental healing through the listening and communicating techniques of Christian psychologists who are biblically sound.

The Characteristics of Biblical Counseling

Even among Christians who acknowledge the place of counseling in the Church, there is much debate about true biblical counseling (what it is, what it's not, who preaches it, who practices it, who doesn't). It's necessary for the many brilliant, godly men and women in the field to exchange views in an effort to arrive at God-honoring methods for helping others. It's not our purpose here, however, to prove, reprove, or improve upon any of those views.

Nonetheless, there are several assumptions that underlie the content and recommendations contained in this book. These assumptions are based on the principles and teachings of the Bible, God's authoritative, infallible Word, which is the ultimate source of healthy living.

1. God is love (1 John 4:16) and God is truth (John 14:6). His love motivates Him to reveal the truth to us. "The major premise of Christian counseling," writes William Backus, "is that truth makes people free when they believe it and obey it (John 8:31–32). . . . [T]he task in counseling is to replace misbeliefs with truth."[3]

2. Though not all crises or problems are spiritual (in their cause or in their correction), they are interrelated with a person's spiritual beliefs and spiritual state. "Because of the Fall," says Dr. Henry Cloud, "*all* of these problems [depression, panic, guilt, addictions, etc.] are related to the underdeveloped image of God within the soul." Cloud believes, "Emotional wholeness lies in the working out of the image of God within us."[4]

3. A crucial (and integrating) factor in achieving healing and wholeness is a personal relationship with the living Christ. "Relationship with Christ," says Larry Crabb, "provides resources that are utterly indispensable in substantially resolving every psychological (i.e., nonorganically caused) problem."[5] Wholeness cannot be achieved apart from Jesus Christ.

4. Healthy relationships are the linchpins of mental, emotional, and spiritual health. Many of the crises faced by today's youth are inextricably related to relationships—with parents, with siblings and other relatives, with friends, with mentors, and even with God. Loneliness, low self-esteem, peer pressure, rebellion, homosexuality, underachievement, and other problems have their basis in unhealthy or broken relationships.

5. Healing of the mind, emotions, and spirit is possible. It will almost certainly require work on the part of the counselor and counselee (and perhaps others in the counselee's circle of family and friends). It will also necessarily involve the work of God through the Holy Spirit. It may take a considerable amount of time. But the God who restored an entire nation that had been conquered and broken[6] can also restore to emotional wholeness a young man or woman who turns to Him.

6. The goal of biblical counseling is not happiness, but Christlikeness. Larry Crabb writes, "Many of us place top priority, not on becoming Christlike in the middle of our problems, but on finding happiness. I want to be happy but the paradoxical truth is that I will never be happy if I am concerned primarily with becoming happy. My overriding goal must be in every circumstance to respond biblically, to put the Lord first, to seek to behave as He would want me to. The wonderful truth is that. . . . if I will obediently abide in truth in order to become more like God and thus make Him known, the by-product will be my eventual happiness."[7]

7. Healing and wholeness will not come without sound biblical teaching and obedience to the Word and will of God. John MacArthur sounds the alarm about those who try to substitute psychological techniques in place of biblical teaching and understanding:

> If one is a truly Christian psychologist, he must do soul work in the realm of the deep things of the Word and the Spirit and not be following around in the shallows of behavior modification. Why should a believer choose to do behavior modification when he has the tools for spiritual transformation? This would be like a surgeon wreaking havoc with a butter knife instead of using a scalpel. The most skilled counselor is the one who most carefully, prayerfully, and faithfully applies the divine spiritual resources to the process of sanctification, shaping another into the image of Jesus Christ.[8]

The man or woman who seeks to help youth in crisis must make every effort to develop sound biblical tenets and techniques for such a ministry of comfort and communication. More important than techniques, however, will be a thorough and constant reliance upon the Holy Spirit of God. As Jay Adams has written:

Methodology and technique, skill and the exercise of gifts are all consonant with the work of the Spirit. What makes the difference is one's attitude and inner motivation: does he do what he does in reliance upon his own efforts, in dependence upon methods and techniques, or does he acknowledge his own inability and ask the Spirit to use his gifts and methods? Gifts, methodology and technique, of course, may be abused; they may be set over against the Spirit and may be used to replace his work. But they may also be used in complete subjection to him to the glory of God and the benefit of his children.[9]

May each caring Christian who uses this handbook so rely on the Holy Spirit to the glory of God and the benefit of His children.

Learning to Offer Christian Counsel

Many years ago, an aging Jew named Paul took an interest in a younger man named Timothy. Over the course of several years, Paul helped his young friend deal with shyness and a reluctance to use his gifts and exert leadership in the church.[1]

Similarly, a successful Christian evangelist named Barnabas took his relative, John Mark, under his wings and shepherded the sometimes inconstant young man until Mark became a respected servant of the church.[2]

Mordecai counseled his young cousin Hadassah, who was also called Esther, even after she became queen of Persia and Media.[3] Naomi helped her widowed daughter-in-law, Ruth, find a loving husband.[4] Moses trained the younger Joshua, the son of Nun, to take over the leadership of God's people.[5]

None of those people were trained in psychotherapy. None of them possessed a graduate degree in counseling. They weren't trained theologians, but they were versed in the Scriptures and led by God in helping younger persons—some of them quite young, perhaps—to overcome difficulties and fulfill God's loving purpose for them.

Many teachers, youth workers, pastors, and parents are in similar positions today. A parent consoles a seventeen-year-old who didn't get asked to the prom. A teacher discovers a seventh-grader is disturbed and distracted by his parents' impending divorce. A pastor prays silently beside the hospital bed of a teenage girl who attempted suicide. A volunteer church youth worker chats over fries and a Coke with a high school senior about his options for college.

Adults in such positions may feel inadequate in knowledge or spiritual experience. They may fear doing or saying something that might end up being harmful to the young person. But many are already performing a crucial ministry of comforting and guiding young people in crisis. They may not be formally trained to handle such situations, but countless Christians are repeatedly called upon to offer godly guidance to a teen or preteen.

The Qualifications for Ministering to Youth

William Backus, a Christian minister and psychologist, says:

> Who can counsel? Doubtless, every human being who has any kind of warm relationship will find himself counseling occasionally, since people naturally help one another, listen to one another, ask and give advice.[6]

No matter how uninformed, ill-equipped, and unqualified we may feel, many of us are confronted with the questions and situations that our youth today are facing. We may not be sure what the qualifications for the job might be, but many of us are utterly convinced that we don't have what it takes.

What *are* the qualifications for ministering to youth? What does it take to comfort and guide hurting fourteen-year-olds and searching eighteen-year-olds? What skills and characteristics should we develop or cultivate in order to more effectively help youth in crisis? Dr. G. Keith Olson writes:

> [Research shows that] counseling is most effective when the counselor possesses three personal characteristics: accurate empathy, non-possessive warmth and genuineness.[7]

Empathy. A parent, youth leader, or other adult who hopes to effectively counsel young people must develop or cultivate "accurate empathy," as Olson terms it. He writes:

> Fifteen-year-old Anne is struggling to tell her story to her counselor. Three days ago she had her first sexual experience. She was raped. Filled with violent conflicting feelings, fighting back uncontrollable nausea and experiencing utter confusion, she haltingly tells her story. How does the counselor help? Platitudes will not work. Reassurances that "everything will be okay" fall meaninglessly to the floor. Reading scripture to her would proba-

bly increase her sense of worthlessness. And praying with her too soon would likely cause her to feel isolated.

> What then can the counselor say to her? Typically, the most helpful initial responses are empathic expressions of understanding: "It's terribly hard to put such strong feelings into words." "It makes you sick to your stomach every time you think about what happened." "Everything seems so confused now." "You were so scared." "You felt so alone, defenseless and helpless." . . .

> The counselor's empathy has a healing impact on the counselee . . . [and reflects] a deep understanding of the troubled counselee's private world [that] engenders a sense that maybe someone really does understand. Maybe someone really does care.[8]

Warmth. "The effective counselor," says Olson, "genuinely cares about the happiness and well-being of the counselee. There is a sense of liking that begins to win the teenager's trust. More importantly, as he or she experiences being valued and cared about, the counselee begins to develop an internal basis for self-value and self-love. 'If my counselor cares about me, then maybe I am worth something after all.'"[9]

Jesus exemplified this type of accepting, caring, loving warmth. He exhibited a sincere interest in the people He met[10] and felt genuine concern and compassion for them.[11] People trusted Him, turned to Him, and confided in Him because the warmth of His care and concern invited them to do so.

Genuineness. Dr. Gary R. Collins cites the same research and the same qualifications for counseling as Olson and says, "The genuine counselor is 'for real'—an open, sincere person who avoids phoniness or the playing of some superior role. Genuineness implies spontaneity without impulsiveness and honesty without cruel confrontation. It means the helper is deeply himself or herself—not thinking or feeling one thing and saying something different."[12]

Beyond these qualifications (which may be possessed by a non-Christian, as well as a Christian, counselor), the adult seeking to effectively counsel youth will also wish to develop or cultivate the following:

A Humble Spirit. Much damage can be done by a counselor who is arrogant or self-centered, or who thinks (or acts like) he or she knows everything. Such a proud and haughty spirit, if it doesn't drive a troubled teenager away, may create far more problems than it solves. A humble spirit, on the other hand, seeks to understand more than to be understood. "A humble spirit," writes Olson, "is not overly eager to give advice. The counselor supports the teenager's search for his or her own answers and direction. A humble spirit focuses the counseling around the thinking and feeling experience of the counselee. Little attention is centered on the skill, expertise or wisdom of the counselor."[13]

Emotional Stability. Perfection is not required of a counselor; if it were, of course, churches and counseling centers would look like ghost towns of the American West. But men or women who hope to effectively counsel youth should be emotionally stable themselves. Adolescents, whether they are visibly in crisis or not, are riding an emotional roller coaster, and they will not be helped by a counselor who is also struggling for control.

Relationship with Jesus Christ. For many reasons, a personal relationship with and reliance upon the Lord Jesus Christ is crucial for anyone who intends to counsel others. There will be times when only the Holy Spirit of God can provide insight into a problem or solution. There will be moments when a supernatural supply of patience or perseverance is needed. There will be situations in which the only prescription is prayer and dependence upon the forgiveness and grace of God. For these and many other reasons, a close relationship with Christ is crucial to an effective ministry of comfort and communication.

Reliance on the Holy Spirit. Any adult who works with youth will encounter questions and situations that tax his or her knowledge and patience. The man or woman who relies on his or her own resources can never be equal to the task. But the caring adult who recognizes his or her inadequacy, who consults God in prayer, and who at every step relies upon the Spirit's wisdom, grace, and power will be a "channel of blessing" to the young person in need of help.

Knowledge of Fundamental Biblical Teaching. A counselor of youth does not need a seminary degree (though it certainly wouldn't hurt), but a knowledge of the Bible and its central precepts and principles is vital. "If you don't know that in God's kingdom it is considered higher and better to serve than to be served," Backus explains, "you're likely going to teach worldly values to others without even knowing the difference. If you haven't discovered that chastening has a primary place in the Christian life, you won't be able to help others who are experiencing such dealings of God. Being well-versed in biblical truth is the most basic requirement [for counseling]."[14] It's important to understand, however, the further necessity of a meaningful and faithful devotional life that includes reading and studying God's Word. It is one thing to know God's Word and another thing entirely to live and experience the Word daily in your own life.

The above are not the only skills or traits that will assist an adult in helping youth; Collins points out that "the good counselor, for example, is able to get along efficiently, having a relative absence of immobilizing conflicts, hang-ups, insecurities or personal problems. The effective counselor is also compassionate, interested in people, alert to his or her own feelings and motives, more self-revealing than self-concealing, and knowledgeable in the field of counseling."[15] However, the seven traits mentioned above (empathy, warmth, genuineness, humility, stability, relationship with Christ, reliance on the Holy Spirit, and knowledge of the Bible's teachings), combined with the information and recommendations contained in this book, can help a concerned pastor, parent, youth leader, or teacher reach out to youth in a way that can prevent or address the many crises today's kids face.

The Object of Ministering to Youth

Larry Crabb says, "As I listen to many patients and introspect about my own goals when struggling with a personal problem, it seems to me that the usual objective so passionately desired is fundamentally self-centered: 'I want to feel good' or 'I want to be happy.'

"Now there is nothing wrong in wanting to be happy. An obsessive preoccupation with 'my happiness,' however, often obscures our understanding of the biblical route to deep, abiding joy."[16]

Many caring adults believe the object of comforting or advising a young person is to make that young man or woman happy. The object of ministering to youth, however, is not happiness but wholeness.

1. Spiritual Wholeness. The first object in working with youth is and must be spiritual wholeness. The centrality of a real, personal, thriving relationship with Jesus Christ cannot be overemphasized. Moreover, as Crabb writes, "Paul wrote in Colossians 1:28 that his verbal interaction with people (counseling?) always was designed to promote Christian maturity. Only the maturing believer is entering more deeply into the ultimate purpose of his life, namely, worship and service. Biblical counseling therefore will adopt as its major strategy the promotion of spiritual . . . maturity. When we talk with other believers, we must always have in our minds the purpose of assisting them to become more mature so they can better please God."[17]

2. Emotional Wholeness. Another purpose of ministering to youth, and one intrinsically related to spiritual wholeness, is the promoting of emotional wholeness. Dr. Henry Cloud points out that emotional problems such as depression, panic, and feelings of guilt are related to "the underdeveloped image of God within the soul." Emotional wholeness, Cloud believes, "lies in the working out of the image of God within us."[18]

Teens or preteens who are being guided to spiritual maturity in Christ can also be helped toward emotional wholeness, toward an understanding and healing of the emotional problems that plague them.

3. Relational Wholeness. Another goal of ministering to youth is the promotion of relational wholeness. So much of the pain and dysfunction suffered by youth today is a result of unhealthy or broken relationships. Key among these is the parental relationship. A major goal of any adult who cares for young people is to achieve healing and restoration of that young person's relationships—first with God, then with parents, then with others.

The Techniques of Ministering to Youth

The English word *technique* is derived from the Greek word *techne*, which means "skill." Any adult who has worked with adolescents will recognize that certain skills are necessary, and anyone who has attempted to offer guidance to another person will acknowledge that how the guidance is given will, in large measure, dictate how well it is received and acted upon.

Gary Collins, a recognized authority in Christian counseling, identifies five basic techniques that will be useful to any person seeking to offer comfort and guidance to another:

1. Attending. The counselor must try to give undivided attention to the counselee. This is done through (a) eye contact, looking without staring as a way to convey concern and understanding; (b) posture, which should be relaxed . . . and often involves leaning toward the counselee; and (c) gestures that are natural but not excessive or distracting. . . .

2. *Listening.* This involves more than giving passive or half-hearted notice to the words that come from another person. Effective listening is an active process. It involves:

- Being able to set aside your own conflicts, biases, and preoccupations so you can concentrate on what the counselee is communicating.

- Avoiding subtle verbal or nonverbal expressions of disapproval or judgment about what is being said, even when the content is offensive.

- Using both your eyes and your ears to detect messages that come from the tone of voice, posture, gestures, facial expressions, and other nonverbal clues.

- Hearing not only what the counselee says, but noticing what gets left out.

- Waiting patiently through periods of silence or tears as the counselee summons enough courage to share something painful or pauses to collect his or her thoughts and regain composure.

- Looking at the counselee as he or she speaks, but without either staring or letting your eyes wander. . . .

- Realizing that you can accept the counselee even though you may not condone his or her actions, values, or beliefs. . . .

3. *Responding.* It should not be assumed that the counselor listens and does nothing else. . . .

Leading is a skill by which the counselor gently directs the conversation. "What happened next?" "Tell me what you mean by . . ." are brief questions that can steer the discussion in directions that will give useful information.

Reflecting is a way of letting counselees know we are "with them" and able to understand how they feel or think. "You must feel . . . " or "I bet that was frustrating," or "That must have been fun" reflect what is going on in counseling. Be careful not to reflect after every statement; do it periodically. . . . The counselor may summarize feelings ("That must have hurt") and/or general themes of what has been said ("From all of this it sounds like you have had a whole string of failures"). Whenever you make a comment, give the counselee time and opportunity to respond to what you have said.

Questioning, if done skillfully, can bring forth a great deal of useful information. The best questions are those that require at least a sentence or two to answer (e.g., ..."What sorts of things are making you unhappy?") rather than those that can be answered in one word (. . . "Are you unhappy?" . . .). . . .

Confronting is not the same as attacking or viciously condemning another person. When we confront, we present some idea to the counselee that he or she might not see otherwise. Counselees can be confronted with sin in their lives, failures, inconsistencies, excuses, harmful attitudes, or self-defeating behavior. Confrontation is best done in a loving, gentle, nonjudgmental manner. . . .

Informing involves giving facts to people who need information. Try to avoid giving too much information at any one time; be clear, and remember that when people are hurting they respond best to information that is relevant to their immediate needs or concerns. . . .

Supporting and encouraging are important parts of any counseling situation, especially at the beginning. . . . Support includes guiding the counselee to take stock of his or her spiritual and emotional resources, and helping with any problems or failures that come as a result of this action.

4. *Teaching.* All of these techniques are specialized forms of psychological education. The counselor is an educator, teaching by instruction,

by example, and by guiding the counselee as he or she learns by experience to cope with the problems of life. . . .

5. *Filtering.* Good counselors are not skeptical people who disbelieve everything a counselee says, but it is wise to remember that counselees don't always tell the whole story and don't always say what they really want or need. . . . As you counsel, therefore, mentally try to sort through the counselee's words. What is he or she really asking? What does this person really want . . . ? Are there problems other than the ones that are being presented? . . .

All of this points again to the counselor's need for wisdom and discernment. Some of this comes with experience, but Christians know that sensitivity more often comes when we pray, asking for the insights, guidance, and accurate perception that comes from the Holy Spirit.[19]

The Limitations of Ministering to Youth

The adult who seeks to comfort, encourage, and minister to youth must be aware of his or her limitations and obligations.

First, in any effort to help a young person manage a crisis or reach a major decision, the involvement of that youth's parents is crucial. A wise pastor, youth pastor, teacher, or youth worker will be extremely sensitive to the parents' biblical and legal authority over the young person. Any effort to advise or guide a teen without the knowledge, approval, and/or involvement of his or her parents is likely to fail or, at the very least, present thorny ethical and practical problems for the youth and the adult. Consequently, except in cases where such involvement is clearly impossible or unwise (as in cases of parental abuse, for example), it should be the youth worker's goal to bridge any gap between parent and child as soon as possible.

The issue of confidentiality may arise in many of the circumstances addressed in this book. In most states and provinces, conversations with members of the clergy are considered privileged and can be kept confidential even in a court of law. For all others, however, the issue of confidentiality can pose problems. A teen who comes to a teacher or youth worker for counsel will most often do so only if he or she is confident that the adult can be trusted with personal information, and caring adults will certainly wish to be worthy of such trust. However, while an adult must exhibit the utmost integrity in such situations, he or she must never promise not to tell anyone without hearing the whole story; in some states and provinces, that adult will be legally obligated to report instances of abuse or illegal behavior, for example.

States and provinces have varying laws addressing the obligation of certain professionals (counselors, pastors, teachers, etc.) to notify parents before any treatment is given to a young person. Collins writes, "Laws covering [various] counseling issues vary from place to place and frequently the statutes change. If you counsel infrequently, informally, or within the confines of a church or educational institution, you probably are exempt from many of the laws that apply to professional counselors. If you counsel frequently, however, it would be wise to check with a lawyer to determine how local laws could influence and perhaps limit your counseling."[20]

Furthermore, anyone seeking to help youth must be aware of the risks involved in such a ministry of comfort and communication and must take steps to minimize risks posed by:

• *Manipulation.* Troubled youth can be adept at manipulating adults. Some youth workers, teachers, parents, and pastors may sometimes find themselves doing all manner of things with and for the young person—things that go far beyond their appropriate roles. Collins suggests asking, "Am I being manipulated?" "Am I going beyond my responsibilities?" and "What does this [person] really want?" This should be done not only to protect the adult but also to promote the best for the young person, because manipulation seldom produces positive results.

• *Dependence.* The development of an attitude of dependence upon the caring person is often the result of a helping relationship. The young person may show an increasing demand for the adult's time and attention and an increasing reliance on his or her approval and advice. Such dependence is contrary to the caring adult's primary objectives of spiritual, emotional, and relational wholeness.

• *Countertransference.* Collins says, "Countertransference occurs when the counselor's own needs interfere with the therapeutic relationship. When the counseling session becomes a place for solving your own problems, counselees are not likely to be helped."[21] This can be especially dangerous when the interaction involves a member of the opposite sex. For this reason, it is strongly recommended that a pastor, youth pastor, teacher, or youth worker limit his or her interaction with members of the opposite sex. A male youth pastor, for example, will be wise to refer girls to his wife or to a mature Christian woman in the church at the earliest possible moment and so avoid not only the appearance of evil,[22] but the opportunity as well.[23]

Several words of wisdom will help a man or woman avoid unnecessary risks in ministering to young people:

• Never counsel anyone—male or female— behind closed doors; meet in public places that offer the opportunity for "private" conversation, such as a school cafeteria, park, or restaurant.
• Set clear limits regarding your involvement, particularly if dependence is beginning to develop; for example, how often do you meet with the young person? Is he or she allowed to call you at home? Anytime? Under what circumstances? For what purpose? Such limits are not intended to separate the adult and the youth but to help

the adult be as objective and, therefore, as helpful as possible to the youth.
• Limit interaction with members of the opposite sex to group settings. If you must interact with a member of the opposite sex, take along a third party, a trusted companion.
• Be alert to signs that you are being manipulated or exploited—Are you doing things for the young person that he could and should be doing himself, for example?—and redefine healthy boundaries in your relationship.
• Make your obligations and limitations clear to the young person. You might say, for example, "No, I can't promise not to tell your parents, but I'll go with you if you would rather tell them yourself." Do not make promises you can't keep, and don't foster expectations you can't meet.

"The counselor must maintain a vigilant attitude," Collins says, "if he or she is to avoid hazards. . . . As Christian helpers we honor God by doing the best job possible, by apologizing when we make mistakes, and by using our mistakes as learning situations and stepping stones to improvement."[24]

The final step in recognizing and handling one's obligations and limitations involves the matter of referral. It will occasionally become apparent, in working with youth, that the crisis is so urgent or complex as to require professional help. At other times, the young person's problems may appear obstinate but not necessarily life-threatening. How does a concerned adult know if (and when) referral to a professional counselor is warranted? While some of the chapters in this book offer direction relative to the specific problem being addressed, Gary D. Bennett offers general guidance:

When should you ask for help . . . ? Whenever the teenager requests or indicates in other ways that he needs help, whenever you feel you can no longer handle the situation, or whenever the teenager's behavior may have harmful long-term consequences. For example, chronic unhappiness, behavior problems (e.g., lying, stealing, running away), feelings of worthlessness, and continuing depression or loneliness may be reasons for referral. Often a few counseling sessions with a professional will be all that is needed.[25]

Sandi Black, a crisis counselor at local and middle schools in Texas, advises referral to a trained counselor if several of the following signs (or a repeated pattern of some of these signs) are present:

Behavioral Signs
- Sudden outbursts of temper
- Repeated stealing, cheating, lying
- Excessive fighting, setting up power struggles
- Hyperactivity/nervousness
- Excessive daydreaming/preoccupation with fantasy
- Excessive blaming of others/irresponsibility
- Compulsive mannerisms
- Constant defiance of rules

Emotional Signs
- Decline in academics, rise in problems at school
- Suspicious and distrusting of others
- Talk about running away
- Preoccupation with physical/sexual topics
- Attention-span difficulty
- Erratic, unpredictable behavior
- New "questionable" friends
- Excessive jealousy toward peers, siblings
- Anger, hitting objects or other people
- Significant change in motivation
- Loss of interest in once enjoyable activities

Physical Signs
- Poor physical hygiene
- Marked change in weight or appearance
- Overly accident prone
- Lack of appetite or overindulgence in food
- Sleep disorders/nightmares
- Frequent illness, headaches, stomachaches[26]

Keep in mind that any of the above conditions—even several of them—do not of themselves indicate the existence of a deep psy-chological problem. When more than a few exist or recur, however, referral may be warranted. Joan Sturkie and Valerie Gibson offer wise guidance to follow when the decision has been made to refer the teen to a professional:

1. Learn what resources are available in your community so the most appropriate place or person may be contacted.

2. Check with the community resources before referring, so you will know that an opening is available for your counselee.

3. Let your counselee know why you feel he or she should be referred while at the same time [giving] as much support as possible.

4. Explain to your counselee the reason for each of the referral options you've shared with him or her.

5. Involve the counselee as much as possible in the decision to refer. If the counselee "claims ownership" for the decision, he or she will probably be more faithful in keeping scheduled appointments.

6. Encourage the counselee to make his or her own appointment, for you may not have the information needed to schedule such an appointment.

7. Help the counselee plan how he or she will get to the appointment, and decide if another person is needed to go along.

8. Show your continuing care for the counselee even after he or she has been referred, and be ready to support the counselee during and after the time he or she is seeing a professional.[27]

The wise parent, teacher, pastor, or youth leader will carefully and prayerfully research community resources and potential counselors. Even highly qualified professionals may not "fit" the needs of a struggling teen or the requirements of the concerned Christian who is referring the young person. The following suggestions may help a caring adult make a wise choice in referral:

1. *Ask for referrals:* Request recommendations from a pastor or a trusted friend—someone

who is nonjudgmental and will not betray the confidence of the person who is asking.

2. *Examine directories:* See a directory of Christian counselors; otherwise, look in the Yellow Pages or telephone a "hotline" (many Christian providers of inpatient therapy also staff hotlines 24 hours a day that can provide names and telephone numbers of Christian counselors in the caller's community or geographical area).

3. *Ask questions on the following topics when arranging an appointment:*

Spiritual qualifications—what does a potential counselor mean by identifying him- or herself as a "Christian counselor"?

Educational and professional qualifications— does the counselor have a graduate degree from an accredited (not just state-approved), reputable university or seminary? In what field of study? Is this person licensed . . . or certified . . . ?

Experience level—how long has the counselor been providing services? . . . What methods does the counselor use? Does he or she have an area of specialty or particular expertise?

Rates—is there a set fee or a sliding scale? Is health insurance accepted? When is payment for services expected? . . .

4. *Pay attention to first impressions.* . . . Is it apparent that the office or counseling center is staffed by Christians? Are clients treated with courtesy, warmth, and respect by everyone from the receptionist to the counselor? Are intake procedures, including forms to be com-

pleted and signed, professional yet clear? Is confidentiality assured?

5. *Ask additional questions.* . . . For example, does the counselor have previous experience with a specific problem? . . .

6. *Above all, pray for wisdom* in locating a Christian counselor who will help carry the burdens of the person in need and help resolve his or her problems.[28]

In addition to the above, the following resources may help concerned adults locate reputable, Christian counseling professionals and treatment centers in their areas:

(800) NEW-LIFE
The Minirth Meier New Life Clinics, a national network of Christian counseling centers

(800) 883-HOPE
New Hope Counseling Centers, a network of twelve Christian counseling centers in the eastern United States

(800) 5-COUNSEL
The American Association of Christian Counselors, an association of nearly five thousand professional, pastoral, and lay counselors

(909) 695-2277
The Christian Association for Psychological Studies (CAPS), an association of approximately twenty-three hundred Christian psychologists, psychiatrists, counselors, pastors, teachers, researchers, and students

EMOTIONAL

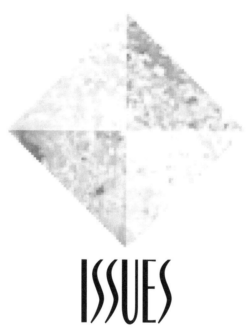

ISSUES

1

LONELINESS

A Synopsis

❖

Introduction

Marie is typical of many freshman girls. She was an only child who grew up with much stress in her home. Her dad was emotionally unstable. Marie tried to be understanding; she reasoned that her dad had enough to worry about just taking care of his own problems, but she often longed for someone who would treat her as a special person. She reached her teen years wondering if a man would ever pay attention to her, let alone love her. When she entered high school, her parents divorced, and she and her mom had to move to a new city so her mom could get a decent job.

"It was hard making friends at my new school," Marie explained later. "Actually, I never did make any girlfriends. And home wasn't much better. Mom was gone most of the time. I thought I would die from the loneliness.

"That's why I was so surprised—overjoyed, really—when Mark asked me out."

Marie and Mark began dating. Mark was older and more experienced, and before long he started pressuring Marie to have sex with him. Marie knew other girls at school who were sexually involved, and this added to her turmoil.

"There was no way I wanted to go back to the way things were before Mark," she says. "If I had lost Mark, I would have been lonelier than before."

Mark had filled a lonely void in Marie's life, so rather than lose him, she consented to have sex with him. Marie needed acceptance, and she thought her physical relationship with Mark would make her feel wanted. She and Mark still date, and they still have sex together. But Marie knows Mark also dates other girls. And she's still lonely.

The Problem of Loneliness

"Loneliness," writes Charles Durham, "is a painful state of mind, a feeling deep in the pit of your stomach. It may be mildly irritating or totally incapacitating."[1] Dr. Gary R. Collins adds:

Loneliness is the painful awareness that we lack meaningful contact with others. It involves a feeling of inner emptiness which can be accompanied by sadness, discouragement, a sense of isolation, restlessness, anxiety, and an intense desire to be wanted and needed by someone.[2]

Loneliness is an uncommonly common problem. It exists everywhere, among all kinds of people. As Durham noted:

One survey revealed that one of every four respondents said they had been lonely within the preceding few weeks, and one out of nine reported severe loneliness in the week immediately past.[3]

A study by psychoanalyst Michael Whitenburgh, who runs stress clinics in Liverpool and London, England, revealed that the greatest fear of Britons—beyond claustrophobia, beyond the fear of insects, beyond the fear of flying—is the fear of loneliness.[4] And one psychologist, when asked about the relation between loneliness and sickness, responded, "That's like asking if *air* is related to health."

As prevalent (and destructive) as loneliness is among the adult population, it is even more pronounced among youth. And loneliness—particularly to a young person—can be overwhelming, consuming, and devastating.

It has been reported that of all people in our nation, the adolescent has the most problems with loneliness. The teen years are the time in life when the need for social acceptance is at its peak. Adolescents regard themselves as no longer children, and most are making efforts to become more independent from their family. Ties with peer groups are extremely important. And the resulting pressure can be tremendous. Even if a teenager has a pleasant family atmosphere, loneliness can be a great problem if there are inadequate ties with other teens.[5]

Psychologist Gary Collins's summary of another Christian psychologist's views offers important insight into the topic of loneliness.

Christian psychologist Craig Ellison has suggested that there are three kinds of loneliness: emotional, social, and existential.

Emotional loneliness "involves the lack or loss of a psychologically intimate relationship with another person or persons. The emotionally lonely person feels utterly alone and can only recover by establishing new in-depth relationships with others.

Social loneliness is the feeling of aimlessness, anxiety and emptiness. The person feels that he or she is "out of it" and on the margin of life. Instead of an in-depth relationship with a specific companion, the socially lonely person needs a supportive group of accepting friends and skill in relating to others.

Existential loneliness refers to the sense of isolation which comes to the person who is separated from God and who feels that life has no meaning or purpose. Such persons need a committed and growing relationship with God, preferably within the confines of a concerned community of believers.[6]

The Causes of Loneliness

Loneliness may have many and varied causes, and identifying the causes in a specific situation is most often a job for a highly trained professional. However, some exposure to the possible influences on a young person who is feeling acute loneliness may nonetheless be helpful for the youth leader or adviser.

◆ Low Self-Esteem

Studies by Levin and Stokes (1986) and Peplau and Perlman (1982) suggest that poor self-concepts and low self-esteem—including "negative evaluations of their own bodies, sexuality, health, appearance, behavior, and functioning"[7]—contribute to a young person's vulnerability to feelings of loneliness. (See also chapter 6, "Unhealthy Self-Esteem.") As Collins writes, "When we have little confidence in ourselves it is difficult to build friendships. The person is unable to give love without apologizing; neither can he or she receive love without cutting oneself down."[8]

◆ Poor Family Relationships

A number of studies suggest that family background is a crucial factor in a young person's vulnerability to loneliness. James J. Ponzetti Jr. writes:

> Lonely students recall poorer relationships with their parents and childhood friends. They also remember less family togetherness (Paloutzian & Ellison, 1982). Mahon (1982) and Hecht and Baum (1984) noted significant correlations between loneliness and disrupted patterns of attachment suggesting that the lack of bonding early in life may contribute to the experience of loneliness.[9]

◆ Societal Factors

In their book *Why Be Lonely?* Carter, Meier, and Minirth write:

> We live in a society that tends to promote loneliness. Our society is fast, mobile, and changing. Every year 20 percent of the families in America move. On Manhattan, one can come in contact with hundreds of thousands of people in a very brief time span. Although we may come in contact with thousands, there is not enough time to build relationships, and so people are lonely.
>
> Also, because of television there is much less time for personal communication. Even what little time people have for each other in our mobile society is often spent in loneliness in front of a television set. Research shows that excessive tele-

vision watching also causes individuals to trust others less and thus promotes even more loneliness. Our changing society also has produced a new set of values, such as excessive individualism and independence, that encourages loneliness.[10]

◆ Temporary or Changing Circumstances

Sometimes youth are lonely because of their circumstances: a girl whose boyfriend "dumps" her; an unathletic boy whose closest friends' time is consumed with football camp, practices, and games; a university freshman who has not yet made new friends; a teen whose family has moved to a new neighborhood, leaving many friends behind. Such situational loneliness is often temporary, however (particularly in the case of youth).

◆ Attitudes

Dr. Paul Tournier, the Swiss psychologist, pointed out in his book *Escape from Loneliness* that loneliness often results from:

- parliamentary attitudes in which we see life as a big tournament with success as the winner's prize and competition as a way of life;

- independent attitudes which cause us to act as if we were each rugged individualists, absolutely autonomous, independent of God and of others;

- possessive attitudes by which we are driven to get what we can for ourselves; and

- demanding attitudes which cause us to fight for our rights and demand "fairness."[11]

◆ Fear

Dr. Gary Collins writes:

> In my office there hangs a plaque which reads, "People are lonely because they build walls instead of bridges." Of course, this isn't the only reason for loneliness, but sometimes individuals do erect barriers to keep others out. Often this is done because of fear of intimacy, fear of being

known, fear of rejection or fear of being hurt—as we may have been hurt in the past. The loneliness is painful but for such people it is no less painful than the fear and insecurity of reaching out to others.[12] [See also chapter 2, "Anxiety."]

◆ Hostility

Some people are lonely because they harbor feelings of anger and bitterness that alienate others and drive them away. Such alienation, of course, often produces further frustration and anger, deepening the person's loneliness in a whirlpool of self-defeating emotions and reactions.

◆ Inability to Communicate

Collins points out that an inability or unwillingness to communicate is sometimes at the root of a person's loneliness:

> Communication breakdowns are at the root of many, perhaps most, interpersonal problems. When people are unwilling to communicate, or when they don't know how to communicate honestly, there is a persisting isolation and loneliness even though individuals may be surrounded by others.[13]

◆ Spiritual Causes

Saint Augustine prayed, "Thou hast made us for Thyself, and the heart of man is restless until it finds its rest in Thee." Some loneliness results from estrangement from God. An individual in open rebellion against God will often feel a deep existential loneliness (to use Ellison's distinction) that can only be corrected by filling that God-shaped void that exists in every human heart "until it finds its rest" in Him. The same loneliness often results from unconfessed sin or even from a casual negligence of God's care and His claims on one's life.

◆ Other Causes of Loneliness

Ellison, in his book *Loneliness: The Search for Intimacy*, lists possible causes of loneliness, from which the following list is adapted:

- Shyness
- Feeling misunderstood
- Unresolved conflict with someone
- Feeling unneeded
- Physical separation from loved ones
- Feeling you don't belong
- Rejection
- Physical illness
- Criticism by an influential person
- Busyness
- Death of a friend or loved one
- Desiring a relationship that isn't happening
- Breakup of a relationship

The Effects of Loneliness

Loneliness affects young people in many and varied ways. The following elaboration of the effects of loneliness may not only serve as warning but may also help equip a youth leader or concerned individual to spot the problem, which may in turn lead to a successful response to the problem.

◆ Physical Effects

Ira J. Tanner's book *Loneliness—The Fear of Love* records some of the physical effects of loneliness:

> Loneliness has a way of infecting every fiber of our being: our hopes, ambitions, dreams, vitality, desires, wants, as well as our actual physical bodies. Eating and sleeping are frequently affected. Obesity and greed may well be symptoms of loneliness, although a loss of weight can also be traced to despair that goes with a feeling of being of no importance or worth to anyone, not even to ourselves. The misery of loneliness may manifest itself in aches (imagined or real) in the body. Weakness in the legs is not uncommon, stemming from the heavy burden of fear that we are carrying on our backs. Stooped shoulders, turned-down corners of

the mouth, a slow and painful walk, silence and withdrawal—all bear testimony to the disease.[14]

◆ Spiritual Effects

Persons suffering with extreme loneliness will often feel out of fellowship with God, estranged from Him, perhaps even deserted by Him. Carter, Meier, and Minirth speak to this in their book *Why Be Lonely?*

> Because of our human imperfections, we are bound to fall short of a state of constant communion with God. However, it is possible to feel a sense of consistency and security when there is a well-established relationship with God through Jesus Christ. Unfortunately, the person who suffers from loneliness does not allow himself to grasp the inner peace found in this relationship. . . . He feels [far] away from God. . . . A person who chronically suffers from spiritual loneliness is either not a Christian, or he is a Christian who is not fully in touch with the saving grace of God that exists in him in the person of Jesus Christ.[15]

◆ Low Self-Esteem

In the cruel cycle that loneliness creates, low self-esteem and a poor self-concept can be not only a cause but also an effect of loneliness. Lonely youth report feelings of emptiness, hopelessness, and worthlessness. As their loneliness deepens, they come to view themselves as unloved and unlovable. They view their lack of friendships as a personal failure, a reflection of their unworthiness. Such people sometimes withdraw into self-pity, self-centeredness, and self-abuse.

◆ Dependence

Carter, Meier, and Minirth write:

> People who have constant bouts with loneliness often fall into the overly dependent style of life. . . . An overly dependent person . . . becomes excessively distraught if he is rejected by someone. He clings to people, sucking up all their emotional energy. He is unaware of the potential strength that lies within himself to make the most out of life, and to withstand trying times. . . . Dependent persons tend to follow a predictable progression in their relationships. They first *discount* their own abilities to take charge of their emotional lives. Second, they *expect* others to fulfill their needs for them. Then they begin to *make demands* of those on whom they depend. Naturally, this causes others to retreat from them, keeping at a distance. The dependent person finds himself back at square one, and usually continues the cycle endlessly.[16]

◆ Depression and Despair

Loneliness breeds depression, which can lead to despair and, in some cases, to suicide. Youth often keep their problems and feelings bottled up inside, fearing to express how they feel or not knowing *how* to express how they feel, increasing their sense of aloneness and heightening the despair they feel. The self-pity and alienation that often characterize chronic loneliness become a cycle of self-defeating attitudes leading the sufferer ever deeper into what seems like a black hole of hopelessness. (See also chapter 5, "Depression.")

◆ Violence

Author W. A. Sadler has suggested violence as an occasional result of loneliness:

> Further investigations will bear out this tentative conclusion: very lonely people, who get angry rather than depressed, will be prone to express their lonely frustration in destructive ways. I do not think it is mere coincidence that we are witnessing an unequalled rise in violence and at the same time loneliness is so pervasive and intense.[17]

◆ Substance Abuse

Alcohol and drugs often seem to be attractive means of escape to a chronic sufferer of loneliness, and many turn to substance abuse in an attempt to "drown their sorrows" or in a misguided attempt to make friends of other abusers. Such behavior, of course, fails to produce the desired result and adds yet another problem to the loneliness. (See also chapters 38, "Alcoholism," and 39, "Drug Abuse.")

The Biblical Perspective of Loneliness

"Loneliness," said the blind poet John Milton, "is the first thing which God's eye named not good." When God surveyed His creation at the dawn of human history, He declared, "It is not good for the man to be alone. I will make a helper suitable for him" (Gen. 2:18). He knew that His crowning creation—like Himself—would desire companionship and fellowship.

With the creation of Eve, God met that need. When the first humans sinned, however, a wedge was driven—for the first time—between them and God, and between husband and wife. Sin—and with it, conflict, selfishness, and loneliness—entered the world. Collins writes:

> Loneliness is rarely discussed in the Bible, but it is seen repeatedly, even in the lives of such giants of the faith as Jacob, Moses, Job, Nehemiah, Elijah and Jeremiah. David once complained that he was lonely and afflicted [Ps. 25:16]. Jesus, who knows all of our "infirmities," surely was lonely in Gethsemane. John ended his life alone in the Isle of Patmos, and the Apostle Paul apparently spent his last days in prison. Writing to Timothy, the aging Paul noted that his friends had left, that some had forsaken him, and that he needed his young colleague to "make every effort to come to me soon" [2 Tim. 4:9–12 NASB].

The entire Bible focuses on our need for communion with God and for people, especially Christians, to love, help, encourage, forgive, and care for one another. A growing relationship with God and with others becomes the basis for any solution to the problem of loneliness.[18]

The Response to the Problem of Loneliness

Listen ◆ Empathize ◆ Affirm ◆ Direct ◆ Enlist ◆ Refer

People suffering from acute loneliness are often counseled to "change jobs, join a club, be positive, become aggressive, get married, get remarried, travel, move, have fun, never be alone . . . listen to [music], watch television, enjoy the movies, read a good book, take up a hobby, pursue cultural interests, expand your horizons, play, increase leisure . . . renew goals, volunteer—and all of these activities may temporarily remedy the pain of loneliness, but they fail to meet the problem on the deepest level and do not produce the desired lasting results."[19] When helping lonely teenagers, however, the wise youth leader or adviser will instead pursue a course such as the following, which may help determine the root problem and address it effectively:

LISTEN. Encourage the young person to talk freely about his or her loneliness. Attempt to help the youth express himself or herself with such questions as:

- Can you describe what you're feeling and thinking?

- Have you struggled with feelings of loneliness for some time?

- When do you feel most lonely?

- When do you feel least lonely?

- Are there times when these feelings go away? Describe them.

- What are some ways you try to cope with your loneliness?

Try to stay away from "Why" questions ("Why do you think you're lonely?" "Why do other kids reject you?") and instead try to focus on the "What" ("What makes you feel better?")

and "How" ("How do you think you can respond when you start to get overwhelmed again?").

EMPATHIZE. As the young person shares his or her feelings of loneliness, communicate your empathy and interest by:

- Leaning slightly forward in your chair.

- Making eye contact.

- Nodding to indicate understanding.

- Reflecting key statements ("You feel . . ." and "You're saying . . .").

- Waiting patiently through periods of silence or tears.

Be careful not to say "I know how you feel," or to relate stories from your past, but try to communicate that the young person is not alone in feeling the way he or she does.

AFFIRM. Be alert to every opportunity to offer sincere and truthful affirmation to the young person, particularly if there is a chance the youth's loneliness is a result of low self-esteem.

Collins says, "Lonely people must be helped to see and acknowledge their strengths, abilities, and spiritual gifts, as well as their weaknesses. . . . Counselees must be reminded that in God's sight every human being is valuable and loved, that every sin can be forgiven, that each of us has abilities and gifts which can be developed, and that all people have weaknesses which can be lived with and for which we can compensate."[20]

DIRECT. Gently but firmly guide the youth to talk through the causes and effects of his or her loneliness, sensitively steering him or her to accept responsibility.

Ellison writes, "Ultimately, we are responsible for our own loneliness. . . . If we sit back passively and wait for a relationship to be restored or a new one to be formed, it won't happen. If we blame our lonely situation on someone else, we'll only feel bitter. If we blame it on ourselves, we'll only feel defeated. The first step in overcoming loneliness is to face it and accept the responsibility for coping with it."[21]

Be especially alert to opportunities to guide him or her to answer the following:

1. Is the loneliness due to a temporary situation? All of us experience occasional situations that cause loneliness, such as the student who stays in a dorm room between semesters while everyone else is gone. Such bouts of loneliness often disappear when the temporary situation is gone.

2. Is the loneliness due to changing circumstances? Life has a way of surprising—or disappointing—us with sudden changes that throw us off balance. A good friend moves to a city six hundred miles away. Mom and Dad announce that they're getting a divorce. The grandparent the teen had always confided in dies. His or her three best friends have begun to do some things the lonely teen can't participate in, and now they're shutting him or her out.

These situations usually take more out of us than temporary events. New adjustments are required that don't come easily. We have to experience the grief of loss. We have to find new friends and build new relationships. And that's not easy.

3. Is the loneliness due to something inside the youth? Perhaps the youth is shy by nature. Maybe he or she has an inner insecurity that makes it hard to make friends. Certain characteristics of the youth's personality may alienate him or her from others. Maybe he or she has dreadful social skills. While this third kind of loneliness may be the most difficult to resolve, it can—once identified—be addressed with honesty and sincere effort.

Most importantly, be careful to include spiritual guidance, pointing out to the young person that, while Christians are not immune from loneliness, he or she cannot overcome loneliness without a personal, thriving relationship with Jesus Christ. Point the youth to Christ and to the local church. If the teen is a Christian, focus his or her attention on the resources of prayer and fellowship with God in private and corporate worship. Pray with him or her, asking for God's comfort and guidance in the young person's battle with loneliness.

ENLIST. Once the primary cause or causes of the loneliness have been identified, enlist the young person's participation in developing a plan of action for overcoming his or her loneliness. Guide him or her to establish specific goals (such as adjusting expectations in a particular way or taking new risks in specific areas). Such an action plan should involve small or manageable steps, it should be specific and measurable, it should be reasonable and workable, and it should be stated positively ("I will invite a friend to a concert this weekend" instead of "I'm not going to hibernate in my room all weekend").[22]

REFER. If the young person's loneliness seems to persist or worsen—particularly if his or her behavior becomes erratic or he or she begins to talk about suicide—refer him or her as soon as possible to professional Christian counseling.

For Further Reading

The following resources may help the concerned parent, pastor, teacher, or youth worker assist a young person who is struggling with loneliness:

Scriptures Cited in This Chapter

- Genesis 2:18
- Psalm 25:16
- Timothy 4:9–12

Other Scripture to Read

- Numbers 11
- 1 Kings 18–19
- Psalm 37:1–4, 23–24
- Psalm 68:5–6
- Psalm 102
- Ecclesiastes 4:9–12
- Isaiah 26:3
- John 8:29, 14:1–27
- Timothy 4:16–18

Further Reading

• W. Leslie Carter, Paul D. Meier, and Frank B. Minirth, *Why Be Lonely? (A Guide to Meaningful Relationships)* (Baker).

• Charles Durham, *When You're Feeling Lonely: Finding a Way Out* (InterVarsity).

• Josh McDowell and Norm Wakefield, *Friend of the Lonely Heart* (Word).

2

ANXIETY

A Synopsis

❖

Introduction

Meghan left home at eighteen for her freshman year in a Christian college about three hundred miles from home. She made several friends her first week of classes and seemed to be coping well with the many adjustments of college life.

Less than four days before her first battery of final exams was to begin, however, Meghan dropped out of school.

"I can't take it anymore," she explained to her roommate. "The professors just keep piling the work on like you have no other class but theirs. I just can't keep up. I think I'm flunking every class. I haven't even *been* to my math class in something like three weeks; I know the professor hates me."

She sniffed loudly and rubbed her nose with the back of her hand. "I can hardly leave my room anymore because I'm afraid I'll meet one of my profs."

"What are you going to do?" her roommate asked.

"I don't know. I can't go home; if my daddy finds out, he'll kill me." Her eyes rimmed with tears. "He's like this big, successful businessman, and he'd go crazy if he knew his only kid flunked her whole freshman year." She pulled a box out of the closet and began stuffing her pictures and posters into it.

"Where are you gonna go?"

Meghan lifted her head and looked at her friend. Tears clouded her eyes, and she pressed her fingers into the corner of each eye and wiped the tears away only to have her eyes fill up again. She shrugged. "I don't know. I have a couple days to clear out of here. Maybe I can find a job and get an apartment. Then I won't have to tell Daddy."

"You'll have to tell him sometime, Meghan."

Meghan shook her head violently from side to side. "No," she answered. "I can't. Never." She struggled to remove a poster from the wall with wildly trembling fingers, but it ripped. She angrily wadded it into a ball and shoved it into the wastebasket.

The Problem of Anxiety

Dr. Gary R. Collins calls it "the official emotion of our age,"[1] and doctors Frank Minirth and Paul Meier call it "the underlying cause of most psychiatric problems."[2]

Anxiety is sadly prevalent among today's youth as well. Psychologist Mary Pipher characterizes adolescents as regularly "overwhelmed by anxiety." Pipher writes, "The kinds of challenges [they] face . . . are just too hard for them to deal with. All of the ways that early teenagers have to prove their adulthood are self-destructive things like drinking, using drugs, sexual activity, smoking. Children who are just putting away their comic books and unicorns are confronted with issues that developmentally they're not ready to handle."[3]

Stress and anxiety become a way of life for many young people today. Dr. G. Keith Olson writes:

> Along with anger and guilt, anxiety and fear are major players in the lives of many teenagers. . . . Anxiety can be defined as the experience of unrest, apprehension, dread or agitated worry. It has been described as a fear in the absence of real danger, or a fear of something that is not clearly understood. . . . Anxiety, fear and worry form a complex system of emotions that make clear differentiation between them quite difficult. They tend to overestimate the negative or threatening aspects of a situation while drawing attention away from the positive or reassuring aspects. The person is left feeling uneasy, concerned, restless, irritable and fidgety.[4]

The Causes of Anxiety

"The causes of anxiety are many," write Minirth and Meier. "It can be the result of unconscious intrapsychic conflicts. It can be learned by example—such as identifying with parents who are anxious. It can come from childhood conflicts. It can come from present-day situational prob-

lems. It can come from being anxious about being anxious. It can come from fears of inferiority, poverty, or poor health."[5]

Collins outlines five broad causes of anxiety: threats, conflict, fear, unmet needs, and individual differences.

◆ Threats

Collins describes anxiety-producing threats as "those which come from perceived danger, a threat to one's feelings of self-worth, separation and unconscious influences. . . ."[6] For example, anxiety may be caused by rejection or harassment from a peer, the possibility of parents' divorcing, the prospect of flunking a course in school, or any number of real or perceived threats.

◆ Conflict

There are three kinds of conflicts that produce anxiety, according to Collins:

> (a) . . . a conflict over the tendency to pursue two desirable but incompatible goals [such as a choice between a great summer job or going on a long-awaited family vacation], either of which would be pleasant. Often making such a decision is difficult and sometimes it is anxiety arousing.
>
> (b) . . . a desire both to do something and not to do it. For example, a person may grapple with [ending a romantic relationship that seems to be going nowhere. Breaking up might bring more freedom and opportunity, but it might also be a traumatic, hurtful experience for both parties.] Making such decisions can involve considerable anxiety.
>
> (c) . . . Here there are two alternatives, both of which may be unpleasant: like having pain versus having an operation which might in time relieve the pain.[7]

◆ Fear

"Fears can come in response to a variety of situations," writes Collins. "Different people are afraid of failure, the future, achieving success, rejection, intimacy, conflict, meaninglessness in life (sometimes called existential anxiety), sickness, death, loneliness, and a host of other real or imagined possibilities. Sometimes these fears can build up in one's mind and create extreme anxiety—often in the absence of any real danger."[8]

◆ Unmet Needs

"For many years psychologists and other writers have tried to identify the basic needs of human beings," writes Collins. He cites Cecil Osborne's conclusion that six needs are fundamental:

- survival (the need to have continued existence)
- security (economic and emotional)
- sex (as an expression of love; as a sexual being)
- significance (to amount to something; to be worthwhile)
- self-fulfillment (to achieve fulfilling goals)
- selfhood (a sense of identity)

If we fail to meet these needs, Osborne believes, we are anxious, "up-in-the-air," afraid, and often frustrated. . . ."[9]

◆ *Individual Differences*

"It is well known, of course, that people react differently to anxiety-producing situations," writes Collins. "Some people are almost never anxious, some seem highly anxious most of the time; many are in between. Some people are made anxious by a variety of situations; others find that only one or two issues trigger anxiety. [Such differences may be due to] the person's psychology, personality, sociology, physiology or theology."[10]

Psychology. "Most behavior is learned as a result of personal experience or teaching by parents and other significant persons. When we have failed and must try again, when we have been hurt in the past, when others have demanded more than we could give, when we have seen anxiety in other people (e.g., the child

who learns to be anxious in thunderstorms because his mother was always anxious) . . . all of these are psychological reactions which arouse anxiety."[11]

Personality. "It may be that some people are more fearful or 'high-strung' than others. Some are more sensitive, self-centered, hostile, or insecure than others."[12]

Sociology. "A past president of the American Psychological Association once suggested that the causes of anxiety rest in our society: political instability, mobility which disturbs our sense of rootedness, shifting values, changing moral standards and religious beliefs, and so on."[13]

Physiology. "The presence of disease can stimulate anxiety, but so can dietary imbalance, neurological malfunctioning and chemical factors within the body."[14]

Theology. "Beliefs have a great bearing on one's anxiety level. If God is seen as all-powerful, loving, good, and in ultimate control of the universe (which is the biblical teaching), then there can be trust and security even in the midst of turmoil. . . . It should not be assumed, however, that nonbelievers necessarily are more anxious than believers. (Some Christians, for example, are so worried about pleasing God that their theology increases anxiety.) Nor should it be concluded that anxiety always reflects a lack of faith. The causes of anxiety are too complex for such a simplistic explanation. Nevertheless what we believe or do not believe does contribute to individual differences in the extent to which we experience anxiety."[15]

False Beliefs. Not only may a person's beliefs contribute to the experience of anxiety; Dr. G. Keith Olson identifies specific false beliefs as a major cause of anxiety among youth:

Many adolescents . . . believe one or more of the following false beliefs:

1. It is essential that I am loved or approved by virtually everyone in my community.

2. I must be perfectly competent, adequate and achieving in order to consider myself worthwhile.

3. It is a terrible catastrophe when things are not as I want them to be.

4. Unhappiness is caused by outside circumstances, and I have no control over it.

5. Dangerous or fearsome things are causes for great concern, and I must continually dwell upon their possibility.

6. It is easier to avoid certain difficulties and self-responsibilities than to face them.

7. I should be dependent on others, and I must have someone stronger on whom I can rely.

8. My past experiences and events are the determiners of my present behavior; I cannot eradicate or alter the influence of my past.

9. I should be quite upset over other people's problems and disturbances.

10. There is always a right or perfect solution to every problem, and I must always find it or the results will be catastrophic.[16]

Parents and youth leaders may recognize such false beliefs as often characteristic of adolescents. Such beliefs can, of course, give rise to considerable anxiety.

The Effects of Anxiety

Anxiety sometimes produces beneficial effects; it can motivate a person, for example. Too much anxiety, however, can produce severe, even crippling, effects.

◆ Physical Effects

It is widely known that great stress and anxiety can produce ulcers, even in young persons. Less well known are the other possible physical effects of anxiety: headaches, rashes, backaches, upset stomach, shortness of breath, sleeping problems, fatigue, and loss of appetite. In addition, the changes in blood pressure, muscle tension, and digestive and chemical changes caused by anxiety can, if they persist over time, cause severe harm.

◆ Behavioral Effects

"When anxiety builds up," writes Collins, "most people unconsciously rely on behaviors and thinking which dull the pain of anxiety and enable us to cope."[17] Such reactions may include seeking relief in sleep, drugs, or alcohol, or trying to deny the reality or depth of the anxiety. Some people may become uncharacteristically disagreeable, blaming others for their problems or throwing childish temper tantrums at the tiniest provocation.

◆ Spiritual Effects

Collins writes,

Anxiety can motivate us to seek divine help where it might be ignored otherwise. But anxiety can also drive us away from God at a time when he is most needed. Fraught with worry and distracted by pressures, even religious people find that there is a lack of time for prayer, decreased ability to concentrate on Bible reading, reduced interest in church worship services, impatience and sometimes bitterness with heaven's seeming silence.[18]

◆ Psychological Effects

It is with reason that anxiety is considered the "most pervasive psychological phenomenon of our time."[19] Anxiety can give rise to a dizzying plethora of disorders, such as:

Separation Anxiety Disorder. This psychological effect is demonstrated in excessive worry or fear of being separated from a parent or other important influence.

Avoidant Disorder of Adolescence. Olson describes this behavior as "when the teenager desires warm, close and affectionate relationships with family members but strongly avoids making contact with strangers"—even peers.[20]

Phobic Reactions. These reactions include fear of crowds and situations in which escape would be difficult (agoraphobia), fear of closed spaces (claustrophobia), fear of heights (acrophobia), and various social phobias.

Anorexia Nervosa and Bulimia. These eating disorders are characterized by anxiety about one's weight and appearance. (See chapters 42 and 43.)

Movement Disorders. Involuntary muscle "tics" can be anxiety-related.

The Biblical Perspective of Anxiety

Collins points out that the Bible uses "anxiety" in two distinct ways: to signify unnecessary worry and to indicate realistic concern. He goes on to offer an insightful overview of the biblical perspective of anxiety:

In his Sermon on the Mount, Jesus taught that we should not be anxious (worrying) about life's basic needs, such as food and clothing or about the future. We have a heavenly Father, Jesus said, who knows what we need and will provide (Matt. 6:25–34). In the New Testament Epistles, both Peter and Paul echoed this conclusion. "Stop perpetually worrying about even one thing," we read in Philippians. Instead, Christians are to bring their requests to God, with an attitude of thanksgiving, expecting to experience the "peace of God which surpasses all comprehension" (Phil. 4:6, 7). We can cast our anxieties upon the Lord knowing that he cares for us (1 Pet. 5:7). . . .

In contrast, *anxiety in the form of a realistic concern* is neither condemned nor forbidden. Although Paul could write that he was not anxious (that is, worried) about the possibility of being beaten, cold, hungry or in danger, he said that he *was* anxious (that is, concerned) about the welfare of the churches. This sincere care for others put a "daily pressure" on Paul (2 Cor. 11:28) and made Timothy "genuinely anxious" (that is, concerned) as well (Phil. 2:20 RSV).

According to the Bible, therefore, there is nothing wrong with realistically acknowledging and trying to deal with the identifiable problems of life. To ignore danger is foolish and wrong. But it is also wrong, as well as unhealthy, to be immobilized by excessive worry. Such worry must be committed in prayer to God, who can release us from paralyzing fear or anxiety, and free us to deal realistically with the needs and welfare both of others and of ourselves.[21]

The Response to the Problem of Anxiety

Listen ◆ Empathize ◆ Affirm ◆ Direct ◆ Enlist ◆ Refer

Trying to help a person suffering from acute anxiety is a difficult task, but one that can be aided by a course such as the following:

LISTEN. Invite the young person to talk about his or her fears and anxieties at length, as much as he or she is capable of expressing such things. Take care, as much as possible, not to interrupt or dismiss the youth's anxieties; a person suffering from acute anxiety will not be convinced by statements like, "Oh, that's nothing to worry about!"

You may consider helping the youth to express himself or herself by asking such questions as the following:

• What things do you worry most about? What things are you most afraid of?

- Which of your worries seem to be unnecessary worries?

- Which seem to be realistic concerns?

- Are you more anxious or nervous at particular times? In particular places? When you're with certain people?

- Are there times when your feelings go away?

- Have you tried to cope with or counter your feelings? How?

EMPATHIZE. One of the greatest challenges in trying to guide a person suffering from acute anxiety is the tendency to become anxious oneself. Anxious people tend to make other people anxious. However, being aware of your own anxiety (even if it is caused by the young person you're trying to help) may help you gain insight into what the teen or preteen is feeling. As a concerned adult, you may express empathy by:

- Nodding your head.

- Making eye contact.

- Leaning forward in your chair to indicate interest and concern.

- Speaking in soothing tones.

- Listening carefully to verbal and nonverbal communication.

AFFIRM. The Bible says plainly, "Perfect love drives out fear" (1 John 4:18). Dr. Jay Adams, writing about that passage, states, "The enemy of fear is love; the way to put off fear, then, is to put on love. . . . Fear and love vary inversely. The more fear, the less love; the more love, the less fear."[22]

The youth leader, pastor, parent, or teacher who wishes to help a young person deal with anxiety may sometimes be able to make significant progress simply by carefully, consistently, and sincerely affirming the young person as one who is valued and loved. Collins writes, "To show love . . . to introduce [young people] to the love of Christ (note Heb. 13:6), and to help them experience the joy of loving others, can all help to cast out fear and anxiety."[23]

DIRECT. The youth leader or parent's goal should not be to eliminate all anxiety from a young person's life; that will not be possible. The goal should be to help the teen or preteen equip himself or herself to cope with anxiety. This may be done by:

1. Helping the youth admit his or her anxiety, understand its cause, and determine (with the support of others) to learn how to cope with it.

2. Challenging the young person to commit his or her fears to God and to find security and peace in the knowledge that God cares for him or her (1 Pet. 5:7).

3. Urging the youth to divert his or her attention from self to others. "As an individual gets his mind off his own problems by helping others," say Minirth and Meier, "his anxiety often decreases."[24]

4. Turning the youth to God in prayer. Pastor and author Barry Applewhite writes, "Prayer provides real relief from anxiety and should be our natural response the moment anxiety begins to build."[25]

5. Guiding the young person to focus on eternal, not temporal, things. Encourage him or her not to lose heart but to recognize that "our light and momentary troubles are achieving for us an eternal glory that far outweighs them all" (2 Cor. 4:16–18).

ENLIST. Enlist the young man or woman's participation, as much as possible, in devising a plan of action to handle stress and anxiety, such as the ten techniques suggested by Minirth and Meier in their book *Happiness Is a Choice:*

1. Listen to Christian music (1 Sam. 16:23).

2. Get adequate exercise—ideally three times per week.

3. Get adequate sleep (Ps. 127:2). Most people need eight hours of sleep per night.

4. Do what you can to deal with the fear or problem causing the anxiety. Examine different alternatives or possible solutions and try one.

5. Talk with a close friend at least once a week about your frustrations.

6. Get adequate recreation—ideally two to three times per week.

7. Live one day at a time (Matt. 6:34). Probably 98 percent of the things we are anxious about or worry about never happen. Learning to live one day at a time is an art that can be cultivated.

8. Imagine the worst thing that could possibly happen. Then consider why that wouldn't be so bad after all.

9. Don't put things off. Putting things off causes more anxiety.

10. Set a time limit on your worries.

REFER. If you are not the young person's parent, take the earliest opportunity to inform and involve parents; such involvement, as explained earlier in this book, is critical. If the youth is hesitant to involve Mom or Dad, try to find out why. Consider asking such questions as:

- Would you rather I talk to your parents?

- Would you prefer to do it yourself?

- Would you like me to accompany you?

If the young person becomes more anxious in spite of the youth leader or parent's sincere and knowledgeable efforts, it may be necessary for the youth and his or her parents to consider involving a professional Christian counselor—particularly if the anxiety is so advanced as to give rise to disorders and panic attacks.

For Further Reading

The following resources may help the concerned parent, pastor, teacher, or youth worker to address anxiety:

Scriptures Cited in This Chapter

- Matthew 6:25–34
- Philippians 4:6–7
- 1 Peter 5:7
- 2 Corinthians 11:28
- Philippians 2:20 RSV
- 1 John 4:18
- Hebrews 13:6
- 1 Samuel 16:23
- Psalm 127:2

Other Scripture to read

- Psalm 131:1–3
- Psalm 139:1–23
- Proverbs 12:25
- Luke 12:22–26

Further reading

- Frank B. Minirth and Paul D. Meier, *Happiness Is a Choice* (Baker).

3

GUILT

A Synopsis

❖

Introduction

Andrew was seven when, one winter morning, he left the house to catch the school bus . . . without his coat. His mother called after him, but he ignored her. Finally, his father began calling, but Andrew could see the school bus coming up the road and didn't want to miss it.

He turned and watched from the school bus stop as his father raced toward him with Andrew's coat in his hands. Moments later, Andrew's dad crossed an icy patch on the sidewalk; his feet flew out from underneath him, and he hit the ground hard, his head making a loud cracking noise as it hit the sidewalk.

His dad's injuries from the fall were severe, and he was rushed to the hospital where, due to complications arising from his fall, he died eleven days later.

After his father's accident, Andrew, a formerly bright and cheerful kid, became dull and morose. At ten, he was nearly killed when he stepped into the path of a car on the street in front of his house. At thirteen, he began suffering from extended bouts of severe depression. At fifteen, he tried to take his life.

Andrew's mother had grieved for years over her husband's death and even longer over the change she had witnessed in her son. She knew her teenage son was suffering deeply, but she couldn't understand why. It came as a total shock to her when she discovered, after attending counseling with her son, that he had been consumed with guilt for most of his life because he blamed himself for his father's death.

The Problem of Guilt

"Guilt is an inescapable fact of human existence," writes Dr. Keith G. Olson in his book *Counseling Teenagers.* It is also an inescapable fact of adolescence. Psychologist Jane Marks says, "Children . . . tend to believe that they are responsible for the events around them."[1] That tendency sometimes continues into adolescence. If a friend gets hurt in their presence, they're apt to feel some degree of guilt about it. If parents argue or fight, they're likely to feel guilt. If they pass a homeless man on the street, they may even feel guilt over his condition. Add to this acute—often unreasonable—sense of culpability the reasonable guilt that results from wrong acts they do commit, and the result is a potent spiritual and emotional mixture.

Olson describes guilt as:

> . . . a very painful, disruptive fact that plays a significant part in many of our psychological, emotional and physical disorders. Christian psychiatrist Quentin Hyder described the complex emotion of guilt in this way: "It is partly the unpleasant knowledge that something wrong has been done. It is partly fear of punishment. It is shame, regret or remorse. It is resentment and hostility toward the authority figure against whom the wrong has been done. It is a feeling of low self-worth or inferiority. It leads to alienation, not only from others, but also from oneself, because of the discrepancy between what one really is and what one would like to be. This leads to loneliness and isolation. Guilt, therefore, is partly depression and partly anxiety."[2]

Olson goes on to point out that Christians often have greater difficulty coping with guilt than non-Christians do, particularly those Christians who are more legalistic in their theology and practice. And Bruce Narramore states:

> It is amazing how consistently the church has taught that guilt feelings experienced by God's

children come from God. I believe the reason the church has equated guilt feelings with the voice of God is due to its failure to distinguish between three different types of guilt and God's method of dealing with Christians and non-Christians. A brief look at these distinctions will help clarify the problem.

The first, *civil or legal guilt,* signifies the violation of a human law. It is a condition or state rather than a feeling or emotion. We can be guilty of breaking the speed limit, for example, even though we may not feel guilty.

Theological guilt, on the other hand, refers to the violation of divine standards or divine law. The Bible indicates that each of us is theologically guilty; we have all "sinned and fall short of the glory of God" (Rom. 3:23). But theological guilt is not a feeling or emotion. It is a condition or state of being in which we are less perfect than God intends us to be, but it is not necessarily accompanied by the emotional aspects of guilt. In a biblical sense, we are all in a continual state of theological guilt. . . . But this doesn't mean that we *feel* guilty.

Psychological guilt is the punitive, painful, emotional experience that we commonly call guilt. In contrast to the legal and emotional types of guilt, psychological guilt *is* an emotional feeling.[3]

Obviously, psychological guilt is the type of guilt that afflicts many teens and preteens, sometimes to an intense degree. Psychological guilt, while it may accompany legal or theological guilt, is highly subjective. Dr. Gary Collins points out that this subjective guilt may be strong or weak, appropriate or inappropriate. It may be beneficial, prompting us "to change our behavior or seek forgiveness from God and others. But guilt feelings can also be destructive, inhibitory influences which make life miserable."[4]

The Causes of Guilt

Collins, in his book *Christian Counseling,* deals at length with the causes of guilt (that is, psychological guilt), citing past learning and unrealistic expectations, inferiority and social pressure, faulty conscience development, and supernatural influences.

◆ Past Learning and Unrealistic Personal Expectations

"Individual standards of what is right and wrong, or good and bad, usually develop in childhood," writes Collins. He adds:

> For some parents the standards are so rigid and so high that the child almost never succeeds. There is little if any praise or encouragement because the parents are never satisfied. Instead the child is blamed, condemned, criticized and punished so frequently that he or she is made to feel like a constant failure. As a result, there is self-blame, self-criticism, inferiority and persisting guilt feelings, all because the child has learned a set of standards, sometimes impossible to reach. While parents most often express these standards, sometimes they come from churches which believe in the attainment of "sinless perfection."
>
> As they grow older, children take over parental and theological standards. They expect perfection in themselves, set up standards which never can be reached, and slide into feelings of guilt and self-blame.[5]

◆ Inferiority and Social Pressure

"It is difficult to determine whether a feeling of inferiority creates guilt feelings, or whether guilt feelings produce inferiority, . . ." writes Collins. However, "social suggestion is . . . the source of innumerable feelings of guilt."[6]

◆ Faulty Conscience Development

Collins continues, "At [an] early stage in life, the child . . . learns about guilt. When the parents are good models of what they want to teach; when the home is warm, predictable and secure, and when there is more emphasis on approval and giving encouragement than on punishment and criticism—then the child knows what it means to experience forgiveness. But when there are poor parental models, and/or moral training which is punitive, critical, fear-ridden or highly demanding, then the child becomes angry, rigid, critical and burdened by a continuing sense of guilt."[7]

◆ Supernatural Influences

"Prior to the Fall it appears that Adam and Eve had no conscience, no knowledge of good or evil, and no sense of guilt," writes Collins.

> Immediately after their disobedience, however, they realized that they had done wrong and tried to hide from God (Gen. 3:8). Objective theological guilt and subjective guilt feelings had entered God's creation.
>
> As the rest of the Bible shows, God's standards are high and people fool themselves if they pretend to be without sin (1 John 1:8-10). An awareness of guilt, therefore, can come from the promptings of the Holy Spirit (John 16:8, 13; 14:26).[8]

Dr. Dwight Carlson points out that guilt can be based on valid or true beliefs (such as guilt that comes from the prompting of the Holy Spirit), but it can also come from false beliefs (such as "the belief that I'm dumb, no good, or ugly, or that I have to be perfect,"[9] which can spring from the other causes mentioned above by Collins). In either case, however—whether the psychological guilt is based on true beliefs or false beliefs—it can be equally harmful.

The Effects of Guilt

There is a difference, of course, between the effects of objective guilt (legal and theological) and the effects of subjective guilt (psychological). Legal guilt may result in prosecution and punishment; theological guilt will, without forgiveness through the atonement of Jesus Christ, bring judgment and death. Subjective guilt, however, may bring several different consequences. Bruce Narramore details the five primary reactions to guilt: condemnation, rebellion, denial and rationalization, confession, and genuine repentance.

◆ Condemnation

Bruce Narramore writes:

> Let's say people . . . berate you, threaten to reject you, and in general let you know they think you're a mess. In other words, they make you feel immensely guilty. Your natural reaction to this guilt might be to give up and agree with their negative evaluation. You may think to yourself, *They're right. I really am a mess.* By agreeing with their evaluation, you participate in their condemnation of yourself.[10]

A young person who reacts to guilt in this way will typically seem sullen and somber. He may often hang his head when speaking to others and exhibit an inability to look others in the eye. She may unconsciously (or, in extreme cases, consciously) inflict punishment on herself by stumbling into frequent "accidents" or gaining weight. Such self-condemnation may also involve "an inability to relax, a refusal to accept compliments, a sexual inhibition, an unwillingness to say 'no' to the demands of others, or an avoidance of leisure activities."[11] It may also lead to severe depression and even suicide attempts.

◆ Rebellion

Narramore continues:

> Some people . . . as soon as they're made to feel guilty, . . . rebel. Someone might tell them, "You're a failure." Their response would be to think, *You haven't seen anything yet!* And they would start to make things worse. They're like a minister's son who told me how frequently he rebelled against his father and the church. During one counseling session, he gleefully told me how, during a drinking spree with some of his buddies,

he lifted a bottle of beer to his lips and yelled, "Here's one for the deacon's board." . . .

> Others don't rebel so openly. They are much like a married person who is passively resistant. Responding to their mate's threats, nagging, or attempts to raise guilt, the husband or wife fights back with passivity. He or she fails to get ready on time, lets household tasks go undone, or gets involved in activities that neglect the family. Unfortunately, such passive rebellion stirs up more anger and guilt and compounds the problem.[12] [See also chapter 23, "Rebellion."]

The teen or preteen who reacts to psychological guilt in this way may exhibit rebellion against his or her parents, church, teachers, or adults in general. Sometimes the rebellion is sharpest against the authority figure who prompts the greatest feelings of guilt—whether by words, attitude, or example.

◆ Denial and Rationalization

Narramore writes:

> [Another] way we react to guilt feelings is to deny them by rationalizing away our failures and our sins. We say things like: "Compared to other people, I'm not so bad." "That's just the way I am" or "That's just human nature." . . . Sometimes we hide our guilt by projecting our sins onto others. We find in them the sins and weaknesses we are hiding in ourselves. By focusing on others, we avoid becoming aware of our failures.[13]

The youth who attempts to deal with guilt by denying and rationalizing it may be extremely critical, especially of parents and siblings. He or she may adamantly maintain innocence when his or her responsibility for some action or attitude is evident to all.

◆ Confession

We turn again to Narramore, who writes:

> Confession is the fourth typical response to guilt. Whenever we feel guilty, we like ourselves

less, feel a sense of alienation from God, and fear His punishment or retribution. Therefore, we learn to admit that we're wrong in order to get relief. We ask forgiveness to overcome our psychic suffering. At first glance, this seems like a positive solution. Confession works like a magic wand; in no time at all, our guilt feelings vanish and we feel better about ourselves, accepted by God, and free from punishment.

But what about the motives for our confession? Were we really concerned about the person we hurt? Were we sorry about doing wrong, or were we just trying to rid ourselves of unpleasant guilt feelings? . . . When this happens, we aren't really experiencing biblical repentance.[14]

The teen or preteen who responds to guilt in this way may be prone to apologize profusely for an action that he or she repeats shortly thereafter. He may often be heard to say, "I *said* I was sorry." She may be prone to feel sorry—not that she did wrong, but that she was caught.

◆ Genuine Repentance

When a young person's guilt is the product of true guilt (guilt that results from true beliefs instead of false beliefs), he or she may respond with true repentance and find forgiveness.

The effects of guilt feelings are not all negative. Some people have learned to accept mistakes, to grow from them, to confess to God and others, and to rest content in the assurance that "if we confess our sins, He is faithful and righteous to forgive us our sins and to cleanse us from all unrighteousness" (1 John 1:9).[15]

The Biblical Perspective of Guilt

"Once we have recognized the harmful effects of guilt feelings," say Bruce Narramore and Bill Counts, "we are free to turn to a constructive alternative."[16] That "constructive alternative" is the key to a biblical view of guilt. Collins points out:

When modern people speak about guilt they usually are referring to subjective guilt feelings, but the Bible never uses guilt in this way. The words which usually are translated "guilt" or "guilty" refer to the theological guilt which was described above. A person is guilty, in the biblical sense, when he or she has broken God's law. In the Bible, therefore, there is little difference between guilt and sin (L. R. Keylock, "Guilt," in *The Zondervan Pictorial Encyclopedia of the Bible*, ed. Merrill C. Tenney, Grand Rapids: Zondervan, 1975, 2:852).

This has significant implications. . . . The Bible does not talk about guilt feelings and in no place does it even imply that we should try to motivate people by making them feel guilty . . . But how can we lead people to a place of repentance without creating considerable guilt feelings? To answer we must understand the concepts of constructive sorrow and divine forgiveness.[17]

Constructive sorrow, as it is explained by Narramore and Counts, is in marked contrast to psychological guilt. They point to Paul's words in 2 Corinthians 7:8–10:

For though I caused you sorrow by my letter, I do not regret it; though I did regret it—for I see that that letter caused you sorrow, though only for awhile—I now rejoice, not that you were made sorrowful, but that you were made sorrowful according to the will of God, in order that you might not suffer loss in anything through us. For the sorrow that is according to the will of God produces a repentance without regret, leading to salvation; but the sorrow of the world produces death. (NASB)

Narramore and Counts consider this passage an illustration of the difference between psychological guilt and constructive sorrow. They go on:

Paul speaks of the "sorrow of the world" (literally "grief") and the "sorrow according to the will of God." He says the sorrow of the world produces nothing positive. It leads only to death. In contrast, the "sorrow according to the will of God" is helpful. It leads to repentance. . . . *Psychological guilt* [the "sorrow of the world"] produces self-inflicted misery. *Constructive sorrow* [the "sorrow according to the will of God"] produces a positive change of behavior. . . . [Psychological] guilt focuses largely

on . . . ourselves and . . . our failures. Constructive sorrow focuses more on the persons we have injured.[18]

Narramore and Counts illustrate the difference between psychological guilt and constructive sorrow with the following chart:

	PSYCHOLOGICAL GUILT	CONSTRUCTIVE SORROW
Person in primary focus	Yourself	God or others
Attitudes or actions in primary focus	Past misdeeds	Damage done to others or our future correct deeds.
Motivation for change (if any)	To avoid feeling bad (guilt feelings)	To help others, to promote our growth, or to do God's will (love feelings)
Attitude toward ourselves	Anger and frustration	Love and respect combined with concern
Result	a) External change for improper motivations) b) Stagnation due to paralyzing effect of guilt c) Further rebellion	Repentance and change based on an attitude of love and mutual respect

From: Narramore and Counts, *Freedom from Guilt* (Santa Ana, Calif: Vision House, 1974).

The Response to the Problem of Guilt

Listen ◆ Empathize ◆ Affirm ◆ Direct ◆ Enlist ◆ Refer

The young man or woman who is struggling with guilt feelings will probably not profit from platitudes or admonitions to "stop feeling guilty" or "just confess your sin and be done with it." It may be possible, however, for the youth to confront and deal with his or her guilt with the help of a youth leader, parent, or con-

cerned adviser. The caring adult who is not a parent should seek to inform and involve the young person's parents (or, ideally, assist the youth in doing so) at the first opportunity. Both parents and other adults can help a young person struggling with guilt feelings by carefully and sensitively leading him or her through a course of action such as the following:

LISTEN. Be careful to listen, not only to the young person's words (though that is vital), but to his or her actions as well. Encourage the youth to talk about what is troubling him or her, perhaps using the following questions suggested by Collins as starting points:

- What were [his or her parents'] expectations of right and wrong?
- Were standards so high that the child could never succeed?
- What happened when there was failure?
- What is the [young person's] experience with forgiveness?
- Were blame, criticism and punishment frequent?
- What did the church teach about right and wrong?
- Was there biblical basis for these teachings?
- Was the [youth] made to feel guilty?
- What makes the [young person] feel guilty today? Be specific.
- Does [he or she] show any of the . . . reactions . . . described above?[19]

EMPATHIZE. The parent, youth leader, or adviser hoping to help a teen or preteen come to terms with feelings of guilt will do well to first examine his or her own experience with the goal of using that experience as an opportunity, not to preach, but to understand the young person's feelings and thoughts. This empathic concern can best be shown by:

- Careful, patient, and thorough listening (not being anxious to speak, reach conclusions, or give advice).
- Observation of emotions, mannerisms, body language—and what they may be revealing.
- Avoiding expressions of judgment or blame.
- Speaking (at first) only to be sure you're hearing and understanding correctly.

AFFIRM. Olson writes,

Teenagers who are suffering from subjective guilt are usually very sensitive to the possibility of being condemned or judged by others. In fact, they often expect it. It takes a great deal of courage for them to disclose their feelings of guilt. Nothing encourages this delicate process more than for the counselor to be genuinely understanding, accepting and non-judgmental. This attitude reassures, "I am not interested in evaluating your behavior or judging your morality. I am interested in helping you to establish and accomplish your own goals."[20]

DIRECT. Though it may take a considerable amount of time, the wise youth leader or parent may do well to offer direction to a young person suffering from guilt feelings, perhaps along the lines suggested by Collins:

First, the [youth] must be helped to reexamine his or her standards of right and wrong. Often people feel guilty about things the Bible doesn't say are sin. Second, [the young man or woman] must learn to ask, "What does God *really* expect of me?" He knows us perfectly. He knows that we are merely dust and he recognizes that we will sin so long as we are on earth (1 Sam. 16:7; Ps. 103:14, 139:1-4; 1 John 1:8). He expects not perfection, but a sincere attempt to do God's will as we understand it and as best we can. God is not so much interested in what we are doing, but in who we are and what we are becoming. He who is compassionate also loves unconditionally and will forgive our sins without demanding atonement and penance. Atonement and penance are no longer necessary because Christ has already paid for human sins "once for all, the just for the unjust, in order that He might bring us to God" (1 Pet. 3:18).

This is basic theology which is so relevant and practical that it can revolutionize and completely free human thinking. The ultimate solution to guilt and guilt feelings is to honestly admit guilt, confess sin to Christ and at times to others (1 John 1:9;

James 5:16), and then to believe with divine help that we are forgiven and accepted by the God of the universe. It is he who in turn helps us to accept, love and forgive both ourselves and others.[21]

Once the youth has developed an understanding of what God truly expects, the caring adult can then lead him or her to investigate whether the youth's guilt feelings are constructive or destructive. If the guilt is true, theological guilt, the young person should be gently encouraged to identify and confess his or her sin, repent of that sin, and trust God to forgive the sin and cleanse the young person of the accompanying guilt (1 John 1:9).

Finally, the youth can be helped to consider ways to counter any false feelings of guilt that may linger or crop up in the future. The parent, pastor, teacher, or youth worker may help by guiding the young person through the following three-step process:

1. Identify guilt quickly. If it is avoided or denied, it will be much more difficult to handle. Treat it like a flu virus; try to identify it early and treat it immediately.

2. Deal with the feelings immediately.
   a. Pray; turn to God for His help in dealing with your feelings.
   b. Read helpful Scripture; let God's Word (e.g., Psalm 32, Isaiah 43:25, Hebrews 8:12, 1 John 1:9) deal with your feelings.
   c. Call a trusted friend or mentor; talk out your feelings.
   d. Talk back to your feelings; speak to your temptations (or to the Tempter) as you would speak to an unruly dog.

3. Prevent and prepare for the next attack.
   a. Identify the things or people that triggered your guilt feelings.
   b. Plan preventive techniques to stay away from that person or avoid that activity or to do something differently the next time you're in a similar situation.

   c. Note your patterns and progress. Recognize—and learn from—your vulnerabilities and your victories; seek to decrease the former and multiply the latter.

ENLIST. Direction such as that suggested above is of no value, of course, if it is not acted upon by the young person. The parent or other adult can suggest, cajole, urge, and advise, but unless the young person makes the decision—and, to some degree, at least—formulates the "plan" for himself or herself, it will meet with limited (or no) success.

The youth leader can help the young person establish reasonable goals, adopt right theology and new attitudes and behaviors, and develop habits that encourage hope and success instead of despair and failure, but unless the young person makes the important decisions himself or herself, freedom from guilt will not result.

REFER. If at any point the young man or woman becomes violent or suicidal (or appears to be approaching that point), or if the young person appears to exhibit symptoms of a serious personality disorder, the youth adviser or parent should immediately notify the youth's parents. The caring adult may also wish to consider consulting or (with the parents' permission) involving a professional Christian counselor.

For Further Reading

The following resources may help the concerned parent, pastor, teacher, or youth worker further assist a young person struggling with guilt:

Scriptures Cited in This Chapter

- Romans 3:23

- Genesis 3:8

- John 16:8, 13; 14:26

- 1 John 1:8, 9
- 2 Corinthians 7:8–10
- 1 Samuel 16:7
- Psalms 103:14; 139:1–4
- 1 Peter 3:18
- James 5:16
- Psalm 32
- Isaiah 43:25
- Hebrews 8:12

Other Scripture to Read

- Psalms 51, 130
- Isaiah 55:7
- Ephesians 4:32

- Luke 12:22–26

Further reading

- Dwight Carlson, M.D., *From Guilt to Grace* (Harvest House).
- Dr. Henry Cloud, *When Your World Makes No Sense* (Oliver Nelson).
- William G. Justice Jr., *Guilt and Forgiveness* (Baker).
- Josh McDowell, *Sex, Guilt, and Forgiveness* (Tyndale).
- Bruce Narramore and Bill Counts, *Freedom from Guilt* (Vision House).
- David A. Seamands, *Healing for Damaged Emotions* (Victor).

4

ANGER

A Synopsis

Introduction

Kevin was the star of his soccer team, but he had not yet entered the game although it was already the second period and his team, the Sharks, were losing, 2–0. He looked down the line of spectators at his mom and stepdad, both of whom had attended every game. He scanned the crowd and finally found his father's face watching the action at the far end of the field. Kevin strode over to his coach.

"C'mon, coach, put me in. I promise, I won't miss another practice."

The coach groaned as his team squandered an opportunity to score.

"Coach, come on. My real dad's here. He's never seen me play all year."

Coach Henson shook his head. "Sorry, Kevin. You know the rules. You'll get your chance."

Kevin started to turn away, but he quickly whipped back around and pushed his face nose-to-nose with the coach, like a drill sergeant. "You can shove your rules—you know that?" he shouted. "You can shove your whole team for all I care!" He spat a stream of violent curses and then began swinging his fists at the surprised man. His first blow landed before Coach Henson could react and connected with the man's nose. Blood began streaming down the coach's face as he and Kevin locked in a struggle and tumbled to the ground, Coach Henson trying to pin the boy down and Kevin punching and kicking wildly.

It was Kevin's stepfather who finally pulled him to his feet, still kicking and struggling. The game had stopped as everyone turned to watch the drama on the sidelines. Kevin was still cursing and trying to break free of his stepfather's grasp when his father strode up to the boy and slapped him in the face.

"What's the matter with you?" he yelled, punctuating his words with profanity. His face was red, and though his arms hung at his sides, his hands were balled into fists. "Get in my car now," he shouted, adding a few more obscenities for emphasis.

Kevin's father glared at his ex-wife and her husband then turned to the coach, who stood wiping his face with a now-bloody handkerchief. "I'm sorry," he said, struggling to control his words. "This should never have happened." He shot a glance at his ex-wife again. "That boy should have been taught better."

The Problem of Anger

"Anger is a very commonly experienced and displayed emotion during adolescence," writes Dr. G. Keith Olson. "Sometimes its occurrence is understandable and predictable; at other times it comes as a surprise and shock to everyone, including the angry individuals themselves."[1]

While extreme mood swings and emotional instability are a natural part of the teen years, temper outbursts and aggressive behavior can be signs that a young person's anger has reached unhealthy proportions and is not being handled appropriately. Psychologist Gary R. Collins writes:

> [Anger] occurs in varying degrees of intensity— from mild annoyance to violent rage. . . . It may be hidden and held inward or expressed openly. It can be of short duration, coming and going quickly, or it may persist for decades in the form of bitterness, resentment or hatred. Anger may be destructive, especially when it persists in the form of aggression, unforgiveness or revenge. . . . Anger, openly expressed, deliberately hidden from others, or unconsciously expressed, is at the basis of a host of psychological, physical and spiritual problems.[2]

Dr. Les Carter outlines three general ways in which people tend to handle anger—repression, expression, and release:

> Repression is a form of denial. If a person denies that he is angry, then he feels no obligation to deal with his anger. The problem is solved (temporarily). Naturally this is a dangerous method of handling anger. Repression may have its short-term rewards, but in the long run repressed anger is usually especially powerful and bitter. By repressing it, a person is pushing anger from the conscious to the subconscious. There it can fester and worsen without that person's knowledge. . . .
>
> [Expression is another way people handle anger.] Anger is not always expressed verbally. It can be expressed through behavior. Well over half of all communication is done through nonverbal means. Nonverbal expressions of anger can include a stern look, a slam of a door, ignoring someone, crying, or giving a cold glare.
>
> Released anger refers to anger that is dismissed, or let go. It is not to be confused with repressed anger. Repressed anger is simply pushed into the subconscious mind. But when anger is released, the person has made a conscious decision that anger is no longer needed and it is therefore dropped. People can gain the ability to release anger only after they first gain some mastery of the art of expressing anger.[3]

The problem many teens and preteens face is that they tend to repress their anger (particularly if their parents or churches have taught them that anger is always bad) or they have never learned how to express anger appropriately, so they express it in inappropriate ways. And, of course, very few young people (or adults) have learned how to release anger when it is warranted. As a result, bitterness, rage, and anger build up until they explode in brawling, slander, or other forms of malice (see Eph. 4:31).

In order to help youth understand and deal with anger, the wise youth leader or parent will first seek to understand its root causes and effects, as well as the biblical perspective on the subject.

The Causes of Anger

There are many reasons anger invades people's lives. Anger is triggered by a vast array of emotions and events. Some of the more prominent and significant are frustration, alienation, hurt or threat of hurt, injustice, fear, or anger as a learned response.

◆ Frustration

There are probably few times in life when a person's frustration level can equal the frustration experienced during adolescence. Teens and preteens are in a very "active, energized, expansive and expressive stage in human development."[4] Consequently, they are extremely likely to experience frustration.

Frustration results when a person's progress toward the attainment of a goal is blocked or interrupted. Collins suggests that "how much [a person feels] frustrated depends on the importance of the goal, the size of the obstacles, and the duration of the frustration."[5] The many goals and passions of the teen years (getting a boyfriend or girlfriend, earning a driver's license, buying a car, getting a date for the prom, even being allowed to stay up late) and the intensity with which teens desire such things make many young people candidates for severe frustration and, therefore, anger.

◆ Alienation

Olson points out:

> During early adolescence, peer group acceptance and involvement is vitally important for healthy adjustment to occur. . . . Teenagers are extremely sensitive to any indication of rejection or isolation from their group or from their special friends. Such isolation brings not only feelings of loneliness, but deeply felt and grave questions about one's own identity, basic okayness and ultimate value as a human being. . . . And when alienation is deeply felt by a teenager, anger reactions are normally expected. They can be outwardly expressed or they can be internally directed in self-destructive, risk-taking substance abuse and even suicide.[6]

◆ Hurt or Threat of Hurt

Anger also arises as a reaction to physical or emotional hurt. When a teammate elbows a basketball player in the nose—whether it was intentional or not—the player is likely to respond in anger. When a parent calls a young person a cruel name, anger will result, though it

may be repressed. When Dad cancels a much-anticipated fishing trip with his daughter, she is apt to be hurt, which will breed anger. When a young man or woman is insulted, made fun of, humiliated, ignored, or threatened, the offended party will respond with anger, expressed or not.

◆ Injustice

Olson writes:

> Adolescents tend to be strongly idealistic and firmly hold to their value system, imposing that system onto others. They are particularly sensitive to any violations of their ethical code or value system because such violations symbolically represent encroachments on their developing autonomy. They are [also] sensitive to perceived injustices that are perpetrated by parents, teachers, political leaders, pastors or other authority figures.[7]

Teens or preteens are likely to react to injustice with anger whether the injustice was done to them, to a peer, or even to a total stranger. Collins points out that injustice "is one of the most valid reasons for anger (perhaps it is the *only* valid reason), yet it probably is one of the least common causes of anger."[8] However, because of their heightened sensitivity, it may be more common among adolescents.

◆ Fear

Fear may also prompt anger among youth. Fear of not making the team, fear of flunking freshman English, fear of what other kids are saying about him or her, fear of not being asked to the prom, fear of being embarrassed in gym class—such a plethora of worries and fears may create high levels of frustration and anger.

◆ Learning

Anger may be a learned response in many cases. A young person may have learned inappropriate ways of handling and expressing anger from parents or others in the family or society. He or she may have learned to harbor hostility, to let bitterness build up into rage, to resent or hate those who are different or express disagreement with him or her.

Olson suggests that the effects of violence in the mass media present role models that, "especially when presented in an attractive, powerful or prestigious fashion embody a strong modeling power."[9] As Collins suggests, "By watching or listening to others, people learn to become more easily angered and more outwardly aggressive."[10]

The Effects of Anger

One writer states emphatically that anger, or hostility, is "a significant factor in the formation of many serious diseases" and is "the leading cause of misery, depression, inefficiency, sickness, accidents, loss of work time and financial loss in industry." In fact, he says, "No matter what the problem—marital conflict, alcoholism, . . . a child's defiance, nervous or physical disease—elimination of hostility is a key factor in its solution."[11]

The effects of anger are widespread—broken relationships, physical impairment, financial hardship, etc. Collins summarizes the effects of anger by describing four effects anger might have on a person, ways that may overlap or alternate from one situation to another: withdrawal, turning inward, attacking a substitute, and facing the sources of anger.

◆ Withdrawal

"Perhaps this is the easiest but least effective way to deal with anger," writes Collins, who adds that withdrawal can take several forms:

- leaving the room, taking a vacation, or otherwise removing oneself physically from the situation that arouses anger;

- avoiding the problem by plunging into work or other activities, by thinking about other things, or by escaping into a world of television or novels;

- hiding the problem by drinking or taking drugs—behavior which also could be used to "get back" at the person who makes us angry; and

- denying, consciously or unconsciously, that anger even exists.[12]

◆ Turning Inward

Sometimes anger is held in and not expressed. "There may be calmness and smiling on the outside but boiling rage within," writes Collins. Internal anger, however, can be a powerful force that may express itself in these ways:

- physical symptoms ranging from a mild headache to ulcers, high blood pressure or heart attacks;

- psychological reactions such as anxiety, fear, or feelings of tension and depression . . . ;

- unconscious attempts to harm [oneself] (seen in accident proneness, in a tendency to make mistakes, or even in suicide);

- thinking characterized by self-pity, thoughts of revenge, or ruminations on the unjustices that one is experiencing; and

- spiritual struggles. . . .[13]

◆ Attacking a Substitute

"Introductory textbooks in psychology often describe the common human tendency to blame innocent people when things are not going well," writes Collins. He notes that the angry person may "verbally, physically, or cognitively attack some largely innocent but accusable person. Sometimes there may even be an illegal or criminal 'acting out' against innocent victims."[14]

◆ Facing the Sources of Anger

The sources of anger can be confronted, says Collins, in either a destructive or a constructive way.

Destructive reactions . . . may include verbal and physical aggression, ridicule, cynicism, refusal to cooperate, or involvement in things which will hurt or embarrass someone else. Drinking [and] failing in school . . . for example, sometimes are really subtle ways to get even with parents. . . .

Much more helpful is an approach which admits that there is anger, which tries to see its causes, and then does what is possible to change the anger-producing situation or perhaps to see it in a different way. This is a constructive, anger-reducing approach, which some people only learn with the help of a counselor.[15]

The Biblical Perspective of Anger

William Backus, the author of numerous books that deal with anger and other subjects, offers an insightful and concise biblical perspective on anger:

> To learn how to apply the truth against anger, we begin with the Scriptures. The word of truth by which God gave us new birth to begin with is a reliable source of power in the control and management of angry impulses and feelings. For instance:
>
> "Of his own will he brought us forth by the word of truth, that we should be a kind of first fruits of his creatures. Know this, my beloved brethren. Let every man be quick to hear, slow to speak, slow to anger, for the anger of man does not work the righteousness of God. Therefore put away all filthiness and rank growth of wickedness and receive with meekness the implanted word, which is able to save your souls" (James 1:18–21 RSV).
>
> "Therefore, putting away falsehood, let every one speak the truth with his neighbor, for we are members of one another. Be angry but do not sin; do not let the sun go down on your anger, and give no opportunity to the devil" (Eph. 4:25–27 RSV).

"The fruit of the Spirit is . . . self-control" (Gal. 5:22–23 RSV).

From these and other materials in the Scriptures, we can learn the following facts about helping [young people] with the management of anger:

1. It is possible to be angry without sin, since anger is an emotion created by God for certain adaptive purposes. Jesus, himself, became angry on occasion—of course, without sin.

2. Counselees should be taught to deal with the issues giving rise to anger as soon as they notice they are angry (before sundown, as Ephesians puts it). Perpetuating anger and not dealing with it creates opportunity for the devil to achieve gains.

3. Not all anger is sinless. Some human anger may inhibit and retard God's righteousness in one's behavior.

4. Such sinful anger is irrational and pointless, accomplishes nothing but strife, and should be dealt with immediately by the application of the truth.

5. Self-control is a primary issue here. The Christian ideal is [to] "Develop self-control in all things, especially in matters of anger."

[Backus suggests considering these] truths about anger, which are related to the above verses:

1. Some anger is to be expressed to the person whose behavior provokes. Here, speaking the truth in love, we seek to involve the other person in changing elements in our relationship which cause difficulty for us.

2. Some anger is not to be expressed, but managed within ourselves. Here, speaking the truth to ourselves, we seek to eliminate our angry feelings and responses, and to replace them with more God-pleasing and effective attitudes and behaviors.

3. Often, the Holy Spirit will lead us to do both of these things, speaking the truth to ourselves until we are no longer angry, bitter, and resentful so that we can effectively speak the truth to the person whose behavior causes problems for us.[16]

The Response to the Problem of Anger

Listen ◆ Empathize ◆ Affirm ◆ Direct ◆ Enlist ◆ Refer

Helping an adolescent or preadolescent who is struggling with anger may be a difficult and lengthy task. However, it is possible to do so, particularly if the following guidelines are kept in mind:

LISTEN. Be careful not to cause new frustration (and anger) by failing to listen. Pay attention to what the young person says (verbally and nonverbally) about how he or she is feeling. "Help the [youth] admit how he or she really feels," suggests Olson. "Gradually breaking down denial and other defenses that prevent [him or her] from self-admission of the anger is often the first goal."[17]

Collins adds, "Such an admission can be threatening, especially for people who are angry at a loved one or who believe that all anger is wrong. It may help to point out that anger is a common, God-given emotion which, for most people, gets out of control periodically. . . . If the counselee persists in denying the anger, even after hearing the evidence, perhaps he or she will admit the *possibility* that anger is present."[18]

EMPATHIZE. The wise youth leader, parent, pastor, or teacher will do well to ask himself or herself, "Have I ever repressed anger or expressed it inappropriately?" "Do I always handle anger in a biblical, Christian way?" "When was I last angry?" "What things do I need to work on?"

Such questions may be a check on harsh or judgmental attitudes, helping the caring adult to empathize with the young person and his or her struggles.

Keep in mind, too, that empathy can be com-

municated in some of the simplest ways. As you listen, try to remember to:

- Lean slightly forward in your chair.
- Make eye contact.
- Nod to indicate understanding.
- Reflect key statements ("You feel . . ." "You're saying . . .").
- Wait patiently through periods of silence or tears.

AFFIRM. Keep in mind at all times that it can be very humbling for a person, regardless of his or her age, to admit that he or she has been angry, has handled it inappropriately, and/or has lost self-control. Consequently, efforts to help a young person confront and deal with anger should be saturated with affirmation and appreciation (the former acknowledging the worth of a person, the latter acknowledging the worth of his or her attributes, actions, and attitudes).

DIRECT. An important step in helping the angry individual is to direct him or her to consider the sources of anger (discussing the roots of bitterness[19] that cause resentment, anger, etc.). Who is he mad at? What is making her angry? Which of the causes discussed above is most pertinent?

Another step, once the source of the anger is identified, is to urge the young person to face the hurt that is causing the anger, invite God into the pain he or she is feeling, and ask God to work through the pain.

Moreover, Ross Campbell offers some helpful advice directed primarily to parents but advice that could also be employed profitably by youth leaders and others:

> You want to *train* [the] teen in the way he should go. First, praise him for appropriate ways he is expressing anger. Then you can talk to him about *one of the inappropriate ways* he is using (like name-calling), asking him to correct

it. You want to choose the best possible moment. . . .

In some cases, it is impossible to resolve anger, as for example, when the person provoking the anger is inaccessible. At these times, the teenager must learn other appropriate ways to ventilate the anger, like exercise, talking it over with a mature person, using diversion such as an enjoyable activity, or spending time alone in a relaxed manner.

Another way to train a teenager in handling his own anger is to teach the art of preventing certain types of anger *cognitively.* This means using active intellectual reasoning to reduce the anger. [Collins calls this "the art of evaluation" and suggests that it involves learning to ask such questions as, "What is making me feel angry?" "Am I jumping to conclusions?" "Is my anger really justified?" and "Are there things I could do to change the situation in order to reduce my anger?"][20]

Patient and sensitive training along the lines Campbell suggests may help a teen learn to express or release his or her anger appropriately, in a biblical manner.

ENLIST. One of the most effective ways of enlisting a young person's participation in resolving a problem with anger is suggested by Richard P. Walters, who prescribes "personal action plans." If possible, the young person should develop his or her own plan for dealing with anger, perhaps along the lines of the following outline adapted from Walters's book, *Anger: Yours and Mine and What to Do About It:*[21]

I. Am I angry?
Identify any active or passive behavior that might indicate anger.

II. What am I angry about?
Evaluate what is causing any anger, bitterness, or resentment.

III. Do I resolve it or not?
Reflect on whether you need to express your anger (appropriately) and seek resolution and reconciliation.

IV. Can I employ "first aid"?
Might any of the following help express or release the anger?

Asking for God's help
1. Recognize that God is in control.
2. Pray with thanksgiving and praise.
3. Pray for peace in your heart.
4. Read, memorize, or meditate upon Scripture.
5. Pray for the person provoking the anger.

Human willful control
6. Measure the issue.
7. Control yourself.
8. Remind yourself that an angry feeling is okay.
9. Divert your attention.
10. Separate yourself from the conflict.
11. Use music.
12. Channel your energy elsewhere.
13. Do something you enjoy.
14. Talk with a friend.
15. Talk with yourself.
16. Laugh.
17. Cry.
18. Write it down.
19. Relax.

REFER. Some adolescent anger possesses such deep and complex roots it requires the expertise of a professional Christian counselor. Be alert to signs of such an instance, and be willing and ready to involve a professional if there is the slightest indication that the young person's history or condition warrants it. (If you are not the young person's parent, keep in mind that the parents should be involved as early as possible and referral should be accomplished with their consent.)

For Further Reading

The following resources may help the concerned parent, pastor, teacher, or youth worker further assist a young person struggling with anger:

Scriptures Cited in This Chapter

- Ephesians 4:31
- James 1:18–21 RSV
- Ephesians 4:25–27 RSV
- Galatians 5:22–23 RSV

Other Scripture to Read

- Psalms 4:4–8, 37:7–8

- Proverbs 12:16, 14:29, 15:1, 16:32, 29:11
- Mark 3:1–5
- John 2:12–25
- Colossians 3:8
- James 1:19–20

Further Reading

- Barry Applewhite, *Feeling Good about Your Feelings* (Victor).

- Les Carter, *Good 'n' Angry: How to Handle Your Anger Positively* (Baker).

- Dr. Henry Cloud, *When Your World Makes No Sense* (Oliver Nelson).

- Tim LaHaye and Bob Phillips, *Anger Is a Choice* (Zondervan).

- Richard P. Walters, *Anger: Yours and Mine and What to Do About It* (Zondervan).

5

DEPRESSION

A Synopsis

❖

Introduction

Seventeen-year-old Melissa had been dating Brian for eight months when he broke up with her—over the phone. The following Monday Melissa sat where she and Brian had eaten lunch together since last September. Her friends sat with her.

"I say you're better off without him," Amy said.

"Yeah," agreed Crystal. "You guys fought all the time anyway."

"I hear Joy and Nathan just broke up," offered Julie with an excited smile. "You've always had a crush on him, haven't you?"

Melissa didn't answer. She lifted her tray and left her friends without a word.

They don't understand, she thought. *They've all had lots of boyfriends.* But Brian was her first *real* boyfriend, and she had entertained fantasies about marrying him ever since they started dating. When they first started going out, Melissa had made up her mind to be everything Brian wanted. She'd lost a little weight and begun dressing with him in mind. She tried so hard to please him; if he showed the slightest pleasure in something she did or said, she would work to do more of the same.

When their relationship became more physically intimate, she determined to give Brian anything, everything; they began having sex after six months as a couple.

When Brian broke up with her, Melissa couldn't believe it. She cried and begged him not to leave her. She told him she'd change; she'd do anything he wanted. But he refused. Her first reaction was anger. *After all I've done to make him happy,* she thought. Then her anger turned inward. *I did everything I know how to do, and it still wasn't enough. I must be totally worthless. I'll never have a man love me. I don't deserve to have a man love me.*

Over the next few weeks, Melissa started spending more time alone in her room. She seldom went out with her friends, preferring instead to stay home, listen to music, and stare at the bedroom walls. She found it difficult to eat, and after a few weeks of having trouble getting to sleep, she began to sleep most of the day, both in class and at home. She began to miss school frequently, and her grades plummeted. When her parents confronted her about her conduct, she shrugged. "I don't care" was her only response.

"I don't understand," her mother told the pastor of their church. "She seems like she's a totally different girl than she was."

The Problem of Depression

Once thought to be a singularly adult problem, depression is a regular state for many teens—and preteens. "Researchers and clinicians now concede that depression frequently occurs in children (Evans, Reinhart, & Succop, 1980; French & Berbin, 1979) and adolescents (Friedrich, Reams, & Jacobs, 1982; Seigel & Griffin, 1984; Teri, 1982a, 1982b)."[1]

While it is difficult to measure how many teens suffer depression, "the findings suggest that a substantial proportion of young people are suffering from strong feelings of unhappiness and despair."[2] One source states, "Nearly 5 percent of all teens are identified as clinically depressed every year."[3]

It is a complex and dangerous condition that often seems to defy description and definition.

This is partly because people use the term *depression* to refer to different things: a general sadness, "the blues," humiliation following failure, or a period of stress and emotional volatility. Even mental health professionals have struggled for years to devise a clear definition.

Webster's Tenth Collegiate Dictionary defines depression as "a state of feeling sad" but adds a second definition: "a psychoneurotic or psychotic disorder marked especially by sadness, inactivity, difficulty in thinking and concentration, a significant increase or decrease in appetite and time spent sleeping, feelings of dejection and hopelessness, and sometimes suicidal tendencies."[4]

Psychiatrist John White, in his book *The Masks of Melancholy*, shares some helpful clarification of the forms depression takes in the following chart:

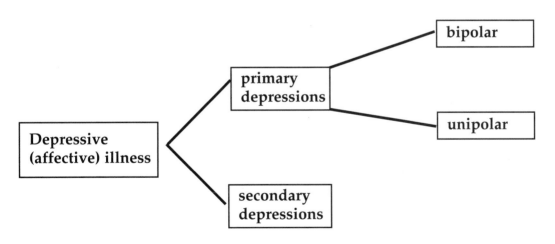

From *The Masks of Melancholy* by John White.

Depressive illness is of two kinds: *primary depressions* or *secondary depressions*. Secondary depressions occur in the course of some other illness or condition, such as alcoholism. Primary depressions, White says, "are mood disorders which are *not* associated with any other form of mental or physical illness."[5]

Primary depressions can also be categorized in two ways: *bipolar* and *unipolar* depressions. Bipolar depression, an illness once referred to as manic-depressive psychosis, is characterized by alternating moods of sadness and happiness. Unipolar depression, by contrast, is a plunge into emotional darkness relieved (if at all) only by restoration to normal moods. "To merit the description of depressive illness," White says, "all of these conditions must last at least a month, and usually last much longer [sometimes years]."[6]

Adolescent depression, as opposed to that experienced and displayed by adults, can be even more difficult to categorize and identify. Dr. Ross Campbell writes:

> Teenage depression is difficult to identify because its symptoms are different from the classical symptoms of adult depression. For example, a teenager in mild depression acts and talks normally. There are no outward signs of depression. Mild teenage depression is manifested in fantasies, in daydreams, or in dreams during sleep. Mild depression is detectable only by somehow knowing the child's thought pattern and thought content. Few professionals even can pick up depression in this state.
>
> In moderate depression, also, the teenager acts and talks normally. However, in moderate depression, the content of the teenager's speech is affected, dwelling primarily on depressing subjects such as death, morbid problems, and crises. Since many adults today seem to dwell on pessimistic trains of thought, the teenager's depression may go unnoticed. . . .
>
> In the vast majority of cases, only in severe depression does the teenager actually appear depressed. . . . There is an exception to this, however. Teenage depression is difficult to identify because teens are good at "masking" it; that is, they can cover it by appearing OK even when they are absolutely miserable. This is often called *smiling depression*. This is a front which teenagers employ unconsciously. . . . primarily when other people are around. When depressed teenagers are alone, they let down or relax the mask somewhat.
>
> This is helpful to parents. If we are able to see our teenagers at times when they believe no one is looking at them, we may be able to identify depression.[7]

Adolescent depression can also be hard to recognize because it can be often mistaken for or accompanied by other things, such as premenstrual syndrome (PMS) in girls.

The Causes of Depression

"Since teenagers are in transition between childhood and adulthood," writes Dr. G. Keith Olson, "it is not surprising that . . . many adolescents' depression relates to developmental struggles. . . . Some depression in adolescence is quite normal, probably more normal during this developmental stage than at any other (except perhaps old age)."[8]

Still, depression can be extremely complex, and the causes may be numerous and varied. Biological factors, ambivalence, parental rejection, abuse, negative thinking, life stress, anger, and guilt are among the causes that may prompt depression in teens.

◆ Biological Factors

Collins writes,

> Depression often has a physical basis. At the simplest level, we know that lack of sleep, insufficient exercise, the side effects of drugs, physical illnesses, or improper diet can all create depression.

Thousands of women experience depression as part of a monthly premenstrual syndrome (PMS) and some are victimized by postpartum depression following childbirth. Other physical influences, like neurochemical malfunctioning, brain tumors, or glandular disorders, are more complicated creators of depression.

There is evidence that depression runs in families and may have a genetic basis. This is difficult to demonstrate conclusively; research reports are sometimes contradictory. Other research has linked depression to brain chemistry that often can be altered by antidepressive drugs.[9]

◆ Ambivalence

Tim LaHaye writes:

> Some psychiatrists, like Dr. Ostow, consider ambivalence "the most common precipitative cause of depression." He defines ambivalence as "the sense of being trapped, that is, being unable to remedy an intolerable situation."[10]

Collins refers to this as "learned helplessness," and says, "When we learn that our actions are futile no matter how hard we try, that there is nothing we can do to relieve suffering, reach a goal or bring change, then depression is a common response. It comes when we feel helpless and give up trying."[11]

◆ Parental Rejection

Researchers Joan Robertson and Ronald Simons reported that, according to a study they conducted, "Perceived parental rejection was significantly associated with both depression and low self-esteem, with low self-esteem showing a strong relationship with depression."[12] Their findings agreed with earlier studies (Brown and Harris, 1978; Brown et al., 1986) that found that young people who experience or sense rejection from their parents are more likely to experience depression. (See also chapter 17, "Inattentive Parents.")

◆ Abuse

K. Brent Morrow and Gwendolyn T. Sorell are among those researchers who have traced a connection between depression and abuse—particularly physical and sexual abuse. They concluded that "severity of abuse was the single most powerful predictor of self-esteem, depression, and negative behavior in incest victims."[13] (See chapters 34, "Sexual Abuse," and 35, "Non-Sexual Abuse.")

◆ Negative Thinking

A young person's mental habits and ways of thinking also can make him or her susceptible to depressive illness. Collins cites psychiatrist Aaron Beck, who says that depressed people show negative thought patterns in three areas:

> First, they view the world and life experiences negatively. Life is seen as a succession of burdens, obstacles, and defeats in a world which is "going down the drain." Second, many depressed people have a negative view of themselves. They feel deficient, inadequate, unworthy and incapable of performing adequately. This in turn can lead to self-blame and self-pity. Third, these people view the future in a negative way. Looking ahead they see continuing hardship, frustration and hopelessness.[14]

◆ Life Stress

Numerous researchers and authors cite stress as a pivotal factor in depression. "When a person encounters stressful events in life that feel overpowering or threatening, one possible reaction is depression," writes Olson.[15] Such events in the life of a teen may include "the rupture of an intense relationship with a peer; family discord; parental separation, divorce, or death of a parent; unwanted pregnancy or abortion; and any event which lowers the teenager's self-esteem such as expulsion from school, failure to make a team, academic failure, or not being invited to a popular social event."[16]

◆ Anger

A young person who has not learned or devised ways of effectively handling and expressing anger is more likely to struggle with depressive illness. Doctors Minirth and Meier write:

> Over and over in the literature on the subject, depression is described as anger turned inward. In the vast majority of cases, anger is very apparent in the facial expressions, in the voice, and in the gestures of depressed individuals. They are often intensely angry, but usually they do not recognize their anger.[17]

A young person may be angry at a friend or loved one who has died, or at an abusive parent, or at his or her own helplessness. If he or she has been taught (by his parents, church, teachers, etc.) that anger is always bad, the youth may repress anger rather than resolving it. (See also chapter 4, "Anger.")

◆ Guilt

Collins writes,

> It is not difficult to understand why guilt can lead to depression. When a person feels that he or she has failed or has done something wrong, guilt arises and along with it comes self-condemnation, hopelessness and other symptoms of depression. Guilt and depression so often occur together that it is difficult to determine which comes first. Perhaps in most cases guilt comes before depression but at times depression will cause people to feel guilty (because they seem unable to "snap out" of the despair). In either case a vicious cycle is set in motion. . . .[18] [See also chapter 3, "Guilt"]

The Effects of Depression

The effects of depression can read like a catalog of physical and psychological afflictions. Among the effects are physical and emotional effects, shortened attention span and/or daydreaming, masked reactions, withdrawal, suicidal behavior, and depressive tendencies in adulthood.

◆ Physical Effects

Minirth and Meier catalog some of the physical ramifications of depression:

> Clinical depression includes the physical symptoms. . . . These biochemical changes have various physical results: The body movements of the depressed individual usually decrease. The quality of his *sleep* is affected. . . . Initially, rather than sleeping too little, he may sleep too much. His *appetite* is also often affected. He either eats too much or too little (usually too little). Thus, he may have either significant *weight loss or weight gain*. He may suffer from diarrhea, but more frequently from *constipation*. In women, the menstrual cycle may stop entirely for months, or it may be irregular. There is often a loss of *sexual interest*. The depressed individual may suffer from tension *headaches* or complain of tightness in his head. Along with *slow body movements*, he may have a stooped posture and seem to be in a stupor. He may have gastrointestinal disturbances. He may have a slow metabolic rate. He may suffer from a *dry mouth*. A *rapid heartbeat* and heart palpitations are fairly common. These physiological changes scare most individuals into hypochondriasis (an overconcern with physical illnesses).[19]

◆ Emotional Effects

While teens may not exhibit the classic signs of adult depression, as mentioned above, they may evidence some emotional effects of depression, such as those described by Minirth and Meier:

> One major symptom of depression is a sad affect (or moodiness). An individual suffering from depression has a sad facial expression. He looks depressed. He either cries often ["the weeps"] or feels like it. His eyes are cast down and sad. The corners of his mouth droop. His forehead is wrinkled. He looks tired, discouraged, and dejected. His features are strained. As the depres-

sion progresses, he gradually loses interest in his personal appearance.[20]

◆ Shortened Attention Span/Daydreaming

Campbell suggests:

> In mild teenage depression, the first symptom generally seen is a shortening of attention span. . . . [The teen's] mind drifts from what he wants to focus on and he becomes increasingly distractable. He finds himself daydreaming more and more. This shortening of attention span usually becomes obvious when the teen attempts to do his homework. He finds it harder and harder to keep his mind on it. And it seems that the harder he tries, the less he accomplishes. Of course, this leads to frustration, as the teenager then blames himself for being "stupid" or "dumb."[21]

◆ Masked Reactions

Researchers Marion Ehrenberg, David Cox, and Ramond Koopman point out that adolescents do not typically express their depression directly but rather through the use of "masks," or "depressive equivalents."[22] Collins lists the following "masked reactions":

- aggressive actions and angry temper outbursts
- impulsive behavior, including gambling, drinking, violence, destructiveness or impulsive sex
- accident proneness
- compulsive work
- sexual problems.[23]

Other masked reactions might include delinquency, school phobias, and poor grades.

◆ Withdrawal

Campbell writes:

> In this miserable state the teenager may withdraw from peers. And to make matters worse, he doesn't simply avoid his peers, but may disengage himself from them with such hostility, belligerence, and unpleasantness that he alienates them. As a result, the teenager becomes very lonely. And since he has so thoroughly antagonized his good friends, he finds himself associating with rather unwholesome peers who may use drugs and/or are frequently in trouble.[24]

◆ Suicidal Behavior

Many studies have linked adolescent depression to suicidal behavior (including Carlson and Cantwell, 1982; Crumley, 1979; Pfeffer, Zuckerman, Plutchik, and Mizruchi, 1984; Simons and Murphy, 1985). Collins writes:

> Not all depressed people attempt suicide but many do, often in a sincere attempt to kill themselves and escape life. For others, suicide attempts are an unconscious cry for help, an opportunity for revenge, or a manipulative gesture designed to influence some person who is close emotionally. . . . While some people carefully plan their self-destructive act, others drive recklessly, drink excessively, or find other ways to flirt with death.[25] [See also chapter 9, "Suicide Thoughts, Tendencies, and Threats."]

◆ Depressive Tendencies in Adulthood

One of the more long-term effects of teenage depression is the well-documented tendency of depressive adolescents to experience major depressive episodes in adulthood (Apter et al., 1982; Kandel and Davies, 1986; Poznanski, Krahenbuhl, and Zrull, 1976). Young people who do not successfully resolve their struggles with depression during their teen years are likely to face further battles with depression as adults.

The Biblical Perspective of Depression

"The Bible speaks of depression," writes authors William Backus and Marie Chapian, "as the 'soul cast down,' and in Psalm 42 we can sense the agony in the words, 'My soul is cast down within me' and 'Why art thou cast down, O my soul?'"[26]

But the Bible doesn't address the subject of depression, per se. The Psalms do include many verses that were apparently written by a human soul who was in the depths of human emotion, however. And Minirth and Meier contend, "The Bible records the depressive symptoms of such men as Job, Moses, Elijah, David, and Jeremiah."[27]

Collins even suggests that the Lord Jesus Himself, though He was perfect and without sin, struggled with depression in the days prior to His crucifixion. His agony in the Garden of Gethsemane is described this way in the Amplified Bible:

> He began to show grief and distress of mind and was deeply depressed. Then He said to [Peter, James, and John], My soul is very sad and deeply grieved, so that I am almost dying of sorrow.[28]

Collins summarizes the biblical perspective of depression by saying:

> Such examples . . . show the realism that characterizes the Bible. But this realistic despair is contrasted with a certain hope. Each of the believers who plunged into depression eventually came through and experienced a new and lasting joy. The biblical emphasis is less on human despair than on belief in God and the assurance of abundant life in heaven, if not on earth.[29]

The Bible does not say that depression is always sinful; it does, however, affirm the possibility of deliverance from depression:

> Why are you in despair, O my soul?
>
> And why have you become disturbed within me?
>
> Hope in God, for I shall again praise Him
>
> For the help of His presence.[30]

God's Word is realistic and straightforward about depression occurring even in the life of the godly, but it also makes it clear that God's will is for "the God of hope [to] fill you with all joy and peace as you trust in him, so that you may overflow with hope by the power of the Holy Spirit."[31]

The Response to the Problem of Depression

Listen ◆ Empathize ◆ Affirm ◆ Direct ◆ Enlist ◆ Refer

"Most people do not 'snap out' of depression," Collins points out. "The road to recovery is long, difficult, and marked by mood fluctuations which come with special intensity when there are disappointments, failures or separations." Still, a patient youth leader, pastor, teacher, or parent can help a young person through a depressive episode by employing a strategy such as the following:

LISTEN. "Fairly early in the treatment of adolescent depression," writes Olson, "the [young person] needs to be able to ventilate or in some way release his or her feelings of anger, guilt and self-doubt. These repressed feelings will block all other efforts at movement out of depression until they are given up. . . . The counselor's task is to encourage such expression, accept it and work toward helping the [young person] channel this released energy into constructive directions."[32] This may be accomplished by:

- *Prayer*, both in preparing to talk to the youth, and in guiding the young person (when he or she is ready) to talk honestly and fervently to God about his or her depression, and to seek His help in conquering it.

- *Patient encouragement* of the young person to talk (without cajoling).

- *Interested questions* (such as, "When do you feel most depressed?" "Do you spend a lot of time alone?" and "What do you usually do when you start feeling depressed?").

- *Frequent reassurances and words of comfort.*

- *Alertness for evidence of anger, hurt, poor self-esteem, etc.*

EMPATHIZE. A parent, youth leader, or adviser will want to empathize with the young person suffering from depression—to try to "walk" with him or her, as authors Don Baker and Emery Nester put it. However, in the case of a depressed person, a warning is also in order:

> Because of the counselee's feelings of helplessness, he or she will probably place on the counselor unrealistic expectations to catalyze a magical cure. . . . The display of inadequacy, dependency and need are partially motivated by conscious or unconscious wishes for the counselor to take care of them. . . . The counselee [may feel] strong dependency on the counselor.[33]

The adult will need to take special care, therefore, to empathize with the young person without letting an unhealthy dependence develop.

AFFIRM. Olson writes,

> The presence of emotional support and reassurance from the counselor is vital when working with depressed adolescents. Complete acceptance of the [young man or woman] is one of the best ways to communicate support. The counselor's realistic optimism that there is "light at the end of the dark tunnel of depression" is often very encouraging to a counselee who feels absolutely hopeless. And when the depressed teenager shows some gains or makes some movement, compliments and statements of encouragement are in order.[34]

DIRECT. David A. Seamands, in his book *Healing for Damaged Emotions*, suggests several directions in which a concerned adult can point a depressed youth:

1. *Avoid being alone.* Force yourself to be with people. This is one of the major areas where you have a definite choice in your depressions.

2. *Seek help from others.* Tell someone how you're feeling. Ask someone for help in combatting your mood. Seek out people and situations which generate joy.

3. *Sing.* Music was the only cure for King Saul's moods of depression (1 Sam. 16:14–23). Use uplifting music to manipulate your moods.

4. *Praise and give thanks.* Paul didn't tell Timothy to "give thanks when you feel like it"; he said, "In *everything* give thanks" (1 Thess. 5:18). Let God minister to your moods by focusing on Him.

5. *Lean heavily on the power of God's Word.* God can use any portion of the Scriptures to minister to you during times of depression, but through the centuries His people have found the psalms to be the most beneficial. Out of the 150 psalms, there are 48 that can speak to your condition: 6, 13, 18, 23, 25, 27, 31, 32, 34, 37, 38, 39, 40, 42, 43, 46, 51, 55, 57, 62, 63, 69, 71, 73, 77, 84, 86, 90, 91, 94, 95, 103, 104, 107, 110, 116, 118, 121, 123, 124, 130, 138, 139, 141, 142, 143, 146, and 147. Read them aloud.

6. *Rest confidently in the presence of God's Spirit.* The psalmist repeatedly affirmed the secret of deliverance from depression. He encouraged himself, "Hope thou in God; for I shall yet praise Him for *the help of His countenance*" (Ps. 42:5 KJV, italics added). God's presence is cause for hope—and the means of deliverance.[35]

ENLIST. As with many other situations in which an adult wishes to influence a young person (or anyone, for that matter), it is crucial to enlist the youth's determination and participation in his or her own recovery, rather than simply preaching to or advising the youth. Don Baker and Emery Nester offer some specific ways to enlist the young person's cooperation:

Encourage the depressed [person] to be involved in some new activity. Help him choose things he has always wanted to do but for which he has never had time. . . . Aim for an activity that is available, geographically and financially. It best serves if it is time-consuming. It should be within the capabilities of the individual. Gardening, painting, photography, or an aerobic sport such as running or swimming are often activities that fit the above criteria.[36]

REFER. If there is any possibility that the depressed young person represents a danger to himself or herself, take immediate steps to obtain intervention by a professional counselor. Be alert for indications such as:

- talk of suicide
- evidence of a "thought-out" plan of action for actually killing oneself
- feelings of hopelessness and/or meaninglessness
- indications of guilt and worthlessness
- recent environmental stresses (such as parental divorce, death in the family, etc.)
- an inability to cope with stress
- excessive concern about physical illness
- preoccupation with insomnia
- evidence of disorientation or defiance
- a tendency to be dependent and dissatisfied at the same time
- a sudden and unexplainable shift to a happy, cheerful mood (which often means that the decision to attempt suicide has been made)
- knowledge regarding the most effective methods of suicide (shooting, drugs, and carbon monoxide work best; wrist slashing is least successful, etc.)
- history of prior suicide attempts (Those who have tried before often repeat their attempt.)

Don't hesitate to ask the young person directly if he or she has contemplated suicide, and take the answer seriously.

Finally, referral to a psychiatrist or physician may be warranted in some cases (with parental permission). As Collins points out:

Nonmedical counselors may want to contact a psychiatrist or other physician who could prescribe [antidepressant] drugs for the temporary relief of a depressed counselee. Also, if a counselee has physical symptoms, referral to a psychologically astute physician is extremely important.[37]

For Further Reading

The following resources may provide further help for a concerned adult or depressive young person:

Scriptures Cited in This Chapter

- Matthew 26:37b–38a AMP
- Romans 15:13
- 1 Samuel 16:14–23
- Psalms 6, 13, 18, 23, 25, 27, 31, 32, 34, 37, 38, 39, 40, 42, 43, 46, 51, 55, 57, 62, 63, 69, 71, 73, 77, 84, 86, 90, 91, 94, 95, 103, 104, 107, 110, 116, 118, 121, 123, 124, 130, 138, 139, 141, 142, 143, 146, 147

Other Scripture to Read

- Genesis 15
- 1 Kings 19
- Psalm 119:25
- Jonah 4
- 2 Corinthians 4:1–18
- Philippians 4:4–8
- 1 Peter 5:7

Further Reading

- Don Baker and Emery Nester, *Depression* (Multnomah).

- Dr. Henry Cloud, *When Your World Makes No Sense* (Oliver Nelson).

- Tim LaHaye, *How to Win Over Depression* (Zondervan).

- Frank B. Minirth and Paul D. Meier, *Happiness Is a Choice* (Baker).

- David A. Seamands, *Healing for Damaged Emotions* (Victor).

- John White, *The Masks of Melancholy* (InterVarsity).

6

UNHEALTHY SELF-ESTEEM

Introduction

O'Neill was raised in a small town in northeast Texas by good parents who loved him. But O'Neill's father could communicate love only by giving to his family materially. He never put his arm around O'Neill. He never told him that he loved him or was proud of him. O'Neill's mother was dominating, controlling, and possessive. The oldest of three children, O'Neill worked hard to gain his parents' acceptance, love, and approval. He became a "mommy's boy"; by the time he reached junior high O'Neill was the school sissy. To make matters worse, O'Neill had a secret fear that someone might find out he was a chronic bedwetter. Until the age of fifteen he could never spend the night at a friend's home, which compounded his loneliness and sense of inferiority. He felt unloved, incompetent, and totally worthless.

O'Neill's college experience was characterized by severe loneliness and times of great depression. At times he sank into almost suicidal depression. He had no close friends. He was afraid to let anyone know the small, frightened boy he was inside. He was certain no one could like him, because he certainly didn't like himself.

The summer after his junior year in college O'Neill heard the gospel of Christ for the first time. He accepted Christ with expectations that at last his life would be completely transformed. Yet nothing seemed to change. His loneliness and sense of inferiority didn't go away. As a result, he was more miserable than before. He knew that Christ was in his life, but his life still wasn't all that different.

At times his struggle with low self-esteem has been almost overwhelming, but a significant turning point in O'Neill's life occurred at a Christian camp in California. He met a counselor there who gave him hope that he could be different. After one brief afternoon session, O'Neill's life began to change dramatically.

In the years since that summer, God has worked to heal him of his pain, loneliness, anger, and feelings of inferiority. He has spent many hours trying to understand himself. He has prayed, studied the Scriptures, and sought counseling from many people. He has come a long way—and still has a long way to go. But today O'Neill is different. O'Neill is learning to like O'Neill.

The Problem of Unhealthy Self-Esteem

As a young person approaches and enters adolescence, he or she faces a brand-new challenge, one that has profound implications for his or her future. That challenge is to answer the questions, "Who am I?" "Where am I going?" and "Where do I belong?"

◆ Three Functional Areas

"The major task of adolescence," writes Dorothy Corkille Briggs, "is the reevaluation of self."[1] This reevaluation uses the teen's past experiences and influences, as well as the messages he or she receives from parents, teachers, friends, and society in general. These all combine to affect three functional areas in the young person's estimation of himself or herself:[2]

The Area of Appearance. Many parents have observed that a frequent side effect of adolescence is an inability to pass a mirror without stopping. Young people are often intensely concerned about their appearance; they worry about their hair, their complexion, their clothes, and their weight. Any imperfection, no matter how small, assumes huge importance to a teen, and any criticism of the youth's appearance is likely to be filed forever in his or her self-concept.

The Area of Performance. A teen's estimate of himself or herself is also formed by how the teen—and others—view his or her developing abilities, skills, and intelligence. "I'm no good at math; I must be dumb." "I stink at sports; I'm such a klutz." "I flunked my driving test; I can't do anything right." Such experiences and sentiments can contribute to a poor self-image.

The Area of Status. The social structure in which a teen lives and functions (or malfunctions) can be complex and unforgiving. Young people are measured according to who they like, who likes them, whether they're popular, what kind of car they drive (or *if* they drive), what their parents do, where they live, etc. While such things may seem trivial to a parent or youth worker, they can be immensely influential in a teen's estimate of his or her own importance and value.

◆ Three Keys to Self-Concept

The areas of influence described above work together to help create the self-concept a teen holds in his or her mind and heart. Maurice E. Wagner points out that that concept consists of three essential elements:

Belongingness. Wagner writes:

> Belongingness is an awareness of being wanted and accepted, of being cared for and enjoyed. . . . Our sense of belongingness is fundamentally established in infancy. Children develop feelings of belongingness when loving parents anticipate their discomforts and affectionately provide for their needs.[3]

Worthiness. Wagner writes:

> Worthiness is a feeling of "I am good" or "I count" or "I am right." We feel worthy when we do as we should. We verify that sense of worthiness when we sense others' positive attitudes toward us and their heart endorsement of our actions. When others do not approve, but criticize us, we feel a loss of worthiness.[4]

Competence. Wagner writes:

> This is a feeling of adequacy, of courage, or hopefulness, of strength enough to carry out the tasks of daily life-situations. . . . True competence acknowledges one's abilities as well as one's weaknesses. . . . Competence begins to develop in preadolescent years, but it grows on to a more fixed attitude as a person finishes his teens. Competence is affected positively by successes, negatively by failures.[5]

Everyone—children, teens, as well as adults—wants to feel accepted, worthwhile, and competent. Unfortunately, the onset of adolescence often wreaks havoc with those feelings. "Youngsters often experience a decline in self-esteem as they enter their adolescent years," writes Bruce Bower. "Social scientists have documented this trend—often more pronounced among girls—over the past 20 years."[6]

The Causes of
Unhealthy Self-Esteem

It is dangerous to oversimplify the many varied factors that contribute to a person's self-image. In fact, many social scientists still argue over the validity of several claims as to its cause. However, while not all contributing factors can be presented here, several are so clearly influential they must be mentioned.

◆ Abuse

A direct correlation between child abuse and low self-esteem has been documented by a number of studies. In fact, K. Brent Morrow and Gwendolyn Sorell say that "severity of abuse was the single most powerful predictor of self-esteem"[7] in their study. (See also chapters 34, "Sexual Abuse," and 35, "Non-Sexual Abuse.")

The link between abuse and self-esteem is not limited to sexual abuse, nor even to physical abuse. Psychologist Irwin Hyman estimates that "50 percent to 60 percent of kids today show some kind of stress as a result of emotional mistreatment at school," such as sarcastic remarks from teachers or disciplinary actions meant to embarrass children in front of their peers.[8] Mary Beth Marklein reported in *USA Today* that "many mental health experts say tactics such as name calling, ridicule or sarcasm can rob children of their self-esteem."[9]

◆ Parental Rejection

Researchers Joan Robertson and Ronald Simons reported that, according to a study they conducted, "Perceived parental rejection was significantly associated with both depression and low self-esteem, with low self-esteem showing a strong relationship with depression."[10]

Young people who were raised in a family environment of excessive parental criticism, belittling, shaming—or of neglect and inattention—are likely to struggle with the adolescent task of reevaluating themselves and their places in the world. (See chapters 16, "Overprotective Parents," and 17, "Inattentive Parents.")

◆ Faulty Thinking

Authors Bruce Narramore and Robert S. McGee are among many who point out that youth with low self-esteem often display wrong assumptions and faulty thinking. Some of those damaging assumptions and concepts are:

I must meet certain standards in order to feel good about myself. Such standards may be the standards of parents, teachers, or friends, or they may be reactions to the standards of those people (like the girl who determined she would never buy secondhand clothes because her parents always did). McGee points out that people who accept this belief respond in one of two ways. Either they become "slaves to perfectionism, driving themselves incessantly toward attaining goals [and basing] their self-worth on their ability to accomplish a goal," or they despair of ever achieving anything good or ever feeling good about themselves. "Because of their past failures, they are quick to interpret present failures as an accurate reflection of their worthlessness. Fearing additional failures, they become despondent and quit trying."[11]

I must have the approval of certain others to feel

good about myself. Acceptance of this false belief will lead young people to bow to peer pressure in an effort to gain approval. They may join certain clubs, "hang around" with certain groups of people, or experiment with drugs and alcohol in an effort to gain the approval of influential others in their lives. Some will do almost anything for a smile from a particular girl, for a laugh from the right crowd, for a nod of approval from a teacher or youth pastor because they base their self-worth on what they think other people think about them.

Those who fail are unworthy of love and deserve to be punished. Narramore writes, "We take in our parents' corrective attitudes and actions just as we take in their goals, ideals, and expectations. To the degree our parents resorted to pressure, fear, shame, or guilt to motivate us, we [develop a false assumption that says], *When I fall short of my goals or expectations, I need to be pressured, shamed, frightened, or punished.*"[12] Because the teen years involve so much trial and error—or failure—this assumption can be devastating to a young person's sense of self-esteem.

I am what I am. I cannot change; I am hopeless. McGee writes, "When past failures, dissatisfaction with personal appearance, or bad habits loom so large in our minds that they become the basis of our self-worth, the fourth false belief becomes established in our lives. . . . If we excuse our failures too often and for too long, we soon find our personality glued to them."[13]

Finally, it must be mentioned that, to some extent at least, the reevaluation of self that characterizes the teen years is often resolved successfully with the passage of time and the development of one's abilities, skills, and intelligence. However, self-esteem is such a crucial element to physical, mental, and spiritual health that the wise parent, youth leader, pastor, or teacher will not neglect any opportunity to help a teen mature in this area as in others.

The Effects of Unhealthy Self-Esteem

◆ Flawed Attitudes

One of the most profound effects of a poor self-image can be seen in the attitude a person develops toward his or her world. Persons with an unhealthy self-image have a fearful, pessimistic view of the world and of their ability to cope with its challenges. They see unexpected or new situations as threats to their personal happiness and security, seemingly planned as attacks on them personally. They see the world closing in on them, pushing and crushing them. Such people tend to receive what the world sends their way without challenging or attempting to change it. They see themselves as victims, helplessly entrapped in a hostile environment, as shown by this graphic depiction:[14]

World

On the other hand, persons with a healthy self-esteem see the world as a challenge to be faced, an opportunity to exercise personal strength and trust in Christ. Such people assume they can have an impact on their world through Christ and that by the grace of God they can effectively change their environment. This attitude is illustrated by the image shown below:

World

Persons with a weak or unhealthy self-image operate in life from any number of these perceived factors and motivations:

1. Pessimistic outlook on life

2. Lack of confidence in social skills

3. Extreme sensitivity to the opinions of other people

4. Self-consciousness about appearance, performance, or status

5. A view of other people as competition to beat, not friends to enjoy

6. A sense of masculinity or femininity felt only through sexual conquests

7. A striving to become something or somebody instead of relaxing and enjoying who they are

8. A view of the present as something to be pushed aside instead of focusing on past achievements or future dreams

9. Fear of God or a belief that He is uninterested or angry with them

10. A habit of mentally rehashing past conversations or situations, wondering what the other person meant

11. A critical and judgmental view of others

12. Defensiveness in behavior and conversations

13. An attitude of carrying a chip on their shoulders

14. Use of anger as a defense to keep from getting hurt

15. A tendency to develop clinging relationships

16. Inability to accept praise

17. Self-defeating habits and behaviors

18. A habit of letting others "walk" on them

19. Fear of being alone

20. Fear of intimacy because it might lead to rejection or a smothering relationship

21. Difficulty believing or accepting God's love or the love of another person

22. Dependence on material possessions for security

23. Inability to express emotions

24. A habit of using negative labels in referring to themselves

25. Anticipation or worry that the worst will happen

26. A tendency to follow the crowd and avoid independent behavior

27. Perfectionistic behavior regarding details

28. Perpetually rigid, legalistic, and ritualistic preferences in worship

29. Interpretation of their world as hostile and overpowering

30. A shifting of responsibility to others for unwanted or negative situations or feelings

31. Need for lots of structure and external control in life

32. Overly sensitive conscience

It must be emphasized that a poor self-image is not the sole cause of all the above factors. There may be many other causes. For example, many of the above tendencies can also be caused by outright unconfessed sin or rebellion. Further, someone who has extremely poor self-esteem will not necessarily exhibit all—or even most—of the above factors.

◆ Quality of Relationships

Low self-esteem also affects the quality of a person's relationships. "Of all the problems with self-esteem," suggests *Psychology Today*, "this may be the worst: people who have it create relationships that tend to perpetuate it. . . . [According to] William B. Swann, Jr., Ph.D., professor of psychology at the University of Texas, people with negative self-views prefer people—even seek them out—who also evaluate them negatively."[15]

◆ Problems in Marital Intimacy

Not surprisingly, then, a poor self-image is also one of the prime causes of problems in marital intimacy. If you do not have a healthy self-acceptance, how can you expect your mate to accept you for who you are? You can't, and so you start to build a facade, and the man or woman who marries you marries the facade, not the real you. When that happens, the facade gets larger and larger, and usually, any intimacy that was in the initial relationship disappears.

◆ Limited Achievement, Satisfaction, and Fulfillment

Low self-esteem bears many results, hampering achievement, satisfaction, fulfillment, and pleasure in school, work, leisure, and marriage and other relationships.

The Biblical Perspective of Unhealthy Self-Esteem

Many Christians are uneasy about the notion of acknowledging *any* self-worth. They are adamantly against the idea of loving or accepting themselves. Because of their theological background, or perhaps other considerations, they constantly see themselves as only insignificant worms to be stepped on, worthless sinners deserving only hell. They have a hard time blending the idea of a good self-image with what they know of the Bible. Quoting Romans 12:3, "Do not think of yourself more highly than you ought, but rather think of yourself with sober judgment, in accordance with the measure of faith God has given you," they say, "You see, you *shouldn't* think highly of yourself."

Contemporary secular psychologists see inconsistencies in such theological thinking. Author Rollo May has said:

In the circles where self-contempt is preached, it is of course never explained why a person should be so ill-mannered and inconsiderate as to force his company on other people if he finds it so dreary and deadening himself. And, furthermore, the multitude of contradictions are never adequately explained in a doctrine which advises that we should hate the one self, "I," and love all others, with the obvious expectation that they will love us, hateful creatures that we are; or that the more we hate ourselves, the more we love God who made the mistake, in an off moment, of creating this contemptible creature, "I."[16]

In Romans 12:3 Paul did not say we should not think highly of ourselves. He said we should not think more highly of ourselves than *what we really are.* In other words, we should be realistic and biblical in our opinions of ourselves. That's why Paul added that we are "to think so as to have sound judgment. . . ."

The verb *to think* in the Greek means "to think or feel a certain way about a person."[17] In Romans 12:3 it means to form an opinion, a judgment, or a feeling about yourself. Paul's point is to form this opinion or self-concept as a result of a realistic appraisal of ourselves.

Christians who believe we should negate self and put ourselves down fail to recognize that humankind has great worth to God. This worth is not from what we have made of ourselves, however, but from what God has done for us and in us. We are fallen sinners, yet we were still created in God's image. We were, in fact, the crown of His creation—which gives all humankind intrinsic worth. And Christians are affirmed by Paul as "God's workmanship,"[18] and as His *poeima* (in the Greek), His poem, His masterpiece, His work of art. Clearly, humankind has worth to God, individually and as a race.

Self-worth is not an idea foreign to Scripture. It is interwoven into the heart of God's redemptive process. The One who bought us with a price knows our true worth. The price He paid for us is *Jesus* (see 1 Cor. 6:20; 1 Pet. 1:18, 19). If we were to place price tags on ourselves, each one would read, "Jesus"; we are "worth Jesus" to God because that is what He paid for us through Jesus' death on the cross to pay for our sins. That is God's statement of our value.

It's important, however, to acknowledge that we have this intrinsic worth because of what God has done and who He made us to be. It is not a worth acquired by us—something *we* did or did not do to deserve it. In Ephesians 1:18, Paul wrote about our intrinsic worth: "I want you to realize that God has been made rich because we who are Christ's have been given to Him" (TLB).

So we see that Scripture validates the concept of self-worth without repudiating human sinfulness. For thousands of years philosophers and theologians have wrestled with these two aspects of our nature. On one hand, human beings created in God's image have great value, intrinsic worth. On the other hand, human beings are fallen, sinful, and have been responsible for history's cruelest events. Humanity's dignity and value, contrasted with its sinfulness, self-centeredness, and pride, are history's great contradiction.

But God's grace is shown in that, even though people are sinners, God considers them valuable enough to be "purchased back," even when the price is something unimaginably precious—the blood of Jesus (see Luke 15). This is the one and only solution for the paradox of human nature, a paradox for which secular psychologists have found no explanation. Only through a loving God's intervention can humankind's two natures be reconciled.

The Response to the Problem of Unhealthy Self-Esteem

Listen ◆ Empathize ◆ Affirm ◆ Direct ◆ Enlist ◆ Refer

A poor self-image is not formed overnight. Neither will it be tempered or corrected overnight. A youth leader, pastor, teacher, or parent can be a vital help to a young person laboring under a weak or unhealthy self-image by pursuing a course like the following:

LISTEN. Some kids don't know what it's like to have an adult listen—really listen—to them. Their parents don't listen, their pastors don't listen, their teachers don't listen . . . or at least the kids don't think they do. It's important to develop a habit of listening closely to the young person who has low self-esteem. Listen to his self-critical statements; listen to the negative labels she uses to describe herself; listen to what he says about his family, his parents, his childhood, his friends, his school, how other people treat him. Just having someone honestly listening can have a salutary effect on a young person.

Use such questions as the following to gently probe the young person's ideas, attitudes, and self-concept:

- How would you describe yourself?
- Do you think you're a valuable person?
- Do you ever call yourself names?
- Do you think other people like you?
- Do you like yourself?
- How do you think your parents feel about you? Your teachers? Friends? Others?
- What things make you feel good about yourself?
- What things make you feel not so good about yourself?

Endeavor, as the young person speaks, to listen not only to his or her words but to the feelings being expressed. And "listen" as well to his or her body language.

Try also to impress on the young man or woman that God is *always* listening and the most important and effective ingredient of a healthy self-concept is to know Him, His love, and His fellowship.

EMPATHIZE. Be careful to empathize with the young person. Examine your own self-concept. What have been your greatest struggles? Do you still struggle with self-esteem? What has helped you accept yourself?

Also strive to communicate warmth and empathy by:

- Leaning forward in your chair to communicate interest.

- Making eye contact with the young person as he or she speaks without staring or letting your eyes wander.

- Avoiding any expression of shock, disapproval, disagreement, or judgment about what is said.

- Waiting patiently through periods of silence or tears.

- Leading the conversation by asking "What happened next?" or "Tell me what you mean by . . ."

- Reflecting the young person's statements by saying, "You must feel . . . ," or "It sounds like you're saying . . ."

AFFIRM. David Seamands writes, "Some parents are afraid to give their children affirmation and encouragement. They think if they praise the children too much, the children will become conceited or proud. . . . [But we] parents are much more in danger of perpetuating our children's fear of failure than of making them unjustly proud."[19]

Whether you're a parent, youth worker, pastor, or teacher, affirmation is critical to the development of self-esteem. Affirm both his or her personhood and his or her performance; try to "catch" the young person doing something right or doing something well, and make sure you comment sincerely on it.

DIRECT. The adult who seeks to influence a young person struggling with low self-esteem should, at an opportune time, sensitively share the biblical truth about that youth's significance in Christ. Some young people, hearing for the first time about their inestimable value in God's eyes, have taken life-changing assurance and confidence from the truth of God's Word.

In addition, the caring adult should seek to counter the sources of the young person's self-esteem. Christian author Tony Campolo suggests two primary emphases in directing a child in ways that will foster healthy self-esteem:

> [Help the youth] develop an area where she is special, unusual, and better than others. Some parents have done this by giving kids music lessons, some by putting children into drama classes, some by focusing on developing children's athletic abilities. You must be very sensitive to the special talents and gifts of the child and then capitalize on them so the child develops them to the utmost. Thus the child feels special, and that feeling enables her to have a sense of worth[20]

Pastors, youth pastors, and teachers can also do this by carefully observing a young person they're concerned about to determine what opportunities and/or training can be offered to the youth. Can she be eased into leading the youth group in worship? Can he be tutored with a view to someday teaching a Sunday school class? Is there an area of responsibility—even a small area—that can allow her to demonstrate that she can handle responsibility and/or perform with competence?

Campolo continues:

> Second, the church youth group at its best can give a child a sense of belonging and acceptance. Very often the child who is not accepted in the larger context of the public school can find affirmation and worth in this small body of believers. Parents need to be willing to change churches as the child comes into those junior-high years, if necessary, to find a church with a youth group [or begin such a group] that will minister to the child's need for affirmation.[21]

ENLIST. Enlist the youth himself or herself in brainstorming ways he or she can work on self-image. Parents can shape it into a project. Youth pastors and youth leaders can use the task of rebuilding self-image as the basis of a weekly Bible study or discipleship meeting with the youth. Tim Hansel suggests the following steps to a healthy self-esteem:

1. Accept yourself.

2. Know yourself.

3. Be yourself.

4. Love yourself.

5. Forget yourself.[22]

Enlist the youth in brainstorming ways to accomplish each of the above, such as the following:

1. Do not label yourself negatively ("I'm such a klutz," etc.). You tend to become the label you give yourself.

2. Behave assertively (but not aggressively) even in threatening situations, particularly when you don't feel like doing so.

3. When you fail, admit or confess it to God, and then refuse to condemn yourself. "Therefore, there is now no condemnation for those who are in Christ Jesus."[23]

4. Be as kind to yourself as you would to any other person.

5. Do not compare yourself with others. You are a unique person. God enjoys you in your uniqueness; have a similar attitude toward yourself.

6. Concentrate and meditate on God's grace, love, and acceptance—not on criticisms from other people.

7. Associate with friends who are positive, who delight in you, and who enjoy life.

8. Start helping others to see themselves as God sees them by accepting them, loving them, and encouraging them. Give them the respect they deserve as one of God's unique human creations.

9. Learn to laugh; look for the humor in life and experience it.

10. Have expectations of others that are realistic, taking into account each person's specific talents, gifts, abilities, and potential.

11. Relax and take it easy. If the sinless Jesus prepared thirty years for a three-year ministry, perhaps God isn't in as much of a hurry with you as you may suppose He is.

12. Do what is right and pleasing in the eyes of God. When our lives reflect God's character, we are a lot happier; obedience to God makes us feel good about ourselves.

13. Be positive (see Phil. 4:8). See how long you can go without saying something negative about another person or situation.

14. Lead others with influence and wise guidance rather than with autocratic power.

15. Love in accordance with God's model of *agape* love and balance love with limits.

REFER. In extreme cases—when a person's self-image is so damaged that it results in serious depression or a total unresponsiveness to counsel and offers of help, for example—it may be necessary to involve a professional Christian counselor. If you are not the child's parent, the parents' early involvement is crucial and their consent to refer is required.

For Further Reading

The following resources may help the concerned parent, pastor, teacher, or youth worker further assist a young person struggling with unhealthy self-esteem:

Scriptures Cited in This Chapter

- Romans 12:3
- Ephesians 2:10
- Ephesians 1:18
- Luke 15
- Philippians 4:8

Other Scripture to Read

- Psalms 91; 116:15
- Ephesians 1:1–14
- 1 Peter 1:18–19

- 1 John 3:1–2

Further Reading

- Dr. Henry Cloud, *When Your World Makes No Sense* (Oliver Nelson).

- Josh McDowell, *Building Your Self-Image* (Tyndale).

- David A. Seamands, *Healing for Damaged Emotions* (InterVarsity).

- Maurice E. Wagner, *The Sensation of Being Somebody* (Zondervan).

7

FACING DEATH

A Synopsis

❖

Introduction

Hannah had lived over half her life in Africa, where her parents were missionaries in Zimbabwe. Two months before her thirteenth birthday, she and her brother Philip returned to the United States with their parents for a two-month furlough.

Upon arrival home in Oklahoma City, Hannah and her family all had to undergo physical examinations. Everyone in the family seemed to be the picture of health . . . except Hannah. The doctor discovered that her spleen was much larger than it should be. He scheduled more tests, and Hannah and her family soon learned she had leukemia, a form of cancer that affects a person's blood and bone marrow.

The doctor explained that Hannah's form of leukemia was somewhat rare and that it's usually discovered much earlier. He also explained the available treatments to the family but added that Hannah might not recover from the disease.

"Am I going to die?" Hannah asked her mother, her eyes wide with fear.

Hannah's mother, who was struggling herself to cope with the news of her child's prognosis, inhaled sharply and wrestled to control her emotions.

"I don't know, Hannah," she answered. "I don't know." She hesitated only a moment before adding, "but it's possible."

Hannah's face flushed red, and she screwed her eyes shut.

Mom, Dad, Philip, and Hannah huddled together in the doctor's office, crying, their arms entwined around each other as if erecting a barrier against the disease that threatened Hannah's life.

The Problem of Facing Death

Most people think of death and dying in relation to adults, particularly to the elderly. But adolescents must often deal with the prospect of death as well.

According to the *Statistical Abstract of the United States,*[1] the leading causes of death among young people in the U.S. (in order) are shown in the table below.

One can see, from the list, that though a large number of children and teens die unexpectedly (that is, as a result of an accident or homicide), many others must face the reality of their own mortality and the prospect of dying at a young age (for example, as a result of heart disease, cancer, or HIV infection).

Such young people are faced with the necessity of coping with a very "adult" problem (in some ways, the ultimate problem) at a very young age, a process that often carries with it many profound and difficult results.

The Effects of Facing Death

A young person who is facing the prospect of death will, like anyone, experience a wide range of varied (and sometimes volatile) emotions. The primary response is likely to be an overwhelming sense of grief, extremely similar to the grief one feels when a loved one dies—except, of course, that in the young person's case, he or she is mourning his or her own impending death.

◆ The Five Stages of Grief

The widely acclaimed work of Elizabeth Kubler-Ross has reflected the five stages of grief, as authors Joan Sturkie and Siang-Yang Tan explain:

1. Denial—The person may refuse to believe that he or she is dying. This stage may vary in length, with some people staying in it longer than others. It is a temporary stage, but it may surface again at any time.

2. Anger—The [youth] may question why this is happening. When the answer is not apparent, he or she may lash out in anger at the seeming unfairness of it all. At the same time [he or she] may feel guilty for feeling angry.

3. Bargaining—This is usually an attempt to postpone death. . . . The dying person often does not tell anyone. The bargaining is usually done in secrecy, with God.

4. Depression—When the dying person faces the reality of his or her death, depression often sets in. It may come when symptoms of terminal illness become impossible to ignore. . . .

5. Acceptance—When the dying person works through the feelings and conflicts that have arisen, he or she may now be ready to accept the fact that death will soon come.[2]

Numerous other effects, physical as well as emotional and psychological, will be experienced at various (or all) points throughout the five stages of grief.

LEADING CAUSES OF DEATH AMONG YOUNG PEOPLE IN THE U.S.	
AGES 5–14	**AGES 15–24**
1. Accidents	1. Accidents
2. Cancer (includes leukemia)	2. Homicide & legal intervention
3. Congenital anomalies	3. Suicide
4. Homicide & legal intervention	4. Cancer (includes leukemia)
5. Heart disease	5. Heart disease
6. Pneumonia & influenza	6. HIV infection[1]

◆ Physical Effects

The physical symptoms of grief described by Erich Lindemann apply not only to a person grieving the loss of a friend or loved one, but to a person facing death himself or herself. Dr. G. Keith Olson lists them as:

- Laborious respiration marked by sighing and tightness in the throat

- Feelings of physical exhaustion and lack of physical strength and endurance

- Digestive symptoms, including altered sense of taste, loss of appetite, insufficient salivary production and hollow feeling in the stomach.[3]

Other physical symptoms are likely to include sleeplessness (or sleeping much more than usual), headaches, and uncontrollable and often unexpected weeping.

◆ Emotional Effects

Facing the prospect of impending death can cause mental turmoil, including these emotional effects:

Fear. Fear will, of course, be a likely response to the prospect of dying. The young person will not only fear the actual death, however (though that will certainly be a great factor that may become overwhelming at times); he or she may (quite naturally) fear what will happen as the illness progresses. He or she also may fear the pain that might be expected. He or she may even fear the effect his or her death may have on others. (See also chapter 2, "Anxiety.")

Guilt. Though a young person may know, cognitively, that the illness or condition threatening his or her life is no one's fault, the inability to accept a seemingly unexplainable event or diagnosis may lead him or her to assume some measure of guilt, to think, *I must have done something to deserve this,* or *I should have been a better daughter,* or even sometimes, *If I had read my Bible*

more, God wouldn't be doing this to me. Such guilt reactions, says Olson, "represent an attempt to again feel in control of life after it has dealt such a painful and shaking blow."[4] (See also chapter 3, "Guilt.")

Helplessness. The prospect of death as the result of a life-threatening disease or condition will likely leave the sufferer (as well as those around him or her) feeling helpless, and Olson points out that "one of the most unacceptable feelings for an adolescent is to feel helpless. To fight against this threatening feeling, the teenager often tries to take on a sense of responsibility for what has happened. In this way, guilt is often selected over helplessness."[5]

Resentment. Frequently a young person who is facing the prospect of a terminal illness and/or death will display resentment, particularly to those who are closest and most helpful. She may resent her friends or siblings because they don't have to go to the hospital, undergo treatments, and face an early death. As the illness progresses, he may resent the fact that he needs help from family members. Mary Beth Moster, the author of *When the Doctor Says It's Cancer,* writes, "The problem of accepting help is tied strongly to the patient's intense desire to be 'normal' and not be different from anyone else. Because there might be times when he is totally dependent on others to help him, his self-esteem can be badly bruised."[6]

Doubt. A common reaction among those facing terminal illness and death is to ask, "Why?" Olson writes:

> Sometimes we ask the question because we really seek an answer. We believe that if we understand a reason, then somehow the pain will be easier to live with. At other times, however, our question is more rhetorical. It yells out an angry protest that wants nothing but to be heard. Pastors and lay counselors, as well as many professional counselors, typically

feel the need to give an answer to the grief-stricken question, "Why?" A better counseling technique is to focus on the future instead of answering the unanswerable. A helpful response might be, "How are you going to deal with this . . . ?"[7]

The above are not, of course, the only effects that will be experienced by a young person facing death, but they are perhaps the most prevalent and profound.

The Biblical Perspective of Facing Death

The Bible is straightforward about death. It presents death realistically, sometimes in gruesome detail. God's Word depicts death as the universal experience of humankind. "Like water spilled on the ground, which cannot be recovered, so we must die,"[8] it says. It describes Job's longing for death, Hezekiah's bargaining to forestall death, Jesus' recoiling in the face of a cruel death (and the accompanying burden of others' sins that He would shoulder as He died), and Paul's facing death reflectively, hopefully. The key, however—for them and for us—was the biblical perspective of death.

Mary Beth Moster shares some key insights:

The Bible teaches that the human spirit does not die. "And the Lord God formed man of the dust of the ground, and breathed into his nostrils the breath of life; and *man became a living soul*" (Gen. 2:7 KJV).

God created man perfect and eternal, and though sin destroyed man's perfection, his spirit remains eternal.

Because of God's holiness, sinful man *cannot* spend eternity with him. To permit this would be totally inconsistent with God's holy nature. Therefore, whoever sins is *alienated* from God during his physical life and separated from God throughout eternity. This state is called "spiritual death."

Every one of us deserves to experience spiritual death, because not one of us can meet God's standards of perfection. "For all have sinned, and come short of the glory of God" (Rom. 3:23 KJV).

The good news is that God loved us so much he sent his Son to die for us and to pay the penalty for our sins.

When a person trusts Jesus Christ to be his own Savior, he is "born again." This spiritual birth transfers him from the state of spiritual death into the state of spiritual life. God himself comes to live in that believer in the person of the Holy Spirit. Consequently a Christian can know (not hope) that if he should die, he would immediately be with Christ (2 Cor. 5:8). . . .

What lies beyond the grave for a believer?

Joseph Bayly, a man who saw three of his sons die, wrote about heaven in *The View from a Hearse*:

I cannot prove the existence of heaven. I accept its reality by faith, on the authority of Jesus Christ: "In my Father's house are many mansions: if it were not so, I would have told you. I go to prepare a place for you."

For that matter, if I were a twin in the womb, I doubt that I could prove the existence of earth to my mate. He would probably object that the idea of an earth beyond the womb was ridiculous, that the womb was the only earth we'd ever know.

If I tried to explain that earthlings live in a greatly expanded environment and breathe air, he would only be more skeptical. After all, a fetus lives in water; who could imagine its being able to live in a universe of air? To him such a transition would seem impossible.

It would take birth to prove the earth's existence to a fetus. A little pain, a dark tunnel, a gasp of air—and then the wide world! Green grass, laps, lakes, the ocean, horses (could a fetus imagine a horse?), rainbows, walking, running, surfing, ice-skating. With enough room that you don't have to shove, and a universe beyond. . . .

Like the fetus, we cannot envision what it will be like on the other side of the tunnel—in heaven.

But from the Bible, God's Word, we can know this much:

- Heaven is a place of rest (Rev. 14:13).

- Heaven is a place without pain, weeping, or mourning (Rev. 21:4).

- Heaven is a place of total joy in the presence of the Lord (Acts 2:28).

- Though we will be changed, we will recognize our loved ones (Matt. 17:3, 4; Peter recognized Moses and Elijah).

- Heaven will be more beautiful than anything we can imagine (Rev. 21–22).

- We will be comfortable in heaven, for it will be *home* (John 14:2).[9]

The Response to a Teen Facing Death

Listen ◆ Empathize ◆ Affirm ◆ Direct ◆ Enlist ◆ Refer

The teen or preteen who faces the prospect of his or her own death is likely to be in a fragile mental and emotional state. The sensitive youth leader, parent, or concerned adviser can best help by pursuing a course of action such as the following:

L ISTEN. Whether you are a parent or other caring adult, the most helpful thing you can do is to offer a listening ear to the young person. Gary R. Collins offers wise guidance:

Make it known [to the youth] that expression of feelings is good and acceptable—but do not pressure [him or her] to show feelings.

Expect outpourings of crying, anger, withdrawal—but still let it be known that you are available.

Be a receptive, careful listener. . . . Guilt, anger, confusion and despair will all be expressed at times and need to be heard by the helper rather than condemned, squelched or explained away.[10]

E MPATHIZE. Olson writes:

Counseling with the dying . . . causes counselors to confront their own attitudes about death. Have we accepted our own mortality? What are our own emotional reactions to the possibilities that we could become seriously ill or suffer a fatal accident? . . . What is our spiritual, psychological and physiological understanding about death? Unresolved feelings within the counselor toward death will probably cause . . . problems in the counseling relationship. . . .

Counselors must have strong capacities for empathic sensing and skills for communicating their empathy to [youth] who are dying. . . . Do we as counselors live our lives as though we are deliberately ignoring the inevitability of our own death? Successful death-related counseling requires counselors to be mindful of their own finitude.[11]

A FFIRM. Olson writes,

An essential ingredient . . . is an open acceptance of the feelings, thoughts and emotional releases expressed by the [teen]. Many are shocked by the intense rage and fathomless anguish that pours forth [at such times]. There is no room for judgmental platitudes such as: "You've cried enough now. It's time to pull yourself together" [and] "You don't have to be so worried. I am sure that everything will be okay." These types of remarks. . . . are most likely to do more damage than good for the counselee, especially with teenagers who tend to hold back their feelings. Instead, the counseling environment needs to be warm and supportive. . . . Teenagers do not need to be invaded or smothered by loving care but they do need to be surrounded by it.[12]

D IRECT. Most of the help a parent, pastor, or other adult can offer a dying young person will be to listen, empathize, and affirm. The concerned adult can also help by directing the young person in the following areas:

- Pray for the youth and comfort him or her with God's Word, being careful not to preach nor to spout pious platitudes.

- Sensitively lead him or her to call upon God's resources in prayer; lead the young person to turn to God, confide in Him, trust Him, and seek strength from Him.

- Help the youth make decisions, particularly those directly related to his or her condition.

- Provide practical help—rides to the doctor, helpful books, etc.

In addition, Collins suggests some other helpful measures, which he offers in the context of preventing unhealthy grieving but which are adapted below to apply to those advising a young person who is dying:

1. *Develop Healthy Attitudes in the Home.* When parents are open and honest about death, children learn that this is an issue to be faced honestly and discussed openly. Misconceptions then can be corrected, and there is natural opportunity to answer questions. It is probably true that a [young person] can never be prepared for death, but an open attitude at home facilitates communication and makes . . . discussions of death more natural.

2. *Anticipating and Learning about Death.* Death education is a relatively new but growing emphasis. In schools, churches, and other places, people are learning to talk about death (including their own deaths), and to discuss such issues as how the terminally ill face death, how people grieve, [etc.].

3. *Anticipatory Grieving.* When people develop terminal illnesses, families and friends frequently pretend that all will be well, and there is no talk of "leave-taking." When patients and families can talk about the possibilities of imminent death and can be honest about their sadness, the subsequent grief process is less likely to be pathological. . . .

4. *Theological Understanding.* . . . The Bible says a great deal about death, the meaning of life, the reality of the promise of eternal life with Christ for believers, and the pain of mourning. These truths should be taught and understood before death occurs.[13]

Such measures will not "solve" the dying person's problems, of course; only eternity will solve the problem of death. They may, however, help a young person better understand and cope with the prospect of his or her own death.

ENLIST. It is important to enlist the participation of a young person—even one who is facing the possibility of death—in his or her own future, regardless of how brief or indefinite that future may be. As soon as is practical (allowing ample time for expression and venting), guide the youth to make some decisions, such as what treatments and/or medications he will or will not use, what she wants to say to family and friends, unfinished projects or unmet goals he wants to complete, even what his or her funeral might be like. The most important decision to be made, of course, is to be sure that the youth is ready for eternity, having trusted Christ for salvation.

REFER. The youth worker, pastor, or teacher should be careful to work in cooperation with the young person's parents, and all concerned adults should be sensitive to the possible contribution that a professional Christian counselor could make to the young person's ability to cope with the prospect of dying—as well as to the possibility that those around the teen (parents, siblings, close friends) may also be well advised to consult a counselor. Such intervention is more effective the earlier it is begun.

For Further Reading

The following resources may help the concerned parent, pastor, teacher, or youth worker further assist a young person struggling with facing death.

Scriptures Cited in This Chapter

- 2 Samuel 14:14
- Genesis 2:7
- Romans 3:23
- 2 Corinthians 5:8
- Revelation; 14:13; 21:4
- Acts 2:28
- Matthew 17:3–4
- Revelation 21–22
- John 14:2

Other Scripture to Read

- Psalm 23:4; 116:15
- Proverbs 14:32
- Romans 14:8

- 1 Corinthians 15:1–58
- Philippians 1:21

Resources to Call

- Compassionate Friends, an organization offering support to parents and siblings grieving a child's death, (312) 990-0010
- Survivors, an organization for those struggling with the death of a loved one, (619) 727-5682

Further Reading

- Joseph Bayly, *The View from a Hearse* (David C. Cook)
- William Fintel and Gerald McDermott, *Living with Cancer* (Word).
- Billy Graham, *Death and the Life After* (Word).
- Mary Beth Moster, *When the Doctor Says It's Cancer* (Tyndale).

8

GRIEF

A Synopsis

Introduction

Fourteen-year-old Greg and fifteen-year-olds Jonathan and Todd squeezed into the backseat of the tiny compact car. Marcus climbed into the front seat, and Matt, who had obtained his driver's license two weeks earlier, slid behind the steering wheel.

The quintet of classmates and teammates headed to a surprise birthday party for a friend. Matt steered the car out of the little town where they all lived and onto a country road heading west. The road soon turned northwest, and the car topped sixty-five miles per hour. Suddenly, the right tires went off the side of the road onto the uneven shoulder; Matt swung the steering wheel sharply to the left. The car immediately went into a slide that carried it across the road, where it slammed into a utility pole and rolled over on its top, crumpling the roof.

At some point, the boys in front were thrown free of the car and received relatively minor injuries; Jonathan, Todd, and Greg, who had been pushed tightly against the rear of the car as it spun off the road, were crushed as the roof crumpled beneath the weight of the car. All three died before help arrived.

The school and the community reeled from the news. The three victims, all A or B students, were well-liked. Their families were highly involved in school and community events. Their friends, classmates, teachers, and coaches sobbed in each other's arms in school hallways on the Monday morning following the accident. Some walked the halls in a daze. Others became physically sick.

The school administration arranged for counselors to be present all day Monday and Tuesday, and students were not required to go to classes; they were permitted to linger in the cafeteria, talking to counselors and friends, for as long as they needed. The school's compassionate response was appreciated by the friends and families of the boys, but the grief felt by so many was nonetheless overwhelming.

"We're a very tight-knit community," the high school principal told the local newspaper, "and it's going to take us all a very long time to completely heal."

The Problem of Grief

Death touches many teens and preteens. Many experience the death of a grandparent. Some lose a parent to cancer or other disease. Some must deal with the loss of a sibling. Others endure the death of a friend, an acquaintance from school, or a teacher.

The grief that attends the death of a friend or loved one is always difficult, but it can present a special challenge in youth. In the midst of a time of life that is characterized by turmoil and crisis—hormonal, psychological, emotional, spiritual, relational—teens are especially vulnerable to the psychological impact of loss.

Psychologist Gary R. Collins discusses grief in this way:

> Grief is an important, normal response to the loss of any significant object or person. It is an experience of deprivation and anxiety which can show itself physically, emotionally, cognitively, socially and spiritually. Any loss can bring about grief: divorce, retirement from a job, amputations, death of a pet or plant, departure of a child to college or of a pastor to some other church, moving from a friendly neighborhood, selling one's car, losing a home or valued object, loss of a contest or athletic game, health failures, and even the loss of confidence or enthusiasm. Doubts, the loss of one's faith, the waning of one's spiritual vitality, or the inability to find meaning in life can all produce a sadness and emptiness which indicate grief. Indeed, whenever a part of life is removed there is grief.
>
> Most discussions of grief, however, concern losses which come when a loved one or other meaningful person has died. Death, of course, happens to everyone and the mourners are left to grieve. Such grieving is never easy. . . . As Christians we take comfort in the certainty of the resurrection, but this does not soften the emptiness and pain of being forced to let go of someone we love. When we experience loss by death grievers are faced with an absolute, unalterable, irreversible situation; there is nothing they can do to, for or about that relationship.[1]

Grief can be devastating. But it is sometimes more so for a young person, due both to the reactions of others and to their own age and relative immaturity. Authors Joan Sturkie and Siang-Yang Tan point out the quandary facing many grieving youth:

> Oftentimes adults forget to consider that a young person is hurting. . . . Somehow, adults seem to think that young people do not feel the pain as much. Of course, this is not true. Unfortunately, to compound the pain, young people often do not have someone who will listen to them talk about how they are feeling. If a father dies in the family, the mother is comforted with many adults who want to help, to listen, to be there for her. But oftentimes the son or the daughter is overlooked, especially if he or she has not reached adulthood.[2]

Young people who are confronted with the death of a friend or loved one face the difficult task of coping with a somewhat "adult" problem while they are still struggling toward adulthood. Though the experience of grief is a natural part of life that every person must deal with at one time or another, the adolescent or preadolescent may be experiencing grief for the first time—using emotional and spiritual resources that may yet be immature and coping mechanisms that may be sorely underdeveloped.

In general, counseling professionals agree that, while grief is natural, understandable, and necessary, it is not always healthy. Normal grief, which can be quite severe, often involves "intense sorrow, pain, loneliness, anger, depression, physical symptoms and changes in interpersonal relations, all of which comprise a period of deprivation and transition that may last for as long as three years—or more."[3]

Normal grief, while sometimes extremely painful—even explosive—runs along fairly predictable lines and leads eventually to restored mental and emotional well-being. The widely acclaimed work of Elizabeth Kubler-Ross has chronicled the five stages of grief, as Sturkie and Tan explain:

1. **Denial**—The person may refuse to believe that [the death has occurred.] This stage may vary in length, with some people staying in it longer than others. It is a temporary stage, but it may surface again at any time.

2. **Anger**—The [youth] may question why the death occurred. When the answer is not apparent, he or she may lash out in anger at the seeming unfairness of it all.

3. **Bargaining**—This is usually an attempt to postpone [an imminent] death [or "cut a deal" that will lessen the pain of grief or the reality of the separation]. . . . The bargaining is usually done in secrecy, with God.

4. **Depression**—When the . . . person faces the reality of . . . [the] death, depression often sets in. . . .

5. **Acceptance**—When the . . . person works through the feelings and conflicts that have arisen, he or she may now be ready to accept the fact [of the] death.[4]

But pathological grief typically differs from normal grief in its depth (the symptoms of grief are much more intense), duration (the grief endures far longer), and destination (it does not lead to mental and emotional health but to further psychological problems). Psychiatrists V. D. Volkan and D. Josephthal[5] point out three key processes that underlie pathological grief:

Splitting is the process by which a "teenager gives intellectual assent to the death while responding emotionally and behaviorally as if nothing has happened,"[6] a process which allows the youth to avoid the mourning process.

Internalization is the process by which the mourner seeks "to preserve [his or her] relationship with the deceased by taking in the lost person and focusing on his or her internal presence,"[7] a process which denies the reality and finality of the death.

Externalization is the process by which the grieving person fixates on an object that is associated with the deceased, such as a photograph or piece of clothing, which serves to postpone the need to admit and cope with the loss.

Collins points out that several things tend to contribute to grieving that is pathological:

- *Beliefs* (the absence of religious beliefs)

- *Background and personality* ("People who are insecure, dependent, unable to control or express feelings and prone to depression often have more difficulty handling their grief."[8])

- *Social environment* (Social attitudes toward death that encourage the denial or quick dispatch of grief—whether communicated by a family, region, ethnic tradition, or society in general—can greatly influence mourners' ability to cope with grief.)

- *Circumstances accompanying the death* (An untimely death, a tragic mode of death, the closeness of the survivor to the deceased, and other circumstances may intensify the grieving process and incite a pathological response.)

The Causes and Effects of Grief

As a young person (or any person) works through the stages of grief, he or she is likely to encounter a widely varying array of emotions and other effects of the process. The effects of grief to be discussed here are not confined to grief that arises from death; many will be experienced whenever loss of any kind occurs (the loss of a romantic relationship, for example). These effects can be intense, but they are nonetheless normal and usually healthy.

◆ Physical Effects

The physical symptoms of grief described by Erich Lindemann (author of a landmark series of interviews, books, and articles on grief) are related by Dr. G. Keith Olson as follows:

- Laborious respiration marked by sighing and tightness in the throat
- Feelings of physical exhaustion and lack of physical strength and endurance
- Digestive symptoms, including altered sense of taste, loss of appetite, insufficient salivary production and hollow feeling in the stomach.[9]

Other physical symptoms are likely to include sleeplessness (or sleeping much more than usual), headaches, and uncontrollable and often unexpected weeping.

◆ Emotional Effects

Fear. "Fear and anxiety," writes Olson, "are common reactions during the grieving process. . . . Anxieties about the future without the deceased reflect the person's dependency and insecurity. Fears about one's own mortality must also be confronted during the bereavement period." The young person may also fear the changes that may result from his or her changing roles: the male teen who must now be "the man in the family," the younger sibling who is now the oldest in the family, etc. (See also chapter 2, "Anxiety.")

Guilt. Olson writes, "Many bereaved individuals experience a deep sense of guilt. Some feel guilty about past experiences or lack of contact with the deceased. . . . Others feel guilty for not being able to prevent the death. Some even blame themselves for the death." Such guilt reactions, says Olson, "represent an attempt to again feel in control of life after it has dealt such a painful and shaking blow."[10] (See also chapter 3, "Guilt.")

Helplessness. Death is irreversible; mourners often become keenly aware of their powerlessness to prevent or reverse it, and Olson points out that "one of the most unacceptable feelings for an adolescent is to feel helpless. To fight against this threatening feeling, the teenager often tries to take on a sense of responsibility for what has happened. In this way, guilt is often selected over helplessness."[11]

Anger. Anger is a normal and frequent reaction to the loss of a friend or loved one. It may be directed at the deceased for dying, for "deserting" the youth. It may be directed at others—particularly adults—who didn't do enough to prevent the death. It may be directed toward God for allowing such a painful thing to happen. (See also chapter 4, "Anger.")

Loneliness. "A deep feeling of having been abandoned leads to an intense sense of loneliness," writes Olson. "To be alone by choice is one thing. To be forced by external events . . . is quite another. The latter is much more conducive to lonely feelings. While some adolescents react to grief with anger, others withdraw into themselves. Karl Menninger asserts that teenagers who withdraw and become more isolated are in worse condition than those who act out their anger aggressively."[12] (See also chapter 1, "Loneliness.")

Doubt. A common reaction to death is to ask, "Why?" It is natural at such times to seek some explanation, some understanding of the possible reasons for our loss. Usually, however, a satisfying answer is elusive, even impossible. Such lack of answers may prompt doubt; a person may doubt God's love, God's wisdom—even His very existence. As real as the questions—and the doubt—may be, most grieving people are helped less by theological and intellectual explanations than by the sensitive comfort and consolation of others.

Relief. When death comes after a period of disability or illness, the mourner often reacts with a sense of relief; the agony of waiting is over. Relief may also be experienced when the deceased was abusive, hostile, or controlling; the agony of the relationship is over. Such feelings of relief are quite normal in some circumstances, but they may lead to or heighten guilt feelings as well.

These emotional and physical effects are not, of course, the only effects that accompany and characterize grief, but they are perhaps the most prevalent and profound.

The Biblical Perspective of Grief

Collins offers insight into the biblical perspective of grief in his book *Christian Counseling:*

The Bible is a realistic book which describes the deaths and subsequent grieving of many people. In the Old Testament, we read of God's presence and comfort as we "walk through the valley of the shadow of death" (Ps. 23:4); we read descriptions of people grieving in times of loss and trouble (Ps. 6:5–7; 137:1, 5, 6; 2 Sam. 12); we learn that God strengthens grievers (Ps. 119:28); and we are introduced to the Messiah as "a man of sorrows, acquainted with grief. . . . Surely our griefs He Himself bore, and our sorrows He carried" (Isa. 53:3, 4).

In the New Testament, a variety of passages deal with death and grief. These might be grouped into two categories, each dealing with the influence of Jesus Christ.

1. Christ has changed the meaning of grieving. There are many nonbelievers who grieve without any hope for the future. For them, death is the end of a relationship—forever.

But the Christian does not believe that. In the two clearest New Testament passages on this subject (1 Cor. 15 and 1 Thess. 4), we learn that "if we believe that Jesus died and rose again, even so God will bring with Him those who have fallen asleep in Jesus" (1 Thess. 4:14). We can "comfort one another with these words" (1 Thess. 4:18), convinced that in the future "the dead will be raised imperishable, and we shall be changed. . . ." (1 Cor. 15:52–54).

For the Christian, death is not the end of existence; it is the entrance into life eternal. The one who believes in Christ knows that Christians will "always be with the Lord." Physical death is still present because the devil has "the power of death," but because of the crucifixion and resurrection, Christ has defeated death and promised that the one who lives and believes in Christ "shall never die" (1 Thess. 4:17; Heb. 2:14, 15; 2 Tim. 1:10; John 11:25, 26).

This knowledge is comforting, but it does not eliminate the intense pain of grief and the need for comfort. In a discussion of death, Paul encouraged his readers to take courage and not lose heart since the person who is absent from the body is present with the Lord (2 Cor. 4:14–5:8). Believers are encouraged to be steadfast, immovable and doing the Lord's work since such effort is not in vain (1 Cor. 15:58) when we have assurance of the resurrection.

2. Christ has demonstrated the importance of grieving. Early in his ministry, Jesus preached his Sermon on the Mount and spoke about grieving: "Blessed are those that mourn," he said, "for they will be comforted" (Matt. 5:4). Mourning was taken for granted. Apparently it was seen as something positive since it is listed among a group of desirable qualities such as meekness, gentleness, mercy, purity of heart and peacemaking. . . .

When Lazarus died, Jesus was troubled and deeply moved. He accepted, without comment, the apparent anger that came from Mary, Lazarus's sister, and he wept with the mourners. Jesus knew that Lazarus was about to be raised from the dead, but the Lord still grieved (John 11). He also withdrew and grieved when he learned that John the Baptist had been executed (Matt. 14:12–21). In the Garden of Gethsemane, Jesus was "deeply grieved" (Matt. 26:38), perhaps with an anticipatory grief, more intense but similar to that experienced by David as he watched his infant son die (2 Sam. 12:15–23).

Even for the Christian, then, grief is normal and healthy.[13]

Grief, as well as death, is a natural and inescapable part of human experience. "To feel a deep sense of grief," says Olson, "to be overwhelmed with pain, to be in utter despair in response to . . . a loss is completely normal, healthy, and in line with God's plan and creation."[14] As "the preacher" said, "There is a time for everything, and a season for every activity under heaven: a time to be born, and a time to die . . . a time to weep, and a time to laugh; a time to mourn, and a time to dance."[15]

The Response to the Problem of Grief

Listen ◆ Empathize ◆ Affirm ◆ Direct ◆ Enlist ◆ Refer

Grief is a painful and difficult experience for the most mature among us; it can be unimaginably more so for an adolescent or preadolescent. The following measures, however, may help a parent, teacher, pastor, or other concerned adult to counsel a grieving teen. The concerned adult who is not a parent should, of course, inform and involve the parents in the ministry of helping a youth through grief.

LISTEN. Grieving youths will not be looking for—and will not be helped by—"convenient, glib answers to ease every question from [their] aching hearts."[16] What they want, and what they need, is someone who is willing to walk through the process of grief with them, always present, seldom talking, always listening. Gary D. Bennett offers wise guidance:

Encourage crying as a legitimate way to show . . . feelings, not as a sign of weakness. Statements such as "Hold your chin up" or "Be

brave" should be avoided. It's better to remain quiet and supportive than to say anything that will interfere with the grief process.[17]

Though Job's friends have been widely criticized and may have been more hindrance than help, it is worth remembering that when they heard of the deaths of his wife and family, "they sat on the ground with him for seven days and seven nights. No one said a word to him, because they saw how great his suffering was."[18]

EMPATHIZE. The parent or youth worker who hopes to help a teen through the grieving process should examine his or her past experiences with—and responses to—death. Is the adult conscious of his or her own finitude? Olson says that "Empathic understanding, one of the most healing dynamics in any counseling relationship, is particularly important when counseling with the bereaved. . . . And empathic expressions of understanding, caring and support have significant healing impact."[19]

God calls Christians to "rejoice with those who rejoice; mourn with those who mourn,"[20] and to point others to "the God of all comfort, who comforts us in our troubles, so that we can comfort those in any trouble with the comfort we ourselves have received from God."[21] Sharing sorrow and sensitively offering comfort are among the simplest and most effective help anyone can offer in times of grief.

AFFIRM. Olson writes,

An essential ingredient in successful grief counseling is an open acceptance of the feelings, thoughts and emotional releases expressed by the [teen]. Many are shocked by the intense rage and fathomless anguish that pours forth from the grieving. . . . The counseling environment needs to be warm and supportive. . . . Teenagers do not need to be invaded or smothered by loving care but they do need to be surrounded by it.[22]

The ministry of prayer is one key way of providing affirmation and comfort to a grieving youth. Pray for him or her; let the youth *hear you* pray for him or her; let your concern and esteem reach the youth by letting him or her listen as you pour out your heart for that young person in prayer.

DIRECT. Most of the help a parent, pastor, or other adult can offer a grieving young person will be to listen, empathize, and affirm. However, some helpful directive measures might include:

• Help the young person to face his or her loss. This can be done by encouraging him or her to talk about the loss, perhaps by asking:

How did it happen?

Where were you when you heard?

Where did it occur?

Who told you about it?

(If the loss was a death) What was the funeral like?

Help the young person identify and express his or her feelings. Typical feelings associated with a loss include anger, guilt, anxiety, and frustration. Keep in mind that most people will not identify and express their feelings when asked directly. Instead, seek to facilitate expression of feelings by responding to the youth: "I can see how that might make you angry," or "You really feel strongly about that, don't you?"

• Help the youth turn to the God of all comfort. Encourage dependence on Him and His limitless resources. Do not preach to or push the young person, but gently remind him or her that God is a "refuge and strength, an ever present help in trouble."[23]

• Help the youth learn to live with the loss. Guide the conversation through the difficulties the young person faces now as a result of

the loss, and walk him or her through various problem-solving approaches (role-playing, playing "what if," listing pros and cons, etc.). Try to steer his or her attention away from the past (the loss itself) and toward the future (What is to be done now?).

• Allow the youth time to grieve. Grieving takes time. Be prepared for the most difficult times in the process:

— the first three months after the loss

— the first anniversary of the loss (in cases of death)

— holidays and special days

• Help the youth examine and admit inappropriate responses to the loss such as withdrawal or resorting to alcohol and drug use as a coping mechanism. Guide him or her to consider appropriate coping devices in place of such things.

• Provide ongoing support to the young person. Help with the many adjustments that follow a loss: changes in relationships, schedules, etc.

ENLIST. As suggested above, one way to help the grieving youth might be to elicit his or her response to the question, "How are you going to deal with this . . . ?" The concerned adult may help facilitate healthy grieving by enlisting the young person's participation in such decisions as, Will he or she attend the funeral? Will he or she participate in the funeral? and Can he or she help others who are grieving (a spouse, family member, or friend of the deceased)? Such activities can be extremely cathartic in working through grief.

REFER. While parents and other caring adults must be involved in helping a young person cope with grief, other resources are often necessary. Olson advises:

Because adolescence is a life stage that is so marked with turmoil and transition, whenever a teenager loses a loved relative or close friend, counseling is advised. Symptoms may or may not be present. Remember, however, that symptom severity is not always a valid indication of the need for counseling intervention. In just a few sessions a counselor can assist bereaved teenagers through their grief process. The counselor can play a crucial role by listening, supporting and empathically caring as the adolescent mourner readjusts and adapts to a future without the presence of the deceased.[24]

For Further Reading

The following resources may help the concerned parent, pastor, teacher, or youth worker further assist a young person struggling with a loss:

Scriptures Cited in This Chapter

- Psalm 23:4
- Psalms 6:5–7; 137:1, 5–6
- 2 Samuel 12
- Psalm 119:28
- Isaiah 53:3–4
- 1 Corinthians 15
- 1 Thessalonians 4
- Hebrews 2:14–15
- 2 Timothy 1:10
- John 11:25–26
- 2 Corinthians 4:14–5:8

- Matthew 5:4
- John 11
- Matthew 14:12–21, 26:38
- 2 Timothy 1:10
- Ecclesiastes 3:1, 4
- Job 2:13
- Psalm 46:1

Other Scripture to Read

- Psalm 116:15
- John 14:1–4
- 2 Corinthians 1:3–7

Resources to Call

• Compassionate Friends, an organization offering support to parents and siblings grieving a child's death, (312) 990-0010

• Survivors, an organization for those struggling with the death of a loved one, (619) 727-5682

Further Reading

• Joseph Bayly, *The View from a Hearse* (David C. Cook).

• Billy Graham, *Death and the Life After* (Word).

• C. S. Lewis, *A Grief Observed* (Bantam).

• Carol A. and William J. Rowley, *On Wings of Mourning: Our Journey Through Grief and Recovery* (Word).

9

SUICIDE THOUGHTS, TENDENCIES, AND THREATS

A Synopsis

Introduction

Fourteen-year-old Lori had been baptized just months before at Blue Springs Community Church, a one-room country church a few miles away from her home. The ceremony was attended by about sixty people, nearly half of them members of Lori's family.

Lori dropped out of church not long afterward, however. The pastor and his wife visited her several times, but they failed to persuade Lori to return to the small church. The entire church was concerned for her, but no one suspected the real reason for her absence. Lori was pregnant.

About a month before she expected to deliver, Lori tidied her room, emptied her school locker, and wrote a note to her mother:

> *"You kept asking me if I was OK and I kept telling you I was, but I wasn't OK. I'm sorry, Mom. I've got too many problems. I am taking the easy way out."*

Lori left that day before her mother arrived home from work. She walked to the railroad tracks near her house, knelt between the rails, and folded her hands over her little round belly as Amtrak 168 barreled down upon her.

The train engineer, a man who had a fourteen-year-old daughter of his own, later said that when he saw Lori, it was too late to stop the train. He watched her cross herself before she died.[1]

The Problem of Suicide

Suicide is the second leading cause of death among teenagers. Youth specialist and lecturer Jerry Johnston writes,

> According to the National Institute of Mental Health, eighteen teenagers per day kill themselves in the United States. Every eighty minutes another teenager takes the suicidal plunge. What a nightmare it is to realize over a hundred teenagers per week kill themselves in our country. In a year's time, the total comes to a staggering sixty-five hundred lives lost. . . .
>
> Reliable sources now say that over a thousand teenagers try unsuccessfully to kill themselves every day! Almost one teen per minute tries to commit suicide.[2]

Dr. David Elkind reports:

> A recent survey of 1,986 teens in *Who's Who Among American High School Students* found that 30 percent of these young people had considered suicide, 4 percent [had] attempted it, and 60 percent said they knew a peer who had attempted suicide or had killed himself.[3]

The statistics do not tell nearly the whole story, however. Many suicides are not even counted in the above statistics due to several factors. Dr. G. Keith Olson points out:

> There are more successful suicides each year that are counted as other forms of death because of lack of knowledge of the victim's intent or motivation. A significant percentage of one-car accidents are actual suicides. . . . Some people who are medically ill die only because they stop taking their medication. And others "flirt with death" by their involvement in high-risk occupations and sports (e.g., sky diving . . .) and life-endangering habits (e.g., smoking, heavy drinking and drug abuse). And finally, Marvin E. Wolfgang has studied a form of suicide that is mainly peculiar to adolescents and young adults. "Victim precipitatal

homicide" occurs when one person provokes or sets up another person to kill him or her.[4]

More importantly, perhaps, statistics alone do not convey the tragedy of teen suicide, nor its epidemic proportions. The human tragedy of promising lives lost in a moment, of parents, siblings, and friends enduring unspeakable grief and sorrow, of families and communities torn apart, cannot be measured.

David Elkind points out that it is often difficult to identify teens who are contemplating suicide partly because "teenagers in particular are often reluctant to reveal the problems they are experiencing or their inner thoughts. Unfortunately many teens also conceal their inner pains and fears so that even their parents and closest friends have no idea that they are suffering and considering suicide.

"Nonetheless," Elkind says, "while many young people often give no implications of an impending suicide attempt, others do."[5] Some of the signs that may alert a parent, teacher, youth leader, pastor or friend to a possible suicide attempt include:

- Previous suicide attempt
- Threats of suicide
- Talking about death
- Preparation for death (cleaning out locker, giving away possessions, etc.)
- Depression
- Sudden change in behavior (acting out, violent behavior, etc.)
- Moodiness
- Withdrawal
- Somatic complaints (sleeplessness, sleeping all the time)
- Fatigue
- Increased risk-taking
- Drafting a suicide note

While it is not always possible to recognize the signs of suicidal tendencies or to prevent a teen from contemplating or committing suicide, a familiarity with the causes and precipitating factors of adolescent suicide can make a crucial difference.

The Causes of Suicide

◆ Societal Factors

"There is a growing consensus," says Bill Blackburn, author of *What You Should Know about Suicide,* about the broader causes of teen suicide, "toward identifying the following influences: (1) the changing moral climate, (2) the high mobility of American society, (3) the high divorce rate, (4) the frequent abuse of alcohol and other drugs, (5) the glorification of violence in the mass media, (6) the easy availability of guns, and (7) the already high suicide rate."

He goes on,

> What remains solid and dependable for young persons in the potentially difficult years of adolescence? Two sources of support are a society where the moral guidelines are firm and a family that you can depend on even though you are breaking away from it. But what happens if the rules of the society keep changing and the morals are objects of debate rather than reliable guideposts? What if the family moves hundreds or thousands of miles from any relatives or mother and father divorce and you see only one of them regularly? The sources of support become shaky foundations.

> When the foundations become shaky, some young people turn to alcohol and other drugs for solace. These agents, when mixed with a teenager's romantic notions of death, a society that glorifies violence, and easy access to the means of suicide, combine into a powerfully lethal mixture that spells death for more and more adolescents. Finally, suicide begets suicide. Suicide attempted

or completed plants the idea of self-generated death in the minds of others[, and] suicide in the family especially pulls other family members closer to that option.[6]

But beyond the societal factors are personal factors. Why do teens try to kill themselves? The following are among the reasons:

◆ Family Disruption

Many researchers have attempted to trace the relationship between family disruption—divorce, moving, etc.—and teen depression and suicide. Although the results are sometimes contradictory, insomuch as family disruption increases a young person's stress, sense of alienation, and perhaps parental rejection, it may be a contributing factor not only to depression but to suicide as well. (See also chapter 19, "Parental Divorce.")

◆ Depression

"A clinically depressed youth may become suicidal," writes author Marion Duckworth, and the experts agree. (See also chapter 5, "Depression.") She cites her own experience:

> I remember writing in my own diary when I was a teenager and angry at my mother, "She'd be sorry if I was dead." But for a seriously depressed youth, the thought of suicide is ongoing and if help is not forthcoming, he may become convinced it's the only way out.[7]

◆ Escape

Blackburn writes,

> Most suicidal persons want to escape from what they consider an intolerable situation. The shape of that situation varies with each person, and many other persons in similar situations do not consider suicide an option. Two important ingredients for those who begin to ponder taking their lives are hopelessness and faulty reasoning. These two are linked: there seems to be no hope of

resolving the situation, but the reason hope does not appear is that the suicidal person is not thinking carefully or clearly. Sometimes this is because of mental illness.[8]

The suicidal person may be intent on escaping a terminal or painful illness, or punishment, or humiliation, or simply the weight of his or her mental and emotional burdens.

◆ Loss

"For some," writes Olson, "the death of a parent, close friend or loved one seems too painful to bear." At such times, the grieving young person will often entertain thoughts of suicide—sometimes simply in an effort to end the seemingly unbearable sorrow and grief (see also chapter 8, "Grief"), and other times, as Blackburn points out, to rejoin the friend or loved one in death:

> To be reunited with one you love by following him through the door of death is one of the most ancient and persistent motives for suicide. . . . The Hindu ritual of suttee called for the widow to sacrifice herself on her husband's funeral pyre. In the Japanese culture, Junshi is a form of suicide for those who wish to join a leader or master in death. Shinju, practiced by the lower classes, is a form of double suicide so the "lovesick" can be joined in death.
>
> Though not ritualized in [Western] society, this is still a compelling motive for many suicidal persons.[9]

◆ Guilt

Guilt feelings often contribute to suicidal tendencies as well. (See also chapter 3, "Guilt.") Olson writes,

> Suicide is often the individual's own attempt to take control of punishment for sins or other misdeeds of which he or she feels guilty. When no punishment has been received from society, friends or family, the individual chooses to be the

victim of his or her own self-punishment. Too often suicide becomes the ultimate punishment.[10]

◆ Attention

Blackburn writes:

> A suicide attempt grabs attention like few other things. People are startled, guilty, concerned, puzzled. Where people previously ignored a person, now they lavish attention on him.[11]

In such an instance, the attempt is often a desperate cry, not only for attention, but for help as well. It may be a teen's way of saying, "I'm hurting, I'm desperate, I don't know how to cope, and I need help. Please, someone pay attention to me!" Tragically, of course, the cry for help sometimes goes too far and becomes fatal.

◆ Manipulation

Blackburn offers insight into this motivation as well:

> Although akin to the attempts to gain attention, this reason for attempting suicide is designed to get more than attention. There is a specific object or action the person is seeking. The desire is to elicit a response that seems otherwise unobtainable. A suicide attempt can be the trump card played after all the other cards have been played.
>
> Manipulation by attempted suicide is used by children against parents, husbands against wives, girlfriends against boyfriends, workers against co-workers.[12]

◆ Revenge

Olson points out:

> People, often young people, feel so overwhelmed by being hurt by another, that their wish to hurt back overrides their wish to live. The suicide of revenge is usually directed toward a lover, parent or parent figure.[13]

◆ Impulsiveness

The teen years are often characterized by experimentation and impulsiveness. Adolescents often display a casual disregard for their life and safety, and also sometimes exhibit a fascination with the unknown, including death. The volatile blend of curiosity, impulsiveness, and feelings of invincibility that exist in the adolescent heart and mind can create a dangerous propensity for suicidal acts.

◆ Expression of Love

Both Olson and Blackburn, among many others, attribute some teen suicides to a desire to express love. Says Olson:

> Loving emotions in adolescents and young adults are often extremely intense and loyal. The breakup of a romantic relationship, a divorce and the death of a loved one deal the rejected or surviving individuals a shattering blow. Their emotions are numbed, their perceptions distorted and their hopes for the future destroyed. Their total focus is on the object of their lost love. Their last self-expression is a twisted proclamation of their love—the ultimate sacrifice of their lives.[14]

The Effects of Suicide

Obviously, the primary, overwhelming effect of a teen suicide is the loss of a young life, with all its promise and potential. But few young people contemplating suicide realize the traumatic effects an act of suicide can have on those around them, principally, grief and the planting of the seeds of destruction.

◆ Grief

The suicide of a friend or family member invariably causes a depth of grief and questioning that surrounds few—if any—other experiences in life. Parents castigate themselves endlessly over their inability to prevent the tragedy, friends feel deserted and sometimes betrayed, pastors question whether they could have or should have done or said something differently, and teachers fervently and futilely wish they had recognized the signs—if, indeed, any were present to recognize.

Don Baker writes:

> Hundreds of times I've watched different degrees of marital disintegration and numerous times I've seen the aftermath of a crushing suicide experience. Inevitably the living never blame the dead—they blame the living—they blame themselves.[15]

The emotional fallout of suicide among the survivors is both deep—the emotional and psychological equivalent of Hiroshima, perhaps—and enduring, affecting people's lives for years, decades, even—in the case of those closest to the victim—lifetimes. (See also chapter 8, "Grief.")

◆ Seeds of Destruction

Suicide not only destroys the person who takes his or her life, but it plants the seeds of destruction in the lives of those around him or her—parents, siblings, friends, and classmates. The *Journal of the American Medical Association* reports "an increased rate of suicidal behavior in the first-degree relatives of suicide attempters."[16] In other words, those closest to a suicide victim are at a higher risk of attempted suicide than others. Some researchers believe this may be due to genetic factors (and it may), but it may also indicate a greater willingness among those whose loved ones have committed suicide to look at suicide as a viable option.

Some communities have experienced what law enforcement officials refer to as "cluster suicides." Jerry Johnston relates:

> In Jefferson County, Colorado, eighteen teenagers killed themselves between January 1985 and June 1986—eighteen deaths in eighteen months! Bryan High School in Omaha, Nebraska, earned the dubious nickname Suicide High when

three students who vaguely knew one another took their own lives in a five-day period. Four other students at Bryan attempted suicide but survived. In Plano, Texas, eleven teenage deaths in sixteen months stunned that city.[17]

As Blackburn says, "Suicide has a ripple effect. Sometimes these ripples become tidal waves that inundate the family and others close by."[18]

The Biblical Perspective of Suicide

The Bible contains many accounts of (and by) individuals who had faced great difficulties and endured great burdens. The psalmist declared, "All day long I have been plagued; I have been punished every morning,"[19] and Job wailed, "May the day of my birth perish. . . . Why did I not perish at birth, and die as I came from the womb?"[20]

The Scriptures even contain a number of accounts of suicides. Samson killed himself along with all the Philistines in the temple of Dagon.[21] King Saul fell on his own sword rather than allow himself to be taken prisoner by the Philistines.[22] Ahithophel, a counselor to King David, "put his house in order and then hanged himself."[23] When he saw that his royal city had fallen to rebel forces, Zimri, king of Israel, set his palace on fire around him and died in the flames.[24] And, of course, Judas—one of the Twelve—betrayed Jesus and later hanged himself.[25]

In none of those cases does the Bible soft-pedal or romanticize suicide, much less endorse it. On the contrary, Scripture repeatedly affirms the sanctity of human life and the conviction that it is the Lord's to give and His to take away: "The Lord brings death and makes alive; he brings down to the grave and raises up."[26]

In light of such principles, suicide is certainly not the Lord's way. He who said, "In this world you will have trouble. But take heart! I have overcome the world"[27] would certainly have His children turn to Him to find hope, strength, and purpose rather than end their lives in despair.

But is suicide the unforgivable sin? It is not the specific act Jesus identified as the unforgivable sin in Matthew 12:31. But does a person who commits suicide end his or her life with a sin that—because it is the final act of that person's life—cannot be confessed and forgiven?

Baker and Nester propose an answer to that question:

> Many feel that suicide is the ultimate sin for which there is no forgiveness. . . . This is obviously a misunderstanding of the gospel of God's grace. The only sin that truly keeps one from God's presence is the sin of unbelief—of not trusting the work of Christ personally. The inability to confess suicide as a sin is not a real issue.
>
> God's forgiveness gives me a position as His child and deals with all of my sin—past, present, and future. If salvation depended upon confessing every sin committed as a believer, no one would qualify! We have all sinned in ways we either were not aware of or were not concerned about enough to confess individually.
>
> > Payment God does not twice demand
> > First at my bleeding Surety's hand
> > And then again at mine.
>
> The unfortunate and sad ending of an individual's life by his own hand does not nullify the effect of the grace of God in his life. Suicide victims who are children of God are redeemed souls in the presence of their Heavenly Father.[28]

The Response to the Problem of Suicide

Listen ◆ Empathize ◆ Affirm ◆ Direct ◆ Enlist ◆ Refer

If a youth has attempted suicide (or is seriously contemplating or threatening an attempt), your responsibility is both urgent and simple: get the young person immediately to a mental health hospital or emergency room; a professional evaluation is absolutely necessary. If you fail to do so and the young person attempts to take his or her life, you may be considered legally responsible.

The following response is designed to help a pastor, youth worker, teacher, or parent offer counsel to a young person who has admitted having passing thoughts of suicide (in contrast to someone who has attempted or threatened suicide). If at any time during the counseling process, you infer or suspect that the youth may be contemplating suicide, do not leave the youth alone until he or she is in the care of a mental health professional.

If at any time you have reason to believe that a young person has given even passing thought to suicide (but has not actually attempted or threatened suicide), you must still proceed to intervene with extreme care and thoughtful prayer. Blackburn advises not to try to shock or shame the person, nor to get into an argument or philosophical discussion or attempt to "mind-read or psychoanalyze" the youth.[29]

Instead, the wise youth worker or parent can help by employing a strategy such as the following:

LISTEN. "Always take every indication seriously that an individual is thinking about suicide," writes Duckworth. Never dismiss, mock, or challenge a youth's statements about contemplating or attempting suicide. "The more concrete their plans," Duckworth continues, "the more dangerous the situation and the more the need for immediate action. Do they have a weapon stashed somewhere? Have they experimented with fashioning a noose? Even if their plans aren't concrete, [keep in mind that] youth are notoriously impulsive."[30] Listen carefully, sensitively, patiently—and take no chances.

EMPATHIZE. Blackburn suggests:

The primary power you have in dealing with a suicidal person is your relationship with him and the way you show interest and concern. . . . Wisely use that power to avert the potential suicide.[31]

Ways to make the most of your relationship may include:

- Making every effort to be available, especially at crisis moments

- Calling periodically to "keep in touch" with the youth's moods and progress

- Praying for the young person (and letting him or her hear your prayers)

AFFIRM. It may be tempting to try to contradict a young person's estimation of how bad things are, how rotten his lot is, etc. While the youth's hopelessness and faulty reasoning should be addressed, it is of primary importance that everything that is said and done by the adult be presented in a way that strongly affirms his or her worth as a person, as a child of God, as a valued and loved family member or friend, and as an individual with capabilities, gifts, and immeasurable potential.

DIRECT. The following imperatives, drawn from the work of Marion Duckworth, Jay Adams, and Bill Blackburn, may present a helpful direction for guiding a teen with suicidal tendencies:

1. Work on relationship. The best resource any parent or other adult has for helping a suicidal youth is a healthy relationship. Work on building your relationship with the youth and on helping him or her to build strong, open relationships with others.

2. Build self-worth. Duckworth writes, "Parents and [others] can ease the struggle for self acceptance by consistently using every method available to teach children . . . two things: Who they really are; How to cultivate a personhood in which they can feel at home."[32] She suggests accomplishing that by reinforcing the child's successes, offering loving reminders that he or she is loved and accepted, and keeping an open dialogue about the things the child faces.

3. Instill hope. "Suicidal persons . . . need hope," writes Adams. "They are preeminently persons with no hope."[33] Duckworth suggests instilling hope by exposing youth to the God of hope (and a hopeful way of looking at Creation, natural laws, etc.), cultivating a sense of wonder that they are children of God, responding to the young person as an individual with a unique personality and unique gifts, working out differences between parents, and involving the positive influences of extended family in the life of the young person.

4. Foster communication. A disturbing percentage of youth—even Christian youth—say they can't talk to their parents about the really important things in life. Duckworth quotes Cathy Benitez's advice to let teens know "they can say whatever they want and they won't be condemned for it. Respect their opinions no matter what they are."[34]

5. Teach coping skills. It's hard to believe in yourself—or in the future—when your world is falling apart, Duckworth says. Many teens lack the skills to cope with the myriad of pressures and problems they face at home, at school, and in their circle of friends. Among her suggestions: majoring in relationships, setting clear boundaries, modeling appropriate ways of solving problems, communicating wisdom wisely and tactfully, entering into the teen's world, and allowing him or her to experience the real world, without illusions.

6. Focus on the available resources. "Most suicidal persons fail to see the resources available to help them cope," says Blackburn. "Not in an argumentative way, but in a vein of gentle exploring, help the person begin to identify clearly the nature of the problems he faces and the alternatives. . . . With some persistence . . . you may be able to spark a flame of hope."[35]

7. Develop a plan of action. Devise a set of practical, concrete steps that will help the youth and his or her circumstances. Foremost among these steps should be the development of a regular, honest habit of fellowship with God, both private and corporate. A helpful plan of action may also include negotiating changes in home and family routines, avoiding certain environments or companions, engaging in some new or favorite hobby or form of recreation, joining a church youth group, entering a mentoring relationship, etc.

ENLIST. Make every effort to enlist the young person's own participation in preventing a suicide attempt. Perhaps the most effective way to do so is to encourage him or her to enter into a contract with you. This can be a verbal or written contract that states:

- The youth agrees to contact you or another person (named in the contract) if he or she begins to think of suicide.

- The youth agrees not to stop trying, even if he or she has trouble reaching you, until the two of you have talked about his or her thoughts of suicide.

- The adult agrees to respond to any call or message immediately upon receiving it and to take time to talk without annoyance or impatience.

- The adult agrees not to leave the young person alone until both parties are confident that the crisis has passed.

REFER. Olson states emphatically, "Once it has been assessed that a teenage counselee is a potential suicide risk, definitive counseling intervention is a must."[36] In other words, consult the young person's parents and get professional help immediately.

The American Association of Suicidology advises:

> The cardinal rule of suicide prevention is this: DO SOMETHING. If someone you know has attempted suicide and has not received professional care: GET HELP. If someone you know threatens to end his life: GET HELP. If someone you know has undergone a drastic change in his life and begins preparing wills or giving away personal possessions: GET HELP. Don't wait to see if other signs develop. Don't decide to consider it for a while. Do it today. Tomorrow may be too late."[37]

Getting help may involve contacting a family physician or taking the young person to a local hospital, calling a suicide crisis center or hotline, involving the local mental health or children's service agencies, or consulting a professional Christian psychologist or psychiatrist. Whatever it takes: GET HELP.

For Further Reading

The following resources may help the concerned parent or other adult further assist a young person who may be contemplating suicide:

Scriptures Cited in This Chapter

- Psalm 73:14
- Job 3:3, 11
- Judges 16:29–30

- 1 Chronicles 10:4–5
- 2 Samuel 17:23
- 1 Kings 16:18
- Matthew 27:45
- 1 Samuel 2:6
- John 16:33b
- Matthew 12:31

Other Scripture to Read

- Psalm 6:4–9
- Psalm 13:2–6
- Psalm 34:18
- Psalms 18, 25, 27, 71, 91, 130, 139
- Psalm 73:28
- Psalm 143:7–11
- 1 Peter 5:7

Resources to Call

- Students Against Suicide, a teen organization to facilitate open communication between parents and teens. (714) 361-9401
- Survivors of Suicide, offering help for families and friends of suicide victims. (414) 442-4638

Further Reading

- Bill Blackburn, *What You Should Know about Suicide* (Word).
- Marion Duckworth, *Why Teens Are Killing Themselves* (Here's Life Publishers).
- Jerry Johnston, *Why Suicide?* (Oliver Nelson).

RELATIONAL

ISSUES

10

LOVE

A Synopsis

Introduction

Rick and Gloria began dating when they were both sixteen. She was a pretty, waifish brunette; he was a blond tennis player. From the time they started dating, neither had ever gone out with anyone else. They began to talk dreamily of marriage when they were both seniors in high school. But Rick had a secret he had never shared with Gloria.

Rick and Gloria often double-dated with Rick's best friend, Justin, and his girlfriend, Amy. The four seemed to have a special bond, a close relationship that forged ties not only between Rick and Justin but between all four of them. Rick and Gloria married at twenty-two on the weekend after Rick's graduation from a small college on the East Coast; Justin and Amy had been married the summer before.

Though the couples seldom saw each other after high school, a bond existed that neither Gloria, Amy, or Justin knew about—until Rick announced to Gloria that he was leaving her less than eight months after their wedding. Rick explained to his new wife that seven years ago—at about the time he and Gloria had begun dating—he had fallen in love with Amy, the girl who was now his best friend's wife.

"I care for you," he told Gloria. "But Amy is the one I love . . . always have." Rick had never dated Amy. He had never before expressed his love for her. "But I'm going to do that now," he said. "I don't expect her to leave Justin. I just have to tell her how I feel, in person. And I have to be around her. I can't live without her."

The Problem of Finding True Love

Everyone wants it. Without it, life would be, at best, incomplete—at worst, desperate. The yearning to give and receive love throbs in the heart of everyone, male and female alike.

People try in many different ways to discover true love, real love, a love that is strong and deep, a love that lasts for all time. Yet the pursuit of love has caused more heartache and pain, more brokenness and bitterness, than all the diseases and all the wars in history.

Many young people struggle mightily to understand what love is and how they can find it. Many are willing to give almost anything in order to experience love, particularly from someone of the opposite sex. To many teens, love *does* make the world go 'round. Yet many—far too many—set themselves up for heartache, disappointment, and tragic miscalculations and mistakes because they lack a clear understanding of what love is—and what it isn't.

The Causes of Not Finding True Love

Youth specialist and author Jerry Johnston writes:

> Sandy is seventeen, with hair the color of her name. She's a junior in high school who makes good grades and seems well-adjusted. But Sandy's story is far from pleasant. . . . Since she became sexually active at thirteen, Sandy has slept with seven or eight boyfriends in addition to numerous one-time dates.
>
> As her story unfolded, I readily sensed the regret and loneliness in her voice. From her vantage point, the future was gray, clouded by the experiences she knew should not have happened. A wish-it-could-be different frustration tugged at her heart as she relived the moments with guys

whose names she was now trying to forget. Each one carried away a fragment of her heart.

> It is over now. The story is finished and there remains nothing but a bitter taste in her heart. So much given away, so fast.
>
> Then, surprisingly, Sandy smiled and said, "All that's changed now. My boyfriend and I have something really special. We make love regularly and it is so wonderfully romantic. I love him dearly and I know he loves me. Our love is different from all the rest."
>
> After a moment of studied silence I ask, "Really? How long have the two of you dated?"
>
> "Two months."
>
> It amazed me that Sandy didn't hear what she was really saying. Her deepest desire, in spite of (or perhaps because of) the other relationships, is to experience true love. Yet . . . how quickly she has forgotten the other guys she thought were *the* one for her. The present love is always the true love for a girl like Sandy.[1]

◆ Teens Don't Know What Love Is

So many teens are making tragic mistakes—some of them over and over again, like Sandy. Very often the reason behind such mistakes is the fact that teens (like many adults) don't really know what love is; they confuse real love with other experiences and emotions. Consequently, they have no basis on which to evaluate the relationships they pursue and the decisions they make in search of real love.

Many public school "sex ed" courses teach kids the mechanics of sex; some even teach kids how to apply condoms. Rock singers and TV stars make public service announcements to warn kids to practice what they call "safer sex." But the politicians, public schools, and pop stars *don't* tell young people what they most need and most want to hear—and what will be most effective in saving them from disappointment and disease—and that is a realistic and biblical understanding of *true love*—what it is and what it isn't.

◆ What Love Isn't

Real Love Isn't the Same As Lust. Rock singer Jon Bon Jovi made an insightful observation when he said, "[Today's] songs are about lust, not love."[2] Lust and love are often confused in our minds, in our music, in our movies, in our magazines—in our whole culture, in fact. But love is much different from lust. Love gives; lust takes. Love values; lust uses. Love endures; lust subsides.

Real Love Isn't the Same As Romance. Some couples experience emotional fireworks when they kiss. Some guys can speak words that make a girl feel so good inside. Some girls can make a guy feel taller and stronger than anyone else just by looking into his eyes. Candlelight dinners, mood music, slow dances, and starry skies can make a moment special. Romance can be wonderful, but it's not love. Romance is a feeling; real love is much more.

Real Love Isn't the Same As Infatuation. Infatuation is a fascination with—an intense interest in—someone of the opposite sex. It can leave a young man or woman feeling breathless, lightheaded, starry-eyed, and addle-brained! Author Joyce Huggett describes infatuation as:

> . . . usually thoroughly "me-centered" rather than "other-centered." You fall for someone, you beguile yourself into believing yourself deeply in love with this person round whom your dreams revolve, you believe yourself ready to renounce your absorption with self for the sake of the well-being of this other person. Then, one morning, you wake up to discover that the euphoria has evaporated in the night. What is more, you find yourself held captive by identical feelings for *another* person.[3]

When people talk about "falling in love" or about "love at first sight," they are usually talking about infatuation. Infatuation can be an overwhelming feeling, but it is not real love.

Real Love Isn't the Same As Sex. Many teens (and many adults as well) confuse the intensity of sex with the intimacy of love. However, the two are distinct. Love is a process; sex is an act. Love is learned; sex is instinctive. Love requires constant attention; sex takes no effort. Love takes time to develop and mature; sex needs no time to develop. Love requires emotional and spiritual interaction; sex requires only physical interaction. Love deepens a relationship; sex (operating alone) dulls a relationship.[4]

Real love is not the same as lust, romance, infatuation, or sex.

◆ What Love Is

"How do I know if I'm in love?" That question is vital to a teenager. It assumes a critical and urgent importance in the hearts and minds of young people. The question is made harder to answer by the fact that few people—adolescents *or* adults—know what real love *is*.

Just as many people confuse love with lust, romance, infatuation, or sex, many also are unaware that there are really three kinds of "love," three ways of behaving that people routinely label as "love."

Love If . . . The first type of love is the only kind many people have ever known. It's what I call "love *if.*" It's the love that is given or received when certain conditions are met. One must *do* something to earn this kind of love:

"If you are a good child, Daddy will give you his love."

"If you get good grades . . ."

"If you act or dress a certain way . . ."

"If you meet my expectations as a lover . . ."

"If you have sex with me . . ."

The love is offered in exchange for something the lover wants. Its motivation is basically selfish. Its purpose is to gain something in exchange for love.

Many young women know no other type of love than the one which says, "I will love you if you will 'put out.'" What they don't realize is that the love they expect to win from someone by meeting his sexual demands is a cheap love that can't satisfy and is never worth the price.

Love *if* . . . always has strings attached. As long as the conditions are met, things are fine. When there is reluctance—to meet expectations, to have sex, to get an abortion—the love is withdrawn.

Many marriages break up because they were built on this kind of love. When the expectations cease to be met, "love *if*" often turns to disappointment and resentment and, tragically, the persons involved may never know why.

Love Because of . . . The second type of love is "love *because of . . .*" In this type of love, the person is loved because of something he or she is, has, or does. This kind of love reflects attitudes, usually unexpressed, such as:

"I love you because you're so beautiful."

"I love you because you're rich."

"I love you because you give me security."

"I love you because you're so funny."

This love may sound pretty good. We want to be loved for what we are and what we do, right? It's certainly preferable to the "*if*" kind of love. The "*if*" kind of love has to be earned constantly, and it requires a lot of effort. Having someone love us because of what we are and what we do seems less demanding, less conditional.

But what happens when someone comes along who is prettier? Or funnier? Or wealthier? What happens when we get older or lose a prestigious job? If such things are the reason another person loves us, that love is temporary and tenuous.

There's another problem with "because of" love. It's found in the fact that most of us are two types of people; we display a "public self," the person everyone knows, but we often hide our "private self," the deep-down-inside person that few others, if any, really know. The man or woman who is loved "because of" a certain trait or quality will most likely be afraid to let the other person know what he or she is really like deep down inside . . . for fear that, if the truth were known, he or she would be less accepted, less loved, or maybe rejected altogether. Much of the love we know in our lives is of this kind, uncertain and impermanent.

Love, Period! The third kind of love is as uncommon as it is beautiful. It is love without conditions. This love says, "I love you in spite of what you may be like deep down inside. I love you no matter what might change about you. You can't do anything to turn off my love. *I love you, PERIOD!*"

"*Love, period*" isn't a blind love. It can know a great deal about the other person. It can know the person's shortcomings. It knows the other's faults, yet it totally accepts that individual without demanding anything in return. There's no way to earn this type of love. Neither can one lose it. It has no strings attached.

"*Love, period*" is different from "love *if*" in that it doesn't require certain conditions to be met before love is given. "*Love, period*" is different from "love *because of*" in that it isn't produced by some attractive quality in the person who is being loved. "*Love, period*" is a giving relationship. It's all about *giving*. The other two kinds of love are all about *getting*.

The Biblical Perspective of True Love

"*Love, period*" is the only real love, the only true love, the only biblical love. According to the Bible, true love is evident when the happiness, health, and spiritual growth of another person is as important to you as your own. The Word of God records the command, "love your neighbor *as* yourself"[5]; it doesn't command us to love our neighbor *more* than ourselves. We are to love *God* more than we love ourselves, but we are to love our neighbor, boyfriend, girlfriend, or our mate in marriage *as* we love ourselves.

Ephesians 5:28 helps us understand the nature of love even better: "So husbands ought to love their own wives as their own bodies; he who loves his wife loves himself." What does it mean to love our own bodies as Scripture commands? The next verse explains: "For no one ever hated his own flesh, *but nourishes* and *cherishes* it, just as the Lord does the church" (emphasis added).

You see, God's definition of true love means to nourish and cherish, that is, to protect (cherish) and provide for (nourish) the happiness, health, and spiritual growth of another person—in the same way you protect and provide for your own happiness, health, and spiritual growth. True love will nurture and cherish, that is, protect and provide for, that other person.

True love will not emotionally or physically exploit or abuse another person, therefore, because that does not nurture him or her; it does not cherish his or her happiness, health, and spiritual growth.

True love will not pressure a boyfriend or girlfriend to have sex outside of marriage, because that does not protect him or her; it does not provide for his or her happiness, health, and spiritual growth.

True love will not insist on the other person's breaking off other healthy friendships, because that will not protect and provide for that person's happiness, health, and spiritual growth.

Authors Stacy and Paula Rinehart define true love with the biblical term *agape.* They write:

> Agape love is an unconditional response to the total person: "I love you in spite of" (the weaknesses I see in you). [It is a] concern for the welfare of someone without any desire to control that person, to be thanked by him, or to enjoy the process. It reaches beyond to a "willingness to give when the loved one is not able to reciprocate, whether it be because of illness, failure, or simply an hour of weakness. It is a love that can repair bonds severed by unfaithfulness, indifference, or jealousy." The best example of this type of love is God himself.

"For God so loved the world that he *gave*" (John 3:16).[6]

The Response to the Problem of Finding True Love

Listen ◆ Empathize ◆ Affirm ◆ Direct ◆ Enlist ◆ Refer

A concerned youth worker, pastor, teacher, or parent can help a young man or woman understand biblical love by pursuing the follow plan:

LISTEN. Encourage the young person to put his or her concept of love into words. Ask questions like:

- What is true love?

- Have you ever been "in love"?

- How do you think a man or woman knows if he or she is in love?

- What do you think being in love feels like or looks like?

EMPATHIZE. Keep in mind the fervency and urgency with which most teenagers approach love issues. Talking about love will probably not be a primarily intellectual or educational exercise for a teen; it will more likely be viewed with the intensity and urgency most adults reserve for life-and-death situations. The empathetic adult will be careful not to dismiss a young person's feelings on this subject but will take the youth seriously and address him or her carefully.

AFFIRM. The tragic mistakes many teens make are a result, not only of not knowing how to give true love, but of not receiving a love that is accepting, affirming, and unconditional (particularly from a parent). Parents and other adults who are concerned for youth must strive to communicate acceptance, affirmation, affection, and appreciation to them at every opportunity.

DIRECT. Take every opportunity to model a biblical concept of love to the young people in your life; let them see you love someone whose happiness, health, and spiritual growth is as important to you as your own. Pray with youth about their love lives; encourage them to involve the Lord in their search for true love. Seek "teachable moments" (television shows, the "soap opera" of relationships at school, the behavior of couples in public, etc.) to communicate a biblical concept of love to the young people in your life so they will know what they are looking for in relationships and be more likely to recognize it when it occurs. Share the content of this chapter, not just once, but repeatedly.

ENLIST. Enlist the young person's participation in evaluating relationships, perhaps using the following twelve questions proposed by Barry St. Clair and Bill Jones in order to determine if a relationship reflects mature biblical love:

1. Do we both know Jesus personally? [See also chapter 11, "Dating."]
2. Is Jesus Christ first in our relationship?
3. Can we be honest with each other?
4. Do we accept each other completely?
5. Do we have our parents' approval?
6. Do we have control over our sex lives?
7. Do we share common values?
8. Can we handle disagreements?
9. Can we handle being apart?
10. Are we really friends?
11. Are we "whole people"?
12. Am I willing to commit myself for life?[7]

REFER. Healthy attitudes about love cannot be fully developed in a Sunday school class or even a weekend youth retreat; they require involvement of and an ongoing commitment from the youth's parents and other significant adults in his or her life. Cooperation among the principal influences in a teen's life is vital to the development of strong, healthy concepts and convictions about love.

For Further Reading

The following resources may help the concerned parent, pastor, teacher, or youth worker further assist a young person who is working through questions about love:

Scriptures Cited in This Chapter

- Matthew 19:19, Mark 12:31, and Luke 10:27
- Ephesians 5:28
- John 3:16

Other Scripture to Read

- John 15:13
- 1 Corinthians 13:1–13
- 1 Timothy 1:5
- 1 John 3:11–20; 4:7–21

Further Reading

- Joyce Huggett, *Dating, Sex and Friendship* (InterVarsity).
- Josh McDowell and Paul Lewis, *Givers, Takers, and Other Kinds of Lovers* (Tyndale).
- Josh McDowell and Bob Hostetler, *13 Things You Gotta Know (to Keep Your Love Life Alive and Well)* (Word).
- Dick Purnell, *Building a Relationship That Lasts* (Here's Life Publishers).
- Dick Purnell with Jerry Jones, *Beating the Breakup Habit* (Here's Life Publishers).
- Stacy and Paula Rinehart, *Choices: Finding God's Way in Dating, Sex, Singleness, and Marriage* (NavPress).
- Barry St. Clair and Bill Jones, *Love: Making It Last* (Here's Life Publishers).
- Tim Stafford, *Worth the Wait* (Tyndale).

11

DATING

A Synopsis

❖

Introduction

You are *so* lucky." Fourteen-year-old Diane sat next to her friend Michelle. They were in the Fireside Room at church, waiting for youth group to start.

"Why?" Michelle responded.

"Only because Lyle Witson asked you out."

"He *is* cute, isn't he?"

"Cute? That doesn't even begin to describe him. Try *perfect*." The girls exchanged short airy giggles. "You are *so* lucky," Diane repeated. Her smile disappeared. "My parents won't even let me date."

"I know," Michelle answered. "Parents can be so impossible."

"They say I have to wait until I'm sixteen."

"That's a whole two years away!"

"I know." Diane's eyes darted around the room to see if anyone else was listening. She lowered her voice. "They say that even *then* I'm only allowed to go on group dates."

Michelle rolled her eyes. "Please!"

"They act like I'm a little kid."

The girls' heads turned simultaneously toward the door as seventeen-year-old Lyle Witson walked in.

"You're *so* lucky," Diane repeated as she and Michelle pinned adoring gazes on Lyle.

The Problem of Premature Dating

Few things occasion as much tension between parents and youth—and within the youth themselves—as the many decisions and dangers surrounding the dating process.

Teenagers invest a massive amount of time, thought, and energy into dating pressures and possibilities. They talk about who's going out with whom, who wants to go out with whom, and who would never go out with whom.

It is ironic, however, that while many young people devote much time and effort to "the dating game," few are prepared for the new stresses and choices that dating presents. Kids face intense pressure from others around them to "go out" with someone; dating can become a badge of acceptance, an evidence of a young person's worth or attractiveness. Author Ann B. Cannon says:

> Many teenagers date because close friends start dating. Some teenagers look for love, security, or support in a date. A few assert their independence by going where they choose and with whom they choose. Many . . . just date because it's expected.[1]

The Causes of Premature Dating

A great many teens set themselves up for danger and disappointment because they begin playing "the dating game" blindly, ignorant of the many decisions to be made in dating, the many dangers of dating, and the advantage of a purposeful design in dating.

◆ Decisions in Dating

The average teen would never dream of going out on a date without spending some time preparing himself or herself in front of a mirror; yet that same teen most often approaches the dating experience with little or no thought about the many decisions to be made—by parents *and* teens—in dating.

When to Start Dating. Few issues cause as much conflict in the home as the question of "How old is old enough to start dating?" Some parents think their children should be a certain age before dating. Some kids think they were born ready to date; others feel they crossed the "date line" when they became teenagers.

However, chronological age is seldom a reliable indicator of a young person's readiness to date. The crucial factor is whether he or she is spiritually and emotionally mature enough to handle the many decisions and dangers of dating. Some people may be mature enough at fifteen or sixteen; others should probably wait longer.

Some of the key indicators of a teen's readiness for dating are:

- Is he or she often influenced by peer pressure?

- Is he or she most attracted to people his or her own age?

- Does he or she intend to date for friendship instead of romance?

- Has the teen committed himself or herself to sexual purity and determined not to compromise that commitment?

- Does the young person have his or her parents' permission to date?

- Is the teen's self-image based on whether or not he or she is dating?

- Is he or she able to resist immediate gratification in other areas? Does he or she display a preference to strive for future satisfaction and fulfillment (over immediate gratification) in other areas?

"No" answers to the above questions should alert a young person (or a caring adult) to areas in which more spiritual and emotional maturity should be allowed to develop before dating.

The Age Factor. "My boyfriend is several years older than I am," one girl wrote author Barry Wood, "and my parents don't want me to date him. Does age make any difference in dating?"[2] While a difference of five years in age may make little difference to a twenty-five-year-old dating a thirty-year-old, for example, it can cause severe problems for a fourteen-year-old dating a nineteen-year-old. The reason for this is that the teen years are a time of major physical, emotional, and spiritual changes; some changes may happen so fast that a teen is ill-prepared to handle them. Of course, once again the central issue is not chronological age as much as spiritual and emotional maturity. Nonetheless, age differences of more than a year or two should be avoided through late adolescence.

Interracial Dating. Though most texts on dating avoid the issue, interracial dating is an issue many young people face. And while many areas of society (and the church) still frown on interracial dating and interracial marriage, the biblical response is clear: "There is neither Jew nor Greek [that is, no racial division] . . . for you are all one in Christ Jesus."[3] Jesus broke down racial barriers between Samaritan and Jew,[4] between Canaanite and Jew,[5] and between Roman and Jew.[6] Young Christian men and women should be aware of the possible social implications of an interracial relationship, but color is not a barrier to God-honoring relationships.

"Missionary" Dating. Should a Christian youth date a non-Christian? Can a Christian teen use the dating experience as a means of witnessing for Christ? The Word of God answers such questions bluntly in 2 Corinthians 6:14, where the apostle Paul commanded Christians, "Do not be yoked together with unbelievers. For what do righteousness and wickedness have in com-mon? Or what fellowship can light have with darkness?"

Paul's warning does not apply only to dating; it refers to any "yoking" of Christian and non-Christian. It applies to business entanglements, for example, as well as to romantic entanglements such as dating and marriage. Barry Wood shows the wisdom of Paul's command:

> What does a believer share in common with a [non-Christian]? There are many areas of common interest. . . . Hobbies, music, sports, politics, intellectual interests, are all elements that could comprise fellowship between Christians and non-Christians. However, can you think of one single eternal value or interest they have in common? No, you can't. On the truly important areas such as God's will, God's ethics, God's Kingdom, God's family values, and God's husband-wife relationships, you find you two are near-strangers. Yet, it's in these areas that love and marriage exist. This is where real communication takes place.[7]

This does not mean that a Christian cannot enjoy fellowship with non-Christians, have fun with non-Christians, share a milkshake with non-Christians, or toss a football with non-Christians. However, the Christian young person who becomes involved romantically with a non-Christian is crossing a line of protection and provision that God's Word has drawn.

◆ Dangers in Dating

Teens who are preparing to date must not only confront the many decisions to be made in the dating experience, they must also be aware of the dangers. Some of these are discussed effectively by Les John Christie in his book *Dating and Waiting: A Christian View of Love, Sex, and Dating*:

> There is the danger of isolating yourself from your friends. Relating with one's own sex is just as important as relating with the opposite sex. But in dating, sometimes your old friends are pushed

into the background, and these are friends who may be needed later, especially if the dating relationship should end. Also, there is the danger of forgetting other important relationships in your life like brothers, sisters, and parents.

There is also the danger of dating for the wrong reasons, [such as] dating to impress your friends, . . . dating to get back at someone, or dating to cause jealousy. In such a case, you are merely using your date, and you don't really care about him as a person.

Many dating relationships are based on power, not on love. The person who loves the least has the most power. Some people prefer power over love; so they withhold love. . . . Dating becomes a power game. The other person is kept on a string like a yo-yo. Love is being used to gain power and prestige. . . .

Another danger is that you become so date conscious that within the church youth group, you only talk with those you feel are potential dates, and you leave the rest alone. This is true for both guys and girls. . . .

There is also the danger of feeling trapped once you start dating a person. . . . There is the danger of getting hurt and hurting someone else. . . . There are also the dangers of mistaking emotional and physical attraction for real love [See chapter 10, "Love."] and the danger of letting sexual desires get out of control. . . .[8]

Far too many teens—especially those who begin dating early—are woefully unprepared for the dangers of dating and, as a result, expose themselves unnecessarily to the worst that the dating experience has to offer.

◆ Design in Dating

Most dating is far from fun because it's so full of sensual ploys and sexual gamesmanship. Even the language surrounding dating reveals this— "Did you get to first base?" "Did you go all the way?" For dating experiences to be fun *and* rewarding, they need to avoid both the pitfalls *and* the ploys. A teen can do both by carefully

thinking through three things: his or her purpose, standards, and plans for dating.

Purpose. Surprisingly few teens give any thought to their purpose in dating. Of course, responding to the basic attraction of a person of the opposite sex is a fundamental reason why many kids date—as is the intense pressure they feel from others. But aside from responding to those influences, most young people never formulate or evaluate their purpose in dating.

One purpose of dating is *socialization*—having fun with other people, getting to know them, enjoying other people's company, learning how to share common interests, and developing conversational and relationship skills. Dating is a means of learning more about oneself and a way to become skilled at sensing the needs and feelings of another person and how to turn that insight into responsive action.

Another key purpose for dating is *mate selection.* Obviously, the person you marry will be someone you've dated. The typical progression is from casual dates to friendship dates to steady dating to engagement and marriage. Dating serves to cultivate and sharpen one's tastes and improve the ability to recognize the character and personality that best meshes with one's own.

A clear understanding of one's purpose in dating is crucial. It should be obvious, of course, that sexual exploration and experimentation are *not* healthy purposes for dating; however, socialization—and even mate selection—are sound purposes for dating.

Standards. A young person who is mature enough to begin dating will be mature enough to establish his or her standards and boundaries in dating—and even to discuss those standards with a date. Parents and other caring adults should help guide a young person to answer such questions as:

- Should I confine my dating activity to double dates?

- Should I frequent only public places?
- What forms of touching and interaction are acceptable?
- What types of activities will I avoid or refuse?

Such questions, if answered *before* temptation comes knocking, can save many problems, misunderstandings, and mistakes later.

Dating standards should certainly include a clear determination of where to draw the line in the following chart of the progression of physical expression and involvement:

Necking	Holding hands
	Hugging
	Casual kissing (peck kissing)
	Prolonged kissing
Petting	French kissing (including last stages of necking—ears, neck, etc.)
	Breasts covered
	Breasts bared
Heavy Petting	Genitals covered
	Genitals bared
	Oral sex
	Genital to Genital
	Intercourse

The wisest place to draw the line in the above progression is after casual kissing. The vast majority of couples in a dating relationship, whatever their age, cannot progress much beyond that point without asking for trouble. The young man or woman who wishes to set helpful dating standards will do well to start there.

Plans. The final step in framing a sound, helpful design for Christian dating is planning. An attractive option is group dating. Ann B. Cannon writes:

> Group dating has been a popular trend for several years. In group dating guys and gals get together to do different activities without pairing up. The group decides where to go and what to do, and everyone goes along. Everyone pays [his or her] own way. Many teenagers like group dating because it removes the sexual pressure of dating just one person.[9]

Another consideration is to plan for a climate in which two people can become friends. Going to a movie on a first date is counterproductive; it offers entertainment but not interaction. A better choice would be to play miniature golf or Frisbee golf, walk around a zoo, or window shop in a quaint section of town. Such activities provide plenty to talk about and allow the participants to discover each other's likes, dislikes, and previous life experiences. Other good dating activities to plan might include:

- table games/jigsaw puzzles
- simple sports like ping pong, croquet, or miniature golf
- sailing, surfing, or other water sports
- a walk through the neighborhood, shopping area, etc.
- people-watching at a mall
- making dinner together
- roller skating/ice skating
- tackling a project together (homecoming float, posters for youth group car wash, etc.)
- going hiking in a local or state park
- making home videos together
- building and flying a kite
- taking a walk in the rain
- planning a party for your friends
- showing off each other's family photo albums
- buying a bus pass and riding all over town
- attending an auction[10]

One more key to planning the dating experience is to map out possible responses to situations that may arise, such as:

- How much money will I need to spend? Will I have enough?

- How will I respond if my date wants to get physical?

- If my date takes me somewhere I don't want to go, what will I do?

- Under what circumstances will I put a stop to the date? To the relationship?

- How will I react if others around me begin to act inappropriately (drinking alcohol or smoking pot, for example)?

- How will I evaluate whether the date was a success?

Some parents help teens in this area of planning by agreeing that if the teen calls home at any time and says simply, "I need to be picked up *now*," a parent will respond without delay and without asking for details. Others impress on their teens the importance of making sure Mom and Dad know (1) who the teen is with, (2) where he or she is, and (3) where he or she is going.

The Response to the Problem of Premature Dating

Listen ◆ Empathize ◆ Affirm ◆ Direct ◆ Enlist ◆ Refer

Is a young man or woman ready to date? Is he or she dating wisely? Is he or she being exposed unnecessarily to the pitfalls and ploys of "the dating game"? A sensitive parent or youth leader can help a young person answer such questions by employing the following strategy:

LISTEN. Take the time to *talk* to the young person about dating and to really listen to what he or she has to say. Try to discern whether he or she possesses the emotional and spiritual maturity to begin dating or to do so in a wise and godly way. Elicit the answers to the questions posed under "When to Start Dating" (page 123)—most likely without asking such questions point-blank—in an effort to evaluate his or her maturity and readiness to date.

EMPATHIZE. Remember your teen years and the importance boy-girl relationships had to you then. Be careful to recognize the urgency and importance that dating issues assume in the hearts and minds of teens. Seek also to understand the emotional and spiritual needs the young person may hope to meet through dating. Whether or not those hopes are realistic, they will be crucial in helping a parent or youth leader to see things through the teen's eyes.

AFFIRM. Too often, young people use dating to try to fulfill needs that are not being met in other relationships, such as those with Mom and Dad. If parents aren't filling the young person's "love tank" (his or her innate need for love and acceptance), the youth will be more vulnerable to the pressures, perils, and pleasures of dating; conversely, dating relationships will be much easier to handle if a young person is receiving affirmation, affection, and appreciation from others—particularly from his or her parents.

DIRECT. Parents, pastors, youth workers, or teachers can help a young person who is approaching the dating experience by:

- Praying for the youth

- Praying with him or her about the dating experience

- Walking him or her through the decisions to be faced in dating

- Informing him or her of the dangers of dating, and

- Helping him or her formulate a purposeful design in dating by sensitively and systematically sharing the content of this chapter.

ENLIST. A concerned parent or other adult may wish to enlist the young person's participation in planning or evaluating his or her dating habits by entering into a "dating contract" similar to the one proposed by Ann Cannon in her book *Sexuality: God's Gift*.[11]

REFER. The youth worker, teacher, or pastor will certainly wish to involve a young person's parents in the process of helping a youth cope with dating pressures. Likewise, parents will be wise to welcome support from a youth pastor, Sunday school teacher, or other concerned adults. In some situations—particularly those in which a young person has already exhibited dangerous habits in dating—it may be helpful for the parents to consult a Christian counseling professional who can offer sound, biblical guidance.

For Further Reading

The following resources may help the concerned parent, pastor, teacher, or youth worker further assist a young person who is preparing to date or struggling with dating issues:

Scriptures Cited in This Chapter

- Galatians 3:28
- John 4:–10
- Matthew 15:21–28
- Luke 7:1–10
- 2 Corinthians 6:14

Other Scripture to Read

- Psalm 119:9–11

- 1 Corinthians 15:33
- Colossians 3:17
- 2 Timothy 2:22
- 1 Peter 5:8–10

Further Reading

- Ann Cannon, *Sexuality: God's Gift* (Family Touch Press).
- Les John Christie, *Dating and Waiting* (Standard Publishing).
- Doug Fields and Todd Temple, *Creative Dating* (Thomas Nelson).
- Doug Fields and Todd Temple, *More Creative Dating* (Thomas Nelson).
- Fred Hartley, *Dare to Date Differently* (Fleming H. Revell).
- Joyce Huggett, *Dating, Sex and Friendship* (InterVarsity).
- Josh McDowell and Paul Lewis, *Givers, Takers, and Other Kinds of Lovers* (Tyndale).
- Josh McDowell and Bill Jones, *The Teenage Q&A Book* (Word).
- Dick Purnell, *Building a Relationship That Lasts* (Here's Life Publishers).
- Dick Purnell with Jerry Jones, *Beating the Breakup Habit* (Here's Life Publishers).
- Stacy and Paula Rinehart, *Choices: Finding God's Way in Dating, Sex, Singleness, and Marriage* (NavPress).
- Barry St. Clair and Bill Jones, *Love: Making It Last* (Here's Life Publishers).
- Tim Stafford, *Worth the Wait* (Tyndale).
- Barry Wood, *Questions Teenagers Ask about Dating and Sex* (Fleming H. Revell).

12

CHOOSING THE RIGHT MARRIAGE PARTNER

A Synopsis

Introduction

She was nineteen, a college freshman. And she'd never been more confused in her life.

Kim sat in her resident adviser's room, folding and unfolding a letter from her boyfriend, who was attending a university more than three hundred miles away.

When she had first pulled the letter from her mailbox and read the return address, she felt certain he was writing to break up, to tell her he had met someone else. That wasn't the reason for this letter, however. He had written to propose to her.

"I know I should do this in person," he had written, "and I really wish I could. But I don't know when we'll see each other again."

The letter went on to suggest that they get married at the end of the school year and that she transfer to his school for her sophomore year.

"What are you going to say to him?" the resident adviser asked.

"I don't know," Kim answered.

"Do you love him?"

"Yes," Kim answered immediately. Then she lowered her gaze and began folding the paper again. "But . . ."

The RA waited while Kim rustled the paper.

"I just don't know if he's the right one," she said finally.

"You don't have to answer him right now," the RA suggested. "You could call him and tell him you're not ready to give him an answer."

"Oh, I couldn't do that to him," Kim said. "I just couldn't."

"Well," the RA said slowly. "What *are* you going to do?"

Kim raised her gaze again and met the RA's eyes with a tortured look. Her eyes welled up, and she began to cry. "I don't know," she said.

The Problem of Choosing the Right Marriage Partner

The two most important decisions of a man or woman's life are usually faced and resolved—for better or worse—in adolescence: whether or not to follow Christ and whom to marry.

The problem of choosing "the right person" to marry can occasion intense struggle—and no little confusion—in a young man or woman's mind. Author Tim Stafford phrases the dilemma in these terms:

> The question of "the right one" comes particularly strongly to those who do not believe in divorce—who want to marry once, for life. If they have doubts, how can they resolve them? How can they know for sure that they have found the right one? Even when a person isn't considering marriage, when he meets someone for the first time the question may cross his mind: Is this the right one?
>
> Out of all the hundreds of people of the opposite sex whom you meet, how will you know the right one? Will some sixth sense tell you? Will you "just know," as some say? Will you feel internal shivers? Or will some rational analysis, using computer matching or values clarification, make the right one obvious?"[1]

Many young people look at the divorces and unhappy marriages that exist all around them and wonder whether they can expect any better. They observe seemingly mismatched couples and worry about making the wrong choice. They witness abusive relationships and fear becoming victims of a poor choice.

In fact, research reveals that, while 90 percent of churched teens believe that God intended marriage to last a lifetime, less than half (48 percent) say they "want a marriage like that of my parents." And 43 percent believe "it is very hard to have a successful marriage" these days.[2]

In such a climate, many young people are intensely concerned with choosing the right marriage partner. Many are motivated by a determination not to repeat their parents' "mistakes." They don't want to become another divorce statistic. They want to "beat the odds" they think are stacked against them. They want to find true, lasting love in marriage. But they're afraid of making a mistake.

The Causes of Problems in Choosing the Right Marriage Partner

Many youth do make mistakes in dating and marriage, and some of their mistakes are tragic. Very often, however, such mistakes are not the result of not finding the right person but result from other causes.

◆ Not Being the Right Person

Teens and young adults routinely make the mistake of looking for and praying for the right person to come along while giving little or no attention to being the right person. The young person who is not surrendered to God, who is not obeying the parts of God's will that have been revealed (See chapter 48, "Knowing God's Will."), who is not becoming the kind of person who could lovingly and selflessly care for "Mr. Right" or "Miss Perfect" is wasting time if he or she is waiting for God to introduce him or her to the "right one."

It is here that so many young people falter. Instead of praying and working to become a young man or woman who is ready to make a lifetime commitment before God, many frantically look for a mate in every date—and so set themselves up (and set their mates up as well) for disappointment.

◆ Looking for the Wrong Person

Similarly, some young men and women look for "the right one" without realizing they're actually looking for the *wrong* one. They paint pictures in their minds of what "the right one" will be like. The list often starts with stunning physical beauty, self-confident charm, and impeccable manners, and may also include spiritual and social characteristics.

Sometimes (often without realizing it) girls imagine that "the right one" will be "just like Daddy." Guys may form a list of qualifications resembling a former girlfriend or the object of an adolescent crush.

In so doing, of course, many young people create an image of Mr. Right or Miss Perfect that is so idealized or romantic that it can blind them to the possibilities all around them. This is not to say that a young person should not look for certain qualities in a potential mate but simply that such qualifications should reflect realistic, godly goals.

◆ Having the Wrong Motives

Mistakes in dating and marriage are often the result of unwise—even ungodly—motives. Even Christian teens and young adults often seek a mate for the wrong reasons. Authors Barry St. Clair and Bill Jones list several of these poor reasons for getting married:

Senior Panic. "Everyone else is getting married right after graduation (high school or college), and I'd better, too." [Some young men and women feel left out as they watch friends and classmates getting married].

Old-Maid Syndrome. "Always the bridesmaid, never the bride." [Some feel like the only single person left, and women particularly seem to fear being alone after all the "good ones" are taken].

The Great Escape. Some marry because of a bad home life. . . .

On the Rebound. Often people marry soon after a painful breakup. They try to fill the emotional vacuum or take revenge. . . .

Pressure Play. When a couple's parents keep pushing them to marry, they often marry. Or when one partner pressures the other one, they often marry. . . . [They marry out of obligation, not love.]

Meet My Needs. Many people marry primarily to have their own needs met, rather than to meet the needs of their spouse. These needs may center on self-esteem, sex, emotions, finances, or other needs. Sometimes there are more deep-rooted needs, such as the need to feel worthwhile or to become someone important.

Crisis Pregnancy. An untold number of couples marry each year because of crisis pregnancy. In some rare situations, this is best, but not in most cases.[3]

The Biblical Perspective of Choosing the Right Marriage Partner

"Success in life consists not so much in marrying the person who will make you happy," says renowned author and Bible teacher Charles Swindoll, "as in escaping the many who could make you miserable."[4]

◆ Three Key Questions

Swindoll's words contain wry wisdom. Many young people agonize over choosing the "right" marriage partner, and of course, that *is* a very important decision. But careful and biblical attention to three questions can help.

Is There Only One Right Person? Tim Stafford writes:

It is my belief that if God has called you to be married, he does have just one person for you. I believe that you can be absolutely certain of finding him or her by walking in the light of God. And you will be able to say for certain, "This woman [or this man] is the only one for me."

Not all Christians see it just this way. Some would say God doesn't have one particular person picked out for you. They would say you might marry any one of a number of people. Perhaps they are right.[5]

Stacy and Paula Rinehart, authors of *Choices: Finding God's Way in Dating, Sex, Singleness, and Marriage*, suggest that it might be more realistic to say "that one should marry *a* right person rather than *the* right person." They write:

> Obviously we're caught in a tension of truths. God is in control, as Job said: "I know that you can do all things; no plan of yours can be thwarted" (Job 42:2). Yet it is equally true that God gives us the freedom to make wise choices within his pre-scribed moral limits. The Bible says a Christian can only marry another believer [2 Cor. 6:14] which in one sense is very limiting (it discounts much of the world), and in another sense is very broad (there are many Christians). From within the body of Christians, then, we must make a spiritually wise choice. We can't ignore either God's sovereignty or our responsibility.[6]

How Do I Know I've Found the Right Person?

Like many decisions, the choice of a mate will affect the rest of a person's life—actually, the rest of two people's lives. And, like any effort to dis-cern God's will, it should be considered prayerfully and biblically. The young man or woman who is contemplating engagement and marriage should certainly apply the biblical process for understanding and following God's will to this important choice. (See chapter 48, "Knowing God's Will.")

The question remains, however: Once a young person has sincerely sought God's guid-ance regarding the choice of a mate, how does he or she know if the right decision has been made? Tim Stafford offers a helpful perspec-tive:

So even if you believe there is a right one, what good does that do you? How can you know for sure who it is?

The answer I'm going to give—it's the Bible's, I believe—may frustrate you. As is so often the case with the Bible, it doesn't solve your problem the way you wanted it solved. Here is its answer: *You know the right one for sure on the day you stand in front of a preacher and say "I do."* Until that day you probably won't know for sure. After that day the issue is settled, forever. . . .

It seems like a trick. You want to know the right one in order to make the choice simple. Instead, the choice becomes more demanding. You make the choice on your own, and then when you've made it you hear the door locking behind you. Your choice has suddenly become God's choice.

I believe we find this frustration because we don't want to face the difficult facts about mar-riage—and about ourselves. We want to reduce marriage mainly to a question of finding the right combination of personalities, like finding the right key for a lock. We hold potential partners up to a list of ideal qualities to see how they rate.

I certainly believe that compatibility is impor-tant. However, it is not the most important criterion in a successful marriage. God's main focus is not compatibility, but a question which cuts to the heart of marriage: *Can you say "I do" and stick with it until death?* If you can, then you have *found* "the right one"—and you have also *become* "the right one."[7]

How Do I Prepare?

Once it becomes clear to a young person that he or she has found someone with whom to share a lifetime, the next steps are, of course, engagement and marriage.

Most couples talk about marriage some time before a formal proposal is made. However, nothing should be taken for granted. Both part-ners should be sure that each understands and agrees to the intention to marry, and they should agree on an engagement period that is comfort-able for both before the wedding. Barry St. Clair and Bill Jones offer wise counsel in this area:

How long should the engagement last? Different couples have different needs, but two guidelines will help. . . .

The engagement should last long enough to prepare. Two big events need preparation—the wedding ceremony and life together after the ceremony. Planning the wedding ceremony usually takes three to six months, depending on the size of the ceremony. . . .

The engagement should be short enough to avoid problems. During engagement the sexual temptation heightens. The longer the engagement, the greater the pressure. . . . A length of three to twelve months gives a good range.[8]

The Response to the Problem of Choosing the Right Partner

Listen ◆ Empathize ◆ Affirm ◆ Direct ◆ Enlist ◆ Refer

A wise parent, pastor, or youth leader can help a young man or woman prepare for engagement and marriage with a strategy such as the following:

LISTEN. Give him or her plenty of time to talk about his or her relationship(s), and listen carefully. Try to gain a helpful perspective on the young person's ideas about dating, marriage, and God's will.

EMPATHIZE. Try to see things through his or her eyes. Remember your teen years; how were you similar to this young person? How were your struggles like his or hers? Seize every opportunity to communicate your empathy and understanding.

AFFIRM. Many youth who are tempted to marry for the wrong reasons are motivated at least partly by insecurity. It can be very helpful, therefore, to carefully and sincerely affirm him or her as a precious child of God who is infinitely valuable. Let him or her know that you enjoy being in his or her company, sharing things you find delightful and worthwhile about him or her. (Be specific.)

DIRECT. Offer guidance, perhaps sharing the content of this chapter and also helping the youth to evaluate his or her motives and readiness for marriage by asking such questions as:

- Are you both Christians? (See 2 Cor. 6:14.)
- Have you sought God's will in a biblical manner? (See chapter 48, "Finding God's Will.")
- Do you love each other with a biblical love? (See 1 Cor. 13; see also chapter 10, "Love.")
- Do your parents approve? (See Exod. 20:12.)

These questions are the biblical bare minimum requirements for a Christian hoping to embark on a godly route toward marriage. Other questions, such as those posed by Tim Stafford in his book *Worth the Wait,* may further help to clarify the depth and breadth of a relationship:

1. Do you help each other grow closer to God?
2. Can you talk?
3. Can you play together?
4. Can you work together?
5. Do you have mutual friends?
6. Are you proud of each other?
7. Are you intellectually on the same level?
8. Do you have common interests?
9. Do you share the same values?
10. Do you feel comfortable about how you make decisions together?
11. Do you help each other emotionally?
12. Do you have absolute trust in each other?

13. Are you more creative and energetic because of each other?

14. Can you accept and appreciate each other's family?

15. Do you have unresolved relationships in your past?

16. Is sex under control?

17. Have you spent time together? [Stafford suggests, "a year of real closeness is the minimum."]

18. Have you fought and forgiven?

19. Have you talked about each area of your future life?

20. Have you had counseling?[9]

ENLIST. It does little or no good for a concerned adult—even one who is trusted—to tell a young person what he or she needs to know about choosing the right marriage partner. Seek instead (or in addition) to cultivate a sense of "ownership" of these ideas in the youth; prompt him (or her) to develop his own convictions and come to his own realizations, based on the Bible, that will guide his (or her) selection of a lifelong mate.

REFER. Premarital counseling by a pastor or Christian counseling professional is recommended for every couple approaching or anticipating marriage. Such counseling should consist of multiple sessions over a period of several months.

For Further Reading

The following resources may help the concerned parent, pastor, teacher, or youth worker further assist a young person who is thinking through questions related to engagement and marriage:

Scriptures Cited in This Chapter

- Job 42:2
- 2 Corinthians 6:14
- 1 Corinthians 13
- 1 Thessalonians 4:3
- Exodus 20:12

Other Scripture to Read

- Genesis 2:18–24
- Proverbs 5, 18–19; 18:22
- Ecclesiastes 9:9
- Ephesians 5:21–28
- Hebrews 13:4

Further reading

- Josh McDowell and Bill Jones, *The Teenage Q&A Book* (Word).
- Josh McDowell, *The Secret of Loving* (Here's Life Publishers).
- Dick Purnell, *Building a Relationship That Lasts* (Here's Life Publishers).
- Stacy and Paula Rinehart, *Choices: Finding God's Way in Dating, Sex, Singleness, and Marriage* (NavPress).
- Barry St. Clair and Bill Jones, *Love: Making It Last* (Here's Life Publishers).
- Tim Stafford, *Worth the Wait* (Tyndale).

13

COPING WITH
SINGLENESS

Introduction

It wasn't like she had never had any offers. Susan was popular and pretty. She had had more than her share of dates. She was a member of the homecoming court her senior year in high school. She was fun to be around, and her yearbook photo boasted the caption, "Most Likely to Have Twelve Children."

But Susan graduated from college at the age of twenty-two with no wedding ring, no engagement ring, not even a serious boyfriend.

That's when the comments started:

"Why are you waiting so long to get married?"

"Why hasn't someone snatched you up yet?"

"Don't you think it's time to grow up and settle down?"

"You're not getting any younger, you know."

"Maybe it's time to stop looking for Mr. Perfect and settle for Mr. Good Enough."

Susan knew that some people wondered if there was something wrong with her. She knew her friends and family meant well, but she quickly became tired of their questions and comments about her singleness. She had even had a couple young men propose to her, but she had turned them down.

"I know a lot of people think I'm some sort of freak because I'm still single. But I don't want to get married because someone else thinks I should. I want it to be because I've found someone to love for the rest of my life. I'm willing to wait forever, if I have to, to find that kind of love."

The Problem of Being Single

Many young people spend their childhoods and teen years thinking, dreaming, and planning for marriage. They imagine who they will marry, what married life will be like, and how many kids they'll have. And, for the vast majority of young people, marriage is in their future. According to the U.S. Census Bureau, 68 percent of American women will have married by the time they're twenty-nine years old. Eighty-one percent will have married by age thirty-four, and 88 percent by the age of thirty-nine.[1]

The number of never-married men and women, however, is on the rise. "In the past 20 years," writes Stephanie Brush, "the percentage of never-married women between the ages of 20 and 44 has more than doubled, rising from 6 percent to 13 percent of the adult female population."[2] Clifford and Joyce Penner offer a profile of this growing demographic group:

> There are those who see themselves as temporarily single. This is the under twenty-five age group who graduated from high school, went off to work or college, and expect that they will be raising a family of their own. Many in the twenty-five- to thirty-five-year age range are focusing on professional goals without great thought or emphasis on marriage. Then there are those singles who intended to marry, but never did. . . . The never-married group includes some who chose not to marry (even if they had the opportunity) or some who chose the celibate life to give their energy to the call of God.[3]

The growing number of never-married singles combined with adults who become single following a death or divorce is reaching sixty-five million and climbing.[4]

While there is a slowly increasing acceptance of (and comfort with) singleness and single lifestyles in Western society, many young men and women still panic at the prospect of singleness. Singles pastor Allen Hadidian writes of one woman who moaned about her singleness, "I am getting so old! I can't handle it! What am I going to do?" When he asked her how old she was, she responded, "Eighteen."[5]

Such panic is not unusual among single men and women, even those who are still in their teens or early twenties. Teens and young adults long to experience intimacy, to belong to someone, and many fear that they will never experience such things. Some become impatient, particularly when they see friends becoming engaged and getting married. A few become morose, convinced they will never be truly and deeply loved; others, while more willing to accept singleness, whether temporary or permanent, come to view their situation as second-best and themselves as second-class.

The Causes of Singleness

◆ Circumstances

Many young men and women are single due to circumstances. They may be pursuing an education or a career that leaves them little time to develop relationships. They may be shy; their family responsibilities (parents or children, for example) may make it difficult to meet new people. They may not have met "the right person" yet. One single woman wrote, "I have lived in a single state for so long, I think, because I value the institution of marriage so much. And I've seen too many people treat it like some kind of dress rehearsal."[6]

The anxiety and uncertainty that often surround the single person are sometimes due, according to Carolyn Koons, to a "lack of developmental information concerning singles and their lifestyles, combined with singles' questions about their goals, needs, and identities." Koons continues:

> Some [singles] fear that singleness might be for a lifetime, leaning toward the fallacy that "the grass is always greener on the other side."

Singleness needs to be viewed more as a season of time. A season is unpredictable, without a specific length, and with various opportunities. And indeed this season, for some, may be for all of life.[7]

♦ Choice

Others are single by choice. They may have consciously determined to wait until after college to marry. They may feel perfectly comfortable living alone; they may like being free to take off for Thailand or France at a moment's notice. Psychologist Dr. Angela Neal says, "People who have a true sense of themselves, who are self-assured and tend to know what's important to them are . . . more likely to remain single."[8]

On the other hand, clinical social worker Don Clarkson suggests that many people who choose the single life do so out of fear, such as a fear of commitment or dependency, or a fear of abandonment. "That's not to say that single people aren't happy," he says, but "one of the larger issues in relationships is the fear of being dependent and being abandoned in the process." It may be more comfortable for some people to keep those fears hidden and remain single, he says, than to risk exposing old wounds and dealing with deep-seated fears.[9]

The Effects of Singleness

It must be stressed here that singleness is not necessarily a problem, except for singles who wish to marry or who allow the reactions of others to make them feel second-rate. There are distinct advantages as well as disadvantages to singleness.

♦ Advantages of Being Single

Singleness Allows for Depth of Character and Personality. Author Gien Karssen quotes Nel, a Dutch social worker, who says:

People often think negatively about being single, but there are advantages as well. You have an opportunity to develop your own personality. If you marry and have children, you may not have time for that.[10]

Singleness Facilitates the Development of Deep Friendships. Hadidian says, "Few realize the extent to which friendships can go toward meeting deep needs that we previously associated with marriage."[11] Single persons can often develop deep, lasting friendships with members of both sexes of a number and type not easily found among married people.

Singleness Allows for Greater Privacy. Single men and women are usually able to enjoy a much higher degree of privacy than married persons. They can think, work, sleep, and create without interruption in an atmosphere of their own choosing.

Singleness Permits Greater Freedom. Single persons can be more mobile in a highly mobile society. They are freer to respond to new job opportunities, to make decisions without consulting someone else, to pursue a variety of interests. They don't have to adjust their schedules or their habits to the demands of a spouse or a child.

Singleness Allows for Simplicity. Beverly Hills attorney Reginald K. Brown claims that what "makes [the single life] good is simplicity. Your life isn't as complicated."[12] And authors Stacy and Paula Rinehart point out that "when a single person decides to buy a car, he usually has only his needs and desires to take into account. A family, however, may invest hours in the discussion of that same purchase. There are more people and more factors to take into consideration. Marriage also introduces a person into a web of relationships (the extended families of each partner) that can be a tremendous blessing or a time-consuming headache at given points."[13]

◆ **Disadvantages of Being Single**

Singleness is not all happiness and light, however. There are disadvantages to being single and to remaining single as well.

Singleness Can Breed Loneliness. Though not all singles are lonely, many do cite loneliness as one of their greatest struggles. "As we talk with single people," write Clifford and Joyce Penner, "especially those who have been single for a number of years, we hear them speak of the hunger they feel for [a] vital connection" with someone, especially someone of the opposite sex.[14] (See also chapter 1, "Loneliness.")

Singleness Can Be Accompanied by a Feeling of Alienation and Non-acceptance. "Most of society," write Clifford and Joyce Penner, "with the exception of those cosmopolitan collections of single people in our major cities, is designed for married people and for families."[15] Singles often feel "left out" by couples, companies, and churches because of their singleness.

Singleness Can Create Sexual Frustration and Pressures. Of course, marriage does not preclude sexual frustrations, but "the lack of physical, sexual fulfillment . . . is an ongoing struggle for many single people. Some will struggle with their sexual frustration on a daily or perhaps hourly basis, while others only wrestle with it on occasion."[16]

Other Struggles of Singleness. Many singles also struggle through "a search for identity in the context of a married society; a tendency toward or preoccupation with self; developing a pattern of going it alone; and outside pressure or criticism and misunderstanding from family and friends."[17]

The Biblical Perspective of Singleness

"Jesus was never married," writes Fred Hartley, "and He was normal. Paul was not married, and he was normal. John the Baptist was single, and he was normal. History is full of normal men and women who were never married. We need to understand that *one is a whole number.*"[18]

In fact, an often-overlooked passage in the Word of God makes it clear that singleness possesses many advantages for the man or woman of God:

> Now about virgins: I have no command from the Lord, but I give a judgment as one who by the Lord's mercy is trustworthy. Because of the present crisis, I think that it is good for you to remain as you are. Are you married? Do not seek a divorce. Are you unmarried? Do not look for a wife. But if you do marry, you have not sinned; and if a virgin marries, she has not sinned. But those who marry will face many troubles in this life, and I want to spare you this.
>
> What I mean, brothers, is that the time is short. From now on those who have wives should live as if they had none; those who mourn, as if they did not; those who are happy, as if they were not; those who buy something, as if it were not theirs to keep; those who use the things of the world, as if not engrossed in them. For this world in its present form is passing away. I would like you to be free from concern. An unmarried man is concerned about the Lord's affairs—how he can please the Lord. But a married man is concerned about the affairs of this world—how he can please his wife— and his interests are divided. An unmarried woman or virgin is concerned about the Lord's affairs: Her aim is to be devoted to the Lord in both body and spirit. But a married woman is concerned about the affairs of this world—how she can please her husband. I am saying this for your own good, not to restrict you, but that you may live in a right way in undivided devotion to the Lord.[19]

Barry St. Clair and Bill Jones offer a helpful and concise perspective on this passage:

Spared of Trouble

Not to put marriage down, but it is a lot of trouble to be married. The apostle Paul says, "But those who marry will face many troubles in this life, and I want to spare you this" (1 Corinthians 7:28). Caring for one person is easier than caring for an entire family. . . .

Released to Minister

Single people have much more free time to give to God's work. Paul points out that the Lord is coming soon and the opportunity to win people to Christ is getting shorter and shorter: "The time is short . . . [and] this world . . . is passing away" (1 Corinthians 7:29–31). When you marry, the time you have to give in ministry to other people gets cut drastically.

Freed from Concerns for a Family

When you marry you have what Paul calls "concerns" (1 Corinthians 7:32–34). As a married person, one of your major concerns is for the welfare of your family.

Are their physical needs being met? . . . Taking care of the physical needs of a spouse and children is much more complicated (not to mention more expensive) than providing for one.

What about your family's spiritual welfare? Many hours are invested in helping our wives and children spiritually. They need constant attention so that they can grow up to love Jesus and follow Him.

The emotional welfare of your family merits concern too. A husband and wife work at meeting the emotional needs of each other. It is the parents' responsibility to "fill up" their children with love, attention and lots of time. And the time fathers invest is practically nothing compared to what moms invest. . . .

Paul summarizes the advantage of singleness in 1 Corinthians 7:35. He says that singleness enables you to live in "undivided devotion to the Lord." Unfortunately, many singles do not see that

as a high calling. . . . But according to 1 Corinthians 7:7, singleness is as much a gift of God as marriage is. Marriage is great and so is being single. Since as a single you can be devoted to Christ without distraction, it is wise to consider whether God wants you married before you even consider who God wants you to marry.[20]

The Response to the Problem of Singleness

Listen ◆ Empathize ◆ Affirm ◆ Direct ◆ Enlist ◆ Refer

A young man or young woman who is comfortable with his or her singleness may need help in practical areas, such as joining or forming a Christian singles ministry, but for the most part the single person needing a caring adult's intervention will be the young person who is struggling with singleness and discouraged by it. A wise parent, pastor, or youth leader can encourage a young man or woman to accept and thrive in his or her singleness with a strategy such as the following:

LISTEN. Demonstrate your interest and concern by carefully listening to the young person's story. Help him or her to express not only his or her fears and concerns, but ask questions designed to prompt thought and elicit discussion of the reasons for those fears and concerns. Be careful, too, not to censure his or her comments; doing so can stifle further disclosure.

Such questions as the following might be helpful:

- What bothers you most/least about being single?

- Do you think there are any advantages to being "unattached"? If so, what?

- What needs do you hope to meet in a romantic relationship?

- What things would be different in your life if you were to become involved in a serious relationship?

- Would a serious relationship make you feel different about yourself? How?

- Do you think your singleness is temporary or permanent?

- Would you do anything differently if you knew your singleness were temporary? If you knew it were permanent? If so, what?

The above questions may reveal that the source of the young person's struggle is not singleness alone but one that involves other issues such as poor self-esteem (see chapter 6, "Unhealthy Self-Esteem") or loneliness (see chapter 1, "Loneliness").

EMPATHIZE. Meet the young person where he is, not where you think he should be or where you hope he will be. Try to see things through his or her eyes; some fears or concerns may seem totally irrational until the caring adult empathizes with the young person and views things from his or her perspective. Seek also to understand the emotional and spiritual needs that cause the young person to be disturbed by the prospect of singleness. Communicate empathy by:

- Careful, non-judgmental listening.

- Leaning forward in your chair to indicate interest and concern.

- Making eye contact.

- Encouraging gestures (nodding the head as if to say, "go on").

- Speaking in soothing tones.

- Reflecting key statements ("You're saying . . ." and "That must have felt . . .").

- Displaying patience during periods of crying or silence.

AFFIRM. "Acknowledge the individual's worth in God's eyes and yours," advises Dan Lundblad, a pastor to single adults and counseling center director. Take every opportunity to sincerely affirm your regard for him or her, being sure to "separate the individual's worth from mistakes and disappointments,"[21] communicating that the latter does not mitigate the former. Be careful not to offer empty flattery, but strive by your words and actions to communicate respect, esteem for, and appreciation of, the young man or woman.

DIRECT. Parents, pastors, youth workers, or teachers can help a young person uncomfortable with or discouraged by singleness by directing his or her energies toward the five areas suggested by Dick Purnell, who writes:

> I had my ups and downs as a single person. But I discovered that certain things kept me on the right path.
>
> The first was the *Word of God*. It gave me a strong foundation for my life. I learned to stand on the truth, no matter what my feelings were or what circumstances confronted me. . . . The Scriptures became my guidebook for living.
>
> The second was *God Himself*. Relating to the Lord was a source of joy and comfort. Prayer became for me a conversation with the God I loved. . . . Openly and honestly, I learned to tell Him all my thoughts and feelings. He was the only lover I had and I poured out my soul to Him. . . .
>
> The third thing was *friends*. Friendship gave me caring companions. They became my "family." Whenever I traveled, I made friends and spent my spare time with them. When I came home, my roommates and the men in my [Bible study] group . . . encouraged me greatly.
>
> The fourth was a *ministry*. There is nothing more fulfilling than meeting the needs of other people. The goal of my life was not to get married or to establish a home. It was to glorify God with my talents. . . . Getting involved in the lives of

others shifted my focus off myself and on to others.

The last was *interesting activities*. These expand a person's mind and make life fun. Being single provided me with the time to become involved in a variety of hobbies and sports.[22]

ENLIST. Make every effort to enlist the young person's participation in outlining a plan to deal with the issues that cause him or her to be uncomfortable about or discouraged by his or her singleness. You will certainly want to help him or her to resolve the problem, but avoid the temptation to do all the thinking and acting—that is his or her job. Ask the young person's opinions and advice. Acknowledge his or her accomplishments. Help him or her to concentrate on improvement, not perfection. And foster a spirit of support and cooperation in ministry between this young person and other singles.[23]

REFER. "Learn to recognize your limitations," writes Lundblad, "and refer to a more qualified counselor, psychologist, or psychiatrist when necessary. If long-term counseling is indicated, refer early so the individual can develop a counseling relationship with someone he will work with for a while."[24] This should be done only with a parent's knowledge and involvement, and should be facilitated by continuing support from parents and other caring adults.

For Further Reading

The following resources may help the concerned parent, pastor, teacher, or youth worker further assist a young man or woman who is contemplating or struggling with singleness:

Scriptures Cited in This Chapter

- 1 Corinthians 7:7

- 1 Corinthians 7:25–35

Other Scripture to Read

- Psalms 38:9; 62:7–8; 142:4–5; 145:17–20

- Proverbs 3:5–6

- Hebrews 4:15

Further Reading

- Douglas L. Fagerstrom, ed., *Singles Ministry Handbook* (Victor).

- Allen Hadidian, *A Single Thought* (Moody).

- Gien Karssen, *Getting the Most Out of Being Single* (NavPress).

- Josh McDowell, *Secret of Loving* (Here's Life Publishers)

- Clifford and Joyce Penner, *A Gift for All Ages* Word). (Contains a helpful section on single sexuality)

- Stacy and Paula Rinehart, *Choices: Finding God's Way in Dating, Sex, Singleness, and Marriage* (NavPress).

14

HANDLING PEER PRESSURE

A Synopsis

❖

Introduction

Randy's thirteenth year was his hardest.

His family moved to a new town the summer before he started eighth grade, and Randy entered a new school.

He might have said no to the cigarette he was offered on the walk home from school—if he were still in his old school.

But he was determined to make friends quickly here, so he took the cigarette and the three new friends that accompanied it. Still, he was careful to let the cigarette burn down between his fingers except when he sensed the other guys were watching him.

When Randy's new friends discovered that both his parents worked, leaving him home alone for several hours after school, they began walking home with him or dropping by soon after school let out. Randy knew his parents didn't allow him to have friends in the house when they weren't home, but he always made sure everyone left in time for him to pick up and straighten the house before Mom and Dad arrived.

One afternoon, Darren, the boy who had first offered Randy the cigarette, brought a six-pack of beer with him when he appeared on Randy's doorstep. Randy was already frustrated at the way things were going, but he didn't want to tell Darren, so he and his friends smoked and drank beer in the house until Randy pleaded with them to leave, warning them that his parents would be home soon.

Randy managed to trash the beer cans before his parents arrived, but the house still smelled of cigarette smoke. His parents accused him of smoking, which he denied. A heated argument ensued, and Randy's father grounded him.

Two days later, while he was still grounded, Randy was arrested at the mall for shoplifting. His friends, who had pressured him into trying to sneak out of a shoe store wearing a pair of expensive boots, had disappeared when the store security person clapped a large hand on Randy's shoulder.

The Problem of Peer Pressure

A disturbing proportion of churched youth—kids from Christian homes who are intensely involved in church activity—are involved in inappropriate, immoral, even illegal behavior. A survey of 3,795 teens in evangelical churches throughout the U.S. and Canada[1] reveals that in the past three months alone:

- Two out of every three (66 percent) lied to a parent, teacher, or other adult.

- Six in ten (59 percent) lied to their peers.

- Nearly half (45 percent) watched MTV at least once a week.

- One in three (36 percent) cheated on an exam.

- Nearly one in four (23 percent) smoked a cigarette or used another tobacco product.

- One in five (20 percent) tried to physically hurt someone.

- One in nine (12 percent) had gotten drunk.

- Nearly one in ten (8 percent) had used illegal, nonprescription drugs.

And over half (55 percent) have engaged in fondling breasts, genitals and/or sexual intercourse by the time they reach the age of eighteen.[2]

Much of this sort of behavior is influenced by peer pressure. Not all, certainly, but much of it. Teens face severe pressure to act in certain ways, to talk in certain ways, to dress in certain ways, to join certain groups, and to try certain things, and any deviation from what is considered the "normal" or popular thing to do can result in ridicule and rejection. (See chapter 15, "Contending with Peer Rejection and Persecution.")

Dr. Bruce Narramore writes:

Few things strike more fear in the hearts of parents than the possibility of peer pressure. We look at the adolescents around our neighborhood or in our local school and quake at the sight. We hear screeching tires as they pull out onto Main Street. We see a gang of slovenly dressed youths hanging out at the local fast-food outlet. We notice some girls wearing seductive clothes or running around dropping a steady stream of profanity from their lips. And we also hear stories of wild parties and the ready availability of drugs on our high school campus. . . .

Even teenagers from "good" families concern us. We wonder about their moral standards, their spiritual commitment, their attitudes toward authority, and their responsibility—or lack of it. And we wonder about their music, dress, and other current fads. We know, whether we like it or not, that what our teenagers' friends say and do will soon influence them as much or more than what we say. . . . [But] teenagers may be just as worried about peer pressure as [their parents]. . . . Steve, a sixteen-year-old high school junior, put it this way: "My friends want to do things that I know are unChristian, and it's hard not to go along. I guess this means my friends aren't good for me, but knowing that doesn't make it easier. No one likes to be the oddball." Janet, a vivacious fourteen-year-old, chimed in, "I know it's stupid but I end up doing things I'd never do by myself. I get caught up in the excitement and just don't think."[3]

The Causes of Peer Pressure

Peer pressure can be both negative and positive. Church youth groups, Christian friends, and older siblings, for example, can exert positive peer pressure. They can "pressure" a teenager to act compassionately toward someone who's hurting. They can "pressure" a young person to attend a Bible study. They can even "pressure" a young man or woman to consider the claims of Christ on his or her life.

But peer pressure can also be negative, and it is such negative pressure that concerns many parents, teachers, pastors, and youth leaders. The causes of negative peer pressure are varied and may be difficult to identify in a specific situation. Nonetheless, the contributing factors can be categorized as external influences and internal influences.

◆ External Influences

Adolescents have always been influenced by peer pressure, but modern pressures, says Sharon Scott, former director of the Youth Diversion Program of the Dallas Police Department, "can be stronger than the child who is not trained to take action to prevent or avoid trouble."[4] She cites "high-tech lifestyle[s that reduce] the quality of adult interaction with children[5] while simultaneously increasing the negative messages and invitations to children." She implicates the influence of the media, changes in family structure, and societal shifts and expectations:

> From our media, children learn more at earlier ages, and of course imitate what they see. The media also reinforces peer pressure: If you want to have a good personality and be popular, you have to wear a certain brand of jeans or use a particular toothpaste. . . .
>
> Our children are not only being bombarded with outside messages and opportunities beyond our control, but in many cases they are not being reinforced sufficiently in the home to withstand negative pressures. Isolation [such as that created by phones and televisions in children's bedrooms] and lack of time for family communication, family work together, and family play is at an all-time high. Our technology has increased our mobility, and our isolation both outside and within the home.
>
> Our children go places at earlier ages, and they are often able to drive cars earlier; so parents have increasingly reduced opportunity to guide the behavior and control the environments of their not-yet-adult offspring. Additionally, the young driving ages and the fact that many families have several cars overbalance the amount of individual leisure at the cost of family activity.[6]

In addition to the above influences, psychological research also consistently reveals lack of family unity as a key factor in a young person's vulnerability to peer pressure. Teens who don't feel understood or appreciated at home, whose parents fight, whose siblings mistreat them, whose parents "work all the time," or whose mom and dad are uninvolved (see chapter 17, "Inattentive Parents") or overbearing (see chapter 16, "Overprotective Parents") are apt to try to fill their needs for acceptance and approval through their friends—no matter what the cost.

◆ Internal Influences

The survey of 3,795 churched youth cited earlier revealed that parents are not among the primary counselors churched youth (ages eleven to nineteen) confide in or turn to for advice. Although the majority of the youth participating in the survey (73 percent) lived in stable homes with both parents and testified to a positive home environment (62 percent), only one in four (26 percent) said they frequently seek advice from their father, and two in five (40 percent) said they frequently seek advice from Mom.[7]

Psychologist Bruce Narramore says that between the ages of twelve and seventeen, the amount of time an average teen spends with Mom or Dad declines by half.[8] Obviously, the teen years are a period of acute susceptibility to the opinions, attitudes, and influences of peers—more so than parents.

But this is a perfectly natural—even desirable—development. Narramore even calls it "a God-given process." He writes:

> The Bible says that every child will eventually leave his mother and father to relate to a mate (Genesis 2:24). Peers are one step in that direction. For years . . . children have grounded their identities in their relationships with [parents]. What [their parents] said and did was pretty much what they accepted as right or true or proper. But the physical and intellectual changes set in motion at

puberty are pressing them toward adulthood. In a sense, peers serve as a kind of a way station or intermediate point between childhood dependency and adult independency and interdependency.[9]

Another internal pressure that makes teens more susceptible to peer pressure is low self-esteem.[10] Teens who see themselves as unintelligent, unpopular, and unattractive are more vulnerable to peer pressure because their hunger for a sense of acceptance and approval compels them to seek such things through conformity. Teens with poor self-concepts also tend to choose friends or acquaintances who reflect or reinforce their own self-image, such as underdogs, drug users, and friends who dominate or bully them.

The Effects of Peer Pressure

Parents and other adults who work with youth are certainly cognizant of the effects of peer pressure. Even young people themselves tend to have a reasonably good grasp on those effects. Most, however, focus on the observable consequences: an arrest, an automobile accident, drug addiction, etc. Such visible consequences of peer pressure comprise just one of five primary results. Other effects include experimentation, fear and frustration, depression, and confusion.

◆ Experimentation

Peer pressure typically prompts a teen to experiment with attitudes and behavior that he or she may not otherwise try. For many teens (and adults), the first puff of a cigarette, the first swig of alcohol, the first exposure to pornographic materials, and the first attempt at shoplifting were prompted by peer pressure. As fourteen-year-old Janet said, peer pressure caused her to do "things I'd never do by myself."

◆ Fear and Frustration

Teens don't like being vulnerable to peer pres-sure. They don't enjoy being persuaded to do risky things. They fear discovery by parents or other authorities, and they experience frustration by their inability to control themselves and their surroundings. Like Randy, the boy whose story introduced this chapter, they often don't want to do the things their friends urge them to do, but they feel trapped into a trade—conformity for acceptance. The "trade," however, results in frustration, because they seldom experience the acceptance they desire.

◆ Depression

Repeated attempts at conformity (which tend to result not in fulfillment but in frustration) often send a teen spiraling into depression.[11] They come to feel more lonely, more helpless, and more hopeless than before because they realize that their efforts to gain acceptance are not working. A subsequent sense of powerlessness, added to an already acute sense of worthlessness, can produce depression. Such depression may be expressed in morose behavior or in anger and agitation.

◆ Confusion

Sharon Scott tells the story of an intelligent and disciplined sixth-grade student who talked and dreamed of being an astronaut. Unfortunately, however, his high grades and efforts to please the teacher earned him the ridicule of the other students in his class. This threat to "his natural need to be liked" prompted him to stop participating in class and start purposely missing questions on tests. Scott writes:

> This child . . . lowered his standards and reduced his chances to meet his goal, which he had once wanted badly to achieve. He became depressed and confused, because he was being offered an impossible choice between reaching his personal goals and achieving peer approval by fitting in.[12]

Youth who succumb to peer pressure can become confused and alienated by the elusive promise of conformity.

◆ Consequences

Most adults and teens recognize the visible results of peer pressure. Few, however, think beyond the most obvious and immediate consequences to the true choice that's being made, as author and speaker Bill Sanders suggests. He proposes that acquiescence to negative peer pressure invariably involves a choice of what to:

1. Act like

2. End up like

3. Be treated like by this group and others

If you choose cigarettes, you choose to: lose over eight years of your life; cough; have bad breath, yellow teeth, and a greater chance of cancer.

If you decide to drop out of school you actually choose: a low-paying job; hard, long hours; ignorance in many areas; and the possibility of friends who can't get ahead either.

If you choose crime, you actually choose: disrespect; a possible prison term; a life of looking over your shoulder.[13]

Peer pressure promises acceptance and approval to young people, but it is an empty promise.

The Biblical Perspective of Peer Pressure

Peer pressure is natural and understandable. It can be positive or negative. And it's unavoidable. Not only do teens face it every day, but their parents, pastors, and teachers do, too. We may surmise that even Jesus struggled with peer pressure, yet without sinning; the Bible says that He was "tempted in every way, just as we are—yet was without sin."[14]

Still, peer pressure—the temptation to conform in attitude or action—must be combatted. Dr. James Dobson writes:

The Scriptures speak very plainly about the dangers of conformity. God in His wisdom knew that social pressure could keep us from doing what is right, and He spoke strongly against it.

Romans 12:2 warns, "Be not conformed to this world [in other words, don't let the world squeeze you into its mold], but be ye transformed [made into something new] by the renewing of your mind, that ye may prove what is that good and acceptable and perfect will of God." That is written in the King James Version of the Bible. Now let me read the same verse from *The Living Bible:* "Don't copy the behavior and the customs of this world, but be a new and different person, with a fresh newness in all you do and think. Then you will learn from your own experience how his ways will really satisfy you."

Another Scripture (First John 3:13) states it even more pointedly. It says, "My brothers, don't be surprised if the world hates you."

It is obvious from these verses (and many others) that God does not want us to follow the whims of the world around us. He expects us to say to ourselves, "I am going to control my behavior, my mind, my body, and my life. I will be like my friends in ways that don't matter, such as wearing fashionable clothes when convenient. But when it comes to being moral and obeying God and learning in school and keeping my body clean and healthy, then I won't let anybody tell me what to do. If they must laugh at me, then let them laugh. The joke won't be funny for very long. I'm not going to let *anything* keep me from living a Christian life. In other words, "I will not conform!"[15]

The Response to the Problem of Peer Pressure

Listen ◆ Empathize ◆ Affirm ◆ Direct ◆ Enlist ◆ Refer

How can a youth leader, parent, teacher, or pastor help a young person handle peer pressure? The task may differ from teen to teen, but it will begin with prayer and a humble dependence on God. Peer pressure is a challenge for everyone, and both youth and caring adult will do well to recognize that will power is not the answer, nor are clever techniques, but a humble reliance on God and His guidance and power is the first and most important step toward handling peer pressure. Other steps will very likely include:

LISTEN. Some teens turn somewhat reluctantly to the influence of their peers (at least in some areas) because they don't think Mom, Dad, or other adults ever really listen to them. It is crucial, especially in early- and mid-adolescence, when reliance on peers reaches its peak, that the young man or woman have a parent or other positive adult influence who will actively and attentively listen to him or her.

You may help a teen talk about peer pressure by asking such questions as:

- Do you have any friends that pressure you in positive ways? Negative ways?

- Have you ever not tried in school or in sports in order to avoid being labeled or ridiculed?

- Are there things you do (or don't do) because of peer pressure? What things?

- Do you ever feel pressure to make fun of someone or be mean to someone because of your friends?

- Do you act differently around family or friends at church than you do at school or among other friends?

- Do you feel like you can talk to your parent(s) about things in general? About things you feel pressured to do?

- Do you ever talk to God about the things you feel pressured to do, say, or be? Why or why not?

The above questions may suggest other ways to help a young person talk about peer pressure and its effects on him or her. As the youth talks, be careful to listen closely, not only to verbal communication but to nonverbal communication and to the emotions that may lie beneath what is said.

EMPATHIZE. Don't be too quick to evaluate or criticize the way the teen is reacting to peer pressure; after all, how do you respond to peer pressure? Do you conform in certain ways in order to be accepted at work? At church? Among friends? An honest appraisal of your own response to peer pressure may help you sensitively and compassionately view the young person's efforts to fit in.

In addition, empathic concern can be communicated by:

- Acknowledging the youth's feelings without censure.
- Body language (leaning slightly forward in your chair, not folding your arms on your chest, nodding, making eye contact, etc.).
- Reflecting key statements (for example, "Let me make sure I understand what you're saying . . .").
- Waiting patiently through periods of silence or tears.

AFFIRM. Like all of us, teens have a "tank" inside them that must be filled in order for them to combat peer pressure. Parents and other caring adults can help a youth cope with peer pressure by filling that tank with acceptance, approval, affirmation, and affection. "A child who feels good about himself on the inside," says Scott, "will have more inner strength and security to help him withstand the knocks of the sometimes harsh outside world. Encouragement for his efforts and praise for his successes are [important] tools [to] use to build his self-esteem."[16]

Affirmation can be offered by:

- Providing a "safe haven" at home from the criticism and ridicule the youth may experience elsewhere.

- Reinforcing the teen's realization of his or her worth in God's eyes (see chapter 6, "Unhealthy Self-Esteem).

- Sincerely complimenting the youth for his or her capabilities and qualities.

- Allowing frequent opportunities for the young person to develop competence and confidence. If he struggles athletically, for example, consider signing him up for horse-riding lessons or teaching him to work on cars; if she is self-conscious about the effect of braces on her appearance, encourage her to develop her basketball game or tutor her in photography to help her feel good about other areas of her life.

- Actively encouraging *positive* peer friendships and associations that will affirm the young person's good qualities and subtly model attitudes and abilities he or she may lack.

DIRECT. In addition to listening, empathizing, and affirming, a caring adult can also offer suggestions and direction to a teen on how to counter peer pressure. Most importantly, gently urge the young person to turn to God, develop his or her relationship with Him, and depend on Him; He is "an ever present help in trouble."[17] In addition, Alison Bell (writing in *Teen* magazine) offers these twenty suggestions:

> *1. Ask 101 Questions. . . .* For example, if a pal pressures you to smoke, ask her why she smokes, how long has she smoked, if she minds having ashtray breath. "Asking

questions puts the other person on the defensive," explains Richard Mills, a consulting psychologist for the Los Angeles Unified School District.

> *2. Say No Like You Mean It. . . .* Make eye contact, then say no forcefully, with authority. The more certain you are in your refusal, the less people will bug you.

> *3. Back Up a No with a Positive Statement. . . .* For example, if you're turning down an offer to smoke pot, say something like, "I like my brain the way it is, thanks." . . .

> *4. Be Repetitive.* Don't hesitate to state your position over and over again. . . .

> *5. Practice Saying No.* Practice saying no in safe environments, like when your big brother asks you if you'd like to spend Saturday night doing his laundry.

> *6. Get Away from the Pressure Zone.* Leave the scene. . . . Make your exit.

> *7. Avoid Stressful Situations in the First Place.* If you know there's going to be alcohol or drugs at a party, make other plans. Or, if you're going out with a guy, avoid being alone with him . . . anywhere he might pressure you to get more physical than you want to be.

> *8. Use the Buddy System. . . .* Find a friend who shares your values and back each other up.

> *9. Confront the Leader of the Pack.* The best way to handle a peer-pressure bully is to nab [him or] her when the two of you are alone and explain how you're feeling [and ask her to] get off your case.

> *10. Consider the Results of Giving In. . . .* Take a moment to think about the consequences of your actions.

> *11. Look for Positive Role Models.* Ever notice that the real popular and successful kids at

your school are the ones who aren't afraid to say what they like and don't like? . . .

12. **Don't Buy the Line That Everyone's "Doing It."** . . . The truth is, everyone's not doing it. . . .

13. **Seek Support.** Talk out any peer pressure you're experiencing with other friends who are also feeling the squeeze. It can be reassuring to know that you're not the only one. . . .

14. **Be Your Own Best Friend.** . . . Remind yourself every now and then that you're special [and] nuke any negative statements. . . .

15. **Find Ways to Excel.** . . . Challenge yourself to do your best. . . . [Focus] your attention on following your personal goals instead of the goals of a group.

16. **Don't Pressure Others.** Watch out for any subtle forms of pressure you may be exerting. . . .

17. **Speak Out!** Fight peer pressure by taking the side of the underdog. . . . Supporting others' opinions will send the message that you think for yourself.

18. **Watch Your Moods.** Be aware that your moods can [affect] your sensibility. . . .

19. **Evaluate Your Friendships.** If your friends are always bugging you to do something you're not comfortable with, remember that true friends like you for who you are, not who they want you to be.

20. **Find New Friends.** If you've decided that your friends don't have your best interests at heart, search out new friends who share your values and interests. . . .[18]

ENLIST. Enlist the young person's participation in battling peer pressure, perhaps by using the technique Scott recommends in her book *PPR: Peer Pressure Reversal*:

1. **Check Out the Scene.** (Notice and identify trouble.)

2. **Make a Good Decision.** (Understand and choose consequences.)

3. **Act to Avoid Trouble.** (Take effective action.)[19]

REFER. Take advantage of all available resources. As with any area of a teen's development, the enthusiastic and sensitive involvement of his or her parents is critical. Parents of youth who are struggling with peer pressure can profit greatly from support groups and informal interaction with other parents of teens. Teens who are struggling with peer pressure can profit from the positive peer pressure of a thriving church and a supportive youth group. Concerned parents may also consider turning to a Christian counseling professional for further help.

For Further Reading

The following resources may help the concerned parent, pastor, teacher, or youth worker to address peer pressure:

Scriptures Cited in This Chapter

- Genesis 2:24
- Hebrews 4:15
- Romans 12:2
- 1 John 3:13
- Psalm 46:1

Other Scripture to Read

- Proverbs 2:20, 13:20, 24:1–2
- 1 Corinthians 15:33
- Ephesians 5:1–7
- 1 Timothy 4:12
- Hebrews 11:24–26

Further Reading

- Neil Anderson, *The Bondage Breaker (Youth Edition)* (Harvest House).**

- Dr. James Dobson, *Life on the Edge* (Word).**

- Robert S. McGee, *The Search for Significance* (Word).**

- Bill Sanders, *Stand Up: Making Peer Pressure Work for You* (Fleming H. Revell).

- Bill Sanders, *Tough Turf: A Teen Survival Manual* (Fleming H. Revell).**

- Sharon Scott, *PPR: Peer Pressure Reversal (An Adult Guide to Developing a Responsible Child)* (Human Resource Development Press, Inc., Amherst, Mass.).

** Contains helpful chapters on peer pressure

15

CONTENDING WITH PEER REJECTION AND PERSECUTION

A Synopsis

❖

Introduction

Mrs. Watkins cried softly; her daughter's diary lay open in her lap. She hadn't intended to read it, but the diary seemed to beckon her as it lay unlocked on Kaitlyn's desk. She recalled how different Kaitlyn seemed recently, and she hoped the diary would offer some clues to her daughter's changes.

She wasn't ready for what she read; it took her breath away and made her nauseous. Kaitlyn's diary described things—sexual things—that were hard for a mother to read.

Kaitlyn's mom knew that the family's move last year from New Jersey had been hard for Kaitlyn; the transition had left her bereft of friends and in a new school, perhaps too vulnerable to withstand the pressures of her peers. But Mrs. Watkins had not suspected the lengths her daughter would go to in her search for acceptance and approval.

She tried hard to sound normal when her daughter arrived home from school that afternoon.

"How was your day?" she asked.

Kaitlyn mumbled a response as she scoured the kitchen for a snack.

"We have something to talk about."

"I have to call Jani."

"I'm sorry, Kaitlyn, but this can't wait. I . . . I read your diary today."

"You what?" Kaitlyn stared at her mother, her eyes filled with rage. Her face reddened as she ranted for several minutes about her mother's shocking behavior.

Kaitlyn finally quieted, and Mrs. Watkins's eyes filled with tears. She didn't look at her daughter as she spoke. "Did you . . . did you really think those kids wouldn't be your friend if you didn't do what they were doing?"

"You think I'm such a kid. You don't even know what it's like. You don't know. You don't know." Kaitlyn began to cry, too, but between sobs she related a story of rejection and cruelty, of classmates' hateful stares and heartless jokes, of being shoved into lockers and doors, of passing students "spilling" food and drink on her as they passed her, seated alone in the school cafeteria.

"I couldn't take it, Mom," she cried. "I just wanted them to think I was cool."

The Problem of Peer Rejection and Persecution

For as long as parents have been raising children the problems of destructive influences outside the home have been met with both protestation and anger by loving parents. Most parents want to protect their children as long as they need it, but many feel helpless to provide what kids need in order to withstand the relentless onslaught of temptation and pressure.

Despite parents' best efforts, many teens are rejected and persecuted. This peer rejection and persecution may occur for a variety of reasons: for religious beliefs, personal appearance, non-compliance to the group, drug use, refusing drug use, academic competence (or incompetence), athletic limitations, compliance to authority, conformity to adult guidelines, language use, physical handicaps, and virtually any conceivable behavior, word, thought, or deed that identifies one as somehow different from the accepted social norm. Some have rightly termed this the "tyranny of the norm."

Even differences in dress between schools can lead to contempt and scorn. This is particularly problematic for teens displaced in the middle of the school year when wardrobes have already been selected with sensitivity to the social norms from the previous school. What is stylish and acceptable in one school can be seen as juvenile and banal in another school—even one within the same city.

The pressure to conform varies from physical attacks to attacks on one's person, from isolating and ostracizing the out-of-step teen to requiring perfect mirroring of the desired peer group. Due to the volatility of teen emotions, these attacks may continue for long periods of time or simply cease for no apparent reason.

Some of the least-enjoyed teens are both the bullies and the bullied. Bullies are often disliked for their cowardly attacks on their smaller and weaker victims. The bullied are often viewed with contempt because of their inability to fend for themselves. They are frequently characterized by an apparent weakness that keeps them from moving away from the role of victim.

Parents have long advised teens to stand up to adverse peer pressure, much like the advice of former first lady Nancy Reagan in her "Just Say No" anti-drug campaign in the eighties.

Unfortunately, as the folks fighting the war on drugs discovered, just saying no is a too-simple approach to a complex problem, one that is rooted in self-image and self-esteem, and complicated by the normal development of adolescence. The impact upon teens can be severe and long-lasting. Teens long remember the embarrassment and pain of peer rejection, abandonment, and grave injuries resulting from trying to fit in.

The common occurrence of teens banding together in groups based upon language, music, and dress testifies to the fact that security needs dominate the life of teens. Their fragile egos are ravaged by social failures and imprinted by grievous memories of ostracism. Many times the reasons for rejection and forced compliance have little to do with the teen's personality and much more to do with appearances . . . some of which are beyond the control of the teen.

Seeing the need for teens to have positive self-esteem and resilience during their teen years, many parents attempt to "peer-pressure proof" their children. By building into their disciplinary actions specific training to withstand outside influences, these well-meaning parents endeavor to equip their teens for the battle for their minds, wills, and emotions. While the research investigating in this area is not abundant, the results are disheartening. The data do not support the notion that we can guarantee our teens will manage peer pressure well in spite of our preventative measures. To the contrary, researchers have discovered that:

. . . by the time they reach high school, no matter how intact they are at 11, some girls will have lost chunks of their vitality and self-esteem, their resilience and their focus, as they realize that, in order to have relationships, they have to give up some central truths about themselves.[1]

Even our relatively intact children are at risk. The pressure to fit in is enormous, and it can exact a heavy toll even on the healthiest teens. At times inexplicable behavior by heretofore well-mannered teens can only be explained and understood by the need to belong and fit into one's peer group. The price of admission is often more than one can pay. Research has shown that social acceptance is a critical factor in predicting emotional problems later on. Peer rejection can wound young kids in such a significant manner that it contributes to feelings of inadequacy, loneliness, and chronic tendencies toward depression.[2]

The Causes of Peer Rejection and Persecution

Many factors contribute to the problem of peer rejection and peer persecution. In order to fully understand the causes, one must examine the teens who are vulnerable to this problem separately from the teens who participate in the problem.

◆ The Vulnerable Teen

Teens who tend to be more vulnerable to this problem range from apparently healthy teens to those who have been identified as high risk for many years by parents, youth pastors, and teachers. The vulnerable teens who are seen as fairly healthy and intact are usually found, upon closer inspection, to have hidden emotional deficits. These are difficult to identify with a superficial evaluation except when they are under stress. At those times their deficits are more easily noticed. Vulnerable teens frequently

have several factors in common that render them susceptible to the influences of others.

Family Factors. Families of teens who struggle with peer rejection and persecution are often troubled themselves. These families will generally be marked by divorce, marital conflict, alcoholism, authoritarianism, and general difficulties providing a secure, safe, and nurturing environment for their children.[3]

Vulnerable teens under authoritarian discipline tend to internalize a conforming, non-thinking, compliance that leaves them prone to blindly follow perceived leadership.

Social Factors. Teens most vulnerable to pressures and rejection tend to be found in two different categories. They are either socially isolated and alone or are relating to groups of peers who are also vulnerable to pressure. These teens are seen by others as ineffective and unattractive, and frequently are the targets of negative attention. In relating to others they find it hard to sustain long-term relationships, are poor at conflict resolution, and seem less likely to appropriately risk social contact due to their history of social failure. Teens with learning disabilities are especially vulnerable to these feelings of failure.

Self-Esteem. Positive self-esteem is one of the best insulators against negative peer pressure. Teens who have self-confidence, a healthy identity, and an accurate estimate of themselves are typically more discerning regarding social conformity. They generally are more capable of independent thinking than those who feel confused about themselves and their place in the world.

Ego Strength. Teens who show deficits in the following areas exposing ego weaknesses are more prone to engage in group behaviors without careful evaluation:

- Teens who are impulsive,
- Teens who show difficulty delaying gratification,
- Teens who demonstrate poor frustration tolerance,
- Teens who have little ability to adapt and cope with changing circumstances,
- Teens with poor ability to tolerate both negative and positive affects,
- Teens with limited ability to think in terms of cause and effect,
- Teens with limited ability to establish true peer relationships, and
- Teens who have some distortion in their sense of reality.

◆ The Participating Teen

Some of the teens who participate in peer rejection and persecution (as opposed to the victims) are identified early in life as they tend to draw school discipline upon themselves. Early-identified teens are typically overt in their intimidation and influence on others; other teens are more clever and exert influence in covert ways, thus limiting their exposure to authority figures. The following factors are common elements of both overtly and covertly controlling teens.

Family Factors. Families of teens who are controlling, both overtly and covertly, are usually characterized by leadership that is authoritarian, controlling, and intimidating. The intimidation is expressed in both physical threats and abandonment threats to force the family members to obey and conform. Teens who use similar tactics seem to have identified with the aggressive parent and now seek to victimize others as they were once victimized. Thus the cycle of control is passed on to the next generation.

The teens who are more overt are teens who found a way to maneuver themselves in their family to their advantage without suffering sanctions.

These families can also be characterized by limited boundaries and chaotic family structure. This can prevent children from exercising self-control and internalizing the value of others, which inhibits their concern for others. In a chaotic home, young people learn that first they must fend for themselves; therefore they develop a more self-absorbed perspective on the needs of others.

Social Factors. Teens who exercise control and influence over others are typically charming, self-absorbed, and have social skills that enable them to convince and persuade others to accept their point of view. They seem to have an uncanny capacity to size up others and find ways to win them over. Many times these teens are considered popular and desirable by the majority of other teens.

Teens who dominate by physical intimidation are generally limited in their social skills, not well-liked by others, and generally have difficulty with authority figures.

Self-Esteem. These teens have underlying poor self-images. However, it often takes a careful analysis to discover this. They are frequently well guarded and deny that they have deficits in this area. Often their use of other teens is a means to bolster up a weak self-image rather than endure the pain and suffering required to resolve the nagging issue of self-doubt.

Superficially these teens look confident and happy. However, their self-appraisal is exaggerated, a defense that protects them from the truth. They are also characterized by constantly changing friends as they feel a need to attract new friends to provide newer emotional supplies when old friends become ordinary. Participating teens who are more physically intimidating have low self-images and are immature, shallow in relationships, and generally fearful of risking true peer relationships. They use intimidation to stave off awareness of the weaknesses they sense in themselves.

Ego Strength. These teens have the same general ego weaknesses mentioned above.

The Effects of Peer Rejection and Persecution

The youth leader or adviser will note that the following effects of peer rejection and persecution are complex and will require careful assistance to accurately assess how to help. Some of the symptoms will no doubt be a consequence of issues that are only tangentially related to the problem of peer persecution and rejection.

◆ Depression

Teens who are struggling with peer rejection and persecution will report feeling lonely, hopeless, and helpless. They may say such things as, "I wish I was dead." In their hopelessness they may take a self-destructive turn and justify their obvious life-risking actions with, "What difference does it make what happens to me? No one will miss me anyway."

Since teens are behavior oriented, they will often express their depression with actions rather than words. They may appear angry and agitated rather than express themselves in words indicating their inner turmoil. The following expressions of depression need to be particularly attended to: extreme moods of crankiness, anger, irritableness, or sadness; irrational displays of emotions; high levels of intensity that are not congruent to environmental precipitators; self-loathing comments; increasing morose ideation and preoccupation; decrease in school performance; and negative moods that last for weeks. (See chapter 5, "Depression.")

Peer pressure, in its most extreme cases, has led teens to commit to suicide pacts. Though this is a rare occurrence, when it does occur it is usually driven by a leader who exerts power and

influence over the others. The group members frequently have in common the above-discussed personal problem areas. An additional consideration one must keep in mind is the close friends of teens who attempt or complete a suicide. These teens are more at risk to attempt suicide than teens who are less close friends.[4] (See chapter 9, "Suicide Thoughts, Tendencies, and Threats.")

◆ Social Isolation

Teens who have suffered from the persecution of peers often abandon efforts to get needs for affection, belonging, love, and acceptance met by their age peers. In dealing with this kind of loss, teens sometimes turn to what they consider safer "objects," such as intense romantic attachments that are characterized by a fused relationship that often blurs the distinctions between the couple, or by turning to less risky companions: animals.

The isolation they feel can be profound, as it leaves teens bereft of the necessary transitional objects (peers) to aid them in leaving their home and moving toward adulthood. In addition, it leaves them with the scars of feeling inadequate, unlovable, and unwanted. These feelings can lead to poor choices for mates and future friendships.

◆ Gang Affiliation

While gang members often refuse to admit the needs that make gang affiliation desirable, many if not most of the teens who join gangs do so for personal security, belonging, and a sense of family. They have failed to find ways to meet these needs in the normal, more-healthy process of relating to their peers. They have thus given up developing real autonomy and adulthood for the short-term sense of power and belonging. They feel they have new power over their situation and a clear understanding of who is good and who is bad.

This helps simplify a complex world for a confused and angry teen. However, the commonly associated criminal behavior, resistance by gang members to let a member leave the gang, and general denial of needs ill prepares the gang members for productive adult lives.

◆ Drug Use

Many teens choose drug use as a way to cope with painful emotions that result from negative peer pressure, persecution, and rejection. They numb personal pain with chemicals rather than risk vulnerability in a relationship or a realistic awareness of their problems. Sometimes they experience a concomitant group affiliation that accompanies their drug use.

The use of personal names for some beverages and drugs attests to the common effort to personalize the chemical as it masks interpersonal needs. Young people need a loving friend who would admonish them when they are unruly, encourage them when they are fainthearted, help them when they are weak, and be patient with them always.[5] Instead they choose a counterfeit that more quickly and easily takes the pain away, albeit not without a terrible price.

Drugs have a seductive quality that enhances the teen's sense that he or she does not need others, thus protecting the youth from the fear that he might become dependent if he acknowledges the need of others. This sense of omnipotence is almost hypnotic and renders teens nearly powerless to resist. Specialized treatment is frequently required to rescue a teen from drug use.

Research has shown that peer influences are different with different kinds of drugs. The more socially used drugs like alcohol and marijuana seem to have greater peer influence with their use. (See chapter 38, "Alcohol Use and Abuse," and chapter 39, "Drug Use and Abuse.")

This influence is frequently misunderstood, however. Peers seldom push drugs with verbal barrages but rather with a subtle influence, indicating what is acceptable and popular.

Positive influences with peers who are exposed to drugs have also been documented.

Researchers have found that peers who associate with non-drug-using peers have a much less likelihood of using drugs themselves.[6]

◆ Sexual Activity

In the last few years information emerged out of a high school in Southern California where a group of male teenagers competed with each other to see who could "hook up" with the most girls. This represents some of the worst effects of peer pressure. As the details of the "Spur Posse's" activity became clear, it was evident that the competition provided acute self-esteem needs and encouraged group members to prey upon needy, less confident females.

In other cases, sexual contact is the price for relationship among teens. It seems a costly price to pay, but it is an example of the power of teens over each other when the playing field is uneven; that is, when predator-like teens prey upon those weaker than themselves; when sexual pleasures substitute for real love, belonging, and acceptance. (See chapter 28, "Premarital Sex.")

◆ Stress

Stress hits many children the day they march off to kindergarten minus Mom and Dad. As kids grow, so do their levels of stress. They start worrying about grades, test scores, sports, and socializing.

Stress is the normal result of any circumstance that threatens (or is perceived to threaten) our well-being. Since peers are an important part of stress reduction and "stress sharing," it is important that the peer group be healthy and supportive and not self-absorbed, robbing the group members of the benefits of growing up together.

Young people who are vulnerable to peer pressure and rejection often find that the only groups they can fit into exact a tremendous toll as they make use of the teen for their own purposes. Instead of mutual support, opportunity for practicing adult coping, and encouragement, teens can be used as scapegoats and all manners of blaming and projecting.

This creates a high level of stress for teens who suffer the ambivalence of wanting to be accepted but finding the price is often giving up their integrity.

The Biblical Perspective of Peer Rejection and Persecution

One of the fundamental truths of Scripture regarding children and the family is found in Genesis 2:24:

> For this reason a man will leave his father and mother and be united to his wife, and they will become one flesh.

Inherent in this reference is the protective and educative nature of the home that prepares the child to leave successfully and start his or her own home. Teens who are vulnerable to peer pressure, persecution, and rejection nearly always come from homes where there is a lack of this preparation. This may be the result of many things, such as family discord, marital conflict, significant losses, and the temperament of the child. The benefits of an intact family are apparent, as it provides adequate training for the children to successfully assume their adult place in the body of Christ and in the world generally.

When proper emotional and spiritual attachment is provided in the home, teens can expect to gain the self-assessment Paul wrote about in Romans 12:3:

> For by the grace given me I say to every one of you: Do not think of yourself more highly than you ought, but rather think of yourself with sober judgment, in accordance with the measure of faith God has given you.

Teens can develop an accurate estimate of themselves that will prevent the puffed-up attitude that leads to preying on peers while also protecting themselves from the negative distortions that make them more vulnerable to peer persecution. Helpers of teens will greatly combat peer pressure by assisting young people to develop an accurate assessment of themselves . . . not too high and not too low. They need to know that they were indeed created in the image of God, as recorded in Genesis 1:26. That created relationship with God is the only place they can truly find out who they are. Relationship with God alone can free us from the bonds of sin and lead us to experience our newness in Christ.[7]

The Bible also explains a way teens can fight conformity to the world and hence the seductions of peer groups:

> Therefore, I urge you, brothers, in view of God's mercy, to offer your bodies as living sacrifices, holy and pleasing to God—this is your spiritual act of worship. Do not conform any longer to the pattern of this world, but be transformed by the renewing of your mind. Then you will be able to test and approve what God's will is—his good, pleasing and perfect will.[8]

By faith we offer ourselves as a holy sacrifice and renew our mind to withstand the conformity of the world. But as we help teens we must realize that they are going through a developmental period that demands a personal touch, a relationship, so that they can experience the love of the incarnate Christ through the person of their parents, pastors, or others who care about them in a noncondemning way as they truly represent the mind of Christ.

The Bible's answer to rejection and persecution is found in a personal relationship to Christ that is worked out daily in the prayers and fellowship of loving believers who support the teenager's development toward the unique plan God has for them during the tumultuous years of adolescence when it is so tempting to try to become what others want us to be instead of what God designed us to be.

The Response to the Problem of Peer Rejection and Persecution

Listen ◆ Empathize ◆ Affirm ◆ Direct ◆ Enlist ◆ Refer

Parents and youth workers who spend time with teens will not escape seeing the ravages of peer pressure and the cruelty of peer persecution and rejection. These teens will be injured and hurt in profound ways. Remember how important it is not to minimize their pain, but give them a chance, in a loving relationship, to express themselves without reproach on either the teen or his/her friends. The following steps should prove to be helpful:

LISTEN. Listen carefully to the young person. Try to help the teen identify the pain without asking too many questions. Remember these will be shameful and embarrassing issues for him or her to express. Be certain to withhold judgment of the persecuting or rejecting teens until you have made a connection with the teen you are helping. Rather than point out the cruelty of the peers, ask the teen how it felt to be left out, persecuted, or rejected. Expect him or her to be very reluctant to admit the social ostracism and embarrassment.

EMPATHIZE. Young people need to know that you care about their pain. They are often convinced that no one really knows how they feel. However, they will appreciate your efforts if they can begin to see that you understand—even if you have little or no common experience. Be careful about jumping into your own history to try and relate too quickly. Teens are somewhat self-focused and aren't sure that adults really can relate to them. They are more touched by

your acknowledgment that you have some sense about what they are going through but will need their help to fully understand. Sometimes a statement about what you think they are going through will help them connect with you. A statement like, "I can see how important it was for you to fit in," can help them see you are understanding.

AFFIRM. Be careful to affirm the teen's value and worth. They don't respond to blithe statements, but they nonetheless need to experience your esteem. This will happen as they find you are not embarrassed or ashamed of their story. They will experience your affirmation by seeing your willingness to protect their worth as you offer them unconditional relationship. They will also feel affirmed if they perceive that you respect their opinions on the options open to them.

Remember, teens are very cautious about becoming vulnerable in exposing their needs. They feel they cannot remain dependent upon adults, and fear any appearance of this. While they are correct that they must gain in independence, they also will need to realize how inter-dependent we all are.

DIRECT. This part of the interaction will be one of the most delicate parts. Assuming you have been able to forge a relatively good relationship with the teen, now you must:

- Encourage the teen to turn to God in prayer and listen to Him through His Word; a thriving relationship with God is an invaluable, irreplaceable resource in times of trouble.[9]

- Offer your resources, but do so in a way that is not experienced as parental and condescending.

- Guide the teens toward open expression of their fears of not belonging, anger at the peers who hurt them, feelings of inadequacy, and the dilemma they face in returning to people and places where the risk of injury is high.

- Be slow to offer ways of handling their peers, but guide them to a realization of helpful techniques and strategies, which may include:

Avoiding potential trouble spots. (Ask, "What can you do the next time trouble starts to develop?")

Devising effective responses to defuse situations. (Ask, "How have you responded in the past? Can you think of any other/better ways to respond, things to say, ways to act?")

Actively countering destructive feelings. (Ask, "Are there any relationships or pursuits you can think of that might help (e.g., developing new friendships, new interests, school activities in an area of proficiency, etc.)?"

Investing yourself. (Ask, "Is there any way you can think of to get your mind off your problems by serving others or helping someone else?")

Seeking positive support. (Ask, "Who are the people who make you feel good about yourself? How can you be around them more? What are the situations that give you confidence? Can you think of ways to get more of that positive support?") (See also suggestions in chapter 14, "Handling Peer Pressure.")

ENLIST. Help build the teen's self-esteem by enlisting him or her in the problem-solving effort. Help the youth discover the causes that left him vulnerable to the problem, but lead him also to find healthy ways to meet needs for love, acceptance, belonging, and understanding. He will probably not be able to simply avoid the problem teens but will need to find peers who will value him and be safe for him. Help him take inventory of the possible people who can be a resource. Teens will not be able to just resist destructive influences without healthy alternatives to replace the old ways.

REFER. Teens who are involved with drugs and gangs nearly always require referral (with parental permission) to a Christian professional. Depressed teens who think about or threaten suicide also require immediate attention. Some of the other issues may require professional assistance, but many churches have effective youth groups that can be of great assistance. Teens who have been hurt by peer rejection and persecution will need a safe, loving peer group to connect with. Church youth groups are excellent places to provide safety for the social needs of teens. Research has validated that children who are involved in activities and get along with others (usually as a result of being involved in activities) are less likely to have the above-mentioned problems, whether the problems are the result of peer pressure, persecution, rejection or other factors.[10]

Family involvement in the caring process is almost always required. Referrals for parenting classes are very helpful in assisting parents to create an environment most conducive to their teen's growth and development.

For Further Reading

The following resources may help the concerned parent, pastor, teacher, or youth worker to address peer rejection and persecution:

Scriptures Cited in This Chapter

- 1 Thessalonians 5:14
- Genesis 1:26, 2:24
- Romans 12:1, 2, 3
- 2 Corinthians 5:17

Other Scripture to Read

- Psalms 9:9–14; 66:16–20; 119:81–88
- Isaiah 53:1–12
- Matthew 5:10–16, 44–48
- John 15:20

- Romans 12:14
- Ephesians 5:1–7
- 1 Timothy 4:12
- Hebrews 11:24–26
- 1 Peter 2:4–10

Further Reading

- Neil Anderson, *The Bondage Breaker (Youth Edition)* (Harvest House).**
- Dr. James Dobson, *Life on the Edge* (Word).**

- Robert S. McGee, *The Search for Significance* (Word).**
- Bill Sanders, *Stand Up: Making Peer Pressure Work for You* (Fleming H. Revell).
- Bill Sanders, *Tough Turf: A Teen Survival Manual* (Fleming H. Revell).**
- Sharon Scott, *PPR: Peer Pressure Reversal (An Adult Guide to Developing a Responsible Child)* (Human Resource Development Press, Amherst, Mass.).

** Contains helpful chapters on peer pressure

FAMILIAL

ISSUES

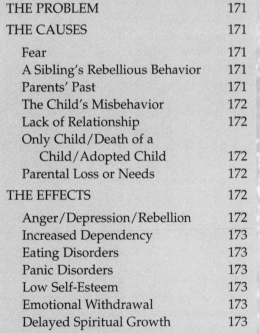

16

OVERPROTECTIVE PARENTS

A Synopsis

❖

Introduction

Lisa could pass for twenty or twenty-one, though she was only thirteen years old. She stood five feet seven inches tall with long dark hair, a well-developed figure, and blue eyes that shone with personality and confidence. Her parents, of course, watched their thirteen-year-old develop the body and personality one would expect in a woman much older than their little girl with more than a little concern. They were worried sick about her.

Not that Lisa never gave her parents cause for concern. She became interested in boys much earlier than her peers. Starting late in her fourth-grade year, her parents began reacting to Lisa's growing independence and maturity by pulling in the reins. As Lisa's peers were beginning to receive more privileges and freedom from their parents, Lisa's mom quit work in order to "be there" for Lisa; Lisa was convinced her mom was intent on "keeping an eye on her."

By her thirteenth birthday, Lisa had devised a system for getting away with things and circumventing her parents' rules. She discovered, for example, that if she asked to spend the night with a friend from church, Mom and Dad would say yes; she could then talk that friend into going to the mall to meet boys.

Lisa's parents felt like they were trying to swim upstream against Lisa's will and her desires; Lisa felt that if her parents were going to such trouble to keep boys away from her, there must be something unimaginably pleasurable that they didn't want her to discover. Little by little, however, Lisa's parents succeeded in monitoring her behavior to such a degree that she stopped planning ways to get around their rules. She stopped engineering ways to meet boys. In fact, she stopped shopping, she stopped dressing for attention, she even stopped bathing.

The Problem of Overprotective Parents

"During my years as a school psychologist," says Dr. Bernice Berk, "I've encountered many overprotective parents. While it's clear they don't want to be overprotective, their concerns about their child prevent them from allowing him to do things that he's perfectly capable of doing."[1]

One of the major tasks of parenting, of course, is to encourage enough confidence and capabilities in a child to equip him or her to leave home and function independently of Mom and Dad when he or she reaches adulthood. But overprotectiveness is a hesitation or inability to do that.

Overprotectiveness is often hard to gauge, but it may be shown in a number of ways:

- Parents will not let the young person out of their sight except at school and, perhaps, at church.

- Parents relate to the teen very similarly to the way they related to the child as an eight-year-old or ten-year-old.

- Parents screen or monitor the teen's phone calls.

- Parents consistently refuse permission for the teen to do things considered age-appropriate by other reasonable parents.

- Parents exhibit a determination to protect the child from *all* harm.

- Parents offer oversight of even the smallest details in the teen's life.

- Parents' actions and decisions seem designed to foster dependence, not independence.

- Parents' rules are applied rigidly and are equally nonnegotiable.

- Parents seem to have difficulty trusting the young person.

The above, of course, are highly subjective measurements of overprotectiveness. The most reasonable parent, for example, will sometimes refuse permission for his son or daughter to do things that other reasonable parents consider appropriate. Generally speaking, however, the above tendencies are typical of overprotective parents.

The Causes of Overprotective Parenting

There are a variety of reasons parents respond to their task in an overprotective manner. Such behavior may be founded upon one or more of the following causes.

◆ Fear

Fear is a common factor among overprotective parents. Today's world is a frightening place in which to raise children, and many parents worry about their children's vulnerability to the dangers they see featured on the evening news. But overprotective parents are sometimes fearful to an irrational degree. "While a certain amount of fear for children's safety is normal and healthy," says Berk, "allowing exaggerated fears to prevent [youth] from engaging in the normal activities of their peers can be harmful."[2]

◆ A Sibling's Rebellious Behavior

Overprotectiveness may also stem from a sense of failure with another (typically older) child. For example, Linda gave her parents every reason to trust her and allow her to attend slumber parties with her middle school friends. But because her older sister's first experience with smoking pot occurred at a middle school slumber party, Linda's parents refused to allow her to attend similar parties, fearing Linda would follow in her sister's footsteps. Linda was not the same sort of person her sister was, but she nonetheless had to pay for her sibling's behavior.

◆ Parents' Past

If one or both of the parents had neglectful or ineffective parenting, they may respond by becoming overly protective. Parenting styles are typically a reflection of—or a reaction to—the way we were parented. Similarly, if one or both parents were rebellious in their childhood or adolescence, they may respond by determining that they will prevent their child from making similar choices.

◆ The Child's Misbehavior or Shortcomings

If a parent views a child as immature, incapable, or limited by physical, mental, or developmental handicaps, he may respond by becoming overly protective. Indeed, at some level there *is* a need to protect such a child; however, an overprotective parent will usually resort to counterproductive control and manipulation rather than healthy support and encouragement based on an understanding of the child's potential to develop and mature. Extra parental precautions may indeed be required for certain children, but there must still be a balance between ensuring safety and allowing our children to try new things and develop new capabilities.

◆ Lack of Relationship

Many parents try to lay down rules without first establishing a real relationship with their children. Mom and Dad may see their parental role as primarily that of a policeman or judge; they focus on rules and may measure how well they are doing by how many rules they have established and how well the children adhere to those rules. Such parents, not knowing how to form and nurture a real relationship, may rely on the good behavior of a child to bolster the parent's own relational needs—a poor and unfulfilling substitute, of course.

◆ Only Child/Death of Child/Adopted Child

Parents of only children may tend toward overprotectiveness, perhaps more so than parents of two or more children. A parent of an only child may focus excessively on the needs of that child and become fearful (consciously or unconsciously)

of losing him or her. There is often a similar reaction by a parent who has lost one child to accidental death or disease; the parent may begin to develop irrational fears about the surviving children that prompt overprotective behavior. Similar unconscious beliefs may be experienced by adoptive parents who may carry a sense that they did not deserve a child and therefore must overcompensate with protective behavior.

◆ Parental Loss or Emotional Needs

Sometimes mothers who feel unfulfilled in their relationships with spouses will divert their pain by focusing obsessively on a child. (This can also be true of fathers, though that is less common.) Some parents become overly protective in an effort to fill their own emotional needs; they are fearful that if they lose the child their own love needs will be unmet. They may also believe that they are protecting the young person from a father's (or mother's) lack of involvement.

The Effects of Overprotective Parenting

"Can overprotectiveness harm a child?" asks Dr. Berk. "Certainly it can," she says, answering her own question. "Children learn not from our experiences but from their own. They need to have opportunities to take reasonable risks, to make mistakes, and to live with the consequences of their own actions. Overprotectiveness on the part of a parent will interfere with that natural learning process."[3] Psychiatrist Michael Liebowitz goes so far as to say that "overprotectiveness brings out the worst in kids."[4] The effects of overprotective behavior in parents vary based on the personality of the child, the degree of connection with or distance from the parent, and the severity of the overprotective behavior.

◆ Anger/Depression/Rebellion

When children feel controlled by a parent, the

most natural response is anger (see chapter 4, "Anger"). They may repress their anger out of fear of Mom or Dad's response, but it will be present nonetheless. The anger can turn inward and become depression (see chapter 5, "Depression") or it can turn outward and be expressed in rebellion (see chapter 23, "Rebellion").

◆ Increased Dependency

Some children of overprotective parents reach their twenties (and beyond) and cannot leave home. The child may get married (the "cleave" mentioned in Genesis 2:24), but never sever his or her dependence on Mom and Dad (the "leave" in Genesis 2:24); some will even live next door to Mom and Dad—or very nearby. The parents' overprotective behavior has stunted the young person's emotional development.

◆ Eating Disorders

There are a variety of contributing factors to eating disorders such as anorexia (self-starvation), bulimia (bingeing and purging), and compulsive overeating. For many children of controlling parents, eating activities become a way to control negative feelings. Bulimia and anorexia become a "tool" a young person uses to regain a sense of control over his or her own life. (See chapter 42, "Anorexia Nervosa," and chapter 43, "Bulimia.")

◆ Panic Disorders

Dr. Michael Liebowitz, the head of Columbia University's unit on panic disorders, has observed that "an unusually high proportion of panic patients report having had overprotective parenting in childhood."[5] Because fear is at the root of the parents' overprotective behavior, the child often picks up on the fear and may develop anxiety disorder or a full-blown panic disorder. Agoraphobia (irrational fear of leaving "home base") is a possibility in some children of overprotective parents.

◆ Low Self-Esteem

Parents don't want to raise proud or arrogant children, yet overprotective parents often make the opposite mistake of unwittingly teaching their children that they (the children) are incapable of caring for themselves and making decisions for themselves. The youth develops a sense that he is incompetent (in his *abilities*) and inadequate (in his *self.*) (See chapter 6, "Unhealthy Self-Esteem.")

◆ Emotional Withdrawal

The way we learn to relate to peers is an important developmental task throughout our lives. When a child is overprotected, peers are usually limited to the people the parents know well and trust; there is usually limited opportunity to develop social skills in various settings, which will often cause insecurity, prompting the young person to withdraw from peers by becoming a "loner."

◆ Delayed Spiritual Growth

Overprotective parents teach children to rely on Mom and Dad. This may prompt the young person to depend less—or not at all—on God. Overprotective parents may teach truths about God, and the child may be well grounded in the foundations of the Christian faith. However, the controlling parent undermines the young person's relationship with God by (perhaps unknowingly) trying to be God to him or her.

The Biblical Perspective of Overprotective Parents

First John 4:18 offers a telling perspective on parenting:

> There is no fear in love. But perfect love drives out fear, because fear has to do with punishment. The one who fears is not made perfect in love.

The overprotective parent is frequently motivated by fear, a fear that may reveal a lack of trust in God, a lack of trust in the young person, or both. Certainly God, our heavenly Father, has ample reason not to trust *us*, but we have no reason not to trust Him. God might be perfectly justified in seeking to control us and to protect us from every mistake, every misjudgment, and every sin we might commit, but He values our growth as well as our safety. He wishes for His children to respond willingly and lovingly to the freedom He has given them but He does not force them to do so.

Similarly, parents (and other adults) must recognize that, as their children grow and mature, they must be granted more autonomy. Doing so may mean sacrificing a measure of safety in exchange for healthy growth toward independence.

It can be difficult, of course, to know just where and how to strike that balance. Children are commanded to honor their parents,[6] but parents are called upon not to "exasperate" their children.[7] This should not be taken to mean giving a child anything and everything he or she wants; but it can serve as a helpful guide: Are the parents' actions fostering healthy development and maturity in the child, or are they simply exasperating him or her? A wise parent will seek to give his or her child two things: roots *and* wings.

The Response to the Problem of Overprotective Parents

Listen ◆ Empathize ◆ Affirm ◆ Direct ◆ Enlist ◆ Refer

A concerned adult has a two-fold task in responding to a young person whose parents may be overprotective: to help the youth by being supportive and encouraging and also (when practical) to help and reassure the parents.

LISTEN. The first step, of course, is to listen to the young person and his or her problems

and frustrations. You may wish to ask such questions as:

- When did you first begin to feel this way (about your parents)?
- Have things gotten better or worse as you've grown?
- (If the youth has siblings) Do your siblings feel the same way? How would you describe their feelings?
- Have you ever tried to discuss this with your parents? If not, why not? If so, with what result?

Don't be too quick to defend the parents, but don't criticize them, either. Let the young person discover that there is (at least) one adult who is interested in his or her thoughts and feelings. Just providing a listening ear can go a long way toward help and healing.

EMPATHIZE. As the teen discusses his or her frustration with the parents, cultivate an atmosphere of empathy toward the youth by:

- Nodding your head
- Making eye contact
- Leaning forward in your chair to indicate interest and concern.
- Speaking in soothing tones.
- Listening carefully to verbal and nonverbal communication.
- Reflecting key statements or gestures ("You seem to be saying. . ." and "You really feel angry about that, don't you?").

Also, consider the prospect that the teen may feel guilty for his anger toward Mom and Dad. Help him acknowledge the bad *and* good feelings he has toward his parents and their behavior.

AFFIRM. Seek to affirm the teen's sense of value and worth without undermining the parents' God-given place in his or her life. Author Dick Foth writes, "We need to hear over and over again that we are valued and valuable. Something fundamental happens when a person says, 'Just being around you is a joy,' or 'When you come into the room, something exciting happens,' or 'You have a great smile.'"8 Display your esteem of the young person not only by your words but by your actions too.

DIRECT. Help the young person consider his or her options within a biblical framework, such as the following:

- Lead the teen into relationship with Jesus Christ or (in the case of a Christian teen) into a deeper relationship with Him, the Lord of life, health, and peace.

- Encourage the youth to turn to God in prayer and rely on Him for the resources he or she lacks.

- She (or he) is likely to know that she is commanded to honor her mother and father; help her brainstorm ways to honor them (and, perhaps, understand them better) while still accurately viewing her own abilities and possibilities.

- Guide the youth to open a respectful, non-threatening dialogue, if possible, with Mom and Dad; one way to accomplish this may be with the method suggested by Ron Hutchcraft, of the teen writing a letter (or a series of letters) to express his or her love and appreciation for his or her parents and then respectfully voicing his or her concerns, frustrations, and even proposals for resolving differences between parent and child.9 (See chapter 18, "Non-Christian Parents," for further reference to this idea.) Such a method, if it is done sensitively and respectfully, can be extremely helpful in opening doors and breaking down walls.

- Brainstorm ways the youth might prove his or her trustworthiness and capabilities to

Mom and Dad and help him or her work toward those goals.

ENLIST. Strive to enlist the teen's participation in the church youth group since this is likely to be a place where parents feel the young person is reasonably safe. Build a relationship with both parents and teen that might encourage Mom and Dad to allow the youth to try new experiences and test a new degree of independence under your supervision. Help the young person aim for improvement, not perfection, in his or her relationship with Mom and Dad.

REFER. If at any time you, as the concerned adult, recognize that the health or long-term well-being of the young person is threatened (by severe depression, panic disorder, eating disorder, etc.), it is time to encourage the family to consult a professional Christian counselor who is qualified to address these specific issues in a biblical manner.

For Further Reading

The following resources may help the concerned parent, pastor, teacher, or youth worker to help a child of overprotective parents:

Scriptures Cited in This Chapter

- Genesis 2:24
- 1 John 4:18
- Exodus 20:12
- Ephesians 6:4

Other Scripture to Read

- Proverbs 17:9
- Philippians 4:5
- Romans 14:13

Further Reading

- Rex Johnson, *Communication: Key to Your Parents* (Harvest House).

- Robert S. McGee, Pat Springle, and Jim Craddock, *Your Parents and You (How Our Parents Shape Our Self Concept, Our Perception of God and Our Relationships with Others)* (Rapha Publishing).

- Paul and Jeanie McKean, *Leading a Child to Independence* (Here's Life Publishers).

- Norman Wakefield, *Listening: A Christian's Guide to Loving Relationships* (Word).

17

INATTENTIVE PARENTS

A Synopsis

Introduction

Mark and Debbie were both professing Christians. They met through the church youth group. Both were sixteen years old when they began dating. They were both sophomores in high school, both had been raised in the same town, and both were good students (though Debbie usually earned better grades than Mark). They had so much in common. But not everything.

Mark was the star basketball player of his high school team and was named to the all-district team. When he won the trophy as the most valuable player for the district championships, he smiled hugely and strode to center court to accept the trophy with a swagger that communicated his sense that he thought he deserved the award—and more. He didn't scan the faces in the crowd to find his parents because he knew they wouldn't be there. They never were.

Debbie didn't understand. She played on the field hockey team, and her parents never missed a game. They seldom missed a practice, in fact. They seemed to take an intense interest in everything she did.

It wasn't just Mark's sports events that his parents missed, though. His dad was a businessman who traveled a lot, and his mom was an obstetrician; they were highly respected in the community. But most mornings, Mark left for school without seeing his parents and usually scrounged in the kitchen to make his own dinner. Mark sometimes commented to his youth pastor that he could probably die and his parents wouldn't discover the body until it began to stink up the house.

The Problem of Inattentive Parents

Neglect can appear in many forms and at different levels of severity. Most authorities consider neglect to be inattention to the basic needs of a child or young person (that is, shelter, food, clothing, medical attention, school attendance, etc.).

The most severe form of neglect, of course, is when a child is physically harmed or dies from lack of nutrition, supervision, or medical attention; a report of the (U.S.) National Committee for the Prevention of Child Abuse showed that 1,299 children died in 1993 as a result of neglect or abuse.[1] (See chapter 35, "Non-Sexual Abuse.")

But some youth suffer a type of neglect that is not so readily recognized, not so easily documented. School and government authorities may not consider Mark's situation (described above) to be a case of neglect or abuse. However, the kind of inattention he suffers, the apparent lack of interest and involvement on the part of his parents, will take a slow but dramatic toll in a young person's life.

Many pastors and youth pastors consider disinterest and uninvolvement on the part of parents a major problem for young people. Seventy percent of the national youth leaders surveyed in preparation for this book rated the problem of inattentive parents as "very important," and 30 percent of those leaders rated the situation of inattentive parents of teens as a "crisis."[2]

The Causes of Inattentive Parenting

Parenting is a difficult job. It is tough enough to juggle the many demands of life without children; many people find giving appropriate attention and care to one or more children—on top of the already considerable responsibilities of marriage and career—a nearly impossible job.

Many succeed admirably, nonetheless, but many—for a variety of reasons—do not.

◆ Poverty

Most experts agree that the most common cause of neglect is poverty. Likewise, poverty is present in many cases in which a child suffers from inattention or apparent unconcern. Many causes related to poverty increase the likelihood of neglect or inattention, such as single-parent households, multiple siblings, lack of education, and lack of proper role modeling for the development of effective parenting skills. Moreover, there is often a general sense of hopelessness in low-income neighborhoods. And, too, parents often lack the knowledge or the will to provide purposeful parenting. However, low-income parents are not alone in this behavior.

◆ Locomotive Lifestyles

Youth in middle-class and upper-class homes usually have their basic needs of food, shelter, schooling, and clothing met. These children of higher-income households are often neglected in different ways, however; they may be starved for attention, affection, and a sense of their parents' interest. Middle-class and upper-class families often suffer from "locomotive lifestyles" in which parents resemble a speeding locomotive, racing the clock while frantically striving to meet the demands of their careers, churches, and communities—while their kids end up feeling like the scenery that gets passed by, blurred and barely noticed at all.

In today's fast-paced world, both parents sometimes feel pressure to work full-time jobs, and some youth are left to fend for themselves after school, sometimes well into the evening. Such times can leave a young person feeling lonely and, not infrequently, afraid, and can also give opportunity for unwise and unhealthy pursuits.

◆ Family Breakup

Divorce and single parenting creates great stress

on parents. The pain and anger a parent experiences from a divorce may overshadow his or her child's needs to grieve the loss of family. Many times after divorce, one parent is left alone to accomplish the complete responsibility for parenting. At the same time, there may be extra financial burdens, the beginning of a new career, new degree, and/or new relationships, all of which distract the parent and make careful attention to the youth seemingly impossible. (See chapter 19, "Parental Divorce.")

Single parenting is an overwhelming task. It is very difficult for a single parent to find the proper balance between his or her needs (which are likely to be acute in the wake of a death or divorce) and the needs of the children. Many single parents are admirably attentive to their children's needs. Too often, however, the young person's emotional needs—for attention, support, and affection—are neglected. (See chapter 20, "Living in a Single-Parent Family.")

◆ Multiple Siblings

It is not difficult to see how multiple siblings in a family can make it harder to invest interest and attention in each child. As one of five kids in the Jones family, Tara never got individual attention from her parents. They were both busy working and trying to keep up with the bills a larger family can so easily incur. Tara's parents were never available or interested in attending any of her school or sports activities and, in fact, did everything they could to discourage her from pursuing extracurricular interests, citing the additional financial burden such involvement would cause. Tara felt she was loved best when she was noticed least.

◆ Parental Preoccupation with the Social Ladder

Parents tend to neglect their children if they are preoccupied with anything, especially social advancement. Marcie's mom and dad were involved in several community activities, and both were constantly vying for advancement. Marcie was left in the care of an aunt, her mom's twenty-year-old sister. Marcie's parents didn't realize that their daughter and her caretaker were smoking pot together every afternoon. Since Mom and Dad usually didn't arrive home until 8 or 9 P.M., the physical evidence was carefully hidden, though the emotional results in Marcie's life were apparent . . . to anyone who cared to notice.

◆ Mental Illness

Schizophrenia, manic depression, postpartum depression, and clinical depression are some of the disorders that might lead to parental inattention. When a parent suffers from one of these disorders and is not being treated appropriately, the disease will sorely inhibit his or her ability to give attention to a child.

◆ Selfishness

Today's society urges men and women to "have it all" and to "have it your way": earn a three-figure income, send your kids to private school, work out every day, vacation in the Bahamas—and, meanwhile, have a happy family. Parents who buy into this "have-it-all" mentality will typically neglect their children's emotional needs, choosing (consciously or unconsciously) to place *their* "needs" ahead of their children's needs.

◆ Lack of Parenting Skills

Kids don't come with a parenting manual. Almost all first-time parents admit that nothing could have prepared them for the demands of parenthood. Some (particularly those whose parents modeled healthy parenting styles and skills) struggle, work, and finally succeed at developing skills that not only provide for their children's physical needs but for their emotional needs as well. Unfortunately, many parents believe that parenting means only providing financially for a family.

The Effects of Inattentive Parents

A young person whose parents seem unconcerned or inattentive is likely to experience hurt, frustration, anger (sometimes resulting in bitterness or rage), as well as feelings of insecurity and loneliness. Reactions such as these may prompt many and various effects.

◆ Low Self-Esteem

When a parent neglects a child (or when a child *perceives* indifference), the young person may develop a sense of worthlessness. Mark, whose story opened this chapter, may have appeared cocky in accepting his MVP award, but his behavior probably masked a critically low selfesteem. He compensated for his parents' indifference to his achievement with a mask of accomplishment and arrogance. (See chapter 6, "Unhealthy Self-Esteem.")

◆ Poor Scholastic Achievement

There is a strong link between parental involvement and academic achievement. When parents are not around, a young person's grades will most likely suffer. (See chapter 45, "Overachievement and Underachievement.")

◆ Poor Peer Selection

Inattentive parents may be the last to know that their child has chosen the "wrong" group to hang out with. A child who feels that his or her parents are indifferent and uncaring will probably be desperate for acceptance; he or she often finds that acceptance in the wrong ways, with the wrong crowd. (See chapter 14, "Handling Peer Pressure.")

◆ Poor Social Skills

Children begin their first social exploration in the family and build confidence and skills with which to reach out to the rest of the world. When

the parents are not available or not interested in the child, the young person's social development will probably be hindered.

◆ Inability to Bond with Others

Bonding is essential to human development and growth. When a teen has not bonded with parents through time, personal interaction, and touch, he or she will be retarded in his or her ability to bond with others, a lack which will show itself in friendships, in dating, in marriage, and eventually in relationships with his or her own children.

◆ Rebellious Behavior

Youth who feel neglected will try to get attention, and they will deem negative attention better than no attention at all. When negative attention achieves the desired results, more negative behavior will follow. A young person may rebel by finding a way (haircut, earrings, profanity, etc.) to embarrass a parent in front of the parent's friends or colleagues, or the youth may become involved in criminal activity (truancy, gang activity, etc.). (See chapter 23, "Rebellion.")

◆ Drug and Alcohol Problems

Neglected teens are more likely to succumb to alcohol and drug abuse because they have more unsupervised time. One researcher reports, "Young teens who come home to an empty house are twice as likely as those supervised by adults to use alcohol, marijuana and cigarettes."[3] (See chapter 38, "Alcohol Use and Abuse," and chapter 39, "Drug Use and Abuse.")

◆ Sexual Acting Out

Teens who feel that their parents are unconcerned or inattentive have both the motivation (seeking intimacy, attention, etc.) and the opportunity (large amounts of free time and unsupervised activities) to act out their frustrations and to seek fulfillment of their needs through sexual behavior. (See chapter 28, "Premarital Sex.")

The Biblical Perspective of Inattentive Parents

Deuteronomy 6:6–7 provides a pattern for godly parenting:

> These commandments that I give you today are to be upon your hearts. Impress them on your children. Talk about them when you sit at home and when you walk along the road, when you lie down and when you get up.

God's model for parenting is a relational model. God commands parents to provide for their children,[4] but He also commands us to teach them and to do so in relationship: when we sit, walk, lie down, and rise up. That attention to relationship is, of course, the very opposite of neglectful parenting.

Jesus set the example by modeling care for and attentiveness to children. When a crowd of children flocked around Jesus, many of them pressed forward by their parents, the disciples wanted to send the kids away, reasoning, perhaps, that Jesus had more important "adult" matters to deal with; but Jesus said, "Let the little children come to me, and do not hinder them, for the kingdom of God belongs to such as these."[5]

God is obviously not unmindful of the many demands and conflicts that arise in living and working and parenting. Surely it was for that reason that He issued commands in His Word for children to honor their parents[6] and for parents not to "exasperate" their children.[7] But the prayer of the concerned adult—pastor, teacher, youth worker, or parent— must be for the Lord to fulfill in every family the promise He made to Israel in Malachi 4:6, when He promised to "turn the hearts of the fathers to their children, and the hearts of the children to their fathers."

The Response to the Problem of Inattentive Parents

Listen ◆ Empathize ◆ Affirm ◆ Direct ◆ Enlist ◆ Refer

A teen who is hurting because of parental indifference or inattentiveness is likely to be in desperate need of an adult who will show interest and offer support; such care and concern will never replace the attention the youth desires from Mom and Dad, but it can certainly help, particularly if the adult responds to the youth in the following ways:

LISTEN. Youth who feel neglected by their parents often yearn for someone just to listen to them; they long to feel that some adult cares about them and their well-being. Careful and patient listening can be very constructive for such a young person. Questions such as the following may encourage the young person to talk, provided they are asked sensitively, without pushing:

- When did you first begin to feel this way?

- Have things gotten better or worse?

- Do your siblings feel the same way?

- Have you ever discussed these things with your parents? If not, why not? If so, with what result?"

Be sure to listen to the youth's feelings, as well as his or her words. Listen (without offering judgment one way or the other) in an attempt to discern whether the parents are being inattentive or whether that is the youth's perception (in either case, the hurt will be real). Listen alertly for any indication of physical neglect or abuse. (These must be reported immediately to authorities; see pages 15–17 in "Learning to Offer Christian Counsel" at the front of this book.)

EMPATHIZE. Come alongside the young person; step out of your "adult shoes" for a moment and try walking in the teen's tennis shoes. Try to see things from her or his perspective. Don't jump to conclusions or offer quick and easy "solutions." Instead, take your time seeing things through the youth's eyes and feeling things with his or her heart. Strive to communicate empathic concern by:

- Being available to the youth
- Making eye contact
- Leaning slightly forward in your chair when he or she is talking
- Nodding to indicate understanding
- Reflecting key statements ("You feel. . ." and "You're saying . . .")
- Waiting patiently through periods of silence or tears

AFFIRM. "Deep down," says author Dick Foth, "we all want to believe that we are likable, worth loving, and valuable to another human being"; a teen whose parents are (or seem to be) unconcerned may have rarely if ever felt that way. One of the deepest needs he or she is likely to have is a need for affirmation; one of the greatest ways a caring adult can help such a teen will be to offer affirmation. Affirmation, says Foth, "is me telling you how I see you in qualitative terms, [not for] what you do, [but for] who you are and what you mean to me. . . . How do we affirm another person effectively? Is it words, actions, or time? The answer is all three."[8]

DIRECT. Sensitively offer the following direction to young persons whose parents are uninvolved or unconcerned:

1. Offer hope. Show them how God sees them; show them that He believes in them and in their future.[9]

2. Lead them into relationship with the Lord. Gently guide them into a deeper relationship with the God who is always there and always has time for them.

3. Direct them to positive peer groups and a community (such as a thriving church or church youth group) that will not neglect their emotional needs. If they have material needs, direct them to resources that will help in those areas too.

4. Get them involved in helping others. Constructive attention can more often be gained through *giving* than through *taking*, through serving instead of being served. Encourage youth to help siblings or friends who may also be feeling neglected or unloved.

ENLIST. Enlist the young person himself or herself in brainstorming and planning ways to cope with the neglect or perceived neglect. Should the teen express his or her feelings to Mom and Dad? Should he or she write a letter (see Ron Hutchcraft's suggestion on page 000)? Can he or she suggest any concrete ways to approach Mom and Dad and suggest ways both parent and child can adjust to make things better?

REFER. Keep in mind that relational problems take time to work out; patience and persistence are called for. Both the caring adult and the young person should be in the process for the long haul. The pastor, youth pastor, teacher, or youth worker should make it a priority to involve the parents in these matters as early as possible. The adult should also be alert to the possible necessity and opportunity for referral of the youth and his or her parents to a competent Christian counselor who can provide family counseling.

For Further Reading

The following resources may help the concerned parent, pastor, teacher, or youth worker to help the child of inattentive parents:

Scriptures Cited in This Chapter

- Deuteronomy 6:6–7
- 1 Timothy 5:8
- Mark 10:14
- Exodus 20:12
- Ephesians 6:4
- Malachi 4:6
- Jeremiah 29:11

Other Scripture to Read

- Deuteronomy 31:6
- 1 Samuel 2:12–36

- 1 Kings 1:5–6
- Psalm 27:10
- Philippians 4:19

Further Reading

- Rex Johnson, *Communication: Key to Your Parents* (Harvest House).
- Norman Wakefield, *Listening: A Christian's Guide to Loving Relationships* (Word).
- Robert S. McGee, Pat Springle, and Jim Craddock, *Your Parents and You (How Our Parents Shape Our Self Concept, Our Perception of God and Our Relationships with Others)* (Rapha Publishing).

18

NON-CHRISTIAN PARENTS

Introduction

Her friends called her Nicki. Her parents called her Nicole.

Nicki became a Christian in the middle of her thirteenth year when a friend invited her to a youth group bonfire. That night, Nicki felt like a mammoth burden of sin had been lifted from her shoulders; for the first time in her life, she felt clean, as though all her troubles were over.

When she arrived home, she began to discover that her troubles were just beginning.

She excitedly shared the news of her salvation with her mom and dad, who greeted her at the door. She expected them to be excited for her. She expected them to congratulate her. She did *not* expect them to be angry.

"Do you know what time it is?" her father asked, glowering at her when she finished her story. "It's after ten o'clock! What did you do all night at that bonfire?"

Nicki didn't understand. She answered her father's anger with anger of her own, stomped up to her bedroom, and slammed the door behind her.

In the weeks and months that followed, Nicki began to grow as a Christian with the help of her friends in the youth group. She had never felt so "at home" with anyone as she did when she was with her Christian friends; nor had she ever felt less "at home" in her own house with her parents.

Nicki's mom and dad showed no interest in her new life. In fact, they seemed determined to thwart her spiritual growth and church involvement at every turn. They discovered that the most severe punishment they could inflict was to ground her from going to church or youth group, and they used that punishment like a sword hanging over her head.

Nicki and her parents seemed to be growing further and further apart until, when Nicki invited them to a parent-child banquet sponsored by the youth group at church, she was secretly happy that they refused. She invited Pam Wilson, her Sunday school teacher, to attend the banquet in her parents' place. After all, Nicki reasoned, Pam was more like a parent to her than her real parents were.

The Problem of Non-Christian Parents

Teens and parents face many obstacles and difficulties in trying to understand and relate to each other. They encounter power struggles, communication breakdowns, disagreement, and defiance—on both sides. It can be difficult for a child of Christian parents. It can be even tougher for a Christian teen whose parents are not Christians.

A 1994 survey of over thirty-seven hundred churched youth revealed that, while three-fourths (74 percent) said they are fairly or very close to their father (a sampling that includes children of both Christian and non-Christian parents), only half (51 percent) claimed that their fathers frequently show love for them. A higher percentage (88 percent) said they are fairly or very close to Mom, while two-thirds (68 percent) said that their mother frequently shows her love to them. The study also indicates that parents are not among the primary counselors churched youth confide in or turn to for advice. Only one in four (26 percent) said they frequently seek advice from their fathers, and two in five (40 percent) said they frequently seek advice from Mom.

Those numbers reflect the opinions and practice of children of Christian *and* non-Christian parents. The experience of many pastors, teachers, and youth workers suggests that many Christian kids whose parents are not Christians face an even tougher time getting along with and confiding in their parents. In fact, 96 percent of national denominational and para-church youth leaders rated disunity among Christian teens and non-Christian parents as an "important" or "very important" issue faced by youth.[1]

Jason and his parents fought frequently, usually over his participation in church events. His parents thought he was spending too much time at church, and they told him often that they wor-ried about some of the things his church was teaching him.

Leesa became a Christian after a high school Young Life meeting; several of her Christian friends invited her to attend church with them, but she wasn't old enough to drive and her parents wouldn't take her. She was too embarrassed to tell her friends why she didn't come, and she resented her parents for their unwillingness to help.

Steven lived with his divorced mother, who supported him and his little sister by bartending. The more involved he became in church, the more ashamed and critical he became of his mother. She, in turn, saw her son's Christian convictions and his church as a threat. Most of the time, Steven and his mom spoke to each other only when they had to, and then it was usually with bitterness and hostility.

Such struggles and troubles are not uncommon among Christian teens and their non-Christian parents. Even in families in which the parents support the young person's convictions and activities, tensions and difficulties can exist that make things difficult for parents and the teen.

The Causes of Difficulties with Non-Christian Parents

Teens and parents often face difficulties in relationships when both parent and teen are in similar spiritual states. Such difficulties can become even more pronounced when a child of non-Christians becomes a Christian. The reasons for this may seem obvious, but they should nonetheless be considered.

In 2 Corinthians 6:14, the apostle Paul commanded Christians not to be "yoked together with unbelievers." The command, of course, seems to refer to romantic, social, and business relationships; it does *not* suggest that a Christian child of non-Christian parents should somehow separate from them. Such an action would contradict Exodus 20:12 ("Honor your father and your mother") and Ephesians 6:1 ("Children, obey your parents in the Lord, for this is right").

However, after giving the command in verse 14, Paul goes on to ask a series of rhetorical questions that may highlight some causes of divisions and differences between Christian youth and their non-Christian parents. Paul asks:

> For what do righteousness and wickedness have in common? Or what fellowship can light have with darkness? What harmony is there between Christ and Belial? What does a believer have in common with an unbeliever? What agreement is there between the temple of God and idols? For we are the temple of the living God.[2]

◆ Stark Differences between Christian and Non-Christian

Paul's words highlight the stark differences that exist between a Christian and a non-Christian, even when they are members of the same family. Authors Stacy and Paula Rinehart discuss the above passage in relation to dating, but their words also describe the spiritual gulf that yawns between a Christian child and a non-Christian parent:

- *"What do righteousness and wickedness have in common?"* These are fundamentally antagonistic forces that cannot be brought into a truly compatible union.

- *"What fellowship can light have with darkness?"* . . . There can be no real fellowship between two people living in two different spiritual conditions, destined for two different spiritual outcomes.

- *"What harmony is there between Christ and Belial (Satan)?"* . . . Each person . . . is controlled by a different power, and harmony is unattainable.

- *"What does a believer have in common with an unbeliever?"* A Christian's citizenship, interest, and inheritance transcends this world. For an unbeliever, this world is the only reality he understands. Thus there's little basis for sharing the most basic issues of life.

- Finally, *"What agreement is there between the temple of God and idols?"* . . . God's temple [the Christian himself or herself] and idols are incompatible; there can be no common purpose. [The authors summarize this comparison in the following table.][3]

	UNBELIEVER	BELIEVER
Destiny	Eternal Judgment	Eternal Life
Source of Power	The Flesh	The Holy Spirit
Source of Control	Satan	The Godhead
Status	Darkness	Light
Condition	Dead in Sin	Alive in God
Allegiance	Worships False Gods	Worships the True God

From *Choices: Finding God's Way in Dating, Sex, Singleness, and Marriage* by Stacy and Paula Rineheart.

◆ Not an Excuse for Disobedience

The reality of this difference between Christian and non-Christian does not suggest that a child should seek to be free of his or her parents' authority, nor does it excuse disrespectful or rebellious behavior on the part of a child. Neither should it be taken to suggest that loving and harmonious relationships are impossible between a Christian child and non-Christian parents. It does, however, underscore the relational obstacles that both parent and child face in such a situation. And it may also illuminate what Jesus meant when He said:

> Anyone who loves his father or mother more than me is not worthy of me; anyone who loves his son or daughter more than me is not worthy of me; and anyone who does not take his cross and follow me is not worthy of me.[4]

The Effects of Having Non-Christian Parents

Disunity among Christians and non-Christians in a family—particularly between non-Christian parents and Christian children—can produce a wide range of effects. The caring adult who seeks to help a Christian teen who is struggling with his or her relationship with a parent should strive not only to be aware of these effects but to make the teen aware of them as well.

Non-Christian parents are likely to react in one of four ways to the news of a teen's decision to follow Christ; they may feel indifferent, confused, threatened, or jealous.

◆ Indifferent

Some parents will hear the news of their son or daughter's spiritual experience with a shrug of the shoulders. They may greet the revelation with the same passivity with which they greeted their son's impassioned replay of the latest teen comedy movie, or their daughter's crush on a teen television star. They may consider the teen's new life in the Spirit to be another passing phase of adolescence or just another point at which parent and teen don't "connect." Such a response may leave a young person to feel unloved or unimportant; the young person may then respond with anger, withdrawal, or in a myriad of other ways.

◆ Confused

Some parents may respond to their teen's decision to follow Christ with confusion, expressed or unexpressed. They may not understand his or her talk of a "new life." They may not understand why he or she needed to be "born again." Their concept of Christianity and salvation may be wrapped up in "doing good" or going to church and so may be sincerely confused by their child's experience. Such a response may cause frustration, anger, or confusion in the young person, who finds it even more difficult than before to communicate with Mom and Dad.

◆ Threatened

Some parents may feel threatened by the change they perceive in their child. They may fear losing control to a pastor, a church—even to God. They may feel that their son or daughter's new convictions implicitly constitute a rejection of their faith system and/or condemnation of them and their lifestyle. This response may cause parents to react angrily or to tighten their family discipline, and it can lead a young person to feel rejected, persecuted, or misunderstood.

◆ Jealous

Some parents who hear of their child's newfound forgiveness and witness his or her joy will respond with jealousy. They may be jealous of their child's experience, secretly wishing for a similar experience but not wishing to "follow" their child into salvation; or they may be jealous of the pastor, youth pastor, church, friends—or, again, even God—who has suddenly occupied a large and important place in their child's life. This response may lead to seemingly irrational behavior on the parents' part which, in turn, may prompt a teen to become frustrated, disillusioned, or depressed.

These are by no means the only responses a parent may feel, but they are basic responses that may cause conflict of many different kinds between the Christian teen and his or her parents.

The Biblical Perspective of Relating to Non-Christian Parents

A teen who is a Christian has journeyed from darkness into light. If his or her parents are not Christians, they are, in many ways, still in the dark. They're in the dark about their child's salvation and about his or her new life in the Spirit, new priorities, new perspective. But even so, they are still the parents and he or she is still their child.

Jim Craddock offers an insightful, biblical perspective for the teen who is struggling with a relationship with non-Christian parents:

In both the Old and New Testaments, the Scriptures direct us to honor our parents:

Honor your father and your mother, that your days may be prolonged in the land which the Lord your God gives you. (Exod. 20:12)

Honor your father and mother (which is the first commandment with a promise), that it may be well with you, and that you may live long on the earth. (Eph. 6:2–3)

What does it mean to *honor* one's parents? There are many misconceptions about this issue.

People who are very conscientious and overly responsible feel that if their parents aren't completely happy with everything they say and do, then they haven't honored their parents. But . . . you are not responsible for making your parents happy. That is between them and the Lord. Their contentment and happiness should not rest on

your shoulders. They need to depend on the Lord, not you, for their security and significance.

Although you are not responsible for your parents' happiness, you are responsible for developing your own separate identity and then extending your love to them. At that point, you should let them respond in any way they choose to respond. Sometimes they will appreciate what you say and do. Sometimes they won't, but you need to do what the Lord wants you to do whether they appreciate it or not.

A very helpful statement in *The Search for Significance* (McGee) gives objectivity and perspective to honoring our parents. As we develop our own identity and then seek to honor them, we should remember: *It would be nice if my father and mother approved of me, but if they don't, I'm still deeply loved, completely forgiven, fully pleasing, and totally accepted by God.* Remember, you are not responsible for their happiness, but you are responsible for acting in a way that pleases God. If your parents are happy with you, fine. If not, be content that you have obeyed and pleased God. After all, He is the Lord, and He deserves our primary affection and obedience.[5]

A Christian teen's devotion to Jesus Christ is not an excuse for disobedience; after all, God Himself has placed those parents in their position of authority. (See Rom. 13:1–2.) A Christian's allegiance to the Lord should, however, place his or her priorities in proper perspective, empowering that young person to relate to his or her parents in the Spirit of Christ, who submitted Himself to His Parent's authority.[6]

The Response to the Problem of Non-Christian Parents

Listen ◆ Empathize ◆ Affirm ◆ Direct ◆ Enlist ◆ Refer

A Christian teen who is trying to cope with differences and disagreements with a non-Christian parent or parents is responsible for how he or she treats Mom and Dad; he is *not* responsible for how Mom and Dad treat him. Jim Craddock, founder of a biblical counseling ministry, says, "Many people expect that treating their parents differently will cause their parents to change and treat them differently. That may happen after a while, but then again, it may not. . . . You can pray for their response. You can love them and accept them unconditionally. You can try to do everything perfectly (but, of course, nobody can do that), and they still may not change their behavior toward you. . . . They may never change—but *you* can!"[7] The sensitive youth leader, teacher, or pastor should foster that realization in a Christian young person by implementing the following steps:

LISTEN. Dr. Norm Wakefield points out two key components of constructive listening. He advises not only listening to a person's words but listening also "for the feelings being expressed and reflect[ing] them back to the speaker in an understanding manner." He also recommends resisting the "tendency to give advice—to moralize, command, criticize, or ridicule, rather than really listen to what the speaker [is] trying to say."[8]

EMPATHIZE. Make every effort to approach the teen and his or her struggles with understanding, compassion, and empathy. "When we empathize with others," says Wakefield, "we try to identify with their feelings, conflicts, and emotions, and we try to relate to them in a caring manner. We may not necessarily agree with their behavior or lifestyle, but we 'weep with those who weep' (Rom. 12:15 RSV). In order to empathize with others, however, we must determine just what they are feeling—and this requires perceptive listening."[9]

AFFIRM. All teens can benefit from sincere acceptance and affirmation, particularly from an adult in a position of influence. A young person who is trying to cope with conflict with a non-Christian parent may need such affirmation even more. Make the most of every opportunity to communicate sincere affection and esteem for him or her as a person of worth for whom Christ died. Seek to impress upon the youth McGee's statement, quoted earlier: *It would be nice if my father and mother approved of me, but if they don't, I'm still deeply loved, completely forgiven, fully pleasing, and totally accepted by God.*

DIRECT. Craddock proposes five extremely helpful principles that may help a Christian young person respond to non-Christian parents:

See yourself as a conqueror, not a victim.

Some people have experienced extraordinarily tragic family situations. . . . Regardless of our backgrounds Christ can bring light out of darkness and purpose out of pain. He can give us hope and confidence because His grace is bigger than our pain. Because we are His children we can be conquerors instead of victims [Romans 8:35, 37]. . . . If we see ourselves as victims we will always be defensive, blaming others for the way we are. If we see ourselves as conquerors we will have a deep sense of both purpose and thankfulness, realizing that God uses difficulties to build character strengths in us. . . .

See your parents as people, not villains.

The truth is: Very few parents intentionally hurt their children. The vast majority . . . simply . . . treat their children in the same way they have been treated by their own parents. . . . Many of them are deeply hurt themselves. They need our understanding and forgiveness, not our criticism and condemnation.

Develop a healthy sense of independence.

Some people base their whole identity on their parents' opinions of who they are. . . . As people mature, [however,] they need to develop their own identities. . . . The failure to establish this kind of objectivity (the ability to see both the good and the bad in our parents) prevents us from establishing a healthy sense of distance and independence from them. Instead, we focus on them and conduct ourselves according to their desires, hoping to secure their blessing and approval. Not only is this harmful to our human development, but it blocks our spiritual growth as well. After all, when we allow our world to revolve around our parents, we effectually serve them instead of Him.

Make godly choices.

. . . . Until we begin to develop our new identity in Christ, we have no choice but to simply try to defend ourselves as best we can and withdraw from or punish those who have hurt us. But when we realize that Christ is our protector, and that He is the complete source of our security and significance, then we can choose to act in a way that is good for us and others, and honoring to Him. . . . The transition may be difficult, [but] life is a series of choices. Will we choose to live by withdrawal and revenge or by the truth of the Scriptures and the power of God's Spirit?

Be prepared.

. . . Fortify yourself with the truth so that when you talk to your parents you can remember that you are deeply loved, completely forgiven, fully pleasing and totally accepted by the Lord, no matter what they (or anyone else) think of you. Then you can make the hard but right choice to love, forgive, and accept them, no matter what their response or your emotions might be.

Responding to parents can be very difficult. Don't be naive about the difficulties. Ask God for His wisdom and power, and be prepared.[10]

ENLIST. Do not simply advise the young person about what he or she should do; seek input from him or her. Enlist his or her active planning and participation in coping with the difficulties between parent and child, guiding him or her to strive for progress, not perfection. One way to enlist the young person's agency is

recommended by Ron Hutchcraft:

> Over and over again I've seen families transformed by a rather simple idea. Here's how it works: A family member makes a conscious decision to take the time to sit down and write a letter to another member of the family. He may even drop it in the mail and have the postman deliver it. . . .
>
> In the letter you can express your love, your appreciation for kindness, your hopes, your frustrations, and your forgiveness—if that's needed. Always try to be candid, but in a framework of love and affirmation for the other person.
>
> Usually a letter is better said, better heard, and better remembered.[11]

REFER. Keep in mind that relational problems take time to work out; patience and persistence are called for. Both the caring adult and the young person should be in the process for the long haul. The adult should also be alert to any opportunity for referral of the youth and his or her parents to a competent Christian counselor who can provide family counseling.

For Further Reading

The following resources may help the concerned parent, pastor, teacher, or youth worker to help the child of non-Christian parents:

Scriptures Cited in This Chapter

- 2 Corinthians 6:14–16
- Exodus 20:12
- Ephesians 6:1–3
- Matthew 10:37–38
- Romans 13:1–2
- Luke 2:51
- Romans 12:15
- Romans 8:35, 37

Other Scripture to Read

- Deuteronomy 31:6
- Psalm 27:10
- Proverbs 20:11, 23:22, 30:17
- Luke 12:51–53
- Philippians 4:19
- Colossians 3:20

Further Reading

- Rex Johnson, *Communication: Key to Your Parents* (Harvest House).

- Robert S. McGee, Pat Springle, and Jim Craddock, *Your Parents and You (How Our Parents Shape Our Self Concept, Our Perception of God and Our Relationships with Others)* (Rapha Publishing).

- Norman Wakefield, *Listening: A Christian's Guide to Loving Relationships* (Word).

19

PARENTAL DIVORCE

Introduction

Fourteen-year-old Megan stormed into the school counselor's office, dropped her books loudly onto the floor, and slumped into the vinyl chair just inside the door. She crossed her arms and glowered at the counselor.

"What's going on with you, Megan?" the counselor asked. The thirty-eight-year-old former science teacher perched on the corner of his desk and crossed his arms on his chest.

When the girl did not respond, the counselor continued. "I've never heard anything but positive reports from your teachers," he said. "Until lately. You've been mouthing off in class, your grades have dropped dramatically in just the last two weeks, and you can't seem to get along with anybody."

The girl said nothing. She fixed her eyes on the picture on the wall over the counselor's left shoulder and stared.

"And now you get into a shoving match with Valerie Evans in study hall? I thought you and Valerie were best friends."

Megan clenched her jaw and stared stubbornly at the wall. She had determined not to say a word. It was hard enough to deal with herself; she didn't want to have to explain to everyone why her parents were breaking up. She didn't want anyone to know. She didn't know how long she could keep it a secret. But she would try.

The Problem of Parental Divorce

In 1900, a year in which the marriage rate in the United States was 9.3 (per 1,000 population), the divorce rate was .7 (per 1,000 population). In other words, at the beginning of the twentieth century, the divorce rate was 8 percent of the marriage rate in the same year. (See Table 19, page 198.)

While the divorce rate climbed slowly (but steadily) throughout the first half of the twentieth century (with a sharp but temporary jump during the World War II period), it remained stable throughout the fifties and most of the sixties. Throughout those two decades, the divorce rate averaged about 25 percent of the marriage rate (compared to less than 10 percent in the years 1900–1910).[1]

A marked and lasting change occurred, however, in the late sixties. The divorce rate began to climb to a level approaching (and sometimes exceeding) 5.0 per 1,000 population, a singular distinction among most nations of the world. (See Table 19B.) In some years the divorce rate equaled 50 percent of the marriage rate, a gigantic shift in just half a century.

While the occurrence of divorce seemed to stabilize toward the end of the twentieth century, it remained at disturbing levels—especially when one considers the effects of divorce upon youth.

The Effects of Parental Divorce

Countless scholars have conducted studies on the effects of divorce on children, identifying a wide range of results and responses, both immediate and long-term. While some mental health professionals believe that a divorce (and the concomitant likely separation of a child's daily life from one parent) is more traumatic at some ages than at others, there is certainly no good time for a young person to endure the divorce of his or her parents.

Youth may respond in multiple and varied ways to the news of their parents' divorce, including denial, shame or embarrassment, blame or guilt, anger, fear, relief, insecurity and low self-esteem, grief, depression, alienation and loneliness, and other effects.

◆ Denial

A common response to pain (especially mental and emotional pain) is denial. Some youth may respond to their parents' divorce by acting as if it isn't happening or by insisting to themselves that their parents won't go through with it. They may say nothing at all to their friends, or they may say their father is simply away on business. This form of denial is often maintained for a long time, continuing even after the divorce is final and new living situations have been formed as a young person entertains a stubborn hope that Mom and Dad will soon get back together.

Another common form of denial manifests itself in a young person's refusal to admit, even to himself or herself, that he or she is upset in any way by the divorce. Such a response is often characterized by an attempt to shrug off the divorce or by a refusal to talk about it because "it's no big deal." While there may be, in rare cases, a degree of relief at the breakup of the parents' marriage (a response discussed later in this section), such casual responses are an indication of the youth's inability or unwillingness to face what's happening to his or her family. Denial may take other forms, such as idealizing the absent parent or even by bragging loudly and frequently about the parents' breakup in order to mask one's own anxiety.

The concerned adult must realize that denial, though usually unhealthy, is a defense mechanism. Youth who resort to denial do so (most often unconsciously) to protect themselves and guard a certain degree of stability in their lives.

Table 19
Marriages and Divorces

Year	Marriage Number	Rate (2)	Divorce (1) Number	Rate (2)
1900	709,000	9.3	55,751	.7
1905	842,000	10.0	67,976	.8
1910	948,166	10.3	83,045	.9
1915	1,007,595	10.0	104,298	1.0
1920	1,274,476	12.0	170,505	1.6
1925	1,188,334	10.3	175,449	1.5
1930	1,126,856	9.2	195,961	1.6
1935	1,327,000	10.4	218,000	1.7
1940	1,595,879	12.1	264,000	2.0
1945	1,612,992	12.2	485,000	3.5
1950	1,667,231	11.1	385,144	2.6
1955	1,531,000	9.3	377,000	2.3
1957	1,518,000	8.9	381,000	2.2
1958	1,451,000	8.4	368,000	2.1
1959	1,494,000	8.5	395,000	2.2
1960	1,523,000	8.5	393,000	2.2
1961	1,548,000	8.5	414,000	2.3
1962	1,577,000	8.5	413,000	2.2
1963	1,654,000	8.8	428,000	2.3
1964	1,725,000	9.0	450,000	2.4
1965	1,800,000	9.3	479,000	2.5
1966	1,857,000	9.5	499,000	2.5
1967	1,927,000	9.7	523,000	2.6
1968	2,069,258	10.4	584,000	2.9
1969	2,145,438	10.6	639,000	3.2
1970	2,158,802	10.6	708,000	3.5
1971	2,190,481	10.6	773,000	3.7
1972	2,282,154	11.0	845,000	4.1

Table 19
Marriages and Divorces (Cont'd)

Year	Marriage Number	Rate (2)	Divorce (1) Number	Rate (2)
1973	2,284,108	10.9	915,000	4.4
1974	2,229,667	10.5	977,000	4.6
1975	2,152,662	10.1	1,036,000	4.9
1976	2,154,807	10.0	1,083,000	5.0
1977	2,178,367	10.1	1,091,000	5.0
1978	2,282,272	10.5	1,130,000	5.2
1979	2,341,799	10.6	1,181,000	5.4
1980	2,406,708	10.6	1,182,000	5.2
1981	2,438,000	10.6	1,219,000	5.3
1982	2,495,000	10.8	1,180,000	5.1
1983	2,444,000	10.5	1,179,000	5.0
1984	2,487,000	10.5	1,155,000	4.9
1985	2,425,000	10.2	1,187,000	5.0
1986	2,400,000	10.0	1,159,000	4.8
1987	2,421,000	9.9	1,157,000	4.8
1988	2,389,000	9.7	1,183,000	4.8
1989	2,404,000	9.7	1,163,000	4.7
1990	2,448,000	9.8	1,175,000	4.7
1991	2,371,000	9.4	1,187,000	4.7
1992	(3) 2,362,000	9.2	1,215,000	4.7

1. Includes annulments.

2. Per 1,000 population. Divorce rates for 1941–46 are based on population including armed forces overseas. Marriage rates are based on population excluding armed forces overseas.

3. Provisional.

Source: *United Nations Monthly Bulletin*, June 1993.

Table 19B. Crude Marriage and Divorce Rates for Selected Countries
(per 1,000 population)

Country	Marriage Rate			Divorce Rate		
	1991	1990	1989	1991	1990	1989
Australia	6.6	6.8	7.0	n.a	2.49	2.46
Austria	5.6	5.8	5.6	n.a.	2.11	2.03
Belgium	6.2	6.6	6.4	n.a.	n.a.	n.a.
Canada	n.a.	7.1	7.3	n.a.	n.a.	n.a.
Czechoslovakia	6.7	8.4	7.5	2.39 {1}	2.61	2.54
Denmark	6.0	6.1	6.0	n.a.	n.a.	2.95
Finland	4.7	4.8	5.1	n.a.	n.a.	2.89
France	4.9	5.1	5.0	n.a.	1.87	1.87
Germany	6.3	6.5	6.7	n.a.	1.94	2.04
Greece	6.0	5.8	6.0	n.a.	n.a.	n.a.
Hungary	5.9	6.4	6.3	n.a.	2.40	2.40
Ireland	4.8	5.0	5.1	n.a.	n.a	n.a.
Israel	6.5	7.0	7.0	n.a.	1.29	1.29
Italy	5.5	5.4	5.4	n.a.	0.48	0.53
Japan	6.0	5.8	5.8	n.a.	1.27	1.28
Luxembourg	6.7	6.2	5.8	n.a.	n.a.	2.27
Netherlands	6.3	6.4	6.1	1.88 {1}	1.90	1.90
New Zealand	6.8	7.0	6.9	2.70 {1}	2.70	2.58
Norway	n.a.	5.2	4.9	n.a.	2.40	2.18
Poland	6.2	6.7	6.8	0.91 {1}	1.11	1.24
Portugal	6.8	7.3	7.4	1.01 {1}	0.93	0.98
Spain	5.6	5.5	5.6	0.59 {1}	n.a.	n.a.
Sweden	4.6	4.7	12.8	2.20 {1}	2.26	2.22
Switzerland	6.8	6.9	6.8	n.a.	1.96	1.91
United Kingdom	6.5	6.8	6.1	n.a.	2.88	2.86
United States	9.4	9.8	9.7	4.73 {1}	4.70	4.70
Yugoslavia	n.a.	6.3	6.7	n.a.	0.81	0.96

1. Provisional.
n.a. = not available.

Sources: Marriage rates: United Nations, Monthly Bulletin of June 1993. Divorce rates: *United Nations, Demographic Yearbook 1991.*

◆ Shame/Embarrassment

"More than anything, I was ashamed," a young woman named Vera related to Anne Clair and H. S. Vigeveno, authors of *No One Gets Divorced Alone*.[2] "Ashamed of living in that crummy place and ashamed of my parents for splitting up. I didn't tell a soul."

Shame and embarrassment are common responses to parents' divorce among teens and preteens. Some are so embarrassed that they don't even tell their closest friends about what is happening in their families . . . even when those friends' parents are also divorced or divorcing.

Such youth typically feel ashamed or embarrassed because they interpret a divorce as an indication that there is something wrong with their family (and assume others will think the same thing). They also may assume that they bear a degree of responsibility for their parents' breakup (discussed later in the "Blame/Guilt" section). They may be embarrassed by what they consider inappropriate conduct on the part of their parents following the divorce (such as Dad dating a younger woman) or by the abrupt changes in their style of living (such as moving into an apartment with Mom).

Such feelings are often intensified among Christian youth. They may feel that biblical teachings regarding divorce condemn their parents and their family. They not only have to face their friends at school and in the neighborhood, but they also have to cope with an entire church (from which they may have reason to fear judgment and censure). If their parents have functioned as leaders in the church, youth may face even greater embarrassment as their parents strive to maintain their positions or relinquish their duties.

◆ Blame/Guilt

Young children often attach huge significance to a single event in their immature attempt to determine the cause of their parents' divorce. They may remember a loud argument Mom and Dad had, or the night that Mom cried alone at the dinner table, and think that must be the reason their parents are getting divorced. Often, of course, the most memorable events in a child's mind are those that pertained to the child: the disagreement over who should take Jennifer to her piano lesson or the time Daddy yelled because Josh strayed from the yard. As a result, children often blame themselves for their parents' divorce. One child psychologist found that "almost three-quarters of the six-year-olds we studied blame themselves for the divorce."[3]

The same thing happens (though at a more sophisticated level, perhaps) among older youth. Preteens and teens may feel that their fights with siblings prompted Mom and Dad's decision to divorce. They may think that their struggle for independence or their teenage rebellion contributed to the split. They may feel responsible because of falling grades, flaring tempers, or failure to communicate their love to one or both of their parents. Some youth have even been told, by parents or other adults, that their attitude or behavior contributed to or caused their parents' divorce.

Youth who blame themselves for their parents' split may also feel a driving, urgent need to engineer Mom and Dad's reconciliation. They may prefer such bearing of responsibility to what they see as the alternative—a feeling of utter helplessness. (See also chapter 3, "Guilt.")

◆ Anger

Anger is among the most common responses to parental divorce. A young person may be angry simply because the divorce disrupts his or her family environment, creating disorder where before there was order. A youth may feel anger because he or she resents being separated from one parent. His or her feelings of abandonment may create anger, or he or she may resent being different from friends who still live in intact families.

Youth may be victims of one parent's resentment toward the other. Sentiments and statements like "Why do you have to be so much like your father?" and "Why do you let her do this to you?" can create a cauldron of anger in an adolescent or preadolescent. Even in the most amicable situations, the turbulence and activity surrounding the divorce may decrease the amount of time and attention the parents are able to give to the family, which may occasion reactions of frustration and anger in the children. And certainly a divorce is likely to cause multiple new resentments and frustrations between the divorcing parents which, added to the disaffection that may already have existed, will make life more stressful on the children.

Physical and financial circumstances may prompt anger as well. If the divorce prompts a family move from a familiar neighborhood, school, and church, or a change to less-than-ideal living circumstances, youth may respond with anger. A teen or preteen may become angry that Mom has to start working (or work longer hours), taking both mother and father away from him or her for long periods of time.

Youth will respond to their anger in various ways. They may repress it and deny it and even feel guilty because they feel angry. They may release it by identifying with others (such as characters in violent movies). They may release it symbolically through passive-aggressive behavior (such as "accidentally" hurting themselves or others, after which they may make effusive attempts at repentance and restitution). They may project their anger onto others, seeing anger in others' words and behavior.

Those young people who suppress their anger may suffer heightened stress. They may experience anxiety attacks, which may include sweating, shortness of breath, body tremors, skin irritations, and even a state of severe, irrational panic. They may experience nightmares at night and/or severe depression and moodiness during the day. (See chapter 4, "Anger," and chapter 5, "Depression.")

The primary purpose of anger, according to Dr. Richard A. Gardner, is to remove a source of irritation and frustration. When anger is directed at a physical threat, it serves a useful protective purpose; anger that is directed at divorcing parents (or something more nebulous, like the divorce itself, or circumstances) creates far more problems than it solves. Anger that is unresolved may lead to rage (a more violent, less directed response) and eventually to fury (an irrational response that is more violent and less directed still).

◆ **Fear**

Like anger, fear is also a common and elemental response to parental divorce. Bowlby (1969) claimed that the loss of anyone to whom an infant is attached produces an instinctive fear response. Such a loss in older children—such as a loss through divorce—will also frequently produce fear.

Adolescents and preadolescents, in addition to experiencing the same instinctive response, will also, because of their age and relative mental maturity, face fears that are more tangible. They may entertain fears about where they will live, where they will go to school, or where they will spend vacations. They may fear the reactions of their friends, family, and church. They may fear total abandonment by one or both parents. They may fear "losing" their grandparents.

Youth who respond to parental divorce in this way may react by withdrawing and becoming less communicative with their parents and/or peers. They may suppress or deny their fears. They may become so frustrated by their fears that they respond angrily and begin to lash out emotionally at parents and others. They may experience nightmares or may be more prone to daydream. Some youth may even be subject to anxiety attacks or panic attacks. (See also chapter 2, "Anxiety.")

◆ Relief

Some adolescents and preadolescents actually experience feelings of relief when their parents announce plans to divorce. Their relief may be occasioned by a variety of factors, but it is most often related to conditions that existed prior to (and may have contributed to) the divorce.

"Anything's better than their constant fighting," they may say.

"I couldn't wait for him to leave," some may say.

"I knew it would happen sooner or later," others may say. "They just never got along."

Such expressions of relief may be a form of denial (discussed earlier in this chapter) intended to mask a young person's pain. Other teens and preteens may use such statements as a means of "getting back" at their parents for the hurt they have caused their children. For others, however, such statements of relief are a sincere and accurate articulation of their feelings.

Divorces rarely occur "out of the blue." They are more often the result of months, perhaps years, of struggles and mistakes. The children in a family are seldom ignorant of those struggles and mistakes. They may have overheard their parents' arguments. They may have witnessed abuse or suffered abuse themselves. They may even have been aware of one parent's infidelity. As a result, for many youth the threat of a divorce is welcomed as the promise of relative peace and harmony.

◆ Insecurity/Low Self-Esteem

Children of divorce are especially vulnerable to feelings of insecurity and low self-esteem. The circumstances that led to divorce, the divorce process itself, and the conditions that commonly follow a divorce often constitute three "strikes" against an adolescent or preadolescent's sense of self-worth.

Children of divorce often reason that their very existence brought about their parents' divorce; "if I had never been born," some may suppose, "Mom and Dad might still be together." Or they may believe that if Mom and Dad had somehow had a different—better—child, the marriage could have been saved (see "Blame/Guilt" discussed earlier in this chapter). Such attitudes, however unreasonable to an objective, adult mind, are intensely real—and reasonable—to many children of divorce, causing a deleterious effect on a young person's self-esteem.

Even if they don't blame themselves for their parents' divorce, teens or preteens may feel different from—and less worthy than—friends whose families are intact. Because in a divorce one parent is largely removed from a young person's daily life and because the circumstances surrounding a divorce often make it harder for either parent to give attention and affection to the children, the younger victims of divorce are likely to feel abandoned to some degree, and many assume that because they have been thus "rejected," they are therefore unlovable.

Many also feel stigmatized by their church or neighborhood because of the family split, and they accept that stigmatization as a reflection of their low worth. Stigmatization may also occur (or be inferred by youth) because of a parent's behavior (alcoholism, promiscuity, abusiveness), which can strike a crippling blow to a young person's self-esteem. Economic changes or hardships can also constitute, in a young mind, evidence of low worth.

The circumstances that follow divorce can also threaten a young person's security and self-esteem (see chapter 6, "Unhealthy Self-Esteem"). If the parents struggle to "make arrangements" for the care and supervision of the children, if one parent is lax in visitation or child-support payments, if the child is made to feel like an inconvenience to Mom and Dad, he or she may believe "I'm nothing but trouble; I'm not worth much to them."

Such situations, because they often breed

insecurity and low self-esteem, may give rise to a plethora of other psychological symptoms.

◆ Grief

After a divorce, children, teens, and adults alike sometimes go through stages of grief much as they would after the death of a loved one. Of course, such grief following divorce is generally not as extreme as grief caused by death, for several reasons: the separation (even when one parent moves far away) is not irrevocable, divorce seldom occurs as suddenly as death often does, and divorce (while it is certainly serious and disturbing) does not often produce quite the same level of upheaval (emotional and otherwise) that death does.

However, a sense of grief is nonetheless real, and often severe, to children of divorce. Grief is a healthy process, providing a period of transition and acclimation to a loss. The grieving process normally includes five stages, as Kubler-Ross identified: denial, anger, bargaining, depression, and acceptance. (See chapter 8, "Grief.")[4] In the case of a divorce, these stages may be less pronounced, but they are often present nonetheless.

While relatively few teens or preteens will mourn overtly, they may experience times of sadness, melancholy, and listlessness. Their tempers and emotions may be unusually volatile. Intense feelings may overcome them at odd moments, and they may have difficulty expressing their feelings or attributing them to any source. They may not connect their grief to their parents' divorce, and they may need guidance to help identify the reasons for the changes in their feelings and behavior.

◆ Depression

Unless the news of a divorce occasions feelings of relief because of prior family conflict and upheaval, most adolescents and preadolescents will experience sadness upon learning of their parents' plans to divorce, and they will endure occasional moments of sadness as they adjust to the new state of affairs.

Depression, however, is a prolonged period of sadness, often intense. (See also chapter 5, "Depression.") It is typically characterized by:

- apathy
- loss of appetite
- loss of interest in and concentration on studies
- loss of ability to enjoy play
- loss of ability to enjoy peer relationships
- helplessness
- hopelessness
- irritability
- obsessive self-criticism
- withdrawal[5]

Other symptoms may include extreme periods of boredom and low frustration tolerance, and extreme cases may be characterized by self-destructive fantasies and threats of suicide (See chapter 9, "Suicide Thoughts, Tendencies, and Threats.")

Such depression may last a few weeks—or months. If circumstances other than the divorce itself (such as pent-up anger or guilt or the prolonged distress of the custodial parent) contribute to the depression, it may last even longer. While a certain degree of depression is natural and understandable among the children of divorce, long-term depression is not a healthy response.

◆ Alienation and Loneliness

Children of divorce—particularly adolescents—often experience a sense of alienation as a result of their parents' decision. They may feel somewhat estranged from one or both parents. They may feel alienated from their church, even when they have experienced no unpleasant or judgmental reaction from church members or leaders. They may feel suddenly distant from their friends.[6] They may feel deserted and rejected by God Himself, and will frequently wonder how God could allow such a thing to happen to their family.

In the wake of such alienation, of course, many teens and preteens experience bouts of extreme loneliness. They may feel friendless, helpless, and alone. They may think that no one understands what they are going through, what they are feeling. They may withdraw physically to their bedrooms, they may withdraw emotionally into fantasy or melancholy, or they may do both. (See also chapter 1, "Loneliness.")

◆ **Other Effects**

The many turbulent feelings a child or teenager may experience in the case of his or her parents' divorce can create other, long-term results which, to a greater or lesser degree, stem from the emotions and responses discussed above. These include academic problems, behavioral problems, sexual activity, substance abuse, or suicide threats and attempts.

Academic Problems. Thomas Ewin Smith (1990) found that adolescent children of single mothers exhibit a lower "academic self-concept" than children living with both biological parents. Furthermore, Shin (1978) and Hetherington, Camara, and Featherman (1981) documented that children from two-parent families have better grades and higher academic achievement than children in one-parent families. Such disparity may be the result of many factors: it is more difficult for children to concentrate on schoolwork in times of family turmoil, slipping grades may be a means of gaining attention or expressing rebellion, and single parents will often find it more difficult to monitor homework, etc. Academic problems may also be an outgrowth of one or more of the problems and emotions mentioned above. (See chapter 44, "Dropping Out," and chapter 45 "Underachievement and Overachievement.")

Behavioral Problems. Some youth exhibit behavioral problems in the wake of their parents' separation and divorce. They may begin smoking or drinking. They may start missing school. They may have trouble getting along with others. They may become disrespectful to schoolteachers and church leaders.

Such behavior is often an expression of anger or confusion, a response to the emotional turmoil they feel—but cannot adequately express—because of their family situation.

Sexual Activity. Research suggests that divorce may also, in the long term, prompt a higher degree of sexual activity and promiscuity. For example, college students with divorced parents have been found to be more sexually active than classmates from intact homes. This is especially true of male children of divorce, who tended to favor "recreational" sex over committed relationships and were most likely to have had more than four sex partners by the time they entered college.[7]

Such activity may be the result of modeling; boys who grow up without a live-in dad "may model more from cultural stereotypes of how a man is supposed to behave, from TV and movies' short-term seductions," says researcher Robert Billingham of Indiana University. Billingham also suggests that such patterns of sexual activity may be—knowingly or not—modeled by single mothers who form multiple short-term relationships.[8] (See also chapter 28, "Premarital Sex.")

Substance Abuse. Researchers have found a linkage between parental divorce and substance abuse. Wilkinson (1980) and Dornbusch and associates (1985) report a correlation between alcohol, marijuana, and tobacco use and the absence of a father from the home. Such behavior may be a simple result of less parental oversight or an expression of anger or rebellion. It may be the action of a young person who feels rejected at home and seeks approval and acceptance with friends and acquaintances. (See also chapter 38, "Alcohol Use and Abuse," and chapter 39, "Drug Use and Abuse.")

Suicide Threats and Attempts. Occasionally, a young person's depression and despair over the breakup of the family will become so severe that he or she will threaten or attempt suicide. The youth may view suicide as a way to avoid the pain and grief engendered by the breakup of the family. He or she may entertain the hope of "reclaiming" Mom and Dad's love and attention by attempting suicide. Suicide may also be (to the youth's imagination) a means of communicating how much his or her parents have hurt him or her, a way of "making them sorry." Regardless of the thoughts and emotions behind the threat or attempt, such statements and actions should always be taken seriously and responded to immediately. (See chapter 9, "Suicide Thoughts, Tendencies, and Threats.")

The long-term effects of parental divorce may also include a fear of betrayal, a fear of commitment, an inability to form close and lasting relationships, and lingering bitterness toward one or both parents.

The Biblical Perspective of Parental Divorce

In the first days of human life, God devised a wonderful plan for humanity. "It is not good for the man to be alone," He declared. "I will make a helper suitable for him."[9] So God created male and female, a man and a woman suited for each other physically, emotionally, intellectually, and spiritually.

After relating the story of humanity's first appearance on the world stage, God's Word then adds one of the earliest precepts of Scripture:

For this reason a man will leave his father and mother and be united to his wife, and they will become one flesh. (Gen. 2:24)

God went on, in His Word, to further explain and amplify that first precept regarding marriage. Jesus, speaking specifically of the marriage commitment, added, "What God has joined together, let man not separate" (Mark 10:9). The apostle Paul, under the inspiration of the Holy Spirit, wrote, "To the married I give this command (not I, but the Lord): A wife must not separate from her husband. . . . And a husband must not divorce his wife" (1 Cor. 7:10–11). Clearly, God intended our marital and familial relationships to be strong, loving, and lasting relationships that reflect the unity of God Himself. (See Deut. 6:4.)

Unity is part of God's nature and character. He is one. And it is that unity that He wishes us to reflect in our marriages and family relationships. When the Bible says that a man and woman shall "be united . . . and . . . become one flesh" (Gen. 2:24), it is saying that marriage should reflect God's nature.

That doesn't always happen, of course; and, more to the point, a child or teenager cannot keep his or her parents' marriage together. Children do not cause divorce. They can also not prevent it; nor does God expect them to. He does, however, command children (of all ages) to "Honor your father and mother" (Exod. 20:12) and to "Obey your parents in the Lord, for this is right" (Eph. 6:1). Divorce and family breakup may make it harder to obey God's commands, but they do not negate them.

Finally, God makes it clear in His Word that the victims of broken families are of special concern to Him. Psalm 68:5 says, "A father to the fatherless, a defender of widows, is God in his holy dwelling," and Psalm 10:14 declares, "But you, O God, do see trouble and grief; you consider it to take it in hand. The victim commits himself to you; you are the helper of the fatherless." God does not frown on those whose parents or spouses have left them; He does not turn a deaf ear to the painful cries of those whose families have been shattered by divorce . . . nor should His people.

The Response to the Problem of Parental Divorce

Listen ◆ Empathize ◆ Affirm ◆ Direct ◆ Enlist ◆ Refer

The youth leader can help an adolescent or preadolescent cope with the tragedy of divorce by implementing the following plan:

LISTEN. Allow the young person to talk freely about his problems, his feelings, his thoughts, his hurts. Don't probe for details of the parents' divorce, but for expression of the young person's thoughts and feelings about it. Perhaps the most important questions to ask at such times are:

- What do you think is happening?

- How does that make you feel?

These questions may help the youth focus on the pertinent issues: the facts (what is *truly* happening) and his or her feelings about the facts.

EMPATHIZE. As you listen, try to see things through the eyes of the young person. Place yourself in his or her shoes; how might you feel in a similar situation? Such empathy can help you understand the young person's responses and reactions to his or her situation. Remember that you can communicate empathetic warmth by:

- Listening carefully to verbal and nonverbal communication.

- Nodding your head.

- Making eye contact.

- Leaning forward in your chair to indicate interest and concern.

- Speaking in soothing tones.

- Reflecting key statements ("So what you're saying is . . .") or gestures ("It looks like that makes you pretty mad.").

AFFIRM. Resist the temptation to tell the young person that his or her feelings or actions are ridiculous or unfounded. Give the young person permission to feel and express his or her feelings. You may say, "What you're going through must be a little scary. I know I would be afraid, not knowing for sure what things would be like now that my parents were divorcing. What's that like for you?" Try to communicate the fact that his or her feelings are natural and understandable and that you accept him or her even when he or she is afraid or angry (for example). Offer affirmation, not only through what you say, but also through faithfulness in prayer for the young person.

DIRECT. A concerned adult should pursue several priorities in offering support and guidance to a youth whose parents are divorcing. These should include:

1. Encouraging dependence on God. Lead the young person into a relationship with Jesus Christ, or encourage frequent prayer and greater dependence on God for the young man or woman who is already a Christian, for God promises to heal, guide, and "restore comfort" to those who are broken and contrite (Isa. 57:18).

2. Try to direct the youth to differentiate between how he *feels* about the divorce and what he *thinks* about the divorce, leading him to evaluate for himself the *reasonableness* of his feelings. Don't discount his feelings, for they are real and powerful, but try to lead him, not only to understand and express himself, but also to temper such feelings according to what he knows objectively to be true.

3. Explore with the youth the difference between things one can control and things one cannot control. For example, one can control whether one hits a brother or sister; one cannot control whether one *has* a sister or brother. One can save for a rainy day; one cannot control on which days it may rain. Help the youth appreciate that parental divorce is among those things that the children in a family—regardless of their age—cannot control.

ENLIST. Enlist the youth's cooperation and participation in acknowledging and devising the things he or she can do to lessen the pain of Mom and Dad's divorce. Focus his or her attention on constructive things that are within his or her power to do, and encourage such things (making the transition to a new lifestyle easier for parent and child, or attending more carefully to the relationship with the absent parent by calling several times a week, for example).

REFER. Strive to facilitate communication and cooperation between the youth and his or her parents. Consider recommending (to parents and child) consultation with a counseling professional who can offer biblical counseling while you continue to offer support and guidance.

For Further Reading

The following resources may help the concerned parent, pastor, teacher, or youth worker assist the young person who is struggling with his or her parents' divorce:

Scriptures Cited in This Chapter

- Genesis 2:18, 24
- Mark 10:9
- 1 Corinthians 7:10–11
- Deuteronomy 6:4
- Exodus 20:12
- Ephesians 6:1
- Psalms 68:5; 10:14
- Isaiah 57:18

Other Scripture to Read

- Psalms 27:10; 147:3
- Isaiah 57:15
- Matthew 5:31–32
- Luke 16:18
- 1 Corinthians 7:1–17

Further Reading

- Andre Bustanoby, *But I Didn't Want a Divorce* (Zondervan). Contains a chapter concerning "Divorce and Your Child."
- Anne Claire and H.S. Vigeveno, *No One Gets Divorced Alone* (Regal).
- Gary and Angela Hunt, *Mom and Dad Don't Live Together Anymore* (Here's Life Publishers).
- Les Woodson, *Divorce and the Gospel of Grace* (Word).

20

Living in a Single-Parent Family

Introduction

Dan's parents had been divorced for almost six months, but a lot had changed in that short time. Fifteen-year old Dan and his thirty-seven-year-old mom moved out of the house they'd lived in since as long as Dan could remember and into a tiny apartment across town. He had to transfer to a new school at the beginning of his sophomore year. And Dan, who had been a solid B student until late last year, was failing most of his classes. He wasn't rebelling or anything; he just didn't feel like doing the work anymore.

When his first report card of the new school year came in the mail, Dan's mom hit the roof.

"What's the matter with you? There's no excuse for you to be getting grades like this!" his mom said. She wasn't used to being the disciplinarian in the family, but she was determined to do a good job as a single parent.

Dan shrugged. "It's no big deal, Mom," he said. "I'll bring 'em up."

"Oh, you bet you will. And you can start tonight. You'll have plenty of time for studying because you're grounded for the next two weeks."

"What? You can't be serious!"

"Well I am. Now march up to your room, young man, and get started on your homework."

"No way! I'm supposed to go to the game with Craig."

"You're not going anywhere." She pointed up the steps.

Dan grabbed his jacket from the doorknob of the hall closet and turned toward the door. His mother blocked the way, her arms folded across her chest.

"You can't stop me, Mom!" he said, pushing her aside and reaching for the door. She pushed him back, and he swung around and threw a punch at her face, knocking her to the floor.

Dan stormed out the door and left his mother lying on the floor of their tiny apartment, crying and rubbing an eye that was already beginning to swell black and blue.

The Problem of Living in a Single-Parent Family

In the post-World War II generation, says journalist Barbara Dafoe Whitehead, "more than 80 percent of children grew up in a family with two biological parents who were married to each other. By 1980 only 50 percent could expect to spend their entire childhood in an intact family. If current trends continue, less than half of all children born today will live continuously with their own mother and father through childhood. Most American children will spend several years in a single-parent family."[1]

Single parenthood may occur because of divorce, desertion, or death, or because a woman has a child outside of marriage. Regardless of the circumstances surrounding the family situation, single parents must face "too many decisions that have to be made without the consultation of another partner, too many jobs to be done by one person, . . . too many tensions and frustrations that seemingly have only intermediate solutions, and too little time apart from child rearing that [can be claimed as one's] own."[2]

Single parents—and their children—face monumental challenges and obstacles, some that are confronted immediately and others that develop over a longer period of time. Among these are: financial struggle as well as the child's academic problems, behavioral problems, and sexual activity.

◆ Financial Struggle

"For the vast majority of single mothers," writes Whitehead, "the economic spectrum turns out to be narrow, running between precarious and desperate. Half the single mothers in the United States live below the poverty line"[3] (compared to one out of ten married couples).

◆ Academic Problems

Thomas Ewin Smith (1990) found that adolescent children of single mothers exhibit a lower "academic self-concept" than children living with both biological parents. Other research indicates that children from two-parent families have better grades and higher academic achievement than children in one-parent families (Shin [1978]; Hetherington, Camara, and Featherman [1981]). Such disparity may be the result of many factors: it is more difficult for children to concentrate on schoolwork in times of family turmoil, slipping grades may be a means of gaining attention or expressing rebellion, and single parents will often find it more difficult to monitor homework, etc. (See chapters 44 and 45 regarding educational issues.)

◆ Behavioral Problems

Some youth exhibit behavioral problems in the wake of their parents' separation and divorce. They may begin smoking or drinking. They may start missing school. They may have trouble getting along with others. They may become disrespectful to schoolteachers and church leaders. Such behavior is often an expression of anger or confusion, a response to the emotional turmoil they feel—but cannot adequately express—because of their family situation.

◆ Sexual Activity

Research suggests that divorce may also, in the long term, prompt a higher degree of sexual activity and promiscuity. Whitehead states that "girls in single-parent families are also at much greater risk for precocious sexuality, teenage marriage, teenage pregnancy, nonmarital birth, and divorce than are girls in two-parent families."[4] And college students with divorced parents have been found to be more sexually active than classmates from intact homes. This is especially true of male children of divorce, who tended to favor "recreational" sex over committed relationships and were most likely to have had more than four sex partners by the time they entered college.[5]

It must be stressed, however, that while adjusting to and living in a single-parent family can create complex problems and considerable challenges, it does not seal a young person's fate. As Nicholas Zill says, "While coming from a disrupted family significantly increases a young adult's risks of experiencing social, emotional or academic difficulties, it does not foreordain such difficulties."[6] The many changes and challenges of living in a single-parent family can produce a number of effects, however, that may recommend or require the attention of a caring adult.

The Effects of Living in a Single-Parent Family

Whatever the circumstances leading to the establishment of a single-parent home—whether it's the death of a parent, divorce, or something else—some of the effects that are likely to be felt by a young person include shame or embarrassment, guilt, rejection, anger, insecurity and low self-esteem, and withdrawal.

◆ Shame/Embarrassment

Shame and embarrassment are commonly felt by teens and preteens living in a single-parent family. They may be embarrassed because of their parents' divorce, interpreting it as an indication that there is something wrong with their family. They also may assume that they bear a degree of responsibility for their parents' breakup. They may be embarrassed by what they consider inappropriate conduct on the part of their parents following the divorce (such as Dad dating a younger woman) or by the abrupt changes in their style of living (such as moving into an apartment with Mom).

◆ Guilt

When the establishment of a single-parent family follows a divorce, many youth are afflicted by guilt. Ronald P. Hutchcraft writes:

Research shows that children of divorce tend to assume blame, or at least part of the blame, for the failure of [their parents'] relationship. They say, "Well, maybe I made too many demands; maybe they spent too much money on me. They argued about me a lot of times."[7]

Even when the single-parent family has been created by the death of a parent, the teen or preteen "may believe himself to be responsible for the death," writes author Clyde C. Besson, "and such a responsibility will create guilt."[8]

Some kids unconsciously prefer such bearing of responsibility to what they see as the alternative—a feeling of utter helplessness. (See also chapter 3, "Guilt.")

◆ Rejection

"One of the deepest feelings a [young person] experiences in a solo-parent situation," writes Besson, "is rejection. Whether the parent has left by death or divorce, the child still experiences a sense of rejection." Teens are acutely sensitive to rejection, either expressed or perceived, and they may even harbor feelings of rejection because their single parent, struggling mightily—and alone—with the demands of parenthood, is not home much of the time, or must occasionally miss important events. The young person may even know, intellectually, that Mom (or Dad) is doing the best he or she can, but emotionally a sense of rejection may persist.

◆ Anger

Besson, founder of Christian Growth Ministries, writes:

In the midst of their confusion, children will feel angry. In the case of a death of a parent, the child will find himself experiencing a sense of anger, feeling that he has been cheated, that he has been deprived of the support and love of that parent. In the case of a divorce, the child will experience anger toward both parents . . . [and particularly] toward the parent who left. Frequently, however, the [youth] will not express his anger toward the missing parent, but rather toward the parent who has custody. Even in a case where the father or mother walks out and never comes back, the anger will be expressed to the parent who remains.[9] [See also chapter 4, "Anger."]

◆ Insecurity/Unhealthy Self-Esteem

Whether the single-parent family is caused by death or divorce, youth in such families may be especially vulnerable to feelings of insecurity and low self-esteem. (See chapter 6, "Unhealthy Self-Esteem.") The circumstances that led to divorce, the divorce process itself, and the conditions that commonly follow a divorce often constitute three "strikes" against an adolescent or preadolescent's sense of self-worth. Teens or preteens may feel different from—and less worthy than—friends whose families are intact; they may feel stigmatized by their church or neighborhood because of the family split and accept that stigmatization as a reflection of their low worth. Stigmatization may also occur (or be inferred by youth) because of a parent's behavior (alcoholism, promiscuity, abusiveness), which can strike a crippling blow to a young person's self-esteem. Economic changes or hardships can also constitute, in a young mind, evidence of low worth.

◆ Withdrawal

"When relationships have hurt us," writes Hutchcraft, "we tend to pull in, withdraw, and not talk, love, or care."[10] Young people in single parent families, he writes, are particularly susceptible to such withdrawal. They may feel somewhat estranged from one or both parents. They may feel alienated from their church, even when they have experienced no unpleasant or judgmental reaction from church members or leaders. They may feel suddenly distant from their friends. They may feel deserted and rejected by God Himself, and will frequently wonder how

God could allow such a thing to happen to their family.

In the wake of such alienation, of course, many teens and preteens experience bouts of extreme loneliness. They may feel friendless, helpless, and alone. They may think that no one understands what they are going through, what they are feeling. They may withdraw physically to their bedrooms. They may withdraw emotionally into fantasy or melancholy. They may do both.

The Biblical Perspective of the Single-Parent Family

God's prescription for the creation and maintenance of a family is recorded in the Creation account:

> For this reason a man will leave his father and mother and be united to his wife, and they will become one flesh.[11]

He ordained that children were to come out of the unity of a man and his wife, and that the mother and father would thereafter cooperate in raising a family.

God created humans as male and female for several reasons, among which is the clear advantages of having a father and a mother in a stable, loving family environment. As Whitehead has said, "The social arrangement that has proved most successful in ensuring the physical survival and promoting the social development of the child is the family unit of the biological mother and father."[12]

However, while Christians must acknowledge God's plan and His ideal, we must also face the fact that the ideal does not always happen. A child is conceived out of wedlock. A parent dies. Mom and Dad divorce. A single-parent family results.

While single parenthood is a less-than-ideal situation, it is not an impossible situation. From all indications, Jesus was the product of a single-parent home! Mary, the mother of Jesus, apparently became a single mother sometime after Jesus' twelfth birthday, for Joseph never appears in the Gospel accounts after that point.[13] Paul's young disciple, Timothy, may likewise have been the product of a single-parent home. In his second letter to Timothy, Paul refers to his friend's "grandmother Lois" and "mother Eunice," but makes no mention of Timothy's father.[14]

God said He was "a father to the fatherless and a judge for the widows" (Ps. 68:5). God loves those who are without parents or spouses too. He made that clear in passages such as the following:

Do not take advantage of a widow or an orphan.[15]

When you are harvesting in your field and you overlook a sheaf, do not go back to get it. Leave it for the alien, the fatherless and the widow, so that the LORD your God may bless you in all the work of your hands.[16]

Learn to do right! Seek justice, encourage the oppressed. Defend the cause of the fatherless, plead the case of the widow.[17]

Do not oppress the widow or the fatherless, the alien or the poor. In your hearts do not think evil of each other.[18]

In addition, Scripture provides another living model of unity—in addition to the traditional family—that can provide some answers for those from broken families.

Scripture instructs husbands to:

Love your wives, just as Christ also loved the church and gave Himself up for her. . . . He who loves his own wife loves himself; for no one ever hated his own flesh, but nourishes and cherishes it, just as Christ also does the church, because we are members of His body. (Eph. 5:25–30)

God's will is for His unity to be expressed in the family; but He has also chosen to reveal His oneness in the institution of the church—His body. Just as a man and woman shall leave mother and father and become one flesh (see Eph. 5:31), so Christ has become one with the church—His body.

Paul, the apostle, said, "This mystery is great," when referring to the oneness of Christ and the church. The person who trusts Christ as Savior is adopted into a living family, a family that is intended to reflect the unity of God Himself. Jesus Christ promised to send the Holy Spirit so that we may experience unity, so that "all of [us] may be one . . . [that we may] be brought to complete unity" (John 17:21, 23).

The single parent who becomes involved in the local body of Christ, a local church, can experience—and expose his or her children to—a living, thriving family that can compensate, in some ways, for the loss of a husband, wife, father, or mother:

For by one Spirit we were all baptized into one body, whether Jews or Greeks, whether slaves or free, and we were all made to drink of one Spirit. . . . God has so composed the body, giving more abundant honor to that number which lacked, that there should be no division in the body, but that the members should have the same care for one another. And if one member suffers, all the members suffer with it; if one member is honored all the members rejoice with it. Now you are Christ's body, and individually members of it. (1 Cor. 12:13 and 24–27)

God wants each of us to suffer when another suffers—to rejoice when another rejoices, he wants us to "bear one another's burdens." Multitudes of broken families have found a great degree of healing, and emotional stability, and an overwhelming sense of belonging as they have experienced the oneness that the unity of the body provides.

The Response to the Problem of Living in a Single-Parent Family

Listen ◆ Empathize ◆ Affirm ◆ Direct ◆ Enlist ◆ Refer

The sensitive pastor, teacher, youth leader, or parent can help an adolescent or preadolescent adjust to and cope with a single-parent situation by implementing a plan such as the following:

LISTEN. Teens in single-parent families need the freedom to express what they are feeling, writes Besson, especially in two areas: he or she needs "the freedom to express his feelings about the missing parent" and "the freedom to express negative feelings without condemnation." If the youth uses inappropriate language, the adult may request more appropriate words, but the adult will be wise to listen closely to the feelings that lay behind the young person's words.

EMPATHIZE. Don't be too quick to judge or correct the young person's reactions, nor to offer a solution. Initially, take time simply to empathize with him or her. Feel with him. Cry with him. Comfort him. Let him know of your care and concern.

AFFIRM. Communicate acceptance and affirmation to the youth. Remember that he or she may be feeling rejected and alienated; the first step toward healing and progress may be for him or her to know that someone believes in him, that someone thinks she's worth something. Remind the youth (particularly by praying with and for him or her) that both God and you highly value and appreciate him or her. Many people who are struggling in difficult circumstances need affirmation—reassurance of their own worth and capabilities—more than anything else.

DIRECT. Some of the following ideas may help a parent or concerned adult to guide a young person struggling with the many adjustments of life in a single-parent family:

1. Encourage dependence on God. Help the teen in a single-parent family learn to turn to God for comfort and fellowship when other relationships fail. He truly is a "father to the fatherless" and a loving parent who can strengthen and sustain the youth through the many difficulties and challenges of life and adolescence.

2. Preserve routines or traditions that are intact. Routine can be reassuring in times of transition; encourage the preservation of bedtimes, mealtimes, school-related routines, etc.

3. Encourage involvement in a church youth group. A healthy and vibrant youth group is an important part of a young person's life—especially for a child from a single-parent home. Youth workers need single parents, and single parents need them.

4. Encourage parent substitutes in the teen's life. Guide the teen boy living with a single mom to male adults who can make regular contributions to his life; help the teen girl who is living with her father to identify female adults in the church who can help answer questions and provide guidance on a regular basis. Try to develop a strong network of families and adopted "uncles" and "aunts" to serve as role models of male and female relationships.

5. Offer hope. Children of divorce and kids in single-parent families do face more obstacles than many other kids, but the majority of kids in single-parent homes do pretty well: they *do* finish high school, they *don't* typically display high levels of emotional distress, and they *don't* get involved in problem behavior.[19] Help the youth understand that there is reason to hope, particularly if he or she trusts God and is supported by a caring, understanding church.

ENLIST. There is much in a single-parent family that no one can change. Mom and Dad probably won't get back together; things will never be like they were. The pastor, parent, teacher, or youth worker can help by enlisting the youth's cooperation and participation in acknowledging and devising the things he or she *can* change, the things he or she *can* improve. Focus his or her attention on constructive things that are within his or her power to do, and encourage such things, which may include:

- Attending more carefully to the relationship with the absent parent (by calling twice a week, for example).
- Recording his or her thoughts and feelings in a journal.
- Helping younger siblings.
- Joining a support group at church or school.
- Seeking support in healthy peer relationships, such as a church youth group.

REFER. Jim Smoke advises, "If [the youth] does not resume normal development and growth in his life within a year of the divorce [or other precipitating event], he may need the special care and help of a professional counselor. . . . If negative patterns continue after a number of months, seek help. A few words by a trained professional can often [help the young person] turn the corner."[20] Such referral, of course, should only be done with parental permission (and, preferably, participation).

For Further Reading

The following resources may help the concerned parent, pastor, teacher, or youth worker assist teens in single-parent families:

Scriptures Cited in This Chapter

- Genesis 2:24
- Luke 2:41–52
- 2 Timothy 1:5
- Exodus 22:22
- Deuteronomy 24:19
- Isaiah 1:17
- Zechariah 7:10
- Ephesians 5:25–31
- John 17:21, 23
- 1 Corinthians 12:13, 24–27

Further Reading

- Clyde Colvin Besson, *Picking Up the Pieces: Successful Single Living for the Formerly Married* (Mott Media, Milford, Mich.). Contains a chapter on "Solo Parenting."
- Andre Bustanoby, *Being a Single Parent* (Zondervan).

21

DEALING WITH STEPPARENTS AND BLENDED FAMILIES

A Synopsis

❖

Introduction

Myra was sixteen when her parents separated because her father was having an affair with Gail, a twenty-five-year-old woman. Following the separation Myra and her two brothers lived with her father because her mother did not feel that she could cope with raising the three children herself. One year later her father married Gail, who had never been married before, and Gail moved into the home.

Since Myra's father was about fifty at the time, Gail was much closer in age to Myra than she was to Myra's father. Gail claimed that she would prefer to be a "friend" to Myra rather than a mother. However, it was quite apparent that Gail was so immature a person herself that it would have been impossible for her to have assumed a mother role. . . . Soon after Gail moved in, she and Myra began lending one another clothing; they confided in one another (even personal matters between Gail and Myra's father) and often enjoyed passing as sisters.

The honeymoon [was short-lived for all three, however]. Myra began to complain that her father took his wife's side over hers whenever there were differences of opinion. Myra resented bitterly when her father and Gail would go out on a Saturday night and couldn't understand why she couldn't go along since she and Gail were such good friends. . . . Within two months of the father's second marriage, bitter fighting between Gail, Myra, and her father became almost incessant. Hardly an issue did not become blown up into a major battle. It was quite clear that Myra was furious at her father for choosing a "peer" over her for a wife. And she was jealous of Gail's intimacy with her father, a jealousy that was made worse by Gail's flaunting her relationship with [Myra's] father to Myra under the guise of divulging intimacies to a close friend.[1]

The Problem of Stepparents and Blended Families

A parent's remarriage and the resulting change in and complexity of relationships can wreak havoc with a child or teenager's mind and emotions. It can ignite reactions that even the youth himself or herself may not fully understand.

In recent years the number of remarried individuals and "blended families" has soared. Over 40 percent of all marriages in the U.S. involve a remarriage of one or both parties. One out of three Americans—sixty million adults and twenty million kids[2]—is a stepparent, a stepchild, or a step-sibling. One out of five children under the age of eighteen is a stepchild.[3] By the year 2000, stepfamilies (involving only one spouse who has children) and complex families (in which both spouses have children) will soon become the majority family type.[4]

A stepfamily presents a considerable challenge, according to Virginia Rutter, writing for *Psychology Today*. "There are attachments that must be maintained through a web of conflicting emotions. There are ambiguities of identity, especially in the first years."[5]

Such adjustments are often hardest, of course, on the kids. "They feel a loss going into a stepfamily," writes Rutter. "It certifies that their original family exists no more."[6] And while a father or mother's remarriage can pose problems for all ages, the formation of a stepfamily is "hardest on children ages 9 to 15."[7] Researcher Mavis Hetherington, professor of psychology at the University of Virginia, attributes this to the fact that "kids in the 9-to-15 age group are struggling with their own independence, and here comes this outsider, interfering. And they are struggling with their own awakening sexuality, and they don't want to think of their mother as a sexual being. It's very difficult not to recognize that when she remarries."[8] These are among the reasons Hetherington warns, "If remarriage occurs in early adolescence, kids respond very negatively."

While research shows that "boys appear to have an easier time with both stepfathers and stepmothers than girls do,"[9] young people of both sexes occasionally face a variety of troubling adjustments and volatile emotions during and beyond the early stages of a stepfamily's formation. Research consistently shows that children of divorce and remarriage have twice as many problems as those from intact families.[10]

Still, many parents and children in stepfamilies manage very well. Hetherington's research indicates that 80 percent of children of divorce and remarriage do not have behavior problems despite all the challenges and difficulties (compared to 90 percent of children of first-marriage families).[11]

However, one thing is extremely clear. Adjusting to the challenges and complexities of a stepfamily is something parents and those involved with youth will need to address, particularly in light of the fact that seven thousand new stepfamilies are being formed every single week.[12]

The Effects of Stepparents and Blended Families

Stepfamilies and step-relationships can be formed in a variety of ways, of course, such as a parent remarrying after the death of a spouse, remarriage after divorce, or marriage following an out-of-wedlock birth. Whatever the precipitating circumstances, however, stepfamilies seldom resemble the Brady Bunch of TV fame. Many are happy and healthy families, but many also encounter some of the following effects of remarriage and complex family relationships:

◆ Grief

As was mentioned above, the formation of a stepfamily often signals the "official" demise of the original family to a child or young person. Family counselor Dr. Kevin Leman points out that such a "destruction of one of the most precious possessions in all the world—a person's original home and family"[13]—can produce grief and the resulting stages of denial, anger, bargaining, depression, and acceptance. (See chapter 8, "Grief.")

◆ Anger

A young person who is mourning the loss of his or her original family (or even his or her most recent family) may become "stuck" in one stage of grief, and Dr. Leman points out a common reaction to the formation of a stepfamily:

> Anger is the most dangerous stage of grief because a person can get stuck there for a long time. It's common for members of a blended family to bury their pain, but sooner or later it bubbles up when they have "had enough."[14]

And Harold Bloomfield, author of *Making Peace in Your Stepfamily,* says that "repressed grief is one of the reasons why stepfamilies are so often troubled by angry outbursts and frequent bickering."[15] (See also chapter 4, "Anger.")

◆ Guilt

Parents are not the only people who struggle with guilt in the wake of divorce or other factors contributing to the formation of a stepfamily; many kids in stepfamilies are afflicted by guilt too. Leman suggests that "[the] children feel guilty, believing, 'If only I had behaved better, Mommy and Daddy wouldn't have gotten divorced.'"[16] He adds that, while all children are susceptible to such feelings, firstborns and only children tend to think that they could have or should have done more to keep the original family together. (See chapter 3, "Guilt.")

◆ Loss of Sense of Control

A significant factor in the difficulties surrounding the formation and functioning of stepfamilies is the loss of a sense of control, a process that may have begun at the time of a parent's death or divorce. The teen may feel that he or she has lost his or her position in the family. He may feel that he can no longer get his dad's attention. She may

think that Mom decided to remarry without sufficient input from her. He may feel that his step-siblings have intruded on his "territory." She may resent the privileges or attention the stepparent or step-siblings claim. Such adjustments can leave a young person feeling as though he or she has no control over his or her own life anymore, and behavioral responses (such as tantrums, even delinquency) sometimes follow.

◆ Stress

Psychologist James Bray of the Baylor College of Medicine says stepchildren report feeling high levels of stress.[17] His findings suggest that the myriad of adjustments stepchildren must face— such as a new adult figure in the house, new siblings in the family, "loyalty conflicts between new parents and old, [moving] to new homes and new schools, leaving old friends behind, new (often improved) financial status and reorganization of household routines"[18]—can result in high (though often temporary) levels of stress.

◆ Loneliness and Depression

The formation and functioning of a stepfamily can leave teens and preteens feeling lonely and left out—even more so at times than life in a single-parent family. The California Children of Divorce Study, directed by clinical psychologist Judith Wallerstein, discovered that nearly half the children in the study said they felt left out in their stepfamilies. And the National Commission on Children, a bipartisan group headed by West Virginia's John D. Rockefeller, reported "that children from stepfamilies were more likely to say they often felt lonely or blue than children from either single-parent or intact families."[19] (See chapter 1, "Loneliness," and chapter 5, "Depression.")

◆ Lower Levels of Parental Involvement

Young people in stepfamilies must sometimes cope with lower levels of parental involvement and support in their lives. Barbara Dafoe Whitehead reports:

> Studies suggest that even though they may have the time, the parents in stepfamilies do not invest as much of it in their children as the parents in intact families or even single parents do. A 1991 survey by the National Commission on Children showed that the parents in stepfamilies were less likely to be involved in a teen's school life, including involvement in extracurricular activities, than either intact-family parents or single parents. They were the least likely to report being involved in such time-consuming activities as coaching a child's team, accompanying class trips, or helping with school projects. According to [sociologist Sara] McLanahan's research, children in stepparent families report lower educational aspirations on the part of their parents and lower levels of parental involvement with schoolwork.[20]

◆ Risk of Sexual Abuse

One of the most severe and disturbing potential effects of remarriage and the formation and function of a stepfamily is the risk of abuse. (See chapter 34, "Sexual Abuse," and 35, "Nonsexual Abuse.") Leslie Margolin and John L. Craft report:

> In a recent study at the University of Iowa of 2,300 cases of sexual abuse within Iowa, researchers found that nonbiological "father caretakers" (stepfathers, foster fathers, and adoptive fathers), were almost four times as likely to sexually abuse children in their care as biological fathers. Likewise, nonbiological "mother caretakers" were almost three times more likely to sexually abuse children in their care than biological mothers.[21]

The Biblical Perspective of Stepparents and Blended Families

Jesus was a stepchild. Few people take time to consider that fact, but the man who helped Mary raise Jesus Christ to adulthood was not Jesus' biological father.[22]

Moses was a stepchild too. Though his natural mother served as his wet nurse, he was raised as the adopted son of Pharaoh's daughter.[23]

God's prescription for the family is for "a man [to] leave his father and mother and be united to his wife, and [for them to] become one flesh,"[24] producing children and cooperating together to raise a family. God's commandments regarding marriage and the family are intended to reflect a universal and eternal principle: unity. In God's eyes, unity is the central element of the marriage relationship.

Similarly, God designed the family as a unity; an unbroken circle of strong, loving, lasting relationships; the primary unit of human society (see Numbers 1); a hedge against loneliness (Ps. 68:6); a defense against poverty and affliction (1 Tim. 5:4–8); and an environment for child-rearing and education (1 Tim. 3:4).

Unity is part of God's nature and character. He is one (Deut. 6:4). And it is that unity that He wishes us to reflect in our marriages and family relationships. When the Bible says that a man and woman shall "be united . . . and . . . become one flesh" (Gen. 2:24), it is saying that marriage should reflect God's nature. When parents obey the divine command to "be fruitful and increase in number" (Gen. 1:28), the family should also reflect the unity that God values.

However, while Christians must acknowledge God's plan and His ideal, we must also face the fact that the ideal does not always happen. A child is conceived out of wedlock. A parent dies. Mom and Dad divorce. A parent remarries. A new household is formed, challenging old loyalties and creating new routines.

While a stepfamily may be a challenging and difficult situation for parents and children alike, it *can* reflect God's unity, even if it was born from brokenness. After all, God Himself is an adoptive parent. He not only accepts all those who come to Him in repentance and faith into His family, but He adopts them as His children:

> Yet to all who received him, to those who believed in his name, he gave the right to become children of God—children born not of natural descent, nor of human decision or a husband's will, but born of God. (John 1:12–13)

> For you did not receive a spirit that makes you a slave again to fear, but you received the Spirit of sonship. And by him we cry, "Abba, Father." (Rom. 8:15)

> "I will be a Father to you, and you will be my sons and daughters, says the Lord Almighty." (2 Cor. 6:18)

> Because you are sons, God sent the Spirit of his Son into our hearts, the Spirit who calls out, "Abba, Father." (Gal. 4:6)

There are no easy answers for young people who are struggling with the many adjustments and complexities of a stepfamily situation. Stepfamilies, like the people who comprise them, are imperfect expressions of God's ideals. But regardless of why or how a stepfamily is formed, God is available to heal the brokenhearted and to help bring unity out of discord.

The Response to the Problem of Stepparents and Blended Family

Listen ◆ Empathize ◆ Affirm ◆ Direct ◆ Enlist ◆ Refer

The sensitive pastor, teacher, youth leader, or parent can help an adolescent or preadolescent adjust to and cope with a stepfamily situation by implementing a plan such as the following:

LISTEN. In all the trials and trauma of adjusting to a stepfamily, many teens are left feeling as though no one listens to them. They feel that their feelings are not being considered. They often need, more than anything else, someone to listen, someone who will allow them the freedom to express what they are feeling without interruption and without condemnation. The pastor, teacher, or youth worker can encourage such expression with questions or statements like the following:

- Tell me what's bothering you.
- How long have you felt this way?
- Have things gotten better or worse?
- How do others in the family feel?
- Have you discussed this with your parents? If not, why not? If so, with what result?

The concerned adult will also be wise to "listen" closely to the young person's nonverbal language as well as to his or her words.

EMPATHIZE. Take as much time as necessary to empathize with the young person and to offer appropriate comfort. Keep in mind that you can communicate empathy by:

- Listening carefully.
- Nodding your head.
- Making eye contact.
- Leaning forward in your chair.
- Speaking in soothing tones.
- Reflecting key statements or gestures.

Resist the temptation to minimize the youth's concerns ("I'm sure things aren't that bad") or to magnify them ("How do you put up with that man?"). Instead, simply try to see things through the eyes of the young person while you listen to him, hurt with him, and cry with him.

AFFIRM. Seize every opportunity to create a climate of acceptance, appreciation, and affirmation. Bathe the young person in prayer, both when you're in his or her presence, and when you're apart. Counter the rejection that he or she may feel in the stepfamily situation with healthy doses of encouragement. Sprinkle every conversation with hope, as well; after all, a whopping 80 percent of stepchildren seem to cope well with a stepfamily situation!

DIRECT. The great difficulty of a child struggling in a stepfamily situation (and one that is keenly felt by the young person himself or herself, you may be sure) is that he or she is relatively powerless to effect change—or so he or she thinks. However, while the parent and stepparent are obviously the ones in the best position to influence the family, the concerned adult can guide a young person in coping with a stepfamily situation with some of the following ideas:

1. Encourage dependence on God. Help the teen in a stepfamily learn to turn to God for comfort and fellowship when other relationships are lacking. He is a loving parent who can strengthen and sustain the youth through the many difficulties and challenges of life and adolescence.

2. Identify the causes of the difficulty. Is the youth grieving? Angry? Feeling guilty? Is the youth responding to a sense that he or she has lost control? Is he or she feeling neglected? Jealous? Help the teen talk through his or her feelings and attitudes in an effort to identify the major sources of problems.

3. Help the youth face reality. Some children in stepfamilies entertain fantasies about their biological parents "getting back together," or of becoming "a real family" (by which they usually mean a family free from the stresses of life in a stepfamily). Such things will not happen; the sooner the youth faces the current situation realistically and determines to make the best of it, the happier he or she is likely to be. Try to accomplish this through the careful use of questions (rather than *telling* the young person how things are): "Do you think that's realistic?"

"What makes you think so?" "What are some more-realistic goals you can set for you and your family?"

4. Brainstorm ways to negotiate the difficulty. A stepfamily, like any family, involves give and take. Help the youth to consider ways to negotiate with parents and/or siblings in areas that will address the causes of his or her struggle, such as agreeing to ask permission before borrowing an item or respecting siblings' privacy by always knocking on closed doors.

5. Involve the parent and stepparent. A pastor, youth pastor, teacher, or youth worker should consider asking the young person for permission to involve the parent and stepparent in addressing the situation. A concerned adult can sometimes facilitate communication and negotiation between parent and child. Such a process, entered cautiously and prayerfully, can often point a stepfamily in the right direction.

ENLIST. Avoid the temptation to let the youth characterize the stepparent or step-siblings as "bad guys" and himself or herself as the "good guy." Enlist him or her in a process of forgiveness, reconciliation, and constructive planning. Encourage the youth to aim for (and contribute to) improvement, not perfection, in the situation.

REFER. The parent, pastor, teacher, or youth worker should be alert to the need for referral. More information on stepfamilies can be obtained from the Stepfamily Association of America, 215 Centennial Mall South, Suite 212, Lincoln, NE, 68508 (402-477-7837). If a concerned adult's efforts show no signs of being effective, or if the situation escalates or deteriorates, parents and children should be encouraged to consult a professional Christian counselor while support from the parent, pastor, teacher, or youth worker is continued.

For Further Reading

The following resources may help the concerned parent, pastor, teacher, or youth worker assist the young person who is having difficulty coping with a stepfamily situation:

Scriptures Cited in This Chapter

- Matthew 1:18–25
- Exodus 2:1–10
- Deuteronomy 6:4
- Genesis 1:28; 2:24
- Numbers 1
- Psalm 68:6
- 1 Timothy 3:4; 5:4–8
- John 1:12–13
- Romans 8:15
- 2 Corinthians 6:18
- Galatians 4:6

Other Scripture to Read

- Exodus 20:12
- Leviticus 19:3
- Psalms 27:10; 68:5–6; 147:3
- Proverbs 23:22
- Isaiah 57:15
- Ephesians 6:1–3
- Colossians 3:20

Further Reading

- Tom and Adrienne Frydenger, *Resolving Conflict in the Blended Family* (Fleming H. Revell).
- Gary and Angela Hunt, *Mom and Dad Don't Live Together Anymore* (Here's Life).
- Dr. Kevin Leman, *Living in a Stepfamily Without Getting Stepped On* (Thomas Nelson).

22

SIBLING RIVALRY

A Synopsis

Introduction

For years, Sabrina and her older brother Mike were best friends. They played football and baseball together. They went bicycling with each other. They were much closer to each other than either was to their older sister.

That all changed, however, around the time Sabrina turned fourteen. Her interests began to change. It wasn't as much fun hanging out with Mike anymore; instead, she found herself drawn to her sister. She suddenly seemed to have much more in common with her than with Mike.

It was around that time that Mike started with the insults.

"He'd call me 'snout,' then 'flea-festation,'" says Sabrina. "I hated it, and I didn't know why he was behaving the way he was—all of a sudden, he wasn't my best friend. If he knew something bothered me, he'd keep going on and on about it until I'd get even more upset and start to cry."

"It really hurt," she says. "I didn't know why it was happening—I was really confused."

The Problem of Sibling Rivalry

Sabrina's experience is not uncommon. Brothers and sisters can be best friends, bitter enemies—or both, depending on the circumstance, the time of day, or their moods. Siblings can be surprisingly loving toward each other, and they can be shockingly cruel.

Trouble between siblings can take many different forms, such as rivalry, strife, or abuse.

◆ Rivalry

Rivalry is natural, perhaps unavoidable, between brothers and sisters. Sibling rivalry is a spirit of jealousy or competition between siblings (or step-siblings) in a family. For example, thirteen-year-old Marc makes a nuisance of himself trying to be a part of his older sister Tiffany's social circle, primarily because he's jealous of the attention she gives to her friends—which she used to give to her brother.

Sibling rivalry can be a devastating factor in family relationships, but it can also be a positive factor. Sixteen-year-old Josh is the starting quarterback on his high school football team, primarily because he always worked hard to compete with his older brother, Justin, who set many school records. "Interaction with siblings is . . . a way to learn how to negotiate, to compromise, to become goal seekers, and to command and give respect to their peers," says Wanda Draper, a child development specialist and professor of psychiatry at the University of Oklahoma Health Sciences Center.[1]

◆ Sibling Strife

Sibling rivalry can become destructive instead of constructive, however, when it begins to create sibling strife. Fifteen-year-old Andrew seemed to take every opportunity to frighten his twelve-year-old brother Todd: teasing the plump boy about his weight, driving him to tears in front of others and then ridiculing him for being a "crybaby," and starting fights for no apparent reason.

◆ Sibling Abuse

Relationships between siblings can sometimes degenerate into abusive behaviors and patterns. Dr. Annaclare van Dalen defines sibling abuse as "an emotional and/or physical assault that makes the victim[s] feel bad about themselves."[2] Siblings are more likely to become abusive if they themselves feel victimized; by turning the tables on a (usually younger) sibling, they regain a sense of power. Such was the experience of Alexis with her brother Ian:

> Although the two of them had never gotten along very well, the summer he was 16 and she was 14 was a nightmare. Alexis explains, "He was an extremely angry guy, really unhappy in school, and he didn't have a lot of friends."
>
> Left alone together over the summer, Ian was like a bomb, waiting to explode. . . . One time, without any provocation, he chased after Alexis with a baseball bat. Alexis was totally terrified: "After I crouched down on the floor in front of him, he was like, 'Okay, okay,' then calmed down and walked away." Another time, Alexis tells, "He was just trying to mess with me, see how far he could go to freak me out, so he came at me with a big kitchen knife. I ran from him until I was backed up against a wall, and he came at me laughing, then veered the knife away."[3]

Van Dalen points out that "Fighting is an effort to try to work out your differences; in abuse, it's one sibling trying to be more powerful than another."[4] Abuse can range from name-calling and inciting fear in a younger sibling to threatening, destroying a sibling's personal possessions, or physically scratching, hitting, or kicking a sibling.

The Causes of Sibling Rivalry

Sibling rivalry has to do with many things. To some extent, it is simply the natural result of multiple children in a family setting, vying for attention and affection. It may also be caused by birth order,[5] by parents' preferential treatment of one sibling, and by a number of other factors, including:

◆ Jealousy

"The underlying source of this conflict," writes family advocate and author Dr. James Dobson, "is old-fashioned jealousy and competition."[6] Jealousy of a sibling's talents, friends, appearance, grades, family privileges, parental attention, etc., will frequently create a sense of rivalry, often leading to sibling strife and abuse. Such feelings may have their roots in events and attitudes that neither sibling remembers or is aware of, yet they are nonetheless real.

◆ Unhealthy or Unfavorable Comparisons

Dr. James Dobson writes:

> Lecturer Bill Gothard has stated that the root of all feelings of inferiority is *comparison*. I agree. . . . This is particularly true in three areas. First, [youth] are extremely sensitive about the matter of physical attractiveness and body characteristics. It is highly inflammatory to commend one child at the expense of another. . . . Second, the matter of intelligence is another sensitive nerve. . . . Third, children (and especially boys) are extremely competitive with regard to athletic abilities.[7]

◆ Changing Roles

Adolescence is, of course, a time of many monumental changes. A young person's body begins to mature, he or she begins to develop new interests, and very often, his or her role in the family takes on a different dimension as well. The young person may have more responsibilities at home; he or she may be entering a new school or starting a part-time job. His or her relationships with friends may become deeper, or broader—with members of the opposite sex, for example.

Such changes can have ramifications within a family. Little brother may feel neglected; little sister may become jealous. Or big brother may move on to college, changing the chemistry of the family. Such changes can create or fuel feelings of sibling rivalry.

◆ Stress

Sibling rivalry can become severe due to stress in a family situation. One social worker described how this happens:

> When you have something that creates tension and conflict—whether it's stress in your parents' marriage, parent/child abuse, an alcoholic parent—and it isn't dealt with, one child may start taking the frustration he or she feels toward their parents out on a weaker or younger sibling.[8]

Rivalry, strife, or abuse may be ultimately directed at someone—or something (such as an undesirable circumstance—other than the sibling; the brother or sister is often simply a convenient target for the release of stress and frustrations.

◆ Selfishness/Difficulty Sharing Limited Resources

From the toddler who doesn't want to share his toys with his little sister to the teen whose arguments with her sister frequently involve the sister's constant "borrowing" of favorite clothes, some of the rivalry and strife among siblings is due to selfishness or having to share limited resources (such as the family car, the parents' time, or money for special purchases). Such situations can be constructive—helping kids learn "how to stand up for [their] rights, how to compete without being hostile, and how to resolve conflict through negotiation and compromise."[9] They can also be destructive, however, creating animosity and hurting the participants.

◆ Desire for Attention

Even in teens (and adults, for that matter), strife between siblings is often a means of manipulating the parents. Dr. James Dobson writes:

> Quarreling and fighting provide an opportunity for [siblings] to "capture" adult attention. It has been written, "Some children had rather be wanted for murder than not wanted at all." Toward this end, a pair of [siblings] can tacitly agree to bug their parents until they get a response—even if it is an angry reaction.[10]

The Effects of Sibling Rivalry

◆ Not Always Deleterious

Sibling rivalry is almost always deeply disturbing to parents and unsettling for the young people involved. However, it is not always deleterious. Draper notes:

> The vast majority of siblings who squabble when they are young outgrow this and become close. The thing to remember is that this is simply another normal aspect of development, and most parents would be wise to back off a bit and let their children develop the ability to handle the situation.[11]

◆ Destructive to Self-Esteem

When the sibling rivalry and strife is particularly severe, however, it can wreak havoc with a young person's sense of self-esteem that may extend even into adulthood. Nancy was constantly berated by her older sister, Nedra. Nedra persistently called her sister "ugly," "clumsy," and "stupid." Though today Nancy is a refined, accomplished, and beautiful adult and mother of three children, she still struggles with feelings of inadequacy and inferiority—particularly following a visit by her older sister.

◆ Effects of Sibling Abuse

Moreover, sibling abuse produces many of the same results as any abuse: guilt, mistrust, aggression, deficient social skills, insecurity and poor self-esteem. (See also chapter 31, "Non-Sexual Abuse.") The physical and emotional scars of sibling abuse are not insignificant because they are inflicted by a brother or sibling; on the contrary, they can make a lasting, tragic imprint on a young person.

The Biblical Perspective of Sibling Rivalry

The Bible contains no discourse or instruction on sibling rivalry. As always, however, God's Word presents an honest and insightful view of family relationships, including those between siblings.

The very first human family, according to the Genesis account, was plagued by sibling rivalry, strife, and abuse: Cain murdered his brother Abel in a fit of jealous rage (see Gen. 4:8). Joseph's brothers were so jealous they conspired to sell him into slavery in Egypt (see Gen. 37:12–36). Abimelech, son of Jerub-Baal, killed seventy of his brothers in order to become king of Shechem (see Judg. 9:5). Absalom ordered the death of his half-brother Amnon (see 2 Sam. 13:29), Solomon ordered the death of his half-brother Adonoijah (1 Kings 2:25), and Jehoram slaughtered all his brothers upon his ascension to the throne of Judah (2 Chron. 21:4).

The Bible clearly—and forthrightly—portrays the tragic results of sibling rivalry, strife, and abuse. In addition, God's Word makes it clear that the root cause of sibling rivalry—jealousy—is not only unacceptable, but undesirable.

> For from within, out of men's hearts, come evil thoughts, sexual immorality, theft, murder, adultery, greed, malice, deceit, lewdness, envy, slander, arrogance and folly. (Mark 7:21–22, emphasis added)

> Let us behave decently, as in the daytime, not in orgies and drunkenness, not in sexual immorality

and debauchery, not in dissension and *jealousy.* (Rom. 13:13, emphasis added)

For I am afraid that when I come I may not find you as I want you to be, and you may not find me as you want me to be. I fear that there may be quarrelling, *jealousy*, outbursts of anger, factions, slander, gossip, arrogance and disorder. (2 Cor. 12:20, emphasis added)

The acts of the sinful nature are obvious: sexual immorality, impurity and debauchery; idolatry and witchcraft; hatred, discord, *jealousy*, fits of rage, selfish ambition, dissensions, factions. (Gal. 5:19–20, emphasis added)

The Bible does not capriciously forbid jealousy and envy; on the contrary, God's purpose in steering His people away from such actions is to avoid the undesirable products they create:

For where you have *envy* and selfish ambition, there you find disorder and every evil practice. (James 3:16, emphasis added)

The biblical antidote to jealousy is prescribed by Paul:

Love is patient, love is kind. It does not *envy*, it does not boast, it is not proud. (1 Cor. 13:4, emphasis added)

Sibling rivalry, while it is quite natural in family relationships, is nonetheless an undesirable and potentially harmful component of those relationships the discerning parent, teacher, youth leader, or pastor will attempt to address.

The Response to the Problem of Sibling Rivalry

Listen ◆ Empathize ◆ Affirm ◆ Direct ◆ Enlist ◆ Refer

Someone has said that the only surefire way to avoid sibling rivalry is to have only one child in each family. Such a solution may be amusing, but it is not very helpful. There are, however, ways to minimize the kind of sibling warfare that plagues so many youth and worries so many parents. The following measures may help a parent, teacher, pastor, or other concerned adult to address sibling rivalry among adolescents or preadolescents:

LISTEN. Often the greatest need felt by a person who is hurting is for someone who will take the time to listen and to care. Let the young person express his or her feelings honestly and openly. Resist the temptation to correct the youth with statements like, "Oh, you don't mean that about your brother," or "She doesn't mean anything by it." Let the young person express himself or herself without censure or correction.

As early and consistently as possible, turn the youth to prayer, reminding him or her that, even when no one else is around to hear and to care, God is (Ps. 34:15–18). Encourage dependence on Him and His resources.

EMPATHIZE. Faber and Mazlish, coauthors of *Siblings Without Rivalry*, suggest that:

Intellectually, [sibling rivalry may not be] hard to understand but, emotionally, many of us have difficulty accepting . . . [young people's] hostile feelings toward each other. Perhaps we might better understand those feelings if we tried to put ourselves in [their] place.[12]

Perhaps some parents or youth workers can recall sibling struggles from their own childhoods; perhaps they can empathize by coming to terms with their own feelings of jealousy and insecurity. Empathetically approaching sibling squabbles will help immensely.

AFFIRM. The wise parent, pastor, teacher, or youth worker will be alert to every opportunity to offer messages of encouragement and affirmation. Take every opportunity to communicate sincere assurances of your esteem for the young man or woman. You may say:

- I enjoy being around you because . . .
- I like the way you . . .
- You have such a terrific smile (voice, sense of humor, etc.)
- You're so good at . . .
- I love you.

Keep in mind the following suggestion as well:

> Remember . . . that siblings are not always fighting. They can be very good friends to each other much of the time. It's very important to notice and praise them when they do something thoughtful for each other. Try to acknowledge [such things].[13]

DIRECT. There are two important directions in which a youth leader, parent, pastor, or teacher can help a young person address sibling rivalry.

1. Within the teen himself or herself. The young person should be encouraged to examine his or her own feelings. Why is there a spirit of rivalry? Does he or she contribute to it? (Remember that even Joseph played a part in his brothers' jealousy [see Gen. 37:1–11.]) What can he or she do to temper the cause(s) of the rivalry?

In the case of sibling abuse, the teen should speak up: he or she should not hesitate to inform the parents (regardless of the threats or intimidation of the sibling) and to continue doing so—loudly—until the abuse is stopped and future abuse is prevented.

2. Within the home. The following tactics may help parents or caregivers prevent or address sibling rivalry:

- *Help youth express themselves.* Help teens and preteens use words to express their feelings; to say, "I feel like you never have time for me anymore," for example, instead of sabotaging an older sibling's friendships.

- *Be careful not to inflame the natural jealousy of siblings.* Resist the urge to compare siblings, particularly in the three areas mentioned above (physical appearance, intelligence, and athletic abilities). Congratulate and appreciate each child without reference to his or her sibling(s). And *never* say, "Why can't you be like your sister?"

- *Treat children uniquely rather than equally.* Children expect equal treatment from their parents, and parents usually respond by trying to prove they're being fair. But children are unique; they have unique interests, gifts, and personalities. Parents should spend time alone with each child as well as together as a family. Strive to love children equally, and to treat them uniquely, enjoying their individual strengths and helping their individual weaknesses.

- *Erect boundaries of respect,* such as a prohibition on name-calling. Dr. Dobson offers several examples he has used in his family:

  a. Neither child is ever allowed to make fun of the other in a destructive way. Period!

  b. Each child's room [or portion of the room if siblings share a room] is his private territory.

  c. The older child is not permitted to tease the younger child.

  d. The younger child is not permitted to harass the older child.

  e. The children are not required to play with each other when they prefer to be alone or with friends.

  f. We mediate any genuine conflict as quickly as possible, being careful to show impartiality and extreme fairness.[14]

- *Intervene when siblings' fighting can't be ignored.*

Do so in a way that will not hand the solution to them on a silver platter but will teach them how to negotiate and resolve conflicts in the future.

ENLIST. Engage the young person himself or herself in solving sibling problems. Encourage him or her to decide, "What will I do the next time? How can I prevent conflict before it occurs? How will I approach disagreements differently? How can I negotiate, compromise, or resolve things better?" If the youth themselves work out a plan for countering sibling rivalry, they will be more satisfied with it, and will be more likely to abide by it.

REFER. The pastor, teacher, or youth leader needs to be sensitive to the home situation of the young person and the necessity of informing or involving the parents in the solution. In severe cases (particularly when sibling abuse is involved), immediate referral to a professional Christian counselor (with parental involvement and permission) is critical.

For Further Reading

The following resources may help the concerned parent, pastor, teacher, or youth worker assist the young person who is struggling with sibling rivalry:

Scriptures Cited in This Chapter

- Genesis 4:8
- Genesis 37:12–36
- Judges 9:5
- 2 Samuel 13:29
- 1 Kings 2:25
- 2 Chronicles 21:4
- Mark 7:21–22
- Romans 13:13
- 2 Corinthians 12:20
- Galatians 5:19–20
- James 3:16
- 1 Corinthians 13:4
- Psalm 34:15–18
- Genesis 37:1–11

Further Reading

- Dr. James Dobson, *The Strong-Willed Child* (Tyndale). Contains a helpful chapter on sibling rivalry.
- Tom and Adrienne Frydenger, *Resolving Conflict in the Blended Family* (Fleming H. Revell).
- Dr. Kevin Leman, *The Birth Order Book* (Fleming H. Revell).

23

REBELLION

A Synopsis

Introduction

Victor was a fourteen-year-old ninth-grader struggling to make passing grades in school. He came from a family that was strongly dependent on Christian values. His parents were well-thought-of by their peers and had positions of leadership in their church and community.

His adolescent years, however, were marked by a spirit of rebellion toward his parents. He deliberately did poorly in school, claiming the classes were useless to him. He used alcohol periodically and seemed to delight in coming home in a drunken stupor occasionally just to prove to his parents that he was bold enough to violate their standards of conduct. He reached a point in his adolescence when he announced his freedom from his religious training and declared that he was not sure God even existed.

He entered early adulthood with feelings of contempt for his parents. Once he was living on his own, however, he discovered that his steadfast rebellious views on life were not as valid as he had once thought them to be. At the age of twenty-two, Victor was willing to reexamine the teachings he had been given by his parents from an early age. Financially broke, educationally untrained, spiritually empty, and deemed irresponsible by his friends, Victor was ready to learn from his mistakes . . . after causing his parents nearly a decade of turmoil and heartache.[1]

The Problem of Rebellion

To some parents and youth workers, the phrase "teen rebellion" may seem redundant. At times, it does seem that adolescence is synonymous with rebellion.

Matt arrives home from school, and his mother greets him by asking, "How was your day?" He spins on his heels and snaps, "Get off my back!"

Darla's mode of dress has bothered her parents for some time, but they've tried to keep their mouths shut. But when she arrived home late one Saturday afternoon with three earrings in one ear and four in the other—and a small silver hoop adorning one nostril—they threw up their hands in disgust.

Julie simply won't go to school. Her parents have tried grounding her, but she just runs away and stays a few nights with friends. She's even been to court for her truancy, but she professes not to care and prefers to hang out at the mall or at friends' houses all day.

Todd, whose father was a deacon in their church, not only refused to go to church with his mom and dad, he managed to get arrested . . . for throwing a brick through a plate-glass window of the church building. He explained to the police that he and his friends were just "looking for something to do" on a Saturday night.

Such instances would be considered mild by some parents who endure physical assault and verbal abuse and watch their kids become involved in dangerous and destructive behaviors on a much larger scale.

According to Dr. Grace Ketterman, behavior that a parent may interpret as rebellion can fit into three categories:

> When parents are obviously too strict, children *rebel* to draw attention to the fact that they are growing up. But the same misbehavior is much more common among children whose parents are terribly inconsistent. I label the actions of these teens *testing-out behavior,* because they aren't actu-

ally rebelling. They are only trying to find out if the parents care enough (and are powerful enough) to stop them. The bad behavior is very similar, but the reason is just the opposite. Rigid parents need to let up a little and be flexible. Inconsistent parents must tighten up and set some standards. The third condition I call *wild behavior,* which is exhibited by some children as an attempt to get away from their emotional pain. Many kids have their own variety of pain—broken homes, loss of a parent, etc., so they act out their feelings, and their actions are interpreted as rebellion.[2]

The Causes of Rebellion

Teenage rebellion occurs for many and varied reasons. In some cases, it is simply an awkward expression of an adolescent's stumbling progress toward adulthood. However, in many cases adolescent rebellion also stems from a number of roots, among which may be a poor relationship with parents, an effort to communicate, a need for control, a lack of boundaries and expectations, an expression of anger and aggression, and the absence of an honest and vulnerable model.

◆ A Poor Relationship with Parents

Rules without relationships lead to rebellion. Parents may consider themselves strict or lenient, but no matter how few or how many rules a teen is expected to observe, the key is the parents' relationship with the teen.

A parent can get a child to "behave" by enforcing a hard-and-fast set of rules; Mom or Dad can control a child by running a "tight ship." But adolescents are often a different matter. When parents try to lay down rules without first establishing a real relationship with their kids, they sow the seeds of rebellion. Sometimes it will be outward rebellion that is easy to spot, but just as often it can be an inward rebellion, in which the young person appears to be obedient but is nursing all kinds of grudges and hang-ups, along with an unhealthy self-image and low self-esteem.

◆ An Effort to Communicate

Rebellion is often a reflection of a teen's effort to communicate what he or she is thinking, feeling, or needing. Dr. William Lee Carter deftly illustrates this fact:

> Several years ago while [I was] teaching a Sunday school class of high school students. . . . one of the teenagers in the class read Colossians 3:8, which states "But now you also, put them all aside: anger, wrath, malice, slander, and abusive speech from your mouth." As soon as these words had been read, another teenage boy, who had a reputation for rebellion, blurted out, "If I quit doing all those things, I'd never get anything across to anybody. No one takes me seriously if I don't force my feelings on them."[3]

Though few teens are as aware of the roots of their rebellion as that young man was—and though they seldom communicate what they consciously or subconsciously intend—many nonetheless rebel in the hope that someone will hear and understand their feelings and their needs.

◆ A Need for Control

Everyone—adults included—needs to feel in control of his or her life to some degree. That is among the reasons we are so deeply disturbed by random killings reported in the news, the burglary of one's own home, and the death of a friend or loved one; they shatter our sense of control.

Adolescents—adults in training—possess the same need for a sense of control. They may respond positively to appropriate parental guidelines and boundaries, but the teen who begins to feel as though his parents control *every*thing he says or does may respond with attempts to shed his parents' control (by repeat-edly breaking curfew, for example) or control things himself (perhaps by using alcohol or doing other things his parents have forbidden). If parents attempt to exert control through threats, coercion, or physical restraint, the teen may feel that he is being forced to either rebel or to sacrifice all control over his own life.

◆ A Lack of Boundaries and Expectations

Dr. G. Keith Olson, author of *Counseling Teenagers,* writes:

> Teenagers raised in overly permissive homes . . . may be just as rebellious as those from restrictive homes, although usually for different reasons. Youth from overly permissive homes may rebel against the lack of codes and expectations. In both home environments, there has probably been a years-long pattern of discouragement, lack of affirmation and direction from family and much self-criticism. By the time these children enter adolescence, they usually have very serious questions about their sense of worth, value and whether they belong.[4]

◆ An Expression of Anger and Aggression

Some psychologists and researchers have linked rebellion and destructive behaviors to "aggressive impulses that are turned inward."[5] The teen may be angry at his or her circumstances (parents' divorce, death of a parent, etc.), at someone in particular (an absent father, an abusive relative, etc.), or even at God. This anger, usually suppressed, can lead to rebellious impulses or acts. (See also chapter 4, "Anger.")

◆ The Absence of an Honest, Vulnerable Model

Ronald P. Hutchcraft writes:

> Kids don't have much respect for parents who are "never wrong." [Parents who] are never wrong, never apologize, or never seek forgiveness . . . seem unapproachable. . . . Another reason

why teens reject parental authority is that they don't think their parents set a good example for them. They feel that parents expect one thing of them but do not practice what they preach. They want their parents to be good models for them—to show them by their own lives how they as children should live and respond to various situations.[6]

The Effects of Rebellion

As has been said, all adolescents are likely to rebel in one way or another. Rebellious thoughts and behavior are not only common, they are natural. Such rebellious tendencies can even be beneficial in helping teens to grow toward independence and their parents to adjust their expectations and practices. However, prolonged rebellion can be both dangerous and deleterious to both parent and child.

◆ Dangerous Pursuits

Rebellion that is expressed in delinquency (alcohol and drug abuse, vandalism, etc.) bears many dangers for youth. The risks of such rebellion are many, as author Linda Peterson makes clear:

> You no doubt remember your own teen turmoil—the arguments with parents over clothes, friends, the state of your room, your schoolwork, your future. Parents and teens are still at it. Only now, the stakes are higher. . . . Today teenagers rock to "I used to love her but I had to kill her" from Guns N' Roses. Fifteen-year-olds are going to "drink-all-you-can" parties, marijuana is five or ten times stronger than it was 15 years ago, and the consequences of casual sex can be deadly.[7]

◆ Depression

In his book *Teenage Rebellion*, Carter writes:

> The typical haughty, arrogant attitude of most rebellious teenagers suggests anything but depression. However, one of the ground rules of human

behavior is that the over-expression of emotions often is a strong indicator of more serious, underlying emotional discomfort. This is the case in the rebellious teenager.

Dissatisfaction is frequently substituted as a synonym for the term *depression*. Rebellious teenagers are frequently dissatisfied with various aspects of their lives. One teenage girl said, "I can't tell you how many things are wrong in my life. I can't get along with my parents. I'm constantly in trouble at home. At school, my teachers act like I'm some sort of snob. They treat me like a juvenile delinquent. . . . I know I'm going nowhere in life, but I don't know how to stop. In fact, I'm not sure I *want* to stop." . . .

Other people characterized her as self-centered, conceited, arrogant, and difficult to manage—and she certainly showed those traits. But the term that described her real feelings was not *arrogant*, but depressed.[8] [See also chapter 5, "Depression."]

◆ Alienation

Rebellious teens also experience a sense of alienation as a result of their attitudes and actions. They come to feel alienated from their parents, from their teachers, from church officials, from society in general—even from their friends. Their behavior and demeanor often cause people to avoid them, and the rebellious teen is seldom oblivious or inattentive to such reactions. The girl quoted by Carter above also said, "The only teenagers who will have anything to do with me are the ones who are always in trouble, just like me."[9] Ironically, such a sense of alienation often leads to more—not less—rebellion.

◆ Guilt

Rebellious teens are often plagued by guilty feelings. They know the wrongness of their actions. They know the pain they cause their parents and others who care about them. They often understand their behavior to be disobedience against God too. But they don't stop their rebellious behavior. They may be determined not to give in to their parents. They may be afraid to show any sign of weakness or vulnerability. They may simply be unable to face the underlying causes of their rebellion. Consequently, they often deny their guilt—and in so doing, invite more of it. (See chapter 3, "Guilt.")

◆ **Anxiety and Fear**

Carter writes:

> Whether or not rebellious teenagers will acknowledge it, they are fearful of many things. . . . [T]hey may fear the eventual results of their rebellious actions. Many rebellious teenagers also fear they will never outgrow their argumentative ways and will find themselves in perennial hot water with others. Some teenagers fear they will never be understood and will be doomed to relationships marred by conflict. . . . Anxiety may be shown as follows:

- Frequent complaints of physical illness, including headaches, stomachaches, and sleep disturbances

- Feelings of panic that result in unbridled emotional expression

- Unrealistic preoccupations or irrational beliefs about others

- Intense emotional displays that go beyond what the situation calls for

- Becoming numb to the emotions of others for fear of further emotional hurt

- Assuming that the worst will always happen

- Holding emotions within to the point that bodily tension becomes uncomfortable[10]

While the reactions listed above do not exhaust the possible effects of rebellion, they do illustrate the unpleasant and destructive potential of teen rebellion—not only to the parents, but to the teen himself or herself.

The Biblical Perspective of Rebellion

The Bible is pretty straightforward about the fact and the effects of youthful rebellion. The classic example, of course, is the story of Absalom's rebellion against his father, King David, recorded in 2 Samuel 15.

A look at Absalom's youth certainly seems to display the seeds of rebellion. He was the product of a polygamous marriage (2 Sam. 3:3) and a turbulent family situation. His youth was marked by tragedy and murder (2 Samuel 13). He was estranged from his father (2 Sam. 14:28) and resorted to arson in an effort to engineer a reunion with his father (2 Sam. 14:29–33).

Absalom's reconciliation with his father, David, was short-lived, however. He returned his father's forgiveness by leading an army against David in an effort to capture the kingdom for himself. Absalom's rebellion was successful in driving David from his capital city, but it ended in Absalom's death (2 Sam. 18:1–18). The result of Absalom's rebellion against his father was his own destruction.

The Word of God is clear about the appropriate behavior of children—not only adolescent children but grown children as well—toward their parents. Deuteronomy 27:16 proclaims, "Cursed is the man who dishonors his father or his mother." And Proverbs 15:20 says, "A wise son brings joy to his father, but a foolish man despises his mother."

More strikingly, Deuteronomy 21:18–21 offers a stern prescription for rebellion against parental authority:

> If a man has a stubborn and rebellious son who does not obey his father and mother and will not listen to them when they discipline him, his father and mother shall take hold of him and bring him to the elders at the gate of his town. They shall say to the elders, "This son of ours is stubborn and rebellious. He will not obey us. He is a profligate

and a drunkard." Then all the men of his town shall stone him to death. You must purge the evil from among you. All Israel will hear of it and be afraid.

Such a response may seem harsh to some parents (and inviting to others!), but God's Word makes it clear that parent-child relationships are a two-way street:

Children, obey your parents in the Lord, for this is right. "Honor your father and mother"—which is the first commandment with a promise—"that it may go well with you and that you may enjoy long life on the earth."

Fathers, do not exasperate your children; instead, bring them up in the training and instruction of the Lord.[11]

Children are to obey; but parents are to relate to their children in a way that encourages obedience rather than inciting rebellion.

One final scriptural model must be cited. Luke 2:41–52 offers the single insight into Jesus' adolescence that is available to us. It depicts the visit of Jesus and His parents to Jerusalem for the Passover observance when Jesus was twelve.

After the Feast was over, while his parents were returning home, the boy Jesus stayed behind in Jerusalem, but they were unaware of it. Thinking he was in their company, they traveled on for a day. Then they began looking for him among their relatives and friends. When they did not find him, they went back to Jerusalem to look for him. After three days they found him in the temple courts, sitting among the teachers, listening to them and asking them questions. Everyone who heard him was amazed at his understanding and his answers. When his parents saw him, they were astonished. His mother said to him, "Son, why have you treated us like this? Your father and I have been anxiously searching for you."

"Why were you searching for me?" he asked. "Didn't you know I had to be in my Father's house?" But they did not understand what he was saying to them.

Then he went down to Nazareth with them and was obedient to them. But his mother treasured all these things in her heart. And Jesus grew in wisdom and stature, and in favor with God and men.

That passage depicts a Jesus of bar-mitzvah age, who is beginning the long, slow route from the dependence of childhood to the independence of adulthood. While that journey apparently caused His parents no little consternation, He managed to assert His growing independence while nonetheless remaining obedient to His parents (Luke 2:51).

Such is the challenge faced by every adolescent both before and since that time.

The Response to the Problem of Rebellion

Listen ◆ Empathize ◆ Affirm ◆ Direct ◆ Enlist ◆ Refer

Olson warns that "counseling rebellious and delinquent youth is a very difficult, slow and often frustrating task. . . . Success might be marginal at best. Counselors will do well to keep an active prayer and fellowship life. Constant contact with God will empower and guide [adults] as they work with these special teenagers." Though attempting to help and guide a rebellious youth is indeed a challenge, the following may help a sensitive, patient youth leader, teacher, pastor, or parent:

LISTEN. Invite dialogue. Allow the young person to vent his or her feelings and to talk without interruption or condemnation. Rebellious teens are unaccustomed to anyone really listening; they expect criticisms, platitudes, Bible verses, and sermons. Surprise him or her by really listening, and listen with the eyes as well as the ears. Look for nonverbal communication; watch the eyes, the gestures, the posture. Use what you see to help the young person better express what he or she feels.

EMPATHIZE. "My characteristic way of approaching behavioral problems," says Carter, "is to consider matters from the teenager's point of view. Although I am not likely to agree with the teen in all areas of concern, my knowledge of his or her viewpoint provides invaluable information that I can eventually use in providing a beneficial response."[12] Try to see things through the eyes of the teen.

Try also to communicate your understanding and empathy by:

- Being available to the youth.
- Listening in order to understand.
- Making eye contact.
- Leaning slightly forward in your chair.
- Nodding to indicate understanding.
- Reflecting key statements ("So, you're saying . . . ." "That must have made you feel . . . .").
- Waiting patiently through silence, anger, or tears.

AFFIRM. Many parents and other adults fear that if they openly express love and appreciation to a rebellious teen it will be misconstrued as endorsement of his or her behavior. On the contrary, sincere affirmation and appreciation is a key to reaching such a young person. You may express appreciation for a rebellious teen's honesty, willingness to talk things out, sense of humor, intelligence, smile, voice, etc. Be prepared, however, for such expressions to be greeted with suspicion or with attempts at manipulation. Still, no matter what happens, seize every opportunity to communicate sincere acceptance and affirmation to the teen.

DIRECT. A rebellious youth is unlikely to acknowledge his or her need of direction, nor to respond to it if it is given. However, the sensitive and discerning adult may be able to offer help in the following ways:

1. Help the youth identify and express the reasons for the rebellion. Patiently talk through the underlying causes (which may come as a surprise to both of you). This may take a long time—months, even years—but it is crucial.

2. Explore with the youth what circumstances might make rebellion unnecessary. The most likely response, of course, is, "When my parents trust me," or "When Mom and Dad get off my back." Help him or her become more searching and more specific than that, however. Under what circumstances might the rebellion conceivably be rendered unnecessary?

3. Involve the parents. Marshall Shelley quotes one pastor who said, "We're finding more and more that we need to get the whole family involved in counseling. For us to deal just with the one who's knocked on the office door or just the one who's being pointed at is not usually helpful at all."[13]

4. Work toward a "negotiated agreement." Help the teen, parent(s), or other significant adults to discuss the following:

   a. *Identifying negotiables and non-negotiables.* For example, premarital sex and drug abuse are nonnegotiable; a loving parent cannot approve or allow such behavior. Curfew, however—or certain music styles or modes of dress—might be negotiable.

   b. *Spelling out expectations.* Parents and teens need to be explicit about their expectations. Parent: "Cathy, I expect you home by eleven o'clock; not eleven-thirty or even eleven-ten." Teen: "Dad, I don't expect you to be at every basketball game, but I think you should make all my home games, at least."

   c. *Attaching specific responses to behaviors.* Parents often set their teens up for rebellion by responding to a teen's behavior out of anger or vindictiveness. By attaching specific responses to behaviors, parents and the teens can sometimes avoid resentment and bitterness. If both parties know that skipping school will result in a teen being grounded for a specific period of time or running away will prompt the parents to call the police, the punishment is not always being meted out by angry parents but is more clearly a choice (albeit a poor one) that the teen himself or herself is making.

d. *Outlining a long-term plan for dealing with the roots of the rebellion.* Remember that addressing teen rebellion is likely to be a long and often frustrating process. Parents and other adults who care about the youth can help over the long run by instituting some long-range plans, such as those suggested by William Lee Carter:

- Show your teen, through words and behavior, that you understand his or her viewpoint.

- Keep criticism to a minimum and use it only after you have actively listened.

- Walk away from arguing, but be firm in your decisions.

- Maintain an open mind. Don't insist you are always right.

- Use proper timing when making negative, but necessary, statements.

- Refrain from trying to emotionally overpower your teen. You won't win.

- Give your teenager a voice in the decision-making process.

- Keep your comments brief.

- Allow your teenager to live with consequences of his or her behavior.

- Show a willingness to approach your child rather than waiting for him or her to approach you.[14]

ENLIST. Keep in mind that a teenager cannot be coerced into submission to his or her parents; he or she must be convinced that rebellion is not the best way to respond to whatever is lacking (nor to fulfill the needs) in his or her life. The young person must become an active participant in addressing the most prominent contributing factors to the rebellion and in eliminating the perceived need for such behavior. This can, of course, be a long (in fact, life-long) process.

REFER. In cases of severe rebellion, particularly rebellion involving alcohol and drug use (see chapter 38, "Alcohol Use and Abuse," and 39, "Drug Use and Abuse"), running away (see chapter 24, "Runaway Threats and Attempts"), premarital sex (see chapter 28, "Premarital Sex") and other dangerous behaviors, a qualified Christian counselor should be involved (with parental permission) at the earliest opportunity.

For Further Reading

The following resources may help the concerned parent, pastor, teacher, or youth worker assist a rebellious young person:

Scriptures Cited in This Chapter

- Colossians 3:8
- 2 Samuel 3:3; 13; 14:28–33; 18:1–18
- Deuteronomy 27:16; 21:18–21
- Proverbs 15:20
- Ephesians 6:1–4
- Luke 2:41–52

Other Scripture to Read

- Exodus 20:12; 34:6–7
- Leviticus 19:3; 20:9
- Luke 15:11–32

- Colossians 3:20

Further Reading

- William Lee Carter, Ed.D., *Teenage Rebellion* (Rapha/Word).

- Jay Kesler with Ronald A. Beers, *Parents and Teenagers* (Victor). Contains several helpful chapters on teen rebellion and related subjects.

24

RUNAWAY THREATS AND ATTEMPTS

A Synopsis

❖

Introduction

She was a smart girl," said Stan Hodges, referring to his stepdaughter, Andrea.

"She got good grades too," Andrea's mother, Lisa, added, "until seventh grade."

Andrea grew up in Fond du Lac, Wisconsin, a town of thirty-seven thousand on the southern shore of Lake Winnebago.

"At first," Lisa said, "she just started skipping school with some friends. They weren't bad kids. Most of them didn't even smoke." Soon, however, Andrea started sneaking out of the house at night to hang out at friends' homes, staying up late, talking, and listening to music.

"We tried everything," Andrea's mother said, "but nothing worked." Finally, her mother and stepfather decided they were unable to control Andrea, and concerned about her influence on her younger brother and two sisters, they allowed the authorities to place her in a foster home.

Andrea ran away from the foster home but was soon caught and placed in a group home, where she met another runaway named Melissa. Andrea and Melissa became fast friends. Two months after Andrea's arrival at the group home, she and Melissa cut a hole in their bedroom screen, crawled out, and crept to the quiet country road that ran by the group home. By the time their absence was discovered, Andrea and Melissa had hitched a ride to Milwaukee.

Melissa took Andrea to an apartment complex she had once lived in, an assortment of dreary, dingy apartments populated by prostitutes, junkies, and runaways.

Melissa left soon after their arrival, but Andrea stayed on. Her pretty face and figure made her the center of attention among the men—many of them two or three times her age—who played cards, drank beer, and smoked pot in the rooms and hallways of the complex.

On September 12, 1995, however, Andrea's mom and stepdad received a call. Andrea had been found dead in a pool of blood on the floor of apartment 113. She had been shot in the head at close range by a nineteen-year-old boy who was high at the time of the shooting.

Andrea was fourteen when she died.[1]

The Problem of Running Behavior

More than one million American teenagers run away from home every year.[2] Some estimates place the numbers much higher, perhaps between two and four million. And the number of runaways and street kids in Canada has been estimated at around two hundred thousand.[3]

The average age of these runaways is fourteen. Seventy percent are white, 16 percent black, and the remaining 14 percent are from Hispanic and other ethnic backgrounds.[4]

"At least half of all youth who run away from home," writes Gary D. Bennett, "stay within the town or vicinity in which they live, many going to a friend's or relative's house. Most runaway episodes seem to be poorly planned, reflecting impulsive behavior, and most runaways return within a week. Generally, the length of time gone from home increases with age."[5]

Keith Wade, a program supervisor at a Minneapolis shelter for runaways, adds, "There is a pattern to running behavior. . . . Kids run for the first time overnight, typically to someone close to them, a friend or a relative. But the more they run the further they go, and the longer they stay."[6]

Wade also observes that the runaway problem is not only becoming more serious and widespread; it is also spreading to younger kids. "The average age of the kids we see here now is 14 $\frac{1}{2}$, and it was 16 when I started. . . . [T]hat's an 18-month decline in the average age in five years, which is significant. . . . Thirteen-year-olds used to be rare; now they are common."[7]

Wade says he has also seen a change in the problems of runaway teens, both before and after their "running behavior" begins. "The kids have worse problems. When I first came, the typical girl we'd see would be experiencing communication problems at home, and maybe there was some abuse. Now we're seeing kids who have already been hospitalized for depression or because of suicide attempts."[8]

Kids who run away from home these days bear little or no resemblance to the comic-strip image of Dennis the Menace with a kerchief on a pole slung over his shoulder. It is an increasingly common and frequently tragic problem.

◆ Three Categories

Dr. James Oraker says, "My experience suggests that teenagers who run away fit into one of three categories: the runaway, the throwaway, or the just-plain-bored." He elaborates:

> The *runaway* is running from a situation he or she can no longer tolerate. Conflict is so great that members of the family can hardly stand each other. . . . The pressure builds until the young person finally leaves home.
>
> Another type of runaway is the young person who lives two lives. One pleases the parents, but a second, secret, life violates what the parents want. Parents become suspicious and begin to ask questions. It becomes more and more difficult to remember what excuse was given. The young person fears that the parents will "find out" and leaves home before the "lid blows."
>
> The *throwaway* was usually rejected as a child. During adolescence, the rejection becomes more and more open and blatant. . . . To escape, the young person may start drifting; he or she leaves home with no resistance or is told to leave home for the sake of the family. . . .
>
> Finally, there is the *just plain bored.* The message I hear from them is, "No big conflict. My parents and I just agreed that home was sort of a 'place to land' for all of us, so I decided to do what everyone else is doing—drift. I really get into looking at people and seeing what's happening in other parts of the country." These young people are difficult to help because they don't want help. . . . Some of them are committed to nothing and desperate for love. This category of runaways is possibly the most frustrating to work with.[9]

The Causes of Running Behavior

Factors contributing to running behavior include abuse, alienation, rebellion, a perceived lack of control, and fear.

◆ Abuse

"Youth don't run for fun or adventure," says Wade. "The majority don't run *to* anything. They run *from* something, usually abuse, emotional, physical or sexual. Or just plain neglect. They are victims when they run, and often they are victimized again."[10]

A study of adolescents and young adults at Toronto's Covenant House, a center for runaway youth, discovered that 86 percent of the runaways they interviewed reported suffering some form of physical abuse in their homes before running away.[11]

◆ Alienation

"Running away is an attempt to solve a problem," says Oraker. The problem, he says, is commonly "alienation—strong feelings of separation or rejection that explode inside. . . . Alienation is usually a family problem that brews for years."[12] He suggests that many teens who run away are simply doing what their parents have been doing for years, except that Mom and Dad may have "run away" into their jobs or into drinking, for example.

◆ Rebellion

Rules without relationships lead to rebellion . . . and running behavior is often an expression of rebellion. (See also chapter 23, "Rebellion.") One mother of a runaway said that her daughter "didn't like rules. That must have been why she ran." The girl's stepfather concurred. "We had rules set up for all the kids, and none of them followed 'em to a T, but she went out of her way to let us know she didn't want to. You couldn't hold her no matter where she was."[13]

A healthy parent-child relationship is no guarantee that a young person will not run away, but it certainly helps temper the adolescent tendency to resist and rebel against rules, which may, in turn, prevent and/or address running behavior.

◆ A Perceived Lack of Control

Billy Best ran away from his suburban Boston home in late 1994 in order to avoid the painful chemotherapy treatments he had been undergoing in order to combat Hodgkin's lymphoma. Best's adoptive parents returned home from Bible study on Wednesday, October 26, to find the note he left behind. "He felt he had no control at all," William Best explained. "We had basically told him, 'You're going to get chemo,' and that was that."[14] Billy's nationally publicized case ended happily four weeks later, when Billy returned home with an agreement to explore less painful treatments.

Adolescents, like adults, need to feel a sense of control over their lives. They may respond positively to appropriate parental guidelines and boundaries, but the teen who begins to feel as though his parents—or someone or something else—control *every*thing he says or does may respond by shedding his parents' control and running away.

◆ Fear

Dr. Oraker describes one teen girl runaway as an example of the fear that is occasionally a factor in a young person's decision to run away. (See also chapter 2, "Anxiety.") He writes:

> She was out of tune with her family and with society. She had deep personal fears of failing and not being able to make it anywhere. For her, drugs, sexual involvement, and running away were ways of coping with those fears.[15]

◆ Other Reasons

Other possible reasons a teen may run from home, according to Gary D. Bennett, include:

- To avoid feeling a lack of love

- To escape a "situation"

- To avoid punishment

- To respond to friends

- To seek attention

- To ease emotional problems

- To act out feelings the teenager has about parents, siblings, or other "important" people in his life

- To find a meaningful family relationship (often a teenager may be detached or rootless)

- To avoid disappointing parents when the teenager feels something he has done will not please them

- To attempt to control; i.e., he exploits the threat of running away in order to manipulate the parent

- To test independence and prove he can make it on his own without parental supervision.[16]

The Effects of Running Behavior

Running away from home seldom—if ever—solves the problems to which the teen is reacting. On the contrary, leaving home is often just the beginning of the teen's problems.

◆ Survival Difficulties

Bennett writes:

Survival becomes a critical dilemma [for many] since most runaway episodes are poorly planned. Food is obtained by panhandling or shoplifting. If shelter isn't available with friends, then a runaway must resort to living and sleeping in cars, laundromats, storm drains, garages, etc. When money runs out, work is usually impossible to find because the runaway is underage and doesn't have

the skills, maturity, or legal acceptability to be hired.[17]

The realities of running behavior and of life on the street make runaways extremely vulnerable to exploitation and abuse. The Canadian news magazine *Maclean's* reports:

◆ Vulnerability to Exploitation and Abuse

Many teenage runaways end up as tragic figures. An internal police report made public in September [1990] said that one female recruiter for a local satanic cult took in runaways and put them to work as prostitutes. Then, in late October, the Youth Victims Project, a joint investigation by Winnipeg social agencies and the police into allegations of abuse of street kids by Asian men issued another . . . report. Project members identified 183 girls, some as young as 10, who had been sexually abused by up to 100 men. . . . Usually, the men picked up the girls at downtown haunts and took them home, where they gave them drugs and alcohol and, in many cases, raped them after the girls were too impaired to resist. Still, many girls clearly went willingly with the men—and declined to report the attacks. "The men provided for the girls at the basic levels: shelter, food, clothing and companionship," said the report. "The victims regarded the sexual exploitation as a small price to pay for the attention they received."[18]

◆ Criminal Behavior

In addition to a heightened vulnerability to exploitation and abuse, running behavior is also often accompanied by criminal behavior. Bennett writes:

Problems with the law are inevitable because running away and the necessities of survival create circumstances which lead to illegal behavior. A runaway may be charged with such offenses as disorderly conduct, hitchhiking, possession and use of alcohol and other drugs, being declared "wayward" or "uncontrollable," and shoplifting.[19]

◆ Other Effects

Runaways also frequently struggle with malnutrition and poor health. They are often plagued by severe feelings of guilt, shame, and low self-esteem. They are susceptible to bouts of depression. Their psychosocial development is typically stunted, and they often become trapped in a cycle of dependency and victimization that can be extremely difficult to break.

The Biblical Perspective of the Runaway

The most famous runaway of all time is the Prodigal Son, whose story is told by Jesus in the fifteenth chapter of Luke's Gospel:

There was a man who had two sons. The younger one said to his father, "Father, give me my share of the estate." So he divided his property between them.

Not long after that, the younger son got together all he had, set off for a distant country and there squandered his wealth in wild living. After he had spent everything, there was a severe famine in that whole country, and he began to be in need. So he went and hired himself out to a citizen of that country, who sent him to his fields to feed pigs. He longed to fill his stomach with the pods that the pigs were eating, but no-one gave him anything.

When he came to his senses, he said, "How many of my father's hired men have food to spare, and here I am starving to death! I will set out and go back to my father and say to him: Father, I have sinned against heaven and against you. I am no longer worthy to be called your son; make me like one of your hired men." So he got up and went to his father.

But while he was still a long way off, his father saw him and was filled with compassion for him; he ran to his son, threw his arms around him and kissed him.

The son said to him, "Father, I have sinned against heaven and against you. I am no longer worthy to be called your son."

But the father said to his servants, "Quick! Bring the best robe and put it on him. Put a ring on his finger and sandals on his feet. Bring the fattened calf and kill it. Let's have a feast and celebrate. For this son of mine was dead and is alive again; he was lost and is found." So they began to celebrate.[20]

Jesus' story can be applied to all of us, adults and youth alike; we all "have gone astray; each of us has turned to his own way."[21] We have all been runaways at one time or another—from God's love, from His commands, from His will. But He, like the waiting father in Jesus' famous story, waited for us and generously accepted us before we could even finish our acts of contrition.

Oraker observes:

Initially, the prodigal son felt that he could do better on his own. To him, freedom was getting away from the family. Soon, however, he was in bondage, a slave to survival and to his boss. Likewise, the young person seeking freedom on the street can almost overnight become a slave to survival, bitterness, drugs, self-centeredness, and insecurity. The pride that drove him or her from home becomes a slave-driver on the street.

Parents also become slaves to control or restrictions as a method of keeping peace in the family. Even after the young person has run away, parents usually refuse to admit any wrong. They continue to deny their part and to realize that most crises are two-sided.[22]

The story of the prodigal son—and his waiting, accepting father—can help us to appreciate God's loving acceptance and restoration of us, and perhaps even emulate it in our relationships with wayward teens and young adults.

The Response to the Problem of Runaway Threats and Attempts

Listen ◆ Empathize ◆ Affirm ◆ Direct ◆ Enlist ◆ Refer

It's not always possible to predict or anticipate

running behavior in teens. The wise parent or concerned adult must be alert to the possible causes of running behavior (abuse, alienation, rebellion, a perceived lack of control, and fear) and seek to address conditions that may contribute to such behavior before the situation reaches a crisis point. In addition, because most teens run to a friend or relative first, it is sometimes possible to prevent further running behavior by addressing the reasons for such behavior as soon as it begins to be evidenced. Some of the following suggestions may help a caring parent, pastor, youth pastor, teacher, or youth worker to reach out to a teen who has shown or is showing signs of running behavior.

LISTEN. William Best, the adoptive father of Billy Best, admits to having learned a valuable lesson from Billy's running behavior: to listen. "You need to really understand what [they're] going through," he said.[23] Allow the young person to talk—at length—about the reason(s) he or she wants to run away. Avoid the temptation to answer or argue what he or she says; criticism or correction will stifle communication and may prevent the concerned adult from discovering the true reason(s) for the behavior.

Some helpful questions may include:

- When did you first think about running away?
- What makes you want to run?
- Can you remember a time when you didn't think about running? What things were different then?
- What do you think running will do for you?
- What things do you think would have to change in order for you to not think about running?

EMPATHIZE. "My characteristic way of approaching behavioral problems," says William Lee Carter, "is to consider matters from the teenager's point of view. Although I am not likely to agree with the teen in all areas of concern, my knowledge of his or her viewpoint provides invaluable information that I can eventually use in providing a beneficial response."[24] Try to see things through the eyes of the teen without taking sides in any disagreement.

AFFIRM. Bennett writes, "At whatever stage one becomes involved in the teenager's return, reassurance and protection should be the message the child receives—certainly not fear of discipline."[25] Strive to communicate unconditional love, acceptance, and esteem—as the father did in Jesus' story of the prodigal son—to the teen.

DIRECT. Successful intervention in the problem of running behavior must involve the teen and the family. Oraker provides a sound and workable outline for helping a family and a teen who exhibits running behavior:

Step 1: Finding an arbitrator agreeable to the family members. Since lack of trust is operating and each person feels abused by the other, the person chosen to help with the healing process must be agreeable to all sides. The arbitrator can be a trusted, sensitive neighbor, a teacher, or a friend. . . .

Step 2: Talking out the problem. A sensitive arbitrator will begin to explore the problem and identify each person's part. As this is accomplished, understanding will begin; things will begin to fit together. This step will take time and energy, but, if done properly, it will provide an adequate foundation for the family work of Step 3.

Step 3: Commitment to a plan. Once understanding has begun and the crisis is resolved, plans must be initiated to work through the problem. A skilled arbitrator will (1) draw out from each family member suggestions to assist in solving the problem; (2) help the family select a concrete plan of action [perhaps even drawing up a contract for each family member to sign]; (3) gain commitment from each member to a plan; (4) provide the tools needed to implement the plan [such as assigning specific rights and responsibilities to each individual]; and (5) establish an evaluation procedure to measure success or failure [such as weekly "family meetings" to discuss progress].[26]

A final—but critical—factor in addressing running behavior is to encourage the family and the runaway to turn to God, to enter into a relationship with Jesus Christ, and to depend on Him for grace and strength in addressing and correcting the problems that have contributed to the behavior. Healing and wholeness cannot be achieved without His involvement in the process.

ENLIST. Oraker also suggests enlisting the parents' and child's participation in the resolution of the problem. "Develop a family strategy without an arbitrator," he writes. "The goals of arbitration are to resolve crisis, initiate solutions, and equip a family with tools so they can work out their own growth. Thus, an arbitrator can withdraw as he teaches the family new skills for relating on their own."[27]

REFER. Do not assume that because a runaway returns home the problem has been solved. It will probably take months, perhaps even years, to fully address the problem. It may also take the intervention of a professional Christian counselor, particularly if running away is a repeated problem. The causes and appropriate responses to running behavior are often complex and may be most effectively addressed by a qualified Christian professional.

For Further Reading

The following resources may help the concerned parent, pastor, teacher, or youth worker assist a young person who is thinking about running away or who has done so:

Scriptures Cited in This Chapter

- Luke 15:11–24
- Isaiah 53:6

Other Scripture to Read

- Exodus 20:12; 34:6–7
- Leviticus 19:3; 20:9
- Hosea 14:1–9
- Isaiah 57:18
- Ephesians 6:1–4
- Colossians 3:20

Further Reading

- Dr. James R. Oraker with Char Meredith, *Almost Grown* (Harper & Row). Contains a helpful chapter on teenage runaways.
- William Lee Carter, Ed.D., *Teenage Rebellion* (Rapha/Word).

SEXUAL

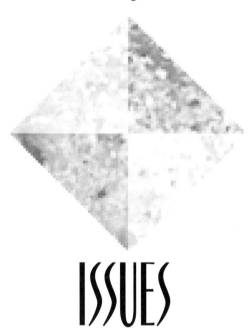

ISSUES

25

LUST

A Synopsis

❖

Introduction

"**I** can't take it anymore!"

Paul flopped into the folding chair in the youth pastor's office, which was littered with books, boxes, and supplies from the youth group's rafting trip on the Whitewater River.

"What's up?" Jim, the youth pastor, responded nonchalantly.

"Man, it's driving me crazy."

"What is?" Jim asked, tilting back in his chair and flopping his size-twelve feet onto his cluttered desk.

Paul glanced around furtively then jumped up from the chair and closed Jim's office door before returning to his seat. Several times he seemed about to say something, but each time he stopped quickly. Finally, he perched on the edge of his chair and told Jim he had to promise to keep secret everything he was about to hear. The youth pastor's smiling demeanor became suddenly more cautious, more serious.

"I sit next to Amanda Huggins in two of my classes," Paul explained, "and she's—well, you know—she's like, really built." He braved a glance at the youth pastor, whose expression hadn't changed. Paul dropped his glance again and stared at his hands, which he clasped tightly in front of him. "And the clothes she wears—well, she's just really nice-looking.

"Anyway, we talk and everything, but we're not really friends or anything, but I think about her all day." Paul shot a quick glance at the youth pastor. "And I—" He stopped. "I daydream about her. I even dream about her." He went on to explain that his dreams—and his daydreams—were explicit and erotic. "It's getting so I spend all my time thinking about her and picturing her naked, and—well, you know."

Paul stopped speaking and began to bite his fingernails while occasionally glancing at the youth pastor.

"Am I—" Paul spoke again, but stopped almost as soon as he had started. His eyes darted all around the room. "Is there . . . Is there something wrong with me?" he asked.

The Problem of Lust

The teen years are characterized by the onset of puberty and many accompanying struggles, including understanding and coping with an awakening sexuality.

Adolescent girls and boys encounter many thoughts and feelings that are both new and disturbing. They begin to notice the physical development and attractiveness of the opposite sex, they develop an intense fascination with romantic and sexual matters, and for the first time they experience sexual arousal, which can be innocent, and lust, which is not.

Dr. Gary Collins addresses the subject of lust in this way:

> It is difficult to give an accurate definition of *lust*. Surely it does *not* refer to normal God-given sexual desires, or feelings of attraction toward sexually stimulating people. God has not given us sexual needs or interests which he then condemns as lust. Lust is a specific desire for the body of another person.[1]

Dr. William Backus defines lust as the "imaginary rehearsal of sinful sexual behavior" and writes:

> Lust needs to be . . . carefully defined. You will find many people feeling guilty about desires which are not, in themselves, lust. . . . It is, therefore, important . . . to understand that lust is not simple sexual drive or desire. A person may be well aware that he finds another person attractive and desirable without committing the sin of lust. Just as one can find another person's car or house attractive and desirable without committing the sin of covetousness, so simple desire is not lust.
>
> Lust goes beyond mere awareness of desire and voluntarily dwells on, fantasizes, or daydreams about lovemaking and sex with an illicit object. This rehearsal of evil behavior in the heart is perhaps the root from which actual overt sinful sexual activity grows.[2]

As the Apostle James wrote, "Each one is tempted when he is carried away and enticed by his own lust. Then when lust is conceived, it gives birth to sin; and when sin is accomplished, it brings forth death."[3]

The Causes of Lust

Lust springs from the sinful human heart, of course. It is a legacy of the Fall. But there are contributing factors that make lust a critical problem for adolescents and an arguably greater problem for today's youth than for the youth of just a generation or two ago.

◆ Physiological Considerations

Teens are not only experiencing various hormonal changes in their bodies, most teens are also largely unprepared for the hormonal surges and surprises that occur as a natural physiological part of adolescence. They have yet to learn how to control and channel their sexual urges, and the frequent, sometimes severe, physical sensations they experience can leave them often bewildered and frightened.

◆ Environmental Influences

Today's teens face a culture that is unabashedly obsessed with sex, sexual attractiveness, and sexual gratification. Television programs, movies, previews, magazine ads, billboards, and commercials as well as styles of clothing are often blatant in their attempt to arouse the viewer sexually. "At a time when sexual urges are most intense and the need for peer approval most pressing, adolescents often succumb"[4] to such environmental pressures to fulfill their sexual desires through lust and through actual sexual encounters provoked by lust.

◆ Curiosity

Adolescence is a time of exploration and discovery, and an awakening sexuality is often accompanied by a strong curiosity that drives the desire to respond to new urges. Curiosity is not wrong, of course, but it does often fuel the fires of lust in a teenager who is naturally anxious to try new and different things.

◆ The Search for Identity

The teen years are typically characterized by a search for self-identity, an effort to discover "Who am I and where do I fit in?" One's sexuality is a part of that mix, of course, and for some teens, lustful fantasies become a salve to their fears and insecurities.

◆ The Search for Intimacy

Like everyone, teens want to be loved. They want to experience intimacy and closeness with others. This natural desire for intimacy leads many adolescents to lustful fantasies, particularly in those who feel lonely, unwanted, and rejected.

The Effects of Lust

While there are many considerable influences that make today's teens vulnerable to lust, it should not be dismissed as a harmless experience of adolescence. The effects of lust are serious and should be understood so that they may be avoided.

◆ Guilt

Lust, like all sin, carries true moral guilt, factual guilt, the invariable result of disobeying God. While lust isn't always accompanied by a sense of guilt in the person committing the sin, it can create an overwhelming sense of "dirtiness" in some and a nagging sense of moral discomfort in others. (See also chapter 3, "Guilt.")

◆ Spiritual Deadness

Collins writes,

Lust and other forms of nonmarital sex are con-

demned in Scripture and described as sin. . . . If [this form] of sexual immorality continues, one's spiritual vitality and influence are certain to decline. Sin must be confessed and forsaken if one is to expect spiritual growth and avoid spiritual deadness.[5]

◆ Overt Sexual Sin

As has been said, lust "is perhaps the root from which actual overt sinful sexual activity grows."[6] The person who harbors habitual lust in his or her heart is, by the frequent rehearsal of other sexual sin, opening the door to the Tempter. Some have suggested that the sin of lust always precedes the sins of adultery, fornication, and deviancy; it certainly makes a young person more vulnerable to those overt sexual sins.

◆ Sexual Addiction

The young person who allows lustful thoughts and feelings to prevail in his or her mind and heart may be setting the stage for sexual addiction. Lustful fantasies increase the person's desire for such stimulation, until the youth is addicted to the fascination and/or release the visual stimulus delivers. An escalation of thought and behavior often follows until the addiction drives the youth to pornography and, perhaps, also to acting on his or her lustful thoughts. (See chapter 27, "Pornography," and other chapters within this "Sexual Issues" section of the book.)

The Biblical Perspective of Lust

Jesus published His own "position paper" on lust in the Sermon on the Mount, when He said:

You have heard that it was said, "Do not commit adultery." But I tell you that anyone who looks at a woman lustfully has already committed adultery with her in his heart.[7]

Jesus did not say that lust was the same as adultery. He did say, however, that lust—the committing of adultery in the heart rather than with the body—is sexual sin.

Collins, in his book *Christian Counseling*, adapts an unpublished paper by four Trinity Evangelical Divinity School students that offers some helpful perspectives that may be applied here to lust:

1. *God made us sexual beings.* Sexual attractiveness and sexual feelings are good, not sinful.

2. *Because all persons, male and female, are created in the image of God, we should have a deep respect for the personhood of each one. Persons* are to be loved; *things* are to be used. To use another person is to violate his/her personality by making that person an object.

3. *Christians must take seriously God's directions for expressing sexuality.* Anything done contrary to God's will as it is specifically revealed in Scripture is sin. The Bible gives us many strong, stern warnings about the misuse of sex: Prov. 5:1–20, Eph. 4:19, 20, Col. 3:5, 1 Cor. 6:9–11. Yet in the right context physical love is a beautiful thing.

4. *God intends his people to live holy lives.* They must be a reflection of his perfect character. The guiding principle in every Christian's life should be, "Whatever you do, do all to the glory of God" (1 Cor. 10:31b).

5. *Sexual sins—be they lustful actions or fantasies, sexual arousal that is defrauding another person, or extramarital sex of any kind—can be forgiven when the person turns to Christ in repentance.* God does not want his people to be burdened with guilt. He freely forgives us on the basis of our faith in Jesus and his redemptive action for us on the cross.

6. *God, through his Holy Spirit, is the source of personal, practical power to help us guide and control our sexuality.* Sex is not a *drive* that we are enslaved to. Instead, it is an appetite that we can feed, either illicitly or spiritually (in the context of marriage). The choice is ours and God helps us along the way by cleansing us on a moment-by-moment basis from wrong attitudes and actions (1 John 1:9; 1 Cor. 6:11).[8]

The Response to the Problem of Lust

Listen ◆ Empathize ◆ Affirm ◆ Direct ◆ Enlist ◆ Refer

How can a youth leader, pastor, parent, or teacher help a young person who is struggling with the sin of lust? Victory must begin—and continue—with prayer, of course, and it may be aided by a plan such as the following:

LISTEN. Collins says that listening with sensitivity "is a basic starting point for all counseling but sometimes it is forgotten when we are presented with sexual issues." He continues:

By listening, we convey our desire to understand and our willingness to help with the counselee's real problem. It is quite appropriate to ask clarifying questions (provided that these are intended to increase our understanding and not to satisfy our curiosity). Try to avoid giving advice, preaching, expressing opinions, or even quoting Scripture, at least until you have a clear perspective on the problem.[9]

Helpful questions may include:

- When did this first become a problem for you?

- Has it become better or worse at particular times?

- When (under what circumstances) do you struggle most with it?

- When did this first become a problem for you?

- Have you tried to cope with it yourself? How? With what results?

- How does it make you feel?

EMPATHIZE. Backus emphasizes the need for getting in touch with our own sinful desires before we can hope to help those struggling with sexual sins. He writes:

> You must get in touch with your own deviant feelings, thoughts, fantasies, and desires. They may or may not be sexual. But they will be sinful. Frankly and honestly own up to them. . . . Let the Holy Spirit convict you [and receive] God's forgiveness. . . . [N]early everyone [has] experienced lust in some form.[10]

Honestly facing our own sin can help us empathize with the young person and approach him or her with compassion and understanding. The wise parent or concerned adult will not need to share his or her own struggles with the youth but will stay focused on addressing the young person's concerns.

AFFIRM. For an adolescent to admit and discuss lustful thoughts and feelings at all is likely to be a difficult endeavor. He or she is likely to feel extremely self-conscious, guilty, embarrassed, and perhaps shameful. Consequently, it is important for an adult who wishes to be helpful to avoid certain attitudes or actions; for example:

> Do not communicate judgment, blame, or disappointment.

> Do not preach; be especially wary of using the words, "You should."

> Do not patronize or sympathize ("I feel so sorry for you").

> Do not cajole or threaten.

Instead, the concerned adult should adopt an attitude of affirmation toward the young person.

Take every opportunity to affirm his or her worth and your regard for him or her. Help the youth realize that sexual desires are normal, that they are especially pronounced in the teen years, and that learning to control and channel them is a primary challenge of adolescence. The caring adult should seek, by his or her actions and attitudes, to communicate three primary messages to the youth:

> You are normal.

> You are valuable.

> You are loved.

DIRECT. Collins writes:

> Counseling is always most effective when we deal with specifics. Sometimes counselees need support and practical suggestions for . . . fleeing temptation. . . .It is not helpful to give advice too quickly, but neither is it helpful to maintain a consistent "nondirective" approach which gives little practical guidance and ignores the clear teachings of the Bible.[11]

The parent, pastor, teacher, or youth leader may suggest some of the following directions for countering lust:

1. *Give careful attention to the devotional life.* "Fellowship with God," says Erwin W. Lutzer, "is the best deterrent for lust."[12]

2. *Steer clear of temptation.* Avoid store displays, magazine racks, television shows, and other things or people that prompt lust. As Ephesians 4:27 says, "Do not give the devil a foothold."

3. *Memorize Scripture to counter temptation* (for example, Ephesians 4:27; James 1:14–15; James 4:7; 1 Peter 5:8–9; Hebrews 4:15–16; and Hebrews 12:2).

4. *Establish accountability.* Enter into an accountability relationship with someone you trust, with the agreement that you will meet

weekly to ask (and give honest answers to) such questions as:

How's your devotional life?

How's your thought life?

Is there any sin in your life?

5. *Make it a habit to begin praying the moment temptation hits.* A temptation can be rendered powerless if it is identified immediately and countered quickly with prayer.

6. *Employ diversions.* Active diversions such as cold showers, fifteen-minute jogs, and playing tennis can effectively redirect a person's thought life.

7. *Identify vulnerable times and plan accordingly.* For example, if a person struggles with lust most often right before bedtime, vigorous exercise right before bed or staying up later might make him or her tired enough to go to sleep quickly and so resist temptation.

8. *When you fail, confess your lust as sin,* repent before God, and ask Him for forgiveness now and victory in the future.

ENLIST. "Remember that people always respond best," Collins writes, "when the desire and motivation for change come from within. Instead of telling counselees what to do, encourage them to think of different courses of action which might work. Point out dangers or problems which counselees might not see, and then encourage commitment to one of the alternatives which does not violate biblical teaching. If such action fails to resolve or reduce the problem, help the counselee find another alternative and keep giving guidance, support and encouragement until the situation improves."[13]

REFER. Be alert to the possibility that the young person may best be helped by professional Christian counseling. Collins again outlines several helpful considerations:

Referral should be considered when counselees appear to have more complicated sexual problems than the counselor can handle, when their sexual problems are accompanied by considerable depression and/or anxiety, when there is great guilt or self-condemnation, when there are extremely disturbed behavior and thinking in the counselee . . . when the counselor is too shocked or embarrassed to continue counseling, or when he or she feels a strong and persisting sexual attraction to the counselee.[14]

While it will likely be difficult for the youth to accept referral, the young person should be shown that the youth leader or adviser considers it in his or her best interests for counseling to continue in that manner.

For Further Reading

The following resources may help the concerned parent, pastor, teacher, or youth worker assist a young person who is struggling with lust:

Scriptures Cited in This Chapter

- James 1:14, 15
- Matthew 5:27, 28
- Proverbs 5:1–20
- Ephesians 4:19–20
- Colossians 3:5
- 1 Corinthians 6:9–11; 10:31
- 1 John 1:9
- Ephesians 4:27
- James 4:7
- 1 Peter 5:8–9
- Hebrews 4:15–16; 12:2

Other Scripture to Read

- Genesis 39:1–12
- Proverbs 6:20–32

- 1 Thessalonians 4:3–7
- 1 Peter 4:1–7
- 1 John 2:15–17

Further Reading

- Verne Becker, ed., *The Campus Life Guide to Surviving High School* (Zondervan/Campus Life Books).

- Erwin W. Lutzer, *Living with Your Passions* (Victor).

- Josh McDowell and Bill Jones, *The Teenage Q&A Book* (Word).

- Josh McDowell, *Why Wait? What You Need to Know about the Teen Sexuality Crisis* (Word).

- John White, *Eros Defiled* (InterVarsity).

26

MASTURBATION

A Synopsis

❖

Introduction

Craig had never told anyone his secret.

It had started when he was twelve or thirteen, and it began almost by accident. Craig had hidden a "dirty magazine" under the covers of his bed and was looking at the pictures by flashlight when he was suddenly aware of a new feeling, a strange sensation that felt good and scary all at the same time. Moments later, he felt another new sensation.

At first he was afraid he'd wet the bed. Then, upon realizing that wasn't it, Craig grew frightened. He feared that something had gone wrong with him; he was even a little scared to go to sleep, afraid it might happen again. He didn't know what to do. But he knew he couldn't tell his mom or dad about it.

In the months and years to come, masturbation became a habit with Craig. He enjoyed it and even planned it, carefully hiding away in a private place where no one would discover his secret. He knew the guys in his gym class would make fun of him if they knew; they talked about it all the time. By the time he reached his junior year in high school, it had become an obsession with Craig. He thought about it all day long. And the slightest stimulation would make him seek release through masturbation, like a drug addict hungry for his next fix.

He tried to tell himself there was nothing wrong with his secret, but sometimes he felt so dirty and guilty he could barely stand it. And he knew he would die of shame if anyone else ever found out what he did when he was by himself.

The Problem of Masturbation

Masturbation—what Christian psychologist Gary R. Collins calls "the self-stimulation of one's genitals to the point of orgasm"[1]—is a common struggle of adolescence. It is joked about, whispered about, and worried about among teenagers.[2] It's also practiced to what many might consider a surprising degree.

Studies reveal that most young people have masturbated at least some time during their adolescence. Though the validity of his famous study has been questioned, Alfred Kinsey reported that 93 percent of adult males and 62 percent of the females he surveyed admitted to having masturbated. More recently, a study conducted by two University of Chicago sociologists and a *New York Times* science writer surveyed 3,432 Americans between the ages of eighteen and fifty-nine and discovered that 60 percent of men and 40 percent of women said they had masturbated within the past year.[3] And one of the authors of that study (with a colleague) reported in a 1967 study that 90 percent of males and 48 percent of females had masturbated during their high school years.

While masturbation certainly does not disappear after adolescence, the practice seems to be most prevalent among adolescents (Dr. Gary Collins says "frequency of masturbation declines following adolescence and after marriage"[4])—particularly among male adolescents. Dr. G. Keith Olson, author of *Counseling Teenagers,* explains:

> With onset of puberty the adolescent male is able to ejaculate, and masturbation from this point on is usually done in order to reach orgasm. Nocturnal emissions and masturbation are the two most common ways that adolescent boys release their rapidly building sexual tensions since heterosexual genital intercourse is not a sanctioned release. . . .

Masturbation has been much more of an issue for adolescent males than it has been for girls for two primary reasons. First, early and mid-adolescent girls typically do not have a strong need for genital sexual release. Their sexual arousal is satisfied for a longer period of time through being held and cuddled. Their stronger sensations of genital arousal begin occurring with more intense petting and foreplay, and especially with genital penetration. A second reason for masturbation being less of an issue for adolescent girls is that their sanctions against masturbation have been much stronger. Until quite recently masturbation in females was thought to be abnormal.[5]

Masturbation is a subject of great confusion and conflict among teens and a subject of much debate and disagreement among Christians. Some condemn it unequivocally as sin; others say it's "not much of an issue with God."[6] The wise parent, pastor, teacher, or youth leader should approach the problem carefully, seeking to understand its causes and effects as well as the biblical perspective of the problem before trying to help a young person who is struggling in this area.

The Causes of Masturbation

Adolescence is a time of monumental physical and emotional upheaval in a person's life. The changes all adolescents encounter often surprise and confuse them, and they are often ill-equipped to understand and cope with them. While this is true of all adolescents, a few factors make masturbation a greater problem for some young people.

◆ Physiological Changes

Some youth do seem to experience the physiological changes of adolescence earlier and more intensely than others. Authors Barry St. Clair and Bill Jones describe these changes as feeling "like the radiator of a car. The more the heat rises in the motor, the more the pressure builds in the radiator, until it finally explodes."[7] The pressures and urges that lead many youth to masturbate are a natural, normal part of growing up.

◆ Unhealthy/Uneducated Views of Sexuality

In addition, some kids have been raised to view any awareness of their bodies—particularly any sexual awareness—as "bad." Their parents may have slapped their hands when they explored their genitals as toddlers, or perhaps the parents avoided any discussion of puberty. Mom and Dad may have communicated that sex and sexuality were "dirty" or "perverted." Or the young people may have gotten those impressions from somewhere else. But an unhealthy and/or uneducated view of puberty and sexuality leaves some kids unprepared for the sexual urges and surges they encounter as adolescents.

◆ Rumors and Secrecy

Finally, the rumors and secrecy that so often surround the subject lead many youth to view the pressures and urges that often lead to masturbation as "weird," "perverted," or "pathetic." Consequently, they avoid confiding in parents, friends, or church leaders about their struggles—at a time when they are ill-equipped to handle such things themselves.

While many Christians view masturbation as a harmless release, the potential effects of the practice warrant serious consideration nonetheless.

The Effects of Masturbation

Teens have long whispered among themselves that the effects of masturbation include insanity and blindness. Some insist that it causes one's face to break out and one's hair to fall out. Others claim it is related to mental illness, tuberculosis, and epilepsy. These claims are, of course, false. The real effects of masturbation are much less dramatic (though perhaps just as damaging).

◆ Guilt

The study of 3,432 adults cited above reported that about half of the men and women who said they had masturbated also said they had felt guilty about it. Though he does not count masturbation as always sinful, Olson says, "The strong feelings of guilt and anxiety that accompany masturbation create problems for many teenagers."[8] (See chapter 3, "Guilt," and chapter 2, "Anxiety.")

◆ Obsession

Some young people, says Dr. Jay Adams, "are so tangled up in the masturbation problem that they hardly can think about anything else but sex all day long." He continues:

> And the more they engage in masturbation, the more they depend upon it, the more they want it, and the more they feed it. And the more they feed it, the more they are trapped by it. They are caught up in one big vicious circle. Masturbation can gain such a tenacious control over them that it saps their energies, takes their minds away from their studies, and sets them to thinking about sex everywhere they go and with every person they see.[9]

"Obsessive behavior built around masturbation and sexual fantasies," writes Dr. James Oraker, "is destructive psychologically because it nudges an individual further and further from reality, until truth itself is a stranger to the person."[10]

◆ Self-Involvement

St. Clair and Jones write:

> Control is the ability to say no to pleasing yourself in order to please another. Masturbation pleases only one person—you. Paul tells Timothy that great stress is caused when people are "lovers of self . . . [and] lovers of pleasure rather than lovers of God" (2 Timothy 3:2, 4). Masturbation is a totally self-centered act and creates more self-centeredness.[11]

◆ Objectification of Others

Since masturbation so often involves images and fantasies, it can result in the transformation of people into things. When masturbation turns a *person* into an *object* that is *used* to achieve orgasm, a destructive and dangerous mental process has begun. Randy Alcorn writes:

> Masturbation can become an obsessive and enslaving habit fueling and refueling the fire of one's lusts and lowering people to sex object status. It can become entangled with the obsessive compulsion of pornography and can lead to increasingly perverse fantasies and desires—and possibly aggression against the opposite sex.[12]

◆ Low Self-Esteem

Masturbation—and the control it can exert over a person—is one of many factors that can cause the self-esteem of a teen who is struggling to form his or her identity to falter and even crumble. Teens who engage in masturbation sometimes hate not only their actions but themselves; they are ashamed of what they do, they feel powerless to control their urges, and their self-images are often damaged by their secret behavior. (See chapter 6, "Unhealthy Self-Esteem.")

The Biblical Perspective of Masturbation

The Bible neither endorses nor condemns masturbation. In fact, it doesn't even mention it. Some passages have been interpreted in the past as accounts and condemnations of masturbation (such as Genesis 38:4–10, in which Onan is condemned for disobeying God and refusing to bear children for his dead brother), but those passages actually address homosexuality or other forms of disobedience or immorality. (See, for example, Rom. 1:24, 1 Cor. 6:9, and 1 Thess. 4:3.)

St. Clair and Jones offer helpful insight by differentiating between natural release and masturbation. They explain:

> When a person goes through puberty, he or she matures sexually. . . . Strong sexual feelings and tensions result.
>
> Many guys experience *nocturnal emissions,* often called "wet dreams". . . . [S]eminal fluid can be released through the penis while a guy is sleeping. . . . If the semen is not released through masturbation or intercourse, then nocturnal emissions are inevitable.[13]

The Bible addresses such "wet dreams" in Leviticus 15:16:

> When a man has an emission of semen, he must bathe his whole body with water, and he will be unclean till evening.

And in Deuteronomy 23:9–11:

> When you are encamped against your enemies, keep away from everything impure. If one of your men is unclean because of a nocturnal emission, he is to go outside the camp and stay there. But as evening approaches he is to wash himself, and at sunset he may return to the camp.

These passages, once thought to refer to masturbation, are recognized now as references to nocturnal emissions, an unavoidable response to a natural body function, one that cannot be controlled by the individual. There is, of course, nothing sinful about such emissions. It is not the physical release accomplished in masturbation that makes it wrong, for a similar release occurs innocently in nocturnal emissions; it is the lust that often facilitates the act of masturbation that makes it wrong. Dr. Jay Adams points out that "[I]n a very young child masturbation may be only exploratory, but before long it gets plugged into fantasizing about sexual relations with imagined sexual partners."[14]

If that occurs—if masturbation involves fantasizing about illicit sex—then it is sinful, because lust is sin.[15] (See chapter 25, "Lust.")

The Response to the Problem of Masturbation

Listen ◆ Empathize ◆ Affirm ◆ Direct ◆ Enlist ◆ Refer

Parents or other adults may believe there are few opportunities to discuss masturbation with a teen. However, the opportunity must sometimes be made. If the subject has not been broached before midadolescence, then there is every possibility that the youth (especially in the case of a male) is already struggling with masturbation. The following outline may help the parent, pastor, teacher, or youth leader deal with the subject sensitively and effectively:

LISTEN. Invite the young person to talk openly and honestly about his or her sexual urges and struggles. Assure the young person of confidentiality. Initially, speak only to make it easier for the youth to speak, never to express shock, outrage, condemnation, or revulsion. Ask questions designed to provide helpful information ("How long has this been a struggle for you?"), not to satisfy curiosity.

EMPATHIZE. It is extremely easy for parents and other adults to forget their own adolescence and minimize the struggles youth endure. But while masturbation does often decrease after adolescence, sexual passions and desires continue. Remember your own weaknesses and struggles in these areas, and use them to gain a compassionate perspective on the difficulties faced by the young person. Understand that a teen is likely to be embarrassed to discuss such matters with an adult, and even more so if he or she is uncomfortable with his or her sexuality and/or behavior. A sensitive adult (of the same sex as the young person) can communicate empathetic warmth by:

- Facing the young person directly (coming out

from behind your desk, for example, if you're in an office).

- Leaning forward in your chair to communicate interest.

- Appropriate touching (a comforting touch on the arm, for example, or a hand on the shoulder).

- Making eye contact without staring or letting your eyes wander.

- Reflecting the young person's statements by saying, "You feel . . ." or "It sounds like you're saying . . ."

- Waiting patiently through silence or tears.

AFFIRM. Adolescents who are struggling with their sexuality are likely to be uncomfortable with themselves, their appearance, and their desires. They may hate their sexual feelings. They may even hate themselves. They will need frequent assurances that they are normal, frequent messages of affirmation, and frequent expressions of appreciation.

Statements such as the following can affirm a struggling youth:

- You're not the only person to struggle with these things.

- Your feelings are normal.

- Just talking to me about this shows remarkable courage.

- I like the way you . . .

- I love you.

DIRECT. "Masturbation can be reduced," writes Collins, "by prayer, a sincere willingness to let the Holy Spirit control, involvement in busy activities involving others, an avoidance of sexually arousing material (such as erotic pictures or novels), a practice of not dwelling on harmful sexual fantasies, and a recognition that sin (including lust) will be forgiven when it is confessed with sincerity and sorrow."[16]

Subtly and sensitively direct the young person in a strategy that will most help his or her specific situation. The following is adapted from a ten-step process prescribed by St. Clair and Jones for addressing masturbation:

1. *Get honest with God.* Realize that the lustful thoughts that lead you to masturbation are a sin against God. Be honest about your sin and ask for cleansing.

2. *Nail down a stake.* A "stake" is a fixed point that marks the start of a journey. Decide that you want to please God more than you want to please yourself and make the decision to "walk by the Spirit, and you will not carry out the desire of the flesh" (Galatians 5:16 NASB).

3. *Plug into power.* Recognize that you cannot win this battle in your own power. Only Jesus Christ living in you can change your desires and habits. Begin now to have a regular, consistent time with the Lord every day.

4. *Renew your mind.* This problem started in your mind, so let God change your mind. God's way of renewing your mind is to get you into the Bible. That's where God's thoughts are found. He wants His thoughts to become your thoughts. Read one chapter of the Bible every day. Memorize one verse a week.

5. *Focus your eyes.* Keep your eyes away from anything that turns you on sexually. Obviously you can't live in a monastery, so your eyes will see sexually stimulating objects. But *don't keep on looking at them*—especially pornographic material, soap operas or R-rated movies.

6. *Control your body.* When your body feels like it will explode if some of the sexual pressure isn't let off, bring it under control with exercise, serving others, or fun physical activities (like riding a dirt bike or playing a game of one-on-one basketball with a friend).

7. *Confide in a friend.* Ask a person of the same sex who is spiritually mature to hold you accountable. Get him or her to ask you regularly if you are avoiding lust.

8. *Avoid tempting situations.* Resist a second look at a sensually dressed person, and avoid magazines and TV shows that stimulate you sexually. Be on guard when you're alone, especially where it's easy to be tempted.

9. *Press on despite failure.* If you fail, don't get discouraged. It took time to get into this habit; it will take time to get out of it. If you fall, don't lie in the dirt, but get up and dust yourself off by immediately confessing your sins and receiving God's forgiveness in faith. Don't, though, accept failure easily.

10. *Go for total victory.* You don't have to sin. You don't have to let the radiator get overheated. As you offer yourself to God (instead of to sin, as an instrument of wickedness), your sexual energy will be channeled to make you a powerful man or woman of God. Trust Christ. Obey Him. He will give you victory.[17]

ENLIST. Enlist the youth to actively respond to his or her own problem by helping him or her formulate a specific plan, complete with action steps, that will serve as a program, or guide for behavior. For example, if his greatest struggles with masturbation occur after going to bed but before going to sleep, he may decide to exercise vigorously or stay up later so that he goes to sleep faster at night. Let the youth suggest his or her own "homework," which will add to the sense of accomplishment, confidence, and reward when progress is made.

REFER. In sexual matters particularly, it is critical that an adult of the same sex as the youth offer the comfort and guidance (if a female teacher is concerned about a young man, for example, she should involve a man in offering counsel to the youth). Offering comfort to a young person of the opposite sex is a dangerous course, both to the adult and to the youth.

In addition, the wise adult will be aware of the fact that sexual problems can be particularly tenacious and can potentially harm a future marriage relationship if they are not addressed early and effectively. Be alert to the need for referral, as Collins suggests:

> Referral should be considered when counselees appear to have more complicated sexual problems than the counselor can handle, when their sexual problems are accompanied by considerable depression and/or anxiety, when there is great guilt or self-condemnation, when there are extremely disturbed behavior and thinking in the counselee . . . when the counselor is too shocked or embarrassed to continue counseling, or when he or she feels a strong and persisting sexual attraction to the counselee.[18]

For Further Reading

The following resources may help the concerned parent, pastor, teacher, or youth worker to offer guidance on the subject of masturbation:

Scriptures Cited in This Chapter

- 2 Timothy 3:2, 4
- Genesis 38:4–10
- Romans 1:24
- 1 Corinthians 6:9
- 1 Thessalonians 4:3
- Leviticus 15:16
- Deuteronomy 23:9–11
- Matthew 5:27, 28
- Galatians 5:16 NASB

Other Scripture to Read

- Job 31:1
- Proverbs 6:20–32
- Philippians 4:8
- 1 Thessalonians 4:3–7
- 1 John 2:15–17

Further Reading

- Randy Alcorn, *Christians in the Wake of the Sexual Revolution* (Multnomah).
- Verne Becker, ed., *The Campus Life Guide to Surviving High School* (Zondervan/Campus Life Books).
- Dr. James Dobson, *Preparing for Adolescence* (Regal).
- Erwin W. Lutzer, *Living with Your Passions* (Victor).
- Josh McDowell and Bill Jones, *The Teenage Q&A Book* (Word).
- Barry St. Clair and Bill Jones, *Sex: Desiring the Best* (Here's Life Publishers).
- John White, *Eros Defiled* (InterVarsity).

27

PORNOGRAPHY

A Synopsis

Introduction

Eleven-year-old Mark was sleeping over at Tim's house when his friend told him about the stack of magazines in the basement. They spent several hours that day thumbing through glossy magazines depicting air-brushed women in various nude and partially nude poses. Mark had never seen such pictures before, and he found himself thinking about Tim's magazines frequently. In the months to come, he seized every opportunity to visit his friend and revisit the secret stack of fantasy women.

He and Tim still played basketball together. They still rode bikes back and forth to each other's house. They still watched cartoons and sitcom reruns together. But they did those things less frequently than before because whenever they had the chance, they would return to the magazines in Tim's basement.

Over the next few years, Mark's interest in such diversions grew. He and Tim raided Tim's father's video collection and devised a way of making copies of the best tapes, which Mark hid under the insulation in the attic. Then one day, Mark unexpectedly hit a gold mine.

Mark liked to "chat" with friends in a "chat room" section of a computer online service his family subscribed to. One day he logged on to the service and discovered E-mail addressed to him from a stranger. The message contained a strange file and included instructions on how to download the file. He downloaded the file, and soon an arrangement of ten photos appeared on his computer screen depicting men and women engaged in various forms of heterosexual and homosexual sex.

Mark saved the images and learned from the author of the E-mail where to find similar—and more perverse—photos, stories, and film clips on the Internet. He shared the materials with his friend Tim, and the two of them quickly began to cultivate another "stash" of pornographic materials—the folders and files of the family's personal computer.

What began as a "harmless" game to eleven-year-old Mark became an obsession by his thirteenth birthday and, when Mark was fourteen, resulted in his disappearance. Authorities later determined that Mark was coaxed into a live meeting by an online acquaintance—a meeting from which he never returned.

The Problem of Pornography

Pornography—"the depiction or portrayal of either sexual activity or the sexual organs for financial gain or reward"[1]—is a multibillion-dollar industry that includes pornographic magazines and novels, X-rated movie theaters and video stores, topless bars and peep shows, "phone sex," and "computer sex." Annual revenues from such products and pursuits are estimated to exceed eight to twelve billion dollars a year, and they're growing.[2] It is so widespread that an investigation by the U.S. Senate Judiciary Committee stated, "Adult bookstores outnumber McDonald's restaurants in the U.S. by a margin of at least three to one."[3]

Pornography is not limited to the air-brushed models depicted in *Playboy* and *Penthouse* either; the vast bulk of pornography is more prurient, more perverse, and more deviant than most people can imagine.

A 1995 study of online porn by a team of researchers at Carnegie Mellon University in Pittsburgh, Pennsylvania, surveyed nearly *a million* sexually explicit pictures, captions, stories, and movie clips. The study revealed a preponderance of examples of pedophilia (pornography featuring children as subjects), hebephilia (pornography featuring youths), and paraphilia (other "deviant" material, including sadism, masochism, urination, defecation, sodomy, and bestiality).

Such material is not purchased, downloaded, or viewed exclusively by adults; a disturbing number of children and young people are exposed to such material:

> In one recent study by Dr. Jennings Bryant, 600 males and females of junior high school age and above were interviewed about their . . . "real life involvement with pornography." He found that 91 percent of the males and 82 percent of the females indicated having been exposed to X-rated hard core pornography.[4]

And churched youth—kids from Christian homes—are involved in pornography to a disturbing degree. The "Right from Wrong" survey of 3,765 churched youth revealed that one in six (16 percent) of Christian teens had watched an X-rated movie in the three months prior to the study.[5]

Many parents and pastors may be surprised at how easy it is for teenagers—even pre-teens—to obtain pornographic material. It is not only *available* in today's youth culture, however—it is *prevalent*.

The Causes of Pornography

◆ Curiosity

Pornography is nothing new. It has been around since ancient times. Humans are naturally curious creatures, and their curiosity extends to sexual matters as well. Xenophon, the Greek general and writer, told of discovering a tribe of people who "freely copulated in the streets like dogs." Xenophon was repulsed by such behavior, yet "even Xenophon," the story concludes, "did not immediately avert his eyes."

◆ Dehumanization of Sex

But curiosity does not account for the recent explosion of circulation and availability of pornographic materials, and the extension of such availability to minors. Other factors are at work as well. Authors Alexandra and Vernon H. Mark suggest:

> One answer is that sex . . . has been dehumanized. It is not regarded as a loving, responsible relationship, but as a sport, and in that light it is not surprising that intercourse and the sexual organs should be thought to be fit for viewing.[6]

◆ Cultural Obsession

Pornography is also fueled by modern culture's obsession with anything sexual and endorsement (tacit, if not active) of all manner of deviancy. In a world that seems to be constantly changing, there seems to be an ever-increasing market for "new" and "imaginative" forms of degeneracy. For many, it seems that initial involvement in pornography is curious and erotic in nature; advanced involvement, however, tends to play "as much on fear, anxiety . . . and taboo as on genuine eroticism."[7]

The Effects of Pornography

Many advocates of pornography (some in the name of free speech) insist that pornography is a harmless diversion, a "victimless" pursuit that has no effect on those involved in it. Professor Norman Anderson of the University of London has said:

> If what men read and view has no effect whatever on them, why do industry and commerce spend millions . . . each year in advertising (and pornography, it may be noted in passing, has more than a little of the nature of advertisement)?[8]

Pornography does indeed affect participants in many and deleterious ways.

◆ Sexual Addiction

Pornography frequently plays a key role in sexual addiction. A person—almost always a male—becomes involved in pornography; with increased exposure comes increased desire for such material, until he is addicted to the release he achieves as a result of the visual stimulus pornography offers. An escalation to more severe, "kinkier" material often follows until his addiction drives him, not only to seek constant release through pornography, but also to seek release by acting out the behaviors that now stimulate him.

Such a cycle may take weeks or months, but it is dangerously common among those who are regularly exposed to pornography. The experi-

ence related below, adapted from testimony presented to the Attorney General's (1986) Commission on Pornography, is typical:

> In 1972, the year we first met, Tom introduced me to pornography. . . . He treated this information as normal, and so I began to read.
>
> We discussed some of the techniques described in the magazines, and eventually Tom began to experiment. . . . For the next 11 years I would wonder what was wrong with me sexually.
>
> In the fall of 1975 I found out Tom was having sex with many of our friends. . . . During this time I felt rejected. . . . Tom swore he did not use prostitutes, but he [admitted he] did fantasize quite a bit with magazines. . . . Once in this sexual dry spell, Tom tried to get me to have sex with one of my friends (his lover). I was so dead inside that all I could do was watch the two of them and feel disgust and contempt for myself because I had allowed my marriage to get to this point.
>
> In 1981 we moved back to Houston, after Tom could no longer function in his job. I thought at the time that his boss was mean to him and that he was overworked. Now I know that he could no longer partake in the daily and hourly use of pornographic magazines, theaters, and shops because he had to account for his time.
>
> The years 1981–1982 were also the beginning of our financial downfall. Money had disappeared mysteriously over the years. Tom would not let me have access to our finances. I thought . . . he liked to pay the bills and keep the records. . . . [But in fact, much] of our joint income was spent on sex in porno houses, porno magazines at $10 per copy, and the hotel rooms and movie theaters he frequented.[9]

Tom's wife went on to relate before the commission how his sexual addiction cost him his job, his home, his wife, and his family.

◆ Sexual Pathology

Individuals who have been exposed to pornography are susceptible to sexual pathology. In the study by Dr. Jennings Bryant cited above:

Two thirds of the males and 40 percent of the females reported wanting to try out some of the sexual behaviors they had witnessed [in pornographic materials]. And 25 percent of the males and 15 percent of the females admitted to actually doing some of the things sexually they had seen in the pornography within a few days after exposure. This powerfully suggests the modeling effect or "imitative learning" effect that pornography can have on human sexual behavior. In addition he found that massive exposure (e.g., over 6 weeks) to pornography was able to change the attitudes and feelings of their subjects in the direction of making sexual improprieties and transgressions seem less bad, the victims of such transgressions were perceived to suffer less, and be less severely wronged.[10]

The above study also showed a correlation between pornography and teen deviancy and promiscuity:

In their study, impressive in its rigorous methodology and statistical treatment, they concluded that, "One finds exposure to pornography is the strongest predictor of sexual deviance among the early age of exposure subjects (young teens). In the early age of exposure (to pornography) subgroup, the amount of exposure was significantly correlated with a willingness to engage in group sexual relations, frequency of homosexual intercourse and serious sexual deviance; and there were trends for the number of both high school heterosexual partners and total homosexual partners to be positively related to (pornographic) exposure."[11]

◆ Undesirable Memories

Exposure to pornographic stimuli can result in vivid memories of the images or experiences, which may surface at unpredictable and undesirable moments. According to the *AFA Journal*:

Epinephrine is a chemical which is secreted into the bloodstream by the adrenal gland when the porn addict indulges in his habit. Epinephrine goes to the brain and locks in the visual (or auditory, e.g. Dial-A-Porn) stimulus present at the time. The addict's mind is polluted with sexually explicit images. Furthermore, he will remember these images without trying, and he will see them regardless of his desire to forget them.[12]

◆ Disrespect toward Women

Psychologist Dolf Zillman of the University of Indiana studied the effects of nonviolent pornographic movies on the viewers. He concluded that:

. . . men began to view women as insatiably sexual playthings; that men become more aggressive toward women; and that they begin to view rape as a trivial offense—something that all women secretly desire. "There can be no doubt," he concluded, "that pornography, as a form of primarily male entertainment, promotes the victimization of women."[13]

Psychologist Edward Donnerstein of the University of Wisconsin, like Zillman one of the country's preeminent researchers, conducted similar research in which he studied the effects of pornographic violence (mutilation, rape, sexual murder, etc.) on men's attitudes toward women. He similarly concluded that a steady diet of such fare desensitizes men to violence and prompts them to trivialize rape.[14]

◆ Unrealistic Expectations

Individuals who have become involved in pornography often exhibit unrealistic expectations, both of their partners' appearance and behavior. The man whose mind has been exposed repeatedly to air-brushed depictions of femininity may be less able to appreciate the unretouched beauty of his wife's form, however attractive she may be.

Exposure to pornography may also foster unrealistic expectations of performance. Unscripted, unstaged moments of intimacy seldom duplicate scenes in a movie or magazine, and the endurance and performance of legitimate partners seldom equal that of porn models and actresses.

Moreover, a person who is indulging in pornography may experience frustration in trying to persuade others to duplicate or equal the scenes and experiences depicted in pornographic materials. Resistance, fear, and discomfort are hardly conducive to maximum sex and intimacy.

◆ Fear, Guilt, and Shame

Added to the other effects of pornography is the experience of fear engendered by involvement with pornography. Young people (as well as many adults) who experiment with pornography do so in secret, and therefore must live in perpetual fear of discovery by parents, teachers, church friends, etc. Such fear not only causes discomfort in the present, but can inhibit wholesome sexual enjoyment in the future, causing such a person to associate fear with sexual pleasure, leading to other sexual pathologies such as voyeurism, exhibitionism, etc.

Guilt also accompanies exposure to pornography.

The Biblical Perspective of Pornography

Our modern word *pornography* actually comes from the ancient Greek word *porne* [por-nay], a noun used to refer to a prostitute (see Luke 15:30, 1 Cor. 6:15, etc.). It was the root of the Greek word for sexual immorality, *pornos*.

However, to arrive at the biblical perspective of the problem, we must consider what pornography accomplishes—sexual titillation and/or release with the aid of someone or something other than a husband or wife. That is the very activity the Bible forbids with the commands, "Flee sexual immorality [*porneian*]" (1 Cor. 6:18) and "abstain from sexual immorality [*porneais*]" (1 Thess. 4:3 NASB).

The "sex without persons" that pornography offers is a dismissal of God's design for sex: "For this reason a man will leave his father and mother and be united to his wife, and they will become one flesh" (Gen. 2:24).[15] God designed sex to be used within the intimacy of a marriage relationship for the purpose of procreation (for the purpose of having children and creating a family),[16] identification (for the purpose of developing "oneness" between a husband and wife in three important dimensions—the physical, psychological, and spiritual),[17] and recreation (for the purpose of pleasure and enjoyment).[18] Pornography accomplishes none of these purposes.

Finally, the values fostered by pornography are anti-biblical and anti-Christ. Dr. Bryant reports that:

> . . . the values which permeate the content of most hardcore pornography [involve] an almost total suspension of the sorts of moral judgment that have been espoused in the value systems of most civilized cultures. Forget trust. Forget family. Forget commitment. Forget love. Forget marriage.[19]

Pornography encourages that which the Bible forbids and eschews that which the Bible commands. In short, involvement in pornography is sin of the most harmful and unhealthy kind. The child or teen who has become involved in pornography must be kindly and carefully counseled away from such involvement.

The Response to the Problem of Pornography

Listen ◆ Empathize ◆ Affirm ◆ Direct ◆ Enlist ◆ Refer

The youth leader can help a young person who has exposed himself (or, in the rare case, herself) to pornography by patiently and sensitively implementing a plan such as the following:

LISTEN. A young person who has been involved in pornography will be unlikely to talk freely, certainly not at first. Be careful and diligent to communicate an attitude of acceptance, understanding, and willingness to listen. Assure the young person of confidentiality.

Patiently encourage him to relate how his involvement began, how it has progressed, and his latest struggles in that area. Especially try to lead him to discuss the *reasons* he turns to pornography.

EMPATHIZE. Try to remember your own experiences as a youth and the struggles you may have faced coping with hormonal changes and the discovery of a sex drive. The young person will most likely feel alone; he may think that no one can truly understand what he is going through. A spirit of empathy can help immensely.

A concerned adult can create an atmosphere of empathic warmth by:

- Facing the young person directly (coming out from behind your desk, for example, if you're in an office).
- Leaning forward in your chair to communicate interest.
- Appropriate touching among persons of the same sex (a comforting touch on the arm, for example, or a hand on the shoulder).
- Making eye contact without staring.
- Nodding your head.
- Reflecting the young person's statements ("You feel . . ." or "It sounds like you're saying . . .").
- Waiting patiently through silence or tears.

AFFIRM. Realize that the young person who has confessed to involvement in pornography may be overwhelmed with shame. Help him realize that sexual desires are normal, that they are especially pronounced in the teen years,

and that learning to control and channel them is a primary challenge of adolescence. Some of the most affirming steps you can take are to:

- Gently lead him or her to confession and repentance of past sin, being careful to let the Holy Spirit (not you) convict of sin.
- Help the young person receive and acknowledge God's love and forgiveness.
- Consistently affirm your acceptance of and love for the youth clearly, verbally.
- Guide the youth to understand that God loves—and *delights in*—him or her. (See Ps. 18:19.)
- Reinforce the young person's positive traits and abilities ("I appreciate your spiritual sensitivity," "You said that so well!").

DIRECT. Once the young person has verbalized his need and his desire to change his behavior and has repented and experienced God's forgiveness and restoration, he may be ready to receive further guidance. Impress upon him that it will not be easy to "abstain from sexual immorality," but that it is God's will for him. (See 1 Thess. 4:3.) Remind him of the reasons he cited for turning to pornography, and help him brainstorm ways to address and/or counter those needs or urges in other ways (exercise, social gatherings, etc.). Ideas may include:

1. Make fellowship with God top priority. A consistent devotional habit is the first line of defense against sin. (See Col. 2:6–15 and Gal. 5:16.)

2. Be transformed by the renewing of your mind. (See Rom. 12:1–2.) High school chemistry taught you that a liquid forces gas out of a test tube; similarly, pure thoughts can force impure thoughts out of your mind. When your mind begins to wander, immediately replace your impure thoughts with pure thoughts. (See Phil. 4:8.) This process can be encouraged by

Christian music and books, by wholesome companions, and through the memorization of Scripture.

3. *Memorize at least one verse of Scripture each week* (for example, Rom. 12:1–2; Ps. 51:10; Col. 3:1–3; Ps. 119:9, 11; 1 Cor. 10:13; and Phil. 4:8). Recite the verses out loud when temptation hits.

4. *Actively flee temptation.* Dispose of all pornographic materials in your possession. Identify (then avoid) places where temptation abounds. Avoid stores that display pornographic material. Give up watching TV talk shows, soap operas, and cable movie channels. Refuse to enter video stores that rent pornographic material. Determine to sign on to the computer interactive service only when Mom and Dad are home. If Mom and Dad are into pornography, consider asking them to lock up all materials, to place a "block" on certain cable channels, etc.

5. *Counter the roots of lust by countering inactivity with exercise and proper diet* and by avoiding large blocks of time alone.

6. *Cultivate healthy friendships with members of the opposite sex* that allow you to see them as people to be respected, not as objects to be used.

7. *Establish accountability.* James 5:16 says, "Confess your sins to each other and pray for each other so that you may be healed." Become accountable to at least one other person with the agreement that you will meet weekly to report on your success or failure in battling pornography.

8. *Plan for victory, but if you fail, remember that you have One who speaks to the Father in your defense, who is faithful and just to forgive you and purify you anew (1 John 1:9, 2:1).*

ENLIST. Subtly guide the young person to devise his own plan for handling temptation. Suggest that the youth write down his or her goals or perhaps even enter into a "contract" of goals with a parent or other adult. Encourage "ownership" of both the problem and the solution.

REFER. In sexual matters particularly, it is critical that an adult of the same sex as the youth offer the comfort and guidance (if a female teacher is concerned about a young man, for example, she should involve a man in offering counsel to the youth). Offering comfort to a young person of the opposite sex is a dangerous course, both to the adult and to the youth. If the youth has been involved in pornography for some time, it may be wise to encourage him to seek out biblical counseling from a professional (with parental permission). The effects of pornography can be tenacious and can cause harm long after the cessation of involvement. It is in the best interests of the youth—and his or her future spouse—to obtain further counseling.

For Further Reading

The following resources may help the concerned parent, pastor, teacher, or youth worker to assist a young person who has been involved in pornography:

Scriptures Cited in This Chapter

- Luke 15:30

- 1 Corinthians 6:15, 18; 10:13

- 1 Thessalonians 4:3 NASB

- Genesis 1:18; 2:24

- Proverbs 5:18–19

- Colossians 2:6–15; 3:1–3

- Galatians 5:16

- Romans 12:1–2

- Philippians 4:8

- Psalm 51:10; 119:9–10

- James 5:16

- 1 John 1:9; 2:1

Other Scripture to Read

- Job 31:1
- Proverbs 6:23–28
- Matthew 5:27–28
- 1 Thessalonians 4:3–7
- 2 Timothy 2:22
- James 1:14–15
- 1 Peter 2:11

Further Reading

- John White, *Eros Defiled* (InterVarsity).

- Erwin W. Lutzer, *Living with Your Passions* (Victor).

- Dr. James Dobson, *Life on the Edge* (Word). Contains a helpful chapter on pornography.

- Josh McDowell and Bill Jones, *The Teenage Q&A Book* (Word).

28

PREMARITAL SEX

A Synopsis

Introduction

Melinda didn't want to go to the party in the first place. She was a Christian, and she knew enough to stay away from places like the party at Matt Barnes's house. But her boyfriend, Jason, had tried hard to persuade her; she finally gave in and agreed to go.

At the party, Jason started acting "weird" and ignored Melinda's repeated pleas to leave. He started drinking beer and even offered a can to Melinda. She refused, but then it seemed like everyone in the house tried to get her to drink, so she finally accepted a can from someone she didn't even know.

Jason had disappeared from her side almost as soon as they entered the house; she finally located him in the kitchen, sipping beer and laughing with Jennifer Crandall, the pretty blonde who made every girl at school flush with jealousy. Moments later, slow music began playing in Matt Barnes's living room, and to Melinda's surprise Jennifer grabbed Jason's hand and led him toward the music. Melinda watched them dancing, slow and close; Jennifer was obviously enjoying it.

Melinda felt like running out, but she couldn't; she had no way to get home unless Jason drove her. *I can't compete with Jennifer Crandall,* she thought.

The dance ended and Jason strode over to her, leaned a hand on the wall above her head, and kissed her on the cheek.

"You don't mind me dancing with Jennifer, do you? *She* asked *me,*" he said.

Melinda shook her head and tried to smile. He held out his hand and asked her to dance. She set the beer can on the floor by the wall and joined him on the dance floor. The music—and the beer—intoxicated her, and she determined to hold on to Jason. She pressed her body against his, and they danced slowly and passionately. She felt the warmth of his body, smelled his cologne, drank in his whispered words, and gripped his shoulders as if she would never let him go. When the music ended and Jason suggested they find someplace to be alone, Melinda didn't hesitate.

Moments later, Melinda dressed in a strange bedroom and fought back tears. Jason kissed her forehead and suggested they join the others downstairs.

"Just take me home," she said.

The Problem of Premarital Sex

According to George Barna of the Barna Research Group, only 23 percent of the post baby boomer generation claim to be virgins. More than three-quarters admit to having sexual intercourse with another single person. Two out of ten single members of that generation say they have had sex with a married person, and of those who are married, one in fourteen has had extramarital sex. Almost half (47 percent) of the babies born to that generation in 1992 were born to unmarried mothers.[1] And the *New York Times* reports that "Some studies indicate three-fourths of all girls have had sex during their teen-age years and 15 percent have had four or more partners."[2]

And girls are having sex much earlier these days; the median age for a young woman's first act of premarital sex has fallen from nineteen in 1960 to seventeen in 1990. Dr. Liana Clark, a Philadelphia physician, says that most of her patients become sexually active at thirteen.[3]

Sexual activity among churched youth is likewise disturbing. By age eighteen, 27 percent have experienced sexual intercourse, and 55 percent have engaged in fondling breasts.

Research indicates that youth apparently become less—not more—resistant as they mature. From the youngest segment (eleven to twelve years old) to the next age category (thirteen to fourteen), the proportion of kids involved in heavy kissing doubles; the fondling of breasts increases fivefold; the fondling of genitals increases by a factor of seven; and the incidence of intercourse (experienced by 1 percent of the youngest age group) increases eight times (to one in eleven) through the course of the teen years.

Activity at each level of sexual involvement—fondling of breasts, fondling of genitals, sexual intercourse—doubles among fifteen- to sixteen-year-olds (compared to those in the next youngest age group). By the age of sixteen, two in five (41 percent) have engaged in (or permitted) the fondling of breasts; nearly one in three (30 percent) have fondled genitals; about one in five (18 percent) have taken part in sexual intercourse (see Table 28A).

TABLE 28A. SEXUAL ACTIVITY WITH PERSONS OF THE OPPOSITE SEX, BY AGE GROUP (CHURCHED YOUTH)[4]

ACTIVITY	ALL	Age 11–12	Age 13–14	Age 15–16	Age 17–18
Held hands	89%	74%	84%	92%	95%
Embracing & some kissing	73%	39%	65%	80%	86%
Heavy "French" kissing	53%	15%	38%	61%	74%
Fondling of breasts	34%	4%	20%	41%	55%
Fondling of genitals	26%	2%	14%	30%	44%
Sexual intercourse	15%	1%	8%	18%	27%

Reprinted from *Right from Wrong: What You Need to Know to Help Youth Make Right Choices* by Josh McDowell and Bob Hostetler (Word, 1994).

A majority are involved in heavy kissing and fondling of breasts by the time they reach the seventeen- to eighteen-year-old age group. About two-thirds of the boys of that age have fondled breasts, an increase of thirty-four percent over the next youngest age group; nearly half of seventeen- and eighteen-year-old boys and girls have fondled the genitals of at least one other person, a 47 percent increase. And, due to a 50 percent rise in the incidence of intercourse among seventeen- to eighteen-year-olds (compared to the next youngest age group), over one in four (27 percent) admit to having gone "all the way."

The Causes of Premarital Sex

It has been said that the typical high school student "faces more sexual temptation on his way to school each morning than his grandfather did on Saturday night when he was out looking for it!"[5] Today's youth do seem to be more aware of sex, more bombarded with sexually oriented messages, and more susceptible to the dangers of illicit sex than previous generations.

The causes of sexual activity among teens are myriad, and trying to untangle why a young person becomes sexually active is often like attempting to untie the Gordian knot. However, while the various causes and influences on sexual activity among youth may be numerous and interrelated, some are more widespread and more significant than others.

◆ Educational and Societal Messages

Youth become sexually involved for many reasons, not the least of which are the messages that are often thrown at them by society in general and by educational programs in particular. The *Playboy* philosophy ("If it feels good, do it") has taken root and born fruit in Western society; youth are routinely exposed to images and messages that encourage sex of all kinds, including adolescent sex and nonmarital sex.

For example, an adolescent curriculum prepared for Planned Parenthood of Alameda-San Francisco referred to the "myth" that "young women who have more than one sexual partner are easy. Some people, both men and women, prefer to relate sexually to more than one person at a time. This is an individual preference." In a magazine published with federal support, Dr. Harvey Caplan wrote, "If we have sex for our own reasons and have carefully considered birth control, VD risks, and other consequences, then there is nothing wrong with sexual activities."[6]

Such messages, of course, may contribute to a young person's decision to become sexually active.

◆ Low Level of Religious Commitment

Thornton and Camburn (1989) documented a two-edged relationship between religious commitment and sexual attitudes and activity. Their research supported the conclusions of earlier researchers that "more frequent attendance at religious services leads to more restrictive attitudes concerning premarital sex and less sexual experience."

They identified also, however, the flip side of that relationship between religious commitment and sexual behavior. Not only does religious commitment affect sexual behavior, but sexual behavior also affects religious commitment. "The empirical estimates indicate that permissive attitudes toward premarital sex reduce attendance at religious services."[7]

◆ Family Structure

The effects of divorce and other family disruption and separation have been documented in numerous studies. One of those effects is sexual activity.

Flewelling and Bauman (1990) concluded "a consistent pattern of significant relationships between family structure and young adolescents' involvement with . . . sexual intercourse."[8] Marital disruption (separation, divorce, etc.) and family structure (single-parent family, step-families, blended families, etc.) play a measurable role in a young person's vulnerability to sexual activity.

Children of intact families are generally more prepared to counter the many influences and enticements to sexual involvement (see chapter 19, "Parental Divorce," and chapter 20, "Living in a Single-Parent Family").

◆ Poor Sex Education at Home

Sociologist Brent Miller reported that the more openly parents discussed their sex-related values and beliefs with teens, the less their children displayed either negative sexual attitudes or promiscuous sexual behavior.[9]

Another publication reports:

> Most parents did not learn about sexuality from their parents and thus lack role models to help them in approaching their own children; they often perceive themselves to be uninformed about sexuality and may be confused about the sexual values they wish to communicate to their children. A survey of 1400 parents of children aged 3–11 found that less than 15 percent of mothers and 8 percent of fathers had ever talked to their children about premarital sex or sexual intercourse[10]

Another researcher found the following:

> In one . . . study, 80 percent of mothers with daughters aged 11–14 had talked about menstruation; however, only 4 percent had explained in any detail the relationship between menstruation and pregnancy.[11]

Kids who don't find the answers at home often learn the answers by painful experience. In the words of one teen, "Teenagers are ignorant about what they are doing. All they know is that they were made with certain body parts, so they might as well find out what they're used for. Sort of like test-driving a car just to see how well it performs."[12]

◆ Relational Needs

Many young people are uncertain of their parents' love. Several thousand high school students were asked, "What one question would you like your parents to answer truthfully?" Fifty percent responded, "Do you really love me?" One teen girl wrote:

> When I was eight years old, I first had sex with a boy of 15. I did it because I lacked love and attention from my parents. I need love, and my parents never show me any. Nothing changed at home, and at 15 I became pregnant. . . . [and] had an abortion. Now I'm afraid to date anyone, and I cry myself to sleep every night.[13]

Kim Cox, a health educator at Balboa High School in San Francisco, says kids are "moved to sex, many of them, not by compassion or love or any of the other urges that make sense to adults, but by a need for intimacy that has gone unfulfilled by their families. . . . Sex is an easy way to get it."[14]

One teen confessed, "We are all running around needing to get hugged. . . . The dilemma for some . . . is that 'if I want to be touched, if I want to be held, I have to have sex.'"[15]

◆ Early Dating

Early dating may lead to early sex, according to research performed by Brent C. Miller of Utah State University and Terrence D. Olsen of Brigham Young University. The researchers studied twenty-four hundred teens, concluding:

> The younger a girl begins to date, the more likely she is to have sex before graduating from high school. It is also true of boys and girls who go steady in the ninth grade. Of girls who begin dating at twelve, 91 percent had sex before graduation—compared to 56 percent who dated at thirteen, 53 percent who dated at fourteen, 40 percent who dated at fifteen, and 20 percent who dated at sixteen. Of boys with a ninth-grade steady, 70 percent said that they'd had sex com-

pared to 60 percent of girls. Of boys who dated occasionally as freshmen, 52 percent had sex compared to 35 percent of girls.[16]

◆ Peer Pressure

A study of a thousand teenagers showed that 76 percent would go far enough sexually to feel experienced and not feel left out.[17] While some teens claim that peer pressure is over-emphasized by adults, most will admit that youths' need for acceptance and affirmation is a driving force behind many of their actions.

Teens who are not sexually active often face overwhelming pressure from friends, media, and others to "join the crowd." Avowed virgins are often made to feel immature or odd. Peer pressure operates as a kind of moral blackmail, using the group's power to accept or reject as a means of producing conformity. A magazine article put the problem this way:

> Once chastity was something to be guarded— or lied about when lost. Now an uncommonly virtuous teenager lies to protect the dirty little secret that she is still a virgin. There is more pressure than ever for a girl to "get it over with."[18]

Regardless of how untrue the perception that "everyone is doing it" may be, peer pressure nonetheless influences many youth into premature sexual involvement. (See chapter 14, "Handling Peer Pressure.")

◆ Alcohol and Drugs

The use of alcohol and other drugs hastens many kids' sexual involvement. (See chapter 38, "Alcohol Use and Abuse," and chapter 39, "Drug Use and Abuse.") One researcher had this to say about the relationship between drugs and teenage sex:

> Perhaps most striking . . . is the association between drinking and loss of virginity.
> Perhaps because alcohol is the most socially acceptable drug, our interviewers found it associ-

ated to a great extent with teens' first intercourse. This was particularly true of unplanned intercourse. . . . Sometimes it was boys who were surprised (a 13-year-old who was "kind of counting on fooling around" lost his virginity after his date "had taken booze out of her parents' liquor cabinet so we got pretty drunk"), but it was more often girls. One New York 15-year-old who had not even been out on a date told us, "I had a party . . . in my house—my mother goes away every weekend and so I have a lot of parties—and so all of us were there, and all our mutual friends and stuff. And four or five people slept over that night, and we were both pretty drunk and sort of just fell asleep together and got more involved as the night went on. I don't think he made the first move; I'm pretty sure I did."[19]

◆ Desire for a Child

Although most youth want desperately to avoid becoming pregnant, some teenage girls are motivated to become sexually active by a desire to have a child. She may feel so bad about herself and so unloved that she tries intentionally to have a child, someone she can love and who will love her back. She may see a child as a "declaration of independence" from her parents, or as a "badge of maturity" among her friends; it may be a means of persuading a boy to marry her or even as a means of revenge against a parent or a former boyfriend. (See chapter 29, "Unplanned Pregnancy.")

The Effects of Premarital Sex

The effects of premarital sex are many and dangerous. The physical consequences can include:

Loss of virginity

An unwanted pregnancy

An illegitimate child

Forced marriage

Abortion

Sexually transmitted diseases

Beyond those tragic physical effects, however, are the devastating psychological and relational problems that often accompany or follow premarital sex, including guilt, emotional distress, broken relationships, self-hatred, sexual addiction, and spiritual bondage.

◆ Guilt

Like any form of immorality and disobedience of God's commands, nonmarital sex results in guilt. One survey of college students reported that nearly 60 percent of those who had nonmarital sex said it produced "tremendous guilt."[20]

As one woman testified, "I became sexually involved with my fiancé. We had convinced ourselves that sex outside of marriage was all right for us since we were engaged, but the Holy Spirit was convicting me that it was wrong. I felt incredibly guilty." (See also chapter 3, "Guilt.")

◆ Emotional Distress

The emotional costs of sexual immorality are immeasurable. One teen explained the effects of her sexual involvement in these words:

Having premarital sex was the most horrifying experience of my life. It wasn't at all the emotionally satisfying experience the world deceived me into believing. I felt as if my insides were being exposed and my heart left unattended. . . . I know God has forgiven me of this haunting sin, but I also know I can never have my virginity back. I dread the day that I have to tell the man I truly love and wish to marry that he is not the only one, though I wish he were. . . . I have stained my life—a stain that will never come out.

Another girl described her experience this way:

After you've done it, you're really attached to that guy. It's as if he's your life; you feel really vul-nerable. [When the relationship ended, I felt] really awful. I can't describe it. About a week after we had sex, we broke up because I found out he was dating other girls. It really hurt.

Sexual immorality (whether premarital or extramarital) breeds suspicion, disappointment, sorrow, stress, emptiness, and many other destructive emotions.

◆ Broken Relationships

The survey cited above reported that 50 percent of males attributed the breakup of a relationship to sexual involvement; 26 percent of females made the same assessment.

In the words of one teen, "Sex . . . hurt[s] a relationship, [and] it also makes it harder for a couple to break up." Premarital sex often makes participants feel trapped; it hinders intimate conversation and trust; it can cause one or both participants to feel used; and, when a breakup does occur, it can be "a terribly tearing experience emotionally."[21]

◆ Self-Hatred

Premarital sex has a serious adverse affect on the self-image of the person engaging in it. As Manhattan sex therapist Shirley Zussman says, "Being part of a meat market is appalling in terms of self-esteem."

Low self-esteem, which is among the causes of premarital sexual involvement, is also among its results. Sexual involvement outside marriage will often exacerbate a person's feelings of self-doubt, insecurity, humiliation, and self-loathing. (See chapter 6, "Unhealthy Self-Esteem.")

◆ Sexual Addiction

The survey of college students cited above also revealed that 44 percent of males and 26 percent of females said that premarital sexual intercourse produced "an intense desire for more."

Trying to fill a spiritual vacuum with physical pleasure (an impossibility), sexually active teens can become swallowed up in their sexual pursuits. The sexuality that started out as a desire soon becomes the master, demanding to be sated, yet never knowing fulfillment.

One young person related his experience:

> I began to notice that the more I had, the more I wanted. I had always heard the excuse that having sex was the way to get rid of sexual tension, but the opposite was true. Having sex increased the desire. It was like a drug. I couldn't stop myself, yet at the same time I wasn't satisfied at all. The people I knew who were outright promiscuous were even worse than I was—it was all they ever talked about and evidently all they ever thought about. It controlled them; they never controlled it. Sex was an all-consuming fire that never burned out, but instead burned them out.[22]

◆ Spiritual Bondage

Sex is often the means by which the adversary (see 1 Pet. 5:8) binds young men and women spiritually and prods them into other risks and behaviors that endanger them physically, emotionally, and spiritually. Sexual involvement hinders a young person's walk with God, sometimes prompts a slackening of religious commitment (see "Low Level of Religious Commitment" earlier in this chapter), and traps him or her in a cycle of pressure and powerlessness.

Furthermore, studies (such as Elliott and Morse, 1989) have charted the relationships between premarital sex and other forms of delinquency and immorality. A teen who engages in illicit sexual activity is more spiritually vulnerable to other temptations as well.

The Biblical View of Premarital Sex

To put sex into God's perspective we need to go back to the beginning: "And the Lord God formed man of the dust of the ground, and breathed into his nostrils the breath of life; and man became a living soul" (Gen. 2:7 KJV). Adam was the culmination of God's creative plan. "God saw everything that he had made, and, behold, it was very good" (Gen. 1:31 KJV).

Yet, after the creation of man, God observed that something was *not* good. "And the LORD God said, It is not good that the man should be alone" (Gen. 2:18 KJV). God's creation, although good, was incomplete. God had "created man in his own image" (Gen. 1:27 KJV). This made man a social being, because God Himself is a social being. Anyone created in "God's image" has the God-given ability to relate to others—to God and to creatures like Himself. Good as God's creation was, it was not good that man was alone.

It is worthwhile noting that God didn't solve Adam's loneliness problem by creating more men. Instead, He created woman. "Eve was like Adam, yet unlike Him. Same humanity, different gender. Man and woman were equal but not the same. Their oneness was not a uniformity stemming from sameness but a unity transcending differentness."[23] With the debut of the second sex, God's creation was complete.

It is important for young people to feel good about being male and female and to accept their sexuality as a gift from God. The psalmist said, "I praise you because I am fearfully and wonderfully made" (Ps. 139:14). The creation of the human body, with its sex drives and organs, is something to thank God for. There are no reasons to be ashamed. From the beginning, human sexuality is seen as a reflection of the character of God and its existence is described as "very good."

Three things form the fundamental biblical perspective of sex:

1. God is pro-sex. He created sex, and He wants people to enjoy it to the fullest.

2. Sexual intercourse is intended to accomplish:

- *Procreation* (for the purpose of having children and creating a family).[24]

- *Identification* (for the purpose of developing "oneness" between a husband and wife in three important dimensions—the physical, psychological, and spiritual).[25]

- *Recreation* (for the purpose of pleasure and enjoyment).[26]

3. God designed sex for marriage. It is meant to take place between a husband and wife. When, according to God's plan, sex is experienced within the context of marriage, the pleasure is maximized. In the commitment of marriage—without guilt, shame, or insecurity—the act of intercourse becomes indescribably enjoyable and beautiful.

The Response to the Problem of Premarital Sex

Listen ◆ Empathize ◆ Affirm ◆ Direct ◆ Enlist ◆ Refer

The youth leader can help a young man or woman deal with premarital sexual activity by implementing the follow plan:

LISTEN. A young person who has become sexually involved may desperately need a listening ear. It will probably not be easy for him or her to talk freely about the activity, so your initial efforts should be focused on helping the youth feel comfortable in your presence. Begin with nonintrusive questions that get the youth talking about himself or herself, or about his or her interests, before moving on to sexual issues.

EMPATHIZE. Be alert for any opportunity to put yourself in the young person's shoes. Try to understand how and why he or she became sexually active. Imagine as the youth talks what you might be thinking and feeling if you were in similar circumstances. Seize every opportunity to communicate your empathy and understanding. Ways to do so may include:

- Face the youth directly (come out from behind your desk).
- Lean slightly forward in your chair.
- Make eye contact.
- Nod to indicate understanding.
- Reflect key statements ("You feel . . ." and "You're saying . . .").
- Wait patiently through periods of silence or tears.

AFFIRM. Keep in mind that the young person's guilt and embarrassment may be overwhelming; he or she may feel dirty and ashamed. Make it a priority to affirm him or her as a precious child of God who is infinitely valuable. Let him or her know that you enjoy being in his or her company, that you find some things delightful and worthwhile about him or her (be specific). Be careful to communicate such things in noncondescending, nonjudgmental ways, such as:

- Carefully and sensitively leading him or her to confession and repentance of past sin, being careful to let the Holy Spirit (not you) convict of sin.

- Helping the young person receive and acknowledge God's love and forgiveness.

- Consistently affirming your acceptance of and love for the youth clearly and verbally.

- Guiding the youth to understand that God loves—and *delights in*—him or her (see Ps. 18:19) . . . even when He doesn't delight in the youth's behavior.

- Reinforcing the young person's positive traits and abilities ("I appreciate your spiritual sensitivity," or "You said that so well!").

DIRECT. A caring, compassionate parent, teacher, pastor, or youth worker can offer valuable direction to a youth who has been sexually active (to whatever degree) in three primary ways:

1. Offer hope. Young people who have been sexually active need a new beginning; they may have given up all hope of ever again living a chaste lifestyle. But one crime does not doom a person to the life of a criminal; therefore encourage the young person to seek a new beginning. God's love and power are so great that He can spiritually restore a young person's virginity. First John 1:9 says that He will "forgive us our sins and purify us from all unrighteousness."

2. Offer loving but firm guidance to the youth, leading him or her to understand and acknowledge God's standards in the area of sexuality. Share the biblical content of this chapter with the young person, being sure he or she understands what God expects.

3. Offer support. Let the young person know that you are willing to listen, talk, cry, worry, pray, hurt, help, and strategize with him (or her) in his efforts to honor God with his or her body (see 1 Cor. 6:20).

ENLIST. Enlist the young person's participation in brainstorming ways of making concrete plans to ensure, as much as possible, a chaste lifestyle in the future. Such plans may include:

1. Rely on God. Victory cannot be achieved apart from God (John 15:5). Guide the young person in establishing and maintaining a healthy devotional life that includes private and corporate prayer, worship, and Bible reading.

2. Set standards beforehand. Encourage the youth to set firm and specific limits for sexual activity before his or her next date. Urge him or her to detail with you how far he or she intends to go on a date, and then to communicate those standards to the person he or she is dating.

3. Set dating goals. Help the young person think

through how he or she wishes to act on a date and what he or she hopes to achieve on a date (possible goals may include "Make my date feel appreciated," and "Learn what makes my date laugh and cry").

4. Make definite plans. Stress the importance of knowing where you're going to go and what you're going to do on a date. It is easiest to stay out of trouble on dates when they're creative, fun, and keep the couple out of situations that can lead to problems.

5. Date only those who have the same convictions. Subtly try to guide the youth to realize the importance of dating only those who have convictions similar to his or her own, those whose faith, moral standards, and dating goals will support—not hinder—those of the youth.

6. Avoid being alone. Steer the youth to the realization that one of the keys to handling temptation is steering away from dangerous situations. Group dates and dates in public, well-lit places are among the ways to avoid danger.

7. Consider taking a break. Sometimes, when teens find themselves unable to break an established habit involving sexual activity, the best thing they can do for themselves is to stop dating for a while. Encourage the youth to consider a "vacation" from the pressures of dating until he or she develops stronger convictions and gains the emotional distance and spiritual maturity needed to put those convictions into practice.

REFER. In sexual matters particularly, it is critical that an adult of the same sex as the youth offer the comfort and guidance. Offering comfort to a young person of the opposite sex is a dangerous course, both to the adult and to the youth; for this reason, it is wise for a male to counsel young men and for a female to counsel young women (see Titus 2:1–8). If at any time it becomes apparent that the young person has more severe sexual problems than the pastor, parent, teacher, or youth worker can effectively handle, referral to a Christian counseling professional (with parental permission) is advised.

For Further Reading

The following resources may help the concerned parent, pastor, teacher, or youth worker to assist a young person who is struggling with premarital sexual activity:

Scriptures Cited in This Chapter

- 1 Peter 5:8
- Genesis 1:18, 31; 2:7, 18, 24
- Psalm 139:14
- Proverbs 5:18–19
- Psalm 18:19
- 1 John 1:9
- 1 Corinthians 6:20
- Titus 2:1–8

Other Scripture to Read

- Psalm 51:10; 119:9–10
- Proverbs 6:23–28
- Romans 12:1–2
- Galatians 5:16
- Philippians 4:8
- 1 Thessalonians 4:3–7
- 2 Timothy 2:22
- James 1:14–15
- 1 Peter 2:11

Further Reading

- Les John Christie, *Dating and Waiting* (Standard Publishing).
- Doug Fields and Todd Temple, *Creative Dating* (Thomas Nelson).
- Doug Fields and Todd Temple, *More Creative Dating* (Thomas Nelson).
- Fred Hartley, *Dare to Date Differently* (Fleming H. Revell).
- Joyce Huggett, *Dating, Sex, and Friendship* (InterVarsity).
- Erwin W. Lutzer, *Living with Your Passions* (Victor).
- Josh McDowell and Paul Lewis, *Givers, Takers, and Other Kinds of Lovers* (Tyndale House).
- Josh McDowell, *Sex, Guilt, and Forgiveness* (Tyndale House).
- Josh McDowell and Bill Jones, *The Teenage Q&A Book* (Word).
- Josh McDowell and Dick Day, *Why Wait? What You Need to Know about the Teen Sexuality Crisis* (Here's Life Publishers).
- Stacy and Paula Rinehart, *Choices: Finding God's Way in Dating, Sex, Singleness, and Marriage* (NavPress).
- Barry St. Clair and Bill Jones, *Love: Making It Last* (Here's Life Publishers).
- Greg Speck, *Sex: It's Worth Waiting For* (Moody).
- Tim Stafford, *Worth the Wait* (Tyndale House).
- Barry Wood, *Questions Teenagers Ask about Dating and Sex* (Fleming H. Revell).

29

UNPLANNED PREGNANCY

A Synopsis

❖

Introduction

Fifteen-year-old Stephanie had told her boyfriend in a quivering voice over the phone that she had something important to tell him. She had insisted on telling him in person. Now, as she faced Brent in the front seat of his car, she struggled to control her emotions. A nervous smile stretched across her lips.

"I have some really great news to tell you," she said, her wide eyes looking into his with a mixture of fear and hope.

Brent's forehead furrowed. He didn't smile. "Yeah?" he said, wondering what this was all about and knowing only that it felt weird.

"I'm—" she stopped herself, almost losing control. But quickly wrestling her emotions like a cowboy roping a calf, she started again. "We're going to have a baby!" She smiled again as broadly as she could and watched his face closely.

Brent's mouth opened, and he peered hard into her face. He had not yet smiled. "You're pregnant?" he asked, his voice squeaking like a choirboy whose voice has just begun to change.

Stephanie nodded vigorously and swallowed before speaking. "Aren't you happy?"

Brent hesitated only a moment this time before answering. "Well, yeah." He licked his lips. "Are you?"

"Yes," Stephanie blurted, desperately wanting to convince Brent—and herself—of the answer. She threw her arms around his shoulders and pressed her face against his neck. "Aren't you?" she asked, her voice barely audible.

Brent slowly wrapped his arms around Stephanie and began to pat her gently as if she were a baby. "Yeah, sure I am. If you're happy about it, then I'm happy too."

Stephanie closed her eyes against the tears that welled inside. She was scared. Scared of being pregnant. Scared of telling her parents. And scared of what Brent was really thinking.

The Problem of an Unplanned Pregnancy

According to research performed by the Guttmacher Institute, one in four teenage girls gets pregnant by age eighteen; half become pregnant by age twenty-one. Eighty-five percent of teen pregnancies are unintended; half end in births, a third in abortion, and the rest in miscarriage.[1]

Every year in America, about one million young women under the age of twenty become pregnant.[2] *Every day* in America, one thousand unmarried teen girls become mothers.[3] In fact, a third of all babies born to unmarried mothers in the U.S. each year are born to teenage girls.[4]

The frequency of teenage pregnancy and teenage parenthood in recent generations has become a fact of life in Western society, but it is no less culturally deleterious and personally disruptive because it has become so common.

The United States spends tens of billions of dollars annually in health care and other services for families started by women who gave birth in their teens,[5] and over half of all mothers on welfare had their first baby while they were still adolescents.[6]

Far more immediate, however, than the drain on economies and cultures presented by teen pregnancy are the individual dramas: the tragedy of interrupted educations, shattered relationships, broken promises, emotional trauma, and unfulfilled potential that often follow the news of an unexpected pregnancy.

The Causes of Unplanned Pregnancy

Unintended teen pregnancy occurs for a variety of reasons, some of which are seldom understood by adults. The teen years are tempestuous for teens and baffling to adults. Adolescence is characterized by new and intense sensations, unpredictable moods, overpowering emotions, and conflicting demands and expectations. Thus, trying to identify the reasons why a teen becomes pregnant (aside from the purely physiological) can be like trying to untie the Gordian knot. However, several factors do seem to contribute more than others.

◆ Lack of Sex Education at Home

There is no substitute for a home in which sex is approached in a frank and sensitive way, in which questions are greeted in an open manner, in which the beauty of sex within marriage and the dangers of sex outside marriage is discussed in a biblical context, and in which an adolescent is calmly prepared for the onset of puberty and the first stirrings of sexual drives and impulses.

Many children, however, don't grow up in such homes. In their homes, the topic of sex is forbidden, either explicitly or implicitly. The parents seem embarrassed—perhaps even afraid—of the subject. The young adolescent's hormonal changes are never (or seldom) discussed.

Even if a child has been educated about the technical aspects of sexual behavior—the reproductive system, the mechanics of sex, the means of birth control—a child whose parents do not "encourage relaxed conversations, calm acceptance of human sexuality, and a loving approach to teen issues"[7] will be far less equipped to avoid premarital sex and pregnancy. (See also chapter 28, "Premarital Sex.")

◆ Inferiority

Dr. G. Keith Olsen points out, in his book *Counseling Teenagers*, that becoming pregnant is "usually quite purposeful." He goes on to suggest that "Pregnancy in adolescent girls often represents an attempt to feel whole and valuable as a woman."[8]

Young women who feel insecure about their bodies, uncomfortable with the physical changes they're experiencing, or uncertain about who they are or where they fit in may turn to sexual involvement and pregnancy as a way of convincing others—and themselves—that they are capable of being wanted and loved, that they are as much a "woman" as anyone else.

Pregnancy may also seem, to an insecure adolescent mind, to be a way to hold on to a boyfriend or to force a boyfriend into marriage. And, of course, a baby she can love—who will love her back—is a promise of love and acceptance to many young women suffering from insecurity and low self-esteem. (See chapter 6, "Unhealthy Self-Esteem.")

◆ Alcohol and Drug Influence

Another factor that adds to the danger of the teen years is, for many, the initial encounter with alcohol and drugs.

Often a young woman who is struggling with the discovery of her sexuality and the power of her first "real relationship" with a boy finds herself at a party or other environment in which alcoholic drinks or drugs are easily accessible. When her third glass of beer is combined with her own raging

hormones and her boyfriend's insistent whispers, her resistance crumbles, and she soon finds herself crossing a line she had not planned to cross. (See chapter 38, "Alcohol Use and Abuse," and chapter 39, "Drug Use and Abuse.")

◆ Contraceptive Failure

Even today, after countless public and private "education" campaigns advising the use of contraceptives to prevent pregnancy and disease, many adolescents still engage in sexual behavior without the so-called "protection" afforded by such devices.

Many of those youth who do use contraceptive devices, however, use them only part of the time and often incorrectly.

Planned Parenthood's research—reported in their own journal, *Family Planning Perspectives*—revealed sobering facts about birth control methods in 1986. The table, reprinted below, identifies some percentages of unplanned pregnancies for single women.[9] *Notice: None of the methods, including the condom, were totally reliable.*

Table 29A. Percentage of Unplanned Pregnancies within the First Year of Contraceptive Use

Age	Pill	IUD	Rhythm	Condom	Diaphragm	Spermicides	None
Under 18	11.0%	10.5%	33.9%	18.4%	31.6%	34.0%	62.9%
18–19	9.6%	9.3%	30.6%	16.3%	28.3%	34.0%	62.9%
20–24	7.2%	6.9%	23.9%	12.3%	21.7%	23.5%	14.2%
25–29	5.0%	4.8%	17.4%	8.6%	15.6%	17.0%	36.3%
30–44	1.9%	1.8%	7.0%	3.3%	6.2%	6.8%	15.7%
All	5.7%	5.4%	23.0%	10.0%	23.3%	19.4%	44.7%

From *Family Planning Perspectives*, Volume 18, Number 5, Sept.–Oct. 1986.

In other words, according to the above research, a teenager expecting to prevent pregnancy with a condom is taking an 18.4 percent chance of being surprised sometime in the next twelve months . . . with a baby!

More recent research reflects similar results, indicating that "150 per 1,000 couples using condoms apparently experience an unplanned pregnancy during the first 12 months of use."[10]

◆ Rebellion

To some girls, pregnancy is the ultimate expression of rebellion against parental authority. (See also chapter 23, "Rebellion.") Most girls may not fully understand their own actions or the motivations behind such actions, but (consciously or subconsciously) their sexual activity and resulting pregnancy become a means of communication.

In the mind of an adolescent girl, her pregnancy may be a means of communicating to her parents, "You can't control me," or "I don't have to do what you say." It may communicate, "I'm grown up; why can't you see that?" Or it may communicate, simply, "Pay attention to me!"

◆ Desire for Freedom

Many adults have expressed bafflement that a teenage girl would choose to endure nine months of pregnancy and the overwhelming responsibility of teen parenthood. "Why would you give up your freedom like that?" they may say. "Why would you tie yourself to a baby?"

Many adolescent girls do not think that way however. They have a notion that pregnancy—and parenthood—will bring them freedom. It will force their parents to accept them as adults. It will enable them to control their own lives. It will get them out of the drudgery of school. It will allow them to make decisions for themselves.

Such reasoning is not entirely fantastic. The research of Stiffman, et al. (1990), indicates that

. . . sexually active, unhappy, and searching youths might conclude that their peers who are

rearing children are not worse off . . . than they are. In fact, as others have suggested, and as our data also indicates, adolescent mothers may seem to be better off than their peers in terms of having achieved independence, having acquired financial resources, and as possessing an infant they can love and be loved by (McAnarny, 1985).[11]

◆ Other Influences

The above do not exhaust the causes of teen pregnancy, of course. There are many and myriad reasons why a girl may become pregnant. Dr. G. Keith Olsen cites just a few others:

Some girls become pregnant because of intellectual inadequacy, an inability to say "no" to a boyfriend's need to prove his potency and sometimes because of an ill-founded belief that God would not let it happen. . . . Some teenage girls have a fantasy that marriage and homemaking will bring them happiness and stability in an otherwise confusing and demanding world. Still other girls have an almost magical notion that they could not become pregnant while others give their boyfriends the complete responsibility by naively believing their assurances that they will take whatever precautions are necessary.[12]

Author Karen J. Sandvig offers a key perspective on the multitude of influences and causes of teen pregnancy:

Why does a teenage girl get pregnant? Often, it happens by virtue of cascading events, one on top of the other, which create a vacuum of existence for her where she does not feel securely loved and valued for just who she is—no matter how irrational or untrue this might actually be. These events can be triggered by the hormonal changes in a girl's body, a lifetime of struggle in a troubled home, or anything in between. Once a young girl is pregnant, there can be no erasing it. It is time now to gather resources, strength, and understanding in order to make the best of a very difficult situation.[13]

The Effects of an Unplanned Pregnancy

In addition to the socioeconomic consequences of teen pregnancy documented by Simkins (1984) and Rutter (1980), among others, including a decreased likelihood of high school graduation and a greater likelihood of divorce, single parenthood, unemployment, and welfare dependency, Stiffman, et al. (1990) have reported that "sexually active youths. . . . [h]ave significant mental health problems that need treatment."[14] While such problems are myriad, it is nonetheless possible to identify a half-dozen or so of the most typical problems faced by a pregnant teen. These include denial, fear, guilt, shame, and regret.

◆ Denial

Denial is common among pregnant teens, even when the pregnancy was not wholly unintentional. Even after the signs of pregnancy would seem incontrovertible to an objective observer, many young women continue to delay seeking a diagnosis, many perhaps hoping that ignoring it will make it go away. The following teen, who was six weeks pregnant before she sought medical care, is typical in many ways:

> I knew something had to be wrong—I was late for my monthly, and I knew it had to be that . . . but I kept putting it off . . . because I knew what that means, you know.[15]

Some take even longer to abandon their denial:

> I started getting sick in the morning, and I was about four and a half months pregnant when I went in to get a test done. At about three and a half months I started to wonder. I knew, but I thought, "Well, maybe not. . . ." I was scared.[16]

◆ Fear

Another common reaction to teen pregnancy (in fact, to nearly all first-time pregnancies) is fear.

A teenage girl who suspects or discovers she is pregnant may fear how her boyfriend will react. She may fear her parents' anger and retaliation. She may be afraid of the changes that will happen in her body or the pain of labor. She may fear censure from her teachers, neighbors, and church. Her fears may be specific, or they may be nameless and shapeless. In either case, her fears may be so severe at times as to induce hysteria or panic attacks and may even produce physical consequences, such as asthma attacks or allergic disorders. (See also chapter 2, "Anxiety.")

◆ Guilt

Unless the conscience has been seared, sin invariably produces guilt, and a teenager who has become pregnant will often be overwhelmed with guilt. (See chapter 3, "Guilt.") In some cases, the guilt becomes so intense that she can barely focus her mind on anything except finding relief for the guilt that afflicts her and that will soon (if it has not already) be apparent to all.

Such a desperate search for relief sometimes prompts a teen to seek an abortion, attempt a self-inflicted abortion, run away, or attempt suicide. The youth leader should be alert to any signs of such desperation, which may include:

- Unusual and/or morbid questions about death

- Extreme depression

- Self-destructive comments or acts

- A manic pretense of joy over her pregnancy

- Sudden concern over money

- Disappearance of money in the home[17]

◆ Shame

Few girls want to be known as *one of those kinds of girls*. Though they may be sexually active, they still want a reputation as a "good girl," a worthwhile, valued, loved, respected human being. For many, therefore, pregnancy represents the end of that "illusion"—pregnancy inevitably publicizes a girl's sexual activity.

Ironically, the same girl who months before may have coyly refused to admit that she was a virgin now recoils *in shame* at the realization that all her friends, teachers, and neighbors will soon know (if they don't already) that she and her boyfriend have "done it."

The shame she feels may be so intense that she is driven either to denial (in which case she may feign elation about her pregnancy and talk excitedly about her baby) or desperation (in which case she may display some of the ideas and behaviors discussed under "Guilt," above).

◆ Regret

Children and teenagers have an imperfect understanding of the irrevocability of certain actions or events. Children may not understand that a broken toy cannot always be repaired or replaced. Even teens may not fully appreciate that some actions cannot be undone, some consequences are irrevocable. For some, pregnancy is a rather rude lesson in irrevocability.

As a result, a pregnant teen may be overcome with regret. She may feel that she has ruined her life or her boyfriend's life. She may think she has shattered her parents' reputation in the church or community. She may—perhaps for the first time—feel the pain of facing the consequence of an action that cannot be undone.

The Biblical Perspective of Unplanned Pregnancy

God's design for humankind included procreation, of course (see Gen. 1:28). Pregnancy—like sex—was God's idea, and we may even infer some of His blessing on that state from the words of Elizabeth (a pregnant woman) to her cousin Mary (another pregnant woman) on the occasion of Mary's visit described in Luke

1:39–45. The manner in which pregnancy occurs, however, is important to God; He made that clear repeatedly in His Word. (See Gen. 1:24, Deut. 5:18, and Col. 3:5.) Sex outside of marriage is sin, and pregnancy outside of marriage is often a visible token of that sin.

Premarital sex is *not* the unforgivable sin, however. (See Matt. 12:31–32.) As disruptive and damaging as it can be, not only to the principals (the girl and her boyfriend) but to the peripherals as well (parents, siblings, friends, other relatives, etc.), repentance is appropriate, and forgiveness is possible.

Regardless of how a pregnancy occurs, however, the life that grows inside a woman's womb is known to God and is precious to Him. God told the Hebrew prophet Jeremiah:

> Before I formed you in the womb I knew you,
> Before you were born I set you apart. (Jer. 1:5)

God's Word clearly emphasizes the value the Creator places on each human life, and His words to Jeremiah (as well as the testimony of David in Psalm 139:13–16) prompt us to believe that His love and concern for us is prenatal in its origins.

While premarital sex is sin that should be repented, the biblical response will also involve concern for the young woman who is pregnant, the boy who has fathered the child, and the child. All three are precious in God's sight. All three should be afforded the best possible protection, counsel, and care in the days to come.

The Response to the Problem of Unplanned Pregnancy

Listen ◆ Empathize ◆ Affirm ◆ Direct ◆ Enlist ◆ Refer

The youth leader can help a young woman (or a boyfriend) cope with an unintended pregnancy by implementing the following plan:

LISTEN. Allow the young person to talk freely about her problems, her feelings, her fears, her guilt, etc. Try to immediately communicate your acceptance and understanding. Help her by your words and your demeanor to communicate calm and hope; help her feel that "all is not lost" and panic is unnecessary. Gentle questions such as the following (when they apply) may help the youth express herself:

- How do you know you're pregnant? Have you missed your period? Have you been tested?

- Who knows about your pregnancy? (If the youth's parents have not been informed, offer to accompany her—perhaps even do the talking—as she tells them; parental notification is critical.)

- How are you feeling right now? What are you thinking?

- How can I help you? How can others help you?

EMPATHIZE. Try to see things from the young person's perspective. Cry with her, feel with her. Communicate your empathy by:

- Facing her directly (coming out from behind a desk).

- Listening carefully to verbal and nonverbal communication.

- Nodding your head.

- Making eye contact.

- Leaning forward in your chair to indicate interest and concern.

- Speaking in soothing tones.

- Reflecting key statements ("So what you're saying is . . . ?") or gestures ("It looks like that makes you pretty mad").

- Waiting patiently through moments of tears or silence.

Be alert for signs of desperation (see "Guilt," discussed above) that might indicate a need for immediate intervention (see the "Refer" section, below).

AFFIRM. A pregnant teen may very well be struggling mightily with her self-esteem and feelings of worth and value. Strive to affirm her in five key ways:

- Communicate God's love to her. Tell her repeatedly that God loves her unconditionally, whether she is pregnant or not, and that He loves her now as much as ever.

- Convince her of your unconditional love with words *and* actions (holding her as she cries, hugging her, etc.).

- Affirm her qualities and abilities. Seize every opportunity to affirm her qualities (sense of humor, sincerity, thoughtfulness, etc.) and abilities (intelligence, musical talent, ability to work with children, etc.).

- Help her realize that God can bring good out of her situation (see Gen. 50:20). Reinforce the fact that, while the teen's problem is serious, it is not something that can't be handled.

- Remind her that she is not alone and that there is time to make decisions carefully and rationally. Help her to specifically acknowledge those who may be ready to reach out to her and help her in practical ways (parents, friends, pastors, etc.).

DIRECT. When she is ready, try to direct the youth in the following ways:

1. Guide the young person toward confession, repentance, forgiveness, and restoration. Sensitively guide her to prayer (perhaps by you praying first) and encourage spiritual restoration.

2. Encourage dependence on God throughout her pregnancy. His resources are limitless, and He can lighten her load immensely. (See 1 Pet. 5:7.)

3. Help her identify the emotional needs and concerns that led to pregnancy. For example, was she rebelling against her parents? Did she hope to hold on to her boyfriend? Did she—consciously or subconsciously—see pregnancy as a means to independence?

4. Help the young woman consider ways to constructively deal with the emotional needs that led to the pregnancy. For example, if she became pregnant in an effort to hold on to her boyfriend, what emotional needs was she trying to meet in him? Did she see that relationship as a way to feel better about herself? If so, what constructive things can she do to fill that need in constructive ways. (See chapter 6, "Unhealthy Self-Esteem," for examples.)

5. Try to identify the predominant threats to the young woman's mental health and well-being: Is she in denial? Is she feeling mainly shame? Is she dominated by fear? Try to understand—and help her understand—her feelings.

6. Prompt the youth to consider her practical options, which include:

Adoption. Adoption is an option that is too often neglected because of the easy availability of abortion. However, it does allow a girl to be responsible to her unborn baby without accepting the burden of parenthood before she is mature enough to handle it. Adoptions can be arranged through the girl's doctor, through an adoption agency, or through friends or relatives (with the help of a lawyer). Of course, such a decision can be emotionally traumatic, marking "the end of what is probably the most intimate of all human relationships."[18]

Marriage. "The benefits are significant if they are fairly mature and deeply love each other," writes Dr. G. Keith Olsen. "Married adolescents sometimes live with one of their families though it is usually preferred for them to be able to have an apartment on their own, even if they require some temporary financial support. This gives them the privacy required for successfully transitioning from being single teenagers to being a young married couple. The major problems with this choice revolve around their relative immaturity, need to finish school, and the severe impact on their peer relationships. These negative impacts become greater with younger teenagers."[19]

Single Parenthood. Some teen mothers decide to keep their babies and raise them alone. Most do so with the assistance of their parents, though some go to live with other relatives and some even attempt to set up housekeeping on their own. Some pregnancy care centers facilitate placement in a "shepherding home" where the youth can be helped and counseled during pregnancy. Single parenthood can be an extremely difficult route, of course, and will necessitate further discussion about completion of school, day care, job, etc. (See also chapter 20, "Living in a Single-Parent Family.")

Abortion. Abortion is not only a biblically abhorrent option, it can also bear deleterious emotional, psychosocial, and physical effects. Dr. Olsen writes, "After an abortion, especially if the girl felt the baby move within her, she is likely to feel murderous and need counseling to help her resolve these feelings. Some girls annually remember the date of their abortion with renewed guilt, remorse and grieving." He further advises, "Christian counselors need to help girls deal effectively with the spiritual aspects of abortion. They need to work sensitively, fully accepting her and communicating no sense of judgment toward her while, at the same time, confronting her with the reality of what abortion really is."[20]

ENLIST. Enlist the young woman's participation, as much as she is able, in planning for her future. Encourage her to write down an "action plan" detailing specific steps to accomplish. Ask her what steps she will be taking to obtain prenatal care. Ask what things she would prefer to do and with what things she would like her parents to help. Ask how she will revise her strategy to accomplish her long-term goals and dreams, and what new hopes and aspirations she has for her child.

REFER. Try to assist the girl's parents in guiding her to medical care for her and the baby and in making them aware of mental health professionals who can offer further biblical guidance to the mother-to-be and the father of the child. If at any time the young woman shows signs of desperation (see "Guilt," page 39), professional intervention should be sought immediately.

For Further Reading

The following resources may help the concerned parent, pastor, teacher, or youth worker to assist a pregnant teen:

Scriptures Cited in This Chapter

- Genesis 1:24, 28
- Luke 1:39–45
- Deuteronomy 5:18

- Colossians 3:5
- Matthew 12:31–32
- Jeremiah 1:5
- Psalm 139:13–16
- Genesis 50:20
- 1 Peter 5:7

Other Scripture to Read

- Psalm 18:16–19; 51:1–17; 130:1–8; 139:13–16
- Romans 12:1–2
- 1 John 1:9

Further Reading

- Stephen Arterburn, *Addicted to "Love"* (Servant).
- "A Dad Named Bill," *Daddy, I'm Pregnant* (Multnomah).
- Donna and Rodger Ewy, *Teen Pregnancy* (Signet).
- Josh McDowell, *Sex, Guilt and Forgiveness* (Tyndale House).
- Josh McDowell and Dick Day, *Why Wait? What You Need to Know about the Teen Sexuality Crisis* (Here's Life Publishers).
- Karen J. Sandvig, *You're What? Help and Hope for Pregnant Teens* (Regal).

30

ABORTION

A Synopsis

Introduction

Brenda had big plans for her senior year in high school. She intended to graduate six months early and begin taking college courses in January at the state university near her home. She had a part-time job in the advertising department at the local newspaper and had even managed to save some money. In June, she planned to attend her high school commencement ceremony with the rest of her class, and then she and her fiancé were going to work at a Christian camp for the summer.

"Then everything fell apart," she says. On October 31, she discovered she was pregnant. And, though she was a Christian, she only considered one option: abortion.

"I was too young to have a baby," she said. "It would have just ruined everything. I mean, we were engaged and everything, but neither one of us was ready for that kind of responsibility. We had college to think about. And I just couldn't put my parents through all that."

Brenda never told her fiancé about the pregnancy or the abortion. She made an appointment at a women's center in a nearby town and withdrew most of her savings to pay the four-hundred-dollar fee. She drove herself to the appointment.

By the time she arrived at the women's center on a Wednesday morning, her hands were shaking so hard she could barely steer the car into the parking lot. She was relieved to see that the sidewalk was empty of prolife protesters or counselors.

Brenda expected the procedure to take about an hour, like a visit to the dentist. That was what the soothing woman's voice had told her over the phone when she had called to make the appointment. But the counseling itself took almost an hour. "I guess they wanted to make sure it was my decision. They explained all kinds of medical stuff to me. I didn't really listen, though; I just wanted to get it over with.

"It didn't hurt at the time," Brenda says now, two years later, "but I was so scared. I mean, it was traumatic.

"I try not to dwell on it now. I still feel ashamed and guilty. I have nightmares. And I worry about things. Like, will I ever have children? Will I ever stop thinking about the one I didn't have? I guess I was lucky because things could've been a lot worse. I just don't feel very lucky."

The Problem of Abortion

Brenda's thinking—and the choice she made—are tragically typical of many teens today. According to research performed by the Guttmacher Institute, one in four teenage girls gets pregnant by age eighteen; half become pregnant by age twenty-one.

Of the more than one million American teens who become pregnant every year,[1] roughly *half choose to have abortions*.[2] Approximately a third of all recorded U.S. abortions—which number in excess of 1.5 million every year—are performed on teenagers. In fact, the abortion rate for eighteen- and nineteen-year-olds is *two times* that of the national average.[3] Dr. M. Balfin states that "More teenagers are having abortions in the United States than in any other country in the world."[4]

Such statistics may only be the tip of the iceberg, however. A rate of 1.5 million abortions figures out to 4,000 abortions a day in the U.S. However, there are at least 4,000 abortion clinics or facilities currently operating in the U.S.[5] It is unlikely that those clinics perform only one abortion per day; consequently, the number of abortions probably far exceeds the oft-quoted figure of 1.5 million, and the number of teens having abortions may be more than half a million. Even Planned Parenthood estimates that nearly two-thirds of teen abortions are never reported: "Respondents aged 15–19 are estimated to have reported only 33 percent of the abortions they obtained."[6]

Like those in America, the number of abortions performed in other countries—from around 70,000 a year in Canada[7] to 180,000 a year in the United Kingdom[8]—continue to increase, adding to the number of babies aborted year after year in worldwide holocaust.

Moreover, one out of every six women who have an abortion describes herself as an evangelical Christian.[9]

The Causes of Abortion

Abortion has become one of the most common surgical procedures in the Western world. It has become tragically common among teens—even among Christian teens—for several reasons.

◆ The Teen Sexuality Crisis

The sexual activity of teens continues at an alarming rate. According to the *New York Times*, "Some studies indicate three-fourths of all girls have had sex during their teen-age years and 15 percent have had four or more partners."[10] And girls are having sex much earlier these days; the median age for a young woman's first act of premarital sex has fallen from nineteen in 1960 to seventeen in 1990. Dr. Liana Clark, a Philadelphia physician, says that most of her patients become sexually active at thirteen.[11]

◆ The Availability of Abortion

Abortion has become a multimillion-dollar industry in many Western countries, and many abortion advocates are committed to making abortion available to every woman—of any age. Planned Parenthood has a full-time *outreach staff* designed to inform teen girls (among others) about the availability of abortion.[12] Many school clinics pay a follow-up visit (often three or four visits) to every teen who comes in for a pregnancy test in order to seek out pregnant girls for abortions.[13] In addition, many states do not have parental consent laws; a teen girl could become pregnant and have an abortion without her parents' knowledge or consent.

◆ The Cultural Climate

While a majority of Americans are opposed to abortion on demand, many people have come to accept abortion. For example, a *Los Angeles Times* poll showed that 57 percent of those interviewed viewed abortion as murder; nonetheless, 74 percent favored abortion if the aborted child had a serious birth defect. And even among evangelical college students, only 71 percent said they opposed abortion in the first trimester of pregnancy.[14] As Operation Rescue director Randall Terry writes:

Many people believe that abortion is just another surgical procedure that removes a piece of unwanted tissue from a woman's body. That puts abortion in the same category as appendectomies, tonsillectomies, and the extraction of wisdom teeth.[15]

Terry goes on to outline two kinds of abortion and the techniques used in performing abortions:

Abortion is expelling a human child from the protection and safety of its mother's womb. Sometimes this is done before the child is capable of sustaining life. Other times, the child would be old enough to survive outside the womb if he or she were not poisoned or burned to death. Hundreds of children survive abortion. Some live; most are denied medical attention and die.

Abortions fall into two categories: *naturally spontaneous* and *artificially induced*. Naturally spontaneous abortions are also known as *miscarriages*. The word *abortion* usually refers to the artificially induced procedure. Depending on the development of the unborn child, any one of six techniques may be used to induce abortions.

Suction Aspiration. In this procedure the cervix is dilated with a series of instruments to allow the insertion of a powerful suction tube into the uterus. The vacuum tears the unborn child and the placenta from the womb and deposits the dismembered child in a container. . . . Ninety percent of all induced abortions use this procedure.

Dilatation and Curettage, or D & C. The cervix is dilated in the same way as for a suction abortion, but a loop-shaped steel knife is inserted to scrape the walls of the uterus. The baby and placenta are sliced to pieces and scraped through the cervix. This method is most commonly used between the seventh and twelfth weeks of pregnancy. . . .

Dilatation and Evacuation, or D & E. A seaweed-based substance is inserted into the cervix to induce dilation. . . . Forceps are inserted into the womb to dissect the child piece by piece. A special tool is used to crush and drain the head, which is usually too large to be removed whole.

Saline Injection. This procedure is used after four months when considerable amniotic fluid has accumulated around the unborn baby. A concentrated salt solution is injected through the mother's abdomen and into the baby's sac. The baby swallows this lethal solution and often reacts violently. For one or two hours he convulses and finally dies of salt poisoning, dehydration, and internal bleeding. Often his entire layer of outer skin is burned off. The mother usually goes into labor within a day or two and delivers a dead, burned, and shriveled baby. Salt poisoning is the second most common abortion procedure.

Prostaglandins. Prostaglandins are hormones that induce labor. Chemicals . . . are injected into the amniotic fluid to induce the birth of a second-trimester infant who is still too young to survive outside the womb. The contractions are so violent that babies have been decapitated during the procedure. Some infants have survived their traumatic entry into the world, so salt or other toxins may be injected with the prostaglandins to prevent a live birth.

Hysterotomy. This procedure is usually used in the last three months of pregnancy or in the event that saline injections or prostaglandins fail to produce a dead baby. Like a Caesarean section, the womb is entered through surgery and the baby is lifted out. Without prompt medical treatment the infant will usually die, although some babies have been born alive.[16]

In addition to the above, abortionists and pharmaceutical companies in the U.S. and abroad are continually working to develop new drugs and new techniques to take advantage of the already-profitable abortion industry.

The Effects of Abortion

The most pertinent effect of abortion, of course, is the willful and cruel loss of human life through the agency of his or her own mother. Such a tragedy has spiritual, medical, emotional, and societal ramifications.

◆ Spiritual Effects

Sin produces guilt, both moral guilt (or true guilt) as well as psychological guilt (guilt feelings).[17] Two researchers reported in the *American Journal of Psychiatry* that patients who "clearly functioned well before the abortion" later "experienced psychoses precipitated by guilt over the abortion."[18] The guilt that results from an abortion may not only produce deep and long-lasting feelings of regret and self-recrimination, it will also harm a young person's relationship with God until the sin is repented and forgiveness is experienced.

◆ Physical Effects

The Institute of Medicine, National Academy of Sciences, reports that "Medical complications associated with legal abortion may occur at the time of abortion (immediate), within 30 days following the procedure (delayed), or at some later time (late)."[19]

In addition, the National Institute of Health, in comparing women who aborted their first babies with women who carried first babies to term, found that women who aborted:

- Had an 85 percent higher miscarriage rate (in subsequent pregnancies).
- Experienced 47 percent higher labor complications.
- Experienced 83 percent higher delivery complications.
- Were 67 percent more apt to have premature babies.
- Miscarried their "wanted babies" twice as often.[20]

Furthermore, the National Center for Health Statistics reported that infertility among American women age twenty to twenty-four has risen from 3.6 percent to 10.6 percent since 1965; probable causes were listed as sexually transmitted diseases, IUDs, and abortion-inflicted uterine damage.

Dr. M. Balfin discovered the following consequences of adolescent abortions:

- Damage to reproductive organs, 42.6 percent
- Uterine rupture or perforation, 5.6 percent
- Endometriosis, 13 percent
- Salpingitis, pyosalpinx, 13 percent
- Cervical lacerations, 11.1 percent
- Hemorrhage, intractable, 13 percent
- Pelvic pain and dyspareunia, 11.1 percent
- Infertility and repeated miscarriage, 7.4 percent
- Incomplete operations; subsequent passage of fetal parts and tissue, 74 percent
- Bowel resection with colostomy, 1.9 percent[21]

Another expert states:

Adolescent abortion candidates differ from their sexually mature counterpart, and these differences contribute to high morbidity. . . . [Adolescents] run the risk of a difficult, potentially traumatic dilation.[22]

Balfin reports that "the most catastrophic complications occur in teenagers,"[23] and adds in another article that serious complications—even deaths—due to abortion may go unreported because (1) there is no mandatory reporting of legal abortions and their consequences in most states, (2) often the abortion doctor never learns of the complication, (3) abortion-related facts may be omitted from death certificates, and (4) the average physician will not report the complication because of the paperwork involved.[24]

◆ Emotional Effects

The Alan Guttmacher Institute, Planned Parenthood's researcher, admitted (in classic understatement), "Pregnancies that end in abortion or miscarriage are, at the least, upsetting and sometimes traumatic to the pregnant woman."[25]

The Institute of Medicine, National Academy of Sciences, asserted that "emotional stress and pain . . . surround the entire [abortion] procedure."[26] And Kumar and Robson report that "eight of 21 women who had obtained a past abortion were found to be clinically depressed and anxious. In contrast, only eight of 98 who had not had abortions were depressed."[27]

Dr. Ann Speckard of the University of Minnesota published a study on the long-term (five to ten years) manifestations of stress from abortion. Although the women she studied came from diverse backgrounds, their reactions were strikingly similar:

- 81 percent reported preoccupation with the aborted child.

- 73 percent reported flashbacks of the abortion experience.

- 69 percent reported feelings of "craziness" after the abortion.

- 54 percent recalled nightmares related to the abortion.

- 35 percent had perceived visitations from the aborted child.[28]

◆ Societal Effects

Abortion carries many effects that will certainly change and may irreparably harm societies and cultures around the world. For example, in some countries where males are highly prized, abortion creates the opportunity for parents to selectively abort female babies (according to one study, for example, out of 8,000 abortions in Bombay, India, 7,999 involved a female fetus).[29] The long-term implications of such trends are obvious.

Moreover, a tragic fact of abortion in the U.S. is that "twice as many black babies are being aborted than white babies. . . . Black women comprise only 12 percent of the female population in the United States, yet they are undergoing approximately 30 percent of the abortions."[30] Hispanic women are "60 percent more likely to have an abortion than non-Hispanic women but are less likely to have an abortion than black women."[31]

In addition, abortion is changing societal attitudes toward the handicapped, the terminally ill, and the elderly. A recent survey of parents discovered that 6 percent would abort a child likely to get Alzheimer's at an old age; 11 percent said they would abort a child predisposed to obesity.[32] Abortion on demand has contributed to a society in which "we educate a generation of young people to 'abort' their unwanted, handicapped, inconvenient and nonproductive children so that their own quality of life will not be impaired or interrupted." Nurses for Life asks the logical question, "How will that generation respond to the economic impact of 70 million senior adults who may be nonproductive, inconvenient, and medically dependent?"[33]

The Biblical Perspective of Abortion

Many helpful treatments of the biblical perspective of abortion have been written. Among the most complete and cogent is Paul B. Fowler's *Abortion: Toward an Evangelical Consensus*. In it, he offers the following perspective:

> While pro-choice advocates try to make light of the significance of conception and deny it as the crucial moment that begins a human life, Scripture places a high importance on conception. . . .
>
> Obviously, people in biblical times did not have the benefit of modern biology. But they did have a basic understanding of the processes of con-

ception and pregnancy as well as birth. The prophetic curse on Ephraim follows the process of life back to its origin: As for Ephraim, their glory will fly away like a bird—No *birth,* no *pregnancy,* and no *conception!* "(Hos. 9:11)

. . . . The biblical writers never say the words, "Life begins at conception." But they consistently refer to conception as the starting point of a person's life, or metaphorically of the life of an idea. The usage is consistent throughout Scripture, even with its many writers extending over a period of some fifteen hundred years. . . .

God is portrayed as active in the event of conception itself. Examples abound, as in the case of Ruth: "The Lord enabled her to conceive, and she gave birth to a son" (Ruth 4:13). And there is Hannah who, after praying for a child, conceives and gives birth: "And she named him Samuel, saying, 'Because I have asked him of the Lord'" (1 Samuel 1:20). . . . Biblical passages revealing the divine role in conception simply serve to confirm that it is more than just a biological phenomenon. The start of a human life is clearly a special occurrence in which God takes part. . . .

That the Bible shows life begins at conception raises an even more important issue: What value does Scripture place upon human life once it has been conceived? Certainly it is a high value—but how high? The value of the unborn in Scripture may be studied in several ways: by their relation to the image of God, by their relation to God, by their continuity with postnatal life, and by the views about their untimely death.

Their Relation to the Image of God. Several verses assume explicitly or implicitly that the fetus is made in God's image. Genesis 5:3 reads: "When Adam had lived one hundred and thirty years, he became the father of a son in his own likeness, according to his image, and named him Seth." Most commentators interpret the phrases, "in his own likeness, according to his image," as meaning the image of God . . .

If this translation is correct, then Adam and Eve were the ones literally created in God's image.

Seth (and all other descendants of Adam and Eve) received the image of God through procreation. Seth's essential humanness was already present at conception. . . .

Their Relation to God. . . . Scripture shows God relating to the fetus in several intimate ways. First, a number of references concur that God oversees the development of the fetus. [See Job 31:13–15; Ps. 119:73, 139:13–16; Jer. 1:5]. A second way God relates personally to the unborn is preparing them as individuals for a specific calling. [See Rom. 9:11; Judg. 13:3–5; Jer. 1:5; and Gal. 1:15.]

Continuity with Life after Birth. A third way Scripture indicates the fetus's value is that a significant continuity between prenatal and postnatal human life is assumed. . . . The biblical writers did not use different words to label prenatal and postnatal life. The same Hebrew and Greek terms are often used to refer both to the born and the unborn. . . . The Bible commonly applies personal language to the unborn. . . .

Their Untimely Death. A fourth, though negative, way of ascertaining the value of the unborn is to look at Scripture's view of their "untimely death." We have seen how conception and birth were viewed as wonderful blessings from the Lord. The opposite was also true; miscarriages and murders of the unborn (pregnant women being ripped open) were viewed as a dreadful curse for any people. [See 2 Kings 8:12; Amos 1:13; and Hos. 9:14, 16; 13:16].

When we apply these texts to our times, it is clear that it is quite a responsibility to make a decision to abort one's own child . . . . Conversely, the decision to care for the "precious ones" of the womb (Hosea 9:16) is in character with the purposes and desires of God.[34]

The Response to the Problem of Abortion

Listen ◆ Empathize ◆ Affirm ◆ Direct ◆ Enlist ◆ Refer

Abortion is such a difficult and sensitive issue because it not only involves an innocent unborn child but also another precious child of God—the mother—who is often confused, frightened, and hurting. The youth leader will most likely encounter one of two situations, pointed out by James Oraker: (1) the young woman who has already had an abortion and is dealing with the consequences, or (2) the young woman who has recently discovered she is pregnant and is contemplating abortion.

LISTEN. Encourage the young person to talk freely about her problems, her feelings, her fears, her guilt, etc. Try to communicate calm and hope; help her feel that "all is not lost" and panic is unnecessary. Some helpful questions for the young woman who is contemplating an abortion may include:

- How do you know you're pregnant?

- How/when did you first learn you were pregnant?

- Who have you told about your pregnancy? (If the youth's parents have not been informed, offer to accompany her—perhaps even do the talking—as she tells them; parental notification is critical.)

- What difficulties do you think the pregnancy will create for you?

- What difficulties do you think an abortion would solve?

- What difficulties do you think an abortion would create?

Questions for a young woman who has already had an abortion may include:

- How long ago did you have the abortion?

- What prompted you to choose that option?

- What have been the emotional effects of that decision? Physical? Spiritual?

EMPATHIZE. Try to react empathically to the youth. Avoid sermonizing or lecturing; instead, try to communicate empathy, not sympathy. Feel with her, not for her. Hurt with her, not for her. Cry with her, not for her. Remember that your empathy can be communicated in many small ways, such as:

- Facing the young woman directly (coming out from behind a desk).

- Listening carefully to verbal and nonverbal communication.

- Nodding your head and using short encouragements ("uh-huh," "I see," etc.) to indicate interest and understanding.

- Making eye contact.

- Leaning forward in your chair.

- Reflecting key statements ("It sounds like . . ." or "So you were afraid when you found out . . .")

- Waiting patiently through tears or silence.

AFFIRM. One of the most beneficial things a youth leader, pastor, or parent can do for a teen contemplating (or recovering from) abortion is to communicate unconditional love and acceptance. If she has already had an abortion, help her understand that she is still loved and esteemed nonetheless—literally, none the less. If she is contemplating having an abortion, communicate the same affirmation. Don't be afraid that accepting her unconditionally may make her more likely to go through with an abortion; on the contrary, withholding affirmation at such a time bears much greater potential for harm.

DIRECT. In the case of a teen who is contemplating having an abortion, the youth leader, pastor, teacher, or parent should strive to offer guidance in the following areas:

1. *Pray with the young woman.* Pray aloud for her, being careful to approach the throne of grace on her behalf (instead of using prayer as a means of delivering a message to the young woman). Encourage her to pray aloud in your presence, casting her cares on God, who cares deeply for her (1 Peter 5:7).

2. *Patiently and sensitively expose her to the biblical perspective of abortion,* as presented earlier in this chapter.

3. *Carefully and sensitively expose her to the effects of abortion,* as presented earlier in this chapter. Impress upon her that part of God's motivation in forbidding certain behaviors is to protect us from harm and to provide good things for us. (See Deut. 10:12–13 and John 8:32.)

4. *Try to foster the realization that, while the teen's problem is serious, it is not something that can't be handled.* Help her understand that God can bring good out of the most desperate situation. (See Gen. 50:20.) Remind her that she is not alone and that there is time to make decisions carefully and rationally. Help her to specifically acknowledge those who may be ready to reach out to her and help her in practical ways (encourage her to list them by name).

5. *Guide her to carefully consider the alternatives to abortion:*

Adoption. Adoption is an option that is too often neglected because of the easy availability of abortion. However, it does allow a girl to be responsible to her unborn baby without accepting the burden of parenthood before she is mature enough to handle it. Adoptions can be arranged through the girl's doctor, through an adoption agency, or through friends or relatives (with the help of a lawyer). Of course, such a decision can be emotionally traumatic, marking "the end of what is probably the most intimate of all human relationships."[35]

Marriage. "The benefits are significant if [the mother-to-be and the father of the child] are fairly mature and deeply love each other," writes Dr. G. Keith Olsen. "Married adolescents sometimes live with one of their families though it is usually preferred for them to be able to have an apartment on their own, even if they require some temporary financial support. This gives them the privacy required for successfully transitioning from being single teenagers to being a young married couple. The major problems with this choice revolve around their relative immaturity, need to finish school, and the severe impact on their peer relationships. These negative impacts become greater with younger teenagers."[36]

Single Parenthood. "Some mothers decide to remain single," writes Gary R. Collins, "and bear the child to maturity. Many find maternity homes, move to boarding homes, go to live with distant relatives or foster parents, or stay at home."[37] Such a route is often difficult, of course, and will necessitate further discussion about completion of school, day care, job, etc.

In the case of a young woman who has already aborted her baby, the caring adult should try to:

1. *Direct the young woman through the stages of repentance* (confession, turning from her sin, accepting God's forgiveness) and restoration. Olsen writes, "Christian counselors need to help girls deal effectively with the spiritual aspects of abortion. They need to work sensitively, fully accepting her and communicating no sense of judgment toward her while, at the same time,

confronting her with the reality of what abortion really is."[38]

2. Encourage the young woman to cry out to God, give Him her broken heart, and depend on Him for healing and restoration, for "The Lord is close to the brokenhearted and saves those who are crushed in spirit."[39]

3. Give special attention to helping the young person deal with psychological guilt, which is likely to recur even after her moral guilt has been erased. (See chapter 3, "Guilt.") If guilt feelings persist, help the young woman address her guilt with the three-step process prescribed in chapter 3: identify guilt feelings quickly, deal with the feelings immediately, and prevent and prepare for the next attack. (See page 39)

4. Try to foster the realization that, while abortion is a tragedy for the unborn child and *the mother, God can bring good out of the most tragic situation.* (See Gen. 50:20.)

ENLIST. In the case of a pregnant girl, enlist her participation, as much as she is able, in planning for her future. Ask her what steps she will be taking to obtain prenatal care. Ask what things she would prefer to do and with what things she would like her parents to help. Ask how she will revise her strategy to accomplish her long-term goals and dreams and what new hopes and aspirations she has for her child. In the case of a girl who has had an abortion, enlist her contribution to strategies that will help remind her of God's forgiveness, alleviate her preoccupation with the abortion (such as volunteering for peer counseling to help other girls avoid the tragic mistake she made), and avoid behavior and thought patterns that contributed to her pregnancy (setting new dating standards, etc.).

REFER. In the case of a young woman who has already had an abortion, professional counseling is strongly urged (with parental permission).

Gently guide the young woman to a Christian counselor who can help her through the post-abortion trauma. In either case, promptly consider immediate medical care (if it has not been started) to diagnose or prevent any post-abortion complications or commence prenatal care.

For Further Reading

The following resources may help the concerned parent, pastor, teacher, or youth worker assist a teen who is contemplating abortion, or a young woman who has already had an abortion:

Scriptures Cited in This Chapter

- Hosea 9:11
- Ruth 4:13
- 1 Samuel 1:20
- Genesis 5:3
- Job 31:13–15
- Psalms 119:73; 139:13–16
- Jeremiah 1:5
- Romans 9:11
- Judges 13:3–5
- Galatians 1:15
- 2 Kings 8:12
- Amos 1:13
- Hosea 9:14, 16; 13:16
- 1 Peter 5:7
- Deuteronomy 10:12–13
- John 8:32
- Genesis 50:20
- Psalm 34:18

Other Scripture to Read

- Genesis 9:6
- Exodus 23:7

- Psalms 18:16–19; 51:1–17; 130:1–8
- Proverbs 6:16–17
- 1 John 1:9

Further Reading

- Stephen Arterburn, *Addicted to "Love"* (Servant).
- "A Dad Named Bill," *Daddy, I'm Pregnant* (Multnomah).

- Paul B. Fowler, *Abortion: Toward an Evangelical Consensus* (Multnomah).
- Josh McDowell, *Sex, Guilt, and Forgiveness* (Tyndale House).
- Karen J. Sandvig, *You're What? Help and Hope for Pregnant Teens* (Regal).

31

HOMOSEXUALITY

A Synopsis

❖

Introduction

Michael began experimenting with homosexuality at a seventh-grade church camp. He'd always suspected he was different from other boys, ever since the time when he was seven that an older boy made him do some things, things that he knew were bad but gave him a mysterious thrill. That week at summer camp simply confirmed it in his mind. Throughout his junior high and high school years, however, Michael played the role he thought others expected of him and even took one of his closest friends, Vanessa Hodges, to the senior prom.

"At times, though," he says now, "the sexual tension would get unbearable. Other guys my age were noticing girls; I felt an attraction to guys. Other guys had posters of girls in their lockers or bedrooms; I hid tiny pictures of male models in the bottom of my dresser drawer. I remember hanging out with one of my friends, wanting to touch him but not daring to give myself away. I had to sit there, pretending like everything was normal, when it wasn't."

When he left home for a Christian college, he was determined to change. "But soon," he said, "I began to notice the men standing in the shadows at the park down the street. I accepted some of their invitations and was amazed to find out that what had caused me frustration for years was suddenly so easy and natural."

Michael carried on a dual lifestyle of Christian student and clandestine lover for his four years of college. Perhaps because he never made a lot of friends, he reached his senior year without anyone knowing of his secret—until the school newspaper published an anonymous interview with a "gay student" at the school.

The article ignited a firestorm. The college president called an assembly and stated emphatically the school's position that homosexual acts were wrong.

When the president finished speaking, Michael stood up.

"I guess I need to tell you that I'm the 'gay student' you're all talking about," he said. "You may not agree with me or with my lifestyle, but I know God loves me just the way I am. If you can't deal with that, then that's your problem."

Michael's short speech didn't make him many friends, but he had few to begin with. Four months later he graduated and vowed never to darken the doors of a church that couldn't accept him for who he was.

The Problem of Homosexuality

Researcher and pollster George Barna, in his book *The Invisible Generation,* refers to the generation now approaching adolescence and adulthood as Baby Busters and writes:

> Relatively few Busters admit to having participated in gay sex: 3 percent, mostly comprised of women. However, the Busters' prevailing views on homosexuality reflect the changing national acceptance of gay lifestyles and practices.
>
> Only one-third of the Busters (32 percent) buy the recent research suggesting that people are born homosexual. A slight majority (55 percent) believe that gay sex is immoral. Half say that opposition to gay rights and lifestyles is evidence of being "close-minded" and half say that such opposition is not being close-minded. . . . More than four out of every ten Busters (44 percent) said that gay couples should be allowed to get married. Nearly as many (38 percent) felt that they should also be allowed to adopt and raise children.[1]

That may be only the beginning. Faced with an onslaught of media images, "gay pride" offensives, and a new climate of acceptance—sometimes open support—at high schools and colleges at a time when many youth are still struggling to come to terms with their sexuality, some young people are confused. Others are playing with homosexuality. Still others are not playing. *Newsweek* magazine has said:

> Teens' eagerness to experiment has made bisexuality almost "cool" in some schools. "From where I sit, it's definitely becoming more chic," says George Hohagen, 20, a Midwestern market researcher not long out of high school himself. . . . At meetings of Boston Area Gay and Lesbian Youth, support-group leader Troix Bettencourt, 19, a public-health intern, has seen an increase in teenagers who identify themselves as bisexual.[2]

The *Newsweek* article goes on to quote Carrie Miller, who operates Generation Q, an informal rap group in Chicago for young homosexuals and bisexuals. "The truth is," Miller says, "[teens are] open to everything."

Another *Newsweek* issue referred to the climate that exists on many college campuses, such as Ohio's Oberlin College, "considered to be a gay mecca by many young homosexuals." The article cited the observance of a "Lesbutante Ball," "Dyke Visibility Day," and numerous college courses on "the homosexual experience" as a reflection of the university climate in many places. The article then stated:

> In today's politically correct atmosphere, say many students, it's become the in thing to experiment sexually. For some, that has meant [homosexual] relations.[3]

Many youth of all ages—youth from Christian families, no less—wage a monumental struggle, not only against such outside influences, but against forces that wage inside their own souls, some of which can be explained and others that cannot.

The Causes of Homosexuality

There have been many proposed (and some vigorously opposed) reasons for homosexuality. Most commonly, it is attributed to genetic factors, disordered family relationships, early sexual abuse or homosexual experiences, and/or the youth's rebellion.

◆ Genetic Factors

The latest and most widely publicized suggestion is that homosexuality has a genetic basis. Stanton L. Jones, chair of the psychology department of Wheaton College, writes:

> The evidence suggests that genetic factors, possibly operative through brain differences, may give some a push in the direction of homosexual preference.[4]

Jones does not suggest, however, that genetic

factors *make* a person homosexual, nor that such factors negate "God's moral call upon our lives."

◆ Disordered Family Relationships

Another often posited contributing factor to homosexuality is disordered family relationships, as John White, author of *Eros Defiled*, explains:

A domineering mother and a passive, ineffectual father are the villains according to some analytic theories (I. Berberet, et al., "The Castration Complex," J. Nerv. Ment. Dis. 129:235 1959). Certainly many homosexual men describe controlling mothers and passive fathers (I. Berberet, et al., "Homosexuality" a Psychoanalytic Study [New York: Basic Books, 1962]).

Mother is the one in command. Like a galleon she may sweep through the household in full sail, lesser vessels (husband and children) trailing in her wake. She may be loud of voice, decisive, determined, ambitious that her children do well in life. . . .

On the other hand her control may be less blatant. She may rule with subtlety but with equal tyranny. . . . But lest we too quickly assign her the role of villain, we must observe that she is only one of several players. . . . Her husband supports her by his abdication. . . . The children may react in different ways as well. But the father-mother model on which they base their reactions is an unhealthy one. They have been denied a day-by-day demonstration of healthy parental behavior. . . .

Out of the many family interactions one may become specially important. If Mother selects one of her sons to be her special confidant, she may lay the groundwork for his future vulnerability to homosexual temptation. He, too, however, must play his part. He must fit into the perplexing pattern she expects of him.

Usually he becomes, not in a physical or sexual but in an emotional sense, the husband she never had. . . . Without realizing what is happening, he

learns to dance to her music and to respond to her moods. . . . Had he a strong father to support him and to model himself on, things might be different. . . .

Such a young man is not a homosexual. Nor is he what Freud termed a latent homosexual (vicious and cruel term). If any term fits, it is Lionel Ovesey's term *pseudohomosexual* (someone who may superficially resemble a homosexual but is not one).

Nevertheless he is more vulnerable to homosexual temptation than other young men might be. He has more learning to do in order to establish a healthy sexual relationship with a woman, and he will find it a tougher job to learn to be a good father.

His deepest problem will be one of loneliness, a loneliness which will drive him in one of several directions. He may stay at home, an aging bachelor, hoping for marriage but finding it strangely elusive, growing increasingly dissatisfied with his relationship with his parents. His sexual solace may be in masturbation or in sexual relations with older women.[5]

White allows that the "analytic theories that try to account for homosexuality by emphasizing the dominant mother and the passive father are by no means the only ones. In any case they fail to explain why many domineering mothers raise heterosexual children or why apparently normal parents rear children who adopt a homosexual way of life." However, there is enough evidence to suggest that dysfunctional family relationships and the lack of healthy male and female role models often play a significant role in homosexual behavior.

◆ Early Sexual Abuse or Experiences

A third contributing factor is suggested by Jerry Arterburn in his book *How Will I Tell My Mother?*:

Early [sexual] experiences with older persons are a key to the development of homosexual behavior. I place this factor as the one link between normal and abnormal development. Shrouded in secrecy and shame, they affect future relationships and desires. . . . [T]he experience of early exposure to homosexual behavior is quite common among many homosexuals I have known.[6]

◆ Rebellion

Finally, as author Kent Philpott points out, homosexual behavior can be a response to rejection, manifested in a spirit of rebellion:

> During the formative years . . . a person [who] experiences rejection. . . . will often rebel. Homosexuality is a result of rebellion. It is in fact the most extreme form rebellion can take because it is acting in exact opposition to the way God created us.[7]

Such rebellion may be a reaction to an overbearing parent. It may be a result of perceived rejection stemming from parental divorce. It may be directed at God, particularly among survivors of abuse. Or it may be more generalized. But anger and a spirit of rebellion can, in some individuals, sow the seeds that grow into homosexual behavior.

The causes described here—genetic factors, disordered family relationships, abuse and/or early exposure to homosexual experiences, and rebellion against authority—are four key factors in homosexual behavior. They are by no means the only factors, nor are they present in every case, and none may be present in a given case. The evidence does suggest, however, that these factors deserve consideration and further investigation.

The Effects of Homosexuality

The effects of homosexuality—on the homosexual himself or herself, on the family of the homosexual, on society in general—could be the subject of a lengthy book. For the purposes of this handbook, however, the most influential effects and potential effects on the homosexual himself or herself will be examined.

◆ Physical Effects

The most obvious (because it has been so widely publicized) effect of homosexuality is AIDS. While AIDS is not limited to the homosexual population, its initial spread and subsequent proliferation is considered by many researchers to be directly related to homosexual behavior. But the physical consequences of homosexual behavior are devastating as well as varied:

> [Homosexuals] represent just 1 or 2 percent of American society, but have 50 percent of syphilis cases and 60 percent of AIDS cases. Between one-half and three-fourths of homosexual men have had hepatitis B, a rate that is 20 to 50 times greater than among heterosexual males. Hepatitis A, amebiasis, shigellosis and giardasis are so common among homosexuals that doctors call these diseases "gay bowel syndrome."[8]

◆ Promiscuity

Sexually transmitted diseases pose such a danger to homosexuals because homosexuality (male homosexuality, particularly) tends to be strongly associated with promiscuity. Stanton Jones writes:

> The famous Bell and Weinberg study (*Homosexualities*) suggested that about a third of gays have had over 1,000 sexual partners in their lifetimes. Very few gays are in committed, long-term relationships; Bell and Weinberg found that less than 10 percent of gays are in such relationships. Those who are in stable relationships do not tend to be sexually monogamous. McWhirter and Mattison (*The Gay Couple*) found that 0 percent of the 100 stable male couples they studied were sexually monogamous after being together for five years. The authors of that study, themselves a gay couple, said that to be gay is to be nonmonogamous.[9]

The *AFA Journal* reported a study of homosexuality that discovered that "43 percent of homosexuals say they have had 500 or more different sexual partners in their lifetime. Only 1 percent of homosexuals said they have had only from one to four different sexual partners in their lifetime."[10]

◆ Descent into Deviancy

The homosexual lifestyle also breeds other forms of sexual deviancy, many of which are abusive and self-abusive. Jones explains:

> It may be that the homosexual community cannot embrace monogamy because homosexual sex can never produce what God made sex for. They turn instead to promiscuity and perversions to create sexual highs. . . . Many know of oral and anal sex, but fewer know of commonly, though not universally, practiced activities such as sadomasochistic practices of inflicting pain on a partner during sex, group sex of all kinds, and more extreme distortions. When sex outside of God's will does not do what God made it to do, many people, gay and straight, search for some way to make sex deliver an ever bigger electric charge, the elusive ultimate orgasm, that can somehow make up for the absence of what sex was meant to create: unity.[11]

◆ Loneliness and Rejection

John White says:
> Homosexuals, by and large, are unhappy people. They are unhappy because however successful their fight against discrimination may be, they will never gain either understanding or acceptance by the straight world. They are also unhappy because they suffer a more than average share of loneliness and rejection—even at times by their gay friends. If inconstancy and infidelity plague the straight world, they plague the gay world to a far greater degree.[12]

◆ Guilt and Self-Hate

No matter how vehemently a practicing homosexual may fight it or try to deny it, he or she is often plagued by an ever-present sense of guilt and shame. He may suppose his sense of guilt to be due to society's "homophobic" rejection of his lifestyle. She may suppose it to be a vestige of her religious upbringing. He may even interpret it as the result of the Holy Spirit's conviction. Or she may completely deny any sense of guilt (and in this, she may be accurate). But guilt is wedded to homosexuality, as it is to all sin. (See chapter 3, "Guilt.") And even if an individual's conscience is silenced or seared, the guilt will sometimes result in low self-esteem and even self-hatred. (See chapter 6, "Unhealthy Self-Esteem.")

The Biblical Perspective of Homosexuality

For the Christian, the correct view of homosexuality does not depend on public opinion, media portrayals, governmental policy, or psychological studies. What matters is the biblical view of homosexuality. Herbert J. Miles writes:

> Genesis 1:28 ties human sexuality to procreation—reproducing after its kind. God said to Adam and Eve: "Be fruitful and multiply, and fill the earth and subdue it . . . have dominion over . . . every living thing that moves upon the earth". . . . The fruit of mankind—husband and wife—is another human being. Thus, homosexuality cannot carry out the first command of God to the human race.
>
> Genesis 2:24 ties human sexuality to a unitive relationship between persons of the opposite sex—husband and wife. "Therefore shall a man leave his father and his mother, and shall cleave unto his wife: and they shall be *one flesh*" (KJV, italics added). This one-flesh unity refers to the spiritual and bodily union of husband and wife in sexual intercourse. . . . Jesus quoted this passage from Genesis as a foundation for his teachings about

marriage (Matt. 19:4–5; Mark 10:7–8). It is obvious that the structural makeup of the physical bodies of two males or two females makes it impossible for them to experience this one-flesh unity. Thus, homosexuality is rejected by the creative and purposive plan of the Creator-God.

In the eighteenth chapter of Leviticus, we are given a list of divine commands designed to protect the sanctity of marriage and to maintain moral respect for the family as a divine institution. These Levitical laws are grounded in the Genesis order of creation. In the midst of this list condemning incest (verses 6ff), and adultery (verse 20), we are told, "You shall not lie with a male as with a woman; it is an abomination" (verse 22). . . .

In the book of Romans, Paul . . . describes the wrath of God against the ungodliness of the Gentiles. Part of this ungodliness was the sin of defiling the human body. In condemning the defilement of the body, Paul singles out homosexuality. He explains that because of their ungodliness:

> Therefore God gave them up in the lusts of their hearts to impurity, to the dishonoring of their bodies among themselves. . . . Their women exchanged natural relations for unnatural, and the men likewise gave up natural relations with women and were consumed with passion for one another, men committing shameless acts with men and receiving in their own persons the due penalty for their error . . . (Rom. 1:24–28). . . .

In writing to the Corinthian Christians, Paul instructed them not to tolerate immorality among their Christian brothers: "Do not be deceived: Neither the sexually immoral nor idolaters nor adulterers nor male prostitutes nor homosexual offenders . . . will inherit the kingdom of God" (1 Cor. 6:9–10 NIV). In writing to Timothy, Paul associated homosexuality with the lawless, the disobedient, the ungodly, the unholy, the profane, and sinners (1 Tim. 1:8–10). There are four other Bible passages that indirectly associate homosexuality

with sinful behavior (Gen. 19:4–9; Judg. 19:1–30; 2 Pet. 2:1–22; Jude 3–23).[13]

Homosexual activists and liberal theologians have challenged these passages, however. Jones offers an overview of "what one will hear from critics of the traditional view":

> They argue that Leviticus 18:22, 20:13, and Deuteronomy 23:18, which condemn male homosexual behavior, are irrelevant because they do not address today's homosexual lifestyles. . . . The only kind of homosexual behavior the Israelites knew, it is argued, was homosexual prostitution in pagan temples. That is what is being rejected here and not the [so-called] loving monogamous gay relationship of persons of homosexual orientation today.
>
> The Genesis 19 story of Sodom and Gomorrah is alleged to be irrelevant because it is a story of attempted gang rape, which was an indicator of the general wickedness of the city. The homosexual nature of the gang rape is seen as an irrelevant detail of the story.
>
> Romans 1 is often reduced to being a condemnation solely of heterosexual people who engage in homosexual acts. They rebel against God by engaging in what is unnatural to them. This passage has no relevance today, it is argued, because modern homosexuals are doing what is natural to them and thus not rebelling against God.
>
> In 1 Corinthians 6:9 and 1 Timothy 1:10, the Greek words that are often translated as referring to homosexual practices are said to be unclear and probably describe and forbid only pederasty, the sexual possession of an adolescent boy by an older adult man of the elite social classes.
>
> Some of these criticisms have an element of legitimacy, but most evangelical biblical scholars concur that every one of them goes too far. . . . Leviticus, Romans, 1 Corinthians, and 1 Timothy are relevant and binding. Archaeological studies confirm that the ancient world knew of homosexual desire and practice, even if the concept of a

psychological orientation was not present. Thus it is striking that *every time homosexual practice is mentioned in the Scriptures, it is condemned*. There are only two ways one can neutralize the biblical witness against homosexual behavior: by gross misinterpretation or by moving away from a high view of Scripture.[14]

However, a final, crucial element of understanding the biblical perspective is offered by Miles:

> Homosexuality is a violation of the direct commandment of the Holy Scriptures. . . . But *homosexuality is not an unpardonable sin nor the greatest sin.* (The greatest sin is the sin of rejecting God.) Homosexuals *can* change their sexual life style and be healed in Christ through repentance and faith. Paul listed homosexuality among the sins of the unrighteous people who would not inherit the kingdom of God (1 Cor. 6:9–10). Then he said to the Corinthian Christians, *"And these are just the characters some of you used to be. But now* you have washed yourselves clean, you have been consecrated, you are in right standing with God, by the name of the Lord Jesus Christ and by the Spirit of God" (1 Cor. 6:11, Williams, italics added).[15]

Christians face a double challenge in dealing with homosexuals and homosexuality, the same balance prescribed in the first letter of John: to balance truth (the truth of God's Word, which clearly condemns homosexuality as sin) and love (love for the individual, who is an unspeakably precious child of God, in need of—and eligible for—forgiveness and regeneration or restoration through the power of Christ and the presence of the Holy Spirit).

The Response to the Problem of Homosexuality

listen ◆ Empathize ◆ Affirm ◆ Direct ◆ Enlist ◆ Refer

Parents, pastors, teachers, and youth leaders can respond to a young person struggling with homosexual feelings or with homosexual behavior by implementing the following:

LISTEN. The adult should strive to create an environment in which sexual issues—including homosexual feelings or practices—can be confronted and discussed openly and sensitively. The adult should determine never to express shock, outrage, condemnation, or revulsion. Listen not only to the young person's words, but give careful attention to his or her moods, attitudes, and emotions as well.

EMPATHIZE. Stanton L. Jones says:

> The key to compassion is to see ourselves in another, to see our common humanity. This is what many of us cannot or will not do. A certain degree of natural revulsion to homosexual acts per se is natural for heterosexuals. All of us should be thankful that there are at least some sinful actions to which we are not naturally drawn. But a revulsion to an act is not the same as a revulsion to a person. If you cannot empathize with a homosexual person because of your fear of, or revulsion to, them, then you are failing our Lord. You are guilty of pride, fear, or arrogance. . . . The homosexual people I know are very much like me. They want love, respect, acceptance, companionship, significance, forgiveness. But, like all of us sinners, they choose the wrong means to get what they want.[16]

AFFIRM. Homosexuals often face rejection—from society, from their families, and from their friends, both gay and straight—and they often expect it from the church. For some, their homosexuality itself is (at least partially) a response to loneliness and rejection. Consequently, it will be difficult if not impossible for them to face their sin and turn from it without a strong sense of acceptance and affirmation from the adult who is committed to helping. He (or she) will need someone who is willing to pray with and eat with him, hug and comfort him, compliment him, be seen with him, and be patient with him through thick and thin. Affirmation can be offered to the youth by:

- Helping the youth receive and acknowledge God's love and forgiveness.

- Communicating unconditional acceptance of and love for the youth clearly and verbally.

- Guiding the youth to understand that God loves—in fact, He *delights in*—him or her.[17]

- Reinforcing the youth's positive traits (sunny disposition, winning smile, healthy sense of humor, etc.) and abilities (athleticism, computer prowess, musical talents, etc.).

DIRECT. The following direction, adapted from the writings of Jay Adams, Jerry Arterburn, and John White, may help a concerned and committed adult to advise a young person struggling with homosexual feelings or behavior:

1. Be sure the young person understands God's view of homosexuality. Call it sin. Guide him or her to call it sin as well.

2. Urge repentance. Gently exhort the young person to confess his or her sin, seek God's forgiveness, and accept His cleansing.

3. Guide him or her to turn from homosexuality. White addresses the youth: "Your practice of homosexuality . . . must stop. *Now.* And if it has not yet started, it must never be allowed to. . . . Whatever God may or may not do for you in the way of changing your sexual orientation, He can and will deliver you from any specific homosexual entanglement and from all homosexual activity. Your part is simply to quit."[18]

4. Exhort him or her to flee temptation. Urge the youth to "break all past associations . . . with other homosexuals."[19] Help him "avoid the company of anyone who specially turns [him] on [and to] avoid places and circumstances which

expose [him] to sexual arousal."[20] Consider suggesting that he tell his gay friends why he is breaking the relationship, explaining that he is not rejecting them, but that he needs to be free from the very powerful influences of the past.[21] (See also suggestions for conquering lust in chapter 25, "Lust.")

5. Advise him or her to avoid "dating" for awhile. Arterburn points out that relationships with the opposite sex can be too frustrating in the early days of the individual's new lifestyle. He says such relationships may fail, causing the young person to justify a return to homosexuality, saying, "I gave it a try."

"In the beginning," Arterburn advises, "it is best to spend some time with new friends while you discover who you really are and who you can become."[22]

6. Recommend prayer and meditation on God's Word. Advise the young person to channel his or her energies into prayer and Bible reading and memorization—not just as a distraction, but as a source of strength. Arterburn suggests, "Make [the Scriptures] a part of your life. Meditate on what they are saying to you. They will allow you to change your entire focus. They will keep you moving toward the goals that God would have you achieve."[23]

ENLIST. Take every opportunity to allow the youth to make his or her own determinations about effecting an exit from the homosexual lifestyle. Enlist his or her involvement in brainstorming each new step to take, remembering that his or her "ownership" of the plan and the process is key to its effectiveness. If the adult is the only one determined to see deliverance take place, it will not happen.

REFER. Arterburn writes:

The issue of sexual orientation is complex. [The youth *and* the youth leader or parent] need help in sorting it all out and making sense of what has happened. I know of no one who has been able to do this alone and not suffer many painful relapses. There are counselors and psychiatrists who specialize in this and can be of great help. The issue is . . . why should [anyone] attempt it alone when help is available?[24]

Some of the resources that are available (in addition to local professional Christian counselors) include:

Minirth Meier New Life Clinics
800-NEW-LIFE

Exodus International
P.O. Box 2121
San Rafael, California 94912
415-454-1017

Worthy Creations Ministry
3601 Davie Blvd.
Ft. Lauderdale, Florida 33312
305-463-0848

Desert Stream Ministries
c/o A.R.M. (AIDS Resource Ministries)
1415 Santa Monica Mall, Suite 201
Santa Monica, California 90401
213-395-9137

Homosexuals Anonymous Fellowship Services
P.O. Box 7881
Reading, Pennsylvania 19603
215-376-1146

For Further Reading

The following resources may help the concerned parent, pastor, teacher, or youth worker assist a young person who is struggling with homosexuality:

Scriptures Cited in This Chapter

- Genesis 1:28, 2:24; 19:4–9
- Matthew 19:4–5
- Mark 10:7–8
- Leviticus 18:6–22
- Romans 1:24–28
- 1 Corinthians 6:9–11
- 1 Timothy 1:8–10
- Judges 19:1–30
- 2 Peter 2:1–22
- Jude 3–23
- Psalm 18:19

Other Scripture to Read

- Psalm 119:9–10
- Psalms 6, 32, 38, 51, 102, 130, 143
- Romans 12:1–2
- 1 Corinthians 6:20
- Galatians 5:16
- 1 John 1:9
- Jude 24–25

Further Reading

- Jerry Arterburn with Steve Arterburn, *How Will I Tell My Mother?* (Oliver Nelson).
- Erwin W. Lutzer, *Living with Your Passions* (Victor).
- Josh McDowell, *Sex, Guilt, and Forgiveness* (Tyndale House).
- Herbert J. Miles, *Singles, Sex, and Marriage* (Word).
- Josh McDowell and Bill Jones, *The Teenage Q&A Book* (Word).
- John White, *Eros Defiled* (InterVarsity).

32

AIDS

A Synopsis

❖

Introduction

Jackie started her freshman year at a small college in Manitoba, Canada, bubbling with optimism and excitement. She had just turned eighteen and felt like the youngest student on campus.

She noticed Zach right away. He was in one of her morning classes, and she thought she noticed him noticing her. He seemed quiet, but he was tall and good-looking. He introduced himself the second or third day of classes, and Jackie discovered that he was a Christian. She was thrilled when he asked her out the second week of classes.

They began dating, and by the end of the term they had become very close. By Christmas, they had begun having sex—not every time they went out, but pretty regularly.

When summer arrived, they separated tearfully, vowing to write each other every day and to remain faithful until they could see each other again in the fall. Zach planned to work all summer at his dad's print shop in Winnipeg, and Jackie was part of a Christian mission group traveling to the Ukraine for six weeks.

She had been dreading the trouble and embarrassment of the physical exam she had to undergo before going on the mission trip, but she had not expected it to change her life. The doctor called her back within a few days of her exam and asked if she could return to the office for a brief visit. When she told him it really wasn't convenient, he gave her the news over the phone: She had tested positive for HIV. He wanted her to take another test.

Jackie was alone in the house when the doctor called; after she hung up the phone, she sat on the edge of her bed, numb with shock. Her chest felt deflated, as if her lungs had collapsed. She sat in silent shock for a half-hour, thinking but not thinking. She couldn't seem to wrap her mind around the doctor's news. The more minutes flipped by on her digital clock, the more distant and unreal the doctor's words seemed.

Suddenly she thought of Zach. *Zach.* She realized with a growing sense of horror what the doctor's words meant for both of them.

Zach was the only sexual partner she'd ever had.

The Problem of AIDS

As of 1994, over a million cases of AIDS (acquired immunodeficiency disease) had been reported to the World Health Organization since the global epidemic began in the late 1970s and early 1980s. Experts estimate that around four million people have contracted AIDS since the disease was first diagnosed, and a total of over sixteen million adults (and one million children) have been infected with HIV, the precursor to AIDS.[1]

While it is difficult to measure the prevalence of the AIDS epidemic (due to under-diagnosis, faulty reporting, and delays in reporting) the number of AIDS cases diagnosed in one year alone topped 100,000 in the United States.[2]

Moreover, HIV infection is occurring among teens in alarming numbers. Pediatrician Mary-Ann Schafer of the University of California's medical school in San Francisco reports, "Teenagers have more STDs [sexually transmitted diseases] than any other group in the United States."[3] About 2.5 million people under the age of twenty are infected with some form of an STD, including AIDS.[4] One panel of experts reported, "Americans under 25, and more specifically those in their teens, are the ones at greatest risk for STDs today."[5] (See chapter 33, "Other Sexually Transmitted Diseases," for more information.)

The Causes of AIDS

Probably no other disease in recent times has caused as much fear or drawn as much of the public's attention as AIDS. This strange and deadly disease—caused by the human immuno-deficiency virus, or HIV—has rather obscure origins. Research indicates that AIDS may have begun in Central Africa.[6] It was in 1978 that the first known case of AIDS was reported to the Centers for Disease Control.[7] The first case among homosexual men was reported in 1979 and among intravenous drug abusers in early 1980; it wasn't until 1981 that the first heterosexual transmission of AIDS was reported.[8]

◆ Teens May Be More Vulnerable Than Adults

Experts say that teens' "sexual behavior, including intercourse with multiple partners and infrequent use of condoms, may make them more vulnerable than many adults to HIV exposure."[9] According to the Centers for Disease Control (as well as the Federal Centre for AIDS in Ottawa), men are far more likely than women to be diagnosed as having contracted AIDS, and female adolescents are more likely than adult females to be diagnosed with the disease.[10] Ellen Flax, writing for *Education Week*, reports:

> The data show that the biggest single source of exposure to the virus reported by female adolescent patients was heterosexual contact, which was cited by nearly four out of ten such patients. Some 72 percent of the female teenagers with AIDS are black or Hispanic.[11]

One-fifth of all the people with AIDS are in their twenties. Many of them were infected when they were in their teens.[12] Dr. Helene Gayle of the Centers for Disease Control revealed that, in 1988, 7 percent of the AIDS cases acquired HIV infection when they were adolescents.[13]

◆ Influence of Multiple Sexual Partners

As might be expected, research has indicated that those who have a lifestyle involving multiple heterosexual partners are much more likely to develop HIV infection than those who have been involved in strictly monogamous heterosexual activity (such as in a marriage where neither partner is unfaithful). Of four hundred heterosexual individuals involved in monogamous relationships only 0.25 percent were HIV positive while 5 percent of the men and 7 percent of the women in a group of four hundred heterosexuals with at least six partners annually for the five years prior to the study were HIV positive.[14]

◆ Sexual Contact, Needle Sharing, Transfusions

The virus is typically spread through sexual contact, needle sharing, and less commonly through transfused blood or related procedures. Infants born to mothers who have the AIDS infection have a 30 to 60 percent chance of testing positive for HIV.[15] And some HIV-infected individuals may not test positive for the AIDS virus "for months or even years."[16]

Contrary to the messages spread by some in government, education, and in the media, condoms do not effectively prevent the spread of AIDS. As former U.S. Surgeon General C. Everett Koop has said, "The only way you can avoid AIDS is through abstinence."[17] And Dr. Thomas Elkins, head of obstetrics and gynecology at Louisiana State Medical School, says that "safe sex for the adolescent is called abstinence in today's world."[18]

The Effects of AIDS

◆ Opportunistic Infections or Diseases

One reference describes the disease and its effects succinctly:

> AIDS is characterized by a defect in natural immunity against disease. People who have AIDS are vulnerable to serious illnesses which would not be a threat to anyone whose immune system was functioning normally. These illnesses are referred to as "opportunistic" infections or diseases: in AIDS patients the most common of these are Pneumocystis carinii pneumonia (PCP), a parasitic infection of the lungs, and a type of cancer known as Kaposi's sarcoma (KS). Other opportunistic infections include unusually severe infections with yeast, cytomegalovirus, herpes

virus, and parasites such as Toxoplasma or Cryptosporidia. Milder infections with these organisms do not suggest immune deficiency.[19]

◆ Early Symptoms

Early symptoms of AIDS include:

- Chronic fatigue lasting for several months.
- Unexplained, progressive weight loss of fifteen pounds or more.
- Swollen lymph glands in the groin, underarms, and neck.
- Chronic diarrhea.
- Chronic fungal infections, which in women often occur in the form of vaginal yeast infections.[20]

◆ Symptoms of Full-Blown AIDS

Symptoms of full-blown AIDS include "a persistent cough, fever, and difficulty in breathing. Multiple purplish blotches and bumps on the skin may indicate Kaposi's sarcoma. The virus can also cause brain damage."[21]

The Biblical Perspective of AIDS

In the earliest days of public awareness of AIDS—when the epidemic appeared to be largely confined to the homosexual community—many preachers and churchgoers expressed the belief that the disease was obviously the curse of God on homosexuals. Some still do.

However, AIDS is not God's judgment on homosexuals. For one thing, the overwhelming majority of people around the world who have AIDS are not homosexual. The disease afflicts heterosexuals too. It has stricken hemophiliacs and others who have contracted it through blood transfusions. It has victimized newborn babies.

But AIDS—as well as other sexually transmitted diseases—does illustrate that God's commandments are like an umbrella. When you put up an umbrella, it shields you from the rain. But if you choose to move out from under that umbrella during a storm, you're bound to get wet.

As long as you stay under the umbrella of God's commands, you'll be shielded from many consequences. However, if you step out from under that protective cover, you should not be surprised if you suffer the consequences. Though sexually transmitted diseases are not a curse from God, they *are* among the many consequences of immoral behavior God wishes us all to avoid.

Dr. S. I. McMillen put it well in his excellent book, *None of These Diseases:*

> Medical science with all its knowledge is inadequate to take care of the world's [sexually transmitted] disease problem. Yet millenniums before the microscope, and before man knew the method of the transmission of [such] diseases, God knew all about them and gave to man the only feasible plan of preventing these universal and blighting killers. Jesus clearly stated that, from the beginning, our Father ordained that one man and one woman should constitute a family unit. This plan of two, and two alone, constituting a family unit is so unique, so different from human plans, and so effective in the prevention of the vast complications of horrible . . . diseases, that again we are forced to recognize another medical evidence of the inspiration of the Bible.[22]

The most casual acquaintance with the effects of sexually transmitted diseases should be enough to convince anyone of the wisdom of God's Word, which says, "Flee from sexual immorality. All other sins a man commits are outside his body, but he who sins sexually sins against his own body."[23]

But the biblical perspective does not only include wisdom which, if it is heeded, may prevent one from contracting a sexually transmitted disease; it also guides us in relating to victims of AIDS:

Do not let any unwholesome talk come out of your mouths, but only what is helpful for building others up according to their needs, that it may benefit those who listen. And do not grieve the Holy Spirit of God, with whom you were sealed for the day of redemption. Get rid of all bitterness, rage and anger, brawling and slander, along with every form of malice. Be kind and compassionate to one another, forgiving each other, just as in Christ God forgave you. Be imitators of God, therefore, as dearly loved children and live a life of love, just as Christ loved us and gave himself up for us as a fragrant offering and sacrifice to God.[24]

And again:

Therefore, as God's chosen people, holy and dearly loved, clothe yourselves with compassion, kindness, humility, gentleness and patience. Bear with each other and forgive whatever grievances you may have against one another. Forgive as the Lord forgave you. And over all these virtues put on love, which binds them all together in perfect unity.[25]

The Lord Jesus Christ, who had compassion on the woman caught in adultery,[26] who healed the woman afflicted with a detestable disease,[27] who accepted the outcast Samaritan woman,[28] would certainly will for His followers to display His likeness in how they relate to people who (even if their condition is the result of their own sin) need compassion, healing, and acceptance.

The Response to the Problem of AIDS

Listen ◆ Empathize ◆ Affirm ◆ Direct ◆ Enlist ◆ Refer

The youth leader or parent can help prevent or address the tragedy of HIV infection with a plan such as the following:

LISTEN. Take the time to understand the teen's comprehension of the disease. Ask questions designed to determine the depth and breadth of his or her education on the subject: what AIDS is, how it is transmitted, how it can be prevented. A young person who has recently learned that he or she is infected may need to vent confusion, frustration, or anger. (The youth leader or parent should review other applicable chapters in this handbook, such as those on anger and on facing death.) Do not pressure the youth to express such feelings, but create a listening atmosphere in which honest expression is welcomed without condemnation.

EMPATHIZE. Don't try to second-guess the youth's state of mind, but do seek to understand his or her reactions. He may think he knows enough about AIDS; he may be tired of hearing it at school and on television. She may be too embarrassed to discuss the matter, or she may wonder why a parent or other adult is broaching the subject. If the young person is infected, he or she is likely to be embarrassed, ashamed, frightened, or in denial. Keep these things in mind. Be aware of how your demeanor can communicate empathic warmth, even in the simplest ways, such as leaning forward in your chair or reflecting key statements. (See the section on "Learning to Offer Christian Counsel," at the front of this book.)

AFFIRM. Be wary of taking an approach that may be interpreted as accusatory or judgmental by the teen. Whether your object is education and prevention or diagnosis and treatment, communicate acceptance of the young person and affirmation of his or her worth in your eyes—and God's. Strive to impress three truths upon the young person: "God loves you unconditionally," "I love you unconditionally," and "You are a person of value and worth." This can be accomplished by:

- What you say ("You are so important to me," "No wonder God thinks you're worth dying for," etc.).

- What you don't say (avoiding condemning or criticizing statements, not dismissing the youth's thoughts or feelings as ridiculous or unimportant, etc.).

- What you do (listening carefully, spending time with the youth, being available, giving weight to his or her ideas, etc.).

- What you don't do (not canceling appointments, not looking bored when he or she is talking, etc.).

DIRECT. If the object in advising a teen is education and prevention, the following direction may prove fruitful:[29]

1. Include and involve parents. Researchers have found that teenage sexual involvement was reduced when parents supervised:

- Who the adolescent dated.

- Where the adolescent went on dates.

- The arrival time back home.

Strong, attentive family relationships tend to reduce sexual activity among teens and, consequently, the incidence of sexually transmitted diseases.

2. Urge the youth to make fellowship with God a top priority. A consistent habit of private prayer, worship, and Bible reading is the first line of defense against sin and its consequences. (See Col. 2:6–15 and Gal. 5:16.)

3. Teach the consequences of promiscuity. Make sure the youth understands the devastating, life-threatening consequences of sexual promiscuity such as those described above.

4. Teach the benefits of abstinence. Emphasize the positive benefits of abstinence—and not just to teen girls but to boys as well.

5. Eliminate or counter mixed messages about abstinence and "safer sex." Take every opportunity to counter dangerous or counterproductive messages from the school, government, or media.

6. *Keep lines of communication open.* Don't let anger, impatience, frustration, or worry clog the lines of communication with a teen. Keep talking—and keep him or her talking.

If the object is diagnosing or responding to a young person who is (or may be) HIV positive, the following course may suggest a helpful starting point:

1. *Respond compassionately.* Hurting people don't need sermons; they need help. Strike an attitude of care and concern, not of disapproval.

2. *Pray.* Pray for and with the young person. Seek God's providential care; ask Him to orchestrate your involvement and those of others in a way that will bear immediate and eternal benefits.

3. *Encourage repentance and restoration (when appropriate).* Lead the young person to verbalize his need and his desire to change his behavior, and try to bring him through repentance to an experience of God's forgiveness and restoration.

4. *Explain the biblical perspective of the problem.* Help the youth understand that AIDS is not a curse from God, but that neither is it a part of God's perfect plan. Be sensitive to any opportunity to convey God's loving motivation in issuing His commands and also to open the young person's eyes to the truth that God is able to bring good out of evil.

5. *Walk with the young person through the stages of grief.* Any time a loss is experienced (such as the loss of one's health), grief is likely to result. Patiently help the youth work through the denial, anger, bargaining, and depression that is likely to precede acceptance of his or her diagnosis. (See chapter 8, "Grief.")

6. *Expose the youth to the available resources for coping with infection.* Foremost among the available resources, of course, is God Himself; encourage the young person, through daily worship and Bible reading, to rely on God and His grace and power. In addition, help the youth

acknowledge (preferably by name) those people who are or may be willing to help in practical ways.

ENLIST. Guide the young person toward a self-initiated course of action for prevention or treatment. Help the youth brainstorm ways to escape temptation; encourage the infected youth to devise his or her own plan for coping with the problem. Lead him or her to consider ways he or she may influence others.

REFER. If the young person has contracted the HIV virus, parental notification and medical attention are, of course, immediate priorities; early diagnosis and ongoing treatment are crucial. There is also an AIDS hotline for recorded information (800-342-2437), as well as a line for specific questions (800-433-0366). The expertise and guidance of a professional Christian counselor is a valuable resource that should not be ignored or postponed.

For Further Reading

The following resources may help the concerned parent, pastor, teacher, or youth worker to educate a young person regarding AIDS or to assist a young person who is infected with AIDS:

Scriptures Cited in This Chapter

- 1 Corinthians 6:18
- Ephesians 4:29–5:2
- Colossians 3:12–14
- John 8:1–11
- Mark 5:25–34
- John 4:1–42
- Colossians 2:6–15
- Galatians 5:16

Other Scripture to Read

- Psalm 34:18

- Psalms 6, 32, 38, 51, 102, 130, 143

- Psalm 103:11–18

- Isaiah 53:4–6

- 1 John 1:9

Further Reading

- Dr. James Dobson, *Life on the Edge* (Word).

- Dan Korem, *Streetwise Parents, Foolproof Kids* (NavPress).

- Josh McDowell, *The Myths of Sex Education* (Here's Life Publishers).

- Josh McDowell and Dick Day, *Why Wait? What You Need to Know about the Teen Sexuality Crisis* (Here's Life Publishers).

33

OTHER SEXUALLY TRANSMITTED DISEASES

A Synopsis

❖

Introduction

Kayla Ross recorded her sexual experiences in a spiral notebook which she kept in the table beside her bed. Her first time occurred when she was twelve years old.

She and her boyfriend had been watching Saturday morning cartoons together at his house. The boy's parents were still in bed.

"I knew it was going to happen." Kayla says now. "We started kissing and then we went up to his bedroom. He got a rubber out of his dresser drawer. I wasn't scared. I wasn't excited, either. I wasn't anything."

Afterward, Kayla says, "I was glad. A lot of girls my age talked about doing it. But I did it."

After that first experience, Kayla started recording her sexual encounters in the notebook. Her large, looping handwriting records nine sexual partners before the age of sixteen, complete with names, dates, and a rating system. Only two of the boys used a condom; from one of the others she contracted chlamydia, a sexually transmitted disease that, untreated, can cause miscarriages, stillbirths, and sterility. One partner beat her up after learning she had the disease.

Kayla had unprotected sex with three boys after discovering her STD. "The doctor gave me some medication and told me I should get checked every six months and tell every guy I've had sex with to get checked—yeah, right. I don't even know where some of them live anymore."

Kayla's mother doesn't know about the notebook, nor about her daughter's disease. When asked if her daughter is sexually active, she answers, "I don't know. I hope not. She's never talked to me about it, but she knows how I feel." She sighs. "Things are different today than when I was in school. You can't keep your kids at home anymore. You can't protect them from everything that's out there.

"I just pray that she's being careful. I don't know what else I can do."[1]

The Problem of Sexually Transmitted Diseases

In recent years, public awareness of and scientific research in sexually transmitted diseases have mushroomed, and with good reason: STDs have reached epidemic proportions. The World Health Organization's *minimal* estimates of the worldwide incidence of the five major bacterial and viral STDs exceed a hundred million cases, and those figures do not include the forty-five other identifiable forms of sexually transmitted diseases.[2]

Statistical breakdowns reveal that 35,616 Americans acquire an STD *every day*. At this rate, one in every four Americans between the ages of fifteen and fifty-five will eventually get a sexually transmitted disease—and the incidence is spiraling upward.[3]

Teens—and even preteens—are contracting STDs at an alarming rate. Pediatrician Mary-Ann Schafer of the University of California's medical school in San Francisco reports, "Teenagers have more STDs than any other group in the United States."[4] About 2.5 million people under the age of twenty are infected with some form of an STD, including AIDS.[5] One panel of experts reported, "Americans under 25, and more specifically those in their teens, are the ones at greatest risk for STDs today."[6]

As mentioned above, over fifty sexually transmitted diseases are known to exist. An overview of some of the more widespread STDs, their causes and effects, follows.

◆ Herpes

Apart from AIDS, perhaps no other disease has jolted the casual-sex movement in America as much as herpes. As recently as the 1950s, the transmission of herpes during sexual intercourse was considered rare. Between 1966 and 1979 the estimated number of consultations with physicians for herpes increased from under 30,000 to over 250,000. By 1984 an estimated twenty million people in America had genital herpes. The National Institute of Allergy and Infectious Diseases now estimates that about "30 million Americans are infected, and that 500,000 more catch the sexually transmitted virus each year."[7] In addition to this huge number of symptomatic cases there are many cases of genital herpes infection in which the individual has no symptoms.

Studies show that 25 to 65 percent of all women carry the virus unknowingly, averaging almost 50 percent of all women over eighteen. *USA Today* reported a study indicating that up to one-third of all adults carry the genital herpes virus in their blood system. One study of pregnant women in several large American cities indicates that up to 65 percent have silent (symptomless) herpes infections.

Herpes can be divided into two types: I and II. In the past, type I was associated with infections above the waist, such as the common cold sore on the lip. Type II was associated with infections of the genital area. However, with the increased practice of oral sex, this distinction has changed. According to one group of studies, from 26 to 40 percent of genital herpes involve type I.

It has been estimated that one-third to one-half of the initial herpes infections are either without symptoms or so mild they go unnoticed. Those victims suffering symptoms typically experience painful blisters beginning two to twelve days after sex with an infected person. The blisters then break down to form ulcers and generally heal within about two weeks. Primary or initial infections can be much more severe, causing swelling, lymph node enlargement, fever, headaches, muscle aches, and discharge or drainage from the genitals. Once the acute infection is over, the herpes virus migrates up the sensory nerve endings to the nerve ganglion and there goes into a latent state.

Later, after some stress, emotional upset, sexual intercourse, menstrual period, or for no apparent reason, the virus will migrate down the sensory nerve endings to the surface of the skin and form new blisters, thus creating a recurrence of the initial herpes infection. The frequency and severity of these recurrent attacks of herpes vary considerably. During the acute attack, it has been recommended by doctors that patients remain sexually abstinent to avoid the spread of the infection. It should be noted, however, that the infection can be passed even when an infected individual has no symptoms, as individuals have been found to shed viruses up to 20 percent of the time, even during symptom-free periods. In fact, according to one medical source, it may be that most herpes infections are passed during these periods.

While condoms offer partial protection against the spread of herpes infection, this protection is not complete. Herpes can be spread even when condoms are used. Also, while the drug Acyclovir may help modify or suppress an infection, it will not completely prevent the transmission of the infection from one person to another.

In addition to the pain and discomfort from the infection itself, herpes can cause other problems. It has been estimated that a baby delivered by a mother with an active infection will have a 40 to 60 percent chance of contracting the disease. Because of their poorly developed immunologic systems, some 40 percent or more of the infants who contract herpes will die, and many of the others will suffer brain damage. To avoid these tragic problems, doctors deliver babies by C-section if the mother has an active infection or is shedding herpes viruses.

Although it is rare, herpes sometimes infects the brain, causing a localized encephalitis that can lead to severe brain damage or death. Also, there is the possibility that herpes may help to cause genital cancers, serving as a cofactor in this regard. In cervical cancer, definite association between herpes viruses and the cancer cells has been noted. Also, more recently an association between herpes viruses and vulvar (external portions of the female genitalia) cancer were noted.

The pain and problems associated with herpes infections point to the importance of avoiding casual sexual encounters, as even one sexual experience with an infected but symptom-free person may lead to years of intermittent suffering and trouble with this infection. Our kids must be taught the truth about herpes.

◆ Chlamydia

This organism is too small to be seen by a light microscope and is difficult to culture, and an infected person may go long periods with no signs or symptoms of the disease. Consequently it has been a difficult organism to detect and report. However, researchers estimate some four million cases of chlamydia occur annually in the U.S.[8] The World Health Organization's minimal estimates place the worldwide incidence of chlamydia at some 50 million cases.[9]

These infections can be so mild that the woman may not even be aware that she has an infection. Nevertheless, over a period of time this infection may lead to a complete blockage of the fallopian tubes and infertility due to the scarring of the infection. Many women in this situation will not know anything is wrong until they try to get pregnant and find that they are unable to.

Chlamydia trachomatis is not only a major cause of pelvic inflammatory disease (PID), but frequently also causes miscarriages and premature labor. Women with this infection also tend to have more stillbirths and postpartum infections. In the newborn child, chlamydia can cause eye infections and pneumonia.

In males, chlamydia can cause chronic prostate infections and other infections of the male genitals, such as epididymitis, which can seriously affect a man's fertility. (The epididymis lies next to the testicles and serves as a storage vessel for sperm cells.) It has been estimated that a quarter of a million cases of acute epididymitis each year are caused by this organism. While most women do not have symptoms with chlamydia, most men develop a milky discharge and pain on urination. It has been estimated that one in twenty adult males is a silent carrier of the infection. There are an estimated several million new cases of chlamydia trachomatis each year in this country. It is more common than gonorrhea and syphilis combined.

◆ Pelvic Inflammatory Disease (PID)

PID is an infectious inflammation of the female organs that strikes approximately one million women in America each year. A number of different kinds of organisms or bacteria can cause this infection, such as gonorrhea or chlamydia trachomatis. In some cases a severe infection forms within the womb and fallopian tubes. If this infection is not treated adequately or in time, a pocket of pus may form that eventually will burst, spreading the infection throughout the abdominal cavity. When this occurs, the victim may first notice a sudden increase in pain and very quickly begin to go into shock. If she does not have surgery quickly to deal with the infection, she may die within a matter of hours. Such surgeries can involve the removal of all of the internal female organs, thus leaving her unable to bear children. In addition, because of the removal of the ovaries, she will need to be on estrogen, a hormone medication, for many years.

In some cases, PID may involve a very mild infection, particularly if chlamydia trachomatis is involved. Of those women who developed PID as a result of chlamydia, gonorrhea, or some other bacterial infection, it has been estimated that 10 to 15 percent who have a first-time infection will become permanently infertile. Those who develop PID a second time have an estimated 30 to 35 percent chance of becoming infertile. And those who have a third episode of PID have an estimated 60 to 75 percent chance of

becoming infertile by this infection.

Infertility, however, is not the only problem these women face. One research study found that women with PID were five times more likely to have abdominal operations and three times more likely to have abdominal pain or pain during intercourse than would normally be expected. Unfortunately, many women do not realize that a single casual sexual involvement can lead to chronic pain and sterility. For teenagers who have multiple sexual partners, their risk of getting PID increases fivefold.

PID can lead to other tragic problems such as ectopic pregnancy. An ectopic pregnancy involves the development of the fertilized ovum or fetus in some other place in the mother's body besides the womb, such as the fallopian tubes. However, the fallopian tubes are unable to expand as the womb is to contain the ever-growing fetus. Usually at around six to eight weeks the developing baby is so large that the fallopian tube suddenly ruptures, leading to rapid bleeding and shock. Typically, the victim experiences severe pain and may even pass out. Without treatment, this condition can lead to death. While ectopic pregnancy can be caused by a variety of medical problems such as pelvic adhesions from previous surgery or endometriosis, some 50 percent of women with this condition appear to have had PID previously.

Due to the tremendous increase in the number of ectopic pregnancies in this country, ruptured tubal pregnancy has now become a major cause of maternal death. The increase in the number of ectopic pregnancies in this country has been so great that it has been referred to as an epidemic. Half of the women who have ectopic pregnancies will be infertile afterward.

It appears that PID can cause ectopic pregnancies by partially blocking the fallopian tubes. In such a case it is possible for the tiny sperm cells to make their way up through the narrowed and scarred fallopian tube to the female egg and fertilize it. But it is then impossible for the much larger fertilized egg to traverse the constricted fallopian tube to the womb where the fetus would normally develop.

It should be noted that surgeons have had only limited success at repairing damaged tubes. It should also be noted that *in vitro* fertilization (fertilizing the woman's ovum with her husband's sperm outside of her body and then placing it back into the womb) has also met with rather limited success.

Although use of condoms has been encouraged as a means of protecting against the spread of STDs, a recent Rutgers University study of students with genital complaints who were seen at the student health center cast doubt on their efficacy in protecting against chlamydial infections. Of those who used condoms, 35.7 percent had chlamydia compared with 37 percent who used oral contraceptives and 44 percent who used no contraceptives.

◆ Cytomegalovirus (CMV)

The risk of infection with cytomegalovirus is an additional reason to avoid casual sexual encounters. While CMV is found in the saliva and apparently can be transmitted in a variety of ways, it is also found in male semen and in female cervical secretions and can be transmitted through sexual intercourse. Frequently CMV infections produce no symptoms, but they may cause illnesses similar to the flu or mononucleosis.

A much more serious situation arises when a pregnant woman becomes infected and then transmits the infection to her unborn child. An estimated forty thousand to eighty thousand babies are born each year with congenital CMV infections. Of these infected children, 10 to 20 percent will have significant and permanent handicaps such as microcephaly (small headedness) or hydrocephalus, seizures, hearing problems, psychomotor retardation, and learning problems.

Other babies infected during pregnancy will die before birth, be born prematurely, or have fatal problems with liver and spleen disease. In the United States, congenital CMV infections are now one of the leading causes of hearing problems in children. Infected mothers can also transmit their infection to their babies during delivery. CMV may also cause pneumonia and respiratory problems in babies.

◆ Hepatitis B

Hepatitis B is another viral infection that can be transmitted sexually. The incidence of hepatitis B rises dramatically with an increase in the number of sexual partners. One study found that those with only one or two sexual partners had a less than 1 percent incidence of hepatitis B, while those with ten or more sexual partners had a 7 percent incidence. Some 60 percent of homosexual men have had hepatitis, while some 85 percent of homosexual males have become infected by age forty. Fortunately a vaccine protecting individuals against hepatitis B became available in 1982, and the U.S. Public Health Services recommended that the high-risk groups, such as prostitutes, homosexually active males, and heterosexually active persons with multiple sexual contact, should receive the vaccine.

Some victims have such mild cases of hepatitis that they are unaware of it, suffering only flu-like symptoms if any. Others experience severe, sometimes fatal liver damage. Hepatitis B virus infection also has been found to lead to primary liver cancer in a significant percentage of cases.

Hepatitis can also be transmitted from a mother to her unborn child, resulting at times in the death of the fetus, a stillbirth, premature delivery, or hepatitis in the newborn child and an ongoing infection through childhood. Other research indicates that 90 percent of the babies whose mothers are chronic hepatitis B virus carriers will be infected at the time of their birth. Of these babies, some 90 percent will go on to become chronic hepatitis B virus carriers. Left untreated, a significant percentage of carriers will eventually develop cancer of the liver. Fortunately, immunization of these exposed babies shortly following their birth can prevent this in a high percentage of cases.

◆ Venereal Warts

In comparison to AIDS and herpes, venereal warts (caused by the human papilloma virus) have received little publicity. Yet in recent years there has been a tremendous increase in the incidence of this disease. Data indicate that during the time that visits to doctors for herpes increased 300 percent, visits for venereal warts increased 1,100 percent.

There are an estimated one million or more cases of venereal warts a year in the United States. It is estimated that some 10 percent of adult men and 5 percent of adult women will have venereal warts, also called VD warts, at some time in their lives.

In one study, 48 percent of the women in an STD clinic (with normal pap smears) had evidence of this infection, and in another study 17 percent of an otherwise normal group of individuals also had evidence of this infection.

Sixty percent or more of the sexual partners of patients with the human papilloma virus infection have the infection themselves.

While VD warts are very common, it is felt that perhaps infections with the human papilloma virus that do not cause warts, or are asymptomatic, are more common than those that do. Evidence also suggests that homosexual males have a higher than average incidence of venereal warts.

Venereal warts are readily passed during sexual intercourse. They typically occur about two to three months after exposure. However, they have been known to occur as soon as a few weeks after sexual contact and as long as two years after exposure.

The warts can occur on different parts of the male or female genitals, even inside a woman's vagina or cervix or inside a man's penis. VD wards grow quickly during pregnancy and may interfere with the delivery of the child. Though it is quite unusual, babies born to mothers with warts may develop warts around their anus or in their vocal cord area, which can cause hoarseness or difficulty with breathing.

In addition to the human papilloma virus, a poxvirus can also cause a different type of wart called *molluscum contagiosum*. This smaller wart usually occurs in clusters, and while it's often no bigger than a fifth of an inch in diameter, it may grow to be as large as an inch in size. This wart can also be found in other parts of the body and be spread by contact. Between 1966 and 1983 the incidence of molluscum contagiosum increased tenfold.

◆ Pelvic Cancer

While doctors used to believe that VD warts were harmless, more recent research indicates that this is not the case. Dr. Ralph Reichert of Columbia University College of Physicians and Surgeons notes that women who have VD warts secondary to the human papilloma virus infection are one thousand to two thousand times more likely to get cervical cancer than women without the warts.[10] One doctor, at the Second World Congress on Sexually Transmitted Diseases in 1986, noted that certain types of the human papilloma virus were found in over 90 percent of the cervical cancers studied.[11] At a state medical meeting of family physicians, another researcher predicted that "an epidemic of cervical cancer among women is likely to occur if liberal sexual life styles continue."[12]

Medical research has indicated that a number of risk factors increase a woman's chance of developing cervical cancer. These include multiple sexual partners, having sex with someone who's had multiple sexual partners, and beginning sexual intercourse at an early age (eighteen to twenty).

The associate chief of staff of the Boston Hospital for women, Dr. Robert Kistner, noted in

1972 that "early and frequent coitus, especially with multiple partners, seems to increase the incidence of this cancer precursor." Dr. Kistner added, "Carcinoma in situ in women under 25 made up only 30 percent of the total cervical cancer cases in 1950–51. However, by 1967–68 this figure had increased in 92.2 percent of the total."[13]

Surprisingly, beginning sexual activity at an early age is considered an even greater risk factor for the development of cervical cancer than having multiple partners. This rather surprising finding seems to be related to the immaturity of the cells that line the cervix in younger women.

Another study found cases of cellular abnormalities in the cervixes to be five times greater in a group of promiscuous teenagers than in a group of virgin teenage girls. Medical researcher I. D. Rathin of the Kaiser Foundation Research Institute reported, "There is enough material in recent literature to caution young women against sexual intercourse at early ages. These several studies are concerned with causation of cancer of the uterine cervix, and results are all in the same direction. . . . All studies agree that cervical cancer risk is increased by . . . first coitus at early ages. . . . By observing abstinence the adolescent female is on reasonably valid biological ground, which requires no moral or religious support."[14]

Another researcher, Rodkin, also reported, "Twice as many patients (i.e., the subjects with cervical cancer) as controls began coitus at ages 15–17. . . . Patients also differed strongly from controls with respect to . . . number of husbands and total number of coital mates. . . . Many more patients than controls had multiple sexual mates."[15]

In regard to women having sex with an individual who has had multiple sexual contacts as a risk factor, women with cancer of the cervix were more likely to have had husbands who had visited prostitutes or who had extramarital affairs. Dr. Irving I. Kessler of Johns Hopkins found that "extramarital sexual practice by either the woman or her spouse is also associated with cervical cancer risk."[16]

In addition to apparently helping to cause cervical cancer, it appears that the human papilloma virus is also associated with increased incidence of vulvar cancer, cancer of the external genitals in women. To a lesser extent, it is associated with penile cancers in men. Furthermore, it appears that cancers of the anal area may be associated with warts, and those who develop warts as a result of oral sex may be at increased risk to get cancers of the esophagus and larynx, or vocal cord area.

Gynecologist Dr. Joe McIlhaney declares, "I have begun telling those patients of mine who seem interested in knowing the cause of their cervical dysplasia, cervical cancer, or venereal warts, that they are sexually transmitted diseases almost entirely."[17]

◆ Syphilis

Syphilis, once hopefully considered to be a conquered disease, has made a global resurgence. While the exact number of syphilis cases is difficult to obtain because of under-reporting, it appears that, with the discovery and use of penicillin, the number dropped dramatically until about 1957. However, between 1957 and 1981 there was an apparent fourfold increase in the number of reported cases. Today, the World Health Organization's minimal estimates place the worldwide incidence of infectious syphilis at 3.5 million cases.[18]

While capable of causing severe disease and complications, syphilitic infections typically begin with rather mild signs and symptoms. In the first of three stages, not including the latent stage that occurs between the second and third, a small bump may appear from nine to ninety days after the transmission of the infection by sexual contact. This bump slowly breaks down, forming a painless ulcer. During the second stage, which often occurs three weeks after the development of the first, the individual may experience a flu-like illness with fever, headache, runny nose, aches and pains, sore throat, and at times, a generalized skin rash. After a while these symptoms disappear and the individual goes into what is called the latent stage, feeling completely free of illness or disease.

Some of these individuals who have a latent infection will go on in time to develop tertiary syphilis. For some this third stage may take the form of destructive lesions, called gummas, which involve the breakdown of tissues, such as skin and bone. As much as ten years after the onset of the latent stage, other infected individuals may develop severe problems with the heart and major blood vessels. Heart valves may be damaged and the aorta, the major artery through which blood flows from the heart, may begin to balloon because of damage, forming an aneurysm. In other cases obstruction of circulation may occur, leading to angina.

In still other patients, severe damage to the brain and spinal cord may occur. Some of these patients may experience marked memory loss and confusion or dementia while others may become psychotic. It appears that syphilis of the brain can mimic almost any psychiatric disorder. Severe damage to the spinal cord may lead to loss-of-position sense in the legs and a very unsteady gait. Spinal-cord damage can also lead to incontinence and impotence. Also disturbing is the data that links syphilic infection with increased rates of HIV (AIDS) infection.

Syphilis in a pregnant woman can lead to disastrous consequences for her unborn child. Studies indicate that approximately one-fourth of these children will die before birth, another one-fourth will die shortly after birth, and still others will develop various complications and medical problems from the syphilis. Fortunately, congenital syphilis, the infection of the baby in the mother's womb, is a rather unusual occurrence. While accurate estimates of the true number of children born with congenital syphilis are difficult to obtain, it appears that the number has been climbing steadily in recent years. These cases tended to involve mostly unmarried young women who received little or no prenatal care.

◆ Gonorrhea

Medical researcher Dr. Gordon Muir reports that gonorrhea has become "the most common reportable disease in school-age children, surpassing chicken pox, measles, mumps and rubella combined."[19] "In 1987," explains *Education Week,* "gonorrhea was reported in more than 1 percent of young people aged 15 to 19. Although people between the ages of 20 and 24 had an infection rate of more than 1.5 percent, the CDC found that when adjusting for sexual-activity rates, adolescents 15–19 actually have the highest rates of gonorrhea of any age group."[20]

H. Hunter Handsfield, director of the sexually transmitted disease control program for the Seattle-King County Department of Health, called the gonorrhea rates "truly phenomenal," especially for black inner-city teenage girls. Handsfield warned, "If a black girl (in King County) becomes sexually active at the age of 13 or 14, her risk of getting gonorrhea is 25 percent every year. If the same girl delays her sexual activity until the age of 15, she has a 50 percent chance of getting the disease by the age of 18."[21]

Unlike syphilis, which causes some of its most severe problems many years after the initial infection, gonorrhea tends to cause problems early on. It commonly causes discharge or drainage from the penis or vagina as well as frequent and painful urination. In females gonorrhea can spread into the uterus and fallopian tubes, causing pelvic inflammatory disease. These infections can lead to infertility, abdominal pain, pain during intercourse, and ectopic pregnancies. Serious and uncontrolled infections may lead to a need for surgery.

According to Dr. Grimes of the University of Missouri at Kansas City School of Medicine, gonorrhea is the primary cause of arthritis in young adults.[22] It is also the most common cause of infectious arthritis in the general population. Although it occurs rarely, gonorrhea may also cause infections of the heart or of the lining of the brain and spinal cord.

In addition to gonorrhea of the genital organs, individuals can develop gonorrhea of the rectum and pharynx (throat) if they're involved in oral or anal sexual practices.

About 60 percent of the women and 20 percent of the men who have a gonorrhea infection will not have any symptoms. This makes it difficult to control the spread of infections, as an infected individual without symptoms may pass it on to somebody else without even knowing he or she had it in the first place.

In the past, gonorrhea was readily treated by a shot of penicillin, but many strains of gonorrhea have become resistant to this medication. In recent years a number of different kinds of resistant strains of gonorrhea have developed, making treatment increasingly difficult.

It is difficult to know the exact number of cases of gonorrhea in this country because of under-reporting, but between 1960 and 1980 the number of reported cases of gonorrhea rose from about 259,000 to slightly over a million. It is thought that there were actually twice that number of cases—two million—in view of the tendency of this disease to be under-reported. The World Health Organization's minimal estimate of worldwide incidence of the disease places the number at twenty-five million.[23]

It is apparent that, although some have had a tendency to think of gonorrheal infections as rather trivial and unimportant, in view of the above facts and data, this is not at all the case. A great many of the more than "70 percent of people who are sexually active by the age of 19 may have an initial exposure to an STD, become infected, and pass the infection on without ever feeling ill or knowing they've been infected."[24]

◆ Miscellaneous STDs

While a complete description of all sexually transmitted diseases is beyond the intent and scope of this chapter, there are several others that should be mentioned: trichomoniasis, T-mycoplasma, scabies, and pediculosis pubis.

Trichomoniasis. Trichomoniasis is a tiny, one-celled protozoa that affects about one-fifth of all women who are sexually active with multiple partners during their reproductive years. There are an estimated 3 million or more new cases of this infection in the United States each year. One study in the Medical Aspects of Human sexuality reports that "an estimated 8 million Americans each year develop trichomoniasis."[25]

Trichomoniasis seems to be easily passed through sexual activity as it is found in 85 percent of the women who are sexual partners of infected males and in 70 percent of the men who are involved sexually with infected females. While men frequently do not have any symptoms, they may develop a discharge from the penis. Research has shown that mobility of the sperm may be decreased by the infection, tending to decrease the ability to father children.

In women this infection is rare in virgins, although it can be transmitted nonsexually. About one-quarter of women do not have any symptoms while others may have a heavy yellowish or greenish malodorous vaginal discharge and also experience severe itching. The infection can cause pain on urination and intercourse as well as menstrual problems. It appears that trichomoniasis can increase infertility in women. Trichomoniasis typically can be successfully treated with Metronidazole. Recently, however, some strains of trichomoniasis have developed resistance to low doses of this drug.

T-Mycoplasma. In spite of the fact that T-mycoplasma infections have received very little publicity, they are very common. This infection is not found in young adults who are virgins, but it has been found in over 40 percent of men and over 70 percent of women who have three to five sexual partners. Recent research indicates that it is at least a temporary cause of infertility in women. T-mycoplasma infections may also play a role in miscarriages.

In men, T-mycoplasma infection is thought to cause some infertility problems as well as penile discharge, pain during urination, and itching. Also in males it appears that this infection may lead to Reiter's syndrome, which involves inflammation of the eye (conjunctivitis), urethritis, and arthritis. The arthritis in this syndrome can sometimes recur for years.

Scabies. Scabies is caused by a tiny eight-legged mite. While this infection is often contracted during sexual intercourse, it can be passed through nonsexual means. Typically the female mite burrows into the skin of the infected individual to lay her eggs in areas of the body such as the male genitals, breasts, buttocks, armpits, wrists, elbows, and near the naval. Itchiness, which is thought to be due to the body's reaction to either the eggs or the mite's feces, which are deposited in the skin, is often very marked at nighttime. Fortunately, prescription lotions are effective in curing this particular infection.

Pediculosis pubis. Pediculosis pubis is an infection similar to scabies, but one that is caused by a tiny, wingless insect called a crab louse, which is barely visible to the naked eye. This louse has claws on the second and third pair of legs that allow it to hold on to pubic hairs while moving about. Frequently there is a one-week to one-month delay between the infestation and the onset of symptoms, which involve itching that at times can be severe. This pubic louse feeds frequently on the blood of the infected individual by sticking its mouth down into tiny blood vessels. Prescription lotions are frequently effective in the treatment of this infection.

The Biblical Perspective of Sexually Transmitted Diseases

Dr. S. I. McMillen, in his classic *None of These Diseases*, details the ravages of sexually transmitted diseases and then states:

> Obedience to God's helpful Guidebook has been and still is the best way to avoid the calamitous effects of venereal disease. Everybody who stubbornly seeks to circumvent his heavenly Father's suggestions will sooner or later have to pay the devil's price. . . . Three thousand years ago our heavenly Father sought to save us from such an end:

> My son, attend to wisdom, bend your ear to knowledge, . . . that they may save you from the loose woman: her lips drop honied words, her talk is smoother than oil itself, but the end with her is bitter as poison, sharp as a sword with a double edge. . . .
> Now listen to me, my son, hold fast to what I say: keep clear of her, never go near her door, lest . . . you are left at last to moan . . . "Ah, Why did I hate guidance, why did I despise all warning?" (Prov. 5:1–12, MOFFATT).

The Lord not only gives many warnings to help mankind, but Jesus so transforms and fortifies one with the energy and power of His Holy Spirit that no [one] has valid excuse for falling into sexual sin. The Apostle Paul expresses the matter forcibly in his Epistle to the Thessalonians:

> God's plan is to make you holy, and that entails first of all a clean cut with sexual immorality. Every one of you should learn to control his body, keeping pure and treating it with respect, and never regarding it as an instrument for self-gratification, as do pagans with no knowledge of God. You cannot break this rule without in some way cheating your fellow-men. And you must remember that God

will punish all who do offend in this matter, and we have warned you how we have seen this work out in our experience of life. The calling of God is not to impurity, but to the most thorough purity. . . .

Medical science with all its knowledge is inadequate to take care of the world's [sexually transmitted] disease problem. Yet millenniums before the microscope, and before man knew the method of the transmission of [such] diseases, God knew all about them and gave to man the only feasible plan of preventing these universal and blighting killers. Jesus clearly stated that from the beginning, our Father ordained that one man and one woman should constitute a family unit. This plan of two, and two alone, constituting a family unit is so unique, so different from human plans and so effective in the prevention of the vast complications of horrible . . . diseases, that again we are forced to recognize another medical evidence of the inspiration of the Bible.[26]

But the biblical perspective does not only include wisdom that, if it is heeded, will prevent one from contracting a sexually transmitted disease, it also guides us in relating to victims of AIDS, chlamydia, herpes, and other STDs:

Do not let any unwholesome talk come out of your mouths, but only what is helpful for building others up according to their needs, that it may benefit those who listen. And do not grieve the Holy Spirit of God, with whom you were sealed for the day of redemption. Get rid of all bitterness, rage and anger, brawling and slander, along with every form of malice. Be kind and compassionate to one another, forgiving each other, just as in Christ God forgave you. Be imitators of God, therefore, as dearly loved children and live a life of love, just as Christ loved us and gave himself up for us as a fragrant offering and sacrifice to God.[27]

And again:

Therefore, as God's chosen people, holy and dearly loved, clothe yourselves with compassion, kindness, humility, gentleness and patience. Bear with each other and forgive whatever grievances you may have against one another. Forgive as the Lord forgave you. And over all these virtues put on love, which binds them all together in perfect unity.[28]

The Lord Jesus Christ, who had compassion on the woman caught in adultery,[29] who healed the woman with a detestable disease,[30] who accepted the outcast Samaritan woman,[31] would certainly will for His followers to display His likeness in how they relate to people who (whether it is the result of their own sin or that of another) need compassion, healing, and acceptance.

The Response to the Problem of Sexually Transmitted Diseases

Listen ◆ Empathize ◆ Affirm ◆ Direct ◆ Enlist ◆ Refer

The youth leader can help prevent or address the tragedy of sexually transmitted diseases with a plan such as the following:

LISTEN. Take the time to understand the teen's comprehension of sexually transmitted diseases. Ask questions designed to determine the depth and breadth of his or her education on the subject: what STDs are, how they are transmitted, how they can be prevented. A young person who has recently learned that he or she is infected may need to vent confusion, frustration, or anger. Do not pressure the youth to express such feelings, but create a listening atmosphere in which honest expression is welcomed without condemnation.

EMPATHIZE. Don't try to second-guess the youth's state of mind, but do seek to understand his or her reactions. He may think he knows enough about STDs; he may be tired of hearing it at school and on television. She may be too embarrassed to discuss the matter, or she may wonder why a parent or other adult is broaching the subject. If the young person is infected with an STD, he or she is likely to be embarrassed, ashamed, frightened, or in denial. Keep these things in mind. Also be aware of some of the practical ways to communicate empathy. For example, try to:

- Face the youth directly (coming out from behind a desk, for example).
- Listen carefully to verbal and nonverbal communication.
- Nod your head.
- Make eye contact.
- Lean forward in your chair.
- Reflect key statements.
- Wait patiently through tears or silence.

AFFIRM. Be wary of taking an approach that may be interpreted as accusatory or judgmental by the teen. Whether your object is education and prevention or diagnosis and treatment, communicate acceptance of the young person and affirmation of his or her worth in your eyes—and God's.

DIRECT. If the object in advising a teen is education and prevention, the following direction may prove fruitful:[32]

1. Include and involve parents. Researchers have found that teenage sexual involvement was reduced when parents supervised:

- Who the adolescent dated.
- Where the adolescent went on dates.
- The arrival time back home.

Strong, attentive family relationships tend to reduce sexual activity among teens and, consequently, the incidence of STDs.

2. Urge the youth to make fellowship with God a top priority. A consistent devotional habit is the first line of defense against sin and its consequences (see Col. 2:6–15 and Gal. 5:16).

3. Teach the consequences of promiscuity. Make sure the youth understands the devastating, life-threatening consequences of sexual promiscuity such as those described above.

4. Teach the benefits of abstinence. Emphasize the positive benefits of abstinence—and not just to teen girls, but to boys as well.

5. Eliminate or counter mixed messages about abstinence and "safer sex." Take every opportunity to counter dangerous or counterproductive messages from the school, government, or media.

6. Keep lines of communication open. Don't let anger, impatience, frustration, or worry clog the lines of communication with a teen. Keep talking—and keep him or her talking.

If the object is diagnosing or responding to a young person who may have a sexually transmitted disease, the following course may suggest a helpful starting point:

1. Respond compassionately. Hurting people don't need sermons; they need help. Strike an attitude of care and concern, not of disapproval.

2. Pray. Pray for and with the young person. Seek God's providential care; ask Him to orchestrate your involvement and those of others in a way that will bear immediate and eternal benefits.

3. Encourage repentance and restoration. Lead the young person to verbalize his need and his desire to change his behavior, and try to bring him through repentance to an experience of God's forgiveness and restoration. Also facilitate the development of a healthy devotional life, incorporating private prayer, worship and Bible reading; a healthy relationship with God is the best line of defense against sin.

4. Explain the biblical perspective of the problem. Help the youth understand that STDs are not a curse from God, but that neither are they a part of God's perfect plan; they are sometimes the natural result of disregarding God's loving commands. Be sensitive to any opportunity to convey God's loving motivation in issuing His commands and also to open the young person's eyes to the truth that God is able to bring good out of evil.

5. Walk with the young person through the stages of grief. Loss (such as the loss of one's health) invariably brings grief, and a young person who has contracted an STD may need help working through the stages of grief (denial, anger, bargaining, depression, and acceptance). (See chapter 8, "Grief.")

6. Expose the youth to the concept of "secondary virginity." If the youth has engaged in sexual intercourse, his or her virginity has been lost. However, with God's help, the young person can begin anew to obey God, to be sexually pure, and to save himself or herself for a future mate. Impress upon him or her that it may not be easy to "abstain from sexual immorality" but that it is God's will (see 1 Thess. 4:3).

ENLIST. Guide the young person toward a self-initiated course of action for prevention or treatment. Help the youth brainstorm ways to escape temptation; encourage the infected youth to devise his or her own plan for coping with the problem. Lead him or her to consider ways he or she may influence others.

REFER. If the young person has contracted a sexually transmitted disease, medical attention is, of course, an immediate priority; early diagnosis and treatment are crucial. The expertise and guidance of a professional Christian counselor is a valuable resource that should not be ignored or postponed.

For Further Reading

The following resources may help the concerned parent, pastor, teacher, or youth worker to educate a young person regarding sexually transmitted diseases or to assist a young person who is infected with an STD:

Scriptures Cited in This Chapter

- Proverbs 5:1–12
- 1 Thessalonians 4:3–7
- Ephesians 4:29–5:2
- Colossians 3:12–14
- John 8:1–11
- Mark 5:25–34
- John 4:1–42
- Colossians 2:6–15
- Galatians 5:16

Other Scripture to Read

- Psalms 34:18; 86:15–17
- Psalms 6, 32, 38, 51, 102, 130, 143
- Psalms 103:11–18; 119:50
- Isaiah 53:4–6
- 1 John 1:9

Further Reading

- Dr. James Dobson, *Life on the Edge* (Word).
- Dan Korem, *Streetwise Parents, Foolproof Kids* (NavPress).
- Josh McDowell, *The Myths of Sex Education* (Here's Life Publishers).
- Josh McDowell and Dick Day, *Why Wait? What You Need to Know about the Teen Sexuality Crisis* (Here's Life Publishers).
- S. I. McMillen, *None of These Diseases* (Fleming H. Revell).

ABUSE

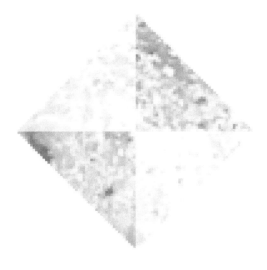

34

SEXUAL ABUSE

A Synopsis

❖

Introduction

It began when Mona was six years old. A nineteen-year-old uncle who lived close by, who was like a big brother to her, would often take Mona with him when he went places, for rides in his car, to friends' houses, and to an occasional movie in town.

Then one day, when they arrived at Mona's house to find her parents gone, her uncle suggested they go out to the barn to play. He offered to show her a secret and exposed himself to her, charging her to keep their "little secret." From that time on, things developed gradually. He began to fondle her and kiss her, and eventually he induced her to fondle him.

Mona knew something wasn't right about the things her uncle was doing, but he promised to never hurt her. He never became violent, and Mona kept their secret, but his abuse did have an effect.

Over the next several years, Mona began to dread contact with her uncle and even began to hate him. She even tried once to tell her mother what was going on, but her efforts only resulted in confusion. She didn't know if her mother disbelieved her, misunderstood her, or blamed her for what was happening.

Mona's family moved away from that uncle when she was nine, but their move didn't end her problems. She began having nightmares and started to withdraw into an emotional shell. By the time she entered her teens, she had few friends at school or at church, and she wrestled with severe depression at times.

When she was fifteen, she began to date—slowly at first—and soon had become sexually involved with several boys at school. Her newfound "popularity" was unrewarding however.

"I felt like I could never be loved," she said. "At least not the way I wanted. It wasn't like I was giving myself away in exchange for love; I didn't feel like I had anything left to give away."

The Problem of Sexual Abuse

A child is molested every two minutes, according to some estimates.[1] More than one out of three adult women and one in seven adult men have been sexually abused before the age of eighteen.[2] The Brooklyn Society for the Prevention of Cruelty to Children has found that as many as 85 percent of reported crimes against children are of a sexual nature,[3] and it is estimated that for every victim known, nine others are hidden.[4]

Sexual abuse is commonly defined as "any form of sexual contact or conversation in which [a] child is sexually exploited for the purpose of bringing sexual gratification to the exploiter."[5] It is a term that covers a broad range of actions and activities, from exposure to actual intercourse, such as:

- An adult showing a child his or her genitals.
- An adult asking a child to undress to be looked at or fondled.
- An adult touching a child's genitals.
- An adult having a child touch his or her genitals.
- Oral-genital contact.
- Forced masturbation.
- Penetration of the anus or vagina with fingers or another object.
- Anal penetration.
- Intercourse.
- Use of children for the production of pornographic materials.[6]

Sexual abuse does not always involve physical harm or even physical contact. "Within a family, there can be incidents that I would label [abuse] even though they don't involve actual contact," says Emily Page, a mental health counselor in Massachusetts. "For example, if a father . . . undresses and masturbates in front of [his daughter], he's creating psychic and emotional pressure in the girl."[7]

Two landmark studies, conducted by David Finkelhor (1978) and Diana Russell (1983) reported the incidence of sexual abuse of children and youth. Finkelhor's study of 530 women found that 14 percent reported intrafamilial sexual abuse (abuse by a family member) before the age of eighteen, and 19 percent reported extrafamilial abuse (abuse by a non-family member). Russell's study of 930 randomly selected women in San Francisco revealed that 16 percent had experienced intrafamilial abuse, and 31 percent had been victims of extrafamilial abuse.

Such statistics reflect unimaginable tragedy, tragedy that is often exacerbated by the fact that sexual abuse of children may be "the most muted crime,"[8] as illustrated in the following account:

> Jill, my sister's daughter, is fourteen. Her stepfather has been [molesting her] and going into her bedroom at night for the past six months. I know she's telling the truth because he did the same to me when I lived with them. Jill couldn't stand it and finally told her teacher. The teacher told the school psychologist, who said that either the child was lying and very sick or the family was in great trouble. The father could go to jail.
>
> When confronted, the stepfather said Jill had lied. Jill's mother believed her husband. Wringing her hands, she pleaded with her daughter to "confess." Otherwise who would support them and her younger brothers? Jill tried to stick to her story, but with persistent pressure and increased guilt at depriving the family of support, she finally "confessed" that she lied. She was denied a request to live with me and placed under psychiatric care.[9]

Such experiences can be extremely damaging to a child or young person and may impose effects that are far-reaching and long-lasting.

The Effects of Sexual Abuse

The effects of sexual abuse of children and youth are so deep and wide that a fair treatment would take hundreds, perhaps thousands, of pages. In this space, however, only an overview of the most common and most significant effects is possible. (See also the effects of nonsexual abuse described in chapter 35.)

◆ Physical and Medical Consequences

A horrific "shopping list" of some of the physical consequences of sexual abuse is offered by Florence Rush in her book (written from a decidedly anti-Christian perspective) *The Best Kept Secrets*:

> Cases of rectal fissures, lesions, poor sphincter control, lacerated vaginas . . . perforated anal and vaginal walls, death by asphyxiation, chronic choking from gonorrheal tonsillitis are almost always related to adult sexual contacts with children. Of twenty cases of genital gonorrheal infection in children aged one to four, nineteen had a history of adult-child sex. A history of adult-child sex was obtained in all twenty-five cases of infected children between five and nine, and the same was true of all 116 cases of children between fourteen and fifteen. In another study, 160 of 161 cases of this illness in children resulted from sexual contacts with adults.[10]

One doctor referred to the damage of child sexual abuse by saying, "Their insides are torn to pieces."[11] The physical and medical consequences of such abuse is severe and, in many cases, irrevocable.

◆ Pregnancy

"Although it is not a common occurrence," state researchers Janice R. Butler of Bucknell University and Linda M. Burton of Pennsylvania State University, "some young girls bear children as the result of sexual abuse. DeFrancis (1969) reported that of 217 victims whose cases went to court, 11 percent had become pregnant as a result of the sexual offense."[12] (See also chapter 29, "Unplanned Pregnancy.")

◆ Guilt

Victims of sexual abuse are prone to crippling guilt. (See also chapter 3, "Guilt.") "If people we trust and need are abusive to us in a way that is an invasion of our person and a deep betrayal of our body, either it's their fault and we'll die—because we depend on them to survive—or it's our fault," says Judith Weiler, a clinical therapist from Stow, Massachusetts. "So most of us make it our fault."[13]

Researchers Butler and Burton reported a not-uncommon response among victims of sexual abuse:

> One young woman, whose abuse by relatives began at the age of 7, remarked, "I feel bad about myself for letting it happen and go on for so many years."[14]

◆ Shame

Shame is a cousin to the emotion of guilt, but whereas guilt focuses on a person's acts, shame points to a person's self. Because sexual abuse is an invasion of an individual's *person*, it is typically accompanied by an overwhelming sense of shame.

Victims often describe their shame with such words as, "dirty," "unclean," "disgusting," and "bad."

"I was molested and raped as a child of eleven years," said one victim. "All my life I have felt dirty, worthless, and no good."[15] Such sentiments are tragically common among victims of sexual abuse.

◆ Feelings of Helplessness

There can be few instances in which a child or adolescent feels so helpless as in cases of sexual abuse when they have guarded a guilty secret and often been locked into a sort of conspiracy—

cajoled, threatened, or perhaps even bribed into silence—by a trusted family member or friend. Such feelings of powerlessness are intensified in those who have tried to tell an adult and been ignored or disbelieved.

Such feelings can become a way of life for victims of abuse, as illustrated by Holly Wagner Green in *Turning Fear to Hope*:

> Counselor Lenore Walker describes experiments in which laboratory animals and human volunteers were confined and then exposed to random, painful stimuli over which they had no control and from which they could not escape. Once they realized their behavior had no effect on what happened to them, their motivation to help themselves seemed to die. They ceased trying to get away or gain relief, actually ignoring obvious avenues of escape, even when these were pointed out. When they had learned they were powerless, they stopped struggling and became passive.[16]

◆ Low Self-Esteem

Long after the abuse has stopped, victims will continue to suffer low self-esteem, "a sad and often crippling loss of self-worth,"[17] as a result. Their feelings of guilt, shame, and helplessness combine to produce low self-esteem, often even so severe as to be accurately called self-loathing and self-hatred. (See chapter 6, "Unhealthy Self-Esteem.")

Such persons often enter adolescence and adulthood convinced that they are unloved, unlovable, and unworthy of love. They find it difficult or impossible to believe that God could love them, that a spouse could love them, even that their own children could love them. Their low self-esteem often leads to other disabilities and dysfunctions, such as eating disorders (see chapters 42, "Anorexia Nervosa," and 43, "Bulimia") and suicidal tendencies (see chapter 9, "Suicide Thoughts, Tendencies, and Threats").

◆ Revictimization

Some research reports that victims of child sexual abuse are almost twice as likely as others to suffer rape or attempted rape later in life, a phenomenon sociologist Diana Russell calls "revictimization."

"If a child is abused," says therapist Linda Schiller, "she may get developmentally stuck at that age, so that if she was abused at age four, she can't protect herself at age fourteen, twenty-four, or thirty-four any better than she could at age four. She didn't learn how."[18]

Author and counselor Jan Frank suggests:

> The victim is drawn to people and/or circumstances she thinks she deserves. Victims are no different from anyone else when it comes to choosing the known versus the unknown. . . . This was demonstrated so clearly to me in my early career as a juvenile hall counselor. I worked with abused and neglected children ranging in ages from birth to seventeen years. Many had been beaten, deprived, or sexually mistreated. . . . When faced with the question of returning to their offender, usually a parent, or to an unknown foster home, most would opt for returning home. They knew what to expect there.[19]

◆ Other Effects

Few—if any—kinds of trauma can produce as many and as severe effects as those produced by sexual abuse, some of which also accompany nonsexual forms of abuse, such as:

Aggression

Mistrust of others

Deficient social skills

Emotional withdrawal

Running away (see chapter 24, "Runaway Threats and Attempts"), and even

Criminal behaviors, such as prostitution.

Other effects of sexual abuse include:

Depression (See chapter 5.)

Anger (See chapter 4.)

Fear (See chapter 2.)

Anxiety (See chapter 2.)

Suicidal tendencies (See chapter 9.)

The Biblical Perspective of Sexual Abuse

It should not need to be said that God abhors sexual abuse. He created sex to be an act of mutual love between a husband and wife (see Gen. 1:24 and Heb. 13:4). Any use of sex outside those boundaries is a transgression of His will and design.

How much more so, however, is the exploitation and victimization of children and youth for the gratification of an adult. Sexual abuse distorts a child's understanding of sex and its wholesome purpose when used within God's design. Sexual abuse interrupts a child's delicate process of emotional, social, and sexual maturation. Sexual abuse "confuses the progression [in a young mind] from accepting healthy human love to knowing the divine love of God."[20]

Most importantly, perhaps, sexual abuse is a transgression against the *image of God* and the *temple of God*, as author and apologist Ravi Zacharias points out (although he is speaking about violence and sex in the media, not about sexual abuse):

> God tells us we are created in His image. In the book of Genesis, He strongly requites the penalty for murder because murder is a direct attack upon the dignity of man, created in the image of God. When we look further into the Scriptures, Jesus reminded His followers that true worship is not in a building of bricks and stones. The human body is itself a temple.
>
> These two truths—that humanity is made in God's image and that the body is the temple of God—are two of the cardinal teachings of

Scripture. . . . Violence defaces the image of God, and sensuality profanes the temple of God.[21]

Sexual abuse incorporates both offenses; it defaces the image of God and profanes the temple of God. It is illicit sexual behavior *directed against a child's very person.*

The abused child can find healing, and the abuser can obtain forgiveness, but neither can happen without recognition of God's standards and commands.

The Response to the Problem of Sexual Abuse

Listen ◆ Empathize ◆ Affirm ◆ Direct ◆ Enlist ◆ Refer

Anyone who has been sexually abused will face enormous difficulties in attempting to cope, let alone be healed. The youth leader who is charged with advising a victim of sexual abuse must face the challenge prayerfully and prudently. The following course may be helpful:

LISTEN. Be slow to speak and quick to listen. Let the young person talk freely about his or her problems, feelings, thoughts, and hurts. Let the youth unfold her story at her own pace, with only the gentlest of urgings from you. Early in the process of intervention, don't try to direct or instruct the young person; instead, concentrate on listening and empathizing (see suggestions below). Try to confine your speech, at least at first, primarily to questions, such as: "Do you think you can talk about it?" "Can you tell me how it started?" "Can you tell me how long it's been going on?" "What happened next?" "How does all this make you feel? (Are you angry? Scared, etc.?)"

EMPATHIZE. At each step along the way, be alert to the effects of abuse (such as guilt, shame, etc.) the youth may be suffering. The last thing hurting people need is instruction; what they need is to have someone to cry with, someone who will love them and hurt with them. Remember that preaching doesn't cast out fear; love casts out fear (1 John 4:18). Remember that instruction doesn't assuage pain; comfort does (2 Cor. 1:1–7). Be especially sensitive to ways you can communicate your empathy and understanding, such as:

- Removing obstacles to the conversation (coming out from behind a desk, for example, or turning music off).

- Leaning forward in your chair.

- Making eye contact.

- Nodding your head, saying "yes," "go on," etc.

- Reflecting the young person's statements ("So you felt . . ." or "And that made you mad," etc.).

- Waiting patiently through silence, anger, or tears.

AFFIRM. A victim of sexual abuse will need frequent—and sincere—affirmation. Statements such as, "I think your feelings are natural," "I'd feel the same way," and "I'm so glad you said that" can affirm a young person and encourage healing. Take every opportunity to express your honest love, esteem, and appreciation for the young person as a person of infinite worth. Reflect often on his or her strengths, concentrating on inner qualities rather than outer ones; affirm his or her personhood more than his or her appearance or behavior.

DIRECT. Keep in mind the words of psychotherapist Susan Forward, who says, "Revealing a major trauma . . . is just the beginning. . . . People sometimes find so much relief in the initial revelation that they leave treatment prematurely."[22] Confiding his or her story in a trusted adviser is a huge step, but it is not the final step. While professional intervention is important and urgent in the event of abuse, a caring teacher, parent, youth worker, or pastor can offer help in the following ways prior to and during professional intervention:

1. Guide the youth to acknowledge (out loud, in his or her own words) that he or she has been abused, and help the young person identify the effects the abuse is having on his or her life. To that end, encourage the youth to talk or write about each abusive experience—even repeatedly—until the abuse is acknowledged and the effects are recognized.

2. If the abuse has not stopped, help the youth take steps to stop it immediately *(by notifying law enforcement or child protection authorities and consulting a professional Christian counselor. [See the "Refer" section, below.] Be aware that silence in this regard may be* illegal.

3. Help the young person return the responsibility for the abuse to the perpetrator and any other contributing sources—not to himself or herself. Gently but consistently challenge any effort to blame himself or his actions, and help the victim accurately identify the responsible persons and other contributing factors.

4. Turn the youth to God as the source of healing and wholeness. Help him or her acknowledge that God did not cause the abuse but that He is the solution to the trauma caused by the abuse. (See Ps. 18:2–6, 25–30.)

5. Walk with the young person through the stages of grief and other emotions and reactions. The loss (of innocence, of wholeness, etc.) experienced as a result of abuse needs to be grieved; a caring adult can help a young person through the stages of grief (denial, anger, bargaining, depression, and acceptance) by helping him or her confront, express, and resolve such feelings, and by accepting the youth with understanding and comfort. (See also chapter 8, "Grief.")

6. Foster a daily partnership of prayer for and with the young person. Encourage the youth to develop and maintain daily fellowship with God in order to rely on His strength, learn from His Word, and counter destructive thoughts and feelings with the mind of Christ. (See Phil. 4:4–9.)

7. Expose the youth to the available resources for coping with the trauma. Help him or her acknowledge (preferably by name) those people who are or may be willing to help in practical ways: an understanding parent, a close friend, hotlines, organizations, pen pals, etc.

8. Encourage the young man or woman to accept the fact that healing will take time. Extend hope to the youth. While the healing process may be painful and may take considerable time, the victim has survived the actual abuse; he or she can also overcome the trauma, with God's help.

ENLIST. Enlist the young person's cooperation and participation in answering the question, "What next?" Elicit suggestions and ideas from the youth, but help him or her understand that under no circumstances should the abuse be allowed to continue, nor should the initial release of confiding the abuse be mistaken for healing. Though healing can be nearly instantaneous, in most cases it is a long and deliberate process. Depending on whether the abuse is current, recent, or further removed in time, engage him or her in actively considering the following forms of intervention:[23]

- Every state in the U.S. has a child abuse and neglect reporting law that requires certain professionals—social workers, medical personnel, educators, child-care staff—to report abuse and neglect. In addition, states either require or suggest that the general public report suspected incidents of abuse. When citizens make such reports in accordance with the law, they are protected from civil and criminal liability. It is critical that you *know the law* in your state or province; if you fail to report abuse or neglect, *you may be breaking the law.* To report abuse or neglect, call your local or state child protection services agency.

- **Childhelp USA** operates a hotline for kids, parents, and others who'd like to help (1-800-4-A-CHILD).

- **Kids Helping Kids** arranges for abused kids to correspond with each other while preserving their anonymity. Write P.O. Box 110, Billerica, Massachusetts 01821.

- **The American Humane Association** (303-695-0811) provides services designed to meet the needs of abused children.

- **Formerly Abused Children Emerging in Society (FACES)** provides support to young adults who suffered abuse as children (203-646-1222).

- Many communities have **Crime Victims Assistance programs** that can provide experienced help in cases of abuse and neglect. Call the local United Way or school guidance counselor.

REFER. Just as severe physical trauma (such as a serious wound or a stroke) requires the assistance of a trained physician to bring about healing, the extreme trauma engendered by sexual abuse calls for the assistance of a Christian counseling professional who can walk the victim through the many steps of healing. Healing from sexual abuse is possible, but it is best accomplished with professional help.

For Further Reading

The following resources may help the concerned parent, pastor, teacher, or youth worker assist a young victim of sexual abuse:

Scriptures Cited in This Chapter

- Genesis 1:24

- Hebrews 13:4

- 1 John 4:18

- 2 Corinthians 1:1–7
- Psalm 18:2–6, 25–30
- Philippians 4:4–9

Other Scripture to Read

- Psalms 34:18; 86:15–17; 103:11–18; 107:20; 119:50; 139:1–24
- Isaiah 53:4–6
- Matthew 5:1–12
- John 14:27
- 1 John 1:9

Further Reading

- Angela R. Carl, *Child Abuse: What You Can Do About It* (Standard Publishing).

- Dr. James Dobson, *When God Doesn't Make Sense* (Tyndale House).
- Jan Frank, *A Door of Hope* (Here's Life Publishers).
- Holly Wagner Green, *Turning Fear to Hope* (Thomas Nelson).
- Dr. Grant Martin, *Please Don't Hurt Me: A Sensitive Look at the Growing Problem of Abuse in Christian Homes* (Victor).
- David Peters, *A Betrayal of Innocence: What Everyone Should Know about Child Sexual Abuse* (Word).

35

NONSEXUAL ABUSE

A Synopsis

❖

Introduction

Thirteen-year-old Brian wanted to get caught. He threw a brick at the windshield of a moving bus and waited at the curb for police to pick him up and take him to the juvenile detention center.

Police, parents, and a court psychologist all asked the same question of Brian: "Why did you throw the brick at the bus?" His answer was the same to everyone: "I don't know." But he did know.

Brian was sick of living with his alcoholic parents. He was sick of waking up in the morning to find them sprawled on the floor or slumped over the kitchen table. He was sick of parents who didn't seem to care whether he went to school or not. Most of all, he was sick of his father's abuse.

When he was younger, his father used to show off in front of his drinking buddies by calling his son over to him and placing a lighted cigarette on Brian's arm or leg to see if he would flinch. Brian never did. He endured the pain, hungry for any sign of approval from his father.

As he grew older, however, the abuse became more unpredictable. His dad would fly into a rage—usually when he was drunk but sometimes while sober—and begin to beat Brian. Brian tried to shelter his face with his hands and arms; he could hide bruises on his body better than he could explain bruises and swelling on his face. He wasn't always successful.

Lately, Brian had begun to fight back, to try to return his father's punches and kicks. But that only enraged his father further; despite his age and poor physical condition, Brian still feared his dad. The worst part about it all, Brian thought, was that his mother didn't stop it. She would watch, flinching and crying, while Brian endured the beating. Sometimes she would flee from the room. Sometimes she would even beg her husband to leave Brian alone. But she never stopped it, and Brian blamed her as much as his father.

"I don't know," he told the authorities when they asked why he had thrown the brick at the moving bus. But he knew why. When the judge announced that he would be sent to a juvenile institution, he left the room without a word—or even a look—to his parents.

The Problem of Nonsexual Abuse

A case of child abuse or neglect is reported every ten seconds in the United States. Many more go unreported.

The number of child-abuse reports reached 2.99 million in 1993, forty-five reports for every thousand children. Over one million cases were verified.[1] An estimated 1,299 children died as the result of neglect or abuse in 1993, and 43 percent of those deaths occurred in families that had previously been reported to child protection agencies.[2] Taking children and youth out of the home isn't always the answer, however; a study by Trudy Festinger, head of the Department of Research at New York University's School of Social Work, revealed that 28 percent of children who are placed in foster care suffer some form of abuse while in the system. And the ACLU's Children's Project estimates that a child in the care of the state is ten times more likely to be abused than those in the care of their parents.

Abuse may take many forms. Author Angela R. Carl defines child abuse as:

> . . . specific acts of commission or omission by parents or other adults . . . that lead to nonaccidental harm or threatened harm to a child's physical, mental, or emotional developmental state.[3]

Physical abuse includes all acts that create injury or a substantial and unnecessary risk of injury. Violent shaking or slapping, shoving, kicking, and punching are all forms of physical abuse. Tying a young person up or locking him or her in a closet are abusive behaviors. Burning a child with a lighted cigarette or match is also abuse. Not all physical contact or corporal punishment is abusive, but any acts that leave bruises, cuts, scars, or welts are certainly abusive, as are physical acts designed to cause harm or humiliation.

Not all abuse is physical however. *Emotional abuse* is defined by Carl as:

> . . . a pattern of blaming, belittling, verbally attacking, or rejecting a child, or demanding that a child assume responsibilities that he is incapable of handling.[4]

Emotional abuse is generally more difficult to identify and to prove, but it is nonetheless abuse and no less harmful because it is less recognizable. It includes words or attitudes intended to provoke, disgrace, or shame a child or young person. It includes verbal abuse such as screaming, insulting, or name-calling. It includes slamming doors and throwing things. It can even include jokes or things said in jest.

"Most parents are guilty of some emotionally abusive behaviors at one time or another," says Carl, "and a certain amount of emotional abuse is accepted by society. For some parents, though, emotional maltreatment of their children becomes a *pattern of life* as opposed to an occasional frustrated outburst followed by an apology and expression of love."[5]

Neglect is another form of abuse, considered by experts to be the most common single form of abuse. Nearly half (47 percent) of verified abuse cases are cases of neglect, and 40 percent of deaths due to abuse are due to neglect. (Fifty-five percent are due to physical abuse, 5 percent to both.) Neglect is the failure of a parent or other caretaker to make *adequate* provision for a child's needs and well-being. Carl defines neglect as failure to provide:

> . . . even a bare minimum degree of care in providing food, clothing, shelter, medical care, education, and supervision. All children skip meals, wear soiled or torn clothing, go to school with runny noses, and experience accidents that might have been prevented by parents from time to time. But neglect involves a chronic inattention to the basic needs of a child.[6]

Parents who leave young children unattended are guilty of neglect. Parents who do not ensure their children's attendance at school or who allow severe illness to go untreated are guilty of neglect. Parents who knowingly allow their children to be placed in danger—with an abusive family member, for example—are guilty of neglect. Parents who ignore their child, failing to express interest and love, are guilty of neglect. Whatever form abuse may take, it must be treated seriously and responded to sensitively.

The Causes of
Nonsexual Abuse

Abuse occurs for many reasons. In most cases, a combination of factors contributes to the abusive behavior. Among them may be substance abuse, an abusive past, anger, and/or poverty:

◆ Substance Abuse

Parents or other caretakers who are impaired by alcohol or drug use frequently neglect or mistreat kids. Sometimes the parents' use of drugs or alcohol is also a factor in the actual abuse, such as parents who prod their children to sip from their whiskey glasses or who use their children to hide or purchase illegal drugs.

◆ An Abusive Past

Children who have been raised in an abusive home, even if they were not themselves a victim, often (not always) emulate that abusive behavior as adults. Many learned violence (whether physical or not) as a way of relating to other people and as a way of "resolving" conflict.

◆ Anger

Some abusive parents are bewildered and surprised by the depth of their anger, says John White, author of *Parents in Pain*. "Their rage often takes them by surprise and humiliates them, bursting like an angry sea over breakwaters they have built to contain it. They grow to be as afraid of their anger as their children are—and deeply ashamed. . . . The more they strive

to control their outbursts, the fiercer the outbursts may become; the greater the parental remorse, the worse the subsequent behavior."[7]

◆ Poverty

"Poverty is strongly linked to neglect," reported *USA Today* in a 1994 story. Numerous studies have documented a correlation between poverty and other forms of abuse as well. However, what is not clear is whether poverty is a cause or whether abuse and poverty are both effects—that often accompany each other—of other conditions or behaviors.

The Effects of
Nonsexual Abuse

The wise youth leader or adviser will seek to develop some understanding of the effects of abuse on the victims in order to offer more competent help.

Aside from the most obvious and immediate effects of abuse (bruises or lacerations in the case of physical abuse, for example), the victim of physical or emotional abuse or neglect will very likely experience any number of the following:

◆ Guilt

Any objective observer could easily see that children and youth who suffer abuse are the victims and bear no blame for their injuries. However, even older children and adolescents are apt to feel guilt as a result of the abuse they suffer.

"I wish I didn't make Mom so mad," he might say.

"If I were a good girl, he wouldn't have done this to me," she might think.

"Why do my parents hate me?" they might wonder.

Such ideas are a common effect of abuse. Sometimes they are conscious; sometimes they exist only in the youth's subconscious. Always, however, they affect the victim's ability to understand and deal with the abuse. (See chapter 3, "Guilt.")

◆ Mistrust of Others

Because of the natural trust children have of their parents (and generally of other adults, particularly other family members), when that trust has been literally abused, it is devastating. A child or teen who has been abused will often vow, "I'll never trust anyone again" and will often live and operate in an attitude of mistrust and suspicion.

Such a young person is often presented with a cruel dilemma: she is starved for affection, for any expression of love or interest, but she feels unable to trust such expressions, no matter who initiates them nor how fervent they may be. The youth will, without intervention, remain skeptical of others' intentions and doubtful of his or her own self-worth.

◆ Aggression

Young victims of domestic violence are more likely to exhibit aggressive and violent behavior "regardless of whether they come from well-off or poor families, live in two- or one-parent homes or regularly observe cooperative or physically violent behavior among adults."

About one-third of such youth "continually express anger and provoke conflict [at school]. Abused children often misinterpret frustrating social encounters, unfailingly attribute hostile intentions to others, and view aggression as the only solution to problems with teachers or classmates."[8]

◆ Deficient Social Skills

Abuse may also lead to deficient social skills among victims. A multi-university study by Kenneth A. Dodge (Vanderbilt University), John E. Bates (Indiana University), and Gregory S. Pettit (Auburn University), concluded that "more than one in three abused children dis-

played unusually high levels of . . . deficient social skills, compared with about one in eight of the other youngsters."[9]

Youth who have suffered abuse may have difficulty relating to others. They may have difficulty understanding the motives and behavior of others. They may find it difficult to trust or confide in others. They may not know how to appropriately handle social situations and may suffer peer abuse as a result of their lack of social skills.

◆ Emotional Withdrawal

Victims of abuse typically show more signs of emotional withdrawal and social isolation than their peers, according to psychologist Kenneth A. Dodge of Vanderbilt University in Nashville. They are less likely to feel comfortable in a group and may enjoy few friendships, even fewer close friendships.

It is a cruel irony that the youths who perhaps most need close, trusted friends are less likely than their peers to develop such associations. Instead, they often isolate themselves and shun (sometimes passively, sometimes actively) the company of others.

◆ Runaway

More than one million teens run away from home every year, and studies show that many of those ran away because of abuse they suffered at home. (See chapter 24, "Runaway Threats and Attempts.")

Research conducted by Mark-David Janus and colleagues at the University of Connecticut reveals that "home" was a dangerous place for the vast majority of the runaways they interviewed. Eighty-six percent reported some form of physical abuse. Half had been hit hard enough (with a hand or belt) to leave a bruise, and 13 percent had been struck with enough force to require a trip to the hospital.

Janus's study suggests that abuse at home may place youth—particularly adolescents—at much greater risk of becoming runaways.[10]

◆ Criminality

There is some evidence, though it is by no means conclusive, that abused or neglected children and youth often become involved in criminal activity. A study by Cathy Spatz Widom of Indiana University shows that "nearly 29 percent of those abused and neglected as children were arrested for a criminal offense as an adult, compared to 21 percent of [those not isolated as victims]."[11]

Though the difference between the two groups reported by Widom is not statistically significant, other studies do infer a correlation, and criminal justice experts often cite the frequency with which accused and convicted criminals cite past experiences of abuse.

The Biblical Perspective of Nonsexual Abuse

Some outspoken voices in the fight to stop child abuse have undertaken to criticize the Bible (and other "religious" writings, such as the Talmud), claiming that it encourages child abuse with such statements as the famous and oft-quoted, "He who spares the rod hates his son, but he who loves him is careful to discipline him" (Prov. 13:24).

However, that verse (and others like it) does not encourage physical abuse of children. It does not exclude corporal punishment but clearly places all forms of child discipline in the context of love.

Nowhere does the Bible advocate or defend abusive behavior, physical or otherwise. On the contrary, it repeatedly presents children as a blessing to be esteemed:

> Sons are a heritage from the Lord,
> children a reward from him. (Ps. 127:3)

Scripture repeatedly portrays the parent-child relationship as one that should be characterized by love, tenderness, and respect:

> Can a mother forget the baby at her breast and have no compassion on the child she has borne? (Isa. 49:15a)

The Bible repeatedly commands parents to sensitively and lovingly care for their children:

> Fathers, do not exasperate your children; instead, bring them up in the training and instruction of the Lord. (Eph. 6:4)

> . . . train the younger women to love their husbands and children. (Titus 2:4)

And God's Word issues dire warnings for those who harm children:

> It would be better for you if a millstone were hung around your neck and you were thrown into the sea than for you to cause one of these little ones to stumble. (Luke 17:2 NRSV)

The serious and sincere student of the Bible will not escape these twin truths: God loves children, commands parents to love and nurture them, and will severely judge those who do them harm.

The Response to the Problem of Nonsexual Abuse

Listen ◆ Empathize ◆ Affirm ◆ Direct ◆ Enlist ◆ Refer

The youth leader who is working with a victim of abuse will be wise to pursue the following course:

L ISTEN. Listen carefully to the young person. Try to elicit all the facts without demanding all the details. Help the youth to communicate clearly and completely all allegations of abuse; be certain (as much as possible) that he or she does not speak vaguely and that you do not misunderstand what he or she is telling you. No matter how alarmed or upset you may be, strive to discover the whole truth. Be careful, however, not to prod or provoke the young person.

Question him or her gently, and listen patiently before asking another question. Questions such as the following may help: "Do you think you can talk about it?" "Can you tell me how it started?" "Can you tell me how long it's been going on?" "What happened next?" "How does all this make you feel? (Are you angry? Scared, etc.?)"

EMPATHIZE. Be sensitive to the likelihood that the youth may not be looking for answers as much as for an understanding, sympathetic, and loving friend. Hurting people don't need instruction as much as they need someone to cry with, someone who will love them and hurt with them. Remember that preaching doesn't cast out fear; love casts out fear (1 John 4:18). Remember that instruction doesn't assuage pain; comfort does (2 Cor. 1:1–7). Also be sensitive to ways you can communicate your empathy and understanding, such as:

- Removing obstacles to the conversation (coming out from behind a desk, for example, or turning music off).

- Leaning forward in your chair.

- Making eye contact.

- Nodding your head, saying "yes," "go on," etc.

- Reflecting the young person's statements ("So you felt . . ." or "You're saying that made you mad," etc.).

- Waiting patiently through silence, anger, or tears.

AFFIRM. Sincere affirmation will be one of the most therapeutic responses to a young victim of abuse. Strive to affirm the young man or woman in ways such as the following:

- *Try not to show embarrassment, incredulity, or offense at the youth's story or experience.* It is

crucial that you take a young person's accounts of abuse seriously, no matter how much shock or incredulity you may feel—and let the youth know that you take his or her account seriously.

- *Protect and enhance the youth's sense of self-worth.* Statements such as, "I think your feelings are natural" and "I'm glad you said that" can affirm a young person and encourage healing. Take every opportunity to express your honest love, esteem, and appreciation for the young person. Reflect often on his or her qualities and abilities. Make sure he or she knows you regard him or her as *a person of worth,* who doesn't deserve the things that have happened or are happening.

- *Offer unconditional relationship.* Let the youth know that God loves him or her unconditionally and that you do too.

DIRECT. While professional intervention is important and urgent in the event of abuse, a caring teacher, parent, youth worker, or pastor can offer direction in the following ways prior to and during professional intervention:

1. Guide the youth to acknowledge (out loud, in his or her own words) that he or she has been abused, and help the young person identify the effects the abuse is having on his or her life. To that end, encourage the youth to talk or write about each abusive experience—even repeatedly—until the abuse is acknowledged and the effects are recognized. Gently and sensitively (allowing as much time as necessary) guide the young person to confess and confront his or her feelings toward the abuser, toward other adults, toward people in general, and toward God. Is he angry at Mom for not stopping the abuse? Is she unwilling to trust anyone? Is he mad at God over what has happened?

2. If the abuse has not stopped, help the youth take steps to stop it immediately *(by notifying law* enforcement or child protection authorities and consulting a professional Christian counselor. [See the "Refer" section, below]. Be aware that silence in this regard may be *illegal*.

3. *Help the young person return the responsibility for the abuse to the perpetrator and any other contributing sources—not to himself or herself.* Gently but firmly challenge any effort to blame himself or his actions, and help the victim accurately identify the responsible persons and other contributing factors.

4. *Turn the youth to God as the source of healing and wholeness.* Help him or her acknowledge that God did not cause the abuse but that He is the solution to the trauma caused by the abuse. (See Ps. 18:2–6, 25–30.)

5. *Walk with the young person through the stages of grief and other emotions and reactions.* The loss (of innocence, wholeness, etc.) experienced as a result of abuse needs to be grieved; a caring adult can help a young person through the stages of grief (denial, anger, bargaining, depression, and acceptance) by helping him or her confront, express, and resolve such feelings and by accepting the youth with understanding and comfort. (See also chapter 8, "Grief.")

6. *Foster a daily partnership of prayer for and with the young person.* Encourage the youth to develop and maintain daily fellowship with God in order to rely on His strength, learn from His Word, and counter destructive thoughts and feelings with the mind of Christ. (See Phil. 4:4–9.)

7. *Expose the youth to the available resources for coping with the trauma.* Help him or her acknowledge (preferably by name) those people who are or may be willing to help in practical ways: an understanding parent, a close friend, hotlines, organizations, pen pals, etc.

8. *Encourage the young man or woman to accept the fact that healing will take time.* Extend hope to the youth. While the healing process may be painful and may take considerable time, the vic-

tim has survived the actual abuse; he or she can also overcome the trauma, with God's help.

ENLIST. Enlist the young person's cooperation and participation in answering the question, "What must be done now?" Elicit suggestions and ideas from the youth, but help him or her understand that under no circumstances should the abuse be allowed to continue. At this point, you will very likely meet with great reluctance. He or she may greet with horror the news that intervention of some kind is necessary, but engage him or her in actively considering the following forms of intervention:[12]

- Every state in the U.S. has a child abuse and neglect reporting law that requires certain professionals—social workers, medical personnel, educators, child-care staff—to report abuse and neglect. In addition, states either require or suggest that the general public report suspected incidents of abuse. When citizens make such reports in accordance with the law, they are protected from civil and criminal liability. To report abuse or neglect, call your local or state child protection services agency.

- **Childhelp USA** operates a hotline for kids, parents, and others who'd like to help (1-800-4-A-CHILD).

- **Kids Helping Kids** arranges for abused kids to correspond with each other while preserving their anonymity. Write P.O. Box 110, Billerica, Massachusetts 01821.

- **The American Humane Association** (303-695-0811) provides services designed to meet the needs of abused children.

- **Formerly Abused Children Emerging in Society (FACES)** provides support to young adults who suffered abuse as children (203-646-1222).

- Many communities have **Crime Victims Assistance programs** that can provide experienced help in cases of abuse and neglect. Call the local United Way or school guidance counselor.

REFER. Many people hesitate to report instances of physical and emotional abuse or neglect. They reason (especially when the family is involved in the church) that a report may be hasty and could cause embarrassment and pain to the family. Angela R. Carl offers counsel for such a situation:

> Certainly, concerned individuals can try to offer assistance to a family before making a report. Frequently, though, abusive families suffer from so many problems that a variety of kinds of professional assistance is needed. Parents may be too frustrated to accept help on their own. An official report is a call for help for both the child and the family.[13]

Moreover, as we stated earlier, a concerned adult's failure to report the abuse may be a crime. Certainly the least that should occur is for the concerned adult to consult a Christian counseling professional who may be able to determine if further intervention or ongoing counseling is advised.

For Further Reading

The following resources may help the concerned parent, pastor, teacher, or youth worker to assist a young victim of sexual abuse:

Scriptures Cited in This Chapter

- Proverbs 13:24
- Psalm 127:3
- Isaiah 49:15a
- Ephesians 6:4
- Titus 2:4
- Luke 17:2 NRSV
- 1 John 4:18
- 2 Corinthians 1:1–7
- Psalm 18:2–6, 25–30
- Philippians 4:4–9

Other Scripture to Read

- Psalms 34:18; 86:15–17; 103:11–18; 107:20; 119:50; 139:1–24
- Isaiah 53:4–6
- Matthew 5:1–12
- John 14:27
- 1 Peter 5:7

Further Reading

- Angela R. Carl, *Child Abuse: What You Can Do About It* (Standard Publishing).
- Dr. James Dobson, *When God Doesn't Make Sense* (Tyndale).
- Jan Frank, *A Door of Hope* (Here's Life Publishers).
- Holly Wagner Green, *Turning Fear to Hope* (Thomas Nelson).
- C. S. Lewis, *The Problem of Pain* (Macmillan).
- Dr. Grant Martin, *Please Don't Hurt Me: A Sensitive Look at the Growing Problem of Abuse in Christian Homes* (Victor).

36

RAPE

A Synopsis

❖

Introduction

Jamie and Todd met at the Campbell College campus mixer in late September and dated through the fall term. Jamie, a freshman, was impressed by Todd's upper-classman sophistication. She was also thrilled to learn that he, too, was a Christian, and they began attending the campus fellowship group together. Just before Jamie left school for Christmas break, Todd kissed her for the first time. By the end of winter term, they were in love.

Campbell's spring formal was their first real "dress-up" date in seven months together. The handsome couple drove to the lakeside country club and danced the evening away starry-eyed. They left at midnight, but instead of heading back to the college, Todd drove slowly along the shore to the far side of the lake and parked overlooking a secluded, moonlit cove. Their customary cuddling session heated up quickly in the romantic setting. In between kisses Todd slipped out of his jacket, unbuttoned his collar, and reclined both of their seats. "I love you, Jamie," he said softly, "and I've wanted to be with you like this for a long time." Then he began kissing and caressing Jamie more intimately than ever before.

Jamie was hungry for Todd's affection, and part of her wanted him to continue. But another part of her realized that Todd was crossing the threshold of intimacy she had reserved for marriage. "I love you, too, Todd," she whispered. "But I think we've had enough for tonight."

Todd didn't seem to hear her. His kissing and fondling became feverish and forceful. Jamie tried to push him away, but he was too strong for her. Suddenly she felt vulnerable and afraid in the presence of the man she loved and trusted. *This can't be happening to me*, she thought frantically. She tried to squirm away from Todd, but he had her pinned to her seat. "Stop, Todd; this isn't right!" she insisted, almost screaming. "I don't want to do this!" But Todd didn't stop.

Several minutes later Todd sat slumped over the steering wheel, dazed and silent with remorse. Jamie huddled in a corner of the back seat sobbing. Her beautiful gown was torn and stained, and her wrists and neck burned from Todd's powerful grip. *Why me, God?* she whimpered inside. *I've always been careful around strangers and maintained my standards on dates. What did I do wrong? What do I do now?*

The Problem of Rape

A recent study conducted by the psychiatric department at the Medical University of South Carolina estimated that 683,000 women are raped each year in the U.S. alone. The study also determined that most rapes are committed by someone known to the woman and that nearly half the victims feared they would be killed during or after the act. Moreover, the study reported that rape is overwhelmingly a "tragedy of youth," as Dean Kilpatrick, coauthor of the study, phrased it; 61 percent of rape victims were first raped before they turned eighteen years old.

There are two categories of rape. The first can be called *stranger rape*, in which the victim does not know her assailant. Stranger rapes, often accompanied by violence and sometimes even by murder, are the kinds you hear about on the eleven o'clock news. It's the fear of stranger rape that drives many women to take self-defense courses, install multiple door locks, buy pistols for the nightstand, and carry Mace self-defense spray in their purses.

The second category is *acquaintance rape*, in which the assailant is known by the victim in some way. He may be a neighbor, a classmate, a coworker, a teacher, or a relative. He may be the brother of a roommate, a boyfriend's best friend, or someone met at a party. He may be a casual date, a steady boyfriend, or even a fiancé. Acquaintance rapes are far more common than stranger rape, though stranger rapes are more often reported (but not often enough).

It's difficult to measure the tragedy of sexual aggression in our society because victims like Jamie are typically hesitant to report such acts, especially when the man involved is someone they know. But several major studies conducted over the last thirty years reveal that date rape and its related offenses are much more common in America than we would like to admit. For example, imagine that fictitious Campbell College is a typical American institution with two thousand students—a thousand men and a thousand women. If we apply the results of the most significant national studies to this small campus, we will discover that:

- About eight hundred of the women at Campbell (that's eight in ten—80 percent!) have been victimized by some form of sexual aggression in their high school and college dating experiences. (Sexual aggression involves unwanted sexual contact, sexual coercion, attempted rape, or rape.) Women aged sixteen to nineteen are the most victimized group, and women aged twenty to twenty-four are a close second. The rate of victimization for these two groups is four times greater than the mean for all women.

- More than five hundred of Campbell's male students (50 percent) have perpetrated some form of sexual aggression in their high school and college dating experience.

- Approximately 250 women (1 in 4) have experienced attempted rape, and 125 (1 in 8) have been raped.

- About 250 Campbell men (1 in 4) have forcefully attempted sexual intercourse against their dates' wishes. Despite the pleading, crying, screaming, and fighting from their dates, about 150 of them—like Todd—succeeded.

- About 100 of those 125 Campbell College rape victims (80 percent) were with a close acquaintance or date, someone they had known an average of almost one year, when they were raped. Nearly half of the men were first dates, casual dates, or romantic acquaintances.

- More than 100 of the 125 date rapes occurred off campus, half of them on the man's turf (his apartment, his car, etc.). About 65 of the victims (over 50 percent) were raped during or at the end of a planned date.

Rape—regardless of whether it's stranger rape or acquaintance rape—is devastating. And the law is clear: Unwanted sexual intercourse—even when perpetrated by an acquaintance, date, or husband—is a felony punishable by imprisonment. Yet rape is the most under-reported of all felonies. Government agencies estimate that three to ten rapes actually occur for every one rape reported to police.[1] One study revealed that only 5 percent of over fifteen hundred women who were victims of rape or attempted rape in college ever reported the crime to law enforcement or college authorities.[2] Other experts estimate that, at the most, half—and possibly as little as 10 percent—of all rapes are reported to the police.[3]

The Causes of Rape

Many people say that men like Todd force themselves on victims like Jamie because they are sex fiends whose desires are out of control. That's not really the case.

◆ Wrong Attitudes

Many significant studies have shown that rapists—including acquaintance rapists—act in response to three identifiable attitudes embedded in their personalities that arm them as walking time bombs of sexual aggression.

The "I Am the King" Attitude. A man who strongly believes in male dominance and female subservience is a potential rapist. This man has oversubscribed to the male role. He accepts as truth the idea that a woman will only respect a man who will "lay down the law" for her. He believes a man must show a woman who is boss or he'll end up henpecked. This man does not rape because he is hungry for sex but because he is hungry for power. His passion is to control and conquer women, whom he sees as his adversaries for superiority. And if this man buys into the use of

force, hostility, and even violence to express his dominance, he's even more likely to hurt and humiliate women in his sexual encounters.

The "Act Now, Think Later" Attitude. Men who commit rape characteristically score very low on personal responsibility. They charge recklessly into situations without pausing to consider the consequences of their behavior. They follow their whims and urges instead of exercising self-discipline and restraint. They can become sexually aggressive tonight without thinking how they will explain their behavior tomorrow or deal with the obvious legal and emotional consequences they may face for months and years to come.

The "Who Cares about You?" Attitude. Men who are prone to rape usually lack social conscience. They act for themselves with little regard for the feelings and well-being of others. "If you get in my way and get hurt," they reason, "that's your tough luck." In a sexual encounter they may be oblivious to the physical and emotional pain they are inflicting on their victim in the process of getting what they want.

◆ Sex Myths

The man who fits the threefold profile of a potential rapist also buys into a number of male sex myths he consciously or subconsciously uses to legitimize his sexual aggression. Here are some of the most common of these myths:

Women Really Want to Be Raped. This myth is an extension of the attitude of male dominance mentioned above. "Entertainment" media often condition men to look at women as objects to be raped, as beings whose sole worth is in their sexual stimulus. Men who accept this myth believe that women enjoy being dominated, including sexually, that they get turned on when men play rough because (consciously or subconsciously) they really want to be conquered. That's a myth, of course. No woman welcomes sexual victimization.

Women Owe Sex to Men Who Spend Money on Them. A survey of junior high students revealed the prevalence of this myth among youth. In the survey, 51 percent of the boys and 41 percent of the girls said a man has a right to force a woman to kiss him if he has spent a lot of money on her. Twenty-five percent of the boys and 17 percent of the girls said forced sex is okay if the man has spent money on her.[4]

Women Can Control Themselves Sexually; Men Can't. Many men claim that they can only "make out" for so long before they "cross the line" and lose control of their sex drive. At that point, they reason, they're not responsible for their actions. In fact, the guy will often blame the girl for an act of date rape, arguing that it was her fault because she took him over that line.

Women May Say No, But Their Actions Say Yes. A lot of men claim that women dress and act seductively in order to turn guys on. When a woman resists his attempts at sex, a man may say, "You tell me to stop, but everything else you do says go. You dress in sexy outfits. You send me those flirty looks across the room. You cuddle with me in the car. I know you're playing hard-to-get with me; that's what girls are supposed to do. I'm only giving you what you really want." In most cases these men are reading messages the women aren't sending. Studies show that men tend to see a woman's friendliness as an interest in sex. Therefore a man may *overrate* a woman's expressions of friendship and *underrate* her verbal protests to his sexual advances.

If the Woman's Not a Virgin, It's Not Rape. Nearly one-third of the junior high students in the survey mentioned above saw nothing wrong with raping a woman who was already sexually active.[5] This response reflects another common myth that dismisses the rape of a non-virgin with, "No harm was done; she was already a 'bad girl.'"

Rape—whether acquaintance rape or stranger rape—is not primarily a sexual act, but an act of aggression. And it is a violent act. One study found that 87 percent of rapists either carry weapons or threaten violence or death.[6] In another study of college women who had experienced sexual aggression, various levels of violence were experienced. Forty-eight percent of the offenders simply ignored the victim's protests and requests to stop. Thirty-two percent verbally coerced their victims into the offensive or displeasing event. Fifteen percent used physical restraint, and 6 percent used various kinds of threats or physical aggression.

The Effects of Rape

◆ Physical Effects

For many victims, the most immediate and noticeable impact of rape is physical. Some have been beaten and injured. Some complain of loosened teeth, bruises, and abrasions suffered either from the attack or from their attempts to escape. Even those who escape obvious injury report that their bodies are sore all over. Others say that certain areas ache more than other areas because of the focus of the assailant's force, such as the neck and throat, chest, ribs, arms and legs, pelvis, or genital area. Some victims report that their sleep is affected, especially if the attack happened at night or in their own bed. They have difficulty falling asleep. They sometimes wake up screaming, tormented by recurring nightmares of the attack, and are unable to get back to sleep. Other victims experience a disturbance in their eating patterns as a result of the assault. Some have reported self-hatred, causing them to abhor their own bodies. When this happens, other problems arise that could include a decrease in appetite, which may lead to compulsive disorders like overeating, bulimia (binge-eating and self-induced vomiting) or anorexia (self-starvation).

Rape victims often succumb to other compulsive physical behaviors as well, such as compulsive exercising, perfectionism, obsessive house-cleaning, overachieving, drug abuse, and others. Some women battle with extreme sexual attitudes or tendencies. Many also suffer from migraine headaches or stomach problems.

◆ Emotional Effects

While the physical effects of rape are traumatic, the emotional wounds and scars such an act of violence leaves are often more horrible and more difficult to overcome. Following are just a few of the responses that victims of rape—both stranger rape and acquaintance rape—are likely to encounter.

Grief. Victims of rape feel deep loss and grief in a number of areas. Perhaps the rapist had been a trusted friend, but now the victim struggles with the fact that she's been betrayed and wonders if she can ever trust again. A rape victim may not only grieve over her loss of trust in the aggressor, but in all men. Victims also struggle because of a loss of self-esteem; the tragic violation of their person causes them to question their value and importance to others. And, last but by no means least, there's the awareness that if the victim was a virgin before the rape, she has lost something she had been saving for the one she would someday marry. With all the losses that accompany rape, a period of deep grieving should be expected. (See chapter 8, "Grief.")

Guilt. One of the most pervasive emotional responses to rape—perhaps date rape in particular—is guilt. Victims often feel partially responsible for what happened to them. They are plagued by a string of guilt-producing "if only's": *If only I hadn't let myself be alone with him*

. . . If only I hadn't worn that dress . . . If only I hadn't led him on . . . If only I hadn't been sexually aroused . . . If only I hadn't cooperated with him . . . The awareness that she has been involved in a wrong—regardless of the fact that *she* was the victim—can produce feelings of guilt in the victim of rape. (See also chapter 3, "Guilt.")

Denial. Many women can't believe that someone they know could have raped them. The idea is too painful. And so emotionally they attempt to bury the episode in their subconscious and deny that it happened. In the case of date rape, a victim will often tell herself, "It wasn't rape. It couldn't have been rape. He wasn't some stranger abducting me at gunpoint; he was my boyfriend. Rapes don't happen between boyfriend and girlfriend."

Fear. Fear, especially related to being with men, is a natural response to a rape experience. Some victims are suddenly afraid of being with any man, being alone, or living alone. If the assailant was tall, the victim will often fear any tall man she meets. If he had a mustache, she may be fearful of any man with a mustache. Even the scent of the cologne worn by the rapist may trigger a panic attack. (See chapter 2, "Anxiety.")

Some women are afraid that their assailant will attack again. One survey noted that 41 percent of raped women expect to get raped again. As a result, many enroll in defense courses, change their phone number, install elaborate locks and alarms, sleep with the lights on, or move in with a friend. When the fear that accompanies a rape experience is not dealt with, it may grow into a serious problem affecting all the woman's future relationships with men, even her husband or father.

Loss of Self-Worth. Many victims of rape sense a deep inner hurt and dismay that causes them to see themselves as "damaged goods." They feel dirty, used, and abused. Their self-images are bruised, and they wonder if they will ever be worth anything again. (See chapter 6, "Unhealthy Self-Esteem.") One study revealed that 30 percent of the rape victims surveyed contemplated suicide after the incident, 31 percent sought psychotherapy, and 82 percent said the experience had permanently changed them.[7]

◆ Social Effects

The victim of rape will also undergo some social responses to her experience. She may find that some people avoid her. Her social involvement—or lack of it—may be governed by her fear that everyone knows she's been raped. She may prefer to stay at home instead of going out with friends. She may feel like cutting classes or not going to work because of the stares or questions she may have to endure. She may want to refuse all dates with men, fearing anything close to a sexual situation. She may avoid church, not wishing to be around people . . . and not wanting to "face" God.

◆ Spiritual Effects

A victim of rape will immediately be faced with the spiritual ramifications of her ordeal. She will quickly start asking questions such as: *Where was God when I was being assaulted? Did He know what was happening to me? Did He care? Did this happen to me because God isn't loving? Or because I'm not lovable?* Such questions not only present problems in themselves to the victim but may also produce more guilt—if the victim tells herself, "I shouldn't be thinking such things; I shouldn't be having such doubts."

The Biblical Perspective of Rape

There are a lot of topics in the Bible that are open to interpretation, but proper sexual behavior isn't among them. God clearly designed sex to be enjoyed by a man and a woman in a loving, committed, monogamous relationship. Any attitude or action that departs from God's standard is sexual immorality, as the following verses declare:

- You shall not commit adultery. (Exod. 20:14)

- You have heard that it was said, "Do not commit adultery." But I tell you that anyone who looks at a woman lustfully has already committed adultery with her in his heart. (Matt. 5:27–28)

- Do not be deceived: Neither the sexually immoral nor idolaters nor adulterers nor male prostitutes nor homosexual offenders . . . will inherit the kingdom of God. . . . Flee from sexual immorality. (1 Cor. 6:9–10, 18)

- But among you there must not be even a hint of sexual immorality, or of any kind of impurity. (Eph. 5:3)

- Put to death, therefore, whatever belongs to your earthly nature: sexual immorality, impurity, lust, evil desires and greed, which is idolatry. (Col. 3:5)

- It is God's will that you should be sanctified: that you should avoid sexual immorality. (1 Thess. 4:3)

- Marriage should be honored by all, and the marriage bed kept pure, for God will judge the adulterer and all the sexually immoral. (Heb. 13:4)

In addition to going against God's guidelines for sexual purity, rape (all violence, in fact) violates God's supreme law: the law of love. The primary word for love in the New Testament is *agape*, a word that signifies the highest form of love. It's an unselfish love, a giving love. *Agape* is the opposite of the lust for power and sex that motivates rape. Lust reaches out to grab what it wants; love reaches out to give what others need.

It is impossible to miss the emphasis on unselfish love in the New Testament. God's law of love leaves no room for the selfishness of rape:

- Jesus taught: "A new command I give you: Love one another. . . . By this all men will know that you are my disciples, if you love one another. . . . Greater love has no one than this, that he lay down his life for his friends" (John 13:34–35, 15:13).

- Paul wrote: "Be devoted to one another in brotherly love. Honor one another above yourselves. . . . The commandments, 'Do not commit adultery,' 'Do not murder,' 'Do not steal,' 'Do not covet,' and whatever other commandment there may be, are summed up in this one rule: 'Love your neighbor as yourself'" (Rom. 12:10, 13:9).

- Peter wrote: "Now that you have purified yourselves by obeying the truth so that you have sincere love for your brothers, love one another deeply, from the heart" (1 Pet. 1:22).

- And John wrote: "Dear friends, let us love one another, for love comes from God. Everyone who loves has been born of God and knows God" (1 John 4:7).

The Word of God makes it clear that the rapist—or attempted rapist—is guilty of an egregious sin. It must be equally emphasized, however, that God holds the rapist—not the victim—accountable. "Acquitting the guilty and condemning the innocent—the LORD detests them both" (Prov. 17:15). The church and the Christian must be careful to do neither in confronting the issue of rape.

Scripture is also clear that God is willing and waiting to extend His love and forgiveness to the rapist who confesses his sin and takes responsibility for his action:

- "Though your sins are like scarlet," the Bible promises, "they shall be as white as snow; though they are red as crimson, they shall be like wool. If you are willing and obedient, you will eat the best from the land; but if you resist and rebel, you will be devoured. . . ." (Isa. 1:18b-20a).

Most importantly, perhaps, God's Word leaves no doubt that He is anxious to extend His hand of love, grace, and comfort on behalf of the victim of rape:

- For he will deliver the needy who cry out, the afflicted who have no one to help. (Ps. 72:12)

- He will defend the afflicted among the people and save the children of the needy; he will crush the oppressor. (Ps. 72:4)

- But you, O God, do see trouble and grief; you consider it to take it in hand. The victim commits [herself] to you; you are the helper of the fatherless. (Ps. 10:14)

The Response to the Problem of Rape

Listen ◆ Empathize ◆ Affirm ◆ Direct ◆ Enlist ◆ Refer

Rape is an unspeakably tragic and traumatic experience, and helping a victim of rape is a challenge for even the most qualified Christian counselor. The youth leader's goal should be to involve a Christian counseling professional as early as possible, but the following steps can be taken preparatory to referral:

LISTEN. It's amazing how many victims of rape fail to tell anyone about it. In one study of women who had experienced an act of rape, 42 percent told no one about the assault. If a young person has confided an experience of rape in you, be careful to:

- Listen attentively and sympathetically.

- Avoid expressing doubt or disbelief.

- Avoid trying to direct or instruct the young person.

- Try to confine your speech initially to gentle questioning, for example, "Do you think you can talk about it?" and "Can you tell me what happened next?" Patiently help the youth to carefully and thoroughly recount the incident. Help her to express not only what happened but how she feels about it and what it has done to her physically, emotionally, and spiritually.

EMPATHIZE. At each step along the way, seize every opportunity to communicate your empathy and nonjudgmental acceptance of the youth's feelings in such ways as:

- Nodding your head.
- Making eye contact.
- Leaning forward in your chair to indicate interest and concern.
- Speaking in soothing tones, quietly prompting ("uh-huh," "go on," "I'm so sorry," etc.).
- Reflecting key statements ("So you're saying . . . ") or gestures ("You felt helpless . . . ").
- Waiting patiently through tears or silence.

The rape victim may be tempted to suppress feelings like anger, helplessness, hatred, fear, embarrassment, or the desire for revenge, thinking that such feelings are evil. Help her understand that feelings are amoral; they're not right or wrong, good or bad. They are merely a God-given warning system indicating that something isn't quite right inside. Emphasize that facing her feelings, expressing them, and responding appropriately to them is the issue.

AFFIRM. Make the most of every opportunity to assure the victim that no matter what she did, said, thought, or how she dressed, she did not ask to be raped. Remind her that she has been criminally victimized, but that her victimization was not her fault. Communicate repeatedly, with words and actions, that she is unconditionally loved by God and by you and that she is a person of infinite worth and value. When appropriate, try to impress the following scriptural realizations on the youth: You are valuable because you are created in the image of God (Gen. 1:27). You are worth so much to God that He gave His Son for you (John 3:16; 1 Pet. 1:18–19). You (if you are a Christian) are God's workmanship, His masterpiece (Eph. 2:10). You are so valuable that God's Word says He is rich because you have been given to Him (Eph. 1:18).

DIRECT. A victim of a traumatic experience such as rape may feel powerless to seek help and make decisions. The caring adult may need to patiently and gently guide the victim through the following steps to recovery:

1. Turn the youth to God as the source of healing and wholeness. A rape victim may find prayer impossible, particularly at first; she may feel as though heaven is closed to her and God's ear is deaf to her. One way to help her through this period is to turn her toward key Psalms; encourage her to read them aloud, to use them to help express her grief and anger and, eventually, to lead her to prayer. Helpful Psalms include Psalms 6, 27, 28, 31, 57, 70, 91, 130, 142, and 143.

2. Walk with the victim through the stages of grief and other emotions and reactions. The loss experienced as a result of rape needs to be grieved; a caring adult can help a young person through the stages of grief (denial, anger, bargaining, depression, and acceptance) by helping her confront, express, and resolve such feelings and accept them with understanding and comfort. (See also chapter 8, "Grief.")

3. Foster a daily partnership of prayer for and with the young person. Pledge your daily prayer support to the victim and encourage her to develop and maintain daily fellowship with God in order to rely on His strength, learn from His Word, and counter destructive thoughts and feelings with the mind of Christ (Phil. 4:4–9).

4. Alert the young person to the possible continuing effects of the rape. Prompt her to be alert to periodically ask such questions as, "Am I more antisocial than usual?" "Am I afraid of men?" "Am I more self-conscious or easily embarrassed?" These questions may help identify unresolved, hidden attitudes or fears resulting from the experience.

5. Expose the youth to the available resources for coping with the trauma. Help her acknowledge (preferably by name) those people who are or may be willing to help in practical ways: an understanding parent, a close friend, hotlines, organizations, pen pals, etc.

6. Encourage the young woman to accept the fact that healing will take time. Extend hope to the youth. While the healing process may be painful and may take considerable time, the victim has survived the actual rape; she can also overcome the trauma, with God's help.

ENLIST. Enlist the young person in several key priorities for recovery:

1. Seeking medical attention. If the rape happened recently, the victim may still be in shock; she may be unaware of some of the physical injuries she suffered. Urge her (with her parents' permission and involvement) to seek the help of her physician, a hospital emergency room, or an urgent-care clinic for a checkup. Most experts recommend that the victim not shower or douche before seeing a doctor because valuable evidence for identifying the attacker may be lost. Also, tests for pregnancy and sexually transmitted diseases are necessary to determine future treatment.

2. Reporting the rape. Be sure the victim understands that filing a police report may lead to an investigation, an arrest, and legal proceedings involving the perpetrator. It may be difficult for her to decide to press charges. But help her understand that the rapist—even if it was some-

one she knew and trusted—committed a crime. Taking legal action may be the only way of ensuring that the offender gets help before he victimizes someone else.

3. Finding a safe place to recover. The concerned adult may wish to suggest a relative or friend stay with the victim until she has overcome the initial shock of the attack—particularly if there is even a remote chance of the offender renewing or repeating the aggression.

4. Pursuing continuing treatment and education. Does the youth want to spend time with a support group of rape victims? Would she profit from a group of godly women who will provide a nurturing atmosphere and support her spiritual growth during her recovery? Does she need to call the Rape Abuse and Incest National Network (800-656-4673)? Would it help to outline (even write down) a specific plan for recovery with her?

REFER. As mentioned above, an urgent priority of the parent, teacher, pastor, or youth leader must be to guide the young victim of rape to professional Christian counseling (with parental permission). The extreme trauma engendered by rape—whether stranger rape or acquaintance rape—calls for the assistance of a counseling professional who can walk the victim through the many steps of healing.

Helping the Offender

A young man who has committed an act of rape—whether stranger rape or acquaintance rape—is in desperate need of wise and godly counsel. If he is guilty of forcing a girl sexually, he has sinned against God and grievously wronged one of God's children. He may be suffering a great deal of hurt himself, hurt that may be both the cause and the effect of his crime. A youth leader who is in a position to help a sexual offender may begin with the following:

LISTEN. Let the young person talk. Allow him to relate what he has done. Don't try to prevent him from offering explanations or defenses, but let him spill his heart without censure.

EMPATHIZE. The listening adult may be overcome with horror and revulsion at the offender's action, but it is important to communicate prayerful support at this time. The youth leader should avoid helping the offender to excuse his actions, but this is not the time for sermons. The offender is likely to be afraid, hurting, and in dire need of loving (but firm) support.

AFFIRM. Try to communicate unconditional love to the offender in such a way that will allow him to distinguish between the concerned adult's acceptance of him (as a person) and acceptance of his crime.

DIRECT. Try to guide the offender through the following steps. (Some—or all—may not be accomplished until after referral to a professional, but they represent a crucial step in helping the offender.)

1. *Get straight with God.* Help the offender understand that his offense against the woman he raped was a sin against God; therefore the first step toward getting things right is to confess that sin to God and receive His forgiveness. You might suggest that the offender sit down with a blank sheet of paper and write a letter of confession to God. You might point him to Psalm 51 as a helpful pattern for a prayer of confession.

2. *Turn around.* Confession is important, but it's not enough. There must also be a change of behavior so the offense is never repeated. The offender must repent. To repent literally means to stop going in the direction you're going, turn around, and head in a new direction. The best way for a rapist to do this is to seek professional Christian counseling.

3. *Engage in a daily partnership of prayer for and with the young person.* Pledge your daily prayer support to the offender, and encourage him to develop and maintain daily fellowship with God in order to rely on His strength, learn from His Word, and counter destructive thoughts and feelings with the mind of Christ (Phil. 4:4–9).

4. *Confess to the victim and, if necessary, to the authorities.* At some point, the offender must decide the best way to apologize to the woman he raped. He may decide to write a letter confessing plainly what he did, expressing his sorrow over it and explaining the steps he is pursuing in order to change, clearly stating that *he* was at fault, not her. In the letter he may also want to offer restitution (such as paying for the victim's counseling, doctor bills, etc.). If the victim elects to press charges, the offender may face punishment at the hands of the court. Guide him to understand the necessity of being entirely truthful and cooperative with the police, attorneys, judge, and other officials. He may alert them to the fact that he is seeking help for his problem, but he should be ready to pay the penalty for his crime.

4. *Pray for reconciliation.* When the offender's confession, repentance, and restitution are met with the victim's forgiveness, reconciliation is possible. This doesn't mean that the young man's relationship with the victim (if there was one) will return to where it was before the attack. It may take years before the woman can even speak to him, let alone have any kind of relationship with him. But if the offender has sincerely sought forgiveness and wholeheartedly done his part, his conscience can be clear and the possibility of reconciliation is real.

ENLIST. Enlist the offender's cooperation in implementing the above steps. As much as possible, let him make the plans and choose the time table. The youth leader may wish to apply gentle pressure and require accountability, but in the final analysis, the offender is the key agent in his own recovery.

REFER. At the earliest opportunity, guide the young offender to involve his parents and commit himself to a Christian counselor who is skilled in working with sex offenders. Such a professional can help the offender deal with the root(s) of his problem, a process that may take several months, a year, or more. However, though the road to recovery may be long, unless the underlying causes of his offense are exposed and treated, the likelihood of it being repeated are great.

For Further Reading

The following resources may help the concerned parent, pastor, teacher, or youth worker assist a rape victim or offender:

Scriptures Cited in This Chapter

- Exodus 20:14
- Matthew 5:27–28
- 1 Corinthians 6:9–10, 18
- Ephesians 5:3
- Colossians 3:5
- 1 Thessalonians 4:3
- Hebrews 13:4
- John 13:34–35, 15:13
- Romans 12:10, 13:9
- 1 Peter 1:22
- 1 John 4:7
- Proverbs 17:15
- Isaiah 1:18b–20a
- Psalms 10:14; 72:4, 12
- Genesis 1:27
- John 3:16
- 1 Peter 1:18–19
- Psalms 6, 27, 28, 31, 57, 70, 91, 130, 142, and 143.
- Philippians 4:4–9
- Psalm 51

Other Scripture to Read

- Psalms 34:18; 86:15–17; 103:11–18; 107:20; 139:1–24
- Isaiah 53:4–6
- Matthew 5:1–12
- John 14:27
- 1 Peter 5:7

Further Reading

- Jennifer Botkin-Maher, *Nice Girls Don't Get Raped* (Here's Life Publishers).
- Dr. James Dobson, *When God Doesn't Make Sense* (Tyndale House).
- C. S. Lewis, *The Problem of Pain* (Macmillan).
- Josh McDowell, *It Can Happen to You* (Word).
- Holly Wagner Green, *Turning Fear to Hope* (Thomas Nelson).

37

RITUAL ABUSE

A Synopsis

Introduction

At age eighteen, Jill felt the courage to recall the nightmare she had as a child. She could not often find restful sleep at night. No words could be spoken to bring necessary comfort. For Jill, nothing could be done to take away the abusive impact of her nightmare. Admittedly Jill's nightmare was different than most. It was not a haunting figment of her imagination that surged forth while she slept. Jill's nightmare was not a dream. It was real.

Jill called herself a survivor of ritual abuse. As a child given up for adoption, Jill endured several years of foster care before she was finally adopted by a couple who were involved in the occult. As part of her family role, Jill was chosen as an integral part of numerous rituals to worship Satan. She was emotionally, physically, and sexually abused. Her adoptive parents sought to guarantee her allegiance to the darkest of forces.

Jill was raped; she had objects inserted into her body. She endured long hours lying in tomb-like boxes filled with fecal matter. Blood was poured over her body. Ghoulish incantations rang loud in her ears. Threats to her life were commonplace. The worst, however, was being forced to watch animal—and human—sacrifices.

By the time Jill became a young adult, the tangible abuse had long stopped. The memories of the actual events had been safely repressed and were no longer attainable to her conscious day-to-day life. Her life was, for the most part, normal. Then one day, unexpectedly, flashbacks of the horrid acts came to her.

Beneath the veneer of a seemingly normal lifestyle lay a fragile person on the verge of total collapse. As the flashbacks continued over the next several weeks, she lived in a constant, ever-growing state of fear and stress. She believed she would be killed if she told anyone of the atrocities she experienced. She wished she could kill herself during times when she felt no hope.

Jill attempted to travel the long road toward recovery; to strengthen herself and regain her life. As a part of her recovery, she cautiously and painstakingly revealed her experience to those she felt trustworthy. Most people could not believe her. At times she doubted it herself.

The Problem of Ritual Abuse

Although the validity of ritual abuse has always been attacked under the guise of false memory syndrome—and false memory syndrome has, in some cases, substantive findings—the nightmare of ritual abuse is indeed real. Numerous published personal accounts, such as those documented by authors Lauren Stratford (1988) and Rebecca Brown, M.D. (1966), support the reality of such abuse. Numerous police reports document the evidence of satanic ritualistic activity. Collaborating medical reports of abused children and the strikingly similar reports received by counselors, psychologists, and psychiatrists across the country lend credence to the claims.

Technically, ritual abuse is not necessarily derived from satanic practices. Yet the goal of ritual abuse appears to reflect the basic foundation of satanic worship and belief. The victim is indoctrinated into a system where good is bad and bad is good. There may also be forced submission to worshiping a designated god. In addition, belief in supernatural powers such as demons and monsters are used to control and terrorize.

Should satanism be implicated? Most definitely. The Church of Satan is alive and well. This fact cannot be denied. Founded by Anton Szannzar LeVey in 1966 and situated in San Francisco, the Church of Satan represents the movement of modern satanism. It is well organized and has a growing membership in the tens of thousands in the United States, not to mention abroad.

There exists a satanic bible, a calendar of satanic ritual holidays, and of course, specific rituals to obtain power and worship. Many rituals involve animal sacrifice, blood, sex, drug usage, and murder. The Church of Satan does not publicly admit or endorse these atrocities, but one does not have to adhere to the nine satanic precepts or espouse satanism as a chosen organized religion to be a perpetrator of ritual abuse.

There are four levels of satanic involvement:

1. Experimentalists and dabblers
2. Self-styled groups
3. Traditional or organized groups
4. International, orthodox, or generational groups

Involvement in ritual abuse at any level is extremely difficult to determine definitively. To avoid incrimination, abusers most often choose victims under the age of six years—a strategy that makes validations and prosecution very difficult, if not impossible.[1] Children seldom have the courage to talk about perpetration of abuse. Some are at first unaware of any wrong action. After all, the abuse is usually done by a trusted adult, and many children simply do not have the words to use to describe such horrific abuse.

Ritually abused children are most often threatened with or have become victims of mind-control techniques. Such techniques are used to convince young victims that if they do disclose any information they, their pets, or their parents will be hurt or killed. If a child does relate any abuse, most accounts are highly scrutinized. Stories from six-year-olds about sacrifices and demons seem incredible. Too often, however, they are not only credible, they are factual.

The Causes of Ritual Abuse

Two questions must be asked. First, why would any person or group ritually and systematically abuse a child? Secondly, how could such horrific abuse occur? The following may help answer such questions.

◆ Why Is There Ritual Abuse?

Evil Is a Reality in Our Hurting World. Satan is real, and his existence, combined with the hurting hearts of mankind, can lead to much cruelty and harm. Specifically, when a person has been abused, he or she has a higher proclivity toward abusing others. If the abuse of that person was extremely severe or perceived to be intentional, the likelihood that he or she will abuse in a systematic manner is greater. It may be suggested that abuse of this type is all the perpetrator knows. In other words, the person only knows how to deal with or relate to others in an abusive manner. It may also be that when a person has been extremely abused, she or he may strive for some retribution or significance. Those once abused may repeat the atrocity perpetrated upon them in a more ritualistic, systematic, or intentional manner.

Satanic Ritual Requires Abuse and Sacrifice. To worship and show loyalty to evil, one must participate in evil. Numerous confessions have revealed the belief (common to ritual abuse) that Satan himself requires brutal acts from his followers. In addition, such acts are often believed to be a means of acquiring greater demonic power for the satanist.

Propagation of Satanism Is International and Well-Organized. Some individuals within the organized satanic church have been designated and identified as recruiters. Their job is to bring new members into Satan's service. They often do so by such means as destroying a child's sense of free will through ritual abuse.

◆ How Does Ritual Abuse Occur?

All Abuse Is Secretive in Nature. Simply stated, no one readily admits to abusing children, and no one enjoys talking about this horrid subject. Be assured that in every case of ritual abuse, children are carefully instructed or manipulated to be secretive. They believe they must hide the incidents of abuse at all costs in order to protect themselves or the people they love and depend upon the most. If they do not, they believe great harm will occur.

Satanism Itself Is Secretive. Traditional Satanism has always been immersed in secrecy. It has only

been since the founding of the Church of Satan in 1966 and the publication of the satanic bible two years later that modern Satanism has received public attention.

Parents May Be Overly Trusting Rather Than Appropriately Vigilant. Too often parents are unaware of the potential dangers of giving an individual or group total care of their child. Parents need to be vigilant in their efforts to reasonably investigate individual and group caregivers, and they need to be sensitive to the warning signs of ritual abuse.

The Effects of Ritual Abuse

There are numerous effects of ritual abuse. In general, children of ritual abuse have great difficulty trusting and relating to others. Victims of such trauma tend to develop emotional and behavioral difficulties that endure for a lifetime as well.

The immediate effects of ritual abuse can serve as warning signs. The categories are listed below and include examples within each. Note that any one symptom or warning sign alone is not conclusive of a ritually abused child.

◆ Change in Bathroom Habits and Hygiene

The child may fearfully avoid the bathroom; he or she may become agitated when entering the bathroom and fearful and agitated when taking a bath. The child may resist being washed in the genital area. He or she may also be preoccupied with cleanliness, changing undergarments excessively, or be preoccupied with urine and feces (even handling them).

◆ Sexual Indications

The child may complain of unusual vaginal or anal pain; vaginal laceration or scarring often exists in the child who has been ritually abused. He or she may use age-inappropriate sexual language not typically used within the specific family. The child may masturbate compulsively or publicly, talk about sexual acts between adults or other children, and/or speak fearfully of things inside the child's body (such as monsters, bombs, insects).

◆ Emotional Changes

The child may exhibit extreme and rapid mood swings of a primarily angry nature. He or she may have intense and frequent nightmares and may be fearful of sleeping or of the bed itself. The child who has been ritually abused may be generally fearful, clingy, withdrawn or depressed, and he or she may regress in developmental behavior (such as in walking or talking).

◆ Relational Fears and Difficulties

The child may fear that his or her parents no longer love or can protect him or her, or the child may fear that the parents may want to kill him or her. He or she may talk of going to people's homes or other locations that are not usual to day-care or school routine. He or she may appear unusually distant and avoid physical contact, seem fearful that someone will take him or her away or intrude in the home and kill the parents. He or she may also talk about "my other mommy" (referring to relationships with abusers).

◆ Shifts in Eating Habits

The child may talk about being forced to eat unusual items and express fear that food may be poisoned. He or she may be resistant to eating certain foods such as meat or red-colored drinks or other foods that are brown or black in color.

These symptoms and signs are not exhaustive, of course; neither are they intended to necessarily suggest ritual abuse in and of themselves. They may, however, in concordance with other changes in behavior, alert a parent or other adult to the possibility of abuse.

The Biblical Perspective of Ritual Abuse

There is no question concerning God's intolerance for the abuse of children. Little ones are His. They are uniquely cherished. Scripture tells us of their value to God and His retribution if harm is perpetrated:

> It would be better for you if a millstone were hung around your neck and you were thrown into the sea than for you to cause one of these little ones to stumble.[2]

God's angry and intolerant view of ritual abuse is similarly clear, as the following Scriptures make clear:

> And he [Manasseh] made his son pass through the fire, [human ritual sacrifices] practiced witchcraft and used divination, and dealt with mediums and spiritists. He did much evil in the sight of the LORD, provoking Him to anger.[3]

> You shall not behave thus toward the LORD your God, for every abominable act which the LORD hates they have done for their gods; for they even burn their sons and daughters in the fire to their gods.[4]

Ritual abuse is clearly an abomination to God. Christian youth leaders, pastors, teachers, and parents must oppose it, prevent it, and seek to overcome its deep and lasting effects with all their energies.

The Response to the Problem of Ritual Abuse

Listen ◆ Empathize ◆ Affirm ◆ Direct ◆ Enlist ◆ Refer

Dealing with a victim—or suspected victim—of ritual abuse is a challenge that any thinking person will approach with much prayer and caution. A youth leader, parent, pastor, or teacher who hopes to help a possible victim of ritual abuse will be wise to pursue the following course:

LISTEN. Listen to the language of the young person. He or she may not communicate directly. Communication may not be verbal but rather symbolic—he or she may talk through actions. Be alert to the signs, symptoms, and symbols he or she uses or displays. Enlist the help of those you can trust who are directly involved with the young person—particularly his or her parents. Allow them to be privy to your concerns and be open to their feedback. Ask questions to verify your concerns and perceptions. Have others seen similar warning signs from the youth? It is often easy to misinterpret kids' comments and behaviors. It might be necessary to enlist the help of a professional or expert in ritual abuse to help you gain more clarifying information. In any case, trust your instincts. If you suspect any wrongdoing, action must be taken. When a verbal report is made, listen without disbelief. Be careful not to ask leading questions. Just listen.

EMPATHIZE. State clearly that you understand the young person's fears, confusions, and other emotions. Be sure not to minimize his or her feelings, perceptions, and experiences. The depth of trauma for the ritually abused is extreme. The youth's perception of your empathy will help establish trust and facilitate communication when otherwise both would be hard to come by. Empathy can often be communicated in the simplest ways, such as:

- Responding to tears or anger with a comforting word and embrace.

- Removing obstacles to intimate conversation (such as a desk, telephone, etc.).

- Listening attentively and nodding your head.

- Making eye contact and encouraging comments (such as "Go on," "I'm so sorry," etc.).

- Appropriate touching (a hug, a hand on the shoulder, etc.).

- Reflecting revealing statements or gestures ("You felt like . . ." "That was difficult for you," etc.).

AFFIRM. Any victim of abuse will need sincere affirmation, affection, and appreciation. These things can be offered in ways such as the following:

- Assuring the young person that his or her story is believed; he or she will be affirmed by being taken seriously.

- Assuring the youth that you are committed to doing whatever you can to help; otherwise, there is no basis for a helpful relationship.

- Communicating that the youth is unconditionally loved by God and by you.

- Communicating through word that the young person is a person of value and worth (for example, "I admire your courage") and through actions (hugs, pats on the back, respecting his or her opinions, etc.).

DIRECT. A concerned adult can help a victim of ritual abuse by offering direction in key areas, such as the following:

1. Guide the youth to acknowledge that he or she has been abused, and help the young person identify the effects the abuse is having on his or her life. Gently and sensitively direct the youth to openly discuss events and feelings with you and other trustworthy adults. Strive to communicate to the youth that, although it may be embarrassing or painful, telling his or her feelings and experiences to others will be helpful.

2. If the abuse has not stopped, help the youth take

steps to stop it immediately. *In fact, the physical or sexual abuse of a minor requires notification of law enforcement or child protection authorities in most states and provinces; be aware that silence in this regard may be* illegal. *Be sure you know—and obey—the laws of your state or province regarding the reporting of abuse.*

3. *Help the young person return the responsibility for the abuse to the perpetrator and any other contributing sources—not to himself or herself.* Gently but consistently challenge any effort to blame himself or his actions, and help the victim accurately identify the responsible persons and other contributing factors.

4. *Turn the youth to God as the source of healing and wholeness.* Help the young person discover that God can be a rock, a fortress, and a deliverer and that He can turn darkness into light. (See Ps. 18:2–6, 25–30.)

5. *Walk with the young person through the stages of grief.* The loss (of innocence, peace, wholeness, etc.) experienced as a result of abuse needs to be grieved; a caring adult can help a young person through the stages of grief (denial, anger, bargaining, depression, and acceptance) by helping him or her confront, express, and resolve such feelings and accepting them with understanding and comfort. (See also chapter 8, "Grief.")

6. *Foster a daily partnership of prayer for and with the young person.* Encourage the youth to develop and maintain daily fellowship with God in order to rely on His strength and learn from His Word, and counter destructive thoughts and feelings with the mind of Christ. (See Phil. 4:4–9.)

7. *Expose the youth to the available resources for coping with the trauma.* Help him or her acknowledge (preferably by name) those people who are or may be willing to help in practical ways: an understanding parent, a close friend, hotlines, organizations, pen pals, etc.

8. *Encourage the young man or woman to accept the fact that healing will take time.* Extend hope. While the healing process may be painful and may take considerable time, the victim has survived the actual abuse; he or she can also overcome the trauma, with God's help.

ENLIST. Enlist the young person's cooperation and participation in answering the question, "What must be done now?" Elicit suggestions and ideas from the youth, but help him or her understand that under no circumstances should the abuse be allowed to continue and that some form of ongoing treatment is necessary. At this point, you may meet with great reluctance. He or she may greet with horror the news that intervention of some kind is necessary, but engage him or her in actively pursuing a plan for treatment and recovery.

REFER. Most states require anyone who suspects any type of child abuse to report it to the proper authorities. When reports are made, anonymity can be maintained. In the case of ritual abuse, the proper agency to be notified is the child protection services designated to serve the area in which the youth resides. In most cases, a report is filed, a case manager is assigned, and an investigation is immediately undertaken.

A referral to a Christian counselor who specializes either in recovery from ritual abuse or in child abuse itself is often necessary. Make sure you know the reputation of any counselor to whom you refer. Do not be afraid to ask questions in order to receive word-of-mouth recommendations.

Finding the right counselor will be extremely instrumental in the young person's recovery. This person may represent the only trusting relationship he or she will have for a long time. The process of healing the scars left by ritual abuse is indeed a life-long journey. It is best not traveled alone.

For Further Reading

The following resources may help the concerned parent, pastor, teacher, or youth worker to assist a victim of ritual abuse:

Scriptures Cited in This Chapter

- Luke 17:2 NRSV
- 2 Kings 21:6 NASB
- Deuteronomy 12:31 NASB
- Psalm 18:2–6, 25–30
- Philippians 4:4–9

Other Scripture to Read

- Psalm 34:18; 44:5; 86:15–17; 103:11–18; 107:20; 139:1–24
- Psalms 6, 27, 28, 31, 57, 70, 91, 130, 142, and 143
- Isaiah 53:4–6

- Matthew 5:1–12
- Luke 10:19
- John 14:27–31
- Ephesians 6:10–18
- Hebrews 2:14–18
- 1 Peter 5:7
- 1 John 3:8
- Revelation 20:1–10

Further Reading

- Holly Wagner Green, *Turning Fear to Hope* (Thomas Nelson).
- Frank and Ida Mae Hammond, *Pigs in the Parlor: A Practical Guide to Deliverance* (Impact).
- Jerry Johnston, *The Edge of Evil* (Word).
- Josh McDowell and Don Stewart, *Demons, Witches and the Occult* (Tyndale House).

ADDICTIONS

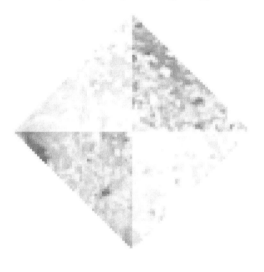

38

A Synopsis

❖

Alcohol Use and Abuse

Introduction

Kevin and Jason tiptoed down the steps a few minutes after 1 A.M. Kevin led his friend into the far corner of the room they called the study, though no one did any studying in there.

A metallic click echoed in the room as twelve-year-old Kevin turned the key in his dad's liquor cabinet.

"He's going to know you got in here," Jason warned.

"No way," Kevin insisted. "I only take what I know he won't miss." He reached around a few bottles in the front and drew out a bottle of vodka. He unscrewed the cap, placed the bottle to his mouth, and swallowed a mouthful of the clear liquid.

He passed it to Jason, and the two drank a few more swallows before returning the bottle to the cabinet.

Kevin's late-night adventure with Jason soon became a regular event when Jason visited or stayed the night. Before long, Kevin snuck liquor from his father's cabinet when he was home alone too. By the time he was fourteen, he was drinking every day.

Kevin had few friends besides Jason, and most evenings he spent alone at home while his father worked late and his mom went to church or Bible study or wherever it was she went when his father wasn't home. It seemed to Kevin like he was always lonely and bored, and the booze somehow helped to fill the void. It made him feel warm and secure, somehow.

Neither his father—whom Kevin suspected was an alcoholic—nor his mother seemed to notice the alcohol that disappeared with regularity from the house. If they did, they never commented on it.

The Problem of Alcohol Use and Abuse

Ninety percent of high school seniors say they've drunk alcohol sometime in their lives[1]; 67 percent say they've used alcohol within the last month, and 38 percent say they've had five or more drinks in a row within the previous two weeks.[2]

Such high degrees of acquaintance with alcohol are not limited to high school students, however. A survey of approximately eleven thousand eighth- and tenth-graders revealed that eight out of nine (88 percent) eighth-graders had tried alcohol. One in four (25 percent) had five or more drinks on at least one occasion in the previous two years, and nearly eight of every nine (84 percent) said it was fairly easy to get alcohol. And 36 percent of American fourth-graders—*nine- and ten-year-old children*—say they have been pressured by their peers to drink alcohol![3]

Former Health and Human Services Secretary Bowen has said that nearly three out of ten adolescents—nearly five million young people—have a drinking problem,[4] and the National Institute on Alcohol Abuse and Alcoholism reports that there are 3.3 million teenage alcoholics in the United States.[5]

Thomas Seessel, executive director of the National Council on Alcoholism, has said, "Adolescent alcohol abuse has become . . . [a] devastating epidemic. Nearly 100,000 ten- and eleven-year-olds get drunk at least once a week."[6]

It begins, of course, with experimentation. A preteen or teen discovers a bottle of wine in the refrigerator or is induced to sample beer at a friend's house. Many young people, after such experimentation, find their curiosity satisfied and thereafter abstain from alcohol. Others, however, continue to drink, sharing a six-pack of beer in a friend's car or sneaking a few swigs from the bottle of champagne in the refrigerator.

Some of those become problem drinkers, occasionally drinking to get drunk, perhaps even driving while intoxicated. Still others succumb to alcoholism.

Frank Moran, manager of adolescent services at the McDonald Treatment Center of Scripps Memorial Hospital in La Jolla, California, summarizes all the statistics and studies with a warning: "It's hard to get an accurate picture of alcohol . . . abuse from kids," he says, "but the reality is that *thousands* of *preteens are halfway down the road to disaster.*"[7] And many teens have already arrived.

The Causes of Alcohol Use and Abuse

Complex problems rarely have simple causes, and alcoholism is a complex problem. Mental health and health care professionals differ as to the primary causes of alcoholism, but the following are generally acknowledged as factors:

◆ Physiology

Numerous studies support the view that alcoholism springs from a physiological source. That is, some people possess an inborn predisposition toward alcoholism. This predisposition may never be discovered in people who never experiment with alcohol; but for physiological reasons, those who do will experience a different reaction to alcohol than many of their friends.

◆ Background

Psychologist Gary Collins points to three factors that can affect the likelihood of alcoholism:

a. *Parental Models.* How parents behave often influences the subsequent behavior of children. When parents drink excessively or abuse drugs, children sometimes vow to completely abstain. More often, however, they follow the parental example. It has been estimated that "without intervention, 40 to 60 percent of children of alcoholic parents become alcoholics themselves."[8]

b. *Parental Attitudes.* Parental permissiveness and parental rejection can both stimulate chemical use and abuse. When parents don't care whether or not the children drink, there is no concern about the dangers of drugs or alcohol and misuse often follows. . . .

c. *Cultural Expectations.* If a culture or subcultural group has clear guidelines about the use of alcohol or drugs, abuse is less likely. Among Italians and Jews, for example, young people are generally permitted to drink but drunkenness is condemned, and the rate of alcoholism is low. In contrast, cultures such as our own are more tolerant of drunkenness. . . . Since "getting high" is the "in" thing to do, conditions are set up which lead many to [alcohol] abuse.[9]

◆ Outside Influences

Another contributing factor to alcoholism is the influence of outside forces such as a dysfunctional family environment, peer pressure, and stress from social problems. Many people, of course, have endured peer pressure or severe stress without becoming alcoholics, but these are among the factors that can influence a young person's abuse of alcohol.

The Effects of Alcohol Use and Abuse

Many people assume they know the effects of alcoholism: drunkenness and debauchery. Such an assumption, however, is not only incomplete, it is incorrect. A drunken person is not always an alcoholic, and some alcoholics are seldom visibly drunk. There are, however, some effects of alcoholism that can be generally applied.

◆ Anguish

Alcoholics frequently experience a combination of physical and mental pain that can only be char-

acterized as anguish. The alcoholic wonders if he or she is going crazy, fearing that he or she has lost control—or will soon. The alcoholic becomes intensely frustrated about his life. He begins to think God has deserted him or is actively seeking to punish him. Steve Arterburn, author of *Growing Up Addicted,* says, "It is as if a big black cloud of everything negative and unpleasant about life is hovering over the alcoholic."[10]

◆ Confusion and Disorientation

The alcoholic will experience a variety of mental effects. A brilliant student may find it difficult or impossible to focus her mind. She may routinely forget names, dates, details, and appointments. She may even experience occasional blackouts (a blackout, not to be confused with passing out, is a state in which a person who appears to be functioning consciously and normally cannot later recall anything that happened during the blackout period). The blackout is considered by many experts to be a primary indicator of alcoholism.

◆ Loss of Control

"Loss of control is the classic indicator for alcoholism," says author Steve Arterburn. He writes further:

> Loss of control is characterized by the inability to predict the drinking behavior once the drinking has begun. It doesn't mean that a person can't stop drinking for two or three weeks. When the drinking does begin, the desired two drinks become the uncontrollable twenty. . . . [It] also refers to the inability to control emotions. . . . The alcoholic may find himself or herself breaking into tears or uproarious laughter at inappropriate times.[11]

◆ Depression

An alcoholic is well acquainted with depression, a bout of severe and prolonged sadness and hopelessness. (See also chapter 5, "Depression.") He feels paralyzed, pathetic, and powerless to regain his grip on life, and that sense of helplessness compels him to drink, which increases his depression. The pain of such emotions, heightened by the chemicals affecting his system, often exceeds that of other forms of depression.

◆ Low Self-Esteem

An alcoholic will typically experience fatal blows to his or her self-esteem. She will feel that her life is a mess, that she made it that way, and that she is powerless to turn it around. She will often conclude that if she were worth anything, if she had any character at all, she wouldn't be in the shape she's in. She feels as though she has no will power, no strength, no worth. She will believe that the friends she's lost, the tests she's failed, the people she's disappointed have all been deserved, because she is worthless. Tragically, such feelings of low self-worth tend only to drive her to drink, which in turn deepens her convictions of worthlessness. (See also chapter 6, "Unhealthy Self-Esteem.")

◆ Personality Distortion

An alcoholic typically becomes nearly unrecognizable to many family and friends, "another person" from the person he or she "used to be." Things that once were priorities are no longer important. Former values and interests are abandoned. A young woman who once took meticulous care of her appearance may often appear frumpy and disheveled; a young man who once seemed devoted to the piano may appear unconcerned with music.

◆ Arrested Maturity

A teen (or preteen) alcoholic will suffer from arrested maturity. "Alcohol stunts emotional growth," says one professional in the field. "Kids who drink heavily don't develop the judgment or coping skills they need as adults."[12] The alcoholic may become easily distressed, easily angered, and easily offended, often like a child many years his or her junior. The path toward emotional and social maturity may not only be stunted; it may actually be reversed.

◆ Guilt and Shame

"In alcoholics undergoing treatment," writes Arterburn, "guilt seems to prevail over all the other emotions."[13] An alcoholic may feel guilt over his conviction (often encouraged by family, church, etc.) that his alcoholism was self-inflicted. His alcoholism may have separated him from family, friends, and even from God. He may know his periodic drunkenness to be a sin forbidden and condemned in Scripture. Such things are likely to engender deep feelings of guilt. (See also chapter 3, "Guilt.") Inasmuch as he equates his *actions* with *himself* and his malady with his person, he will also feel shame—shame because he is an alcoholic, because he is a "drunk," because he is a "failure," because he's not "normal"—in his own eyes and often in the eyes of others.

◆ Remorse

An alcoholic will frequently be overcome with remorse. Whereas guilt focuses on a person's acts and shame focuses on the person's self, remorse focuses on the harm the person has caused something or someone else. She may be remorseful over the tears her mother has shed on her behalf. She may feel remorse for the lies that have hurt her friends. She may deeply regret the embarrassment she has caused her family or the trouble she feels she's caused her pastor. Such remorse, combined with guilt and shame, can prompt a person to sincere repentance—or total despair.

◆ Alienation and Isolation

Many of the above effects—low self-esteem, depression, guilt, shame, remorse—can create a crippling sense of alienation in the young alcoholic's mind and heart. He or she feels alone, unable to get close to anyone, unable to seek help from anyone. Arterburn writes:

The alcoholic, alienated from God and others, is left to suffer alone. . . . "They don't really care." "He hasn't been through what I've been through." "How could you help someone like me?" All become the battle cries of continued alienation. One by one the alcoholic figures out some excuse to push everyone out of his or her life.[14]

◆ Despair

A young person who is in the advanced stages of alcoholism will sooner or later succumb to despair. The situation appears hopeless. Life is effectively over. There seems to be no way out. Many alcoholics at this point succeed at suicide. Even if they do not, however, the outlook—apart from intervention—is bleak. "The progression," Arterburn says, "100 percent of the time, ends in death from disease, an accident, suicide, or total insanity."[15]

The Biblical Perspective of Alcohol Use and Abuse

"The Bible quite clearly pronounces the evils of drunkenness," writes Stephen Arterburn, "[but] it is silent on alcoholism and addiction."[16]

Many Christians and preachers, however, have alienated some people and perhaps harmed others by condemning what the Bible does not condemn and endorsing what the Bible does not endorse. Yet the biblical perspective of alcoholism is helpful in what it forbids and in what it allows.

The Bible does not explicitly condemn alcoholic drinks. Though there were many cultural differences between biblical days and ours, it must be granted that the Bible does not condemn alcohol. On the contrary, Psalm 104 includes "wine that gladdens the heart of man" in a listing of God's blessings. It is likewise obvious that Jesus drank wine. (See John 2:9, Matt. 26:27–29, and Luke 7:33–34.) The apostle Paul even prescribed wine for its medicinal benefits to a young pastor. (See 1 Tim. 5:23.)

The Bible strongly condemns alcohol abuse. "Wine is a mocker and beer a brawler; whoever is led astray by them is not wise," Proverbs 20:1 says. Proverbs 23:20a enjoins, "Do not join those who drink too much wine." Paul commanded, "Do not get drunk on wine, which leads to debauchery. Instead, be filled with the Spirit" (Eph. 5:18). Dr. Anderson Spickard Jr. of Vanderbilt University Medical Center outlines the biblical stance on alcohol abuse:

Alcohol abuse, [even that which] may not lead to serious consequences, is addressed very pointedly in the Scriptures. Both Jesus and Paul warn us repeatedly that drunkards will not inherit the kingdom of God (Luke 21:34, 1 Cor. 6:10, Gal. 5:21). It's not hard to figure out why they speak so strongly: alcohol abuse is involved in most murders, most assaults, most child abuse cases, most traffic fatalities—the list is endless. We do ourselves and our entire society a great disservice when we laugh at drunkenness or treat it lightly.[17]

The Bible endorses abstinence. While the responsible drinking of wine was not prohibited, the Bible does take a favorable position on abstinence. The Nazirite vow (Num. 6:2–4), in which a man "dedicate[d] himself to the Lord," included abstinence from wine and strong drink. The Rechabites were commended by God for their faithfulness to their ancestor's charges, specifically the charge never to drink wine (Jer. 35:1–19). John the Baptist (who may have taken the vow of a Nazirite), "drank no wine" (Luke 7:33). Gary R. Collins says, "Many Christians today would conclude that moderation is good, but abstinence is better, especially in view of the clear dangers inherent in drinking."[18]

The Bible does not directly address the state of alcoholism or the plight of the alcoholic. The Bible soundly forbids drunkenness and condemns the drunkard. However, not all drunkenness proceeds from alcoholism, and not all alcoholics are "drunkards." Furthermore, while some Christians contend that all the alcoholic needs is to repent and get right with God, many professionals insist that, because alcoholism involves physiological and emotional—as well as spiritual—components, the solution is not quite so simple. Again, Dr. Spickard offers a reasoned response in the absence of biblical imperative:

> Alcohol abuse—drunkenness—is a sin. The Scripture is clear on this point. But once a person is an alcoholic, once he has allowed his will to be captured by alcohol through abuse, he is sick. He can no longer help himself. To tell an alcoholic to shape up and stop drinking is like telling a man who has just jumped out of a nine-story building to fall only three floors. It just isn't going to happen.
>
> If we defined alcoholism as a physical disease, without a spiritual dimension, that might be humanism. [But alcoholism affects a person] physically, mentally, and spiritually. He will not get well unless he is treated in all three areas.[19]

The Response to the Problem of Alcohol Use and Abuse

Listen ◆ Empathize ◆ Affirm ◆ Direct ◆ Enlist ◆ Refer

A young person who is struggling with alcoholism is in acute and urgent need of help. Even if the youth has not progressed far into alcoholism, even if he or she does not perceive his or her own need of help, the youth leader must wisely and diligently seek to bring help and healing. Before detailing a plan of response, it might be helpful to quote Collins's list of things that will not help: criticism, coaxing, making the person promise to stop, threats, hiding or destroying the alcohol . . . urging the use of will power, preaching, or instilling guilt.[20] The following suggestions may, however, assist the youth leader:

LISTEN. Listen closely, not only to what the young person says but to what his or her words and actions indicate. Keep in mind that alcoholics (even young ones) are often masters of denial and manipulation. Resist the temptation to preach or argue; instead, try to communicate nonverbally ("If the addict collapses on the living room floor," Collins suggests, "leave him or her there rather than helping the person into bed.") or by the use of nonthreatening questions ("Can you tell me more?" or "Why are you angry?").

EMPATHIZE. Try to see beyond the young person's words or actions to imagine what he or she is feeling and thinking. Strive to focus (at least initially) on understanding, not on correction. "Let your gentleness be known"[21] to the young man or woman, and be alert to ways to communicate your empathy and willingness to understand, such as:

- Being available to the youth.
- Making eye contact.
- Leaning slightly forward in your chair as he or she talks.
- Nodding to indicate understanding.
- Reflecting key statements.
- Waiting patiently through silence, anger, or tears.

AFFIRM. Be very careful to remember that most alcoholics experience intense anxiety and low self-esteem. Consequently, be careful not to criticize or condemn the young person; instead, communicate your acceptance of and appreciation for him or her (although not of his or her behavior). Be gentle, accepting, affirming—but not gullible—in your approach.

DIRECT. The concerned adult can most help a young person struggling with alcohol abuse by offering the following direction:

1. Gently but firmly guide the young person to recognize and admit the problem. The following eight questions may help:

- Do you sometimes look forward to drinking when you should be doing something else?

- When you are drinking, do you drink as much as you can as quickly as possible?

- Do you ever end up drinking more than you (or others) think you should? (A "yes" answer to this question indicates a 90 percent likelihood of a drinking problem.)

- Do you ever drink alone (not necessarily physically alone; others may be present but not involved with the drinker)?

- Do you try to protect your supply of alcohol in order to make sure you're not "short" when you need it?

- When you're upset or sad, do you ever think, "If I could just have a drink, I'd feel better"?

- Are you able to drink more than you used to while remaining remarkably functional?

- Do you ever have trouble remembering things you did or said while drinking?

If the young person answers "yes" to four or more of the above questions, it is likely that he or she has a drinking problem. If the youth refuses to answer honestly or is resistant, offer calm but consistent evidence, sticking as much as possible to a nonthreatening questioning style. Present specific examples ("Did you intend to lose control last night?") rather than general accusations ("You're never sober anymore!").

2. *Turn the young person toward God.* Lead him or her to confession and repentance of sin, and help the young person receive and acknowledge God's love and forgiveness. Impress upon the youth that there is grace and strength in a relationship with God through Jesus Christ. Guide him or her to the establishment of a daily habit of prayer and Bible reading.

3. *Inform and involve the youth's parents.* As early as possible, the young person's parents must become involved. Though sometimes parents are reluctant to face the truth of a son or daughter's problem, their cooperation and support will be central to effective treatment and recovery.

4. *Review the options for treatment.* Help the youth (and parents) to consider medical intervention, support groups (such as Alcoholics Anonymous), and other forms of treatment. One of the most effective ways of accomplishing this is by suggesting "either/or" options ("Would you feel more comfortable seeing your family physician about the problem or would you like me to suggest someone?").

ENLIST. Once the youth has faced his or her problem (which may take considerable time and effort—for both of you), concentrate your efforts on enlisting him or her in planning for recovery. Offer gentle prodding and guidance, as warranted, but gain as much participation from the youth as possible. Though he or she may at first feel powerless, steer the teen toward solutions, but be sure the youth "owns" whatever decisions are made.

REFER. Teen alcoholism is a complex and critical problem. It is imperative that, as quickly as possible, the youth be referred to a qualified professional who can offer biblical counsel and guidance. Under no circumstances should you let an alcoholic try to overcome his or her alcoholism without considerable and professional help. There is a wide variety of organizations (like Alcoholics Anonymous) and treatment programs that can help, and an informed physician or psychologist can help the youth and the youth leader connect with such resources.

For Further Reading

The following resources may help the concerned parent, pastor, teacher, or youth worker to assist a young person who is struggling with alcohol use or abuse:

Scriptures Cited in This Chapter

- Psalm 104:15
- John 2:9
- Matthew 26:27–29
- Luke 7:33–34
- Proverbs 20:1; 23:20a
- Ephesians 5:18
- Luke 21:34
- 1 Corinthians 6:10
- Galatians 5:21
- Numbers 6:2–4
- Jeremiah 35:1–19
- Philippians 4:5

Other Scripture to Read

- Proverbs 21:17; 23:29–31

- Ecclesiastes 10:17
- Isaiah 5:11
- Luke 21:34
- Romans 6:12; 13:13
- Galatians 5:16–25
- Ephesians 6:10–18
- 1 Thessalonians 5:4–11
- James 3:2
- 2 Peter 1:5–7

Further Reading

- Stephen Arterburn and Jim Burns, *Drug-Proof Your Kids* (Focus on the Family).
- Stephen Arterburn, *Growing Up Addicted* (Ballantine).

39

DRUG USE AND ABUSE

Introduction

Twelve-year-old Justin Sawyer rode his ten-speed toward the shopping center down the street from his home. He and several seventh-grade friends would often meet in the parking lot to ride bikes and skateboards on the inviting acres of asphalt. That's where he had told his parents he was going, and they had given him permission; the shopping center was not far from home, and Justin always managed to return before nine o'clock.

But Justin did not stop at the shopping center that night. He rode past the vast parking lot toward the convenience store on a busy corner a block from the shopping center.

Justin had been saving his money for several weeks and had managed to collect fifty dollars. He was intent on discovering for himself what some of the kids at school talked about. He wanted to know what they knew. He wanted to feel what they felt. He wanted to wear his accomplishment like a badge. He wanted to try crack.

He skidded to a stop in front of a man who stood talking on a pay phone at the edge of the convenience store parking lot. The man glanced toward Justin and, when Justin nodded, hung up the phone.

The convenience store cashier would later tell authorities she had seen something change hands between Justin and the man before Justin pedaled away.

At 9:30 that night, just three hours after he left home, two teenagers discovered Justin's body at the bottom of a dry concrete drainage ditch. Two empty vials, a glass pipe, and a cigarette lighter were found next to Justin, indicating the cause of death even before his body was delivered to the coroner.

Justin had died of an overdose the first time he had tried crack; the purity of the cocaine was too high, producing a physiological reaction too intense for Justin's heart to withstand.

The man who had sold the crack to Justin was apprehanded, tried, and convicted; he served two and a half years of a five-year sentence. Justin will never finish serving his sentence.[1]

The Problem of Drug Use and Abuse

One out of every ten high school seniors uses marijuana on a daily basis.[2] Almost one in six high school seniors has tried cocaine or crack.[3] Nearly one out of twenty sixth- to twelfth-graders have used cocaine sometime in the past year.[4] Every day in America, five hundred adolescents begin using drugs.[5]

The National Institute on Drug Abuse reports that 30 percent of all college students will use cocaine at least once before they graduate and that as much as 80 percent of the entire population will try an illicit drug of some kind before their midtwenties.[6] Two in three American kids will use illicit drugs before their high school graduation.[7]

Drug use is not confined to high school and college-age youth, however. A *Weekly Reader* survey of a half-million young students discovered that 39 percent of *fourth-graders* say that "using drugs is a big problem among kids our age."[8] According to a Gallup poll, "The average age at which children first try alcohol or marijuana is twelve."[9] And 12 percent of kids from ages twelve to seventeen are regular (at least twenty times a month) marijuana users.[10] Nearly one in ten kids involved in an evangelical church or Christian youth group admits to having used illicit drugs in the past three months.[11]

Drugs have become increasingly available and visible among youth. Gallup reports that "more than four million youngsters between thirteen and seventeen years of age said they have been offered illicit drugs in the last thirty days."[12] More than half of high school seniors surveyed said that it would be "fairly easy" or "very easy" to obtain marijuana or cocaine.[13] And more than one in four sixteen- and seventeen-year-olds report that they have been exposed to the use *and* sale of drugs.[14]

An illicit drug is an addictive, mood-altering substance, the use of which is either controlled (such as prescription drugs) or banned (such as heroin or LSD). Illicit drugs come in many forms: inhalants (fumes from glue, typewriter correction fluid, spray paint, etc.), narcotics, hallucinogens, stimulants, and depressants. Table 39 on page 404 gives an overview of some of the most prevalent drugs.

The Causes of Drug Use and Abuse

Youth become involved in drugs for a variety of reasons. Though the reasons for teenage drug use are often varied and complex, many are strikingly consistent, such as:

◆ Peer Pressure

"Drugs are such a pervasive part of our culture," writes Dr. Armand M. Nicholi Jr., "that students now assume everyone takes drugs, and if you don't take them you indeed are part of the minority."[15] One young man explained the influence of peer pressure on his first experience with drugs: "I never wanted to smoke even one joint, let alone get high every day, but I was offered a joint at a blast [party] by a neat chick, and I couldn't refuse it. I've been smoking ever since."[16] (See also chapter 14, "Handling Peer Pressure.")

◆ Sexual or Physical Abuse

The *AFA Journal* has reported that "Among young people who have been physically or sexually abused, many turn to drugs. In a recent study of four hundred youth in a juvenile detention center in Florida, a team of researchers established a strong correlation between child abuse and later drug use."[17] (See also chapters 34, "Sexual Abuse," and 35, "Nonsexual Abuse.")

◆ Latchkey Kids

Researcher Jean Richardson of the University of Southern California reported that "young teens who come home to an empty house are twice as likely as those supervised by adults to use alcohol, marijuana and cigarettes."[18]

◆ Parental Example

A report of the San Diego County Grand Jury stated, "It is difficult for children to say no to drugs and alcohol when they find that their parents and relatives are using them."[19] Youth lecturer and author Bill Sanders quotes the sentiments of one youth who said, "My parents drink booze every time they go out to dinner or have friends over. So I drink and do dope. What's the difference?"[20]

◆ The Need to Escape

The complexity and turbulence of adolescence and modern life cause some teens to look to drugs as a means of escape. "When I get high," one teen explained, "it's like there's no school, no zits, and no worries. It's just me and no one bugging me. It's great."[21]

Psychologist Gary Collins cites five considerations that make a person more prone to drug abuse and addiction:

1. Personality, Heredity, and Physiology. . . . There are some traits which appear with above average frequency in those who abuse drugs. These include a high level of anxiety, emotional immaturity, problems in accepting authority, a low ability to tolerate frustration, low self-esteem. . . . [f]eelings of isolationism, perfectionism, guilt and compulsiveness. . . . In spite of these conclusions, not all specialists would agree on the personality characteristics of drug abusers. There is no such thing as a typical alcoholic or drug-abusing personality . . . Personality, heredity, and physiology may make some people more prone to become drug abusers, but in themselves these factors do not cause drug addiction.

2. Past Background and Culture. The family environment and society in which we are raised also can increase or decrease the likelihood of addiction.

    a. Parental Models. How parents behave often influences the subsequent behavior of children. . . .

    b. Parental Attitudes. Parental permissiveness and parental rejection can both stimulate chemical use and abuse. When parents don't care whether or not the children drink, there is no concern about the danger of drugs or alcohol and misuse often follows. If parents neglect the children or are excessively punity, the children rebel. Delinquency, excessive drug abuse, and alcoholism often follow.

    c. Cultural Expectations. If a culture or subcultural group has clear guidelines about the use of alcohol or drugs, abuse is less likely. [However, if] teenage and college drinking is winked at as a sign of growing up and . . . "getting high" is the "in thing" to do, conditions are set up which lead many to drug abuse.

3. Present Stress. The roots of addiction most often are found in the teenage years. . . . [Drugs are used as] a way to escape pressures temporarily and enjoy a feeling of tranquility or euphoria [which later becomes] an indispensable crutch by which people deny stress and dull the pains of life.

4. Perpetuating Influences. In understanding addiction it is important to consider what makes some people vulnerable (including personality, culture, and background), what motivates people to start taking the drug (primarily peer pressures and stresses), and what keeps the addiction going.

At some stage in the addiction process endocrine and biochemical changes occur which make withdrawal very difficult. Even more powerful are the psychological changes which have built up over the years. The drug has become the core around which life is organized. . . .

[Other perpetuating influences include] the

addict's family. Alcoholism and, to a lesser extent, drug addiction have been described as family diseases. . . . Treatment will be delayed if families or employers perpetuate the problem by denying its reality, hiding it from others, and protecting the addict from facing the consequences of his or her irresponsible and self-centered behavior.

5. Spiritual Influences. One Christian writer has emphasized that

by far the most important cause of drug abuse . . . is the existence of a spiritual, religious, and existential vacuum. . . . Stated concisely, human beings have an inner need for a real and growing relationship with God. When this craving is denied, unrecognized, and unfilled, there is a search for something else which will fill the vacuum. No more clearly is this stated than in the Bible: "Don't drink too much wine, for many evils lie along that path; be filled instead with the Holy Spirit, and controlled by Him." Here in one sentence, is a warning, an implied cause, and and answer to the problem of addiction.[22]

The Effects of Drug Use and Abuse

Discussing the effects of drug abuse requires a distinction between the physiological effects produced by various substances and the long-term effects—physical, spiritual, and social—of drug abuse and addiction.

Dan Korem, author of *Streetwise Parents, Foolproof Kids,* has developed a helpful table detailing the physiological effects of various controlled substances (see Table 39) that affords a quick overview of the relationship between specific drugs and their basic characteristics.

The long-term effects may include physical ramifications; guilt, shame, and remorse; sexual activity; dropping out of school; problem behaviors; depression; suicide; and delinquency.

◆ Physical Ramifications

Physical effects of drug abuse and addictions include dry skin, chronic sore throats, liver and pancreas disease, among many others. But other long-term effects of drug use are not so easily detected. In addition to the risk of overdose for the abuser and the tragic consequences of drug use for expectant mothers and their babies, the drug abuser faces such physical ramifications as leukemia, heart attack, infertility, tissue damage, and malnutrition.

Leukemia. A study funded by the National Cancer Institute suggested that marijuana use raises the risk of nonlymphoblastic leukemia by eleven times![24]

Heart Attack. A study conducted by Dr. David Hills of Texas Southwestern Medical Center found that even small amounts of cocaine can decrease blood flow to the heart, increasing the risk of a heart attack.[25]

Infertility. A study reported in the journal *Fertility and Sterility* suggested that long-term use of cocaine may be a major contributor to infertility in men.[26]

Tissue Damage. Inhalants destroy brain cells and damage tissue; cocaine is among the drugs that causes long-term lung damage, leading to emphysema.

Malnutrition. Use of certain drugs such as cocaine results in the loss of appetite, which sometimes results in malnutrition.

◆ Guilt, Shame, and Remorse

A drug abuser and/or addict will often experience feelings of guilt, shame, and remorse. Regardless of how vehemently or cavalierly a drug abuser or addict may explain or defend his behavior, he will often be haunted by feelings of guilt (an inner response to a wrong act), shame

Table 39. Controlled Substances, Uses and Effects [23]

	DRUGS/CSA SCHEDULES		TRADE OR OTHER NAMES	MEDICAL USES	DEPENDENCE Physical	Psycho-logical
NARCOTICS	Opium	II III V	Dover's Powder Paregoric Parepectolin	Analgesic, antidiarrheal	High	High
	Morphine	II III	Morphine, MS-Contin, Roxanol, Roxanol-SR	Analgesic, antitussive	High	High
	Codeine	II III V	Tylenol w/Codeine Empirin w/Codeine Robitussin A-C Fiorinal w/Codeine	Analgesic, antitussive	Moderate	Moderate
	Heroin	I	Diacetylmorphine, Horse, Smack	None	High	High
	Hydromorphone	II	Dilaudid	Analgesic	High	High
	Meperidine (Pethidine)	II	Demerol, Mepergan	Analgesic	High	High
	Methadone	II	Dolophine, Methadone Methadose	Analgesic	High	High-Low
	Other Narcotics	I–V	Numorphan, Percodan Percocet, Tylox, Tussionex Pentanyl, Darvon, Lomotil Talwin *	Analgesic, antidiarrheal, antitussive	High-Low	High-Low
DEPRESSANTS	Chloral Hydrate	IV	Noctec	Hypnotic	Moderate	Moderate
	Barbiturates	II III IV	Amytal, Butisol, Fiorinal Lotusac, Nembutal, Seconal Tuinal, Phenobarbitol	Anesthetic, anti-convulsant, sedative, hypnotic veterinary euthanasia agent	High-Mod.	High-Mod
	Benzodiazepines	IV	Ativan, Dalmane, Diazepam Libruim, Xanax, Serax Valium, Tranxexe, Veratran Versed, Halcion, Paxipam Restoril	Antianxiety, anticonvulsant, sedative, hypnotic	Low	Low
	Methaqualone	I	Quaalude	Sedative, hypnotic	High	High
	Glutethimide	III	Doriden	Sedative, hypnotic	High	Moderate
	Other Depressants	III IV	Equanil, Miltown Noludar, Placidyl, Valmid	Antianxiety, sedative, hypnotic	Moderate	Moderate
STIMULANTS	Cocaine**	II	Coke, Flake, Snow, Crack	Local anesthetic	Possible	High
	Amphetamines	II	Biphetamine, Delcobese, Desoxyn, Dexedrine, Obetrol	Attention deficit disorders, narcolepsy weight control	Possible	High
	Phenmetrazine	II	Preludin	Weight control	Possible	High
	Methylphenidate	II	Ritalin	Attention deficit disorders	Possible	Moderate
	Other Stimulants	III IV	Adipex, Cylert, Didrex, Ionamin, Melfiat, Plegine Sanorex, Tenuate, Tepanil, Prelu-2	Weight Control	Possible	High
HALLUCINOGENS	LSD	I	Acid, Microdot	None	None	Unknown
	Mescaline and Peyote	I	Mexc, Buttons, Cactus	None	None	Unknown
	Amphetamine Variants	I	2.5-DMA, PMA, STP, MDA, MDMA, TMA, DOM, DOB	None	Unknown	Unknown
	Phencycliding Phencyclidine	II	PCP, Angel Dust, Hog	None	Unknown	High
	Analogues	I	PCE, PCPy, TCP	None	Unknown	High
	Other Hallucinogens	I	Bufotenine, Ibogaine, DMT, DET, Psilocybin, Psilocyn	None	None	Unknown
CANNABIS	Marijuana	I	Pot, Acapulco Gold, Grass Reefer, Sinsemilla Thai Sticks	None	Unknown	Moderate
	Tetrahydrocannabinol	I II	THC, Marinol	Cancer chemotherapy anti-nauseant	Unknown	Moderate
	Hashish	I	Hash	None	Unknown	Moderate
	Hashish Oil	I	Hash Oil	None	Unknown	Moderate

*   Not designated a narcotic under the CSA.

** Designated a narcotic under the Controlled Substances Act (CSA).

	TOLER-ANCE	DURATION (Hours)	USUAL METHODS OF ADMINIS-TRATION	POSSIBLE EFFECTS	EFFECTS OF OVERDOSE	WITHDRAWAL SYNDROME
NARCOTICS	Yes	3–6	Oral, smoked	Euphoria, drowsiness respiratory depression, constricted pupils, nausea	Slow and shallow clammy skin, convulsions coma, possible death	Watery eyes, runny nose, yawning, loss of appetite, irritability, tremors, panic, cramps, nausea, chills and sweating
	Yes	3–6	Oral, smoked, injected			
	Yes	3–6	Oral, injected			
	Yes	3–6	Injected, sniffed, smoked			
	Yes	3–6	Oral, injected			
	Yes	3–6	Oral, injected			
	Yes	12–24	Oral, injected			
	Yes	Variable	Oral, injected			
DEPRESSANTS	Yes	5–8	Oral	Slurred speech disorientation, drunken behavior, without odore-of alcohol-	` Shallow respir-ation, clammy skin, dilated pupils, weak and rapid pulse, coma, possible death	Anxiety, insomnia tremors, delirium, convulsions possible death
	Yes	1–16	Oral			
	Yes	4–8	Oral			
	Yes	4–8	Oral			
	Yes	4–8	Oral			
	Yes	4–8	Oral			
STIMULANTS	Yes	1–2	Sniffed, smoked, injected	Increased alert-ness, excitation, euphoria, increased pulse rate and blood pressure, insomnia, loss of appetite	Agitation, increase in body temperature, hallucinations, convulsions, possible death	Apathy, long periods of sleep, irritability, depression, disorientation
	Yes	2–4	oral, injected			
	Yes	2–4	Oral, injected			
	Yes	2–4	Oral, injected			
	Yes	2–4	Oral, injected			
HALLUCINOGENS	Yes	8–12	Oral	Illusions and hallucinations, poor perception of time and distance	Longer, more intense "trip" episodes, psychosis, possible death	Withdrawal syndrome not reported
	Yes	8–12	Oral			
	Yes	Variable	Oral, injected			
	Yes	Days	Smoked, oral, injected			
	Yes	Days	Smoked, oral, injected			
	Possible	Variable	Smoked, oral, injected, sniffed			
CANNABIS	Yes	2–4	Smoked, oral	Euphoria, relaxed inhibitions indreased appetite, disoriented behavior	Fatigue paranoia, possible psychosis	Insomnia, hyperactivity, decreased appetite occasionally
	Yes	2–4	Smoked, oral			
	Yes	2–4	Smoked, oral			
	Yes	2–4	Smoked, oral			

[23]Table from *Streetwise Parents, Foolproof Kids*. Dan Korem, Colorado Springs, CO: NavPress, 1992, pp. 198–199.

(a feeling of personal inadequacy or unworthiness in response to a wrong act), and remorse (a feeling of regret for the harm the person has caused something or someone else). Such feelings may lead to repentance—or to despair and more abuse. (See also chapter 3, "Guilt.")

◆ Sexual Activity

Researchers Elliott and Morse of the University of Colorado have documented a correlation between drug use among youth and teen sexual activity. They reported that "the risk of engaging in sexual intercourse is highly dependent on one's . . . drug use status. Similarly, among those who are sexually active, the frequency of sexual intercourse is consistently higher for those who are involved in . . . drug use."[27] (See also chapter 28, "Premarital Sex," and chapter 29, "Unplanned Pregnancy.")

◆ Dropping Out of School

A study by Jeffrey Fagan of Rutgers University and Edward Pabon of Columbia University established a correlation between substance use and school dropout. "Both male and female dropouts have more serious and frequent involvement in substance abuse," the researchers reported. Although few of the dropouts admitted to having drug problems, drug use among male dropouts was nearly triple that of male students, and "female dropouts were more seriously involved in substance use than either male or female students"[28] (See also chapter 44, "Dropping Out.")

◆ Problem Behaviors

Ralph and Barr (1989) identified what they called "adolescent behavioral chemical dependency syndrome," a condition that may include increased defiance toward parents, rejection of parental values, decline in school achievement, truancy, compulsiveness, depression, and hyperactivity. Such behaviors are sometimes a result of more (or other) things

than drug use, but they are often associated with it.

◆ Depression

A number of researchers, among them Norbert Ralph and Kimberly Ann Morgan, have documented a correlation between drug abuse and depression. While drug use is often *caused* by depression, depression can also be a *result* of drug abuse. (See chapter 5, "Depression.") The mood changes induced by the drug can lead to severe and prolonged depression that, heightened by the effects of the drug and/or withdrawal from the drug, can provoke an almost unimaginably deep depression.

◆ Suicide

The depression and despair that often accompany drug use can lead to suicidal thoughts, threats, and actions. Medina, Wallace, Ralph, and Goldstein (1982) showed that chemical abuse is a major contributor to adolescent mortality (drunk-driving fatalities and suicides). More recently, Peggy Mann's *Marijuana Report* writes:

> According to the Surgeon General's Report, *Healthy People*, American teenagers are the only age group in the United States whose mortality rate has gone up during the past two decades. The chief reasons for this are due to drink- and drug-impaired driving and drug-related suicide. The suicide rate among 10- to 14-year-old children has risen almost as fast as the rate among 15- to 24-year-olds. Furthermore, there are a hundred attempted suicides among young people for every one that succeeds. Suicide rates among teenagers have tripled in the last two decades—which coincides with the epidemic of marijuana use among our young people.[29] [See also chapter 9, "Suicide Thoughts, Tendencies, and Threats."]

◆ Delinquency

Drug use and abuse often breeds delinquency and criminality, not only among adults, but among youth as well. *The Economist* reported: "About two-thirds of the people arrested in the larger cities for felonies such as robbery test positive for illegal drugs, *and about half the juveniles in prison are there for a drug offense.*"[30]

The Biblical Perspective of Drug Use and Abuse

The Bible does not specifically address drug use and abuse. It is silent, of course, on the subject of all drugs other than alcohol, primarily because most modern drugs were unknown or uncommon in the biblical era. Such silence, however, does not mean that God's Word leaves us without direction. On the contrary, the Bible offers several very clear perspectives on the subject of drug abuse.

The Bible explicitly condemns substance abuse. Drunkenness is condemned in no uncertain terms (Prov. 20:1 and 23:20) and is listed as evidence of the sinful nature (Gal. 5:21). Paul writes that drunkards will not inherit the kingdom of God and issues the straightforward command, "Do not get drunk with wine" (Eph. 5:18). Substance abuse—whether the substance is wine or crack, whiskey or smack—is contrary to scriptural principles.

The Bible's commands are incompatible with drug abuse. God's Word clearly commands attitudes and behaviors that are compromised or negated by drug use and abuse. For example, Paul's letter to the Corinthian church records his determination that "I will not be mastered by anything" (1 Cor. 6:12); yet the person who abuses drugs will invariably be mastered by them. Drug abuse is likewise incompatible with scriptural commands to avoid excess (Eph. 5:18), practice self-control (1 Pet. 5:8), obey the law (Rom. 13:1–5), and honor God with the body, which is His temple (1 Cor. 6:15–20).

The Bible makes it clear that comfort is found only in Christ. Many young people turn to drugs in an effort to escape their problems, but drugs are not an escape, they're a trap. "Come to *me*," Jesus says to the person who seeks relief through drugs, "and I will give you rest" (Matt. 11:28; see also Jer. 6:16 and Isa. 55:1–3).

The Bible prescribes an alternative to substance abuse. "Do not get drunk on wine, which leads to debauchery," Paul wrote. *"Instead, be filled with the Spirit"* (Eph. 5:18). The young man or woman who is living by the Spirit will not gratify the desires of the sinful nature (Gal. 5:16). While drug addiction is a complex and challenging problem, it can be best prevented—and overcome—with the power of God through life in the Spirit.

Finally, the Bible commands a compassionate but firm approach to the addict. "Be merciful to those who doubt," Jude wrote; "snatch others from the fire and save them; to others show mercy, mixed with fear" (Jude 22–23). Christians are called to gently restore those who have stumbled and are struggling (Gal. 6:1), a charge that certainly includes the young man or woman who has fallen into addiction.

The Response to the Problem of Drug Use and Abuse

Listen ◆ Empathize ◆ Affirm ◆ Direct ◆ Enlist ◆ Refer

"No one should expect addicted people," writes counselor and author Stephen Arterburn, "to be able to pull themselves out of an addiction problem and into recovery." A young person who is involved in the use and abuse of drugs is in critical need of help, and while there must be no wasted time in getting help to the youth, the pastor, teacher, youth worker, or parent will not succeed by preaching to the young person nor by urging him or her to "get a grip on yourself." The following plan may be pursued with better effect:

LISTEN. "He who answers before listening—that is his folly and his shame," Solomon said (Prov. 18:13). Resist all temptations to offer advice or criticism. Try to lead the youth to discuss his or her drug use, keeping in mind that addicts are often masters of denial and manipulation. Gently but firmly guide the young person to recognize and admit the problem, perhaps by posing the following eight questions:

- Do you occasionally look forward to "using" or getting high when you should be doing something else?

- When you are using, do you take as much as you can as quickly as possible?

- Do you ever find yourself using more than you (or others) think you should? (A "yes" answer to this question indicates a 90 percent likelihood of a drug-abuse problem.)

- Do you use alone (not necessarily physically alone; others may be present, but not involved with the user)?

- Do you try to protect your supply to make sure you're not "short" when you need it?

- When you're upset or sad, do you ever think, "If I had it, I'd feel better?"

- Are you able to take more than you used to while remaining remarkably functional (not applicable to marijuana, which usually has the opposite effect)?

- Do you ever have trouble remembering things you did or said when you were using (only applicable for sedative drugs)?

If the young person answers "yes" to four or more of the above questions, it is likely that he or she is addicted. If the youth refuses to answer honestly or is resistant, offer calm but consistent evidence, sticking as much as possible to a non-threatening questioning style.

EMPATHIZE. Instead of trying to make sense of the young person's behavior, strive to understand (at least somewhat) the pain and turmoil the youth is experiencing. What are his hurts? What are her insecurities? What are his fears? What are her frustrations? Until you gain some insight into such things, you are not prepared to help. Also keep in mind that empathy can be communicated in simple, practical ways, such as listening carefully, making eye contact and nodding as the youth speaks, facing the young person directly (instead of from behind a desk), and making empathetic gestures, such as placing a hand on his or her shoulder as the youth cries or waiting patiently as he or she struggles to find words.

AFFIRM. Remember that addicts typically experience intense anxiety and low self-esteem. Consequently, be careful not to criticize or condemn the young person; instead, communicate your acceptance of and appreciation for him or her (although not of his or her behavior). Be gentle, accepting, affirming—but not gullible—in your approach. Aim to facilitate three affirming realizations in his or her mind:

- God loves the youth unconditionally.
- You love the youth unconditionally.
- He or she is a person of inestimable worth in God's eyes and in yours.

DIRECT. The concerned adult can be most helpful by offering the following direction to a young person who is involved with drugs:

1. Turn the youth toward God. Lead him or her to confession and repentance of sin, and help the young person receive and acknowledge God's love and forgiveness. Impress upon the youth that there is grace and strength in a relationship with God through Jesus Christ. Guide him or her to develop and maintain daily fellowship with God in order to rely on His strength, learn from His Word, and counter temptation with the mind of Christ (Phil. 4:4–9).

2. Inform and involve the youth's parents. As early

as possible, the young person's parents must become involved. Though sometimes parents are reluctant to face the truth of a son or daughter's problem, their cooperation and support will be central to effective treatment and recovery.

3. Review the options for treatment. Stephen Arterburn identifies three important elements of treatment that are essential for an addict to recover:

> First, the person must get the [drug] out of the system. The body must be allowed to return to normal. The second element involves a positive support system. This support system must educate, provide therapy, and reinforce the recovery process. The third aspect of treatment involves the establishment of rewarding things to do, things that provide meaning and satisfaction. If the person is not going to get high, something must fill the void. All three elements of treatment are very important in establishing a strong recovery program.[31]

ENLIST. While no one should expect an addict to "pull himself up by the bootstraps" and climb out of addiction himself, the enlistment of the youth in planning for recovery is crucial. The concerned adult may need to make the arrangements and even provide firm and insistent direction, but an attempt should be made at every opportunity to allow the youth to make decisions and determinations about his or her recovery. Review the options for treatment (which will certainly include the three elements mentioned above), but be sure the youth "owns" whatever decisions are made. One of the most effective ways of accomplishing this is by suggesting "either/or" options ("Would you feel more comfortable seeing your family physician about the problem or would you like me to suggest someone?").

REFER. Under no circumstances should a parent or youth leader attempt to lead an addict through recovery without professional help. At the earliest opportunity, get the young person involved with a professional in the field of addiction. There is a wide variety of organizations (like Narcotics Anonymous) and treatment programs that can help, and an informed physician or psychologist can help the youth and the leader connect with such resources.

For Further Reading

The following resources may help the concerned parent, pastor, teacher, or youth worker to assist a young person who is involved with drugs:

Scriptures Cited in This Chapter

- Proverbs 20:1; 23:20
- Galatians 5:16, 21; 6:1
- Ephesians 5:18
- 1 Corinthians 6:12, 15–20
- 1 Peter 5:8
- Romans 13:1–5
- Matthew 11:28
- Jeremiah 6:16
- Isaiah 55:1–3
- Jude 22–23
- Proverbs 18:13
- Philippians 4:4–9

Other Scripture to Read

- Romans 6:12; 13:13
- Galatians 5:16–25
- Ephesians 6:10–18
- 1 Thessalonians 5:4–11
- 2 Peter 1:5–7

Further Reading

- Stephen Arterburn and Jim Burns, *Drug-Proof*

Your Kids (Focus on the Family).

- Stephen Arterburn, *Growing Up Addicted* (Ballantine).

- Dr. Joel C. Robertson, *Kids Don't Want to Use Drugs* (Oliver Nelson).

- Dan Korem, *Streetwise Parents, Foolproof Kids* (NavPress).

- Bill Sanders, *Tough Turf: A Teen Survival Manual* (Fleming H. Revell).

40

GAMBLING

A Synopsis

❖

Introduction

It began quite innocently: card games in junior high for small change and betting a few bucks here or there while playing pool at a neighbor's house. But David never realized the effect winning would have on him.

By the time he entered high school, David was already placing wagers on multiple professional sports games at his part-time job. Soon, someone gave him the number of an actual bookie. He began placing his own bets with his new contacts. The more he won, the more he wanted to win; the more he lost, the more he felt compelled to recoup his losses. He began to lose control.

During his freshman and sophomore years, David was lucky more often than not. He boasted of his winnings to his friends. His habit boosted his ego and gave him a sense of power and control over his life. In the middle of his junior year, however, David began to "bottom out." His luck ran out one too many times. The weekend before Thanksgiving, David's parents received a call from their local police department informing them that their son—straight-A student, star quarterback, and sterling church youth group member—had been arrested for burglarizing a motor vehicle.

His mother, on the verge of panic, and his father, literally on the verge of a heart attack, called the church youth leader and asked him to go with them to bail David out; he agreed. On the dreary drive home, David kept telling his Mom and Dad, "I only did it to protect you." Neither David's parents nor the youth minister understood what he meant until David asked to spend some time alone with Scott, the youth minister. David confessed his secret to Scott. He admitted that he had been into small-time theft, off and on, for over six months to fund his gambling habit. He explained that he tried to steal the car because he had somehow managed to rack up a ten-thousand-dollar gambling debt. David's bookie had threatened to bring harm to his family if he didn't pay up—quickly.

Through the financial sacrifice of his parents and the prayers, support, and counseling of others, David not only managed to walk the aisle at his high school graduation—he also began walking the long road to recovery.

The Problem of Gambling

Gambling among teens is not a new problem, but experts agree that it is on the rise. A 1992 report by Chicago's Better Government Association estimates that seven million juveniles gamble in the United States.[1] In the northeast part of the United States, as many as 50 percent of high school students reported gambling for money in a one-year period.[2]

A recent Harvard Medical School survey found that between 6.4 and 8.5 percent of suburban Boston high school students surveyed were classified as compulsive gamblers. Among the 75 percent who said they had gambled, 32.5 percent placed their first bet before the age of eleven. Fifty-six percent started between the ages of eleven and fifteen.[3]

The first U.S. review of teenage gambling, a study of youths in California, Virginia, New Jersey, and Connecticut, was done a decade ago at Loma Linda University Medical School in California by Durwood Jacobs, vice president of the National Council on Problem Gambling. According to Jacobs, "Our initial findings were that 4 to 6 percent of high school age youngsters, average age 16, were probable pathological gamblers at the time we surveyed them."[4]

Follow-up studies have produced similar findings, but a more recent study in Ontario, Canada, after the legalization of casino gambling, showed an increase in teenage gambling.[5] According to Jacobs, as teens move into college, the problem tends to increase for a variety of reasons:

> They have more money, they're out of parental supervision, they have more freedom of action. That's been true a good long time. Gambling tends to level off generally when men get into their late 20s and early 30s. Because at that time they really have to come to grips with the world. It's time to grow up. College is just an extension of adolescence.[6]

The problem of teenage gambling is both deep and wide in the U.S. and Canada, and it is getting worse. "We are absolutely seeing more teenage gamblers," reports Tony Milillo, coordinator of the Compulsive Gambling Program at the Belmont Center for Comprehensive Treatment in Philadelphia. Such news would not be surprising to police in New Jersey; not long ago, they broke up a teen sports betting ring of thirty to forty high school kids who were wagering *five thousand to seven thousand dollars a week.*

The Causes of Gambling Addiction

Experts believe teen gambling is fed by an increasing acceptance of it in society. Casinos and state lotteries abound. Bookies give easy credit to teens. And mortified parents are paying off their kids' gambling debts, concerned about the risk of reprisals.

◆ Primary Social Reasons

The primary social reasons for the increase in teen gambling are fivefold: a breakdown in our national morals, the availability of gambling opportunities and the "get-rich-quick" syndrome that pervades Western society, the legalization of gambling, the failure to educate teens about the dangers of gambling, and the failure to control or break up illegal gambling operations that are open to all ages.

Teens become addicted to gambling for a variety of reasons. Many, like David, get started by betting on sports events. The potential of gaining nine dollars for risking one dollar can be very appealing. Moreover, many teens seem to thrive on risk, which is an inherent factor in gambling. There tend to be five characteristics common to teens who become compulsive gamblers:

◆ Teens Who Gamble Compulsively . . .

Are Often Troubled to Begin With. Teens who gamble compulsively were often troubled to begin with, and gambling provides an escape. Gambling often acts as an anesthetic for a teenager who has problems with school, friendships, family, or self-esteem. The teen who is failing in school gains a sense of accomplishment from winning a bet. The young woman who has no friends will have no trouble finding them in the gambling world. The young man who has severe family problems may find a temporary oasis of escape in gambling—and a sense of having control over something. A young person who has no sense of self-worth occasionally finds his or her ego boosted by the "accomplishment" of a win. (See chapter 6, "Unhealthy Self-Esteem.")

Often Display Addictive Behavior Already. Teens who gamble compulsively often have an addictive character already. Alcoholism and drug addition are heavily tied to the gambling syndrome. Teens who gamble compulsively share common addictive traits, which are easily identifiable:

1. Their answer to any conflict, problem, or pain is "escape."

2. They feel the need for something in their lives that they can "absolutely control."

3. They are egocentric and cannot delay gratification.

4. They are impulsive, seldom thinking before acting.

5. They see life in black-and-white terms; they have a "winner or loser" mentality.

6. "Denial" is their most cherished defense when confronted.

Tend to Be Depressed. Teens who gamble compulsively tend to be depressed. Researchers are currently not certain whether the depression is a cause or a symptom, but most agree that a correlation exists between depression and compulsive gambling. (See also chapter 5, "Depression.")

Tend to Be Predisposed to "Sociopathy." Teens who gamble compulsively tend to have a predisposition toward "sociopathy." A sociopath is a person who does not profit from trial and error, lacks personal and group loyalty, shows poor judgment and responsibility, rationalizes inappropriate behavior, and has a mind that will not tell him or her when he or she is wrong.

Are Usually Thrill/Action Seekers. Teens who gamble compulsively are usually "action" or "thrill" seekers. These teens crave an adrenaline high. Normal daily life is boring to them. Their significance in life is found through primitive physical stimulation.

The Effects of Gambling Addiction

Examining the effects of compulsive gambling on teens is best accomplished by looking at how compulsive gambling develops. The typical progression comprises three recognizable phases: the winning phase, the losing phase, and the desperation phase.

◆ The Winning Phase: The Search for Action or Escape

Gambling is fun, exciting, and enjoyable for teens. They want the excitement more than anything else. "Winning"—even at a game of chance—is attractive, and most teenage gamblers see their wins as a reflection of their own abilities. The risk only adds to the excitement. And gambling also provides an escape, allowing them to forget or avoid "real life."

◆ The Losing Phase: The Chase

Continued gambling ultimately brings increased losses, which threaten self-esteem. To salvage his or her self-esteem, to get back lost money and to hide losses, the gambler must find ways to get more money. As a result, gambling can push teens to extremes: to cover large losses, teens may "start to borrow money from their girl-friends, then steal money and jewelry from their parents, and then start to break into houses and cars," says Edward Looney, executive director of the Council on Compulsive Gambling of New Jersey, Inc.[7] Teens may also resort to:

- Getting advances from a parent's credit cards.
- Dealing drugs.
- Becoming bookies themselves.
- Robbing and stealing.
- Haunting pawn shops.
- Working overtime hours at a job.

◆ The Desperation Phase: Panic and the End of the Line

Desperation develops as the teenage gambler becomes obsessed with getting even and paying off debts. Now betting with borrowed or stolen money, however, and often losing money intended to pay off debts, the teen gambler digs an ever-deepening hole; IOUs begin to mount. At this point gambling completely takes over a teen's life, and he or she will tend to exhibit the following symptoms:

- Losing time from school; poor grades.
- More lying.
- Alienation from family and friends.
- Blaming others.
- Strong guilt and anger.
- Panic/anxiety.
- Increased drug or alcohol use.

- Increased borrowing and increased level of stealing.
- Emotional breakdown.
- Hopelessness and depression.
- Suicidal thoughts or gestures.
- Problems with the law.

A young person's gambling is out of control when it reflects three of the following ten criteria for compulsive gambling:

1. Frequent preoccupation with gambling or obtaining money to gamble.

2. Loss of control (via repeated unsuccessful attempts to cut down or stop gambling).

3. Tolerance (once wagering is done for large amounts of money, bets at smaller amounts fail to produce the desired excitement).

4. Withdrawal (including restlessness and irritability, cravings and psychological signs).

5. Returning another day in order to get even ("chasing" one's losses).

6. Gambling as a means of escaping from problems or intolerable feelings.

7. Lying to family and others about the extent of gambling.

8. Jeopardizing relationships, education or career in order to pursue the activity.

9. Engaging in illegal activities in order to finance gambling or pay gambling-related debts.

10. Reliance on others or institutions to relieve a financial situation produced by gambling.[8]

The Biblical Perspective of Gambling

The Bible does not specifically address the subject of gambling, nor does it call gambling a sin or explicitly forbid its practice. However, gambling does involve several biblical issues.

The Bible explicitly condemns greed. Gambling is predicated upon the love of money and the desire for more, which the Bible clearly identifies as "a root of all kinds of evil" (1 Tim. 6:10). Gambling encourages such "kinds of evil" as greed, materialism, and covetousness, which are contrary to biblical commands (Luke 12:15, Prov. 15:7).

Gambling is contrary to the biblical work ethic. God intended honest wages to be gained through honest work (Luke 10:7; Exod. 20:9; Eph. 4:28; 2 Thess. 3:10–12), not through games of chance.

Gambling is destructive and addictive for "people who want to get rich fall into temptation and a trap and into many foolish and harmful desires that plunge men into ruin and destruction" (1 Tim. 6:9). Nowhere is the truth of Paul's words to Timothy more evident than in the foolish and harmful desires that often plunge compulsive gamblers into hopelessness, depression, and suicidal thoughts or gestures.

The Bible prescribes an alternative to gambling. God has already blessed the Christian with "every spiritual blessing in Christ," and has lavished "the riches of God's grace" on him or her (Eph. 1:3, 7). Whatever the young person's motivation in turning to gambling—escape, control, a "high"—God can "meet all [those] needs according to his glorious riches in Christ Jesus" (Phil. 4:19). While compulsive gambling is a complex and challenging problem, it can be best prevented—and overcome—with the power of God through life in the Spirit (Gal. 5:16).

Finally, the Bible commands a compassionate but firm approach to the compulsive gambler. Christians are called to bear one another's burdens and to gently restore those who have stumbled and are struggling. (See Gal. 6:1–2.) Though a young person who has fallen into compulsive gambling may require a firm response, he or she must still be treated lovingly and compassionately.

The Response to the Problem of Gambling Addiction

Listen ◆ Empathize ◆ Affirm ◆ Direct ◆ Enlist ◆ Refer

The parent or youth leader who is working with a teenager who is a compulsive gambler will be wise to pursue the following courses:

LISTEN. When dealing with a teenage gambler, the first goal is to get the facts in order to determine the level of his or her problem. This might be done by asking the following questions (seven yes answers qualify one as a compulsive gambler):

1. Do you ever lose time from work (or school) due to gambling?

2. Does gambling ever make your home life unhappy?

3. Does gambling affect your reputation?

4. Do you ever feel remorse after gambling?

5. Do you ever gamble to get money with which to pay debts or otherwise solve financial difficulties?

6. Does gambling cause a decrease in your ambition or efficiency?

7. After losing do you feel you must return as soon as possible and win back your losses?

8. After a win do you have a strong urge to return and win more?

9. Do you often gamble until your last dollar is gone?

10. Do you ever borrow money to gamble?

11. Do you ever sell anything in order to gamble?

12. Are you reluctant to spend "gambling money" for normal purchases?

13. Does gambling make you careless of the welfare of your family, friends, or self?

14. Do you ever gamble longer than you had planned?

15. Do you ever gamble to escape worry or trouble?

16. Do you ever commit, or consider committing, an illegal act to finance gambling?

17. Does gambling cause you to have difficulty sleeping or functioning at school?

18. Do arguments, disappointments, or frustrations create within you an urge to gamble?

19. Do you ever have an urge to celebrate any good fortune by a few hours of gambling?

20. Do you ever consider self-destruction as a result of your gambling?[9]

EMPATHIZE. As the helper in a case involving a teenager who is a compulsive gambler, you may literally be his or her lifeline. Suicide may indeed be an option for a gambler who is in the desperation phase (the level at which help is most often sought). The gambler at this point has likely bottomed out and is reaching out for help, not condemnation. Do not sermonize; instead, empathize to the point where you can build a bridge of trust. After all, the teenage gambler will have to trust you in order to agree to involve parents and legal authorities if necessary.

AFFIRM. A teenage compulsive gambler needs several things if he or she ever hopes to escape addiction. Love, grace, and patience should be the caring adult's starting point, since the lack of these in his or her life may be the deeper underlying cause of the gambling. Give praise for the gambler's courage to face the problem and ask for help. Always let the gambler know that by admitting the problem, he or she has taken the most difficult step. Offer encouragement and affirmation at every sign of progress.

DIRECT. The caring parent, teacher, pastor, or youth worker must be gentle to the teenager and firm with the addiction. Being directive involves several specific phases:

1. Gently but firmly guide the young person to recognize and admit the problem. Break through the gambler's denial system. If the youth refuses to answer honestly or is resistant, offer calm but consistent evidence, sticking as much as possible to a nonthreatening questioning style. Present specific examples ("What happened to the money from the sale of your car?") rather than general accusations ("You're out of control!"). Sensitively but firmly share the information in this chapter regarding the effects of gambling with the youth.

2. Encourage the youth to turn to God for help. Lead the young man or woman to confession and repentance of sin, and help him or her receive and acknowledge God's love and forgiveness. Impress upon the youth that there is grace and strength in a relationship with God through Jesus Christ. Guide him or her to establish a daily habit of prayer and fellowship with God, which will both meet the inner needs the youth formerly sought to meet through gambling *and* supply strength against temptation.

3. Inform and involve the youth's parents. As early as possible, the young person's parents must become involved. Though sometimes parents are reluctant to face the truth of a son or daughter's problem, their cooperation and support will be central to effective treatment and recovery.

4. Review the options for treatment. Help the youth (and parents) to consider professional counseling, support groups, and other forms of treatment.

ENLIST. If the youth has admitted that a prob-lem exists and is willing to seek help, the concerned parent, pastor, youth worker, or teacher must allow him or her to be instrumental in planning each successive step. Resist the temptation to do the thinking and the work for him or her; enlist the teen's active participation in devising and implementing a plan for help and recovery.

REFER. Most cases of compulsive gambling will have to be referred to licensed compul-sive gambling counselors, which most gambling states must provide by law. Your job, however, is crucial in convincing the teen who is struggling with gambling that he or she needs help, partic-ularly professional help. If you determine that your gambler does not meet the criteria for com-pulsive gambling, you may handle the situation with education or information on the dangers and myths of gambling. If the gambler you are helping will not go to a treatment facility or counselor, you might be able to refer him or her to your local Gamblers Anonymous program. In all cases, referral must be accomplished with parental permission and preferably with family support. Unless you are an expert on gambling or gambling addiction, be prepared to enlist the help of several agencies in the areas of treat-ment, information, education, and support. The following is a list of sources:[10]

National Organizations

Gam-Anon International Service Office, Inc.
P.O. Box 157
Whitestone, NY 11357
718-352-1671

Gamblers Anonymous International Service Office
P.O. Box 17173
Los Angeles, CA 90017
213-386-8789

National Council on Problem Gambling
445 West 59th Street
New York, NY 10019
212-765-3833
800-522-4700

Canadian Foundation on Compulsive Gambling
505 Consumers Road, Suite 605
Willowdale, Ontario M2J 4V8
Canada
416-499-9800
416-222-7477

Treatment Programs for Compulsive Gamblers

California
CPC Westwood Hospital
Los Angeles, CA 90025
213-479-4281

Connecticut
Connecticut Compulsive Gambling
  Treatment Program
Greater Bridgeport Community
  Mental Health Center
Bridgeport, CT 06606
203-579-6934

Florida
The Treatment Company
North Miami, FL 33161
305-893-7640

Iowa
St. Luke's/Gordon Recovery Center
Sioux City, IA 51104
712-279-3960

Broadlawns Medical Center
Des Moines, IA 52801
800-BETS-OFF

Eastern Iowa Center for Problem Gambling
Davenport, IA 52801
319-322-2535

Maryland
Taylor Manor Hospital
Ellicott City, MD 21043
301-465-3322

Washington Center for Pathological Gambling
College Park, MD 20740
301-345-6623

Massachusetts
Mount Auburn Hospital
Center for Problem Gambling
Cambridge, MA 02238
617-499-5194

Minnesota
Lake Superior Area Family Services
Duluth, MN 55802
218-722-2273

Montana
Rocky Mountain Treatment Center
Great Falls, MT 59401
406-727-8832

Nevada
Charter Hospital
Las Vegas, NV 89117
702-876-4357

New Jersey
Compulsive Gambling Treatment Center
John F. Kennedy Medical Center
Edison, NY 08818
201-321-7189

New Hope Foundation
Marlboro, NJ 07746
201-946-3030

St. Clares Riverside Medical Center for
Pathological Gambling Services
Boonton, NJ 07005
201-316-1896

New York
South Oaks Gambling Treatment Program
Amityville, NY 11701
516-264-4000

St. Vincent's North Richmond Gambling
Treatment Center
Staten Island, NY 10310
718-876-1285

Westchester Jewish Community Services
Hartsdale, NY 10530
914-949-6761

Compulsive Gambling Treatment Program
Metro Center
Rochester, NY 14620
716-423-9490

Ohio
Richland Hospital
Mansfield, OH 44901
419-589-5511

Pennsylvania
Valley Forge Medical Center and Hospital
Norristown, PA 19403
215-539-8500

Treatment for compulsive gamblers is also available at the following Veterans Administration Medical Centers:

California
Loma Linda (714-825-7084)

Florida
Bay Pines (813-398-6661)
Miami (305-324-4455)

New Jersey
East Orange (201-676-1000)
Lyons (201-647-0180)

New York
Brooklyn (718-836-6600)

Ohio
Brecksville (216-526-3030)

Affiliate Councils of the National Council on Problem Gambling

California Council on Compulsive Gambling
435 N. Roxbury Drive, Suite 403
Beverly Hills, CA 90210
800-FACTS 4 U (in California only)
408-TRY-9099

Canadian Foundation on Compulsive Gambling
505 Consumers Rd., Suite 605
Willowdale, Ont. M2J 4V8, Canada
416-499-9800 (business hours)
416-222-7477 (after hours)

Connecticut Council on Compulsive Gambling
P.O. Box 6244
Hamden, CT 06517
800-34-NO BET (in Connecticut only)

Delaware Council on Gambling Problems, Inc.
113 West 8th Street, second floor
Wilmington, DE 19801
302-655-3261

Florida Council on Compulsive Gambling, Inc.
P.O. Box 947664
Maitland, FL 32794–7664
800-426-7711

The Council on Compulsive Gambling of Illinois, Inc.
401 Schroeder Hall
Illinois State University
Normal, IL 61761–6901
309-438-7626

Iowa Problem Gambling Council, Inc.
321 E. Walnut, Suite 370
Des Moines, IA 50309
515-281-8802

Maine Council on Compulsive Gambling, Inc.
P.O. Box 11034
Portland, ME 04104
207-490-1505

Maryland Council on Compulsive Gambling, Inc.
1712 Arabian Way
Fallston, MD 21047
410-879-8460

Massachusetts Council on Compulsive Gambling
190 High Street, Suite 6
Boston, MA 02110
800-426-1234 (in Massachusetts only)

Minnesota Council on Compulsive Gambling
702 Torrey Building
314 W. Superior Street
Duluth, MN 55802
800-541-4557 (in Minnesota only)

Nebraska Council on Compulsive Gambling
703 West 24th Avenue
Bellevue, NE 68005
402-291-0980

Nevada Council on Compulsive Gambling, Inc.
4535 W. Sahara St., Suite 112-H
Las Vegas, NV 89102
800-729-GAMB

Council on Compulsive Gambling
of New Jersey
1315 West State Street
Trenton, NJ 08618
800-GAMBLER (in New Jersey only)

Council on Problem and Compulsive
Gambling of North Dakota
P.O. Box 10292
Fargo, ND 58107
701-293-1887

Ohio Council on Problem Gambling
P.O. Box 41262
Brecksville, OH 44141
800-457-7117 (in Ohio only)

Oregon Council on Problem Gambling
410 Oxford St. S.E.
Salem, OR 97302–5252
503-581-8104

Council on Compulsive Gambling of
Pennsylvania
2319 South St.
Philadelphia, PA 19146
215-744-1880

Texas Council on Problem and Compulsive
Gambling, Inc.
5501 LBJ Freeway, LB 23, Suite 602
Dallas, TX 75240
800-742-0443 (in Texas only)

Washington State Council on Problem Gambling
P.O. Box 55272
Seattle, WA 98155–0272
800-547-6133

For Further Reading

The following resources may help the concerned parent, pastor, teacher, or youth worker assist a young person who is struggling with a gambling problem:

Scriptures Cited in This Chapter

- 1 Timothy 6:9–10
- Luke 10:7; 12:15
- Proverbs 15:7
- Exodus 20:9
- Ephesians 1:3, 7; 4:28
- 2 Thessalonians 3:10–12
- Philippians 4:19
- Galatians 5:16; 6:1–2

Other Scripture to Read

- Isaiah 58:11
- Jeremiah 6:16
- Romans 6:12; 13:13
- Galatians 5:16–25
- Ephesians 6:10–18
- Philippians 4:4–9
- 1 Thessalonians 5:4–11
- 1 Peter 5:8

Further Reading

- William Backus and Marie Chapian, *Why Do I Do What I Don't Want to Do?* (Bethany House).
- Joel C. Robertson, *Kids Don't Want to Use Drugs* (Thomas Nelson). Contains a helpful approach to addictions (not just drugs).

DISORDERS

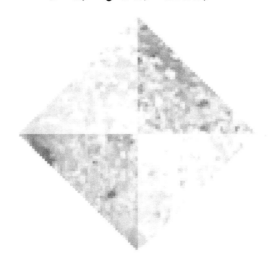

41

A Synopsis

❖

ATTENTION DEFICIT DISORDER

Introduction

Drew Dawson was a high-spirited, fun-loving kid. But at times he also appeared to be a magnet for trouble. His dimpled cheeks, olive skin, and deep-brown eyes made the fifteen-year-old an attractive boy, even though he wasn't quite as tall or developed as other boys his age. He had friends, but he would have had more if he hadn't displayed an uncanny knack for irritating people. Sometimes it seemed that whatever thought popped into his head came out his mouth. Usually he phrased things in a funny way that made others overlook his tactlessness; still, there were times when he seemed oblivious to the irritation he caused people.

School was a struggle for Drew. He was disorganized and sloppy in his academic work. His teachers used words like *distractible, lazy,* and *forgetful* to describe him. Although he showed remarkable insight from time to time, he usually tested poorly. His citizenship grades were often C or below because he couldn't seem to stay quiet and settled in class.

Drew's parents were Christians who had attempted to set good guidelines for Drew. They had used these guidelines with great success for Drew's older brother and sister, and although Drew did seem to want to obey his parents, his impulsive nature often got the best of him. If an unexpected request was made of him, Drew could easily lose his temper. He seemed to have no concept of time and was habitually late. He was so "now" oriented that a virtue like saving money felt like punishment to him.

Drew's mother and father approached his problems from different ends of the spectrum. His mother often made excuses for him, accepting her role of running forgotten materials to school, constantly picking up after Drew yet continually nagging him about his shortcomings. Drew's father, on the other hand, was a busy man who paid little attention to his younger son unless a crisis arose; then he was likely to explode in anger over the problem, making strict and sometimes unreasonable demands. Drew would quickly accept the challenge of seeing who could yell the loudest, and a power struggle would ensue with Drew always on the losing end, it seemed. The happy, free-spirited youngster was rapidly becoming a bitter, frustrated teenager, tuning out his parents' words . . . and slowly rejecting their values.

The Problem of Attention Deficit Disorder

Kids like Drew are misunderstood by many people. Adults assume that such children willingly choose to allow their impulses to control them. Actually, Drew and others like him (to a varying degree, two out of every ten people) struggle with attention deficit disorder. This disorder is foundationally a biological problem. Children and adults (people do not outgrow this problem) with ADD function primarily out of the right side of the brain. This area of the brain houses our creativity and problem solving, our intuitive thinking, our feelings and impulses, our ability to see the "whole picture." On the other hand, the left side of the brain houses our logical thinking, linear or ordered thinking (Step 1, Step 2, Step 3, etc.), our ability to pay attention to detail, and our value systems. People with attention deficit disorder are not totally lacking in these left-brain skills, but the neurotransmitters that connect the two sides of the brain are only sporadically working—or there may be a pocket of left brain saturation while other areas do not function well. Therefore, we occasionally see a person who is extremely gifted in one particular area, such as math, while the rest of his processing is guided by the right brain.

Since the neurotransmitters between the two lobes are "down," so to speak, people with ADD have a difficult time attending selectively to the most important aspects of their environment. Many describe their minds as racing, hazy, or overwhelmed by incoming stimuli. Their impulses, feelings, and creativity play the dominant role in their thought patterns. Step-by-step thinking and order are more difficult for them; values, consequences, and goals do not automatically race to the forefront of their minds in tense or crucial situations. People with ADD typically exhibit a majority of the following characteristics:

1. Unable to concentrate (long-term).
2. Bored easily, restless.
3. Disorganized.
4. Impulsive.
5. Intuitive.
6. Poor anger control.
7. Creative.
8. Uses loop thinking rather than linear thinking.
9. Sees the whole picture quickly.
10. Not sensitive to detail.
11. Problems with self-esteem.
12. May be coupled with hyperactivity.
13. Distractibility.
14. Low frustration level.
15. Poor short-term memory.
16. Risk-taking mentality.
17. Auditory-kinesthetic learning style (learns best by listening and/or while in motion).

The Causes of Attention Deficit Disorder

Unfortunately, many Christians tend to label kids like Drew as troublemakers, or even "unregenerate," and wash their hands of them. Or they may blame poor parenting, lack of discipline, or peer pressure for these young persons' conduct. Such labels, however, are woefully inadequate—and usually incorrect—for teens with ADD.

◆ Biological Problem

Attention deficit disorder is a biological problem that can usually be traced back through a family to parents, uncles, aunts, or grandparents who struggled with the same symptoms. In other words, ADD is usually transmitted through the gene pool. The problems engendered by attention deficit disorder can be intensified, of course, when an ADD child has an ADD parent.

◆ Historical Roots

There are people who question why the United States seems to have so many people who struggle with ADD while countries such as Germany and Japan seem to have so few problems with it. The answer may be twofold, dealing with both history and environment.

The types of early explorers and settlers who chose to make North America their home were (generally speaking) men and women of vision who were willing to take risks and accept new ideas and ways of doing things. They often needed creativity for every area of life in order to survive. It is easy to see that many people who today might be diagnosed as having ADD would find such a lifestyle to their liking; it is possible that, for this reason, the American gene pool has a higher concentration of ADD than other nationalities.

◆ Environmental Roots

But why has ADD suddenly become such a popular diagnosis? Some would argue that we are simply making excuses for overly permissive parenting. However, before accepting this statement as fact we must take a good look at our environment today. In the largely rural societies of yesteryear, folks with ADD probably had much less trouble fitting comfortably into the culture. In fact, their energy and creativity and their need for lots of different activities to discourage boredom would have been seen as great assets on most farms and ranches.

However, as society becomes more and more specialized, most people find themselves necessarily concentrating their efforts in one area for many hours, a task that is very difficult for a person with ADD.

Besides this narrow focus, so much of our lives has become automated, and our level of physical activity has sharply decreased. Thus, the natural energy of the person with ADD has no outlet. This is especially hard on those with ADHD (attention deficit hyperactive disorder). Sitting on a school bus for the ride to school, sitting in a classroom all day, and then coming home to sit in front of a TV or video game—or homework assignments—is a recipe for trouble for the youth with ADD. When we add to this mixture all the distracting and violent influence society serves up to many children in the form of broken homes, movies, TV, and gang-filled streets, it is little wonder that their learning and relating difference becomes a disorder of enormous proportions.

The Effects of Attention Deficit Disorder

A child with ADD begins to feel like the only runner in a race who's forced to run with leg weights on. He begins to ask himself why other people seem to run the race so effortlessly while he lags behind, struggling to keep up the pace.

◆ Creative, Ingenious

Anyone who cares about these young people experiences that struggle as well. The family of an ADD child soon discovers that he or she lives in an interesting but volatile world. Early on, parents may enjoy their child's creativity and ingenuity, but such traits may be the cause of despair in some instances as well. Since their ability to consider consequences, access their value system, or adhere to long-term goals is often negligible, these kids need much more parental/adult guidance and control in their formative years.

◆ Seemingly Bent on Destruction

Even with plenty of supervision, ADD kids may seem bent on destruction. They may also seem bent on disobeying (or at least seem very hard of hearing). Sometimes it may seem as if they see

Mom and Dad's lips move but are totally unaware of the meaning of their words. Actually, that is a pretty fair assessment. Their thoughts are distracted elsewhere, and they are truly processing very little of what is being said. Angry outbursts, sensitivity to sugar, an inability to settle down at night or get up in the morning—all are common to ADD kids. As a result, their parents are often exhausted, frustrated, increasingly desperate people who feel like failures in the most important area of life.

Carolyn and Bill expressed feelings of guilt, confusion, and even fear concerning the way their son, Chris, responded during family devotions. Though they had tried to make their family devotional times creative and enjoyable, Chris often appeared to purposely ruin the atmosphere. As a young Christian, Carolyn had daydreamed about those special family times around the fireplace, sharing together the truth and joy of God's Word. But her reality is a restless, disruptive kid, seemingly uninterested in spiritual things. Carolyn has begun to give up on having meaningful family devotions.

◆ **Academic Difficulties**

If a parent can get to the point of "giving up," it is easy to see how teachers and schools can as well. If these children do find success, it may only be on the athletic field or in the role of class clown. Their forgetfulness and poor organization often earn them low marks, even if their IQs are high (which is often the case). One out of every four ADD kids is a girl, but often she will go undiagnosed and be simply labeled a daydreamer because she is usually quieter and tries harder to please than her male counterparts. As their school career continues, year upon year of failure and frustration in a left-brained world cause many ADD folks to fall into a second level of problems related to low self-esteem. (See chapter 6, "Unhealthy Self-Esteem.") They may become depressed (see chapter 5, "Depression,") or defiant and are at greater risk for addictions,

prison and suicide (see chapter 9, "Suicide Thoughts, Tendencies, and Threats").

◆ **Frustrating, Embarrassingly Honest**

The church often reacts unsympathetically to the ADD child. Sunday school workers and elders are likely to label such disruptive children as "bad seed." ADD kids can be frustrating and embarrassingly honest; whereas other teens have learned to cover their boredom or true feelings of any nature, the impulsive, feeling-oriented ADD teens will "let it all out." They are not as skillful as left-brained kids at saying the right thing at the right time.

Jesus once told His disciples a parable about two brothers. The father asked both to go and work in the vineyard. The first said, "Yes, I will go" but later decided not to. The second said, "No, I don't want to go" but went anyway. Then Jesus asked which one did the Father's will. Of course, it was the brother whose first response was negative. Lots of ADD kids are like that brother. Their hearts are sensitive, but their impulsive responses can get them in trouble in the very ordered structure of the church and the wide range of specific responses expected there.

The Biblical Perspective of Attention Deficit Disorder

Is there a biblical perspective of attention deficit disorder? The Bible predates the clinical diagnosis of ADD by a couple thousand years; could it possibly offer any insight into or guidance on the problem?

To answer that question, let's consider whether we should label the impulsiveness, easy boredom, and forgetfulness that is typical of ADD kids (and adults) as rebellion. A case can be made for that; perhaps they don't enjoy reading and memorizing Scripture because they simply don't have a heart for God. Perhaps they act up in church because they are irreverent and lack discipline at home. That's the easy way out, but it soothes the conscience of many Sunday school teachers and youth workers and enables them to feel more comfortable when they find themselves secretly hoping that little Johnny Cutup drops out of the church youth group.

However, it may help to look at Jesus' response to His brash, impulsive disciple named Peter. Peter may not have had attention deficit disorder, but he appeared to have much in common with young people today who are diagnosed with ADD. The big fisherman, whose mouth was often moving before his brain was in gear (Matt. 16:21–23), probably was the despair of the synagogue youth group; he was a risk-taker (Matt. 14:28–30) who vowed one thing and did another (Luke 22:33–34, 54–62), struggled to control his angry outbursts (John 18:10–11), and *ran* where others tiptoed (John 20:1–6).

But Jesus did not throw up His hands in despair over Peter's disposition; the Lord was patiently loving, encouraging, and correcting toward His impetuous disciple. On the contrary, Jesus saw promise in the Galilean fisherman, and it appears that the Lord was determined to chisel Simon, son of Jonas, into Peter, the rock Jesus knew he would one day become (Matt. 16:17–18).

Concerned Christian adults will do well to cultivate a similar perspective with ADD kids. Each one has remarkable creativity, ability, insight, and boldness. It is our job as youth workers and parents to patiently disciple, believe in, and correct these kids. ADD is never an excuse for sinful behavior, but the wise parent, pastor, teacher, or youth worker will distinguish between the behavior and the disorder.

We need not excuse disruptive or immoral behavior in these young people, but neither should we demand that they conform completely to our left-brained world. God made them different for a purpose. They—and their special gifts—are of immense value to Him and to His

church. Who knows whether God will one day use their boldness to bring revival? Who knows whether He will use their ready faith and boundless energy to take giant strides for the cause of Christ?

The Response to the Problem of Attention Deficit Disorder

Listen ◆ Empathize ◆ Affirm ◆ Direct ◆ Enlist ◆ Refer

LISTEN. When an ADD youth comes for counsel, a wide range of problems might be the precipitator. A child may have a more common set of problems, such as trouble interacting with peers and parents. Or he or she may have already headed into a second tier of troubles that include illicit sex, drug addiction, and other troubles with the law resulting from impulsive, poor choices. Allow this young person to vent his or her feelings in safety. Some may seem to enjoy attempting to shock or challenge you; show them that nothing they can say or do will change the love God has given you for them, nor change your belief in their ability to now make good choices.

EMPATHIZE. If you have always seen life from a left-brained perspective, it will be difficult for you to empathize with an ADD kid. He or she may appear not to be trying very hard; this is usually because of defense mechanisms the young person uses for daily emotional survival. Listening to his or her frustrations in a nonjudgmental way can begin to soften that outer layer of defense mechanisms.

ADD kids are very perceptive; if they see you care, if they know you are being real, you will win their confidence. Your empathy for an ADD youth can be communicated in practical ways, such as listening patiently, making (and holding) eye contact, gently steering the youth back to the point when he or she wanders, and keeping your comments short and to the point (no long lectures, please). If it is appropriate, placing your face close to the youth's face as you speak (even gently holding his or her face in your hands, perhaps) may help him or her focus.

AFFIRM. Most ADD kids are like grass growing in sand; they will grow well with plenty of watering—the water of encouragement. In almost every case, the more encouragement and positive affirmation an ADD child gets, the better he or she will do in any area, whether it is academics, social situations, sports, or work. Affirmation makes them blossom and keeps them blossoming. Of course, the opposite side of the coin is also true. If they perceive your attitude toward them is negative, they are more likely than most kids to "act out" that negativity. This is not to say that the guiding adult must in any way try to eliminate the consequences for negative behavior. Natural consequences are among the most valuable teaching tools we have for these children, especially if the adult lovingly and patiently helps the young person to see the connection between a particular behavior and a specific consequence.

DIRECT. ADD youth generally need more correction and guidance than other teens whose left brain is more often at the controls. A compassionate adult can help by keeping the following in mind:

1. Coach, don't nag. Fix your mind on coaching these young persons rather than nagging them. Think of the most positive way to give direction or to request a change of behavior. Try to catch them doing something right, then offer praise rather than waiting until they do something wrong and offering criticism or correction.

2. Use guiding questions to get them to think about necessary attitude or behavior changes, especially "would you rather" questions ("Would you

rather help me decorate the room or do something by yourself?"). Questioning comes from the right side of the brain and helps the ADD person tune in to what you are saying. Be very careful, however, to avoid sarcasm or "talking down" to them.

3. Encourage dependence on God. Attention deficit disorder does not rule out a meaningful relationship with God. Help the youth discover prayer skills and techniques that are not frustrated by ADD (such as pacing the floor while praying aloud, observing shorter but more frequent prayer times, using Christian music and music videos, etc.). Help him or her rely on God to cope with ADD and conquer temptation (Gal. 5:16).

4. Seize on activities and pursuits in which the youth displays interest and direct his or her attention and energies to those areas. It will be more effective to steer the youth *to* positive pursuits than constantly trying to steer him or her *away* from negative behavior.

5. Help the youth focus on improvement, not perfection. A young man or woman with ADD can become very frustrated trying to meet everyone's expectations and demands; yet "We all stumble in many ways" (James 3:2). Guide the young person to take one day at a time and strive for improvement (which is attainable), not perfection (which is not).

6. Treat the youth as a person who is worthy of respect and responsibility, and he will very likely do his best to rise to that challenge.

ENLIST. Seek to draft the young person himself or herself onto the team; involve him or her in identifying problem behaviors and brainstorming possible solutions. Also, enlist the help of spiritually mature young people to be unofficial accountability partners. Ask them to help remind the ADD young person of dates, times, and other details that may easily slip his or her mind. Ask them to help you encourage the positive behaviors of which the young person is capable. When the ADD person begins to feel that he is understood and accepted, his natural enthusiasm for life will encourage others to come and enjoy all that is happening.

REFER. There are times when behavioral and academic problems seem so deeply rooted that attitudes and actions are hard to change. When parents or teens are at an impasse in their struggle with ADD, they may benefit from the food supplements and/or medications that are available. These, however, require a medical doctor or licensed nutritionist for specific diagnosis and prescription. Drugs such as Ritalin, Cylert, Tofranil, and several others have been used with great success for ADD people. Basically, these medications simply stimulate the neurotransmitters between the right and left sides of the brain so that ADD people can more quickly access things like memory, logic, organizational skills, and ingrained values. Sometimes a regiment of food supplements can achieve similar results. It is also important to realize that certain allergies and mental conditions (such as depression and manic/depressive disorder) can mimic attention deficit disorder. This is why definitive diagnosis should always be made by a licensed professional counselor.

For Further Reading

The following resources may help the concerned parent, pastor, teacher, or youth worker assist a young person with attention deficit disorder:

Scriptures Cited in This Chapter

- Matthew 14:28–30; 16:17–18, 21–23
- Luke 22:33–34, 54–62
- John 18:10–11; 20:1–6
- Galatians 5:16
- James 3:2

Other Scripture to Read

- Colossians 1:9–12
- 1 Thessalonians 5:14
- 1 Peter 5:6–10

Further Reading

- Paul Warren, M.D., and Jody Capehart, M. Ed., *You and Your ADD Child* (Thomas Nelson).

42

ANOREXIA NERVOSA

A Synopsis

Introduction

Ever since she was a baby, Linda had been fat. Her parents used to call her their little teddy bear because she was so cuddly and pudgy. One of their favorite scrapbook pictures of Linda showed her grinning from ear to ear, her arms puffed out of a sleeveless shirt that was partially buttoned over a pregnant-looking tummy. Linda hated that picture and all the memories attached to being known as a "fat kid." She swore that someday she was going to take that picture out of the scrapbook and burn it.

Months before Linda first sought treatment, she tried out for cheerleader. Her close friends told her she was the most skilled of all those competing. When the big day of tryouts came, she performed perfectly. Everyone, including Linda, thought she would be selected.

The next morning she left for school, excited as she anticipated seeing her name on the list of the new rally squad members. Then came the shocking truth. Her name wasn't on the list. She couldn't believe it. What had gone wrong? She knew she had done better than the other girls at tryouts. Why wasn't her name posted?

Linda ran down the hall to find the cheerleading adviser—maybe she could give her some answers. Mrs. Anderson stood up as Linda walked into her office in tears.

"Why didn't I make the squad when everyone, including you, said I was so good?" Linda cried.

Mrs. Anderson's frank reply made a scarring impression on Linda. "You're good," she said, "but you're also overweight. We can't put fat cheerleaders out in front of everyone. Besides that, we don't have a uniform big enough to fit you."

Stunned, Linda turned and walked out of Mrs. Anderson's office. She hated herself. She hated her fat. She determined at that moment never to put another fattening food into her mouth. During the following weeks, she lived on water, lettuce, and celery.

Two months later, Linda had lost forty pounds and had gone from a size thirteen to a size four. At five feet seven inches tall, she weighed 102 pounds. She had become anorexic at fifteen years of age.[1]

The Problem of Anorexia Nervosa

About eight million people in the United States suffer from an eating disorder such as anorexia nervosa.[2] Anorexia, characterized by extreme, purposeful weight loss greater than 25 percent of the person's original body weight, occurs most often among adolescent girls, affecting about one in every 100 to 200 young women. The highest incidence, says Dr. Liliana R. Kossoy, is among sixteen- to eighteen-year-olds from middle- to upper-class backgrounds.[3]

But males may also be victims. About a million of the eight million victims of an eating disorder in the U.S. are males. Cynthia Adams, professor of allied mental health at the University of Connecticut, points out that young athletes—who often develop disorders in an effort to compete and achieve a certain weight—are especially at risk of developing an eating disorder.[4]

"The term eating disorder," write authors Joan Sturkie and Siang-Yang Tan, "refers to the misuse of food which includes undereating, overeating and self-imposed vomiting. . . . Any normal person may engage in one of these behaviors temporarily, but when the choices become habitual, they become eating disorders."[5]

Robert S. McGee, founder and president of Rapha (a Christian health care and recovery organization), clarifies the term "eating disorder" by first establishing what eating disorders are *not*:

> Eating disorders are not the strange food cravings women may experience during pregnancy. Eating disorders are not personal habits of overeating with consequential weight gains, nor are they necessarily the habits of skipping meals with consequential weight loss. An eating disorder is not the inability to stick to a diet. . . . Eating disorders are compulsive-addictive behavioral patterns in which a person's substance of choice for abuse is food.[6]

Anorexia nervosa, to be more specific, is "addictive dieting, deliberate self-starvation, comprising one part of the compulsive drive for perfection and control common to all addictions."[7] Sturkie and Tan list several characteristics of anorexia:

- Anorexics practice self-starvation, and the body takes on the look of a starving person. The anorexic always feels he or she is not thin enough.

- An anorexic has an exaggerated interest in food, but at the same time will deny being hungry.

- By concentrating on his or her fatness (or thinness), the anorexic avoids dealing with problems relating to self, relationships with others, emotions, and intellectual abilities and limitations.

- Anorexics believe that losing just a few more pounds will solve their problems. They believe they will be more attractive and, therefore, more popular.

- Anorexics may develop unusual eating preferences and will often restrict their diet to only certain foods. They put a lot of emphasis on counting calories.

- Anorexics [tend to be] high achievers and want to be the best at what they do.

- Anorexics may exercise to excess in an effort to lose weight. Their exercise routines go well beyond normal physical conditioning. . . .

- The anorexic may prepare elaborate meals for the family but will choose not to eat with them and will prefer to eat alone.[8]

Vivian Meehan, founder of the National Association of Anorexia Nervosa and Associated Disorders, refers to anorexia as something that "starts out as a way to deal with life [and] then takes hold of [a person]."[9]

The Causes of Anorexia Nervosa

There are many factors that may cause an adolescent to become anorexic, but the following are the most prominent:

◆ Sociocultural Influences

Approximately seven times as many women as men suffer from an eating disorder.[10] The reasons for that imbalance may be debated, but Dr. Arnold Anderson, a psychiatry professor at the University of Iowa, suggests that sociocultural influences play a significant role. "There's clearly less general reinforcement for slimness and dieting for males than for females," he says. "But when subgroups of males are exposed to situations requiring weight loss—such as occurs with wrestlers, swimmers, runners and jockeys—then a substantial increase in the behaviors of self-starvation and bulimia follows, suggesting that behavioral reinforcement, not gender, is the crucial element."[11]

In a culture in which physical beauty—particularly for women—is emphasized and prized so highly, being thin and trim is associated with being loved, accepted, and valued as a person of value and importance.

◆ Pain

"Food is not the issue with anorexics," say the authors of *The Thin Disguise: Understanding and Overcoming Anorexia and Bulimia.* They go on:

> The cycle always begins with pain. That pain can have its origin in some major life trauma, family issues, or low self-esteem.[12]

Anorexia is sometimes related to childhood abuse or neglect (see chapter 34, "Sexual Abuse," and chapter 35, "Nonsexual Abuse"), to a dysfunctional family situation, or to insecurity and unhealthy self-esteem (see also chapter 6, "Unhealthy Self-Esteem").

◆ Perfectionism

McGee points out that one of the "key emotional and spiritual components [that] inaugurate and sustain all eating disorders [is] *perfectionism.*"[13] The anorexic believes he or she should be—*must be*—perfect: attractive, thin, athletic, popular. Such perfectionism is often communicated by the parents, as Dr. G. Keith Olson points out:

> Often the mothers [of anorexics] are perfectionistic. They have a lot of goals for their daughters: to be successful, articulate, the most popular girl. [And] the fathers of these girls are often very successful in their occupations.[14]

The perfectionism engendered in such an environment often adds to a young person's frustration, contributing to the cycle of pain that leads to the development of an eating disorder.

◆ Need for Control

The eating disorder also often represents a symbolic expression of the need for control, even if it is control only over the youth's own body. To the anorexic, obsessive and sometimes highly ritualistic patterns of eating—or not eating—sometimes represent a way of bringing order out of chaos. This is especially true of the anorexic who has been a victim of abuse. (See chapters 34, "Sexual Abuse," and 35, "Nonsexual Abuse.")

◆ Faulty Thinking

The authors of *The Thin Disguise* outline a dozen "irrational beliefs" that typically fuel an anorexic's obsession with food and weight loss:

1. "The best way to stay thin is the way I'm doing it now."

2. "The worst thing that could happen to me would be to gain weight or become fat."

3. "This eating behavior is my life. If I give it up, I will have nothing to do."

4. "My favorite escape from my problems is food. If I give up this area of my life, I'll

have to deal with those other sore spots, and I don't want to."

5. "I'm happy with my life the way it is."

6. "I have to continue this pattern because my friends won't care about me if I'm well and don't have this problem anymore."

7. "I don't want sensual advances from the opposite sex. If I give up my eating disorder, I may become more appealing, and I'm not sure I could handle a come-on. This way I can avoid my sexuality."

8. "My family is so preoccupied with the way I eat that if I start eating again, everyone will be on my back about everything I put in my mouth."

9. "I can use my eating disorder as a scapegoat now. If people reject me, I can say it's because I'm anorexic. . . . If I give up this eating disorder, I'll have nothing safe on which to blame rejection."

10. "I would be better off killing myself than trying to fight this eating disorder."

11. "My eating disorder doesn't affect other people."

12. "I just don't want to try to quit this behavior because I know it will just happen again."[15]

The Effects of Anorexia Nervosa

Many people erroneously assume that the effects of anorexia nervosa are plainly visible. In reality, beyond the obvious weight loss are many more and greater physical and psychological effects.

◆ Physical Effects

The physical effects of anorexia are both numerous and serious. They include:

Amenorrhea. Anorexia nervosa may cause the disruption of normal menstrual cycles. "Anorexics often skip three or more menstrual periods."[16]

Anemia. Anemia (decreased red blood cell count) or decreased white blood cell count are frequent results of anorexia.

Glandular Malfunctioning. Problems such as thyroid abnormalities and other glandular malfunctions have been connected to anorexia and other eating disorders.

Constipation. The failure to take in or retain sufficient foods and fluids can cause anorexics to suffer problems with constipation.

Malnutrition. Malnutrition may occur with accompanying lethargy and water retention.

Kidney Dysfunction and Failure. As the person's weight loss becomes extreme, the risk of kidney failure—as the kidneys and other organs are deprived of vital nutrients and proteins—presents itself.

Seizures. "For some reason not fully understood," write the authors of *The Thin Disguise,* "seizures occur in persons with eating disorders at a higher rate than in the general population."[17]

Osteoporosis. Caused by vitamin deficiency (as well as other musculoskeletal problems), osteoporosis can result from anorexia.

In addition to the above physical consequences, the following problems may occur:

Dry skin is common. Head hair may be thin (and also fall out when it is washed or combed), and downy fuzz may appear on other parts of the body. . . . Many anorexics' hair is limp and thin, and [the] downy fuzz will appear on their bodies to insulate them from cool weather because the natural fat layer has been depleted. The anorexics' hands, feet, and other parts of the body are always cold. . . . Broken blood vessels in the face and bags under the eyes are two other physical symptoms of this disease. Fainting spells and rapid or irregular heartbeats are also common.[18]

◆ Psychological Effects

Though the lines between physical and psychological effects of anorexia are sometimes blurred and some of the physical consequences listed above may have medical origins, the following are symptoms generally counted among the psychological ramifications of anorexia:

Impulse Control Disorder. This problem is "loss of control of oneself, which results in impulsive actions and extreme emotions, such as anger and rage."[19] It may be as much a cause of anorexia as an effect; or it may be both.

Guilt and Shame. Guilt and shame are also powerful effects of anorexia. Anorexics feel intense guilt over their behavior, as well as intense shame. They typically hate themselves and their behavior. They try to hide their behavior. They try to stuff their guilt and shame deep inside themselves, hoping it will go away. But, of course, it doesn't. It only produces more pain and more severe problems. (See also chapter 3, "Guilt.")

Impaired Judgment. Another common problem among anorexics is impaired judgment. Whether the source is physical or psychological is a subject of debate, but it is well known that a five-foot-five anorexic who weighs ninety pounds can stand in front of a mirror and steadfastly maintain that she is fat. Such faulty functioning extends to other areas as well, causing some anorexics to seem disoriented, forgetful, etc.

Social Withdrawal. Anorexics routinely hide their eating habits and often lie about them as well. The cycle of deceit, as well as the guilt and shame the behavior produces, lead many to withdraw from friends and family. They become loners, preferring to eat—or not eat—alone.

The Biblical Perspective of Anorexia Nervosa

It is certainly not God's desire for any of His children to suffer the ravages of anorexia. Our bodies are temples of the Holy Spirit, and the Word of God commands us to honor God with our bodies[20]—what we do with them and how we treat them. Anorexia is a form of self-abuse and therefore is a violation of God's will. He wishes for our bodies to be offered "as living sacrifices, holy and pleasing to God" (Rom. 12:1), not to be starved in an effort to ease pain or wasted in the pursuit of unrealistic ideals.

However, the anorexic's problem will not be solved by sermonizing because at its root anorexia is a response to pain. Such pain may have been caused by abuse, neglect, or some other trauma. It may be related to perfectionism or low self-esteem and is often a result of a dysfunctional family situation. Tragically, the pain that leads to anorexia often impedes a biblical understanding of the problem. The authors of *The Thin Disguise* write:

> [Anorexics] frequently have trouble picturing God as a companion and friend. They see Him as a black-robed judge (or as a critical parent) who blames them for their problems. An anorexic or a bulimic has difficulty understanding that God loves her even when she is starving herself. . . . Unconditional love is a foreign concept to almost anyone raised in a dysfunctional family, but when that concept is understood and appropriated, it is a tremendous point of release. . . .[21]

The anorexic's pain is understood by God. "For we do not have a high priest who is unable to sympathize with our weaknesses, but we have one who has been tempted in every way, just as we are—yet was without sin" (Heb. 4:15).

The anorexic's pain is felt by God. The Bible calls Jesus "a man of sorrows," and states that "he took up our infirmities and carried our sorrows" (Isa. 53:3–4). Jesus is not only familiar with the anorexic's pain, He carries it. He grieves with God's children whose lives have been broken; He is close to those whose spirits have been crushed.[22] He longs to heal their broken hearts and restore their lives to wholeness.

The anorexic's pain can be healed by God. "He heals the brokenhearted and binds up their wounds" (Ps. 147:3). As the authors of *The Thin Disguise* say, He can take the rubble of our lives and transform it "into something strong and beautiful. [He] can take the very areas of our lives that have been rendered seemingly useless through years of brokenness and destruction, and restore them."[23]

The Response to the Problem of Anorexia Nervosa

Listen ◆ Empathize ◆ Affirm ◆ Direct ◆ Enlist ◆ Refer

A youth leader, pastor, parent, or teacher who suspects or knows a young person is suffering from anorexia should first approach God in prayer for wisdom and sensitivity and then implement the following response:

LISTEN. Talk to the young person; ask how she feels about herself. Gently and sensitively ask about her eating habits. She may be manipulative and hide the fact that she doesn't eat. Talk with her parents; ask them what patterns they have seen, if they have talked to the youth about her eating habits, and with what result. Use questions, not to accuse the young person, but to try to direct his or her attention, to open

his or her eyes (or those of parents). Listen closely to the youth (and, if applicable, to the parents), and be alert not only to what is said verbally, but to what is said nonverbally as well. The following questions, suggested by McGee, may help:

- (For women) Do you have irregular periods, or have you experienced total loss of menstruation for at least three cycles when it should otherwise have been expected?

- Have you been dieting, not because you are overweight (according to standards based on your age, sex, and height), but because you desire to be more slim in your appearance?

- Do you claim to "feel" fat when others tell you that you obviously are not overweight?

- When others tell you that you are not overweight, do you ever feel annoyed or irritated, perceiving that they are trying to control your body, that they are jealous, or that they just cannot understand the needs of your life and your body?

- Do you often think about food, calories, body weight, nutrition, and cooking, to the extent that such thinking distracts you from other important, though unrelated, responsibilities and tasks?

- Does physical exercise occupy a disproportionate amount of your time each day?

- Do you weigh yourself frequently, even going out of your way in order to get on a set of scales and check your weight one more time during the day?

- Do you fast, induce vomiting, or use laxatives or diuretics in order to lose weight?

- Do you go to the bathroom immediately after meals? Do you get angry or irritated if it is occupied or if you must delay for some other reason?

- Do you often hide or hoard food or act out

some other type of food-related behavior that you think is sensible, but which you prefer others not know about?

- Do you feel nauseated or bloated when you eat as much as or less than others your own age and size at a normal mealtime without prior snacking?

- Do you occasionally binge on food and then feel ashamed of yourself and atone for your overeating by subsequently starving yourself totally for a period of time?[24]

EMPATHIZE. Avoid arguing with the youth; instead try to come alongside him or her in a spirit of love and understanding. Don't get into power struggles over food. Don't try to motivate the youth with guilt or shame. Don't offer pat answers. Concentrate instead on understanding and communicating empathy. Some practical ways to do so include:

- Speaking softly and slowly.

- Making eye contact.

- Leaning slightly forward in your chair when he or she is talking.

- Nodding to indicate understanding.

- Reflecting key statements ("You feel . . ." or "You're saying . . .").

- Waiting patiently through periods of silence or tears.

AFFIRM. Since the source of the anorexic's disorder may be a self-image and self-esteem problem, carefully and prayerfully focus on affirming the young person's sense of value and worth. It will do little good to insist that the youth is pretty or thin enough; instead, try to concentrate on creating an accepting, loving relationship in which the youth can develop a sense of security and belonging.

DIRECT. Anorexia is a complex problem and presents considerable challenge for the most competent professional counselor; the following direction should not be pursued in lieu of professional intervention. It may, however, help the parent or other caring adult who is preparing a youth for referral:

1. Prompt the youth to recognize and admit the problem. It may take some time to do this, but the concerned adult should be patient and persistent (without nagging).

2. Encourage dependence on God. If the youth is not a Christian, turn him or her to accept forgiveness of sins and salvation through Christ, a necessary first step toward wholeness. Help the youth develop and maintain daily fellowship with God in order to rely on His strength, learn from His Word, and counter destructive thoughts and feelings with the mind of Christ. (See Phil. 4:4–9.) Propose a prayer partnership in which the youth and the caring adult pray for (and with) each other.

3. Involve the young person's parents. If you are not the youth's parents, make every effort to inform and involve them at the earliest possible moment. Their insight, support, and approval will be crucial to effectively helping the youth.

4. Help the young person discuss the causes of the problem. What prompts his or her behavior? Is it a way of dealing with pain? Does she feel the need to be perfect in her mother or father's eyes? Does her behavior reflect a craving for control? Help the youth talk these issues out and try to foster an understanding of the reasons for her behavior.

5. Prompt recognition of the false beliefs that promote her behavior (see pages 436–437). Encourage the young person to talk honestly about her beliefs, and help her evaluate each one.

6. Help the young person formulate a daily plan for

combating his or her disorder. Urge her to develop a daily plan for success that includes three healthy meals (a written menu of what she plans to eat the next day) and a set of workable strategies for healthy eating habits (such as "I will eat only at the dining table," "I will remember that it's normal to feel full after a meal," and "I will leave the bathroom scale in the closet").

7. *Encourage the youth to identify vulnerable times and develop a battle plan for such times.* For example, does the company of certain people trigger feelings that contribute to her problem? How can she avoid or better respond to those people? Is she beset with "body hate" first thing in the morning? Would it help to remove the full-length mirror from the bathroom? Is there a key person she can call when she's feeling her worst? Encourage her to *write down* specific plans for handling vulnerable times.

8. *Enlist the support of others.* Alert other family members, close friends, teachers, etc., to the ways they can help: being honest about the youth's appearance ("You look much healthier," "You look emaciated, sweetheart—are you eating?"), avoiding comments about one's own weight ("I need to lose ten pounds"), offering affirmation to the youth ("You have a wonderful sense of humor"), etc.

9. *Help the youth accept the fact that change will take time.* Promote patience, perseverance, and hope. Encourage the young person to "Be strong and courageous. . . . For the Lord your God goes with you; he will never leave you nor forsake you."[25]

ENLIST. Whether you are a youth worker, pastor, parent, teacher, or grandparent, you cannot hope to effect change in an anorexic's life unless the young person himself or herself enlists in the cause. You cannot force an anorexic to recover; he or she must be an active participant. By helping the youth talk freely, affirming

him or her, and directing him or her to recognize the problem, you may be able to enlist the young person in a determination to seek help. That will be a major accomplishment, one that could potentially be life-saving.

REFER. It is of utmost and urgent importance to involve medical and mental health professionals (as well as parents) in an anorexic's recovery. Hospitalization in a unit for eating disorders may be necessary, but release from the hospital will not signal completion of treatment; the young person will need ongoing counsel from a professional Christian psychologist to prevent a relapse. In addition to professional attention on a local, personal level, some of the following resources may be helpful:

- American Anorexia and Bulimia Association (201-836-1800).

- American Anorexia Nervosa Association, Inc. (212-734-1114).

- Anorexia Nervosa and Associated Disorders, Inc. (847-831-3438).

- National Anorexic Aid Society, Inc. (614-436-1112).

For Further Reading

The following resources may help the concerned parent, pastor, teacher, or youth worker to assist an anorexic youth:

Scriptures Cited in This Chapter

- 1 Corinthians 6:19–20
- Romans 12:1
- Hebrews 4:15
- Isaiah 53:3–4
- Psalms 34:18; 147:3

- Philippians 4:4–9
- Deuteronomy 31:6

Other Scripture to Read

- Psalms 62:5–8; 63:1–5

- Luke 12:22–31

- 1 Corinthians 10:31

- Ephesians 6:10–18

- Philippians 4:6–8

Further Reading

- Shannon Christian, *The Very Private Matter of Anorexia Nervosa* (Zondervan).

- Robert S. McGee and William Drew Mountcastle, *Overcoming Eating Disorders* (Rapha/Word).

- Dr. Frank Minirth, Dr. Paul Meier, Dr. Robert Hemfelt, Dr. Sharon Sneed, and Don Hawkins, *Love Hunger* (Thomas Nelson).

- Pam Vredevelt, Dr. Deborah Newman, Harry Beverly, and Dr. Frank Minirth, *The Thin Disguise* (Thomas Nelson).

43

BULIMIA

A Synopsis

❖

Introduction

It started in her senior year at Harvard. Ellen Hart ran on the track team, and her coach suggested that she lose some weight over the Christmas break. It would help her compete, the coach said. . . .

From that moment, the young runner's eating habits changed. She would eat little and spend all her free time running. "But then I'd have this uncontrollable, demonic urge to eat ice cream, cookies, doughnuts—anything high-calorie. And I'd eat until I couldn't eat anymore. Afterward, I couldn't bear the thought that it would stay in me and turn to fat, so I'd have to purge. During the worst periods, I'd binge and purge four or five times a day, from the moment I woke up until I went to sleep. By April, I was down to 110, and I looked like a cadaver . . .

By the time she graduated in June, Ellen knew she had a problem. It affected her physically, it affected her relationships, and it affected her emotionally to the degree that she said, "Sometimes I was actually sorry that the eating disorder wouldn't kill me and I'd think, 'Please just let me out of this.'"

All her efforts to control her problem met with failure, until—five months after her marriage to Federico Pena—Ellen learned she was pregnant. She continued to binge and purge during her pregnancy, and six months into her pregnancy she began to have contractions. "That was the moment when I said, 'Stop. You have to take care of your body, and your body is now carrying a baby.'" Still, she says, "I'm absolutely convinced that if I hadn't [already] been in therapy for a long time, I wouldn't have been able to turn the corner."

Today Ellen—a world-class runner who set an American women's record in the thirty-kilometer run in 1982 and wife of the U.S. secretary of transportation—says, "I'm running and even competing again, but for the first time I can run just for the enjoyment of it. I've also learned to manage my weight, which is now 125, without getting totally compulsive. . . . There are still times when I'm tempted to binge and purge, and I think, 'Maybe just today . . .' But I'm strong enough to resist it. I'm not walking near that cliff again because going over the edge was my private hell. I can't go back."[1]

The Problem of Bulimia

Ellen Hart Pena suffers from bulimia, an eating disorder that is estimated to affect 3 percent of all American women between the ages of fourteen and forty. While the vast majority of diagnosed bulimics (85 percent)[2] are women, males—particularly young wrestlers, runners, jockeys, and other athletes—can also be victims.[3]

About eight million people in the United States suffer from an eating disorder, the most common of which is bulimia nervosa.[4] Eighty-six percent of sufferers report the onset of the disorder before the age of twenty; only half report being cured. Six percent of serious cases die of the disorder.[5]

Bulimia "is a psychiatric disorder whose victims engage in uncontrollable binge eating to relieve anxiety and hunger, then induce vomiting, abuse laxatives or exercise excessively to counteract weight gain," says Dr. Katherine Halmi, director of the Eating Disorder Program at Cornell University Medical Center, Westchester Division. She says that a key difference between bulimia and anorexia is "that bulimics stay close to their normal weight and continue to menstruate, while anorexics lose a great deal of weight and stop menstruating. About half of anorexia patients also suffer from bulimia."[6]

The Causes of Bulimia

Among the many factors that may cause an adolescent to become bulimic are the following:

◆ Sociocultural Influences

The authors of *Love Hunger*, a book about eating disorders, attribute the problem at least partially to cultural influences that constantly bombard people with twin—and conflicting— messages:

> Never before in history have so much time, money, and energy gone into urging people to eat

and yet at the same time demanding that they be slim. Psychiatrists call these push/pull messages double-bind messages, paradox messages, or best of all: "crazy-making messages." And these crazy-making messages have led us to become the most food-obsessed, obesity-plagued society in the world.[7]

The tragic and frequent incidence of bulimia is not surprising in a culture in which physical beauty—particularly for women—is emphasized and prized so highly, and eating is pushed and pursued so fervently.

◆ Abuse

Women with bulimia are three times more likely to have been sexually abused as children than women who do not suffer from the eating disorder, according to a study conducted through the mental health portion of the Ontario (Canada) Health Survey. Paul Garfinkel, president of Toronto's Clarke Institute of Psychiatry, explains, "Abuse leads to feelings of helplessness in the world and disgust about their bodies. They feel that somehow, if they can change the outside, the inside will feel better."[8]

Other studies show that nonsexual abuse may also contribute to the likelihood of bulimia in women. One such study, conducted by Joel Yager of the University of California, Los Angeles, suggests that prolonged physical and psychological abuse are characteristic of the early family experiences of many bulimics.[9] (See chapter 34, "Sexual Abuse," and chapter 35, "Nonsexual Abuse.")

◆ Trauma

Bulimia may be fostered by other trauma in addition to the trauma of abuse in the home. Dr. Katherine Halmi says that "up to 50 percent of bulimics have had traumatic and stressful problems in their families or earlier lives [such as the] death of a family member, [or] a traumatic event at home or school."[10]

◆ Perfectionism

Counselor and author Robert S. McGee points out that one of the "key emotional and spiritual components [that] inaugurate and sustain all eating disorders [is] *perfectionism*."[11] Bulimics have often been raised by successful parents in family atmospheres of high expectations. This perfectionism can lead to a compulsion about weight and appearance.

◆ Need for Control

"The major problem [that feeds bulimia]," according to Dr. Peter D. Bash, an assistant clinical professor of medicine at UCLA, "invariably concerns a need to feel in control."[12] Ellen Hart Pena said that her eating problems began as a result of "changes happening [which] I couldn't control." The bulimic's need for a sense of control soon develops a problem that, ironically, quickly spins out of control.

◆ Faulty Thinking

Psychologists Barbara Bauer and Wayne Anderson have identified nine irrational beliefs that are commonly held by people with bulimia:

1. "Becoming overweight is the worst thing that can happen to me."
2. "I believe there are good foods, such as vegetables and fish, and bad foods, such as sweets and carbohydrates."
3. "I must have control over all my actions to feel safe."
4. "I must do everything perfectly or what I do is worthless."
5. "Everyone is aware of, and interested in, what I am doing."
6. "Everyone must love me and approve of what I do."
7. "External validation is crucial to me."
8. "As soon as a particular event such as graduation or marriage occurs, my bulimic behavior will disappear."
9. "I must be dependent and subservient yet competitive and aggressive."[13]

◆ Low Self-Esteem

The authors of *Love Hunger* point out that many people become bulimic in an effort, conscious or unconscious, to dull the pain caused by low self-esteem. (See also chapter 6, "Unhealthy Self-Esteem.")

> In searching for a way to make the pain bearable, people turn to a narcotic agent that will anesthetize their pain, even for a short period of time. For some it's alcohol; for others, drugs or sex or rage or spending. For still others . . . it's food.[14]

The above discussion clearly does not include the only causes of bulimia, nor will all of the above symptoms necessarily characterize a person suffering from bulimia, but the research indicates that they are frequently and typically present in many bulimics.

The Effects of Bulimia

In contrast to anorexia nervosa, which can often be identified by the victim's rapid loss of weight, bulimia does not show up readily; bulimics are generally not excessively thin. However, alertness to the following effects of the disorder may help a concerned parent, pastor, youth leader, or teacher identify and/or counsel a young person:

◆ Social Effects

Some of the effects of bulimia are apparent in the young person's behavior. Many bulimics will become secret bingers; increasingly they may withdraw from interaction with their friends and family. Most surprisingly, perhaps, bulimics in many cases resort to stealing to support their behavior.

Secrecy. Bulimics will often refuse to eat—or will eat very little—when with friends and acquaintances. They will pick at their food and often move it around the plate to make it look as though it's been eaten; the real eating they do is done in secret, often in mind-boggling amounts. Prior to the end of the meal—or just after it—they will often excuse themselves to go to the bathroom, where they can purge themselves of what they have eaten behind a locked door.

Withdrawal. Bulimics will often begin to avoid the company of others, even their closest friends, in order to (literally) feed their disorder. While they may date, they will tend not to allow themselves a close relationship and will sometimes inexplicably break off an apparently thriving relationship, fearing the discovery of their habits.

Stealing. The authors of *The Thin Disguise* report that "research indicates that 24 percent of those with eating disorders steal compulsively."[15] They may steal laxatives or diet pills, or they may steal food; after all, binges are expensive, as are the "aids" bulimics often use in their periods of purging.

◆ **Physical Effects**

The physical effects of bulimia include:

Amenorrhea. Bulimia may cause the disruption of normal menstrual cycles.

Anemia. Anemia (decreased red blood cell count) or decreased white blood cell count are frequent results of bulimia.

Constipation. The failure to take in or retain sufficient foods and fluids can cause bulimics to suffer problems with constipation.

Dental and Periodontal Problems. Bulimics' frequent vomiting results in the erosion of tooth enamel, discoloration of the teeth, and periodontal disease caused by the hydrochloric acid

from the stomach. Damage to the esophagus is another frequent result.

Glandular Malfunctioning. Problems such as thyroid abnormalities and other glandular malfunctions have been connected to bulimia and other eating disorders.

Hypoglycemia. "A person with an eating disorder may have a low blood sugar count (hypoglycemia) in response to a binge intake of high-calorie, simple-sugar foods. The body overcompensates by releasing excessive insulin, which then drives the blood sugar too low. As a result, the body craves more sugar. Hypoglycemia may manifest itself by fatigue and feelings of anxiety. Complaints of dizziness and headaches are common."[16]

Malnutrition. Malnutrition may occur with accompanying lethargy and water retention.

Kidney Dysfunction and Failure. As the person's weight loss becomes extreme, the risk of kidney failure—as the kidneys and other organs are deprived of vital nutrients and proteins—presents itself.

Seizures. "For some reason not fully understood," write the authors of *The Thin Disguise*, "seizures occur in persons with eating disorders at a higher rate than in the general population."[17]

Osteoporosis. Caused by vitamin deficiency (as well as other musculoskeletal problems), osteoporosis can result from bulimia.

Other dangers. Other dangers associated with bulimia include ulcers, stomach and bowel disorders, [and] mouth and throat irritations. . . . Regular purging can upset the body's chemistry and cause the heart to become irregular. The esophagus can rupture, and the bulimic can bleed to death.[18]

◆ **Psychological Effects**

Bulimia shares many of the psychological effects of anorexia and, as is the case with anorexia, some of the psychological effects of bulimia may have medical origins. The following are generally counted among the psychological ramifications of bulimia:

Impulse Control Disorder. This problem is "loss of control of oneself, which results in impulsive actions and extreme emotions, such as anger and rage."[19] It may be as much a cause of bulimia as an effect; or it may be both.

Guilt and Shame. Guilt and shame are also both a cause and an effect of bulimia. In fact, the authors of *Love Hunger* state that "most doctors believe that at some level all addictions are shame-based." Bulimics carry "a double burden of guilt . . . because they have the shame of the obesity and the overeating itself plus the old shame from their family of origin. The two flood in together, and the shame is overpowering."[20] (See also chapter 3, "Guilt.")

Depression and Anxiety. Dr. Paul Garfinkel says bulimics are "people who are really suffering. These are not people who are throwing up once in a while and then going on their merry way. They have significant problems with depression [and] anxiety."[21] (See also chapter 2, "Anxiety," and chapter 5, "Depression.")

The Biblical Perspective of Bulimia

The Christian's body is a temple of the Holy Spirit, and the Bible commands us to honor God with our bodies[22]—what we do with them and how we treat them. Bulimia is a form of self-abuse and therefore is a violation of God's will.

But the bulimic's problem is not about food; it is not simple gluttony (Prov. 23:20–21). The bulimic uses food to mask another, deeper, problem—usually the pain caused by abuse, trauma, perfectionism, or low self-esteem.

The bulimic's pain, however, is not beyond the reach of a loving and compassionate God. "He heals the brokenhearted," the Bible says, "and binds up their wounds."[23] He grieves over His children whose lives have been crushed, whose hearts have been broken. As the authors of *The Thin Disguise* have written, "His desire is to see their lives rebuilt and restored to His original purpose and design. . . . [He] longs to see [the bulimic] healed and restored.[24]

God is the God of all comfort (2 Cor. 7:6). But He also calls His children to respond compassionately to those around them, especially to those who are hurting, whose lives have spun out of their control, who find themselves in the grip of a destructive disorder. "Comfort, comfort my people, says your God."[25] And, in the words of Paul to the church at Thessalonica, "we urge you, brothers . . . help the weak [and] be patient with everyone."[26]

Bulimics need comfort and help to overcome what can be a life-threatening disorder. It can be overcome, however, with trust in God and wise help from His people.

The Response to the Problem of Bulimia

Listen ◆ Empathize ◆ Affirm ◆ Direct ◆ Enlist ◆ Refer

A youth leader, pastor, parent, or teacher who suspects or knows that a young person is suffering from bulimia should first approach God in prayer for wisdom and sensitivity and then implement the following response:

LISTEN. Talk to the young person and "find out how she feels about herself. Find out how she feels about eating and how often she eats. She may be very manipulative and hide the [truth about her eating habits]. A talk with the parents is very much in order. What patterns have they seen? Have they talked to her about it? Is there a physical problem?"[27] Use questions, not to accuse the young person, but to try to direct his or her attention, to open his or her eyes (or those of parents). The following questions, suggested by McGee, may help:

- Are you fearful of being fat, believing that body fat is a "sin"?

- Do you try to diet repeatedly, only to sabotage your plans by binging activities for which you feel great shame?

- Do you frequently tend to overestimate your needs for food intake for a given meal or snack, especially "oversnacking" when under stress?

- Do you hide and hoard private stashes of food for later binging?

- Do you binge on high-calorie, sugary, "forbidden" foods, or on "safe" foods, such as salads?

- Do you shroud your eating (especially binges) in secrecy, fearing anyone's scrutiny of your eating behavior?

- Do you often feel ashamed and/or depressed when you eat?

- Do you spend much time thinking about your next binge, planning it (perhaps in detail), when you should be engaged in other tasks and activities?

- Do thoughts about food occupy much of your time?

- Does any interruption of this thinking result in your feeling cross, irritable, and angry, all of which you must hide from anyone else's notice?

- Do you induce vomiting in order to get rid of "binge food"?

- Do you exercise to work off a binge?

- Do you use laxatives and/or diuretics in ways other than prescribed to eliminate food you have eaten?

- Do you also engage in any of these behaviors especially to discharge feelings of anger or anxiety that may have accompanied the binge?

- Do you disappear to the bathroom or to another available, hidden source of plumbing immediately after meals? Do you become anxious or angry if it is occupied or if you cannot use it for any other reason?

- If you have been living in a college dorm room with a sink or other source of plumbing, have you ever had to make maintenance calls to repair the plumbing system due to your purging?

- Do you binge/purge more than three times a week?

- Have you been confronted by others about your behavior (and denied all) and then resolved to start keeping more distance from friends or family members to avoid future confrontations about your food behavior?[28]

If it is determined that the young person does show signs of bulimia, it is important to involve professional help as soon as possible.

EMPATHIZE. Try to come alongside the young person in a spirit of understanding (rather than confronting him or her in an attitude of authority). Avoid arguing with the youth. Avoid power struggles. Don't try to motivate him or her with guilt or shame. Don't offer pat answers. Concentrate instead on understanding and communicating empathy. Some practical ways to do so include:

- Leaning forward in your chair to communicate interest.

- Making eye contact with the young person as he or she speaks without staring or letting your eyes wander.

- Avoiding any expression of shock, disapproval, disagreement, or judgment about what is said.

- Waiting patiently through periods of silence or tears.

- Leading the conversation by asking "What happened next?" or "Tell me what you mean by . . ."

- Reflecting the young person's statements by saying, "You feel . . . ," or "It sounds like you're saying . . ."

AFFIRM. Joan Sturkie offers a reminder "to be nonjudgmental when dealing with the person with an eating disorder. The attitude of 'the counselee brings it on himself or herself' is not acceptable. Lonely, isolated and hungry people need support."[29] Since the source of the bulimic's disorder may be a self-image and self-esteem problem, make a special effort to carefully and prayerfully focus on affirming that young person's sense of value and worth. It will do little good to insist that the youth is pretty or thin enough; instead, try to concentrate on creating an accepting, loving relationship in which the youth can develop a sense of security and belonging.

DIRECT. Bulimia is a complex problem and presents considerable challenge for the most competent professional counselor; the following direction should not be pursued in lieu of professional intervention. It may, however, help the parent or other caring adult who is preparing a youth for referral:

1. Prompt the youth to recognize and admit the problem. It may take some time to do this, but the concerned adult should be patient and persistent (without nagging).

2. Encourage dependence on God. If the youth is not a Christian, turn him or her to accept forgiveness of sins and salvation through Christ, a necessary first step toward wholeness. Help the youth develop and maintain daily fellowship with God in order to rely on His strength, learn from His Word, and counter destructive thoughts and feelings with the mind of Christ (Phil. 4:4–9). Propose a prayer partnership in which the youth and the caring adult pray for (and with) each other.

3. Involve the young person's parents. If you are not the youth's parents, make every effort to inform and involve them at the earliest possible moment. Their insight, support, and approval will be crucial to effectively helping the youth.

4. Help the young person discuss the causes of the problem. What prompts his or her behavior? Is it a way of dealing with pain? Does she feel the need to be perfect in her mother or father's eyes? Does her behavior reflect a craving for control? Help the youth talk these issues out and try to foster an understanding of the reasons for her behavior.

5. Prompt recognition of the false beliefs that promote her behavior. (See "Faulty Thinking" page 446.) Encourage the young person to talk honestly about her beliefs, and help her to rationally and biblically evaluate those beliefs.

6. Help the young person formulate a daily plan for combating her disorder. Urge her to develop a daily plan for success that includes three healthy meals (a written menu of what she plans to eat the next day) and a set of workable strategies for healthy eating habits (such as "I will eat only at the dining table," "I will remove my favorite binge foods from the house," and "I will leave the bathroom scale in the closet").

7. Encourage the youth to identify vulnerable

places and times and develop a battle plan for them. For example, are certain times of the day or week harder than others? How can she prepare for those times? What does she plan to do when the urge to binge hits (take a walk, read an engrossing book, call a friend)? Is there a key person she can call when she's feeling her worst? Encourage her to *write down* specific plans for handling difficult times.

8. Enlist the support of others. Alert other family members, close friends, teachers, etc., to the ways they can help: Parents may remove the lock from the bathroom door (to prevent purging), friends might avoid comments about their own weight ("I need to lose ten pounds"), and others might offer occasional affirmation to the youth ("You have a wonderful sense of humor"), etc.

9. Help the youth accept the fact that change will take time. Promote patience, perseverance, and hope. Encourage the young person to "Be strong and courageous. . . . For the Lord your God goes with you; he will never leave you nor forsake you."[30]

ENLIST. Whether you are a youth worker, pastor, parent, teacher, or grandparent, you cannot hope to effect change in a bulimic's life unless the young person himself or herself enlists in the cause. You can help him or her recognize and/or admit that he or she has a problem, but you cannot force the youth to recover; he or she must be an active participant. Prompt the youth to take responsibility for his or her actions. Let him or her make as many of the key decisions as possible. Involve the young person in choices regarding ongoing treatment.

REFER. It is of utmost and urgent importance to involve medical and mental health professionals (as well as parents) in a bulimic's recovery. Hospitalization in a unit for eating disorders may be necessary, but release from the hospital will not signal completion of treatment; the young person will need ongoing counsel from a professional Christian psychologist to prevent a relapse. In addition to professional attention on a local, personal level, some of the following resources may be helpful:

- American Anorexia and Bulimia Association (201-836-1800).
- American Anorexia Nervosa Association, Inc. (212-734-1114).
- Anorexia Nervosa and Associated Disorders, Inc. (847-831-3438).
- National Anorexic Aid Society, Inc., (614-436-1112).

For Further Reading

The following resources may help the concerned parent, pastor, teacher, or youth worker to assist a bulimic youth:

Scriptures Cited in This Chapter

- 1 Corinthians 6:19–20
- Proverbs 23:20–21
- Psalm 147:3
- 2 Corinthians 7:6
- Isaiah 40:1
- 1 Thessalonians 5:14
- Philippians 4:4–9
- Deuteronomy 31:6

Other Scripture to Read

- Psalms 62:5–8; 63:1–5
- Luke 12:22–31
- 1 Corinthians 10:31
- Ephesians 6:10–18
- Philippians 4:6–8

Further Reading

- Robert S. McGee and William Drew Mountcastle, *Overcoming Eating Disorders* (Rapha/Word).

- Dr. Frank Minirth, Dr. Paul Meier, Dr. Robert Hemfelt, Dr. Sharon Sneed, and Don Hawkins, *Love Hunger* (Thomas Nelson).

- Pam Vredevelt, Dr. Deborah Newman, Harry Beverly, and Dr. Frank Minirth, *The Thin Disguise* (Thomas Nelson).

EDUCATIONAL

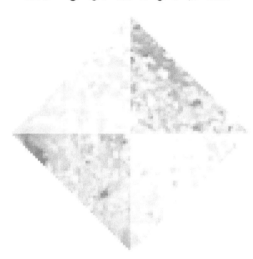

ISSUES

44

44

DROPPING OUT

Introduction

The conflict in Ray's mind had been brewing for some time. With poor grades and numerous detentions, his mother was at her wit's end trying to force him to pay attention and cooperate with his teachers. Dad was nowhere to be seen, and with the bills to pay, his mother worked at nominal jobs. The money was tight, and Ray had no allowance of money to spend on himself. He saw school as a boring waste of time.

Ray's best friend had dropped out of high school two months ago to work full-time at Superior Auto Trim, and he already had a new car and was talking about buying a snowmobile.

Ray figured if he could drop out and get his own job he could finally do the things he wanted to do. It would be so great to be free of the hassles: no more fights at school, no more arguments with Mom, no more boring classes. The temptation was overwhelming; the benefits were clear. Soon he was going to be his "own man."

The Problem of Dropping Out

A 1986 report of the U.S. Department of Education indicated the national average for dropping out of school in the United States to be 25 percent. Since that time over twenty-six hundred programs, both public and private, have addressed the question of why young men and women choose to leave school, with the goal of reducing dropout rates. Many of these programs, however, have met with failure.

The dropout rate is much higher in urban schools; some communities report as high as a 50 percent dropout rate. Studies have indicated that schools with the lowest dropout rates clearly emphasize the value of academic learning with accountability, rewards for achievements in school, and strong parental support of school objectives. Statistics show that inner-city schools that seriously focus on discipline, character, orderliness, accountability, and academic excellence have significantly lower failure and dropout levels.

Though dropout rates have been declining over the past forty years, this problem still poses serious social consequences. With ever-increasing technological advances and a greater-than-ever need for vocational and occupational training, students who drop out of school will find themselves on the fringe of society. The inability to market even basic skills puts the dropout at serious risk of facing serious financial struggles and severely limiting his or her potential for advancement and accomplishment—both of which can bear unfortunate consequences should the dropout marry and raise a family.

The Causes of Dropping Out

◆ Academic Demands, Social Requirements

School presents a set of challenges, frustrations, and tensions that even the best of students often find difficult. The academic demands of algebra, chemistry, even basic courses like English and history (particularly for a generation raised on MTV and *Short Attention Span Theater*) can produce frustration. The social requirements of dressing, speaking, and acting just right can be tiresome, even befuddling, to many teens. The need to relate to male and female, younger and older kids, peers and authority figures, can be extremely difficult for some adolescents.

However, the challenges faced by potential dropouts is, in most cases, identical to that faced by those students who complete their academic programs. What is different is the intensity of frustration, discouragement, and eventual rejection of "the system" that dropouts experience.

◆ Experimental Curricula, Ineffective Teaching Methods

Many educators and sociologists have implicated the experimental curricula that were born during the 1960s and 1970s as disruptive to learning and counterproductive to maintaining graduation rates among students. Students who have been handicapped by ineffective teaching methods are at greater risk for dropping out.

◆ Boredom and Frustration

Students who drop out see their decision as a solution to a long history of boredom and frustration. One study revealed that half of the dropouts surveyed left school in response to school-related problems, such as repeated failure, consequences to disruptive behavior (i.e., suspensions and expulsions), and perceived rejection by school personnel.

◆ Other Problems

The concerned adult must also be alert to the presence of other problems that put the student at risk for withdrawing from school. Academic problems have always been symptomatic to larger and weightier issues of life experienced by teenagers. Substance abuse (see chapters 38, "Alcohol Use and Abuse," and 39, "Drug Use and Abuse"), associations with other youth who reinforce nonachievement, and the fallout that comes from membership in a dysfunctional family can also alert a sensitive adult to the possibility of a problem that might lead a student to drop out. A young person who is receiving insufficient encouragement and guidance with his or her academic frustrations will also be more likely to consider discontinuing his or her studies.

The question of what causes a student to drop out begs another—and perhaps more significant—question: What factors contribute to a student's success in school? This becomes the main issue in preventing and correcting the problem of kids dropping out of school.

The Effects of Dropping Out

◆ Poor Earning Power

A student who views dropping out as a solution to academic frustration will soon learn the painful effects of his or her decision. The poor earning power and inevitable lifestyle that accompanies marginal earnings generate more frustration, disappointment, and stress than most teens can imagine. Studies show that dropouts are not only less likely to *win* in the job market, they are less likely to *participate* in the labor force. Dropouts display a proportionately higher dependence on general relief and welfare programs than the rest of the population.

◆ Functional Illiteracy

Sociologists view dropping out of school as a unique social problem that generates a set of far-reaching consequences. Researchers estimate that 13 percent of the U.S. population has less than a sixth-grade reading level. Twenty-three million adults have failed to develop the necessary reading and writing skills to adequately function in society. An additional thirty million are characterized as marginally literate.

◆ Loss of Desire to Achieve in Other Areas

Despite the large-scale impact of school failure, however, the most significant failure is in the individual lives of those who drop out. Often one experiences the loss of desire to achieve in other arenas of life. A pattern of indifference, a loss of potential, and undeveloped individual abilities often develop among those who left school early.

It is encouraging to note that many dropouts apparently come to realize that the decision to drop out was a poor one. The surveys that examine dropout rates report that, in time, 40 percent will eventually return to the educational system. While that figure certainly provides a ray of hope, it is obvious that prevention is still better than correction.

The Biblical Perspective of Dropping Out

God has given every human being an inquisitiveness and the desire to learn. There is satisfaction and joy when one discovers something new and learns more about the environment God has created. The capacity to think and learn is among His sweetest and most precious gifts, and God expects man to use his gift to the greatest of his ability.

Paul wrote Timothy:

> Don't let anyone look down on you because you are young, but set an example for the believers in speech, in life, in love, in faith and in purity. Until I come, devote yourself to the public reading of Scripture, to preaching and to teaching. *Do not neglect your gift*, which was given you through a prophetic message when the body of elders laid their hands on you. [Emphasis added.][1]

While Paul's exhortation to Timothy not to neglect his gift referred specifically to a supernatural gift that was given to him for use in

458

ministry, Paul's words do make it clear that God gives gifts *to be used*—and that would certainly include the gift of intellect.

God's Word clearly places a premium on study and education:

> Blessed is the man who finds wisdom, the man who gains understanding.[2]

> A wise man has great power, and a man of knowledge increases strength.[3]

> Do your best to present yourself to God as one approved, a workman who does not need to be ashamed and who correctly handles the word of truth.[4]

Anything short of an individual's true ability is wasteful and unproductive. However, it must also be recognized that the decision to drop out of school does not make a person stupid or worthless; he or she still has infinite worth and boundless potential in God's eyes. It is possible—and biblical—to confront the *issue* without attacking (in fact, while *affirming*) the person.[5]

The Response to the Problem of Dropping Out

Listen ◆ Empathize ◆ Affirm ◆ Direct ◆ Enlist ◆ Refer

LISTEN. Problems with school are often an indication of problems in other areas of the youth's life. Establish good rapport with the young person and exhibit a willingness to listen without criticism or correction. No matter how simple the solution may seem to you, adopt a listening attitude. The use of active listening will give you, in time, a better understanding of the teen and his or her problems.

EMPATHIZE. Schoolwork is difficult for most youth. Rarely does learning come easily, even for the best of students. By empathizing with the student who finds school a challenge or a bore, you afford an opportunity to create hope. This does not mean you must agree with all the teen's complaints; it means identifying with his or her feelings and frustrations and acknowledging that learning problems exist for many and that some students do have legitimate gripes about teaching styles and techniques. Establish a rapport, listen to the frustrations and problems, empathize with the emotional expressions of these frustrations, and finally, take action to correct learning problems. Empathy is the bridge between the problem and the solution.

AFFIRM. Strive to communicate to the teen that the goal of schooling is not perfection but development. Education is a process that (if cooperatively joined with) does produce success, fulfillment, and satisfaction in life. Give the uninterested student a clear signal that he or she does belong in school and has every right to expect good results.

When learning behaviors are applied and a support system is used to hold the student accountable, there is no limit to what can be accomplished. Affirm the young person's worth, qualities, and strengths, being careful not to place on the youth any undue pressure to perform above his or her level of ability. Often, if a young person is pressured to perform above the level of his ability, feelings of inadequacy, loss of hope, and pessimism emerge, and he or she gives up. On the other hand, be careful not to direct the student to an inferior course of study that falls below his or her level of ability.

DIRECT. Once a concerned adult has established a strong foundation of trust by listening carefully, empathizing, and affirming the young person, he or she might profitably proceed to offer some direction. The following may serve as a helpful outline:

1. Involve the young person's parents. If you are

not the youth's mother or father, make every effort to inform and involve the parents at the earliest possible moment. Their insight, support, and approval will be crucial to effectively helping the youth.

2. *Involve God.* Place God in charge of your efforts to help the young man or woman, and trust His wisdom and power. Urge the young man or woman to likewise turn to God, asking Him for help in the present and future. (See James 1:5.) Help the youth develop and maintain daily fellowship with God in order to rely on His strength, learn from His Word, and seek His will. Propose a prayer partnership in which the youth and the caring adult pray for (and with) each other.

3. *Encourage the young person to discuss the causes of the problems.* Invite the young person to freely ventilate the issues that contribute to his or her dissatisfaction with school. To a frustrated adolescent, the call for independence from school and the lure of an income (even from a low-paying job), presents a strong temptation. Verify and acknowledge the particulars of school problems and frustrations.

4. *Facilitate negotiation to address the problems.* If the student is bored, meet with a school counselor about a schedule change that will stimulate more interest. If the student struggles with written tests, consider negotiating oral exams with his or her teachers. Strive to find ways to address the student's valid concerns.

5. *Help the student assess his or her needs and goals.* Invite the young person to talk about his or her interests and goals. As you explore the youth's plans for the future (and his or her aptitudes), you will be in a better position to clarify the role of education and the responsibility of the learner to prepare for these interests. Many times the frustrations of school can be tolerated if and when the student gets a bigger picture of what an education can afford.

6. *Help the young person formulate a plan.* Encourage him or her to draw up a clearly defined set of purposes, objectives, and goals. Purposes define the youth's aspirations (for example, "Purpose: to become a pro tennis player"). Objectives define major steps the youth must take to realize his aspirations ("Objectives: make the high school tennis team; become captain of the high school tennis team," etc.). Goals define the intermediary steps that must be taken before meeting the objectives (Goals: "Stay in school; carry a C average; find a regular tennis partner," etc.). Eliminate the notion of failure; what is needed is a plan that appeals to the interest of the young person.

7. *Offer practical encouragement.* Consider arranging a visit to a company or industry that offers careers similar to the interests of the student. Arrange for a tour and allow the student to meet with adults who can stimulate interest in a career and also create an awareness of the educational requirements for that career and its attendant benefits (salary, benefits, etc.). Consider the possibility of a work-study or vocational program.

8. *Consult with others.* Involve the youth's guidance counselor, parents, teachers, pastors, and others in an effort to generate a creative alternative to the student's problems.

ENLIST. Resist any temptation to coerce the youth to remain in or return to school (an impossible task, anyway). Instead, seek to enlist his or her participation in communicating what changes, adjustments, and motivations will make remaining in school attractive and rewarding.

REFER. A psycho-educational battery of testing is certainly very important. An educator or school psychologist who is familiar with problems of nonachievement is best suited to assess the achievement and ability levels of the student; this information can provide useful feedback to all parties concerned in reformulating a learning program. One must keep in mind that many possibilities exist in explaining the cause of learning problems. It is not always a lack of motivation that stonewalls learning. With the test results in hand, counselors and psychologists can give clear directives on how to correct the problem.

Schools often sponsor seminars and workshops on how to improve reading skills and study skills. Libraries also carry an assortment of reference materials and guides for improving school performance.

For Further Reading

The following resources may help the concerned parent, pastor, teacher, or youth worker assist a dropout or potential dropout:

Scriptures Cited in This Chapter

- 1 Timothy 4:12–14

- Proverbs 3:13; 24:5
- 2 Timothy 2:15
- John 8:1–11
- James 1:5

Other Scripture to Read

- Proverbs 1:7, 22; 8:10; 17:16
- Philippians 1:9–11
- Titus 3:14

Further Reading

- Verne Becker, ed., *The Campus Life Guide to Surviving High School* (Zondervan).
- Dan Korem, *Streetwise Parents, Foolproof Kids* (NavPress). Contains a helpful chapter on public school trends.

UNDERACHIEVEMENT AND OVERACHIEVEMENT

45

Introduction

Jo Mendoza is an only child. She's also a prodigy.

Jo and her family live in El Paso, Texas. For most of her young life, she lived in a house without running water. Her father is a farmworker; her mother works in a laundry.

Jo began reading primary books at age two, devouring them the way most kids watch cartoons on television. By age five, she was reading romance novels. Her mother found it difficult to fill Jo's voracious appetite for books.

By the time she entered fourth grade, Jo was enrolled in pre-algebra. She tackled three years of math at a summer camp for gifted students—in three weeks. She graduated from high school at the age of fifteen. She is currently attending college on a full academic scholarship. She plans to be a writer.

Patrick Borders of Terre Haute, Indiana, was acknowledged by his parents, teachers, and friends as a smart kid—some would say brilliant. His intelligence was accompanied by striking good looks and a charming personality. He seemed to have everything . . . except passing grades in school.

Patrick seemed to have little difficulty with his studies—when he applied himself—and his teachers often lectured him and pleaded with him to begin achieving his potential. He always listened politely and would continue neglecting his homework, turning in appallingly poor assignments and failing nearly every test and quiz he took.

Patrick managed to complete high school four months before his twentieth birthday through a vocational program and landed a job installing car stereos at AutoSound. Though he shows no interest in the financial and management matters at the store, he hopes to become manager and perhaps even own his own business someday.

The Problem of Underachievement and Overachievement

What made Daphne and Patrick so different? The major difference between them was not intelligence; both had considerable mental abilities. What brought about such different results then? And what can parents, teachers, pastors, and youth workers do to help young people achieve both academic and personal satisfaction?

An important developmental task for youth is to discover and develop their God-given talents and abilities. Their potential strengths, interests, and aptitudes are exposed and exercised through various opportunities to achieve at home, at church, and in school.

Some youth seem to mature with little difficulty and gain a clear understanding of their potentials and limitations. Others resist the challenge to develop their potential. An underachiever will not only fail at school but will usually experience a number of other problems that may last a lifetime. Overachievement is a condition in which perfectionism, fear of failure, compulsive behavior, and anxiety drive a student to exhaustion and eventual inefficiency. While overachievement is typically treated as cause for celebration, the consequences can be quite destructive.

The Yerkes-Dodson Law (sometimes called the "inverted U" scale), which shows a curvilinear relationship between one's level of arousal and one's level of performance, illustrates the need for balance and moderation. Suppose three students of equal ability and knowledge are compared by their performance in school. One student has no interest in how well he or she does. The second student wants to do well and is somewhat relaxed but still feels pressured to do his or her best. The last student is very motivated, tense, and anxious, feeling that if he or she does poorly (on a test, for example), it will

reflect badly on his or her self-esteem and worth as a human. Which of the three would perform most competently? The second student, because students will perform most effectively when the level of arousal is moderate. One who is both motivated and confident will do far better in school compared with students who are bored or unmotivated and students who are overanxious or feel intense pressure to perform well. (See Figure 45.)

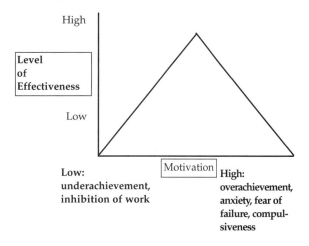

Figure 45.

It is estimated that the performance of 20 percent of the American school population is inhibited in some way. Seventy-five percent of those underachieving students are males. These students do not have cognitive or central nervous system dysfunctions, nor do they possess learning disabilities. They are capable; their achievement simply doesn't match their capabilities.

Three things are necessary for good performance in school: ability, good work methods, and interest. Ability, of course, differs from one person to another. Good work methods or study skills are learned, however, and as they become "second nature" to the student, that young person becomes more efficient in the use of time and in the ease of study. The third requirement for success in school is interest and motivation.

A common problem with nonachievers is that they have not gained a true knowledge of their abilities and strengths, nor of the "how to" of study skills, techniques, and shortcuts, nor have they developed the interest and motivation that are requisite for achievement. Many educators agree that a failure to apply oneself in school is strong indication of poor self-definition, inferiority, and poor identity development. (See chapter 6, "Unhealthy Self-Esteem.") These are among the root causes of poor achievement. Overachievers, while they may exhibit mastery of the requirements for achievement, may yet lack confidence and healthy self-definition. They tend to link their self-worth directly to academic perfection. Consequently, the slightest failure is a threat to their integrity and identity, which produces anxiety, guilt, and eventually, unproductivity.

The Causes of Underachievement and Overachievement

Academic problems are frequently indicators of larger problems, often having to do with personality and lifestyle, societal and economic factors, and the family.

◆ Personality, Lifestyle Factors

Studies of the personality and lifestyle factors of underachievers indicate that nonachievers generally display some or all of the following characteristics:

- Emotional immaturity
- Inability to adjust
- Excessive fear and anxiety
- Low self-esteem
- Deep-seated feelings of hostility
- Resentment

- Negativism
- Perceptions of unfair treatment
- Rejection of adult authority

◆ Societal, Economic Factors

Most adolescents, of course, struggle with most or all of the above at one time or another. They are hesitant to comply with requests made of them on *their* time schedule. They want to assert their independence and often boast an attitude of "I know what's good for me." Yet the natural struggles and stresses of adolescence do not always hamper achievement. They can be exacerbated, however, by other factors.

Richard Jaeger, professor of educational research at the University of North Carolina, cites societal and economic factors such as poverty, unemployment, and parental divorce as impediments to adolescent achievement. According to Jaeger, "economic support and family stability are . . . essential to school success."[2]

◆ Family Factors

Family factors play a critical part in a young person's success in school. A study of family patterns of interaction among nonachieving students in middle-class communities identified four patterns of interaction that created hazards for students.

Parental Disharmony, Conflict. The first pattern was an overall disharmony between the parents as to standards of child discipline and child-rearing practices. The confusion in the family resulted in negativism, emotional immaturity, and poor grades in school. The basic needs of children were simply not met by the parents who spent more energy quarreling than parenting.

Parental Indifference. A second family pattern contributing to work inhibition were parents who were indifferent to the accomplishments of their children. (See chapter 17, "Inattentive Parents.")

By focusing on their own careers and interests, the parents prompted the child to feel unloved and unappreciated. Children achieve when basic needs are met. When these needs are ignored or denied, the resulting symptoms of a troubled child in school are expressed in poor grades or dropping out of school altogether. The symptoms include disrespect, inability to concentrate, a power struggle against authority, withdrawal from performing in school, poor self-motivation, and an unwillingness to stay on learning tasks.

At the very heart of the cause for nonachievement or overachievement are unmet emotional needs of children. Parents who expect too much or who are too lenient often fail to foster a healthy sense of achievement among their children. When young people are responded to in a fashion that meets their emotional needs, one can expect good results to occur in school. Note these important emotional needs:

1. *Unconditional love.* A child can depend on the parent for continued support and approval.

2. *Consistency and predictability.* Inconsistency can be unsettling to a child of any age. Unpredictable behavior can lead to confusion about acceptable and unacceptable behavior.

3. *Congeniality.* Children need the freedom to laugh, to be happy, and to be relaxed; such freedom can help them adjust to the pressures and demands placed on them in (and out of) school.

4. *Approval.* Giving recognition for personal achievements sets the stage for a sense of pride and accomplishment. A sense of accomplishment and approval can foster a strong self-esteem.

5. *Accountability.* The development of character comes when children are given godly guidance and required to accomplish goals, such as school achievement, that honor the Lord.

6. *An example of excellence.* Young people observe and copy the lifestyles set before them. The influence of attitude and behavior lie squarely on the shoulders of adults who set the example. Parents and teachers who exhibit negativism, perfectionism, indifference, or cynicism tend to generate the same attitudes in children.

Parental Pressure. The third family pattern contributing to achievement problems is seen in parents who are overprotective, perfectionistic, domineering, and over-directing. (See chapter 16, "Overprotective Parents.") The constant expectation for children to do better and better without ever giving attention to their achievements and capabilities does great harm. If a child is pressured to perform above the level of his or her ability, feelings of inadequacy, loss of hope, and pessimism emerge.

Parental Uninvolvement. The fourth family interaction style harmful to developing achievement motives in students is the uninvolved parent. (See chapter 17, "Inattentive Parents.") Some such parents may be interested in and concerned for a child's academic success but may be unable or unwilling to take the necessary steps to stimulate achievement. A clear sense of vision, confidence building, and directive leadership is necessary to build the right type of achievement motives in young students.

The Effects of Underachievement and Overachievement

◆ Poor Grades, Limited Options

Underachievement in school carries many effects, some of which seem obvious. A teen who is performing poorly in school will receive poor grades, and his or her options for college acceptance, college scholarships, choice of vocation, jobs, and future income will be sorely limited.

◆ Loss of Confidence, Self-Esteem

The emotional and psychological effects, which go beyond such obvious consequences, may in the long run be even more severe. A young man or woman who does poorly in school may lose all confidence in his or her ability to achieve (a condition that has been called "student alienation"). He or she is likely to struggle with feelings of worthlessness (see chapter 6, "Unhealthy Self-Esteem"), meaninglessness, and powerlessness. He or she is likely to suffer social estrangement.

◆ Social Problems

The widespread decline in academic achievement in recent decades has also generated serious social problems. A cycle of nonachievement is often created in families and communities that leads to unemployment (or underemployment), poverty, and other problems. Unfulfilled potential in young people translates to a loss of effectiveness and competitiveness in many ministries, industries, and businesses.

◆ Other Problems

For the overachiever, a chronic obsession with being perfect in school can lead to exhaustion and eventually to ineffectiveness. The emotional compulsions and insecurities that sometimes lead to overachievement can also cause alienation from others and can plague a young man or woman's relationships for the rest of his or her life.

The Biblical Perspective of Underachievement and Overachievement

The Word of God speaks about spiritual gifts in Romans 12:6–8, but what is true of spiritual gifts is also true of intellectual gifts:

> We have different gifts, according to the grace given us. If a man's gift is prophesying, let him use it in proportion to his faith. If it is serving, let him serve; if it is teaching, let him teach; if it is encouraging, let him encourage; if it is contributing to the needs of others, let him give generously; if it is leadership, let him govern diligently; if it is showing mercy, let him do it cheerfully.

Not everyone possesses an aptitude in math. Not everyone can excel in music or science. Not everyone can get an A in English literature or even a B.

But God does desire for each of His children to use the gifts (spiritual and intellectual) He has given them. If it is performing mathematical calculations, let them do that. If it is writing poetry, let them do that. If it is memorizing or conceptualizing or reading or singing, let them do that. And let them do it as well as they are able:

> Study to shew thyself approved unto God, a workman that needeth not to be ashamed, rightly dividing the word of truth.[3]

However, it must also be stressed that "the Lord does not look at the things man looks at. Man looks at the outward appearance, but the Lord looks at the heart."[4] God gives different intellectual gifts and aptitudes to each of us, but neither those gifts nor our use of them is a reflection of our value and worth in His eyes.

The underachiever is called to accept and use all God's gifts—intellectual as well as spiritual, physical, and emotional. The overachiever is called to remember that God's love—and the individual's worth—are unconditional; he or she cannot earn it nor lose it.

The Response to the Problem of Underachievement/Overachievement

Listen ◆ Empathize ◆ Affirm ◆ Direct ◆ Enlist ◆ Refer

Many resources are available to the young person who is drifting in a sea of academic expectation and confusion. School may seem too difficult or boring to a young person—and it may be true—but that is no excuse for laziness, apathy, indifference, or carelessness. Despite the problems in learning or in attitude, help is available.

LISTEN. Since underachievers are in part maladaptive to working independently in school and employ any number of defense mechanisms, the concerned adult must afford the student an opportunity to express whatever dislike or frustration exists toward school. Does he or she exhibit hostility? Immaturity? Anxiety? The use of open-ended questions ("Why do you think you feel that way?") and either/or questions ("Do you feel more afraid or angry?") can help the youth express his or her feelings.

Listen with an open heart. Hear the pains and key into the hurts that, although they may be signs of immaturity, are significant to the young person. Parents must be encouraged to rethink their patterns of communication. Keep conflict and the level of objection to a minimum.

EMPATHIZE. It is so easy for adults to miss the real point as they listen to a teen's complaints about school. Many concerned adults listen in order to talk; it is much more helpful to listen in order to understand. A caring parent, teacher, or other adult will certainly want to help the teen with his or her problem, but empathy must come first. Pray for compassion and for the ability to respond to the youth's problems empathetically; then trust the Spirit to lead you moment by moment.

AFFIRM. Parents of achievers give praise, show approval, demonstrate interest, and show understanding to their kids. They give children a sense of belonging and identification. Accountability, respect, and encouragement are woven into the fabric of a young student's academic life.

Another important step in responding to achievement problems is affirming the individual student's aptitudes and capabilities. Once the student has verbalized his or her hurt and a caring adult has empathized with those feelings and affirmed the teen and his or her capabilities, the student can begin to realize the possibility of achievement. The first three steps are critical and may take some time, but unless they are accomplished first, the next phases cannot be accomplished.

DIRECT. The first step in directing young people to achieve in school is to develop the proper attitudes and motives for study. There must be the desire for wanting to do well in school and the belief that he or she can succeed. One must form a positive attitude and self-discipline in order to attain full benefit from one's education. Any resentment, unresolved frustration, or poor attitude will cancel out any attempts to do well in school.

1.Take the time and effort to assess what the student is capable of doing. Compare this to his or her current level of achievement.

2. Define the academic problem in terms of a goal. Take one goal at a time and explain what the student can expect to do and *how* the student can expect to accomplish this goal. Tutoring and the development of study skills can be applied to the specifically defined problem areas.

3. Acquaint the student with other people who are enthusiastic, interested, and excited about school achievements. Disinterested students are (for the most part) unhappy, bored, and uninvolved. When parents, teachers, and other concerned adults acquaint the child with wholesome and exciting influences, the student is more apt to excel.

4. Follow through with patience, loving firmness, and support when the child makes mistakes. Give praise and approval when he or she succeeds.

The disinterested child who experiences genuine success in school finds it easier to comply and move up the ladder of academic achievement.

5. *Once the student has established good habits in school, be alert for the next time he or she succeeds on his or her own.* Seize the opportunity to reinforce this success.

6. *Focus on developing learning behaviors.* Use charts and checklists to identify productive learning behaviors.

7. *Aid the development of good study habits.* The next step in directing a young person to work up to his or her ability is to closely examine the study habits and skills employed by the student. There are time-proven techniques to actually shorten the study time while improving the quality. Educators tell us that the *quality* of studying is more important than the *quantity* of study time. Everyone wants a shortcut, especially students who are active. One can actually study less if certain organizational strategies and study skills are used. The following principles, faithfully implemented and diligently observed, are likely to bring measurable improvement:

- Study in a location free from distractions, interruptions, and noise (no radio, CD players, television, etc.).

- A clean desk, adequate lighting, and good posture are important. Clear your desk of distractions like pictures, toys, mementos, and clutter.

- Make studying a joy, not a chore! Be positive in your approach. Begin your study session in prayer that God will use this time for the betterment of your mind.

- Personalize and apply what you are learning as much as you can to your life.

- Do your hardest and most difficult assignments first. Easier work should be done last, when you are more tired.

- Allow yourself rest periods, or breaks. Study for thirty minutes, then take a five-minute break. Return to your work promptly after five minutes.

- Realize that the most difficult part of studying is *getting started*. Do not wait for inspiration. Start it NOW and you will be inspired by the progress you make as you study.

- Study as rapidly as is comfortable to you. Do not go too slowly; be active in your study and apply yourself. Be sure of your work, then keep going!

- Observe the general rules of good health so that you are physically able to study. Get eight hours of sleep, eat well, exercise daily, and keep spiritually in tune with God.

- Look at school as a preparation for a good life. Each assignment is a step closer to success.

- Be organized. Listen in class; take good notes. Concentrate and plan ahead.

- Study with a questioning mind. Always ask: WHO, WHAT, WHEN, WHERE, WHY, and HOW?

- Take pride in your schoolwork for, while it does not reflect on your worth as a human being or child of God, schoolwork done well does exhibit admirable qualities.

- The key to learning is repetition, review, and reinforcement.

- Even if you do not understand, make an effort.

- Be aware of what the teacher is trying to accomplish. Demonstrate to your teacher that learning is going on. Show your teacher that you are progressing.

ENLIST. There is a necessity for working intensively both with parents and teachers if the patterns of nonachievement or overachievement are to be corrected; most importantly, however, improvement cannot be effected without the participation of the youth himself (or herself). Dr. Foster Cline and Jim Fay say, "Teenagers must be taught to view their own success or failure in school as belonging directly to them. Many children have problems in school out of conscious or unconscious rebellion, thinking that if they fail, their parents—not they themselves—will suffer."[5] The teen himself (or herself) must be enlisted in the determination and plan to change his or her school performance.

REFER. It is imperative to refer a student with achievement problems to a qualified professional such as a guidance counselor or Christian psychologist. Any number of tests to assess mental ability, cognitive ability, achievement grade levels, study attitudes, and other problem areas are available. The information supplied by these psycho-educational test batteries are valuable in forming an individualized learning plan. School guidance counselors possess a wealth of information on seminars, references, and literature to assist the parent and student in improving study skills. Tutoring is advisable when achievement grade levels fall below the student's grade placement.

Additional programs to improve reading skills and develop a stronger memory are also advised if the student will agree to participate.

For Further Reading

The following resources may help the concerned parent, pastor, teacher, or youth worker assist a student with achievement problems:

Scriptures Cited in This Chapter

- Romans 12:6–8
- Timothy 2:15
- Samuel 16:7

Other Scripture to Read

- Proverbs 1:7, 22; 3:13; 8:10; 17:16; 24:5
- Philippians 1:9–11
- 1 Timothy 4:12–14
- Titus 3:14
- James 1:5

Further Reading

- Verne Becker, *The Campus Life Guide to Surviving High School* (Zondervan).
- Dan Korem, *Streetwise Parents, Foolproof Kids* (NavPress). Contains a helpful chapter on public school trends.

PHYSICAL

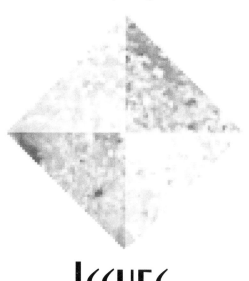

ISSUES

46

LIVING WITH A DEFORMITY OR DISABILITY

Introduction

Stacy Brennan has had twenty operations. And she's not done yet.

She was eight years old when she began to complain to her parents about her jaw hurting. A visit to the family doctor revealed that the pain was caused by a tumor. Stacy was diagnosed with Ewing's sarcoma, a rare and often fatal form of cancer.

The family followed their doctor's recommendations and scheduled an operation to remove the tumor. That first operation disfigured Stacy's face and the years of chemotherapy and radiation treatments resulted in the temporary loss of all her hair. Stacy felt hideous.

Stacy dreaded the painful chemotherapy treatments she had to endure five days a week, but she considered them preferable to the treatment she received at school. Her third- and fourth-grade classmates called her names. One boy seemed to delight in pronouncing her "the ugliest girl in the world." She became a loner, isolated from the other kids her age. Even her parents, overwhelmed by their daughter's sickness, became distant from her and from each other; they divorced when she was thirteen.

At the age of fifteen, Stacy began a series of bone and tissue grafts intended to correct her facial deformity. She entertained high hopes for each operation, praying that she would emerge whole, with a face that people could look at without cringing or laughing. The first series of grafts were unsuccessful, however; with each one, Stacy's bitterness and hopelessness only increased.

Today, after twenty operations, Stacy's face is still misshaped. The right side of her smile droops, and her lower lip is only slightly thicker than a pencil line. But Stacy, who teaches music at a state university, is no longer bitter.

"It took a long time," she says, "but I'm learning to find happiness in other things—things that don't depend on being picture perfect. I know I'll never be a model, I guess, but I'm learning to like what I am." [1]

The Problem of Living with a Deformity or Disability

Millions of people around the world suffer some form of deformity or disability that affects their appearance and/or severely limits their abilities to manage their daily activities. Many such deformities and disabilities are related to birth defects, disease, accidents, and other injuries. Visible disabilities may take the form of blindness, deafness, facial disfigurement, immobility, and paralysis, among many others. Disabilities that are not as visible include developmental disabilities, learning disabilities, and diseases (such as diabetes or arthritis).

An estimated 200,000 teens in Canada[2] and well over that number in the U.S.[3] suffer some form of disability. Teens with deformities or disabilities—even seemingly "minor" forms—often face titanic struggles in addition to the already-difficult tasks and adjustments of adolescence. The impact of a deformity or disability can be critically heightened by the passions and pressures of the teen years. David Veerman writes:

> During adolescence the emotions are focused on identity. This is the "self-search" time of life, when teens are trying to discover "who I am" and "where I fit in." These are years of doubts and "moments of truth." Consider the girl who heard dozens of relatives remind her of how pretty she was—but now in high school, a less than average complexion has rendered her "plain." Or the boy, pushed into football to meet the needs of a frustrated father—he's fine until his pituitary refuses to cooperate. While everyone else adds height, weight, and muscle, Johnny becomes one of the little guys, a "has-been" at fifteen.[4]

If acne or small stature wreaks such havoc in the mind and heart of a teen—and it does—then a serious deformity or disability is likely to cause extreme difficulties, foster acute inferiority, and create serious problems.

The Causes of Not Coping with a Deformity or Disability

While the physical or medical cause of a young person's deformity or disability may be obvious—cancer, perhaps, or spina bifida, for example—the challenges and problems posed by the youth's condition are exacerbated by four key factors:

◆ Societal Pressures

Modern society places a premium on physical fitness and beauty and devalues those who don't fit the "Hollywood mold" of perfect teeth, perfect hair, perfect physique, and perfect coordination. Society encourages abortion of babies who are likely to be born with a defect, endorses (at least tacitly) the assisted suicide of elderly people who have outlived their usefulness to society, and in a myriad of other ways conveys contempt for those who don't "measure up." Author Les John Christie writes:

> Think of the stories we teach our children: "The Ugly Duckling" (but what about kids who remain ugly ducklings?), "Sleeping Beauty," "Snow White," "Cinderella." All have beautiful girls. Or how about "Rudolph the Red-Nosed Reindeer," or "Dumbo the Elephant"? They both had physical problems and had to prove their value to society by doing something spectacular to make up for their deformities. Kids get the message loud and clear from age four.[5]

◆ Adolescent Search for Identity

Teens are obsessed with appearance and ability because the adolescent mind (and some people never outgrow this, even in adulthood) equates "what I look like" and "what I can do" with "who I am." Consequently, the teen years often comprise an unending, often internal, competition to establish a sense of identity. Like his or her peers, the youth who is coping with a deformity or disability tends to measure himself or herself against others and then uses the results of that comparison to form a "working hypothesis" of his or her identity. Unfortunately, the teen's disability often clouds his or her true identity to such a degree that the answer to the question "Who am I?" often comes out sounding like, "I am a cripple," or "I am weird," or "I am ugly."

◆ Unrealistic Expectations

Well-intentioned adults often place unrealistic expectations on individuals with a disability. Parents may be struggling almost as much as the child to cope with their son or daughter's condition. They may grow impatient with prolonged treatments, or they may be unconvinced by their teen's cries of pain or frustration. They may urge the young person to "try harder." They may admonish him or her not to "let it get you down." They may be embittered by the evaporation of the hopes and dreams they had for their child. Such reactions and expectations make it even more difficult for the teen to cope with a deformity or disability.

◆ Reactions of Peers

Veerman writes, "The problem is exacerbated by peers. They are struggling, too, with egos 'on the line,' and the competition becomes brutal. Peer approval means so much, but kids can be so cruel."[6] The teen with a deformity or disability will often be the victim of peer persecution and ridicule, silent rejection and exclusion, well-meaning condescension, and thinly-masked pity—all of which are severely damaging.

The Effects of Not Coping with a Deformity or Disability

Dr. James Dobson suggests that "Beauty, intelligence, and money are the three attributes valued most highly in our society. And when [young people] first discover that they are lacking in one (or all three) of these characteristics, they begin sliding downward in despair."[7]

The young man or woman who is coping with a deformity or disability *may not truly be lacking in any of those areas.* However, the four factors mentioned above may produce a sense in the young person that he or she is lacking in beauty and perhaps also in intelligence. This perceived lack—whether or not it is grounded in fact—will affect three primary areas:

◆ Self-Identity

Tom Perski, writing in the helpful book *Parents and Teenagers*, says, "One of the most difficult 'growth' combinations is trying to form one's identity while having a physical handicap. Answering 'Who am I?' is an important task for the young person throughout adolescence and well into his twenties."[8] The teen may associate his identity solely in terms of his deformity or disability: "I am ugly," or "I am stupid." Or he may try to deny the disability in formulating his or her identity: "I could run just as fast as Tony if I wanted to," or "I could look like Cindy if I wore as much makeup as she does." The healthy approach, of course, is neither to deny nor to focus on the disability, but to accept it *and* acknowledge its irrelevance to "who I am."

◆ Self-Esteem

Christian counselor and author Jay Kesler says, "All young people have to face a certain amount of teasing and ridicule."[9] Some may face such self-esteem-shattering abuse for something they have some control over, such as failing a class or booting a ground ball in a baseball game. Teens with deformities and disabilities, however, face mistreatment as a result of something they cannot control. "Ridicule," Kesler states, "is usually aimed at producing conformity."[10]

But a disabled person cannot conform; consequently, he or she is likely to strongly take to heart the criticism or ridicule and interpret it as a reflection of his or her worth as an individual. (See also chapter 6, "Unhealthy Self-Esteem.")

◆ Mental and Emotional Outlook

The pressures stated above will often have a deleterious effect on the mental and emotional outlook of the young person who is struggling with a disability or deformity. He or she may respond with anger, viewing much of life and his or her relationships with others through a lens of resentment, ready to take offense at the first sign of criticism or rejection. On the other hand, he or she may react with despair, withdrawing from relationships, nursing depression and giving up all hope of a "normal" life. Some youth may actually alternate between these reactions, though it is more common for one to predominate.

The Biblical Perspective of Deformity or Disability

God does not cause deformities or disabilities. He does not afflict babies with spina bifida. He does not smite nine-year-old girls with Ewing's sarcoma. He does not torment teenage boys with juvenile-onset diabetes. But neither does He promise that any of us will escape such things. He does not promise that germs will not invade our bodies, that tornadoes will not assail our homes, that we can expect to escape injury, calamity, deformity, or disability.

The Word of God makes it clear that Christians and non-Christians, men and women, children and adults, good people and bad people alike suffer the effects of a fallen world. "Time and chance happen to [us] all," wrote Solomon[11]; we all suffer the ravages of time and the hazards of chance.

That realization, of course, seldom makes it any easier—particularly for a teen—to endure a deformity or disability. But God's Word is also explicit about what God considers most important. First Samuel 16:7 records the Lord's words to Samuel:

Do not consider his appearance or his height. . . . The Lord does not look at the things man looks at. Man looks at the outward appearance, but the Lord looks at the heart.

This does not suggest that God considers the pain of a person coping with a deformity or disability to be unimportant. On the contrary, He is "a compassionate and gracious God . . . abounding in love and faithfulness."[12] He does, however, consider what's *inside* a person to be far more important than a person's appearance or physical ability.

God looks at the heart. He is impressed by a heart of love. He is stirred by a responsive spirit. He looks for traits like self-control, joy, peace, patience, kindness, goodness, faithfulness, and gentleness.[13] He knows—as Christians should—that, "Our days on earth are like a shadow,"[14] that our bodies are mere "jars of clay," and that the real treasure is *inside*.[15] And that, of course, is *who we are*—the treasure God sees on the inside, not the earthen vessel people see on the outside.

The Response to the Problem of Living with a Deformity or Disability

Listen ◆ Empathize ◆ Affirm ◆ Direct ◆ Enlist ◆ Refer

The young person who is trying to cope with a deformity or disability will not be helped with platitudes or pat answers. He or she faces a situation with which few adults could effectively cope. However, a sensitive and patient parent, pastor, youth leader, or teacher may be able to help by prayerfully and carefully pursuing the following plan:

LISTEN. A young person with a disability or deformity may object to an adult's efforts to help or understand. "You don't know how I feel!" he may say. And he's right. No one can know how he feels. For that reason, the best place to start (and end) with a disabled young person is to encourage honest expression of his or her thoughts and feelings (perhaps with such open questions as "What's that like?" "How does that make you feel?" and so on). Don't give advice in an effort to help; listen in an effort to understand.

EMPATHIZE. Veerman advises, "Feel their hurt. It's easy to dismiss their situation [and offer easy solutions], but the pain is real."[16] Put yourself in the young person's place and try to see things through his or her eyes. God calls Christians to "Rejoice with those who rejoice; mourn with those who mourn;"[17] simply sharing sorrow and sensitively offering comfort are among the simplest and most effective ways to minister to someone with a disability or handicap. In addition, be sensitive to practical ways to communicate your empathy, such as:

- Removing hindrances (sitting or kneeling beside a person in a wheelchair, for example, or learning simple sign language for a hearing-impaired person).

- Nodding your head.

- Making eye contact.

- Leaning forward in your chair.

- Speaking in soothing tone.

- Quiet prompting.

- Reflecting key statements or gestures.

- Waiting patiently through tears or silence.

AFFIRM. Donald Mardock emphasizes that teens . . .

must know that they are unique. That helps them to stop comparing their beauty, athletic ability, intelligence, and personality with that of others. . . . We must [also] help each young person realize that he is accepted as he is. He doesn't have to imitate another person to have value. We must acknowledge teens as persons with unique abilities and talents. No two are alike, and God had each person in mind when He knit him together in his mother's womb (see Ps. 139:13, NIV). . . . [Finally,] we must appreciate them for what they are and for what they do. How often we criticize our kids when we think they could do better, but yet forget to tell them that we appreciate what they do well.[18]

DIRECT. A caring pastor, parent, teacher, or other adult can guide a young person who is trying to cope with a physical deformity or disability in the following ways:

1. Partner with the parents. A teen or preteen's parents are the most critical component of success in helping a youth with a physical deformity or disability. If you are not the young person's parent, be sure that you consult with them and involve them as much as possible in responding to the youth's struggles, keeping in mind that parents of such youth are often exhausted and in need of compassion and understanding themselves.

2. Encourage dependence on God. If the youth is not a Christian, turn him or her to the God who promises health and wholeness of the most important kind (spiritual) through Christ. Help the youth develop and maintain daily fellowship with God in order to rely on His strength, learn from His Word, and find solace in prayer. Teach the youth to use the Psalms as a prayer book, praying aloud the words of such Psalms as 31, 41, 42, 61, 62, and 71, to name a few. Propose a prayer partnership in which the youth and the caring adult pray for (and with) each other.

3. Emphasize God's total acceptance and love. Veerman suggests, "To most teenagers, God is a concept, and that's tough to love or to care about. But God is a Person who created, accepts and loves them, and wants the very best for their lives. Jesus, God in the flesh, was the epitome of unconditional love. He touched lepers, prostitutes, and other outcasts. Quiet and loving reminders of these realities (not preaching) will bring understanding and healing to our young people."[19]

4. *Encourage the cultivation of deeper qualities.* Help the young person recognize and cultivate the deeper qualities. Facilitate the development of traits such as kindness, communication, honesty, and discipline, and affirm those qualities in their lives whenever and however they are displayed.

5. *Steer the young person into areas of affirmation.* There are many fulfilling and affirming pursuits that might be accessible to a disabled youth. Veerman suggests identifying creative alternatives: "Most high schools," he says, "provide a smorgasbord of extracurricular activities, many of which provide excellent training for the future (for example, debate, publications, music, and drama). Hobbies such as collecting and [fishing] can help, and youth clubs like Campus Life, Young Life, and Campus Crusade for Christ as well as the church youth group will offer acceptance by peers *and* caring adults."[20]

ENLIST. Dr. Foster Cline and author Jim Fay advocate letting teens "own their own problems, their own feelings, their own disappointments, their own rewards. . . . It's the teen's responsibility to own the problem and find a solution."[21] Do not simply advise the teen; as early as possible, prompt recognition of the need for him or her to become the agent in working out a strategy that will bring improvement.

REFER. The problems and challenges of disability are sometimes extensive and consequently are best addressed with the help of a trained professional. A professional Christian counselor should be involved as early as possible (with parental permission and involvement), and assistance from state and local agencies should be sought. In addition, the following resources may be helpful:

The Clearinghouse on Disability Information Program
U.S. Dept. Of Information
Room 3132
Mary Switzer Building
Washington, DC 20202-2524
202-732-1723, 202-732-1241

The National Rehabilitation Information Center (NRIC)
8455 Colesville Road
Suite 935
Silver Spring, MD 20910
800-346-2742

For Further Reading

The following resources may help the concerned parent, pastor, teacher, or youth worker to assist a student with a deformity or disability:

Scriptures Cited in This Chapter

- Ecclesiastes 9:11
- 1 Samuel 16:7
- Psalm 86:15
- Galatians 5:22
- 1 Chronicles 29:15
- 2 Corinthians 4:7
- Romans 12:15
- Psalm 139:13
- Psalms 31, 41, 42, 61, 62, 71

Other Scripture to Read

- Psalms 16, 18, 40, 57, 86, 88, 91, 102, 116, 121, 139, 142
- Ecclesiastes 3:1–11; 4:9–12
- Lamentations 3:22–33
- Isaiah 53:4–6

Further Reading

- Dr. James Dobson, *When God Doesn't Make Sense* (Tyndale House).

- Jay Kesler with Ronald A. Beers, *Parents and Teenagers* (Victor). Contains several helpful chapters on this subject.

- Josh McDowell and Bill Jones, *The Teenage Q&A Book* (Word). Contains a helpful section on self-image.

47

COPING WITH LONG-TERM ILLNESS

Introduction

Susan was a beautiful girl with eyes that talked and a smile that elicited genuine warmth. She seemed, at seventeen, to have it all. She came from a loving family with a strong Christian heritage. She was an honor student, played the French horn in the school band, and was voted most popular by her peers.

Susan's senior year in high school went perfectly. Everything seemed to be going her way. She finished high school, took a job for the summer, and began to prepare for her long-awaited desire, attending college.

The Christian college she chose also saw her as a jewel, and, because of her academic achievement and character, she received a full-tuition grant. Susan was now on her way to a promising major and a career in the field of elementary education. As August rolled around, Susan headed off to college with high expectations.

Susan's college success picked up where her high school career left off. She was the professors' favorite and was feeling more confident each day. Each day, that is, until November 12. November 12 was a day Susan will never forget.

That morning, she awoke with a "tingly" feeling in her feet. She shrugged it off at first, but the sensation persisted as the day progressed. Susan began to be concerned and called her folks for advice. They advised her to see a physician, and after enduring a battery of tests, Susan discovered that she had lupus.

Lupus is a progressive disease. This crippling infirmity can be rapid in its attack on the body though it can go into periods of remission. When lupus attacked Susan, it not only affected her ability to walk, it also created havoc on her facial skin. To make matters worse, the medical treatment caused some severe swelling.

Susan's exciting dreams were brought to a skidding halt; she was forced to drop out of school (at least for a while). She was unable to walk without a cane. Susan became dejected and depressed, and her difficult situation produced relational tensions with friends and family members.

Susan and her family recognized their need to make some changes. Wisely, they did not wait too long. They consulted a Christian counselor, and though the disease still haunts her, Susan and her family are learning to adjust to the reality of a long-term illness.

The Problem of Coping with a Long-Term Illness

The onset of a long-term illness dashes the hopes, dreams, and illusions of many teenagers. Contracting such a condition can present a daunting challenge to a teen, whether it is occasioned by biological or environmental factors.

The teen years comprise a time when most individuals struggle mightily simply to maneuver the apple cart of adolescence—acne, hormonal changes, awakening interests, and formulation of a healthy self-image and self-identity; this is a time of change and challenge; the "'self-search' time of life, when teens are trying to discover 'who I am' and 'where I fit in'. . . . years of doubts and 'moments of truth.'"[1] The addition of a long-term illness to that volatile mix can turn the whole apple cart upside down—and a surprising number of youth have had to endure such an upsetting, sometimes traumatic, experience, as Table 47 indicates:

The problems listed in Table 47 do not exhaust the long-term illnesses that afflict many youth, of course, but the list does provide statistical insight into the prevalence of some physical illnesses and difficulties.

The Effects of a Long-Term Illness

A constellation of problems is likely to appear when a young person is confronted with the prospect of a long-term illness such as lupus or diabetes, for example. The obvious effects are physical, of course, but it is estimated that in over half the cases seen in a counseling setting, the physical problem itself is not the major cause of stress in the patient's life; quite often a crisis not only creates new problems, it also exposes old ones.

◆ Physical Effects

The physical consequences of a long-term illness often reach beyond the obvious physical effects that are intrinsic to the illness or condition itself. Hartman-Stein and Reuter, for example, point out that "the disfigurement of her insulin shot sites" may prompt a teenage girl with diabetes to feel less attractive than her peers.[3]

Diabetes also places a pregnant woman and her unborn baby at risk for various anomalies and abnormalities. Each of the physical conditions in Table 47 bears physical implications beyond the symptoms of the condition itself.

Table 47. Chronic Conditions Among Youth Under 18[2]
(Prevalence rate of existing cases per 1,000 population)

Arthritis	15.0	Heart Disease	18.9
Chronic Sinusitis	56.7	Hearing Impairment	21.0
Dermatitis	31.0	Orthopedic Impairment	28.8
Diabetes	0.6	Ulcer	1.6

From: *Health Care Book of Lists*, 1993.

◆ Psychological Effects

Perhaps the most predictable response following a crisis is *a period of numbness*. And if the event has been preceded by a difficult period of waiting or uncertainty, there is often a paradoxical sense of relief when reality replaces anxiety. Doctors have discovered that during a time of extreme crisis, the human body often produces a drug similar to Valium. A person under the influence of what one woman described as "God's emotional Novocain" may smile bravely and hold up well. Friends may comment that "she's doing so well emotionally" and go back to their normal routine as much as possible. Later, reality sets in, and the person spirals downward emotionally, spiritually, and/or physically.

The loss of one's health invariably occasions a degree of *grief.* Each person handles the five stages of grief (denial, anger, bargaining, depression, and guilt) differently and on a different timetable, but each stage is necessary to eventual emotional health and wholeness. (See chapter 8, "Grief.") Because the early grieving process is usually marked by extremes, friends and relatives should keep in mind that finding a balance may take awhile and therefore not take behavior during this time too seriously.

Another common effect of a long-term illness is seen in *strained relationships.* The confidence or insecurity of the individual and his or her friends and family, as well as prior communication patterns and the impact of past conditioning and experiences, are common causes of discord. Choosing to cope with problems through denial is a common survival mechanism that can also create new problems and disrupt relationships. If family members deny what is going on or deny the hurt of what is happening, the relationships will be strained.

When individuals refuse to acknowledge the impact of significant events on their lives, communication becomes superficial and phony.

Denying the problem will only create misunderstanding and distance in relationships.

A *tendency to relational extremes* is also a frequent effect of the period of adjustment to a long-term illness or condition. The young person may exhibit a tendency to withdraw and isolate himself or herself from others; some, however, tend to become overly dependent on others during this period, so the need exists to establish a social routine that adds stability—for example, church every Sunday, lunch with a friend on Tuesday, etc.

Like Susan, most people tend to be extremely sensitive to real or perceived slights as they adjust to their situation. Susan recalled that in the days following her coming home from college, the greatest stress came from well-meaning friends, acquaintances, and relatives. "They gave me their genuine condolences," she said. "But in the majority of cases, they added, 'are you ever going to drive again?' or 'I hope you will still date,' or 'What are you going to do now that college is not an option?' I needed their love and understanding; instead, their remarks lowered my self-esteem and made me feel inferior. I now recognize that at the time of bereavement, any sensitive issue becomes more sensitive than ever—and learning to drive was the subject where I felt most vulnerable."

Finally, another common effect following a significant medical hardship is a *vulnerable sense of identity and self-esteem.* (See chapter 6, "Unhealthy Self-Esteem.") A person under pressure becomes increasingly sensitive to the perceptions and judgments of others. This can be a time of shifting identity. The individual may begin to act out a drama that can last for years, using roles picked up quickly in crisis. Those with a strong established social network before the crisis are less susceptible to the problem. For example, if we as children were loved for our achievements and our performance rather than unconditionally accepted, we may feel anxiety, self-doubt, or even worthlessness when our achievements or performance are threatened. The problem then becomes one of perceived loss of identity or selfhood, not just the external loss of health, a college degree, or a job.

◆ Financial Effects

Millions of Americans have no health insurance. Even those who do often find that certain conditions and contingencies are not covered. As a result, many families must cope not only with a difficult diagnosis but also with financial hardship caused by the condition. Financial strain can prompt considerable emotional stress and relational difficulties as well.

◆ Theological Effects

Very often the onset of diabetes, arthritis, or other physical conditions will prompt a young person to question God, His love, His judgment, even His existence. A young man or woman who is struggling to cope with what will be an enduring difficulty may very naturally wonder why God has "chosen" to let such a thing happen to him or her. Some youth will go beyond questioning and actively rebel against God. A few may remain in rebellion, but many will, after a period of questioning, resolve their questions and—even if they don't know the answers—trust God, who *does* know the answers.

Tension and struggle are natural, even healthy, results of the onset of a long-term illness. The young person can expect to have good and bad times; recovery from the shock of a disheartening diagnosis generally consists of gradual progress interspersed with temporary setbacks.

The Biblical Perspective of Coping with a Long-Term Illness

Individuals who have never encountered tragedy on a personal level usually have a gen-

eral faith in good fortune, a carefree lack of anxiety based on the unspoken assumption that "it will never happen to me." When a crisis, like a long-term illness, does occur, something momentous happens to such a person.

Several years ago Elizabeth Berg was diagnosed with immune system cancer. In an article entitled "Moments of Ease," she wrote:

> You look at photographs of yourself from before, aching. It is as though the essence of you has moved away, leaving behind a fragile shell that waits in vain to be what it used to be. You think you'll never be careless again, and that you'll never laugh all the way, or lean back in your chair sighing and smiling, eyes closed, arms loose at your sides, full of some naive sort of confidence you didn't know you had until you lost it.[4]

Even mature Christians can subtly confuse that breezy, "naive sort of confidence" with faith. When they can no longer accept that everything is going to work out right, they think they have lost their faith in God. Some people confuse God with life; when they become disappointed with life, they become disappointed with God too. When life is not good, they conclude that God is not good.

Although we may feel vulnerable and badly shaken when our sense of security is lost, the loss of our false confidence need not interrupt our relationship with God. God never gave a lifetime guarantee of good health. On the contrary, no less an authority than Job said, "Man born of woman is of few days and full of trouble."[5]

While anyone afflicted with a long-term illness or condition may understandably cry, with the psalmist, "Relent, O Lord! How long will it be?"[6] And though our God is "an ever-present help in trouble"[7] and the God "who comforts us in all our troubles,"[8] a mature faith has to rest on a deeper level of loving God for who He is and not just for what He does or does not do in this particular moment to ease our pain.

Critical illness strips away the veneer of perception that falsely concludes we are in control of our lives. It uncovers our complete dependence upon the Creator of life. During that fragile time of sorting through emotions and working through our questions about God's involvement, God is present (whether His presence is felt or not), and His grace is sufficient,[9] for:

The LORD is good to those whose hope
    is in him, to the one who
      seeks him . . .
It is good for a man to bear the yoke
    while he is young.

Let him sit alone in silence,
    for the Lord has laid it on him.
Let him bury his face in the dust—
    there may yet be hope.
Let him offer his cheek to one who would
      strike him,
    and let him be filled with disgrace.

For men are not cast off
    by the Lord for ever.
Though he brings grief, he will show
      compassion,
    so great is his unfailing love.
For he does not willingly bring affliction
    or grief to the children of men.[10]

The Response to the Problem of Coping with a Long-Term Illness

Listen ◆ Empathize ◆ Affirm ◆ Direct ◆ Enlist ◆ Refer

A teen who is diagnosed with an illness or condition that promises to last a long time—perhaps his or her whole lifetime—is forced to cope with a situation that would prove daunting for most adults. However, a sensitive and patient parent, pastor, youth leader, or teacher may be able to help by prayerfully and carefully pursuing the following plan:

LISTEN. A primary need of anyone who is trying to cope with a disheartening diagnosis is for a listening ear. The young person will probably react to advice or expressions of comfort with "You don't know how I feel!" (which is true; no one can know how he or she feels). The teen will not be helped—at least initially—by knowing what you think; he will be helped, however, if you are simply willing to hear how he or she feels.

EMPATHIZE. David Veerman advises people who work with youth to "feel their hurt."[11] Let yourself see things through the eyes of youth and through the eyes of this youth. Don't be in a hurry to advise; be patient and empathize with him or her. Also be sensitive to ways you can communicate your empathy and understanding, such as:

- Removing obstacles to the conversation (coming out from behind a desk, for example, or kneeling beside the youth's wheelchair).

- Leaning forward in your chair.

- Making eye contact.

- Nodding your head, saying "yes," "go on," etc.

- Reflecting the young person's statements ("So you're saying . . ." "That made you feel . . ." etc.).

- Waiting patiently through silence, anger, or tears.

AFFIRM. A young person in pain is unlikely to be convinced (at least at first) by oral expressions of affirmation; instead, until he or she is able to accept your affirmation ("Your friendship is a gift of God to me," "I thank God for you"), let the youth see your affirmation. Show how highly you prize and esteem him or her; let the teen feel your regard by treating him respectfully, like an adult, as someone who is lovable and capable.

DIRECT. To "win" in a seemingly "no-win" situation, Susan chose to deal with her illness in a "pro-active" manner. "I suggest to those who are going through a major illness not to continue to fantasize about the 'good ol' days,'" she says. Learning to live with an ongoing illness requires realism spiced with hope. A parent, pastor, teacher, or youth worker can offer helpful direction such as the following:

1. Help the youth understand that he or she is not responsible for the illness or condition. Many people assume the blame for their condition, reasoning (consciously or subconsciously) that this has happened to them because they deserve it. Gently but firmly challenge any such notions and help the youth understand and adopt a biblical perspective of his or her illness or condition.

2. Turn the youth to God as the source of peace and comfort. Help the young person cry out to God, who is a father to the fatherless,[12] a defender of the helpless,[13] a Comforter in sorrow.[14]

3. Walk with the young person through the stages of grief and other emotions and reactions. Loss needs to be grieved, and the loss of time, health, and wholeness that is often felt as a result of a long-term illness or condition is no different; a caring adult can help a young person through the stages of grief (denial, anger, bargaining, depression, and acceptance) by helping him or her confront, express, and resolve such feelings and accepting them with understanding and comfort. (See also chapter 8, "Grief.")

4. Foster a daily partnership of prayer for and with the young person. Encourage the youth to develop and maintain daily fellowship with God in order to rely on His strength and experience His help. (See Isa. 41:10.)

5. Expose the youth to the available resources for coping with the trauma. Help him or her acknowledge (preferably by name) those people who are or may be willing to help in practical ways: an understanding parent, a close friend, hotlines, organizations, pen pals, etc.

6. Assist the youth in careful planning—including a revision of plans, if necessary. Susan eventually managed to return to college, though she had to commute from home and could only handle two courses at a time. Help the young person decide (a) what prior plans and goals can still be pursued, (b) which plans and goals must be revised or postponed, and (c) what new plans and goals should be formulated to help him or her cope with the situation *and* to persevere through it.

7. Foster realistic hope. Help the youth to understand that it is probably unrealistic to expect to get back to "the way things used to be"; instead, strive to foster the realization that the goal is not total recovery or perfection, but progress.

8. Steer the young person toward service. Susan said that when she assisted others in need, the "sting" of her long-term illness seemed to fade. Help the youth realize that God "comforts us in all our troubles, so that we can comfort those in any trouble with the comfort we ourselves have received from God."[15] Allow plenty of time, of course, to allow emotions to stabilize; unlike television drama, real-life crises are seldom resolved in thirty minutes.

ENLIST. Do not simply advise the teen; strive to get him or her (as early as possible) to "own" the process of recovery, to "take charge" of the plan. One effective way of doing this is to encourage the young person to keep a spiritual journal. According to Susan, doing so helped her "tie the whole recovery process together." Here are other suggestions you might make to the youth:

1. Begin writing down major stressors in your life; problem areas, personal goals, emotional struggles, etc.

2. Every day read short portions of Scripture

for fifteen to twenty minutes specifically for the purpose of finding at least one "golden nugget" that will provide insight to at least one of the major stressors you've identified.

3. Record the date of the reading, verse reference, and/or insight in the journal (placing them in the proper categories of your concerns).

4. Before retiring for the night, list all the pluses and minuses of that day. Make sure the pluses outweigh the minuses two-to-one! (Susan had to force herself to do this at first because she felt that so much of her life was negative.) Then, beside the minuses write an antidote for each ("If it were to happen again, how should I respond?").

5. At least once each week, review those golden nuggets and antidotes.

REFER. The teen's doctor and hospital should be able to provide resources (such as support groups, local agencies, and national organizations) that can provide further help. In addition, a professional Christian counselor should be involved as early as possible, with the permission and participation of the youth's parents.

For Further Reading

The following resources may help the concerned parent, pastor, teacher, or youth worker assist a student with a long-term illness:

Scriptures Cited in This Chapter

- Job 14:1
- Psalm 90:13
- Psalm 46:1
- 2 Corinthians 1:4, 12:9
- Lamentations 3:25–26, 28–33
- Psalm 68:5
- Proverbs 23:10, 11
- Jeremiah 8:18
- Isaiah 41:10

Other Scripture to Read

- Psalms 16, 18, 31, 40, 41, 42, 57, 61, 62, 71, 86, 88, 91, 102, 116, 121, 139, 142
- Psalm 145:17–18
- Isaiah 53:4–6
- Ecclesiastes 3:1–11; 4:9–12
- Lamentations 3:22–33

Further Reading

- Dr. James Dobson, *When God Doesn't Make Sense* (Tyndale House).
- Jay Kesler with Ronald A. Beers, *Parents and Teenagers* (Victor). Contains several helpful chapters on this subject.
- Josh McDowell and Bill Jones, *The Teenage Q&A Book* (Word). Contains a helpful section on self-image.

VOCATIONAL

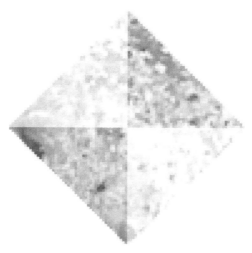

ISSUES

48

KNOWING GOD'S WILL

Introduction

The rest of the church youth group had cleared out of the local McDonald's where they had all stopped for shakes and sodas after their Sunday night meeting. But Brenda and Marty stayed behind, facing each other across a table.

Marty slurped the last little bit of his shake and sighed. "Thanks for sticking around," he said to Brenda. "I really need to talk to somebody."

Brenda said nothing but leaned forward to indicate she was ready to listen. She and Marty had been friends since sixth grade; they were both high school seniors now.

"It's this college thing," he said, wrinkling his brow and setting his plastic cup down on the table. "I have no idea what to do. I mean, this decision is going to affect the rest of my life, you know? I guess it's good to have scholarship offers from so many schools, but it makes it so confusing. How am I supposed to know whether I should go to Duke or Georgetown or one of the others? I mean, I've prayed and prayed about it, but I have no idea what God wants me to do. I've even asked him for a sign, but . . ." His voice trailed away as a uniformed teenager started mopping the floor around them.

"I know exactly what you mean," Brenda answered. "You know Jim has asked me to marry him, and I love him and everything, but how am I supposed to know if he's the one God wants me to marry?"

Marty nodded. They exchanged doleful looks.

"So," Brenda said, slowly. "What are you going to do?"

"I don't know," Marty answered. "I don't know."

The Problem of Discerning God's Will

"How do I know God's will?" That is one of the four or five questions most frequently asked of Christian leaders, particularly those who work with teenagers and young adults.

A lot of young people have sincere, serious questions about God's will. The subject presents no small struggle for many youth. They talk about it, they worry about it—even lose sleep over it.

This is largely because the years of adolescence and young adulthood are the period during which most people face the three greatest decisions of life: "their salvation decision, their marriage decision, and their life's work decision—master, mate, and mission."[1] It is easy for adults to forget or dismiss the pressure and urgency many kids feel on this subject; it is real, however, and must be addressed as early and as thoroughly as possible.

The Causes of Not Discerning God's Will

Many young people do not even realize that God has a will for their lives. Adrian Rogers writes:

> The starting place for teenagers who want to find God's will is the parents, not the teenagers themselves. . . . It's highly important for parents to teach their children that God does indeed have a will for everyone's life. Many young people go through life without this awareness.[2]

Yet the Bible says, in Psalm 32:8:

> I will instruct you and teach you in the way you should go;
> I will counsel you and watch over you.

Some Christian kids may be aware that God does have a will for their lives, but they're at a loss as to how or where to discern His will. Many of them will say, "I don't think I've ever known the counsel of God. I go through day after day without the counsel of God." Yet God's will—His counsel—is available. But it is often missed, ignored, or misunderstood as a result of several faulty attitudes people have concerning God's will. These attitudes may be stated differently, but they are often expressed as follows:

God's will is "lost" and I have to find it. Rogers writes:

> Finding God's will is not like going on an Easter egg hunt, with God hiding it somewhere and you trying to discover it. It is not our job to find God's will. It is God's job to reveal it, and our job to be receptive and ready.[3]

I don't really want to know God's will because I'm afraid of it. Some people, in their heart of hearts, are afraid of God's will. They're afraid that He may demand something they can't give or send them somewhere they can't go. But Romans 8:32 speaks volumes about God's attitude toward His children:

> He who did not spare his own Son, but gave him up for us all—how will he not also, along with him, graciously give us all things?

God does not play games with our lives. He does not want us to submit to His will so He can take good things away from us and make us miserable; He wants to graciously *give* us all things that will fulfill our deepest desires.

I want to do part of God's will and ignore the rest. The young person who possesses this attitude will probably never know God's will—until he or she desires to do the *whole* will of God. Such an approach is like driving a car by simultaneously stepping on the gas pedal and applying the brake—one moment saying, "Lord, show me Your will," and the next moment saying, "I don't want to do that part of Your will." The person who is not doing that which he or she knows to be God's will *right now* should not expect Him to reveal more of His will.

I want to know God's will so I can decide whether or not I want to do it. Seeking God's will is not like shopping for a new car; a person can't "test-drive" God's will and then decide if he or she wants to "buy" it. If that's taking place in a young person's life, he or she will never know God's will—until the person begins to truly desire *God's* will instead of his or her own.

I am willing to do God's will whatever it is. The appropriate attitude toward God's will—and the only one that will be rewarded—is to be willing to accept God's will even before it's known. It is the attitude the psalmist expressed when he said, "I desire to do your will, O my God; your law is within my heart." Otherwise, why should God bother to reveal His will? Why should God give His counsel if it's going to be disregarded or discarded?

The Biblical Perspective of God's Will

God's will can be divided into two distinct categories: His universal will, which applies to everyone, and His specific will, which applies to an individual. Most people seem earnestly concerned with the latter and more or less indifferent about the former. But the two, while distinct, are intricately intertwined.

◆ God's Universal Will

God's universal will is clear and indisputable because it is spelled out in God's Word. For example, it is God's will that His children pray. First Thessalonians 5:17 says, "Pray without ceasing." God wants us to develop a constant, consistent attitude of prayer and fellowship with Him. Jesus' words in John 13:34–35 likewise point out something that all of us know is God's universal will:

A new command I give you: Love one another. As I have loved you, so you must love one another. By this all men will know that you are my disciples, if you love one another.

Another area of God's universal will is spending time in the Bible. Second Timothy 3:16–17 makes it clear that reading and studying God's Word is His will for every believer.

Most people don't realize that the main portion of God's will is already revealed. We don't even have to pray about it or seek it. The main points of God's universal will—salvation, submission, obedience to parents, sharing the faith, sexual purity, and being filled with the spirit—are explicitly stated in God's Word.

Salvation. The first aspect of God's revealed will is for all men and women to be saved, to trust Christ as Savior and Lord. First Timothy 2:3 states:

This is good, and pleases God our Savior, who wants all men to be saved and to come to a knowledge of the truth.

Submission. God's will for every nonbeliever who becomes a believer is commitment, the submitting of one's life, one's future, one's will to Christ. That's the next step in the revealed will of God for everyone. Romans 12:1–2 reads:

Therefore, I urge you, brothers, in view of God's mercy, to offer your bodies as living sacrifices, holy and pleasing to God—this is your spiritual act of worship. Do not conform any longer to the pattern of this world, but be transformed by the renewing of your mind. Then you will be able to test and approve what God's will is—his good, pleasing and perfect will.

Obedience to Parents. God's will for every believer is that he or she live in obedience to his or her parents. The reason for that is that God sometimes reveals His will to a person through the counsel or example of his or her parents. If that person is not obedient to his or her parents, then that relationship can't act as a channel of God's will. Ephesians 6:1 says:

> Children, obey your parents in the Lord, for this is right.

Sharing the Faith. It is the universal will of God for Christians to share their faith with others. The Christian young person need never pray, "Should I witness to my friend?" or "Should I share my faith with this person?" God's will is already revealed in that area—for all believers. It is His will that we share our faith with *all* nations—not just with those across the ocean but also with those across the hall and those across the lunch table as well. Matthew 28:19–20 states:

> Therefore go and make disciples of all nations, baptizing them in the name of the Father and of the Son and of the Holy Spirit, and teaching them to obey everything I have commanded you. And surely I am with you always, to the very end of the age.

Sexual Purity. A Christian young person need not seek God's will about his or her sexual involvement with a boyfriend or girlfriend; that has already been revealed in His Word. His will is for His children to be sexually pure, not sexually immoral. First Thessalonians 4:3 asserts:

> It is God's will that you should be sanctified: that you should avoid sexual immorality.

Be Filled with the Spirit. God's will is for His people to be filled with the Holy Spirit. The Holy Spirit enters every believer's life at the moment of salvation. The believer does not need to seek "more" of the Holy Spirit; the Holy Spirit seeks to control more of the believer. God desires to *permeate* the Christian, to control every part, every corner of his or her life through the Holy Spirit, which is already in him or her. It is

God's universal will for the Christian young person to be filled with the Spirit. Ephesians 5:17–18 reveals:

> Therefore do not be foolish, but understand what the Lord's will is. Do not get drunk on wine, which leads to debauchery. Instead, be filled with the Spirit.

◆ God's Specific Will

Of course, most young people are anxious about knowing God's will *for them.* They want to know:

- Who God wants them to date,
- Who God wants them to marry,
- What school God wants them to attend,
- What major God wants them to declare,
- What classes God wants them to take,
- Where God wants them to go for summer recess,
- What career God wants them to choose . . .

and God's perspective on a hundred other seemingly important and urgent decisions they face.

It's important, first, to understand that God most often reveals His will a day at a time. Many people want to know God's will for the distant future. "What is Your will," they may pray, "for next month, next year, *for my life?*" But God seldom works that way.

In John 16:12, Jesus told His disciples:

> I have much more to say to you, more than you can now bear.

Few of us could bear to know God's will for the next fifteen years; it might very well overwhelm us. But God mercifully times the "much more" of His will for a time when we can bear it and reveals His will to us a day at a time, a step at a time.

It is also important to understand that God's specific will is *contingent* upon His universal will. The young woman who is not obeying God's universal will is wasting her time praying for God to choose a boyfriend or husband for her. The young man who is not obeying God's universal will is wasting his time wondering whether God wants him to go to Daytona or Myrtle Beach for spring break. If a young person is ignoring God's will that is common to everyone, why should God get more particular with that person?

However, the young person who *is* responding obediently to God's universal will—the young man or woman who desires God's will regarding salvation, submission, obedience to parents, sharing the faith, sexual purity, and life in the spirit—can then begin to seek God's will that relates specifically to him or her. This can be done most effectively through a four-step process:

1. Scripture. A knowledge of the Scriptures is foundational in seeking and discerning God's will. It is not necessary, for example, for a young Christian to wonder whether God wishes her to marry a non-Christian; God's Word is clear on that matter. (See 2 Cor. 6:14–15; see also chapter 11, "Dating.") God will never prompt a young man or woman to do something that is contrary to His Word.

2. Prayer. In Matthew 6:8–10, Jesus instructed His disciples:

Do not be like [pagans], for your Father knows what you need before you ask him. This, then, is how you should pray:

"Our Father in heaven, hallowed be your name, your kingdom come, your will be done on earth as it is in heaven. . . ."

Jesus sought the will of the Father through prayer. Likewise, the seeking Christian can seek to discern—and conform to—God's will through prayer, as He did (Matt. 26:39).

3. Counsel. Another step in discerning God's will is seeking spiritual counsel from mature believers. Counsel helps the believer in a couple

ways: it helps to prevent a purely emotional decision (offering an objective viewpoint), and it helps to overcome a lack of experience (offering a mature viewpoint).

4. Circumstance. God often directs through external circumstances. In Romans 1:13, Paul wrote:

I do not want you to be unaware, brothers, that I planned many times to come to you (but have been prevented from doing so until now) in order that I might have a harvest among you, just as I have had among the other Gentiles.

God closed doors to Paul; He directed the apostle through circumstances. Of course, caution is in order in evaluating circumstances because they do not always clearly indicate God's will; if the going gets rough in a particular path or pursuit, for example, that doesn't necessarily mean that thing is not God's will. The reverse is true as well; if the going is smooth, that's not necessarily an indication of God's will. Circumstances must be balanced with a knowledge of the Scriptures, with sincere prayer, and with wise counsel.

The young man or woman who is conforming to God's universal will (salvation, submission, obedience to parents, sharing the faith, sexual purity, and life in the spirit) *and* who has sought His specific will by evaluating a particular choice or decision in light of Scripture, prayer, counsel, and circumstance, can then take the next step: *Do what you want to do.*

Psalm 37:4 promises:

Delight yourself in the LORD
and he will give you the desires of
your heart.

When a Christian believer faces a specific decision *and has conformed to God's universal will and sincerely sought His will in light of Scripture, prayer, counsel, and circumstance,* the final step is to do what he or she wants, to follow the desires of his or her heart. The man or woman who is delighting in the Lord and in the will of the Lord will desire what God desires; that person is therefore free to walk by faith, believing that if his or her desire is not God's will, *He* will make that clear.

The Response to the Problem of Discerning God's Will

Listen ◆ Empathize ◆ Affirm ◆ Direct ◆ Enlist ◆ Refer

A youth leader, pastor, parent, or teacher who is called upon to offer counsel to a young man or woman who is seeking God's will may wish to implement the following response:

LISTEN. As always, it will be necessary to listen—really listen—to the young person. Occasionally a young man or woman seeking counsel "about God's will" is merely wanting someone to endorse his conduct or make her choices for her. Let the adolescent or young adult talk, and listen carefully.

EMPATHIZE. Many adults forget how urgent things seemed as a teen; the adults forget how impatient they themselves became to make decisions and how difficult it was to "wait on God" while everyone around them seemed to be getting engaged, getting married, choosing a college, entering the ministry, etc. The wise adult will strive to remember such feelings and let those memories contribute to a spirit of empathy for the young person.

AFFIRM. Resist the temptation to steer a young person toward the ministry or to advise him or her in what you think is best; instead, concentrate on creating an accepting, loving relationship in which the youth can feel comfortable making a decision.

DIRECT. The concerned parent or other adult can offer helpful guidance in four primary ways:

1. Be conformed to the universal will of God. Challenge the young person to conform to God's revealed will regarding salvation, prayer, life in the Spirit, sexual purity, etc.

2. Be informed regarding the specific will of God. Share the perspective of this chapter with the youth. Help him or her submit any prospective decision to the four-step process outlined above (Scripture, prayer, counsel, circumstance).

3. Submit to the revealed will of God, then do what you want. Help the young person cultivate a daily walk of faith, believing that if his or her desire is not God's will, *He* will make that clear.

4. Relieve the pressure. Once a youth has sincerely done the above, he or she should stop worrying; the pressure is off. Bill Bright (founder of Campus Crusade for Christ) advises telling a young person, "You don't really have to figure out what to do with your life. . . . If God is sovereign, if the steps of a good man [or woman] are ordered by the Lord, all you really have to do for the rest of your life is just be sure every day that you are doing what He wants you to do that day. Do not worry about marriage or your profession. Simply say, 'Lord, I want to do what You want.' Then it is up to Him to work in you to will and to do."[4]

ENLIST. Challenge the seeking teen or young adult to apply himself or herself, first, to obey God's universal will, and second, to sincerely seek His specific will in light of Scripture, prayer, counsel, and circumstance. If he or she is not actively enlisted in these endeavors, your counsel is likely to be ineffectual.

REFER. Consider enlisting the aid of a spiritually mature prayer partner who can meet regularly with the young person, corporately seeking God and His will in prayer and holding each other accountable.

For Further Reading

The following resources may help the concerned parent, pastor, teacher, or youth worker to assist a student seeking to know and obey God's will:

Scriptures Cited in This Chapter

- Psalm 32:8
- Romans 8:32
- 1 Thessalonians 5:17
- John 13:34–35
- 2 Timothy 3:16–17
- 1 Timothy 2:3
- Romans 12:1–2
- Ephesians 6:1
- Matthew 28:19–20
- 1 Thessalonians 4:3
- Ephesians 5:17–18
- John 16:12
- 2 Corinthians 6:14–15
- Matthew 6:8–10; 26:39
- Romans 1:13
- Psalm 37:4

Other Scripture to Read

- Psalm 40:8; 143:10
- Hebrews 13:20–21
- 1 John 2:17

Further Reading

- Jay Kesler with Ronald A. Beers, *Parents and Teenagers* (Victor). Contains several helpful chapters on this subject.
- Josh McDowell, *Knowing God's Will* (audiotape) (Tyndale House).
- J. I. Packer, *Knowing God* (InterVarsity). Contains a helpful chapter on this subject.
- Charles R. Swindoll, *Stress Fractures* (Multnomah). Contains a helpful chapter on knowing God's will.

49

CHOOSING A MINISTRY OR CAREER

A Synopsis

❖

Introduction

Dad, listen—"

Denny Matthewson's six-foot-four frame towered over the pay phone in the dim hallway of his college dorm. His eyes scanned the hallway; he was fearful of being overheard.

"Look, Dad, I know you want me to be an optometrist like you, but—"

Denny grimaced as the voice on the other end of the line interrupted him again.

"Yeah, sure, that would be really cool," he said when he had the opportunity to speak again. "Okay, so it would mean a lot to work with you in your practice."

Denny fell silent again. Finally, he said, "No, it's not just my grades, Dad. How many times do I have to tell you that? I'm flunking those classes because they're boring! I don't give a flying leap for that stuff. *That's* what I'm trying to tell you. I don't want to spend my whole life doing a job that bores me."

The metal door to the staircase swung open and three seniors burst through, laughing hysterically. They brushed past Denny, seemingly without noticing him, and disappeared down the hall at the opposite end of the building from Denny's room.

"No, I couldn't hear you, that's all," Denny said after a moment. "What?" He listened. "No, I *don't* know what I want to do with my life. I just know what I *don't* want to do.

"Yes," he sighed into the phone after another moment. His voice took on a dejected tone. "Yes sir." He leaned his back against the wall next to the phone, switching the phone to his other ear. "Yeah, I guess. Okay. Let me talk to Mom."

The Problem of Choosing a Ministry or Career

It starts around the age of four or five. "What do you want to be when you grow up?" Ironically, most kids seem to have a more fixed idea at that age than they do later, when they're eighteen or twenty, on the threshold of a career.

For some youth, career or ministry choices are made in mid- to late adolescence, in the latter years of high school. They enter college or the work force with a firm idea of where they are headed.

Many others, however, graduate from high school and enter college with little or no sense of where they want to go. They may change majors several times in college. They may drift from job to job. Or they may make a hasty choice that leaves them feeling trapped and regretful later on. Dr. Gary Collins writes:

> [Vocational] choices are crucially important, [and] frequently difficult. . . . They are important because career choices largely determine one's income, standard of living, status in the community, general satisfaction with life (it is hard to be happy if one hates one's job), social contacts, emotional well-being, feelings of self-worth and use of time (how we will spend at least one-third of our waking hours as adults). Career choices are frequently difficult because of the many available careers, the staggering array of jobs and the great potential for making mistakes.[1]

The choice of a ministry or career is one of many significant choices that must be faced in the years of adolescence or young adulthood. It is a choice that weighs heavily on many young minds, and one in which mature, godly guidance is warranted.

The Causes of Difficulty in Choosing a Ministry or Career

Many young people attach not only importance to the choice of a career, but an urgency as well. The choice of a career or ministry is already fraught with anxiety and a degree of hopelessness among youth; many fear that "all the good jobs are taken," and that they will have to settle for far less fulfillment and reward than their parents did.

The choice of a career is influenced by several key factors, including family pressures, societal pressures, circumstances, and past performance.

◆ Family Pressures

Though much has changed in recent generations—sons are no longer routinely expected to follow in their fathers' footsteps— outside expectations do still play a large part in the choice of a career. Many young people feel pressured, "at a time when they are immature, idealistic, [and] inexperienced,"[2] to choose a career path as early as possible. Even if they don't insist that a child follow Mom or Dad's footsteps, parents often push for early decisions (mindful, as they are, of such things as scholarship opportunities and competition). While research does show that youth who choose a career path early generally enjoy more success, unreasonable pressure from Mom and Dad can deter thoughtful planning and lead to hasty or ill-advised choices.

◆ Societal Pressures

Dr. James Dobson writes:

> I remember a college senior who came to see me about her plans after graduation. We talked about various job opportunities and the possibility of her going to graduate school. Then she suddenly paused and looked over her shoulder. She leaned

toward me and said, almost in a whisper, "May I be completely honest with you?" I said, "Sure, Debbie . . ."

"Well," she continued in a hushed tone, "I don't want to have a career at all. What I really want is to be a full-time wife and mother."

I said, "Why do you say that like it's some kind of secret? It's your life. . . ."

"Are you kidding?" she said. "If my professors and my classmates at the university knew that's what I wanted, they'd laugh me out of school."[3]

Societal pressures often bear a powerful influence on young people's career choices. Friends may tease a young person who is still vacillating about his or her vocation. High school counselors may stress the importance of an early start. A church or ministry group may apply high-pressure recruiting tactics to persuade a promising youth to enter the ministry.

◆ Circumstances

Some young people choose a college or career path based on circumstances. They may be motivated by familial circumstances; an unhappy or stressful home situation may prompt a young person to choose a path that is readily available, one that offers a quick escape. They may be spurred by financial pressures; early entry into parenthood or a teen marriage may persuade a young person into a choice that offers what seems at the time to be a high pay and benefit level.

◆ Past Performance

A young person who struggled academically through high school is often hesitant to pursue a college education or a challenging career. Poor performance in high school and/or college can limit—or appear to limit—a person's choices. Conversely, a successful high school or college record—involving both academic and nonacademic pursuits—opens doors to a wider array of career options.

While a wise career choice is often predicated on some of the factors described above (which routinely characterize a hasty or ill-advised choice), it is often also influenced by other factors as well, such as personality, interests and abilities, values, and theology.

◆ Personality

An individual's personality is an essential element of his or her career choice. If the youth possesses a highly social personality, for example, he or she may wish to pursue a different vocation than the person who is dominantly analytical or entrepreneurial.

◆ Interests and Abilities

It has become axiomatic that people do best in occupations that are suited to their interests, aptitudes, and abilities. If a young man thinks books and magazines are a boring waste of his time, he will probably not thrive as an editor. If a young woman demonstrates no propensity for math or science, she may want to think twice before entering med school.

◆ Values

Collins writes, "One early study found that three values influence the career choices of college students: helping people, earning money or attaining status, and having opportunity to be creative. Others want to change society, attain maximum independence, find the best working conditions, or have the greatest possible influence for Christ."[4]

◆ Theology

For the Christian young person, a key factor in the choice of a career or ministry should be openness and/or obedience to God's will. (See chapter 48, "Knowing God's Will.") Some will enter a career convinced that God has personally made the choice for them. Others will submit themselves and their choice totally to God and then pursue "the desires of [their] heart[s]."[5] In either case, a sensitivity to God's leading can produce freedom and confidence in the process of choosing a ministry or career.

The Mistakes in Choosing a Ministry or Career

A young man or woman who makes an ill-advised career choice will feel the effects in many ways, but the most significant effects will be shown in five areas: dissatisfaction, instability, emotional difficulties, low self-esteem, and spiritual consequences.

◆ Dissatisfaction

The effects of a poor career choice will be felt, not only in dissatisfaction with the job itself, but in a more general way as well. As Collins says, "People who do not like their work are often unhappy with life in general. When a person is not happy at work, this unhappiness can permeate his or her whole life."[6]

◆ Instability

An individual who begins poorly on a career path is far more likely to change jobs—and careers—frequently. Such instability has come to mark a whole generation of youth entering the work force. Pollster and researcher George Barna states (of the children of baby boomer parents): "[T]hey are expected to change careers (not just employers, mind you, but career paths) up to six times during their working years."[7]

◆ Emotional Difficulties

A man or woman who does not feel fulfilled and rewarded in his or her career or ministry is likely to experience higher levels of stress, frustration, resentment, and regret than the individual who is content with his or her choice of career. Such emotions can create or exacerbate emotional problems.

◆ Low Self-Esteem

An individual who is unfulfilled and frustrated in his or her work is vulnerable to a deteriorating sense of self-worth. Some men or women find it more difficult to excel in a job they do not enjoy, and even those who manage to perform well may be tempted to discount their performance, reasoning that their lack of satisfaction reflects a deficiency in themselves. (See also chapter 6, "Unhealthy Self-Esteem.")

◆ Spiritual Consequences

"The nature of our work and the degree of our success," Collins says, "affects many areas of life and even has an impact on our spiritual development. When we believe that God is leading us in a vocation, we can be more content on the job and better able to handle the complexities of life."[8] Conversely, a sense that one has "blown it" or that God has failed to "come through" can have a deleterious effect. Meredith Long once wrote in *HIS* magazine that he "had been holding a grudge against God" because Long, a man with extensive education, had to work as a salesman in a hardware store.[9] And that resentment, of course, affected his spiritual life.

The Biblical Perspective on Choosing a Ministry or Career

The Bible portrays the world of work and career in many different ways. Adam was a gardener then a farmer. Noah was a shipbuilder, among other things. Joshua was a soldier. David was a shepherd who rose to the highest office in the land. Joseph, Esther, and Daniel made their mark in government. Matthew was a tax collector who entered full-time ministry late in life. Luke was a physician and historian. Paul was a tentmaker and missionary. Work has been a part of God's plan from the beginning. (See Gen. 2:15.)

The Bible offers a clear perspective on the subject:

1. *Work is commanded; laziness is condemned.* Even before the Fall, "the Lord God took the man and put him in the Garden of Eden to work it and take care of it" (Gen. 2:15). The Bible strongly condemns laziness (see Prov. 6:6–11, 13:4, 20:4 and 2 Thess. 3:10–12) but commands and exalts hard work (see Prov. 14:23 and 1 Thess. 4:11).

2. *Honest work is honorable.* Those who work with their hands (Eph. 4:28 and 1 Thess. 4:11) and those who work in the home (Prov. 31:10–31), and those who work in the ministry are commended in Scripture as being worthy of honor (1 Tim. 5:17–18). As Jesus said (and Paul quoted), "The worker deserves his wages" (Luke 10:7 and 1 Tim. 5:18).

3. *Work is not meant to be unremitting.* God "rested from all his work" on the seventh day of Creation, not because He was tired but to ordain the Sabbath. (See Gen. 2:2–3 and Exod. 20:8–11.) God commanded work, but He also ordained rest from work, a biblical pattern that was observed by Jesus and those who followed Him.

4. *Work should employ an individual's gifts and temperaments.* The Bible makes it clear that individuals are given differing gifts (Rom. 12:3–8, 1 Cor. 12:4–31, and Eph. 4:7–13). At its best, work should employ those gifts. Though this is not necessary for work to be honorable and blessed, it is certainly preferable. (See Isa. 55:2.)

5. *A Christian's work should be marked by excellence.* "Whatever you do," the Bible says, "work at it with all your heart, as working for the Lord, not for men" (Col. 3:23). Shoddy workmanship, halfhearted effort, and dishonest practices are clearly unbiblical. (See Eph. 6:5–9, Col. 3:22–25, and 1 Thess. 4:11–12.)

6. *The choice of a vocation can be guided and blessed by God.* God called Isaiah and Jeremiah to be prophets before they were even born. (See Isa. 49:1, 5 and Jer. 1:5.) John the Baptist's work as the forerunner of the Messiah was announced to his father before John was conceived. (See Luke 1:11–24.) Though Saul had trained as a rabbi and later paid the bills by working as a tentmaker, God called him (as an adult) to be the apostle to the Gentiles. (See Acts 9:1–19.) Though the Bible does not clearly say that such is always the case, it is apparent that God does call men and women to specific tasks and vocations. It is also apparent that, whatever an individual's career choice may be, God desires him or her to use it as a means of honoring Him. (See Col. 3:23.)

The Response to the Problem of Choosing a Ministry or Career

Listen ◆ Empathize ◆ Affirm ◆ Direct ◆ Enlist ◆ Refer

The choice of a career or ministry is an intensely personal decision; no one should make that decision for another person. Still, a youth leader, pastor, parent, or teacher can help a young man or woman clarify his or her options and make a wise choice by remembering the following outline:

LISTEN. The first step is to listen to the young person. Personality and vocational tests are largely devoted to getting to know an individual through his or her responses to many questions. Seek to do something similar by asking about his or her desires, interests, abilities, hopes, and dreams, and listen not only to the answers but to the emotions—fear, anxiety, guilt, etc.—being expressed as well.

EMPATHIZE. Strive to see things from the young person's perspective. How would you feel in his or her situation? How did you feel at his or her age? What understanding and compassion can your experience prompt?

Remember, too, that you can communicate empathetic warmth by:

- Listening carefully to verbal and nonverbal communication.

- Nodding your head.

- Making eye contact.

- Leaning forward in your chair to indicate interest and concern.

- Speaking in soothing tones.

- Reflecting key statements ("So what you're saying is . . .") or gestures ("It looks like that makes you pretty mad.").

AFFIRM. Seek to identify—and affirm—the youth's personality, interests, aptitudes, and abilities. David L. McKenna writes, "When we do career counseling, we first ask if students want to work with things, numbers, or people. Usually this interest can be ascertained early. . . . Each of these areas is valuable, so don't force a "numbers" child to work with people. Begin to encourage your teen in the area [in] which he feels comfortable. Praise any evidence of success in that field."[10]

DIRECT. Jon Clemmer advises, "When counseling . . . on issues surrounding career choice, evaluation, and change, try to focus in on the following issues:

- Discussing God's will according to biblical principles. (See chapter 48, "Knowing God's Will.")

- Including personal enjoyment as a criterion.

- Handling inappropriate pressure from [society, family, and others].

- Evaluating past experiences in the job market.

- Soliciting the opinions of close friends and relatives.

- Getting sophisticated *personality* testing done through a reputable Christian counselor.

- Getting sophisticated *vocational* testing done through a reputable counselor.

- Considering any limitations in ability or education.

- Determining whether further training is needed.

- Getting the hard facts regarding the current job market.

- Keeping your walk with Christ strong. (See James 1:6–8.)

- Knowing the principles behind a call to full-time ministry.[11]

ENLIST. "It is not the counselor's job to tell the counselee what to do vocationally," Collins says. "Instead, the counselee must be helped to make and evaluate his own decisions based on the available information. It should not be expected that counseling will reveal the 'one true job' for the counselee. Instead, such counseling will narrow the career opportunities down to a few categories of potentially satisfying kinds of work. Educational opportunities, counselee desires and motivation, job availability, and similar circumstances then determine the type of work that may be chosen."[12]

REFER. As mentioned above, personality and vocational testing and further counseling by a Christian counseling professional may be warranted. The involvement of parents, high school counselors, college counselors and deans, and individuals employed in the young person's areas of interest may prove helpful.

For Further Reading

The following resources may help the concerned parent, pastor, teacher, or youth worker offer counsel in the matter of choosing a career or ministry:

Scriptures Cited in This Chapter

- Psalm 37:4
- Genesis 2:2–3, 15
- Proverbs 6:6–11; 13:4; 14:23; 20:4; 31:10–31
- 2 Thessalonians 3:10–12
- 1 Thessalonians 4:11–12
- Ephesians 4:7–13, 28; 6:5–9
- 1 Timothy 5:17–18
- Luke 1:11–24; 10:7
- Exodus 20:8–11
- Romans 12:3–8
- 1 Corinthians 12:4–31
- Isaiah 49:1, 5; 55:2
- Colossians 3:22–25
- Jeremiah 1:5
- Acts 9:1–19
- James 1:6–8

Further Reading

- Jay Kesler with Ronald A. Beers, *Parents and Teenagers* (Victor). Contains several helpful chapters on this subject.
- Josh McDowell, *Knowing God's Will* (audiotape) (Tyndale House).

50

CHOOSING A COLLEGE

A Synopsis

❖

Introduction

Sandy watched the tall buildings and green lawns of the university campus disappear in the rearview mirror. She was leaving . . . for good. Sandy had begun her freshman year of college with high hopes, determined to excel in all her classes, make a dorm-ful of new friends, and graduate at the top of her class.

Less than three weeks into her first semester, though, Sandy knew she'd made a terrible mistake. It wasn't just that she was homesick, though she was. It was a lot of other things too. She was doing okay in most of her classes—though all but one of the classes she wanted to take were already full when she tried to register—but she hadn't made a single friend on campus. Her roommate, Terri, was into a lot of weird stuff—tarot cards and seances, stuff like that; most nights, Terri didn't even sleep in her own bed . . . which was just fine with Sandy.

Worse still, Sandy was afraid to leave her dorm after dark (her quad was on the south edge of the campus, next to a pretty seedy neighborhood). As a result, Sandy's social life was practically nonexistent, consisting of brief conversations between classes and at the cafeteria.

For a while, she had called her parents every Friday night, but she felt like they got tired of her crying over the phone, begging them to let her come home. They just encouraged her to "stick it out," promising that things would get better if she would just be patient.

That morning, a Sunday, she had made her decision. She had walked seven or eight blocks to a brick church near the campus, hoping to find some Christian fellowship, maybe meet a few other Christian students. She entered the church, sat through the formal worship service, and left—without a single soul greeting her or even meeting her eye.

It took her less than an hour to pack; she'd never really settled in anyway. She loaded her boxes into her car and left without arousing any notice or comment from the other students in her dorm. She didn't look forward to breaking the news to her parents that she was quitting, but the seven-hour drive home would give her a chance to figure out what she would say.

The Problem of Choosing a College

Nearly three million Americans a year choose a college.[1] Approximately two million of those are freshmen entering college for the first time.[2] And statistics indicate that "a distressingly high percentage of incoming college students discover that they picked the wrong school. In a 1987 nationwide poll conducted by the Higher Education Institute at UCLA, nearly one in three students said they would not select their current college if they had the choice to make over again."[3]

In other words, statistically speaking, young men and women preparing for college stand almost a one-in-three chance of being disappointed or disillusioned by their choice. Some of those young people stay in school and learn to live with a regretful choice. Others struggle through four years of a college experience that limits not only their enjoyment but their performance—and future opportunities—as well. Some change schools, usually losing some credits in the transfer process. Still others drop out.

The Causes of Mistakes in Choosing a College

Why do so many teens and young adults make regrettable choices and experience such dismal results in the process of selecting a college? While the possible reasons are myriad, there are a few that seem notable.

◆ Parental Pressure

Parental pressure plays a significant part in some kids' selection of a college. The young man or woman may be persuaded to attend Mom or Dad's alma mater. He or she may be pressured to attend a school primarily because it is close to home or less expensive than others. The young person may be pushed to attend a denomination college or a well-regarded Christian college. Some parents even select the school *for* the child. David Elkind addresses parents of college-bound youth:

> Try to stay on the sidelines while your child makes her choices. . . . You can and should provide guidance, but it is important to resist the urge to dictate which schools are acceptable. . . . You may have to swallow hard and accept some of your child's seemingly irrational reasons for liking or disliking a school. . . . Bear in mind that your child may be in a better position than you to know what she wants to study and where she'll feel most comfortable.[4]

◆ Poor Research

Some high school juniors and seniors select a college based on limited research. Many approach the choice of a school with nonchalance. Some have been known to select a college solely because a parent or older brother attended or because a friend has applied to the same school. "I went to Cornell because my father had gone there, and I never thought much about going anywhere else," says author Janet Spencer.[5] Others base their decision largely on a single factor such as a sports team's winning season or convenience to home.

◆ Slick Salesmanship

An article in *Money* magazine stated the matter bluntly:

> Virtually all schools tend to paint themselves as the full-color ideal . . . while playing down the black-and-white reality—whether it is overcrowded classes, the incidence of date rape, or the lack of student housing. "With declining enrollments, admissions officers are like hotel desk clerks," warns C. Wayne Griffith, head of a computerized college-search service in Natick, Mass. "Their priority is to fill up space."[6]

◆ Limited Resources

Particularly in this era of spiraling tuition and related costs, many students and families are forced to select a school primarily or solely on the basis of its affordability. While cost will certainly be a factor—and a major one, at that, for most families—allowing financial considerations to supersede all others can, in the long run, be a much more expensive route than anticipated (if it results in poor performance, transfer, or dropping out, for example).

Preventing Mistakes in Choosing a College

Young men and women preparing for college need guidance in three primary areas: making application, making a choice, and making ends meet financially.

◆ Making Application

Sometime prior to the beginning of a student's senior year in high school (or, at the latest, early in the fall of that year), he or she should contact a number of schools that interest him or her (the high school library or counselor's office should have college catalogs and reference books, such as *Peterson's Guides*, that list colleges). Requests for applications should be sent or phoned to these colleges (contacting a dozen or more is not excessive).

Application should be made approximately ten to twelve months before the date the student wants to start (for four-year colleges; community colleges and junior colleges often accept applications much closer to the start of the school year, such as in the spring). The student should apply to as many colleges as interest him or her; though application fees can be twenty dollars or more, this is not the time to cut corners. The ideal situation, of course, is for a young man or woman to be accepted by several schools, allowing him or her to compare the advantages of each before making a selection.

Ferne Cherne offers helpful information on improving the chances of acceptance in an article that appeared in *Teen* magazine:

1. Improve your chances for acceptance (and scholarships) early on. Make good grades a priority—your GPA will be your calling card for scholarships.

2. Master the SAT. Sign up to take it (or the ACT) early, so that if at first you don't succeed . . . you can take it again! Taking a prep course beforehand will give you an added advantage.

3. Be well-rounded. Colleges want students who not only earn good grades but are involved. This can mean sports participation, church-related activities, student clubs or part-time work.

4. Get set on the right class course. See your school counselor to be sure you're taking the classes you need.

5. Look into college choices. Check out books available through your counselor, or computer programs (like EUREKA and DISCOVER). Attend college fairs or events where college representatives are present. Find out about admissions requirements, prerequisites, financial aid and ask any questions you may have about each campus.[7]

◆ Making a Choice

The most often cited criteria for choosing a college are location, cost, and reputation. Each of these is extremely important, of course, and will be considered by any thoughtful student, parent, or caring adult. However, there are numerous other important factors to consider:

Faculty. Many schools boast a fine faculty, but a listing of respected names in a college catalog does not necessarily reflect the quality of teaching at a school. Lani Luciano advises, "Ask specifically whether the superstars teach only graduate seminars or lecture in huge amphitheaters. Do the faculty rosters include professors on sabbatical? Those who only conduct research? Some courses may even be run by graduate students."[8]

Course Offerings. A student will want to attend a college that is strong in his or her area of interest, of course: art, for example, or theology. However, a consideration of the curriculum should delve below the surface. Luciano explains: "Lotteries and long waiting lists for sought-after classes are common at even the priciest private schools. And because of budget constraints, not all classes are offered every semester. In some cases, a student could be forced to spend an extra year in school just to take courses required for graduation."[9]

Campus Atmosphere. The atmosphere of the campus should be taken into consideration. This should include not only a safe, attractive, comfortable campus that faculty and students seem to take pride in, but the social environment as well. "All campuses have their particular social ethos," writes R. Judson Carlberg, president of Gordon College. "Some, especially in the secular environment, get a reputation as 'party schools,' where studies are incidental. Others, though having a reputation for academic stimulation, may have residence halls in which life is an ongoing bacchanalia."[10]

Available Housing. "Dorms are the center of college social life," writes Luciano, "and can provide a protective environment for youngsters not quite ready to live on their own. Yet many freshmen face a NO VACANCY sign. While literature from the University of California at Berkeley concedes that there is 'a high demand for on-campus or near-campus housing,' it does not state that nearly one in five entering students will be forced to live elsewhere."[11]

Safety. A recent survey conducted by Towson State University's Center for the Study and Prevention of Campus Violence found that more than a third of the respondents reported being the victims of a theft and/or an assault on campus during their college years.[12] Many schools are extremely reluctant to discuss or reveal the extent of the crime problem on campus, of course, but some states—Pennsylvania was the first—require colleges to compile such statistics and provide them on request.

Intangibles. The hardest things to measure—and anticipate—about a college are the many intangibles that can contribute to (or detract from) a positive learning and growing experience. Seemingly small but surprisingly influential things such as the quality of the cafeteria food, the cleanliness of the locker rooms, the lighting on the campus, and the sense of community among students, staff, and faculty, can only be gauged by a visit to the college. Jessica Aldock wrote in *USA Today*:

> Students today visit an average of 10 colleges [before making a selection]. . . . Janet Spencer, co-author of *Visiting College Campuses* [says], "It's a costly undertaking and it's not for everybody, but getting a feel for campus life can make a difference in deciding whether a particular college is the right match."[13]

Aldock offers nine suggestions for making the most of a college visit:

> Contact the admissions office at least a week before your visit. This is important if you want an interview or to stay overnight in a residence hall.

> —Attend an information session and student-guided tour at each college.

> —Allow plenty of free time to stroll around the campus.

> —Eat a meal in a campus dining hall.

> —Attend at least one class in an academic area of interest.

—If you play a sport, try to arrange a meeting with the coach.

—Pick up recent copies of the student newspaper and alumni magazine.

—Talk to as many students as possible. Ask lots of questions.

—Take notes on your impressions of each college. Take photographs.[14]

Attention to the above—in addition to careful consideration of cost, location, and reputation—can greatly assist a young person in making a wise choice.

◆ Making Ends Meet

Students preparing for college face a seeming mountain of financial need—usually with a molehill of resources to draw from. While a college education is an increasingly steep financial challenge, there are ways to make ends meet. Cherne makes the following recommendations to financially strapped applicants:

If you think you'll need financial aid, check off the boxes on your college applications indicating that you'll be applying for financial aid or scholarships. [In the U.S.,] federal financial aid is available in the form of FAFSA, or the Free Application for Student Aid. Applications are available in December and due between January and March. Some words of wisdom: apply early, and get your parents' help (the application requires their tax and income information). For help in filling out the form, contact the college financial-aid office, or call the Federal Student Aid Information Center at 1-800-433-3243.

Beyond federal aid, you're likely to need more cash. What can you do?

- Most states [in the U.S.] have supplemental programs for low-income students. These programs provide book monies, sometimes transportation funds, and generally another $1,000 per semester or $2,000 per year.

- Colleges often have financial-aid programs targeted for specific groups. There may be programs that you are eligible for. Often, these programs give grants, meaning the money does not have to be paid back. If you check the appropriate boxes on your college application, you will receive information about what's available.

- Find out about scholarships you may be eligible for through your counselor, your college application and scholarship computer programs. Scholarships can be based on grades; your plans to study in a specific field; artistic, musical or athletic talent; financial need; leadership ability; ethnic or cultural background; gender; religious affiliation; state residency; rural residency; or any number of other specific criteria.

- Look into military programs such as the ROTC. You receive assistance with your college expenses with the agreement that you will give a specific amount of military service. Military recruiters and the ROTC office at the college can give you information.

- Find out about work-study and coop programs. With cooperative learning, you work in your field of interest in exchange for college credits. Some schools arrange a program where you attend school for a year or a semester and then work in your related field for a year or a semester.

- Get a part-time job. Try not to work more than 20 hours per week or your grades may take a dive. You must keep your grades at a satisfactory level, usually a 2.00 GPA or your financial aid can be canceled.

- Loans are another option. Students can borrow up to $15,000 for four undergraduate years. Keep in mind that if you borrow several thousand dollars, when you graduate and get a job, loan repayments of $200 or more per month will take a big chunk out of your salary.[15]

Paying for college requires persistence and creativity, but it can be done. A surprising array of financial sources and resources are available for the diligent student.

The Biblical Perspective on Choosing a College

Should a Christian young person attend a Christian college or a secular university? The question incites much controversy within the church. Of course, Moses was schooled in a pagan environment. (See Acts 7:22.) The apostle Paul attended a highly regarded Jewish institution. (See Acts 22:3.) Peter and John were graduates of the first Christian institute of higher learning. (See Acts 4:13.) Still, the Bible offers no specific guidance as to whether a Christian should attend a secular or Christian college; it is probable that no one can answer that question better than the young person (and perhaps his or her parents). A few guidelines can be offered here, however, about the family's resources, the student's goals and personality, and the advantages of the school.

◆ The Family's Resources

As stated above, not all families can support a son or daughter's college education irrespective of considerations surrounding cost or location. Christian colleges are often more expensive and less convenient than federal- and state-supported schools, and that fact will present an impediment to some young people. However, families are often surprised at the affordability of fine Christian institutions once the full range of options and aid are considered.

◆ The Student's Goals

A student who is planning for a career in animation or veterinary science may find few Christian schools offering degrees in his or her field. On the other hand, a Christian who is hoping to pursue biblical studies, archaeology, music, or education can find many quality programs among Christian colleges, and may in fact be hindered (or his faith or principles undermined) by attendance at a secular school.

◆ The Student's Personality

A strong, witnessing Christian may flourish in a secular environment where another Christian might falter. Conversely, a college environment that one young Christian may find stimulating may seem stifling to another. Tim, who attended a Christian college, said his school offered "'a different type of peer pressure'. . . one in which you are encouraged to follow the Lord."[16] Linda, who attended a non-Christian school, said, "'I had fears about falling away from the Lord and getting into the party scene.' But at her secular school, she found an active, though small, group of believers. 'It was strong because of the forces against it,' she says."[17]

◆ The School's Advantages

Some "Christian" schools are little different from many secular universities. Many, however, not only offer a wholesome atmosphere and exceptional academic programs but combine several other advantages as well. R. Judson Carlberg, president of Gordon College in Massachusetts, cites four reasons to choose a Christian college:

1. *Faculty outlook.* Secular higher education today has deeply imbedded assumptions about life and learning; Christianity just isn't in the loop. . . . The president of a major campus ministry put it bluntly in a recent letter to his supporters: "The sad truth is the university in America today is one of the most hostile places in the world to the gospel of Jesus Christ. . . ."

2. *Biblical study and understanding.* . . . [A] biblically guided college holds the historic Christian faith as a valid standard to test ideas and

claims of truth [and] is committed to building community based on Christian principles of love, grace, justice, and peace.

3. Responsible living. . . . [R]esidential life at a Christian college is part of the learning experience. Students living together in an atmosphere free from alcohol and drug abuse learn responsible interpersonal relationships, how to get along in community, and respect for the rights of others.

4. Christian faculty. The kind of faculty students study with is crucial. What teachers believe, the life choices they model, their commitment to students, their ability to communicate in the classroom or in one-on-one discussion, and their personal worldview—all should be vital considerations when choosing a college.[18]

The Response to the Problem of Choosing a College

Listen ◆ Empathize ◆ Affirm ◆ Direct ◆ Enlist ◆ Refer

How might a caring youth leader, pastor, parent, or teacher help a young man or woman to make a wise decision in choosing a college? It will require much prayer and sensitivity to the Holy Spirit, of course, and may also incorporate the following:

LISTEN. Listen carefully to the young person. Probe his or her thoughts about what he or she considers important in a college, what his or her interests and priorities are, what his or her fears are. Listen not only to what the young person says but how he or she says it (consider the emotions and motivations behind the words).

EMPATHIZE. If you have taken time to listen and tried to understand the youth, you will be in a better position to empathize. Strive to see things from the young person's perspective. How would you feel in his or her situation?

How did you feel at his or her age? What factors guided your selection of a college? Let your experience prompt understanding and compassion more than advice.

AFFIRM. A youth whose college choices are limited by poor performance or slight involvement in high school may feel a sense of embarrassment. Similarly, a young person who has been rejected by his or her top college choice(s) will probably feel rejected. Elkind says:

A rejection is a blow to the self-esteem of even the most blasé teenager. It is especially important at this time that she knows that you love and believe in her, no matter where she goes to school. [Parents] may be able to be more understanding if [they] keep in mind that a rejection is not a reflection on [their] success as a parent. And [the youth] can take strength from the truth that, in the end, we are measured not by the schools we attend but, rather, by what we do with the education we receive.[19]

DIRECT. A caring, involved adult can offer guidance to a college-bound youth in ways such as the following:

1. Involve the youth's parents. If you are not the young person's mom or dad, gain the parents' support and input in the process.

2. Pray for and with the youth. Pray for wisdom. (See James 1:5.) Encourage him or her to submit to God and seek His will in the matter. (See also chapter 48, "Knowing God's Will.") Consider forming a prayer partnership with the young person to support him or her through this period of decision.

3. Expose the college-bound youth (and his or her parents) to the content of this chapter in subtle and sensitive ways. Gently guide him or her to grasp and grapple with each of the factors that must be considered before making a decision.

ENLIST. It is crucial not only to enlist the young person's participation in the decision of which college to attend but to ensure that it is indeed his or her decision. Elkind offers a helpful perspective for parents (some of which may also guide other caring adults):

> Once you have set the financial parameters, try to stay on the sidelines while your child makes her choices. Remember, she has been practicing for this through the many decisions she has made during adolescence. . . . By making such a decision for her, you may strike a blow to her emerging sense of autonomy and identity. Instead, try to see her choice in a positive light: It shows she knows what she wants and is willing to take a stand.[20]

REFER. Don't hesitate to take advantage of the many resources that exist to aid a young person's decision. The involvement of parents, high school counselors, college counselors, current students at prospective colleges, alumni, and individuals employed in the young person's areas of interest may prove helpful.

For Further Reading

The following resources may help the concerned parent, pastor, teacher, or youth worker to offer counsel in the matter of choosing a college:

Scriptures Cited in This Chapter

- Acts 4:13; 7:22; 22:3
- James 1:5

Other Scripture

- Psalms 32:8; 37:4; 40:8; 143:10
- Proverbs 1:7, 22; 3:13; 8:10; 17:16; 24:5
- Matthew 6:33
- 2 Timothy 2:15
- Hebrews 13:20, 21

Further Reading

- *Choose a Christian College* (handbook) (Peterson's Guides).
- Dr. James Dobson, *Life on the Edge* (Word). Contains a helpful chapter on "Choosing a College."
- Josh McDowell, *Knowing God's Will* (audiotape), (Tyndale House).

Notes

Introduction

1. These statistics are compiled from figures published by the Children's Defense Fund, from information in the book *13th Generation* by Neil Howe and Bill Strauss, and from a special report, "Struggling to Save Our Kids," in *Fortune* magazine, 10 August 1992.

2. Cited in "Struggling to Save Our Kids," *Fortune*, 10 August 1992, 38.

3. Ibid., 34.

4. This written survey of twenty-three national youth leaders was conducted by the Josh McDowell Ministry in 1993.

5. 2 Cor. 4:6

Laying the Foundation

1. Tim Stafford, "The Therapeutic Revolution," *Christianity Today* 37, no. 6 (17 May 1993): 24.

2. Gary R. Collins, *Christian Counseling: A Comprehensive Guide* (Waco, Tex.: Word, 1980), 16.

3. William Backus, Ph.D., *Telling the Truth to Troubled People* (Minneapolis: Bethany House, 1985), 20.

4. Dr. Henry Cloud, *When Your World Makes No Sense* (Nashville: Oliver Nelson, 1990), 17.

5. Lawrence J. Crabb Jr., *Understanding People: Deep Longings for Relationship* (Grand Rapids, Mich.: Zondervan, 1987), 21.

6. Israel; see Ezra 8:35.

7. Lawrence J. Crabb Jr., *Effective Biblical Counseling* (Grand Rapids, Mich.: Zondervan, 1977), 20–21.

8. John F. MacArthur Jr., "The Psychology Epidemic and Its Cure," *The Master's Seminary Journal* 2, no. 1 (Spring 1991): 7.

9. Jay E. Adams, *Competent to Counsel* (Grand Rapids, Mich.: Baker, 1970), 24–25.

Learning to Offer Christian Counsel

1. 2 Tim. 1:6–8 and 1 Tim. 4:12–14.

2. Acts 15:36-40; Col. 4:10; 2 Tim. 4:11.

3. Esther 4:1–17.

4. Ruth 3:1–18.

5. Deut. 31:1–8.

6. Backus, *Telling the Truth to Troubled People*, 15.

7. Dr. G. Keith Olson, *Counseling Teenagers* (Loveland, Colo.: Group Books, 1984), 3.

8. Ibid., 3, 5.

9. Ibid., 5.

10. Matt. 8:5–13 and Mark 5:30.

11. Mark 1:41 and Luke 8:13.

12. Collins, *Christian Counseling*, 25.

13. Olson, *Counseling Teenagers*, 9.

14. Backus, *Telling the Truth to Troubled People*, 16.

15. Collins, *Christian Counseling*, 25.

16. Crabb, *Effective Biblical Counseling*, 20.

17. Ibid., 22–23.

18. Cloud, *When Your World Makes No Sense*, 17.

19. Collins, *Christian Counseling: A Comprehensive Guide*, rev. ed. (Dallas: Word, 1988), 42–45.

20. Ibid., 48–49.

21. Ibid., 29.

22. 1 Thess. 5:22 KJV.

23. 1 Cor. 10:12; 16:13.

24. Collins, *Christian Counseling*, rev. ed., 28.

25. Gary D. Bennett, "When to Seek Professional Help," in Jay Kesler with Ronald A. Beers, *Parents and Teenagers* (Wheaton, Ill.: Victor Books, 1984), 526.

26. Sandi Black, "Does Your Teen Need Counseling?" *Living with Teenagers*, July 1994, 29.

27. Adapted from Joan Sturkie and Valerie Gibson, *The Peer Counselor's Pocket Book* (San Jose, Calif.: Resource Publications, 1989), 32–33.

28. These suggestions are adapted from "How to Choose a Counselor" (special advertising section), *Christianity Today* 37, no. 6 (17 May 1993): 58.

Chapter 1 ❖ Loneliness

1. Charles Durham, *When You're Feeling Lonely: Finding a Way Out* (Downers Grove, Ill.: InterVarsity Press, 1984), 15.
2. Collins, *Christian Counseling*, 72.
3. Durham, *When You're Feeling Lonely: Finding a Way Out*, 15.
4. "Loneliness Called Britons' Biggest Fear," *Washington Times*, 13 September 1993, A15.
5. Rubin Zick, "Seeking a Cure for Loneliness," *Psychology Today*, October 1979, 82-90, cited in Leslie W. Carter, Paul D. Meier, and Frank B. Minirth, *Why Be Lonely? (A Guide to Meaningful Relationships)* (Grand Rapids: Baker, 1982), 75.
6. Craig W. Ellison, "Loneliness: A Social-Developmental Analysis," *Journal of Psychology and Theology* 6 (1978):3–17, cited in Collins, *Christian Counseling: A Comprehensive Guide*.
7. Cited by James J. Ponzetti in "Loneliness Among College Students," *Family Relations*, no. 39 (July 1990): 337.
8. Collins, *Christian Counseling*, 75.
9. Ponzetti, "Loneliness Among College Students," 337.
10. Carter, Meier, and Minirth, *Why Be Lonely? (A Guide to Meaningful Relationships)*, 50.
11. Paul Tournier, *Escape from Loneliness*, trans. John S. Gilmour (Philadelphia: Westminster Press, 1962).
12. Collins, *Christian Counseling*, 76.
13. Ibid., 75.
14. Ira J. Tanner, *Loneliness—The Fear of Love* (New York: Harper & Row, 1973), 11.
15. Carter, Meier, and Minirth, *Why Be Lonely? (A Guide to Meaningful Relationships)*, 92.
16. Ibid., 98–99.
17. W. A. Sadler, "Cause of Loneliness," *Science Digest* 78 (July 1975): 58–66.
18. Collins, *Christian Counseling*, 73.
19. Richard Wolff, *The Meaning of Loneliness* (Wheaton, Ill.: Key Publishers, 1970), 45.
20. Collins, *Christian Counseling*, 79.
21. Craig W. Ellison, *Loneliness: The Search for Intimacy* (Chappaqua, N.Y.: Christian Herald, 1980), 154.
22. Based on insights from Ellison, *Loneliness: The Search for Intimacy*, 154.

Chapter 2 ❖ Anxiety

1. Gary R. Collins, *Overcoming Anxiety* (Santa Ana, Calif.: Vision House, 1973), 11.
2. Frank B. Minirth and Paul D. Meier, *Happiness Is a Choice* (Grand Rapids, Mich.: Baker, 1978), 168.
3. Psychologist Mary Pipher, quoted in Nicole Carroll, "The Rocky Road to a Girl's Adolescence," *USA Today*, 27 April 1994, 7D.
4. Olson, *Counseling Teenagers*, 331.
5. Minirth and Meier, *Happiness Is a Choice*, 168–9.
6. Collins, *Christian Counseling*, 63–65.
7. Ibid.
8. Ibid.
9. Cecil Osborne, *Release from Fear and Anxiety* (Waco, Tex.: 1976), cited by Collins, *Christian Counseling, A Comprehensive Guide*, 63–65.
10. Collins, *Christian Counseling*, 63–65.
11. Ibid.
12. Ibid.
13. Ibid.
14. Ibid.
15. Ibid.
16. Olson, *Counseling Teenagers*, 331.
17. Collins, *Christian Counseling*, 66.
18. Ibid.
19. Collins, *Overcoming Anxiety*, 11.
20. Olson, *Counseling Teenagers*, 336.
21. Collins, *Christian Counseling*, 60–61.
22. Jay E. Adams, *The Christian Counselor's Manual* (Grand Rapids: Baker, 1973), 414–15.
23. Collins, *Christian Counseling*, 67.
24. Minirth and Meier, *Happiness Is a Choice*, 170.

25. Barry Applewhite, *Feeling Good About Your Feelings* (Wheaton, Ill.: Victor, 1980), 77.

Chapter 3 ❖ Guilt

1. Jane Marks, "We Have a Problem," *Parents* magazine, March 1992, 50.
2. O. Quentin Hyder, *The Christian's Handbook of Psychiatry* (Old Tappan, N.J.: Fleming H. Revell, 1971), cited in Olson, *Counseling Teenagers*, 324.
3. Bruce Narramore, *You're Someone Special* (Grand Rapids: Zondervan, 1978), 144.
4. Collins, *Christian Counseling*, 117.
5. Ibid., 119–122.
6. Ibid.
7. Ibid.
8. Ibid.
9. Dwight Carlson, M.D., *From Guilt to Grace* (Eugene, Oreg.: Harvest House, 1983), 42–43.
10. Narramore, *You're Someone Special*, 145.
11. Collins, *Christian Counseling: A Comprehensive Guide*, 122–123.
12. Narramore, *You're Someone Special*, 145–6.
13. Ibid., 146–7.
14. Ibid.
15. Collins, *Christian Counseling*, 123.
16. Bruce Narramore and Bill Counts, *Freedom from Guilt* (Santa Ana, Calif.: Vision House, 1974), 123.
17. Collins, *Christian Counseling*, 118.
18. Narramore and Counts, *Freedom from Guilt*, 123–25.
19. Collins, *Christian Counseling*, 124.
20. Olson, *Counseling Teenagers*, 329.
21. Collins, *Christian Counseling*, 125.

Chapter 4 ❖ Anger

1. Olson, *Counseling Teenagers*, 313.
2. Collins, *Christian Counseling*, 100.
3. Les Carter, *Good 'n' Angry: How to Handle Your Anger Positively* (Grand Rapids: Baker, 1983), 93–99.
4. Olson, *Counseling Teenagers*, 314.
5. Collins, *Christian Counseling*, 104.
6. Olson, *Counseling Teenagers*, 315–16.
7. Ibid., 315.
8. Collins, *Christian Counseling*, 104.
9. Olson, *Counseling Teenagers*, 317.
10. Collins, *Christian Counseling*, 105.
11. Milton Layden, *Escaping the Hostility Trap* (Englewood Cliffs, N.J.: Prentice-Hall, 1977).
12. Collins, *Christian Counseling*, 106–108.
13. Ibid.
14. Ibid.
15. Ibid.
16. Backus, *Telling the Truth to Troubled People*, 157–58.
17. Olson, *Counseling Teenagers*, 322.
18. Collins, *Christian Counseling*, 108.
19. Heb. 12:15
20. Ross Campbell, M.D., *How to Really Love Your Teenager* (Wheaton, Ill.: Victor, 1987), 71–72.
21. Richard P. Walters, *Anger: Yours and Mine and What to Do About It* (Grand Rapids, Mich.: Zondervan, 1981), 152–55.

Chapter 5 ❖ Depression

1. John W. Maag, Robert B. Rutherford Jr., and Bradford T. Parks, "Secondary School Professionals' Ability to Identify Depression in Adolescents," *Adolescence* 23, no. 89 (Spring 1988): 73.
2. Joan F. Robertson and Ronald L. Simons, "Family Factors, Self-Esteem, and Adolescent Depression," *Journal of Marriage and the Family* 51 (February 1989): 126.
3. Julie Monahan, "True Stories Dealing with Depression," *'Teen* magazine, October 1993, 42. Reprinted courtesy of *'Teen* magazine.
4. *Merriam-Webster's Collegiate Dictionary*, 10th ed. (Springfield, Mass.: Merriam-Webster, 1993).
5. John White, *The Masks of Melancholy* (Downers Grove, Ill.: InterVarsity Press, 1982), 63.
6. Ibid.

7. Campbell, *How to Really Love Your Teenager*, 89–91.

8. Olson, *Counseling Teenagers*, 354.

9. Collins, *Christian Counseling: A Comprehensive Guide Guide*, rev. ed., 107.

10. Tim LaHaye, *How to Win Over Depression* (Grand Rapids: Zondervan, 1974), 52.

11. Collins, *Christian Counseling: A Comprehensive Guide*, 87.

12. Robertson and Simons, "Family Factors, Self-Esteem, and Adolescent Depression," 134.

13. K. Brent Morrow and Gwendolyn T. Sorell, "Factors Affecting Self-esteem, Depression, and Negative Behaviors in Sexually Abused Female Adolescents," *Journal of Marriage and the Family* 51 (August 1989): 683.

14. Collins, *Christian Counseling*, 87.

15. Olson, *Counseling Teenagers*, 353.

16. Cited by Cathie Stivers, "Parent-Adolescent Communication and Its Relationship to Adolescent Depression and Suicide Proneness," *Adolescence* 23, no. 90 (Summer 1988): 292.

17. Minirth and Meier, *Happiness Is a Choice*, 99.

18. Collins, *Christian Counseling*, 89.

19. Minirth and Meier, *Happiness Is a Choice*, 26.

20. Ibid., 24.

21. Campbell, *How to Really Love Your Teenager*, 91–2.

22. Marion F. Ehrenberg, David N. Cox, and Ramond F. Koopman, "The Million Adolescent Personality Inventory Profiles of Depressed Adolescents," *Adolescence* 25, no. 98 (Summer 1990): 416.

23. Collins, *Christian Counseling*, 90.

24. Campbell, *How to Really Love Your Teenager*, 91.

25. Collins, *Christian Counseling*, 90.

26. William Backus and Marie Chapian, *Telling Yourself the Truth* (Minneapolis: Bethany House, 1980), 36.

27. Minirth and Meier, *Happiness Is a Choice*, 20.

28. Matt. 26:37b–38a AMP.

29. Collins, *Christian Counseling*, 86.

30. Ps. 42:5 NASB.

31. Rom. 15:13.

32. Olson, *Counseling Teenagers*, 363.

33. Ibid., 357.

34. Ibid., 361–62.

35. Adapted from David A. Seamands, *Healing for Damaged Emotions* (Wheaton, Ill.: Victor Books, 1981), 128–9.

36. Don Baker and Emery Nester, *Depression: Finding Hope and Meaning in Life's Darkest Shadow* (Portland, Oreg.: Multnomah, 1983), 147–48.

37. Collins, *Christian Counseling*, 91–92.

Chapter 6 ❖ Unhealthy Self-Esteem

1. Dorothy Corkille Briggs, *Your Child's Self-Esteem: The Key to Life* (Garden City, N.Y.: Doubleday, 1970), 154.

2. Suggested in Maurice E. Wagner's *The Sensation of Being Somebody* (Grand Rapids, Mich.: Zondervan, 1975), 31.

3. Wagner, *The Sensation of Being Somebody*, 33–34.

4. Ibid., 34.

5. Ibid., 36.

6. Bruce Bower, "Teenage Turning Point: Does Adolescence Herald the Twilight of Girls' Self-esteem?" *Science News*, 23 March 1991, 184.

7. K. Brent Morrow and Gwendolyn T. Sorell, "Factors Affecting Self-esteem, Depression, and Negative Behaviors in Sexually Abused Female Adolescents," *Journal of Marriage and Family* 51 (August 1989): 683.

8. Mary Beth Marklein, "Sarcasm, Humiliation Wound Kids' Esteem," *USA Today*, 18 December 1990, 10D.

9. Marklein, "Sarcasm, Humiliation Wound Kids' Self-Esteem," 100.

10.. Joan F. Robertson and Ronald L. Simons, "Family Self-Esteem, and Adolescent Depression," *Journal of Marriage and the Family*, 51 (February 1989): 134.

11. Robert S. McGee, *The Search for Significance* (Dallas: Word, 1987), 35.

12. Narramore, *You're Someone Special,* 87.

13. McGee, *The Search for Significance,* 83.

14. The two images depicting poor and healthy self-esteem are reprinted from Josh McDowell, *Building Your Self-Image* (Nashville: Thomas Nelson).

15. "Mired in Misery," *Psychology Today,* July–August 1992, 16.

16. Rollo May, *Man's Search for Himself* (New York: W. W. and Co., 1953), 100.

17. Walter Bauer, *A Greek-English Lexicon of the New Testament,* trans. William F. Arndt and F. Wilbur Gingrich (Chicago: University of Chicago Press, 1957), 874.

18. Eph. 2:10.

19. David Seamands, "Affirm the Present Achievement" in *How to Get Your Teenager to Talk to You,* (Wheaton, Ill.: Victor Books, 1984), 134.

20. Tony Campolo, "Developing High Self-Esteem" in *How to Get Your Teenager to Talk to You,* 137.

21. Ibid.

22. Tim Hansel, "Five Steps to A Healthy Self-Esteem" in *How to Get Your Teenager to Talk to You,* 134.

23. Rom. 8:1.

Chapter 7 ❖ *Facing Death*

1. *Statistical Abstract of the United States,* 1994.

2. Joan Sturkie and Siang-Yang Tan, *Advanced Peer Counseling in Youth Groups* (Grand Rapids, Mich.: Youth Specialties, 1993).

3. Olson, *Counseling Teenagers,* 487.

4. Ibid., 489.

5. Ibid., 490.

6. Mary Beth Moster, *When the Doctor Says It's Cancer* (Wheaton, Ill.: Tyndale, 1979), 27.

7. Olson, *Counseling Teenagers,* 488.

8. 2 Sam. 14:14.

9. Moster, *When the Doctor Says It's Cancer,*

50-53. The passage Moster quotes is from Joseph Bayly, *The View from a Hearse* (Elgin, Ill.: Cook, 1969), 88.

10. Collins, *Christian Counseling,* 420.

11. Olson, *Counseling Teenagers,* 497.

12. Ibid., 497–98.

13. Collins, *Christian Counseling,* 423–24.

Chapter 8 ❖ *Grief*

1. W. A. Miller, *When Going to Pieces Holds You Together* (Minneapolis: Augsburg, 1976), cited in Collins, *Christian Counseling,* 411–12.

2. Sturkie and Tan, *Advanced Peer Counseling in Youth Groups.*

3. Collins, *Christian Counseling:* 414.

4. Sturkie and Tan, *Advanced Peer Counseling in Youth Groups.*

5. V. D. Volkan and D. Josephthal, "The Treatment of Established Pathological Mourners," *Specialized Techniques in Individual Psychotherapy,* eds. T. B. Karasu and L. Bellak (New York: Brunner/Mazel, 1980).

6. Olson, *Counseling Teenagers,* 494.

7. Ibid., 494.

8. Collins, *Christian Counseling,* 415.

9. Olson, *Counseling Teenagers,* 487.

10. Ibid., 489.

11. Ibid., 490.

12. Ibid., 490.

13. Collins, *Christian Counseling,* 412–13.

14. Olson, *Counseling Teenagers,* 486.

15. Eccles. 3:1, 4.

16. Vance Havner, *Though I Walk Through the Valley* (Old Tappan, N.J.: Revell, 1974), 67.

17. Gary D. Bennett, "Dealing with Death" in Kesler, *Parents and Teenagers.*

18. Job 2:13.

19. Olson, *Counseling Teenagers,* 498.

20. Rom. 12:15.

21. 2 Cor. 1:4–5.

22. Olson, *Counseling Teenagers,* 497–98.

23. Ps. 46:1.

24. Olson, *Counseling Teenagers,* 500.

Chapter 9 ❖ *Suicide Thoughts, Tendencies, and Threats*

1. Based on an actual newspaper account of a teenage suicide. Names and details have been changed to protect identities.

2. Jerry Johnston, *Why Suicide?* (Nashville: Oliver Nelson, 1987), 34.

3. David Elkind, "The Facts About Teen Suicide," *Parents* magazine, January 1990, 111.

4. Olson, *Counseling Teenagers*, 369. The reference to "precipitatal homicide" is from Marvin E. Wolfgang, "Suicide by Means of Victim-Precipitated Homicide" in *Suicidal Behavior*, ed. H. L. Resnick (Boston: Little, Brown, 1968).

5. Elkind, "The Facts About Teen Suicide," 111.

6. Bill Blackburn, *What You Should Know about Suicide* (Waco, Tex.: Word, 1982), 31.

7. Marion Duckworth, *Why Teens Are Killing Themselves* (San Bernardino, Calif.: Here's Life Publishers, 1987), 35–36.

8. Blackburn, *What You Should Know about Suicide*, 20–21.

9. Ibid., 23.

10. Olson, *Counseling Teenagers*, 371.

11. Blackburn, *What You Should Know about Suicide*, 22.

12. Ibid., 23.

13. Olson, *Counseling Teenagers*, 371.

14. Ibid., 373.

15. Baker and Nester, *Depression: Finding Hope and Meaning in Life's Darkest Shadow*, 49.

16. Editorial, "Youth Suicide: The Physician's Role in Suicide Prevention," *JAMA* 264, no. 24 (26 December 1990): 3195.

17. Johnson, *Why Suicide?* 36.

18. Blackburn, *What You Should Know about Suicide*, 62.

19. Ps. 73:14.

20. Job 3:3, 11.

21. Judg. 16:29–30.

22. 1 Chron. 10:4–5.

23. 2 Sam. 17:23.

24. 1 Kings 16:18.

25. Matt. 27:5.

26. 1 Sam. 2:6.

27. John 16:33b.

28. Baker and Nester, *Depression: Finding Hope and Meaning in Life's Darkest Shadow*, 180-81.

29. Blackburn, *What You Should Know about Suicide*, 90.

30. Duckworth, *Why Teens Are Killing Themselves*, 147–48.

31. Blackburn, *What You Should Know about Suicide*, 90.

32. Duckworth, *Why Teens Are Killing Themselves*, 77–84.

33. Adams, *The Christian Counselor's Manual*, 45.

34. Duckworth, *Why Teens Are Killing Themselves*, 81.

35. Blackburn, *What You Should Know about Suicide*, 83.

36. Olson, *Counseling Teenagers*, 380.

37. "Before It's Too Late," The American Association of Suicidology, in cooperation with MSD Health Information Services, 8.

Chapter 10 ❖ *Love*

1. Jerry Johnston, *Going All the Way* (Waco, Tex.: Word, 1988), 154-55.

2. Jon Bon Jovi quoted in Anthony Carr, *Liberty Report*, February 1987, 3.

3. Joyce Huggett, *Dating, Sex, and Friendship* (Downers Ill.: InterVarsity, 1985), 68–69.

4. Adapted from Dick Purnell and Jerry Jones, *Beating the Breakup Habit* (San Bernardino, Calif.: Here's Life Publishers, 1984), 76.

5. Matt. 19:19, Mark 12:31, Luke 10:27.

6. Stacy and Paula Rinehart, *Choices: Finding God's Way Dating, Sex, Singleness, and Marriage* (Colorado Springs, Colo.: NavPress, 1982), 139. The quoted passage is from Robert K. Kelley *Courtship, Marriage, and the Family* (New York: Harcourt, Brace, Jovanovich, 1974), 214.

7. Barry St. Clair and Bill Jones, *Love:*

Making It Last (Bernardino, Calif.: Here's Life Publishers, 1988), 110–19.

Chapter 11 ❖ Dating

1. Ann B. Cannon, "The Dating Game: Is Your Teen Ready?" *Living with Teenagers,* July 1994, 11.

2. Barry Wood, *Questions Teenagers Ask about Dating and Sex* (Old Tappan, N.J.: Fleming H. Revell Co., 1981), 33.

3. Gal. 3:28.

4. John 4:1–10.

5. Matt. 15:21–28.

6. Luke 7:1–10.

7. Wood, *Questions Teenagers Ask about Dating and Sex,* 144.

8. Les John Christie, *Dating and Waiting: A Christian View of Love, Sex, and Dating* (Cincinnati: Standard Publishing, 1983), 12–14.

9. Cannon, "The Dating Game: Is Your Teen Ready?" 11.

10. See Doug Fields and Todd Temple's excellent books, *Creative Dating* and *More Creative Dating,* for many helpful date ideas (Thomas Nelson Publishers).

11. Ann Cannon, *Sexuality: God's Gift* (Nashville: Family Touch Press, 1993).

Chapter 12. ❖ Choosing the Right Marriage Partner

1. Tim Stafford, *Worth the Wait: Love, Sex, and Keeping the Dream Alive* (Wheaton, Ill.: Tyndale, 1988), 106.

2. Josh McDowell and Bob Hostetler, *Right From Wrong: What You Need to Know to Help Youth Make Right Choices* (Dallas: Word, 1994), 294.

3. St. Clair and Jones, *Love: Making It Last,* 139–40.

4. Charles R. Swindoll, *Singleness* (Portland, Oreg.: Multnomah, 1981), 13.

5. Stafford, *Worth the Wait: Love, Sex, and Keeping the Dream Alive,* 107.

6. Rinehart and Rinehart, *Choices: Finding God's Way Dating, Sex, Singleness, and Marriage,* 142.

7. Stafford, *Worth the Wait: Love, Sex, and Keeping the Dream Alive,* 111.

8. St. Clair and Jones, *Love: Making It Last,* 141–142.

9. Ibid., 115–21.

Chapter 13 ❖ Coping with Singleness

1. Figures cited in Stephanie Brush, "Still Single at 38," *McCall's,* April 1993, 86.

2. Ibid.

3. Clifford and Joyce Penner, *A Gift for All Ages: A Family Handbook on Sexuality* (Waco, Tex.: Word, 1986), 154.

4. Cited in Carolyn Koons, "The Single Adult Identity," *Singles Ministry Handbook,* ed. Douglas L. Fagerstrom (Wheaton, Ill.: Victor, 1988), 43.

5. Allen Hadidian, *A Single Thought* (Chicago: Moody Press, 1981), 15.

6. Brush, "Still Single at 38," 86.

7. Koons, "The Single Adult Identity," 46–47.

8. Dr. Angela Neal, quoted in Lisa C. Jones, "Single Satisfaction: Unmarrieds Sing Praises of Uninhibited, Unhitched Lifestyle," *Ebony,* November 1994, 164.

9. Don Clarkson, quoted in Jones, "Single Satisfaction: Unmarrieds Sing Praises of Uninhibited, Unhitched Lifestyle," 164.

10. Nel, a Dutch social worker, quoted in Gien Karssen, *Getting the Most Out of Being Single* (Colorado Springs, Colo.: NavPress, 1982), 53.

11. Hadidian, *A Single Thought,* 104.

12. Reginald K. Brown, quoted in Jones, "Single Satisfaction: Unmarrieds Sing Praises of Uninhibited, Unhitched Lifestyle," 164.

13. Rinehart and Rinehart, *Choices: Finding God's Way In Dating, Sex, Singleness, and Marriage,* 122.

14. Penner and Penner, *A Gift for All Ages: A Family Handbook on Sexuality,* 159.

15. Ibid.

16. Ibid., 158.

17. Koons, "The Single Adult Identity," 46.

18. Fred Hartley, *Dare to Date Differently* (Old Tappan, N.J.: Fleming H. Revell, 1988), 98.

19. 1 Cor. 7:25–35.

20. St. Clair and Jones, *Love: Making It Last,* 138-39.

21. Dan Lundblad, "Counseling the Discouraged," *Singles Ministry Handbook,* ed. Douglas L. Fagerstrom (Wheaton, Ill.: Victor, 1988), 145.

22. Dick Purnell, *Becoming a Friend and Lover* (San Bernardino, Calif.: Here's Life Publishers, 1986), 212–13.

23. These four suggestions are drawn from Lundblad, "Counseling the Discouraged," 146-47.

24. Ibid., 146.

Chapter 14 ❖ Handling Peer Pressure

1. See Josh McDowell and Bob Hostetler, *Right From Wrong: What You Need to Know to Help Youth Make Right Choices.*

2. Ibid., 8–9.

3. Narramore, *Adolescence Is Not an Illness* (Tarrytown, N.Y.: Fleming Revell, 1980), 47–48.

4. Sharon Scott, *PPR: Peer Pressure Reversal* (Amherst, Mass.: Human Resource Development Press, 1985), 6.

5. See chapter 17, "Inattentive Parents."

6. Scott, *PPR: Peer Pressure Reversal,* 7.

7. McDowell and Hostetler, *Right From Wrong: What You Need to Know to Help Youth Make Right Choices,* 283–89.

8. Narramore, *Adolescence Is Not an Illness,* 48.

9. Ibid., 48–49.

10. See chapter 6, "Unhealthy Self-Esteem."

11. See chapter 5, "Depression."

12. Scott, *PPR: Peer Pressure Reversal,* 3.

13. Bill Sanders, *Tough Turf: A Teen Survival Manual* (Old Tappan, N.J.: Fleming H. Revell 1986), 89.

14. Heb. 4:15.

15. Dr. James Dobson, *Preparing for Adolescence* (Santa Ana, Calif.: Vision House, 1978), 60–61.

16. Scott, *PPR: Peer Pressure Reversal,* 102.

17. Ps. 46:1.

18. Alison Bell, "Twenty Ways to Fight Peer Pressure," *'Teen* magazine, August 1993, 73. Reprinted courtesy of *'Teen* magazine.

19. See Scott, *PPR: Peer Pressure Reversal.*

Chapter 15 ❖ Contending with Peer Rejection and Persecution

1. Judith Timson, "Adolescent Girls: World-Beaters at 11," *Chatelaine,* April 1994, 58.

2. "Peer Rejection: Of Bullies and the Bullied," *Psychology Today,* January-February 1993.

3. "Children at Risk: I. Risk Factors and Child Symptomatology," *Journal of the American Academy of Child and Adolescent Psychiatry* 29, no. 1 (1990): 51–59.

4. "Risk, Protective Factors, and the Prevalence of Behavioral and Emotional Disorders in Children and Adolescents," *Journal of the American Academy of Child and Adolescent Psychiatry* 28, no. 6 (1989): 918–24.

5. 1 Thess. 5:14.

6. "Alcohol and Drug Use by 3rd, 4th, and 5th Graders in Town of 20,000," *Sociology and Social Research* 76, no. 3 (1992): 156–60.

7. 2 Cor. 5:17.

8. Rom. 12:1–2.

9. See Ps. 46:1.

10. "Risk, Protective Factors, and the Prevalence of Behavioral and Emotional Disorders in Children and Adolescents," 262–68.

Chapter 16 ❖ Overprotective Parents

1. Bernice Berk and Patricia Owen, "Are You an Overprotective Parent?" *Good Housekeeping,* September 1990, 100.

2. Ibid.

3. Ibid.

4. "The Age of Anxiety," *Psychology Today,* Sept-Oct 1994, 18.

5. Ibid.

6. Exod. 20:12.

7. Eph. 6:4.

8. Dick Foth, "The Power of Affirmation," *Moody,* July/August 1995, 54.

9. Suggested in Ronald Hutchcraft, "The Power of a Letter," *How to Get Your Teenager to Talk to You* (Wheaton, Ill.: Victor Books, 1984), 50.

Chapter 17 ❖ Inattentive Parents

1. "Child Abuse: A Trust Betrayed," *USA Today,* 8 April 1994, 8A.

2. Written survey of twenty-three national youth leaders conducted by Josh McDowell Ministry, 1993.

3. *USA Today,* 6 September 1989.

4. 1 Tim. 5:8.

5. Mark 10:14.

6. Exod. 20:12.

7. Eph. 6:4.

8. Foth, "The Power of Affirmation," 53.

9. See Jer. 29:11.

Chapter 18 ❖ Non-Christian Parents

1. Written survey of twenty-three national youth leaders conducted by Josh McDowell Ministry, 1993.

2. 2 Cor. 6:14b-16a.

3. Rinehart and Rinehart, *Choices: Finding God's Way Dating, Sex, Singleness, and Marriage,* 72-73.

4. Matt. 10:37–38.

5. Jim Craddock, "Breaking the Cycle: Responding to Your Parents," in Robert S. McGee/Pat Craddock, *Your Parents and You* (Houston: Rapha Publishing, 1990), 166–67.

6. Luke 2:51.

7. Craddock, "Breaking the Cycle: Responding to Your Parents," 168.

8. Norman Wakefield, *Listening: A Christian's Guide to Relationships* (Waco, Tex.: Word, 1981), 36.

9. Ibid., 37.

10. Craddock, "Breaking the Cycle: Responding to Your Parents," 168–74.

11. Hutchcraft, "The Power of a Letter," 50.

Chapter 19 ❖ Parental Divorce

1. Note that these statistics are not correlated. That is, they only compare the number of marriages in a given year with the number of divorces in that same year. No other relationship between the two figures can be inferred.

2. Anne Clair and H. S. Vigeveno, *No One Gets Divorced Alone* (Ventura, Calif.: Regal, 1987), 75.

3. Neil Kalter in "Young Children of Divorce: Depressed, Wary, Subdued," *USA Today,* September 1987, 10.

4. Elisabeth Kubler-Ross, *On Death and Dying* (New York: Macmillan, 1969).

5. Richard A. Gardner, *The Parents Book about Divorce* (New York: Bantam, 1977), 123.

6. Research in this area indicates that, while Smilanski and Weisman (1981) found children of divorce to be less popular and more "rejected," Allers (1982) and Hetherington, et al. (1979), showed that school-age youth often turn to their friends for emotional and relational support as they adjust to the divorce.

7. Marilyn Elias, "Parents' Divorce Affects Sex Lives of Collegians," *USA Today,* 8 November 1989, 1D.

8. Ibid.

9. Gen. 2:18.

Chapter 20 ❖ Living in a Single-Parent Family

1. Barbara Defoe Whitehead, "Dan Quayle Was Right," *The Atlantic Monthly,* April 1993, 47.

2. Jim Smoke, *Growing Through Divorce* (Irvine, Calif.: Harvest House, 1976), 58.

3. Whitehead, "Dan Quayle Was Right," 62.

4. Ibid., 66.

5. Elias, "Parents' Divorce Affects Sex Lives of Collegians," 1D.

6. Nicholas Zill, quoted in Whitehead, "Dan Quayle Was Right," 66-70.

7. Ronald P. Hutchcraft, "Life As a Single Parent," in Jay Kesler with Ronald A. Beers, *Parents and Teenagers* (Wheaton, Ill.: Victor, 1984), 471.

8. Clyde Colvin Besson, *Picking Up the Pieces* (Milford, Mich.: Mott Media, 1982), 144.

9. Ibid., 142.

10. Hutchcraft, "Life As a Single Parent," 471.

11. Gen. 2:24.

12. Whitehead, "Dan Quayle Was Right," 48.

13. Luke 2:41–52.

14. 2 Tim. 1:5.

15. Exod. 22:22.

16. Deut. 24:19.

17. Isa. 1:17.

18. Zech. 7:10.

19. Whitehead, "Dan Quayle Was Right," 70.

20. Smoke, *Growing Through Divorce*, 66.

Chapter 21 ❖ *Dealing with Stepparents and Blended Families*

1. This case study is reprinted from Gardner, *The Parents Book about Divorce*, 358-59.

2. Myriam Weisang Misrach, "The Wicked Stepmother and Nasty Myths," *Redbook*, July 1993, 88.

3. Connie Schultz, "Separating Fact, Fiction of Blended Family," *Cleveland Plain Dealer* 28 January 1995, 1E.

4. Virginia Rutter, "Lessons from Stepfamilies," *Psychology Today*, May-June 1994, 30.

5. Ibid.

6. Ibid.

7. Joshua Fischman, "Stepdaughter Wars," *Psychology Today*, November 1988, 38.

8. Mavis Hetherington, quoted in Fischman, "Stepdaughter Wars," 38.

9. Fischman, "Stepdaughter Wars," 38.

10. Lynn Smith, "Stepfamilies Still Face Many Woes," *St. Louis Post-Dispatch*, 10 November 1993, 4F.

11. Mavis Hetherington, quoted in Rutter, "Lessons from Stepfamilies," 30.

12. Rutter, "Lessons from Stepfamilies," 30.

13. Leman, *Living in a Step-Family without Getting Stepped On* (Nashville: Thomas Nelson, 1994), 237.

14. Ibid., 238.

15. Harold H. Bloomfield with Robert B. Kory, *Making Peace in Your Stepfamily* (New York: Hyperion, 1993), 26.

16. Leman, *Living in a Step-Family without Getting Stepped On*, 240.

17. James Bray, quoted in Fischman, "Stepdaughter Wars," 38.

18. Ibid.

19. Both findings cited in Whitehead, "Dan Quayle Was Right," 71–72.

20. Whitehead, "Dan Quayle Was Right," 72.

21. Leslie Margolin and John L. Craft, "Child Sexual Caretakers," *Family Relations* 38 (1989): 450–55.

22. Matt. 1:18–25.

23. Exod. 2:1–10.

24. Gen. 2:24.

Chapter 22 ❖ *Sibling Rivalry*

1. Wanda Draper, quoted in "Sibling Rivalry Is Perfectly Normal," *USA Today Magazine*, August 1994, 3.

2. Dr. Annaclare van Dalen, Ph. D., quoted in "Oh Brother (and Sisters!): When Sibling Stress Strikes," *Teen*, April 1994, 40.

3. Van Dalen, quoted in "Oh Brother (and Sisters!): When Sibling Stress Strikes," 40.

4. Van Dalen, quoted in "Oh Brother (and Sisters!): When Sibling Stress Strikes," 40.

5. See Dr. Kevin Leman's *The Birth Order*

Book (Tarrytown, N.Y.: Fleming H. Revell, 1985).

6. Dr. James Dobson, *The Strong-Willed Child* (Wheaton, Ill.: Tyndale, 1978), 128.

7. Ibid., 128–29.

8. Perlmutter, a Certified Social Worker in Mineola, New York, quoted in, "Oh Brother (and Sisters!): When Sibling Stress Strikes," 40.

9. Nancy Samalin and Patricia McCormick, "How to Cure Sibling Fights," *Parents* magazine, May 1993, 146.

10. Dobson, *The Strong-Willed Child*, 133.

11. Quoted in "Sibling Rivalry Is Perfectly Normal," 3.

12. Adele Faber and Elaine Mazlish, "Wouldn't You Like Your Kids to Be Closer?" *Redbook*, February 1989, 98.

13. Samalin and McCormick, "How to Cure Sibling Fights," 146.

14. Dobson, *The Strong-Willed Child*, 132.

Chapter 23 ❖ *Rebellion*

1. Based on and largely excerpted from an account related in William Lee Carter, Ed.D., *Teenage Rebellion* (Houston/Dallas: Rapha Publishing/Word, 1991), 9–10.

2. Grace Ketterman, M.D., "Rebellion: Can It Be Prevented?" in Jay Kesler with Ronald A. Beers, *Parents and Teenagers* (Wheaton, Ill.: Victor, 1984), 483-84.

3. Carter, *Teenage Rebellion*, 20–21.

4. Olson, *Counseling Teenagers*, 476.

5. Ibid.

6. Ronald P. Hutchcraft., "Why Teens Reject Parental Authority," in Kesler and Beers, *Parents and Teenagers*, 171, 173.

7. Linda Peterson, "Teen Rebellion: the Good, the Bad, and the Healthy," *Redbook*, January 1992, 125.

8. Carter, *Teenage Rebellion*, 30–31.

9. Ibid.

10. Ibid.

11. Eph. 6:1–4.

12. Carter, *Teenage Rebellion*, 3.

13. Marshall Shelley, *Helping Those Who Don't Want Help* (Waco, Tex.: Word, 1986), 148.

14. Carter, *Teenage Rebellion*, 52–53.

Chapter 24 ❖ *Runaway Threats and Attempts*

1. Adapted from an actual family's story. Names and details have been changed to protect identities.

2. Paul Chance, "Running from Home—and Danger," *Psychology Today*, September 1989, 10.

3. Myrna Kostash, "Surviving the Streets," *Chatelaine*, October 1994, 103.

4. *USA Today*, 18 October 1989, 5D, cited in the *Josh McDowell Research Almanac and Statistical Digest*, 1990, 117.

5. Gary D. Bennett, "Runaways," in Kesler and Beers, *Parents and Teenagers*, 487.

6. Keith Wade, quoted in Rubenstin, "Erica Who Hated Rules," *Minneapolis-St. Paul Magazine*, June 1993, 64.

7. Ibid.

8. Ibid.

9. Dr. James R. Oraker with Char Meredith, *Almost Grown* (San Francisco: Harper & Row, 1980), 153–55.

10. Keith Wade, quoted in Rubenstin, "Erica Who Hated Rules," 64.

11. Chance, "Running from Home—and Danger," 10.

12. Oraker and Meredith, *Almost Grown*, 152.

13. Quoted by Bruce Rubenstein, *Minneapolis-St. Paul Magazine*, June 1993, 64.

14. Marjorie Rosen, "Road Warrior," *People*, 12 December 1994, 48.

15. Oraker and Meredith, *Almost Grown*, 151.

16. Bennett, "Runaways," 487.

17. Ibid.

18. Brian Bergman, "Hell on the Streets: Winnipeg Tries to Cope with Runaways," *Maclean's*, 19 November 1990, 21.

19. Bennett, "Runaways," 488.
20. Luke 15:11–24.
21. Isa. 53:6.
22. Oraker and Meredith, *Almost Grown*, 156.
23. Rosen, "Road Warrior," 48.
24. Carter, *Teenage Rebellion*, 3.
25. Bennett, "Runaways," 488.
26. Oraker, *Almost Grown*, 158–59.
27. Ibid., 159.

Chapter 25 ❖ Lust

1. Collins, *Christian Counseling*, 284.
2. Backus, *Telling the Truth to Troubled People*, 240.
3. James 1:14, 15, NASB.
4. Collins, *Christian Counseling*, 286.
5. Ibid., 289.
6. Backus, *Telling the Truth to Troubled People*, 240.
7. Matt. 5:27–28.
8. "Dating and Heavy Petting," an unpublished 1977 paper by Trinity Evangelical Divinity School students Joan Barlett, Marty Hansen, Isolde Anderson, and Jay Terbush, adapted by Collins, *Christian Counseling*, 294.
9. Collins, *Christian Counseling*, 290-91.
10. Backus, *Telling the Truth to Troubled People*, 237.
11. Collins, *Christian Counseling*, 291.
12. Erwin W. Lutzer, *Living with Your Passions* (Wheaton, Ill.: Victor, 1983), 155.
13. Collins, *Christian Counseling*, 291.
14. Ibid., 292.

Chapter 26 ❖ Masturbation

1. Collins, *Christian Counseling*, 285.
2. From J. Allen, "The 'M' Word: It's Joked About, Whispered About, Worried About, But It's Hardly Ever Talked About," *Chicago Tribune* Tempo section, 30 January 1995, 1.
3. Ibid.

4. Collins, *Christian Counseling*, 295.
5. Olson, *Counseling Teenagers*, 403.
6. Dobson, *Preparing for Adolescence*, 83.
7. Barry St. Clair and Bill Jones, *Sex: Desiring the Best* (San Bernardino, Calif.: Here's Life Publishers, 1987), 110.
8. Olson, *Counseling Teenagers*, 403.
9. Adams, *The Christian Counselor's Manual*, 400.
10. Oraker and Meredith, *Almost Grown*, 52–3.
11. St. Clair and Jones, *Sex: Desiring the Best*, 116.
12. Randy Alcorn, *Christians in the Wake of the Sexual Revolution* (Portland, Oreg: Multnomah, 1985), 215.
13. St. Clair and Jones, *Sex: Desiring the Best* 113–14.
14. Adams, *The Christian Counselor's Manual*, 400.
15. Matt. 5:27–28.
16. Collins, *Christian Counseling*, 296.
17. St. Clair and Jones, *Sex: Desiring the Best*, 118–22.
18. Collins, *Christian Counseling*, 292.

Chapter 27 ❖ Pornography

1. Alexandra Mark and Vernon H. Mark, *The Pied Pipers of Sex* (Plainfield, N.J.: Haven, 1981), 112.
2. "Report of the Attorney General's Task Force on Family Violence," U.S. Department of Justice, Washington, D.C., 112, and Mark and Mark, *The Pied Pipers of Sex*, 113.
3. U.S. Senate Judiciary Committee, Subcommittee on Juvenile Justice, *Effect of Pornography on Women and Children*, 98th Congress, 2d sess., 1984, 227.
4. Dr. Jennings Bryant study cited by Victor B. Cline, University of Utah Department of Psychology, "Correlating Adolescent and Adult Exposure to Sexually Explicit Material and Sexual Behavior" (paper presented at the National Conference on Human Immunodeficiency Virus).

5. McDowell and Hostetler, *Right from Wrong: What You Need to Know to Help Youth Make Right Choices*, 258.

6. Mark and Mark, *The Pied Pipers of Sex*, 115.

7. Philip Elmer-DeWitt, "On a screen near you: Cyberporn—It's popular, pervasive, and surprisingly perverse," *Time*, July 1995, 38.

8. Quoted in *Pornography: The Longford Report* (London: Coronet, 1972), 412.

9. Quoted in "A Disrespector of Persons," *Christianity Today*, 7 March 1986, 18.

10. Cline, "Correlating Adolescent and Adult Exposure to Sexually Explicit Material and Sexual Behavior."

11. Ibid.

12. *AFA Journal*, February 1989, cited in *Josh McDowell Research Almanac and Statistical Digest*, 1990, 89.

13. Study by psychologist Dolf Zillman of the University of Indiana, cited in Tom Minnery, "Pornography: The Human Tragedy," *Christianity Today*, 7 March 1986, 20.

14. Psychologist Edward Donnerstein of the University of Wisconsin, cited by Minnery in "Pornography: The Human Tragedy," 20.

15. Rabbi Akiba, who lived about a century after Christ, taught that the phrase, "and be united to his wife" meant also "but not to his neighbor's wife, nor to a male, nor to an animal," thus at once prohibiting adultery, homosexuality, and bestiality.

16. Gen. 1:28.

17. Gen. 2:24.

18. Prov. 5:18–19.

19. Bryant study cited by Cline, "Correlating Adolescent and Adult Exposure to Sexually Explicit Material and Sexual Behavior."

Chapter 28 ❖ Premarital Sex

1. Figures cited in *Baby Busters: The Disillusioned Generation* (Chicago: Northfield Publishing, 1994), 122–23.

2. Warren E. Leary, *New York Times*, 9 February 1989.

3. Dr. Liana Clark, quoted in Doug Levy, "Doctors Hope to Bring a Healing Touch to Social Ills," *USA Today*, 6 July 1995, 3D.

4. This table is reprinted from McDowell and Hostetler, *Right from Wrong: What You Need to Know to Help Youth Make Right Choices*, 269.

5. Nadine Brozan, "New Look at Fears of Children," *New York Times*, 2 May 1983, 85.

6. Quoted from "Teenage Pregnancy: National Policies at the Crossroads," *Family*, The Family Research Council, November/December 1989, 3.

7. Arland Thornton and Donald Camburn, "Religious Participation and Adolescent Sexual Behavior and Attitudes," *Journal of Marriage and the Family* 51 (August 1989): 651.

8. Robert L. Flewelling and Karl E. Bauman, "Family Structure as a Predictor of Initial Substance Abuse and Sexual Intercourse in Early Adolescence," *Journal of Marriage and the Family* 52 (February 1990): 178.

9. As reported by Greer L. Fox in "The Family's Role in Adolescent Sexual Behavior," *Teenage Pregnancy in a Family Context*, Theodora Ooms, ed. (Philadelphia: Temple University Press, 1981).

10. E. S. Roberts, D. Kline, and J. Gagon, *Family Life and Sexual Learning of Children*, vol. 1 (Cambridge, Mass.: Population Education, 1981).

11. Lewis J. Lord, "Sex, with Care," *U.S. News and World Report*, 2 June 1986, 53–57.

12. Josh McDowell and Dick Day, *Why Wait? What You Need to Know about the Teen Sexuality Crisis* (San Bernardino, Calif.: Here's Life Publishers, 1987), 92.

13. Teenager quoted in Ronald S. Toth, "Teen Pregnancy," *Plain Truth*, September 1986, 5.

14. Josh McDowell, *The Myths of Sex Education* (San Bernardino, Calif.: Here's Life Publishers, 1990), 20.

15. Ibid.

16. Research cited in Jeannie Echenique, "Early Dating May Lead to Early Sex," *USA Today*, 12 November 1986, D1.

17. Leslie Jane Nonkin, *I Wish My Parents Understood* (New York: Penguin, 1982), appendix II, 58.

18. David Gelman, "The Games Teenagers Play," *Newsweek*, 1 September 1980, 48–53.

19. Robert Coles and Geoffrey Stokes, *Sex and the American Teenager* (New York: Harper and Row, 1985), 79.

20. Jerry Peyton, unpublished surveys of University of Arizona students in 1970, 1975, and 1980.

21. McDowell and Day, *Why Wait? What You Need to Know about the Teen Sexuality Crisis*, 256.

22. Ibid., 200.

23. Alcorn, *Christians in the Wake of the Sexual Revolution*, 176.

24. Gen. 1:18.

25. Gen. 2:24.

26. Prov. 5:18–19.

Chapter 29 ❖ Unplanned Pregnancy

1. Kim Painter, "Teens and Sex a Fact of American Life," *USA Today*, 7 June 1994, 6D.

2. Cited in Naomi B. Farber, "The Process of Pregnancy Resolution Among Adolescent Mothers," *Adolescence* 26, no. 103 (Fall 1991): 697.

3. From statistics published by the Children's Defense Fund.

4. *Statistical Abstract*, 1989, 454–56, cited in *Josh McDowell Research Almanac and Statistical Digest*.

5. "Pregnancy Problem Is Real," *Dallas Morning News*, 19 February 1987.

6. Kristin Moore, "Teenage Motherhood: Social and Economic Consequences," The Urban Institute, Washington, D.C., 1979, 32.

7. Karen J. Sandvig, *You're What? Help and Hope for Pregnant Teens* (Ventura, Calif.: Regal,

1988), 12.

8. Olsen, *Counseling Teenagers*, 409.

9. *Family Planning Perspectives* 18, no. 5 (Sept./Oct. 1986): 204, 207.

10. Elsie F. Jones and Jacqueline Darroch Forrest, "Contraceptive Failure Rates Based on the 1988 NSFG," *Family Planning Perspectives* 24, no. 1 (Jan./Feb. 1992): 12–17.

11. Arlene R. Stiffman, et al., "Pregnancies, Childrearing, Mental Health Problems in Adolescents," *Youth & Society*, no. 4 (June 1990): 492–93.

12. Olsen, *Counseling Teenagers*, 409.

13. Sandvig, *You're What? Help and Hope for Pregnant Teens*, 22–23.

14. Stiffman, et al., "Pregnancies, Childrearing, Mental Health Problems in Adolescents," 491.

15. Farber, "The Process of Pregnancy Resolution Among Adolescent Mothers," 702.

16. Ibid.

17. Some of these signs were suggested by Sandvig in *You're What? Help and Hope for Pregnant Teens*, 49.

18. Olsen, *Counseling Teenagers*, 411.

19. Ibid., 409.

20. Ibid., 411.

Chapter 30 ❖ Abortion

1. Cited in Farber, "The Process of Pregnancy Resolution Among Adolescent Mothers," 697.

2. Cited in Marcus, Tarshis, and Whiteford, "The Most Difficult Decision," 6.

3. Eloise Salholz and Ann McDaniel with the assistance of Patricia King, Nadine Joseph, Gregory Cerio, and Ginny Carroll, "The Battle Over Abortion," *Newsweek*, 1 May 1989, 31.

4. M. Balfin, M.D., "A New Problem in Adolescent Gynecology," *Southern Medical Journal* 72, no. 8 (August 1979).

5. According to an NBC special on *Roe v. Wade*.

6. Deborah Anne Dawson, "The Effects of

Sex Education on Adolescent Behavior," *Family Planning Perspectives* 18, no. 4 (July/August 1986).

7. According to the *1991 United Nations Demographic Yearbook,* 70,705 abortions were performed in Canada in 1989.

8. According to the *1991 United Nations Demographic Yearbook,* 180,622 abortions were performed in the United Kingdom in 1989; 184,092 in 1990.

9. Salholz and McDaniel, et al., "The Battle Over Abortion," 31.

10. Leary, *New York Times,* 9 February 1989.

11. Dr. Liana Clark, quoted in Doug Levy, "Doctors Hope to Bring a Healing Touch to Social Ills," *USA Today,* 6 July 1995, 3D.

12. Edward A. Brann, et al., "Strategies for the Prevention of Pregnancy in Adolescents," reprinted by the U.S. Dept. of Education and Welfare, Public Health Service from *Advances in Planned Parenthood* 14, no. 2 (1979).

13. Ibid.

14. *Christianity Today,* 14 July 1989.

15. Randall A. Terry, *Operation Rescue* (Binghamton, N.Y.: Operation Rescue, 1988), 256.

16. Ibid., 256–258.

17. See chapter 3, "Guilt," for more on the distinction between moral guilt and psychological guilt.

18. Spaulding and J. Cavernar, "Psychoses Following Abortion," *American Journal of Psychiatry* 135, no. 3 (March 1978): 364.

19. "Legalized Abortion and the Public Health," a report of a study by the Institute of Medicine, National Academy of Sciences, Washington, D.C., May 1975.

20. Cited in the *Illinois Right to Life Committee News,* July-September 1988.

21. Balfin, "A New Problem in Adolescent Gynecology."

22. C. Cowell, "Problems of Adolescent Abortion," Ortho Panel 14, Toronto General Hospital.

23. M. Balfin, M.D., *OB-GYN Observer,* October-November 1975.

24. M. Balfin, M.D., "A New Problem in Adolescent Gynecology."

25. "Teenage Pregnancy: The Problem That Hasn't Gone Away," Alan Guttmacher Institute, 1981, Section 5, 28.

26. "Legalized Abortion and the Public Health."

27. R. Kumar and K. Robson, *Psychological Medicine* 8 (1978): 711–15.

28. Anne Catherine Speckhard, "The Psycho-Social Aspects of Stress Following Abortion," a thesis submitted to faculty of the Graduate School of the University of Minnesota, May 1985, 69.

29. *Newsweek,* 30 January 1989.

30. *All About Issues,* October 1989, 34.

31. Salholz and McDaniel, et al., "The Battle Over Abortion," 31.

32. Source: New England Regional Genetics Group.

33. "The Economic Factor of Abortion," Nurses for Life, Atlanta, Georgia.

34. Excerpted from Paul B. Fowler, *Abortion: Toward an Evangelical Consensus* (Portland, Oreg.: Multnomah Books, Questar Publishers, 1987) 135–147. Used by permission. Fowler also gives a sound exposition of the oft-cited Exodus 21:22–25.

35. Olsen, *Counseling Teenagers,* 411.

36. Ibid.

37. Collins, *Christian Counseling,* 449.

38. Olsen, *Counseling Teenagers,* 411.

39. Ps. 34:18.

Chapter 31 ❖ Homosexuality

1. George Barna, *The Invisible Generation* (Glendale, Calif.: Research Group, 1992), 145–46.

2. David Gelman with Debra Rosenberg, Vicki Quade, Elizabeth Roberts, and Danzy Senna, "Tune In, Come Out," *Newsweek,* 8 November 1993, 70–71.

3. Melinda Beck with Daniel Glick and Peter Annin, "The Power and the Pride," *Newsweek,* 21 June 1993, 58.

4. Stanton L. Jones, "The Loving Opposition," *Christianity Today,* 19 July 1993, 23.

5. John White, *Eros Defiled* (Downers Grove, Ill.: InterVarsity, 1977), 114–16. Used by permission.

6. Jerry Arterburn with Steve Arterburn, *How Will I Tell My Mother?* (Nashville: Oliver Nelson, 1988), 45.

7. Ken Philpott, *The Gay Theology* (Plainfield, N.J.: Logos International, 1977), 99.

8. Brad Hayton and John Eldredge, "Homosexual Rights: What's Wrong?" *Focus on the Family Citizen,* 18 March 1991, 7.

9. Jones, "The Loving Opposition," 23.

10. "Study on Homosexuals Released," *AFA Journal,* February 1990, 3.

11. Jones, "The Loving Opposition," 23.

12. White, *Eros Defiled,* 119.

13. Herbert J. Miles, *Singles, Sex, and Marriage* (Waco, Tex.: Word, 1983), 72–73.

14. Jones, "The Loving Opposition," 20.

15. Miles, *Singles, Sex, and Marriage,* 79.

16. Jones, "The Loving Opposition," 25.

17. Ps. 18:19.

18. White, *Eros Defiled,* 132–33.

19. Adams, *The Christian Counselor's Manual,* 408.

20. White, *Eros Defiled,* 133.

21. Arterburn, *How Will I Tell My Mother?* 152.

22. Ibid., 151–52.

23. Ibid., 151.

24. Ibid., 150.

Chapter 32 ❖ AIDS

1. According to World Health Organization (WHO) figures in "The Global AIDS Situation," *Information Please Almanac* (Boston: Houghton-Mifflin, 1995).

2. According to the Centers for Disease Control, the number of AIDS cases diagnosed in 1993 was 106,618, a figure cited in Dante Ramos, "A Second Wave," *The New Republic,* 5 June 1995, 29.

3. Mary-Ann Schafer, quoted in William Hines, "Other sex diseases dwarf AIDS," *Chicago Sun Times,* 21 May 1989, 28.

4. Anita Manning, "Teens and sex in the age of AIDS," *USA Today,* 3 October 1988, 2D.

5. Hines, "Other sex diseases dwarf AIDS," 28.

6. Peter A. Selwyn, M.D., "AIDS: What Is Now Known," *Hospital Practice,* 15 June 1988, 150-51.

7. "MD's suggestions are invited in research on prevention of AIDS," *American Medical News,* 4 May 1984, 27.

8. Ibid.

9. Ellen Flax, "Explosive Data Confirm Prediction: AIDS Is Spreading Among Teenagers," *Education Week* 9, no. 8 (October 1989): 1, 12.

10. Shaffin Shariff, "The Hidden Toll: More Women Are Victims of AIDS," *Maclean's,* 13 May 1991, 56.

11. Flax, "Explosive Data Confirm Prediction: AIDS Is Spreading Among Teenagers," 1, 12.

12. Manning, "Teens and sex in the age of AIDS," 2D.

13. Helene Gayle, cited by M. F. Goldsmith, Speakers on Adolescents AIDS, Reports from the Fourth International Conference on AIDS, *Journal of the American Medical Association* 260, no. 6 (August 1988).

14. W. H. Masters, V. E. Johnson, and R. C. Kolodny, *Crisis: Heterosexual Behavior in the Age of AIDS* (New York: Grove Press, 1988), cited in Robert C. Kolodny, M.D., and Virginia Johnson, DSC, "New Directions in the AIDS Crisis: The Heterosexual Community," *Medical Aspects of Human Sexuality,* April 1988, 83.

15. Chuck Talbert, "Sexually Transmitted Diseases—What Teachers, Counselors, and Parents Should Know," *Adolescent Counselor,* February/March 1990, 33–37.

16. Patricia Kloser, M.D., "AIDS News: Special Report from the Fourth International AIDS Conference, Stockholm, June 12–16," *Medical Aspects of Human Sexuality,* August 1989, 15.

17. C. Everett Koop, quoted by William Bennett, then U.S. secretary of education, "AIDS: the Ongoing Debate," 1987 Conference on AIDS, Washington, D.C.

18. "A Decade of Denial: Teens and AIDS in America," Minority Dissent, Select Committee on Children, Youth, and Families, 10 April 1992.

19. "Understanding AIDS," *General Almanac*.

20. Lisa Holland, "Women, Children & AIDS: The Latest News," *Good Housekeeping*, November 1990, 271.

21. "Understanding AIDS," *General Almanac*.

22. S. I. McMillen, *None of These Diseases* (Old Tappan, N.J.: Fleming H. Revell, 1984), 44.

23. 1 Cor. 6:18.

24. Eph. 4:29–5:2.

25. Col. 3:12–14.

26. John 8:1–11.

27. Mark 5:25–34.

28. John 4:1–42.

29. See Josh McDowell, *The Myths of Sex Education* (San Bernardino, Calif: Here's Life Publishers, 1990) for detailed elaboration on these points.

Chapter 33 ❖ *Other Sexually Transmitted Diseases*

1. This composite account was developed from a 1990 magazine article describing the growing problem of teenagers having sex.

2. "Other Sexually Transmitted Diseases," *Information Please Almanac* (Boston: Houghton-Mifflin, 1994).

3. Lewis J. Lord, with Jenny Thornton and Joseph Carey, "Sex, With Care," *U.S. News and World Report*, 2 June 1986, 53.

4. Hines, "Other sex diseases dwarf AIDS," 28.

5. Manning, "Teens and sex in the age of AIDS," 2D.

6. Hines, "Other sex diseases dwarf AIDS," 28.

7. *New England Journal of Medicine*, 6 July 1989.

8. Ann P. Stein, M.D., "The Chlamydia Epidemic: Teenagers at Risk," *Medical Aspects of Human Sexuality*, February 1991, 26.

9. "Other Sexually Transmitted Diseases," *Information Please Almanac*.

10. "Cervical neoplasia caused by Condyloma virus," *Medical Aspects of Human Sexuality* 19, no. 10 (October 1985): 150.

11. "Several types considered genital cancer risks," *Sexually Transmitted Diseases Bulletin* 6, no. 5 (October 1986): 6.

12. "Cervical Cancer Epidemic with Current Lifestyles," *Family Practice News* 14, no. 15 (1–14 August 1984): 3.

13. "Medical Aspects of Human Sexuality," *Contemporary Ob/Gyn*, September 1972. (An expanded version appeared in the same publication, September 1974.)

14. *Journal of the American Medical Association*, 17 February 1962, 486.

15. *Cancer Research*, April 1967, 603.

16. "Venereal Factors in Human Cervical Cancer," *Cancer* 39 (1977): 1912–19.

17. Joe S. McIlhaney, M.D., *CMS Journal* 18, no. 1 (Winter 1987): 28–30.

18. *Information Please Almanac*, Houghton-Mifflin Co., 1994.

19. *All News*, 28 July 1989. Sources: *Journal of the American Medical Association*, 23–30 June 1989; *Washington Times*, 12 June 1989; *Washington Post* Health section, 11 July 1989.

20. Flax, "Explosive Data Confirm Prediction: AIDS Is Spreading Among Teenagers," 1, 12.

21. Ibid.

22. "Spreading the Word on Disseminated Gonorrhea," *Emergency Medicine*, 15 May 1983, 71.

23. *Information Please Almanac*, Houghton-Mifflin Co., 1994.

24. Marsha F. Goldsmith, "'Silent Epidemic' of 'Social Disease' Makes STD Experts Raise Their Voices," in the "Medical News and Perspectives"

column, *Journal of the American Medical Association* 261, no. 24 (23–30 June 1989): 3509.

25. Mark G. Martens, M.D., and Sebastian Faro, M.D., Ph.D., "Update on Trichomoniasis: Detection and Management," *Medical Aspects of Human Sexuality*, January 1989, 73.

26. McMillen, *None of These Diseases*, 44.

27. Eph. 4:29–5:2.

28. Col. 3:12–14.

29. John 8:1–11.

30. Mark 5:25–34.

31. John 4:1–42.

32. See Josh McDowell, *The Myths of Sex Education* (San Bernardino, Calif.: Here's Life Publishers, 1990) for detailed elaboration on these points.

Chapter 34 ❖ *Sexual Abuse*

1. Cheryl McCall, "The Cruelest Crime— Sexual Abuse of Children: The Victims, the Offenders, How to Protect Your Family," *Life*, December 1984, 35.

2. *Glamour* magazine, cited in *Signs of the Times*, December 1989, 6.

3. Brooklyn Society for the Prevention of Cruelty to Children Annual Report, 1977.

4. Lois Timnick, "22 Percent in Survey Were Child Abuse Victims," *Los Angeles Times*, 25 August 1985.

5. Penner and Penner, *A Gift for All Ages*, 224.

6. Maxine Hancock and Karen Burton Mains, *Child Sexual Abuse: A Hope for Healing* (Wheaton, Ill.: Harold Shaw), 5–6.

7. Emily Page, quoted in Marcia Yudkin, "The Nightmare of Child Sexual Abuse: Survivors Speak Out," *Cosmopolitan*, May 1992, 246.

8. Florence Rush, *The Best Kept Secret: Sexual Abuse of Children* (New York: McGraw-Hill, 1980), 4.

9. Cited in Rush, *The Best Kept Secret: Sexual Abuse of Chidlren*, 3–4.

10. Rush, *The Best Kept Secret: Sexual Abuse of Children*, 6.

11. Ibid., 4.

12. Janice R. Butler and Linda M. Burton, "Rethinking Teenage Childbearing: Is Sexual Abuse a Missing Link?" *Family Relations*, January 1990, 73.

13. Judith Weiler, quoted in Yudkin, "The Nightmare of Child Sexual Abuse: Survivors Speak Out," 246.

14. Butler and Burton, "Rethinking Childbearing: Is Sexual Abuse a Missing Link," 77.

15. Hancock and Mains, *Child Sexual Abuse: A Hope for Healing*, 24.

16. Holly Wagner Green, *Turning Fear to Hope* (Nashville: Thomas Nelson, 1984), 78.

17. Hancock and Mains, *Child Sexual Abuse: A Hope for Healing*, 24.

18. Linda Schiller, quoted in Yudkin, "The Nightmare of Child Sexual Abuse: Survivors Speak Out," 34–35.

19. Jan Frank, *A Door of Hope* (San Bernardino, Calif.: Here's Life Publishers, 1987), 34-35.

20. Hancock and Mains, *Child Sexual Abuse: A Hope for Healing*, 88.

21. Ravi Zacharias, *Can Man Live Without God?* (Dallas: Word, 1994), 100.

22. Susan Forward, quoted in Hancock and Mains, *Child Sexual Abuse: A Hope for Healing*, 72.

23. Adapted from "How to Help: Tips, Telephone Numbers," *USA Today*, 8 April 1994, 8A.

Chapter 35 ❖ *Nonsexual Abuse*

1. Report of the National Committee for the Prevention of Child Abuse, cited in "Child Abuse: A Trust Betrayed," *USA Today*, 7 April 1994, 8A.

2. Ibid.

3. Angela R. Carl, *Child Abuse: What You Can Do about It* (Cincinnati: Standard Publishing, 1985), 16.

4. Ibid., 20.

5. Ibid., 20–21.

6. Ibid., 21.

7. John White, *Parents in Pain* (Downers Grove, Ill.: InterVarsity, 1979), 78, 81.

8. "Charting the Aftermath of Child Abuse," *Science News*, 12 January 1991, 29.

9. Ibid.

10. Cited in Paul Chance, "Running from Home—and Danger," *Psychology Today,* September 1989, 10.

11. Study cited in "Child Abuse: a 'cycle of violence'?" *Science News,* 22 July 1989, 61.

12. Excerpted from "How to Help: Tips, Telephone Numbers," *USA Today,* 8 April 1994, 8A.

13. Carl, *Child Abuse: What You Can Do About It,* 66.

Chapter 36 ❖ Rape

1. As reported in *Violence in Dating Relationships.*

2. Dr. Mary P. Koss, as reported in "Date Rape: When Sex Is a Weapon," the Orange County Sexual Assault Network (OSCAN).

3. Laura Mansnerus, "The Rape Laws Change Faster Than Perceptions," *New York Times*, 19 February 1989.

4. As reported by columnist Claude Lewis, "Distorted Attitudes Reinforced," in the *Philadelphia Inquirer.*

5. Ibid.

6. "Date/Acquaintance Rape: What You Need to Know . . . " from the Rape Crisis Center of the Center for Women's Study and Service.

7. As reported in *Violence in Dating Relationships.*

Chapter 37 ❖ Ritual Abuse

1. Children's Institute International, Marshall Resource Center, Southern California Training Center, 1989.

2. Luke 17:2 NRSV.

3. 2 Kings 21:6 NASB.

4. Deut. 12:31 NASB.

Chapter 38 ❖ Alcohol Use and Abuse

1. Reported in *Group Members Only*, cited in *Josh McDowell Research Almanac and Statistical Digest* (Josh McDowell Ministry, 1990), 147.

2. A 1987 report by Monitoring the Future, cited in "It Is Time to Ban the Advertising of Alcohol from Broadcasting," *AFA Journal,* January 1990, 12.

3. A National Adolescent School Survey 1987, cited in "It Is Time to Ban the Advertising of Alcohol from Broadcasting," 12.

4. Cited in "It Is Time to Ban the Advertising of Alcohol from Broadcasting," 12.

5. Johnston, *Why Suicide?* 54.

6. Ibid.

7. Frank Moran, quoted in Stephen Phillip Policoff, "Bottle Babies," *Ladies Home Journal,* May 1989, 182.

8. Robert J. Ackerman, *Children of Alcoholics* (Holmes Beach, Fla.: Learning Publications, 1978), cited in Collins, *Christian Counseling*, 380.

9. Collins, *Christian Counseling*, 380.

10. Steve Arterburn, *Growing Up Addicted* (New York: Ballantine, 1987), 129.

11. Ibid., 131.

12. Policoff, "Bottle Babies," 182.

13. Arterburn, *Growing Up Addicted*, 137.

14. Ibid., 138.

15. Ibid., 139.

16. Ibid., 294.

17. Quoted in Barbara R. Thompson, "Alcoholism: Even the Church Is Hurting," *Christianity Today,* 5 August 1983.

18. Collins, *Christian Counseling*, 379.

19. Quoted in Thompson, "Alcoholism: Even the Church Is Hurting."

20. Collins, *Christian Counseling*, 388.

21. Phil. 4:5.

Chapter 39 ❖ Drug Use and Abuse

1. Adapted from an account in Arterburn, *Growing Up Addicted*, 257–8.

2. Kesler and Beers, *Parents and Teenagers*, 502.

3. *USA Today*, 13 September 1989, 1D.

4. *USA Today*, 27 September 1989, 1D.

5. McDowell and Hostetler, *Right from Wrong*, 6.

6. Johnston, *Why Suicide?* 63.

7. Ibid., 59.

8. Study cited in Johnston, *Why Suicide?*, 58.

9. "How to Beat Drugs," *U.S. News and World Report*, 14 August 1989, 70.

10. Johnston, *Why Suicide?* 59.

11. McDowell and Hostetler, *Right from Wrong*, 9.

12. "How to Beat Drugs," 70.

13. "Drugs and White America," *U.S. News and World Report*, 18 Sept. 1989.

14. "Teenage Drug Use Alarming," *USA Today*, 15 August 1989, 6A.

15. Armand M. Nicholi Jr., "Commitment to Family," *Family Building*, ed. Dr. George Rekers (Ventura, Calif.: Regal, 1985), 55.

16. Sanders, *Tough Turf: A Teen Survival Manual*, 129.

17. *AFA Journal*, September 1989, 18.

18. *USA Today*, 6 September 1989.

19. "Drug Abuse through the Umbilical Cord," Report #6, 1989–90, San Diego County Grand Jury, April 1990. 9.

20. Sanders, *Tough Turf: A Teen Survival Manual*, 129.

21. Ibid., 129.

22. Collins, *Christian Counseling: A Comprehensive Guide*, 380–84.

23. This table is from Dan Korem, *Streetwise Parents, Foolproof Kids*, 2d. ed. (Richardson, Tex.: International Focus Press, 1996). Used with permission.

24. *USA Today*, 16 October 1989, 1.

25. "Cocaine: A Little Can Hurt Heart," *USA Today*, 7 December 1989.

26. "Cocaine Use Linked to Infertility," *USA Today*, 13 February 1990, 1D.

27. Delbert S. Elliott and Barbara J. Morse, "Delinquency and Drug Use as Risk Factors in Teenage Sexual Activity," *Youth & Society* 21, no. 1 (September 1989): 56.

28. Jeffrey Fagan and Edward Pabon, "Contributions of Delinquency and Substance Use to School Dropout Among Inner-City Youths," *Youth & Society* 21, no. 3 (March 1990): 330.

29. Peggy Mann, *Marijuana Alert* (New York: McGraw-Hill, 1985), 18–19.

30. *The Economist*, 21 January 1989, 25–26.

31. Arterburn, *Growing Up Addicted*, 273.

Chapter 40 ❖ Gambling

1. Cited in "Against All Odds: Will Christians reclaim the high ground in a battle to fight America's recreational pastime?" *Christianity Today*, 14 November 1994, 58–60, 62.

2. Ibid.

3. Ron Scherer, "Easy Credit and Sheepish Parents Add to the Rise of Underage Gambling," *The Christian Science Monitor*, 19 May 1995, 3.

4. Durwood Jacobs, quoted in Steve Wilstein, "Colleges Deal with Gambling," *The Arizona Press*, 31 March 1995, 01.

5. Ibid.

6. Ibid.

7. Edward Looney, quoted in Scherer, "Easy Credit and Sheepish Parents Add to the Rise of Underage Gambling," 3.

8. Symptoms described in the *American Psychiatric DSM IV* (Diagnostic Statistical Manual) edition 0004 (Washington, D.C.: American Psychiatric Press, 1996).

9. A nonclinical survey instrument used by Gamblers Anonymous.

10. Excerpted from "Understanding Compulsive Gambling," Hazelden Foundation, 1993.

Chapter 42 ❖ Anorexia Nervosa

1. Pam Vredevelt, Dr. Deborah Newman, Harry Beverly, Dr. Frank Minirth, *The Thin*

Disguise: Understanding and Overcoming Anorexia and Bulimia (Nashville: Thomas Nelson, 1992), 48–49.

2. Based on figures cited in Leslie Knowlton, "Silence and Guilt: Eating Disorders Have Long Been Associated with Women," *Los Angeles Times*, 23 May 1995, E1.

3. Liliana R. Kossoy, "Detecting the Hidden Eating Disorder," *Medical Aspects of Human Sexuality*, August 1991, 46.

4. Quoted in Knowlton, "Silence and Guilt: Eating Disorders Have Long Been Associated with Women," E1.

5. Sturkie and Tan, *Advanced Peer Counseling in Youth Groups*.

6. Robert S. McGee, *Overcoming Eating Disorders* (Houston and Dallas: Rapha/Word, 1990), xiii.

7. Ibid.

8. Sturkie and Tan, *Advanced Peer Counseling in Youth Groups*.

9. Vivian Meehan, quoted in Knowlton, "Silence and Guilt: Eating Disorders Have Long Been Associated with Women," E1.

10. Based on figures cited in Knowlton, "Silence and Guilt: Eating Disorders Have Long Been Associated with Women," E1.

11. Dr. Arnold Anderson, quoted in Knowlton, "Silence and Guilt: Eating Disorders Have Long Been Associated with Women," E1.

12. Vredevelt, Newman, Beverly, and Minirth, *The Thin Disguise: Understanding and Overcoming Anorexia and Bulimia*, 51.

13. McGee, *Overcoming Eating Disorders*, xiv.

14. Olson, *Counseling Teenagers*, 396.

15. Vredevelt, Newman, Beverly, and Minirth, *The Thin Disguise: Understanding and Overcoming Anorexia and Bulimia*, 51.

16. Ibid., 35.

17. Ibid., 44.

18. Ibid., 42.

19. Ibid., 40.

20. 1 Cor. 6:19–20.

21. Vredevelt, Newman, Beverly, and Minirth, *The Thin Disguise: Understanding and Overcoming Anorexia and Bulimia*, 77.

22. Ps. 34:18.

23. Vredevelt, Newman, Beverly, and Minirth, *The Thin Disguise: Understanding and Overcoming Anorexia and Bulimia*, 78–80.

24. McGee, *Overcoming Eating Disorders*, 2–3.

25. Deut. 31:6.

Chapter 43 ❖ Bulimia

1. From "Hitting Her Stride," *People* magazine, 10 April 1995, 115–19.

2. "An Expert Confronts the Complex Challenges of Bulimia Nervosa," *People* magazine, 3 August 1992, 70.

3. Quoted in Knowlton, "Silence and Guilt: Eating Disorders Have Long Been Associated with Women," E1.

4. Based on figures cited in Knowlton, "Silence and Guilt: Eating Disorders Have Long Been Associated with Women," E1.

5. Leslie Knowlton, "Basic Facts about Bulimia and Anorexia," *Los Angeles Times*, 23 May 1995, E1.

6. Quoted in "An Expert Confronts the Complex Challenges of Bulimia Nervosa," 70.

7. Dr. Frank Minirth, Dr. Paul Meier, Dr. Robert Hemfelt, Dr. Sharon Sneed, and Don Hawkins, *Love Hunger* (Nashville: Thomas Nelson, 1990), 20.

8. "Many Bulimic Women Were Abused as Kids, Study Says," *Chicago Tribune*, 10 July 1995, News Section, 6.

9. Reported in Bruce Bower, "Tracing Bulimia's Roots," *Science News*, 5 June 1993, 366.

10. Dr. Katherine Halmi, quoted in "An Expert Confronts the Complex Challenges of Bulimia Nervosa," 70.

11. McGee, *Overcoming Eating Disorders*, xiv.

12. Quoted in Marjorie Rosen, "Eating Disorders: A Hollywood History," *People* magazine, 17 February 1992, 98.

13. Cited in Pamela Kind, "Turning Around Bulimia with Therapy," *Psychology Today,* September 1989, 14.

14. Minirth, Meier, Hemfelt, Sneed, and Hawkins, *Love Hunger,* 57.

15. Vredevelt, Newman, Beverly, and Minirth, *The Thin Disguise: Understanding and Overcoming Anorexia and Bulimia,* 70.

16. Ibid., 40

17. Ibid., 44.

18. Sturkie and Tan, *Advanced Peer Counseling in Youth Groups.*

19. Vredevelt, Newman, Beverly, and Minirth, *The Thin Disguise: Understanding and Overcoming Anorexia and Bulimia,* 40.

20. Minirth, Meier, Hemfelt, Sneed, and Hawkins, *Love Hunger,* 59–60.

21. Dr. Paul Garfinkel, quoted in "Many Bulimic Women Were Abused as Kids, Study Says," 6.

22. 1 Cor. 6:19–20.

23. Ps. 147:3.

24. Vredevelt, Newman, Beverly, and Minirth, *The Thin Disguise: Understanding and Overcoming Anorexia and Bulimia,* 78–80.

25. Isa. 40:1.

26. 1 Thess. 5:14.

27. Olson, *Counseling Teenagers,* 397.

28. McGee, *Overcoming Eating Disorders,* 3–4.

29. Sturkie and Tan, *Advanced Peer Counseling in Youth Groups.*

30. Deut. 31:6.

Chapter 44 ❖ Dropping Out

1. 1 Tim. 4:12–14.
2. Prov. 3:13.
3. Prov. 24:5.
4. 2 Tim. 2:15.
5. See John 8:1–11.

Chapter 45 ❖ Underachievement and Overachievement

1. Adapted from an actual magazine account. Names and details have been changed to protect identities.

2. Cited in "The Dunce Gap," *Psychology Today,* Nov.-Dec. 1992, 9.

3. 2 Tim. 2:15 KJV.

4. 1 Sam. 16:7.

5. Foster Cline, M.D., and Jim Fay, *Parenting Teens with Love and Logic* (Colorado Springs: Pinon Press), 207.

Chapter 46 ❖ Living with a Deformity or Disability

1. Based on an actual magazine account. Names and details have been changed to protect identities.

2. *Demographic Yearbook, United Nations.*

3. *Statistical Abstract of the United States, 1994.*

4. David Veerman, "Skin Deep," in Kesler, *Parents and Teenagers,* 180.

5. Christie, *Dating and Waiting: A Christian View of Love, Sex, and Dating,* 18.

6. Veerman, "Skin Deep," 180.

7. Dobson, *Preparing for Adolescence,* 27.

8. Tom Perski, "Handicapped, But Complete," in Kesler, *Parents and Teenagers,* 521.

9. Jay Kesler, "Handling the Sting of Ridicule and Teasing," in Kesler, *Parents and Teenagers,* 284.

10. Ibid., 284.

11. Eccles. 9:11.

12. Ps. 86:15.

13. Gal. 5:22.

14. 1 Chron. 29:15.

15. 2 Cor. 4:7.

16. Veerman, "Skin Deep," 180.

17. Rom. 12:15.

18. Donald Mardock, "What Teens Don't Like about Themselves," in Kesler, *Parents and Teenagers,* 189.

19. Veerman, "Skin Deep," 180–81.

20. Ibid.

21. Cline and Fay, *Parenting Teens with Love and Logic,* 51–52.

Chapter 47 ❖ Coping with Long-Term Illness

1. Veerman, "Skin Deep," 180.
2. Source: *Health Care Book of Lists, 1993.*
3. Paula Hartman-Stein and Jeanette M. Reuter, "Developmental Issues in the Treatment of Diabetic Women," *Psychology of Women Quarterly* 12 (1988): 421.
4. Elizabeth Berg, "Moments of Ease," *Special Report on Health,* January 1991, 9.
5. Job 14:1.
6. Ps. 90:13.
7. Ps. 46:1.
8. 2 Cor. 1:4.
9. 2 Cor. 12:9.
10. Lam. 3:25, 27–33.
11. Veerman, "Skin Deep," 180.
12. Ps. 68:5.
13. Prov. 23:10–11.
14. Jer. 8:18.
15. 2 Cor. 1:4.

Chapter 48 ❖ Knowing God's Will

1. Adrian Rogers, "Letting God Be Your Guide," in Kesler, *Parents and Teenagers,* 353.
2. Ibid.
3. Ibid.
4. Bill Bright, "Knowing God's Will," in Kesler, *Parents and Teenagers,* 352.

Chapter 49 ❖ Choosing a Ministry or Career

1. Collins, *Christian Counseling,* 235.
2. Ibid., 238.
3. Dr. James Dobson, "Dr. Dobson Answers Your Questions," *Focus on the Family* magazine, November 1995, 5.
4. Collins, *Christian Counseling,* 240.
5. Ps. 37:4.
6. Collins, *Christian Counseling,* 241.
7. Barna, *The Invisible Generation,* 123.
8. Collins, *Christian Counseling,* 241.
9. Meredith W. Long, "God's Will and the Job Market," *HIS,* June 1976, 1.
10. David L. McKenna, "Guiding Your Teen to the Right Career," in Kesler, *Parents and Teenagers,* 670.
11. Jon Clemmer, "Goal- and Career-Planning," in *Singles Ministry Handbook,* ed. Douglas L. Fagerstrom (Wheaton, Ill.: Victor, 1988), 105.
12. Collins, *Christian Counseling,* 243.

Chapter 50 ❖ Choosing a College

1. Lani Luciano, "What Colleges Don't Tell You," *Money,* April 1990, 128.
2. Jessica Aldock, "Check Out the Campus," *USA Today,* 19 July 1995, 4D.
3. Luciano, "What Colleges Don't Tell You," 128.
4. David Elkind, "Getting Into College," *Parents* magazine, November 1991, 251.
5. Janet Spencer, quoted in Jessica Aldock, "Check Out the Campus," 4D.
6. Luciano, "What Colleges Don't Tell You," 128.
7. Ferne Cherne, "Cash for College," *Teen,* magazine, July 1995, 46.
8. Luciano, "What Colleges Don't Tell You," 128.
9. Ibid., 128.
10. R. Judson Carlberg, "Why Christian Colleges Make Sense for Christians" (special advertising section), *Christianity Today,* 14 November 1994, 121.
11. Luciano, "What Colleges Don't Tell You," 128.
12. Cited in Luciano, "What Colleges Don't Tell You," 128.
13. Aldock, "Check Out the Campus," 4D.
14. Ibid., 4D.
15. Cherne, "Cash for College," 46.
16. Quoted in Anne Williman, "Home Where You Belong," *Young Salvationist,* February 1988, 7.
17. Quoted in Lisa Manning, "Wanted: Christians on Campus," *Young Salvationist,*

February 1988, 6.

18. Carlberg, "Why Christian Colleges Make Sense for Christians", 121.

19. Elkind, "Getting Into College," 251.

20. Ibid., 251.

Expand Your Counseling Reach with this New, Interactive Audio Resource for Youth

Youth leaders, pastors, Christian educators—anyone ministering to youth—will benefit from this comprehensive, interactive "Youth in Crisis" resource designed by Josh McDowell. This unique program provides a step-by-step guide to help a youth through the first 48 hours of a crisis.

Josh McDowell's Counseling Youth in Crisis Resource identifies 24 of the most troubling issues facing youth today—all discussed in this Handbook. This extended program offers a wealth of additional information and resources, including:

- Discussion Guidesheets (for step-by-step use with the student)
- 24 Audio Tapes (for the student to take home)
- Students' Interactive Worksheets
- The Book: *Josh McDowell's Handbook on Counseling Youth*

ISBN 0-8499-1153-2

Available through your favorite source for Christian products.

WORD PUBLISHING

CAMPAIGN **RIGHT FROM WRONG** RESOURCES

Passing on the Truth to Our Next Generation

The "Right From Wrong" message, available in numerous formats, provides a blueprint for countering the culture and rebuilding the crumbling foundations of our families.

Read It and Embrace a New Way of Thinking

The Right From Wrong Book for Adults

Right From Wrong - What You Need to Know to Help Youth Make Right Choices
by Josh McDowell & Bob Hostetler

Our youth no longer live in a culture that teaches an objective standard of right and wrong. Truth has become a matter of taste. Morality has been replaced by individual preference. And today's youth have been affected. Fifty-seven percent (57%) of our churched youth cannot state that an objective standard of right and wrong even exists!

As the centerpiece of the "Right From Wrong" Campaign, this life-changing book provides you with a biblical, yet practical, blueprint for passing on core Christian values to the next generation.

Right From Wrong, Trade Paper Book
ISBN 0-8499-3604-7

The Truth Slayers, Trade Paper Book
ISBN 0-8499-3662-4

The Truth Slayers Book for Youth

The Truth Slayers - The Battle of Right From Wrong
by Josh McDowell & Bob Hostetler

This book–directed to youth–is written in the popular NovelPlus format and combines the fascinating story of Brittney Marsh, Philip Milford and Jason Withers and the consequences of their wrong choices with Josh McDowell's insights for young adults in sections called "The Inside Story."

The Truth Slayers conveys the critical "Right From Wrong" message that challenges you to rely on God's word as the absolute standard of truth in making right choices.

103 Questions Book for Children

103 Questions Children Ask About Right From Wrong
Introduction by Josh McDowell

"How does a person really know what is right or wrong?" "How does God decide what's wrong?" "If lying is wrong, why did God let some people in the Bible tell lies?" "What is a conscience and where does it come from?" These and 99 other questions are what kids ages 6-10 are asking. The *103 Questions* book equips parents to answer the tough questions kids ask about right from wrong and provides an easy-to-understand book a child will read and enjoy.

103 Questions, Trade Paper Book
ISBN 0-8423-4595-7

Hear It and Adopt a New Way of Teaching

The Right From Wrong Audio for Adults

What You Need to Know to Help Youth Make Right Choices
by Josh McDowell

What is truth? In three powerful and persuasive talks based on the book *Right From Wrong*, Josh McDowell provides you, your family, and the church with a sound, thorough, biblical, and workable method to clearly understand and defend the truth. Josh explains how to identify absolutes and shows you how to teach youth to determine what is absolutely right from wrong.

Right From Wrong, Audio–104 min.
ISBN 0-8499-6195-5

The Right From Wrong Musicals for Youth

The Truth Works Musical by Dennis and Nan Allen
The Truth Slayers Musical by Steven V. Taylor and Matt Tullos

The *Truth Slayers* Musical for junior high and high school students is based on the *Truth Slayers* book. The *Truth Works* Musical for children is based on the *Truth Works* Workbook. As youth and children perform these musicals to their peers and families, it provides a unique opportunity to tell of the life-changing message of Right From Wrong.

Each musical includes complete leader's instructions, songbook of all music used, dramatic script, and accompanying soundtrack on cassette or compact disc.

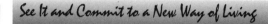

See It and Commit to a New Way of Living

Video Series to Adults

Truth Matters for You and Tomorrow's Generation
Five-part Video Series featuring Josh McDowell

Josh McDowell is at his best in this hard-hitting series that goes beyond surface answers and quick fixes to tackle the real crisis of truth. You will discover the reason for this crisis, and more importantly, how to get you and your family back on track. This series is directed to the entire adult community and is excellent for building momentum in your church to address the loss of values within the family.

This series includes five video sessions, a comprehensive Leader's Guide including samplers from the five "Right From Wrong" Workbooks, the *Right From Wrong* book, the *Truth Slayers* book, and a 8-minute promotional video tape to motivate adults to go through the series.

Truth Matters, Adult Video Series
ISBN 0-8499-8587-0

Video Series to Youth

Setting Youth Free to Make Right Choices
Five-part Video Series featuring Josh McDowell

Through captivating video illustrations, dynamic teaching sessions, and creative group interaction, this series presents students with convincing evidence that right moral choices must be based on a standard outside of themselves. This powerful course equips your students with the understanding of what is right from what is wrong.

The series includes five video sessions, Leader's Guide with reproducible handout including samplers from the five "Right From Wrong" Workbooks, and the *Truth Slayers* book.

*Setting Youth Free to Make
Right Choices*, Youth Video Series
ISBN 0-8499-8585-4

Practice It and Make Living the Truth a Habit

Workbook for Adults

Truth Matters for You and Tomorrow's Generation
Workbook by Josh McDowell with Leader's Guide

The "Truth Matters" Workbook includes 35 daily activities that help you to instill within your children and youth such biblical values as honesty, love, and sexual purity. By taking just 25 - 30 minutes each day, you will discover a fresh and effective way to teach your family how to make right choices–even in tough situations.

The "Truth Matters" Workbook is designed to be used in eight adult group sessions that encourage interaction and support building. The five daily activities between each group meeting will help you and your family make right choices a habit.

Truth Matters, Member's Workbook ISBN 0-8054-9834-6
Truth Matters, Leader's Guide ISBN 0-8054-9833-8

Workbook for College Students
Out of the Moral Maze
by Josh McDowell with Leader's Instructions

Students entering college face a culture that has lost its belief in absolutes. In today's society, truth is a matter of taste; morality of individual preference. "Out of the Moral Maze" will provide any truth-seeking collegiate with a sound moral guidance system based on God and His Word as the determining factor for making right moral choices.

Out of the Moral Maze, Member's Workbook with
Leader's Instructions
ISBN 0-8054-9832-X

Workbook for Junior High and High School Students

Setting You Free to Make Right Choices
by Josh McDowell with Leader's Guide

With a Bible-based emphasis, this Workbook creatively and systematically teaches your students how to determine right from wrong in their everyday lives–specifically applying the decision-making process to moral questions about lying, cheating, getting even, and premarital sex.

Through eight youth group meetings followed each week with five daily exercises of 20-25 minutes per day, your teenagers will be challenged to develop a life-long habit of making right moral choices.

Setting You Free to Make Right Choices, Member's Workbook
ISBN 0-8054-9828-1
Setting You Free to Make Right Choices, Leader's Guide
ISBN 0-8054-9829-X

Workbook for Children

Truth Works - Making Right Choices
by Josh McDowell with Leader's Guide

To pass on the truth and reclaim a generation, we must teach God's truth when our children's minds and hearts are young and pliable. Creatively developed, "Truth Works" is two workbooks, one directed to younger children grades 1 - 3 and one to older children grades 4 - 6.

In eight fun-filled group sessions, your children will discover why such truths as honesty, justice, love, purity, self-control, mercy, and respect work to their best interests and how four simple steps will help them to make right moral choices an everyday habit.

Truth Works, Younger Children's Workbook ISBN 0-8054-9831-1
Truth Works, Older Children's Workbook ISBN 0-8054-9830-3
Truth Works, Leader's Guide ISBN 0-8054-9827-3

Contact your Christian supplier to help you obtain these "Right From Wrong" resources
and begin to make it right in your home, your church, and your community.